Experience Humanities

Experience Humanities

VOLUME I: BEGINNINGS THROUGH THE RENAISSANCE

Roy T. Matthews & F. DeWitt Platt
MICHIGAN STATE UNIVERSITY

Thomas F. X. Noble
THE UNIVERSITY OF NOTRE DAME

McGraw Hill

Connect
Learn
Succeed™

Connect
Learn
Succeed™

EXPERIENCE HUMANITIES

Published by McGraw-Hill, a business unit of The McGraw-Hill Companies, Inc., 1221 Avenue of the Americas, New York, NY, 10020. Copyright © 2014 by The McGraw-Hill Companies, Inc. All rights reserved. Printed in the United States of America. Previous editions © 2011, 2008, and 2004. No part of this publication may be reproduced or distributed in any form or by any means, or stored in a database or retrieval system, without the prior written consent of The McGraw-Hill Companies, Inc., including, but not limited to, in any network or other electronic storage or transmission, or broadcast for distance learning.

Some ancillaries, including electronic and print components, may not be available to customers outside the United States.

This book is printed on acid-free paper.

1 2 3 4 5 6 7 8 9 0 DOW/DOW 1 0 9 8 7 6 5 4 3

ISBN   978-0-07-337665-3 (complete)
MHID   0-07-337665-5 (complete)
ISBN   978-0-07-749470-4 (volume I)
MHID   0-07-749470-9 (volume I)
ISBN   978-0-07-749471-1 (volume II)
MHID   0-07-749471-7 (volume II)

Senior Vice President, Products & Markets: *Kurt L. Strand*
Vice President, General Manager, Products & Markets:
   Michael J. Ryan
Vice President, Content Production & Technology Services:
   Kimberly Meriwether David
Director: *Christopher Freitag*
Brand Manager: *Laura Wilk*
Managing Development Editor: *Nancy Crochiere*
Development Editor: *Arthur Pomponio*
Editorial Coordinator: *Jessica Holmes*
Director of Development: *Rhona Robbin*
Digital Development Editor: *Betty Chen*
Marketing Manager: *Kelly Odom*

Lead Project Manager: *Susan Trentacosti*
Content Project Manager: *Emily Kline*
Senior Buyer: *Carol A. Bielski*
Designer: *Debra Kubiak*
Cover/Interior Designer: *Pam Verros*
Cover Image: *The Arch St. Louis Missouri Gateway Monument:*
   © Phil Degginger/Alamy; The Ishtar Gate: © bpk, Berlin/Vorder-
   asiatisches Museum, SMB/Olaf M. Teßmer/Art Resource, NY
Senior Content Licensing Specialist: *Lori Hancock*
Photo Researcher: *Robin Sand*
Typeface: *9.5/12 Palatino*
Compositor: *Thompson Type*
Printer: *R. R. Donnelley*

All credits appearing on page or at the end of the book are considered to be an extension of the copyright page.

The Library of Congress has catalogued the complete edition as follows

Matthews, Roy T.
   [Western humanities]
   Experience humanities / Roy T. Matthews & F. DeWitt Platt, Michigan State University; Thomas F. X. Noble, The University of Notre Dame. — Eighth Edition.
      pages cm
   Revised edition of: The Western humanities. 7th edition. New York : McGraw-Hill, 2010.
   Includes bibliographical references and index.
   ISBN-13: 978-0-07-337665-3 (complete edition : alk. paper)
   ISBN-10: 0-07-337665-5 (complete edition : alk. paper)
   ISBN-13: 978-0-07-749470-4 (volume I : alk. paper)
   ISBN-10: 0-07-749470-9 (volume I : alk. paper)
   [etc.]
   1. Civilization, Western—History.   I. Platt, F. DeWitt, author.   II. Noble, Thomas F. X., author.   III. Title.
CB245.M375 2014
909'.09821—dc23

2012043014

The Internet addresses listed in the text were accurate at the time of publication. The inclusion of a website does not indicate an endorsement by the authors or McGraw-Hill, and McGraw-Hill does not guarantee the accuracy of the information presented at these sites.

www.mhhe.com

To LeeAnn, Dixie, and Linda

There is nothing nobler or more admirable than when two people who see eye to eye keep house as man and wife, confounding their enemies and delighting their friends, as they themselves know better than anyone.

—Homer, *Odyssey*

Contents

11 The Late Middle Ages

Crisis and Recovery
1300–1500 262

12 The Early Renaissance

Return to Classical Roots
1400–1494 294

13 The High Renaissance
and Early Mannerism
1494–1564 322

Experience Humanities
and Connect® Humanities

The humanities are alive. We see the great pyramids in contemporary design, we hear Bach in hip-hop and pop music, and we feel ancient religious themes and philosophies in our impassioned contemporary dialogues. *Experience Humanities* invites students to take note of the continual evolution of ideas and cross-cultural influences to better understand the cultural heritage of the West, and to think critically about what their legacy will be for future generations.

Together with Connect® Humanities, a groundbreaking digital learning solution, students not only experience their cultural heritage, but develop crucial critical reading, thinking, and writing skills that will prepare them to succeed in their humanities course and beyond.

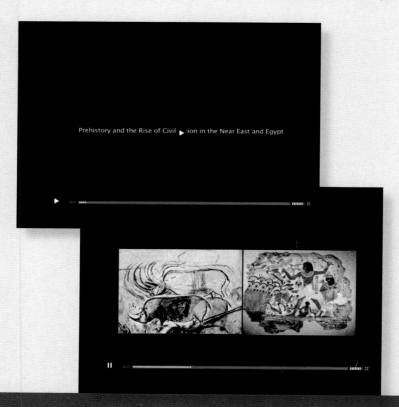

Connect to Engage

Dynamic video previews of each chapter immerse students in the sights and sounds of artistic contributions over time and across continents. Key ideas, people, and events that shaped the time period are introduced to provide historical context and prepare students for the discussions to come in each chapter.

Connect to Analyze

Cultural artifacts come to life in Connect Humanities. Interactive assessments guide students through the process of analyzing art, literature, music, and other primary source documents from each chapter to build critical reading and analysis skills.

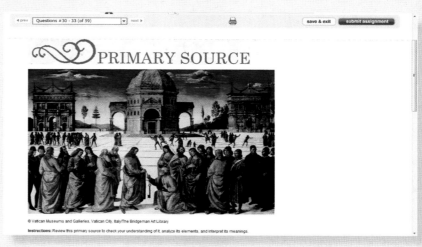

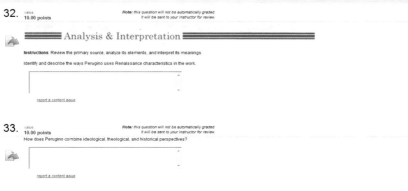

Connect to Experience

Interdisciplinary activities challenge students to explore connections across artistic genres, and begin to develop and express informed opinions on how ideas evolve over time and across cultures.

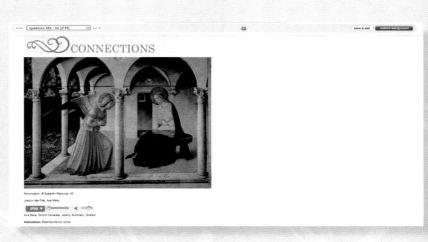

Experience Humanities Features

Interpreting Art

Twenty-three Interpreting Art examples—one per chapter in each volume—focus on a great work of art (painting or sculpture) or architecture, using a set of six call-outs that highlight both formal qualities (how it *is* a work of art) and historical context (how it *reflects* the historical moment). Students who master this feature will be able to apply the approach to understanding any work of art that they encounter.

Industrialism: The Shrinking Globe After its beginnings in England in the 1700s (see Chapter 18), industrialism started to take root in France in the 1830s, and a short time later Belgium entered the industrial age. For the next forty years, Belgium and France were the chief economic powers on the Continent, with factory and railway systems radiating from Paris and Brussels to Vienna and Milan by 1871. The expansion of rail lines meant that factories no longer needed to be near coal mines or clustered in urban areas. Inventions in communications, such as the telegraph, made it easier for industrialists to take advantage of distant resources and markets, and in 1866 engineers laid a transatlantic telegraph cable, linking Europe and America. Further shrinking of the globe occurred with the founding of national postal systems. The United Kingdom led the way (1839), cre-

Global Encounter

In Chapter 11 in Volume I and in most chapters in Volume II, this feature shows the West interacting with the rest of the world. These encounters, which show cultural influences flowing in either direction, are highlighted in the text in two different ways: either as a shaded section or denoted by a symbol.

The West and Islam: The Ottoman Empire in Retreat, 1700–1830

After the Treaty of Karlowitz, in 1699 (see Chapter 15), by which Ottoman rule over most of the Christian peoples of the Balkans was ended, the Ottoman Empire was never the same. For centuries, the empire had been the major power in the Middle East and the Arab world. Now, it was a weakened force in the region, racked by internal strife and threatened by western invaders. At home, the battles were now between reformers, who wanted to westernize the Ottoman world, and a renewal movement based on Islamic law. In foreign affairs, the perennial issue was the threat of European states intent on expanding their political and commercial influence across the Middle East and North Africa.

Between 1699 and 1830, Ottoman rulers made a se-

The West and Islam

In seven chapters in volume II, this feature helps students understand the forces at play between the West and Islam. Discussions cover the Ottoman Empire, showing its complicated relations with the West, down to the empire's abolition in 1923 and the consequent rise of a new system of Islamic states.

Legacy

The Western arts and humanities influence not only high culture but also today's mass culture. The Legacy feature draws from sources across the cultural spectrum to help readers recognize that today's culture did not emerge in a vacuum but that it grew from the matrix of the Western tradition.

Legacies from Prehistory and Near Eastern and Egyptian Civilization

Today one cannot turn on the news without being deluged with stories about the Near East or the Middle East. There was no "news" in antiquity, but things would have been the same. This old, vast, rich, and complex region has been simultaneously at the root and at the forefront of the West. Greeks, Romans, Muslims, Crusaders, and modern European imperialists have continually warred, traded, and exchanged ideas with the lands of Gilgamesh and the pharaohs. Apart from the vast forces of history, we have inherited much else from these people. Students still go to school to lean their "a, b, c's." High school and college students study circles by means of *pi*. The ancients used lunar calendars and most people today use solar ones. But the ancients gave us sixty-second minutes and sixty-minute hours. The Egyptians remain perennially fascinating. If a museum has a display of mummies, there will be lines at the door. We no longer bury people in pyramids, but the distinguished architect I. M. Pei built a glass one to serve as an entrance to the Louvre Museum in Paris. And in 1986 a rather forgettable rock group, the Bangles, had a hit song called "Walk Like an Egyptian." For a while, lots of young people gallivanted around imitating poses from Egyptian art.

Louvre Pyramid, Paris. 115' on each side, 70' high. This glass and steel pyramid designed by I. M. Pei (1917–) opened in 1989 as the main entrance to the Louvre Museum. Pei's pyramid was in part a homage to the precise geometric designs of the great French landscape architect, André LeNotre. And, in part, the pyramid's geometric planes echoed the articulated planes of the Louvre's roof and surrounding buildings.

Chapter Opening

Each chapter opening is organized around a specific artwork—either a painting, a sculpture, or a building. The artwork is carefully selected to embody many of a chapter's themes. The chapter opening sets the stage for a particular cultural period and draws readers into the text.

Temple of Hera, Paestum. Ca. 560–550 BCE. Limestone. Archaic temples set p used by the Greeks. The buildings were aligned east-west, with the entrance in altar stood before the entrance, and people gathered around it to share a sacrific enclosed space inside the temple's colonnade was off-limits except to the priests

The Aegean
The Minoans, the Mycenaeans, and the Greeks of the Archaic Age

Preview Questions

1. *What* key aspects of the Minoan and Mycenaean cultures lived on among the later Greeks?

2. *What* were the principal political and social achievements of the Greek Archaic period?

3. *How* do epic and lyric poetry differ from each other?

4. In *what* ways do Greek religion and philosophy differ from each other, and how do both differ from the achievements of the Mesopotamians and Egyptians?

Three significant peoples thrived in the Aegean basin: the Minoans, the Mycenaeans, and then the Greeks. The former two were the first to achieve civilization in Europe from about 2000 to 1200 BCE. On the island of Crete and in southern Greece, these peoples built complex societies only to fall, the Minoans to the Mycenaeans and the Mycenaeans to the Dorians. For about three centuries after 1100 BCE the Greek world was poor, isolated, and a cultural backwater. Then, between about 800 and 500 BCE the Greek world entered the Archaic period. *Archaios* in Greek means "ancient," or "beginning," and this was indeed the beginning of Greek history and culture in the strict sense (Timeline 2.1, Map 2.1). On rocky coasts and rugged islands and peninsulas, the peoples of the Aegean basin coaxed a subsistence living from the thin, stony soil and turned to the sea for trade, conquest, and expansion. From the Bronze Age to the Iron Age, Minoans, Mycenaeans, and Greeks interacted with and learned from the cultures that surrounded them, chiefly those of the Hittites and the Egyptians, but whether it was in systems of writing or forms of sculpture, Aegean peoples were never content merely to borrow. They always adapted, blended, and, finally, superseded the contributions of other cultures. The Greek genius was partly a matter of stunning originality and partly a matter of creative synthesis.

Preview Questions and Summary

Each chapter begins with a series of Preview Questions and ends with a Summary. This twin feature guides students to an understanding of cultural achievements within their historical setting—the thrust of the *Experience Humanities* program—and helps students master the complexities of the humanities story.

SUMMARY

Civilization arose in Europe in the Aegean world in the second millennium BCE, first on the island of Crete and then on the adjacent Greek mainland. The Minoans, peaceful folk and avid traders, built a complex society, erected majestic palaces, and created beautiful artworks. Influenced themselves by the Hittites and Egyptians, they in turn influenced the Myceneans. At several sites in the Peloponnesus the Mycenaeans, led by kings and warriors—the people we meet in Homer's *Iliad*—also built palaces and created works of art that still dazzle the eye. The identity of the Mycenaeans is still a little mysterious, but they did speak Greek and bequeathed to the later Greeks religious, mythical, and political ideas. After about 1100 the Greek world

plunged into darkness. Around 800 BCE the Archaic period opened and, over the next several generations, the Greek polis took shape and political power, no longer confined to kings and mounted warriors, came to be shared with farmers and merchants. Intercity rivalries and a rising population led many Greeks to leave home and settle in colonies around the Mediterranean shores. The polis was dynamic not only in political life but also in literature and the arts. Epic and lyric poetry flourished. Philosophy, as a rational way of understanding the world, appeared in several places. Sculptors began to capture the human form and to invest it with motion, with life. Builders created flexible, adaptable models.

Learning Through Maps

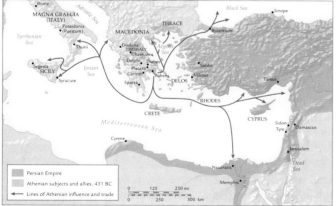

MAP 3.1 THE ATHENIAN EMPIRE, 431 BCE
This map shows the Athenian and Persian Empires on the eve of the Peloponnesian War. *1. Compare* the Athenian and Persian Empires, with respect to size and sea and land configuration. *2. Notice* the difference between Athenian and Spartan influence in the eastern Mediterranean. *3. How* did the locations of Athens and Sparta influence their respective naval and military policies? *4. In what way* did the distance between Sicily and Athens affect the course of the Peloponnesian War? *5. Observe* that Macedonia's proximity to Greece helped in its conquest of the late fourth century BCE.

This feature encourages students to develop geographical skills—highly desirable in this age of globalization. By interacting with map exercises and answering map-related questions, students learn to read maps and understand historical and cultural developments within a specific geographic setting.

Slice of Life features

The Slice of Life boxes offer students the opportunity to hear the voices of eyewitnesses to the historical and cultural events described in the text. These excerpts from primary sources and original documents bring history to life.

SLICE OF LIFE
A College Student's Letter Home

MARCUS, SON OF CICERO

Cicero's son Marcus, having spent all his money, wrote in 44 BCE to his father's secretary Tiro. Because of the press of public life, Cicero often relied on Tiro to handle his correspondence. Knowing that Tiro will relay a message to his father, Marcus offers assurances that he has mended his ways and describes his schoolwork.

That the rumors, which reach you about me, are gratifying and welcome to you, I have no doubt at all, my dearest Tiro; and I shall make every effort to guarantee that this opinion of me which is springing up more distinctly every day becomes twice as good. For that reason you may with unshaken confidence fulfill your promise of being the trumpeter of my reputation. For the errors of my youth have caused me such grief and agony that not only do my thoughts shrink from what I have done, but my very ears shrink from hearing it talked about.

I must tell you that my close attachment to Cratippus is not so much that of a pupil as that of a son. For not only do I attend his lectures with enjoyment, but I am greatly fascinated also by the charm of his personality. I spend whole days with him, and often a part of the night. Indeed, I implore him to dine with me as often as possible. Now that we have become so intimate,

he often strolls in upon us when we least expect him and are at dinner, and throwing to the wind all austerity as a philosopher, he bandies jokes with us in the most genial manner possible.

As to Bruttius, why should I mention him at all? There is never a moment when I allow him to leave my side. He leads a simple and austere life, but that the same time he is a most delightful man to live with. For there is no ban upon merry talk in our literary discussions and our daily joint researches. I have hired lodgings for him next door, and, as far as I can, alleviate his penury out of my own narrow means.

Besides all this I have begun to practice declaiming in Greek with Cassius; but I like practicing in Latin with Bruttius.

I beg of you to see that a secretary is sent to me as quickly as possible—best of all a Greek; for that will relieve me of a lot of trouble in writing out lecture notes.

Interpreting This Slice of Life

1. *How* was education conducted in Greece and Rome?
2. *How* credible does Marcus's letter to his father strike you?
3. *Compare and contrast* the life of a typical student today with that of Marcus.

Why Study Cultural History?
A Letter from the Authors

To be ignorant of what occurred before you were born is to remain always a child.

— CICERO, FIRST CENTURY BCE

Anyone who cannot give an account to oneself of the past three thousand years remains in darkness, without experience, living from day to day.

— GOETHE, NINETEENTH CENTURY CE

The underlying premise of this book is that some basic knowledge of the Western cultural heritage is necessary for those who want to become educated human beings in charge of their own destinies. If people are not educated into their place in human history—five thousand years of relatively uninterrupted, though sometimes topsy-turvy, developments—then they are rendered powerless, subject to passing fads and outlandish beliefs. They become vulnerable to the flattery of demagogues who promise heaven on earth, or they fall prey to the misconception that present-day events are unique, without precedent in history, or superior to everything that has gone before.

Perhaps the worst that can happen is to exist in a limbo of ignorance—in Goethe's words, "living from day to day." Without knowledge of the past and the perspective it brings, people may come to believe that their contemporary world will last forever, when in reality much of it is doomed to be forgotten. In contrast to the instant obsolescence of popular culture, the study of Western culture offers an alternative that has passed the unforgiving test of time. Long after today's heroes and celebrities have fallen into oblivion, the achievements of our artistic and literary ancestors—those who have forged the Western tradition—will remain. Their works echo down the ages and seem fresh in every period. The ancient Roman writer Seneca put it well when he wrote, in the first century CE, "Life is short but art is long."

When people realize that the rich legacy of Western culture is their own, their view of themselves and the times they live in can expand beyond the present moment. They find that they need not be confined by the limits of today but can draw on the creative insights of people who lived hundreds and even thousands of years ago. They discover that their own culture has a history and a context that give it meaning and shape. Studying and experiencing their cultural legacy can help them understand their place in today's world.

THE BOUNDARIES OF THE WEST

The subject of this text is Western culture, but what exactly do we mean, first, by "culture" and, second, by the "West"? *Culture* is a term with several meanings, but we use it here to mean the artistic and intellectual expressions of a people, their creative achievements. By the *West* we mean that part of the globe that lies west of Asia and Asia Minor and north of Africa, especially Europe—the geographical framework for much of this study.

The Western tradition is not confined exclusively to Europe as defined today, however. The contributions of peoples who lived beyond the boundaries of present-day Europe are also included in Western culture, either because they were forerunners of the West, such as those who created the first civilizations in Mesopotamia and Egypt, or because they were part of the West for periods of time, such as those who lived in the North African and Near Eastern lands bordering the Mediterranean Sea during the Roman and early Christian eras. Regardless of geography, Western culture draws deeply from ideals forged in these lands.

When areas that had been part of the Western tradition at one time were absorbed into other cultural traditions—as happened in the seventh century in Mesopotamia, Egypt, and North Africa when the people embraced the Muslim faith—then they are generally no longer included in Western cultural history. Because of the enormous influence of Islamic civilization on Western civilization, however, we include both an account of Islamic history and a description and appreciation of Islamic culture. In this edition, we have added a feature called The West and Islam to show the difficult relations between these two worldviews over the centuries. Different in many ways from our own, the rich tradition of Islam has an important place in today's world.

After about 1500, with voyages and explorations reaching the farthest parts of the globe, the European focus of Western culture that had held for centuries began to dissolve. Starting from this time, the almost exclusively European mold was broken, and Western values and ideals began to be exported throughout the world, largely through the efforts of missionaries, soldiers, colonists, and merchants. Coinciding with this development and further complicating the pattern of change were the actions of those who imported and enslaved countless numbers of black Africans to work on plantations in North and South America. The interplay of Western culture with many previously isolated cultures, whether desired or not, forever changed all who were touched by the process.

The Westernization of the globe that has been going on ever since 1500 is perhaps the dominant theme of our time. What human greed, missionary zeal, and dreams of empire failed to accomplish before 1900 has been achieved since through modern technology, the media, and popular culture. The world today is a global village, much of it dominated by Western values and styles of life. In our time, Westernization has become a two-way interchange. When artists and writers from other cultures adopt Western forms or ideas, they are not only Westernizing their own traditions but also injecting fresh sensibilities and habits of thought into the Western tradition. The globalization of culture means that a South American novel or a Japanese film can be as accessible to Western audiences as a European painting, and yet carry with it an intriguingly new vocabulary of cultural symbols and meanings.

HISTORICAL PERIODS AND CULTURAL STYLES

In cultural history, the past is often divided into historical periods and cultural styles. A historical period is an interval of time that has a certain unity because it is characterized by the prevalence of a unique culture, ideology, or technology, or because it is bounded by defining historical events, such as the death of a military leader like Alexander the Great or a political upheaval like the French Revolution. A cultural style is a combination of features of artistic or literary expression, execution, or performance that defines a particular school or era. A historical period may have the identical time frame as a cultural style, or it may embrace more than one style simultaneously or two styles successively. Each chapter of this survey focuses on a historical period and includes significant aspects of culture—usually the arts, architecture, literature, religion, music, and philosophy—organized around a discussion of the relevant style or styles appropriate to that time.

The survey begins with prehistory, the era before writing was invented, setting forth the emergence of human beings from an obscure past. After the appearance of writing in about 3000 BCE, the Western cultural heritage is divided into three sweeping historical periods: ancient, medieval, and modern.

The ancient period dates from 3000 BCE to 500 CE (Timeline 1). During these thirty-five hundred years the light of Western civilization begins to shine in Mesopotamia and Egypt, shines more brightly still in Greece and Rome, from the eighth century BCE, until it begins to dim with the collapse of the Roman Empire in 500 CE. Coinciding with these historical periods are the cultural styles of Mesopotamia; Egypt; Greece, including Archaic, classical (or Hellenic), and Hellenistic styles; and imperial Rome.

The medieval period, or the Middle Ages, covers events between 500 and 1500 CE, a one-thousand-year span that is further divided into three subperiods (Timeline 2). The early Middle Ages (500–1000) is typified by frequent barbarian invasions and political chaos so that civilization itself is threatened and barely survives. No single international style characterizes this turbulent period, though several regional styles flourish. The High Middle Ages (1000–1300) is a period of stability and the zenith of medieval culture. Two successive styles appear, the Romanesque and the Gothic, with the latter dominating culture for the rest of the medieval period. The late Middle Ages (1300–1500) is a transitional period in which the medieval age is dying and the modern age is struggling to be born.

The modern period begins in about 1400 (there is often overlap between historical periods) and continues today (Timeline 3). With the advent of the modern period, a new way of defining historical changes starts to make more sense—the division of history into movements, the activities of large groups of people united to achieve a common goal. The modern period consists of waves of movements that aim to change the world in some specific way.

The first modern movement is the Renaissance (1400–1600), or "rebirth," which attempts to revive the cultural values of ancient Greece and Rome. It is accompanied by two successive styles, Renaissance and

Timeline 1 THE ANCIENT WORLD

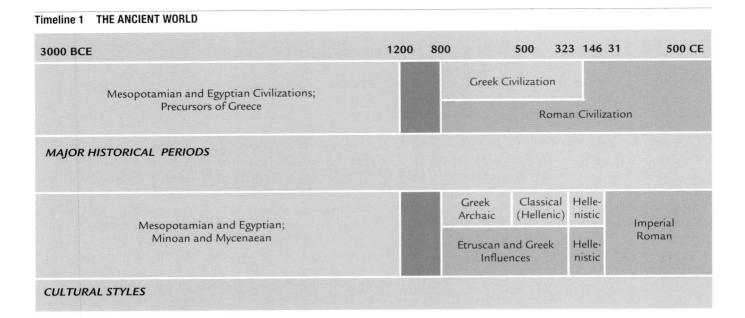

3000 BCE	1200	800	500	323	146	31	500 CE

Major Historical Periods

Mesopotamian and Egyptian Civilizations; Precursors of Greece

Greek Civilization

Roman Civilization

MAJOR HISTORICAL PERIODS

Cultural Styles

Mesopotamian and Egyptian; Minoan and Mycenaean

Greek Archaic | Classical (Hellenic) | Helle-nistic

Etruscan and Greek Influences | Helle-nistic

Imperial Roman

CULTURAL STYLES

mannerism. The next significant movement is the Reformation (1500–1600), which is dedicated to restoring Christianity to the ideals of the early church set forth in the Bible. Although it does not spawn a specific style, this religious upheaval does have a profound impact on the subjects of the arts and literature and the way they are expressed, especially in the mannerist style.

The Reformation is followed by the Scientific Revolution (1600–1700), a movement that results in the abandonment of ancient science and the birth of modern science. Radical in its conclusions, the Scientific Revolution is somewhat out of touch with the style of its age, which is known as the baroque. This magnificent style is devoted to overwhelming the senses through theatrical and sensuous effects and is associated with the attempts of the Roman Catholic Church to reassert its authority in the world.

The Scientific Revolution gives impetus to the Enlightenment (1700–1800), a movement that pledges to

reform politics and society according to the principles of the new science. In stylistic terms the eighteenth century is schizophrenic, dominated first by the rococo, an extravagant and fanciful style that represents the last phase of the baroque, and then by the neoclassical, a style inspired by the works of ancient Greece and Rome and reflective of the principles of the Scientific Revolution. Before the eighteenth century is over, the Enlightenment calls forth its antithesis, romanticism (1770–1870), a movement centered on feeling, fantasy, and everything that cannot be proven scientifically. The romantic style, marked by a revived taste for the Gothic and a love of nature, is the perfect accompaniment to this movement.

Toward the end of the nineteenth century, modernism (1870–1970) arises, bent on destroying every vestige of both the Greco-Roman tradition and the Christian faith and on fashioning new ways of understanding that are independent of the past. Since 1970, postmodernism has emerged, a movement that tries

Timeline 2 THE MEDIEVAL WORLD

500	1000	1150	1300	1500

Early Middle Ages | High Middle Ages | Late Middle Ages

MAJOR HISTORICAL PERIODS

Regional Styles | Romanesque | Gothic

CULTURAL STYLES

Timeline 3   THE MODERN WORLD

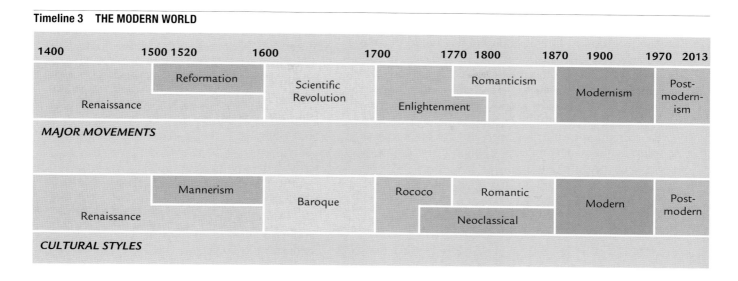

to make peace with the past by embracing old forms of expression while adopting a global and multi-voiced perspective. Although every cultural period is marked by innovation and creativity, our treatment of them in this book varies somewhat, with more space and greater weight given to the achievements of certain times. We make these adjustments because some periods or styles are more significant than others, especially in the defining influence that their achievements have had on our own era. For example, some styles seem to tower over the rest, such as classicism in fifth-century BCE Greece, the High Renaissance of sixteenth century Italy, and modernism in the mid–twentieth century, as compared with other styles, such as that of the early Middle Ages or the seventeenth-century baroque.

AN INTEGRATED APPROACH TO CULTURAL HISTORY

Our approach to the Western heritage in this book is to root cultural achievements in their historical settings, showing how the material conditions—the political, social, and economic events of each period—influenced their creation. About one-third of each chapter is devoted to an interpretive discussion of material history, and the remaining two-thirds are devoted to the arts, architecture, philosophy, religion, literature, and music of the period. These two aspects of history do not occur separately, of course, and one of our aims is to show how they are intertwined.

As just one example of this integrated approach, consider the Gothic cathedral, that lofty, light-filled house of worship marked by pointed arches, towering spires, and radiant stained-glass windows. Gothic cathedrals were erected during the High Middle Ages,

following a bleak period when urban life had virtually ceased. Although religion was still the dominant force in European life, trade was starting to flourish once again, town life was reviving, and urban dwellers were beginning to prosper. In part as testimonials to their new wealth, cities and towns commissioned architects and hired workers to erect these soaring churches, which dominated the landscape for miles around and proclaimed the economic well-being of their makers.

We adopt an integrated approach to Western culture not just in considering how the arts are related to material conditions but also in looking for the common themes, aspirations, and ideas that permeate the artistic and literary expressions of every era. The creative accomplishments of an age tend to reflect a shared perspective, even when that perspective is not explicitly recognized at the time. Thus, each period possesses a unique outlook that can be analyzed in the cultural record. A good example of this phenomenon is classical Greece in the fifth century BCE, when the ideal of moderation, or balance in all things, played a major role in sculpture, architecture, philosophy, religion, and tragic drama. The cultural record in other periods is not always as clear as that in ancient Greece, but shared qualities can often be uncovered that distinguish the varied aspects of culture in an era to form a unifying thread.

A corollary of this idea is that creative individuals and their works are very much influenced by the times in which they live. This is not to say that incomparable geniuses—such as Shakespeare in Renaissance England—do not appear and rise above their own ages, speaking directly to the human mind and heart in every age that follows. Yet even Shakespeare reflected the political attitudes and social patterns of his time. Though a man for the ages, he still regarded monarchy as the correct form of government and women as the inferiors of men.

A CHALLENGE TO THE READER

The purpose of all education is and should be self-knowledge. This goal was first established by the ancient Greeks in their injunction to "Know thyself," the inscription carved above the entrance to Apollo's temple at Delphi. Self-knowledge means awareness of oneself and one's place in society and the world. Reaching this goal is not easy, because becoming an educated human being is a lifelong process, requiring time, energy, and commitment. But all journeys begin with a single step, and we intend this volume as a first step toward understanding and defining oneself in terms of one's historical and cultural heritage. Our challenge to the reader is to use this book to begin the long journey to self-knowledge.

ACKNOWLEDGMENTS

We are grateful to many people for their help and support in this revision of *Experience Humanities.* Roy Matthews and DeWitt Platt continue to appreciate the many insightful comments of students and former students at Michigan State University over the years. Tom Noble is grateful to his thousands of students for all they have taught him over thirty-eight years. He is also pleased, and humbled, at being asked to lend a hand in crafting another new edition of a wonderful and successful book.

This edition is built on the mutual respect and friendship we three authors forged when we became a writing team in the previous edition. Once again, we are grateful to Art Pomponio for his reasonable responses, calming voice, and steady guidance as we met various deadlines. To our McGraw-Hill handlers, we are especially grateful to Nancy Crochiere for her smart leadership. From the start of this project, Nancy was on top of things, ably answering our many questions or helping us to find quick solutions to issues outside her sphere. Great job, Nancy! We also praise Susan Trentacosti, Lead Project Manager, for her skill in guiding us through the production process. We profited from the splendid work of Robin Sand, our Photo Researcher, and Jenna Caputo, our Literary Researcher. The finalizing of this revision was complicated by the impact of Hurricane Sandy, but the production team never wavered in its ability to prevail against the fallout from that storm. To Laura Wilk, we give a shout-out for her lead role in helping us transform our project in *Experience Humanities.* Thanks, Laura.

ACKNOWLEDGMENT OF REVIEWERS

This edition continues to reflect many insightful suggestions made by reviewers. The current edition has benefited from constructive and thorough evaluations offered by the faculty listed below. We believe that, because of the changes their reviews inspired, we have produced a better, more usable textbook. Reviewers, we salute you! The reviewers include the following:

Jonathan Austad, Chadron State College

Richard Baskin, Gordon College

Penelope A. Blake, Rock Valley College

Kurt Blaugher, Mount Saint Mary's College

Dan Brooks, Aquinas College–Michigan

John Chamberlain, Saint Petersburg College–Gibbs

Cynthia Clements, Richland College

Kevin DeLapp, Converse College

May Dubois, West Los Angeles College

Andrew J. Grover, Thiel College

Richard Hall, Texas State University–San Marcos

John Hardin, Hillsborough Community College–Brandon

Jason Horn, Gordon College

Luke Howard, Brigham Young University–Provo

Cheryl Hughes, Tulsa Community College

Derek Jensen, Brigham Young University–Idaho

Prudence Jones, Montclair State University

Susan Jones, Palm Beach Atlantic University

Kim Justesen, Utah Career College

Richard Kortum, East Tennessee State University

Barbara Kramer, Santa Fe Community College

Connie LaMarca-Frankel, Pasco-Hernando Community College

Diana Lurz, Rogers State University

Ruth Miller, Diablo Valley College

James Mock, University of Central Oklahoma

Margaret Worsham Musgrove, University of Central Oklahoma

Victoria Neubeck-O'Connor, Moraine Valley Community College

Kaliopi Pappas, San Joaquin Delta College

Douglass Scott, Chattanooga State Tech

Sonia Sorrell, Pepperdine University

Deborah Sowell, Brigham Young University–Provo

Michael Sparks, Wallace State University

Alice Taylor, West Los Angeles College

Margaret Urie, University of Nevada–Reno

Theresa A. Vaughan, University of Central Oklahoma

Paul B. Weinstein, The University of Akron Wayne College

Jason Whitmarsh, St. John's River Community College

TEACHING AND LEARNING WITH *EXPERIENCE HUMANITIES*

Online Learning Center

(www.mhhe.com/matthewsEH)

The Online Learning Center for *Experience Humanities* includes a variety of helpful teaching resources: Instructors Manual, PowerPoint Presentations, and Test Bank

CourseSmart

This text is available as an eTextbook at www.Course Smart.com. At CourseSmart, students can take advantage of significant savings off the cost of a print textbook, reduce their impact on the environment, and gain access to powerful Web tools for student learning. You can view CourseSmart eTextbooks online or download them to a computer. CourseSmart eTextbooks allow students to do full text searches, add highlighting and notes, and share notes with classmates. Visit www.CourseSmart.com to learn more and try a sample chapter.

create (www.mcgrawhillcreate.com)

Design your own ideal course materials with McGraw-Hill's Create™. Rearrange or omit chapters, combine material from other sources, upload your syllabus or any other content you have written to make the perfect resource for your students. Search thousands of leading McGraw-Hill textbooks to find the best content for your students; then arrange it to fit your teaching style. You can even personalize your book's appearance by selecting the cover and adding your name, school, and course information. When you order a Create book, you receive a complimentary review copy. Get a printed copy in three to five business days, or an electronic copy via e-mail in about an hour. Register today at www.mcgrawhillcreate.com.

Tegrity campus

Tegrity is a service that makes class time available around the clock. It automatically captures every lecture in a searchable format for students to review when they study and complete assignments. With a simple one-click start-and-stop process, you capture all computer screens and corresponding audio. Students can replay any part of any class with easy-to-use browser-based viewing on a PC or Mac. With Tegrity Campus, students quickly recall key moments by using Tegrity Campus's unique search feature, which lets them efficiently find what they need, when they need it, across an entire semester of class recordings. To learn more about Tegrity, watch a two-minute Flash demo at http://tegritycampus.mhhe.com.

Campus

McGraw-Hill Campus is a new one-stop teaching and learning experience available to users of any learning management system. This institutional service allows faculty and students to enjoy single sign-on (SSO) access to all McGraw-Hill Higher Education materials, including the award-winning McGraw-Hill Connect® platform, from directly within the institution's Web site.

Readings to Accompany *Experience Humanities*

The selections of primary source materials are arranged chronologically to follow the twenty-three chapters of the text, and are divided into two volumes. Volume I covers ancient Mesopotamia through the Renaissance; Volume II, the Renaissance into the twenty-first century. This anthology gives students access to our literary and philosophical heritage, allowing them to experience firsthand the ideas and voices of the great writers and thinkers of the Western tradition.

A Humanities Primer
How to Understand the Arts

INTRODUCTION

We can all appreciate the arts. We can find pleasure or interest in paintings, music, poems, novels, films, and other art forms, both contemporary and historical. We don't need to know very much about art to know what we like, because we bring ourselves to the work: What we like has as much to do with who we are as with the art itself.

Many of us, for example, will respond positively to a painting like Leonardo da Vinci's *The Virgin of the Rocks.* The faces of the Madonna and angel are lovely; we may have seen images like these on Christmas cards or in other commercial reproductions. We respond with what English poet William Wordsworth calls the "first careless rapture," which activates our imaginations and establishes a connection between us and the work of art. However, if this is all we see, if we never move from a subjective reaction, we can only appreciate the surface, the immediate form, and then, perhaps subconsciously, accept without question the values it implies. We appreciate, but we do not understand.

Sometimes we cannot appreciate because we do not understand. We may reject Picasso's *Les Demoiselles d'Avignon,* for it presents us with images of women that we may not be able to recognize. These women may make us uncomfortable, and the values they imply may frighten us rather than please or reassure us. Rather than rapture, we may experience disgust; but when we realize that this painting is considered a groundbreaking work, we may wonder what we're missing and be willing to look deeper. (*The Virgin of the Rocks* and *Les Demoiselles d'Avignon* are discussed in the text on pages 317–318 and pages 551–552, respectively.)

To understand a work of art (a building, a poem, a song, a symphony), we need to keep our "rapture" (our emotional response and connection) but make it less "careless," less superficial and subjective, less restricted to that which we recognize. We need to enrich our appreciation by searching for a meaning that goes beyond ourselves and which involves understanding:

- The intent or the goal of the artist
- The elements of form present in the work
- The ways in which the various elements contribute to the artist's goal

Leonardo da Vinci. *The Virgin of the Rocks.*

- The context within which the artwork evolved
- The connections of the work to other works

APPROACHES TO THE ANALYSIS OF LITERATURE, ART, AND MUSIC

To analyze a work of art, we want to identify the intent of the work, and we want to evaluate its execution. Thus, we can examine the formal elements of the work—an approach known as formalism—and we can explore its context—known as contextualism.

Formalism

A formal analysis is concerned with the aesthetic (artistic) elements of a work separate from context. This type of analysis focuses on medium and technique:

- A formal analysis of a painting, sculpture, or architectural structure examines its line, shape, color, texture, and composition, as well as the artist's technical ability within the medium used; it is not concerned with anything extraneous to the work itself.
- A formal analysis of a literary work, such as a short story or novel, explores the relationships among theme, plot, characters, and setting, as well as how well the resources of language—word choice, tone, imagery, and symbol—are used to support the other elements.
- A formal analysis of a film explores theme, plot, characters (as developed both verbally and nonverbally), and setting, as well as how the resources of cinematography—camera techniques, lighting, sound, editing, and costumes—support the other elements.

A formal analysis of *The Virgin of the Rocks* examines the artist's use of perspective, the arrangement of figures as they relate to each other and to the grotto that surrounds them, the technical use of color and line, and the dramatic interplay of light and shadow (known as *chiaroscuro*). The same technical considerations are explored in a formal analysis of *Les Demoiselles d'Avignon*. That the two paintings were completed in 1483 and 1907, respectively, is important only in terms of the technology and mediums available to the artists. In a formal analysis, time and place exist only within the work.

Contextualism

Unlike formalism, contextualism requires that a work be understood in its time and place. Contextual analysis focuses on what is outside the work:

- The artistic, social, cultural, historical, and political forces, events, and trends

- The artist's intent and motives in creating the work
- How the work fits in with other works of the same genre of the same or different eras
- How the work fits in with the rest of the artist's body of work

A contextual analysis of the da Vinci and Picasso paintings would include information about where and when each painting was completed, the conditions from which it arose, the prevailing artistic styles of the times, the life circumstances of the artists, and so on. The paintings alone do not provide enough information for contextual inquiry. Similarly, contextual analysis of a novel by Dostoyevsky would consider both his personal circumstances and the conditions in Russia and Europe when he wrote. A contextual analysis of a chorale and fugue by Bach would include information on Bach's life, his religious beliefs, and the political climate of Germany in the eighteenth century.

An Integrated Approach

In a strictly contextual analysis of an artwork, the work itself can sometimes be lost in the exploration of context. In a strictly formal analysis, important knowledge that can contribute to understanding may remain unknown. The most effective analyses, therefore, combine and integrate the two approaches, examining the formal elements of the work and exploring the context within which it was created. A work of art, whether a poem or a painting, a cathedral or a cantata,

PABLO PICASSO. *Les Demoiselles d'Avignon.*

is a complex entity, as are the relationships it fosters between the artist and the art and between the art and its audience. The integrative approach recognizes these relationships and their complexity. This is the approach to artistic and cultural analysis most frequently used in *Experience Humanities.*

A Variety of Perspectives

Many students and critics of culture are also interested in looking at things from a particular perspective, a set of interests or a way of thinking that informs and influences their investigations and interpretations. Common perspectives are the psychological, the feminist, the religious, the economic, and the historical.

- A *psychological* perspective looks for meaning in the psychological features of the work, such as sexual and symbolic associations—in effect, a kind of retroactive psychological analysis of the artist. This perspective might also examine the facial expressions, gestures, and body positions of Mary and the angel in *The Virgin of the Rocks,* or it might be interested in da Vinci's attitudes toward women and his relationship with them.

- A *feminist* perspective examines the art itself and the context in which it arises from a woman's point of view. This perspective also asks how the work depicts women, what it says about women and their relationships in general, and how it may or may not reflect a patriarchal society. Many critics have discussed the apparent hatred of women that seems evident in Picasso's *Les Demoiselles d'Avignon.* At the same time, the work, in its size (8 feet by 7 feet 8 inches) and in the unblinking attitude of its subjects, suggests that these women have a kind of raw power. Feminist critics focus on such considerations.

- A *religious* perspective is often appropriate when a work of art originates in a religious context. The soaring spires and cruciform floor plans of medieval cathedrals reveal religious meaning, as do Renaissance paintings depicting biblical characters. Religious analyses look to the use of symbolism, the representation of theological doctrines and beliefs, and intercultural connections and influences for meaning.

- An *economic* perspective on a work of art focuses on its economic content—the roles and relationships associated with wealth. Often drawing upon Marx's contention that class is the defining consideration in all human relationships and endeavors, an economic analysis examines both purpose and content: the artwork created as a display of power by the rich, as a depiction of people of different classes, and as an indicator of the distribution of wealth.

- Perhaps the most encompassing of all perspectives is the historical, because it includes explorations of psychological, religious, and economic issues, as well as questions about class and gender in various times and places. Historical analysis requires an understanding of the significant events of the time and how they affect the individual and shape the culture. *Experience Humanities* most often takes a historical perspective in its views of art and culture.

The Vocabulary of Analysis

Certain terms and concepts are fundamental to the analysis of any artwork:

- **Audience** is the group for whom a work of art, architecture, literature, drama, film, or music is intended. The audience may be a single person, a small group of people, or a special group with common interests or education.

- **Composition** is the arrangement of constituent elements in an individual work. In music, composition also refers to the process of creating the work.

- **Content** is the subject matter of the work; content can be based on mythology, religion, history, current events, personal history, or almost any idea or feeling deemed appropriate by the artist.

- **Context** is the setting in which the art arose, its own time and place. Context includes the political, economic, social, and cultural conditions of the time; it can also include the personal conditions and circumstances that shape the artist's vision.

- A **convention** is an agreed-upon practice, device, technique, or form. A sonnet, for example, is a fourteen-line poem with certain specified rhyme schemes. A poem is not a sonnet unless it follows this formal convention. A convention of the theater is the "willing suspension of disbelief": we know that the events taking place before our eyes are not real, but we agree to believe in them for the duration of the play.

- **Genre** is the type or class to which a work of art, literature, drama, or music belongs, depending on its style, form, or content. In literature, for example, the novel is a genre in itself; the short story is another genre. In music, symphonies, operas, and tone poems are all different genres.

- The **medium** is the material from which an art object is made—marble or bronze, for example, in sculpture, or watercolors or oils in painting. (The plural of *medium* in this sense is often *mediums;* when *medium* is used to refer to a means of mass communication, such as radio or television, the plural is *media.*)

- **Style** is the combination of distinctive elements of creative execution and expression, in terms of both form and content. Artists, artistic schools, movements, and periods can be characterized by their style. Styles often evolve out of existing styles, or in reaction to styles that are perceived as worn out or excessive.

- **Technique** refers to the systematic procedure whereby a particular creative task is performed. For example, a dancer's technique is the way he or she executes leaps and turns; a painter's technique is the way he or she applies paint to a canvas with broad, swirling brushstrokes.

- The **theme** is the dominant idea of a work, the message or emotion the artist intends to convey. The theme, then, is the embodiment of the artist's intent. In a novel, for example, the theme is the abstract concept that is made concrete by character, plot, setting, and other linguistic and structural elements of the work.

These general concepts and terms are supplemented by the more specific terms that will be introduced in the following literary, artistic, and musical sections.

LITERARY ANALYSIS

Literary analysis begins with a consideration of various literary genres and forms. A work of literature is written either in **prose,** the ordinary language used in speaking and writing, or in **poetry,** a more imaginative and concentrated form of expression usually marked by meter, rhythm, or rhyme. Prose is often divided into nonfiction (essays, biography, autobiography) and fiction (short stories, novels).

In literature, *genre* refers both to form—essay, short story, novel, poem, play, film script, television script—and to specific type within a form—tragedy, comedy, epic, and lyric.

- **Tragedy,** according to Aristotle, must have a tragic hero—a person of high stature who is brought down by his or her own excessive pride *(hubris);* this person doesn't necessarily die at the end, but whatever his or her greatness was based upon is lost.

- **Comedy** is a story with a complicated and amusing plot; it usually ends with a happy and peaceful resolution of any conflicts.

- An **epic** poem, novel, or film is a relatively long recounting of the life of a hero or the glorious history of a people.

- A **lyric** poem is a short, subjective poem usually expressing an intense personal emotion.

- **Theme** is the message or emotion that the author wishes to convey. In an essay the theme is articulated as the thesis: the idea or conclusion that the essay will prove or support. In a novel, story, or play, we infer the theme from the content and the development of ideas and imagery.

- **Plot,** in fiction, is the action of the story. There may be a primary plot that becomes the vehicle by which the theme is expressed, with subplots related to secondary (or even tertiary) themes. Plot can be evaluated by how well it supports the theme.

- **Characters** provide the human focus, the embodiment, of the theme; they act out and are affected by the plot. The protagonist, or primary character, of the work is changed by the dramatic action of the plot and thus is a dynamic character; static characters remain unchanged throughout the story. An antagonist is a character in direct opposition to the protagonist. Some characters are stock characters, representing a type rather than an individual human being.

- The **setting** is the background against which the action takes place. It can include the geographical location, the environment (political, social, economic) in which the characters live, the historical time in which the action takes place, and the culture and customs of the time, place, and people.

- The **narrator** tells the story or poem from his or her point of view. The narrator is not necessarily identical with the author of the work. The narrator (or **narrative voice**) can be examined and analyzed like any other element of the work. When a narrator seems to know everything and is not limited by time or place, the work has an omniscient point of view. Such a narrator tells us what everyone is thinking, feeling, and doing. When the story is told from the perspective of a single character who can relate only what he or she knows or witnesses, the work has a first-person point of view. Such a narrator is limited in his or her understanding. Thus, we need to consider the narrator in order to judge how accurate or complete the narrative is.

A literary analysis of a drama, whether a play for the stage or a film script, will consider not only the elements already mentioned—theme, plot, character, setting, language, and so on—but also the technical considerations specific to the form. In theater, these would include the work of the director, who interprets the play and directs the actors, as well as stage design, light and sound design, costumes, makeup, and so on. In film, technical considerations would include direction, editing, cinematography, musical score, special effects, and so on.

Let's turn now to a poem by Shakespeare and see how to approach it to enrich our understanding. Identifying a poem's intent and evaluating its execution is called an *explication*, from the French *explication de texte*. An explication is a detailed analysis of a poem's meaning, focusing on narrative voice, setting, rhyme, meter, words, and images. An explication begins with what is immediately evident about the poem as a whole, followed by a more careful examination of its parts.

William Shakespeare (1564–1616) was not just a great playwright; he was also a great poet. His works portray human emotions, motives, and relationships that we recognize today as well as the conditions and concerns of his time. In this sense, they are an example of aesthetic universality, the enduring connection between a work of art and its audience.

Shakespeare's sonnets are his most personal work. Scholars disagree about whether they are generic love poems or are addressed to a specific person and, if the latter, who that person might be. Formally, an English (or Shakespearean) sonnet is a 14-line poem consisting of three 4-line stanzas, or quatrains, each with its own rhyme scheme, and a concluding 2-line stanza, or couplet, that provides commentary on the preceding stanzas. The rhyme scheme in a Shakespearean sonnet is abab cdcd efef gg; that is, the first and third lines of each quatrain rhyme with each other, as do the second and fourth lines, though the rhymes are different in each quatrain. The last two lines rhyme with each other.

The meter of most Shakespearean sonnets is iambic pentameter; that is, each line has five feet, or units ("pentameter"), and each foot consists of an iamb, an unaccented syllable followed by an accented syllable (as in *alone*). An example of iambic pentameter is "My mistress' eyes are nothing like the sun"; each foot consists of an unaccented and an accented syllable, and there are five feet. Unrhymed iambic pentameter—the verse of most of Shakespeare's plays—is known as **blank verse.**

Sonnet 130 ("My mistress' eyes are nothing like the sun") is a poem that not only illustrates sonnet form but also showcases Shakespeare's wit and his attitude toward certain conventions of his time. The poem was originally written in Elizabethan English, which looks and sounds quite different from modern English. We reproduce it in modern English, as is customary today for Shakespeare's works.

Sonnet 130

My mistress' eyes are nothing like the sun;
Coral is far more red than her lips' red;
If snow be white, why then her breasts are dun;
If hairs be wires, black wires grow on her head.
I have seen roses damask'd, red and white,
But no such roses see I in her cheeks,
And in some perfumes is there more delight
Than in the breath that from my mistress reeks.
I love to hear her speak, yet well I know
That music hath a far more pleasing sound;
I grant I never saw a goddess go,
My mistress when she walks treads on the ground.
And yet, by heaven, I think my love as rare
As any she belied with false compare.

Because the poet's intent may not be immediately evident, paraphrasing each line or stanza can point the reader to the theme or meaning intended by the poet. Let's begin, then, by paraphrasing the lines:

My mistress' eyes are nothing like the sun;
The speaker's lover's eyes are not bright.
Coral is far more red than her lips' red;
Her lips are not very red, certainly not as red as coral.
If snow be white, why then her breasts are dun;
Her breasts are mottled in color, not as white as snow.
If hairs be wires, black wires grow on her head.
Her hair is black (not blond, as was the conventional beauty standard then, when poets referred to women's hair as "golden wires").
I have seen roses damask'd, red and white,
But no such roses see I in her cheeks,
Her cheeks are not rosy.
And in some perfumes is there more delight
Than in the breath that from my mistress reeks.
Her breath doesn't smell as sweet as perfume.
I love to hear her speak, yet well I know
That music hath a far more pleasing sound;
Her voice doesn't sound as melodious as music.
I grant I never saw a goddess go,
My mistress when she walks treads on the ground.
Although the speaker has never seen a goddess walk, he knows his lover does not float above ground, as goddesses are supposed to do, but walks on the ground, a mortal woman.
And yet, by heaven, I think my love as rare
As any she belied with false compare.
His lover is as rare and valuable as any idealized woman glorified by false poetic comparisons.

Remember that to analyze a poem, we ask questions like, What is the theme of the poem, the poet's intent? How does Shakespeare support his point with specific images? From the paraphrased lines it is clear that the narrator is stating that his love is a real woman who walks upon the ground, not an unattainable ideal to be worshiped from afar. Idealized qualities are irrelevant to how he feels about her; the qualities he loves are the ones that make her human.

Closely examining each line of a poem helps to reveal the rhyme scheme (abab cdcd efef gg), the meter (iambic pentameter), and thus the form of the poem (sonnet). Explication of the formal elements of the poem would also include examining the use of language (such as word choice, imagery, comparisons, metaphors), the tone of the narrative voice, and so on.

To understand the context of the poem, we would consider the cultural climate of the time (was "courtly love" a prevalent cultural theme?); common contemporary poetic conventions (were many other poets proclaiming their eternal love for idealized women?); and the political, social, and economic conditions (what roles were open to women in Elizabethan England, and how were they changing? What influence might Queen Elizabeth have had on the poet's point of view? What comments about his society is Shakespeare making?).

Finally, we might consider how honest and accurate we find the emotional content of the poem to be, how relevant its truth. Are Shakespeare's observations germane to today, a time when the mass media present us with a nearly unattainable ideal as the epitome of female beauty?

FINE ARTS ANALYSIS

As with literature, knowledge of a particular vocabulary helps us "speak the language" of art critics. The terms introduced here are in addition to those discussed earlier, such as *medium* and *technique*. They apply to all the visual arts, including drawing and painting, sculpture—the art of shaping material (such as wood, stone, or marble) into three-dimensional works of art—and architecture—the art and science of designing, planning, and building structures, usually for human habitation. In architecture, the critic would also pay attention to the blending of artistry and functionality (how well the structure fulfills its purpose).

- **Representational art** is true to human perception and presents a likeness of the world much as it appears to the naked eye.
- **Perspective** is the appearance of depth and distance on a two-dimensional surface.
- **Abstract art** presents a subjective view of the world, the artist's emotions or ideas; some abstract art simply presents color, line, or shape for its own sake.

The formal elements of visual art include the following:

- **Line** is the mark made by the artist, whether with pencil, pen, or paintbrush. Lines can be straight or curved, thick or thin, light or dark, spare or plentiful.
- **Color** is the use in the artwork of hues found in nature; color can enhance the sense of reality presented in a visual image, or it can distort it, depending on how it is used. The primary colors are red, blue, and yellow, and the secondary colors are orange (a combination of red and yellow), green (a combination of yellow and blue), and purple (a combination of blue and red).
- **Composition** is the artist's arrangement of elements within the artwork. Through the composition the artist leads us to see the artwork in a particular way.
- The **setting** of an artwork is the time and place depicted in a representational work, as defined by visual cues, such as the people, their dress, their activity, the time of day, and the season of the year.

Interpreting Art

The Interpreting Art feature helps students to understand the visual arts and architecture. Drawing on the analytical terms and categories of the fine arts,

which are set forth above, this feature serves as a tool to further unify the text. Following an integrative approach to an understanding of a work of art or architecture—blending formal analysis with contextual analysis—our Interpreting Art feature offers a model that students can apply to any work of art, whether in the textbook or when they visit art galleries and museums. To demonstrate this new feature, we offer the example of *Cow's Skull with Calico Roses* by the American artist Georgia O'Keeffe (1887–1986), painted in 1931.

MUSICAL ANALYSIS

Like literature and art, music has its own vocabulary, and we need to be familiar with it in order to analyze a composition.

- **Sacred music** refers to religious music, such as Gregorian chants, Masses, requiems, cantatas, and hymns.
- **Secular music** is the term used to describe symphonies, songs, operas, dances, and other nonsacred musical works.
- **Vocal music** is music that is sung and generally has lyrics (words).
- **Choral music** is vocal music performed by a group of singers.
- **Instrumental music** is music that is written for and performed on instruments.
- **Form,** in music, means the particular structure or arrangement of elements by the composer in the musical composition. Musical forms include symphonies, songs, concertos, string quartets, sonatas, Masses, and operas.
- **Tone** is a musical sound of definite pitch (pitch is determined by the frequency of the air waves producing the sound). The term *tone* can also refer to the quality of a sound.
- A **scale** is a set pattern of tones (or notes) arranged from low to high (or high to low). The modern Western scale is the familiar do, re, mi, fa, sol, la, ti, do, with half steps in between the tones. In other cultures, more or fewer tones may be distinguished in a scale.
- **Tempo** is the rate of speed of a musical passage, usually set or suggested by the composer.
- **Texture** describes the number and nature of the voices or instruments employed and how the parts are combined. In music, a theme is a characteristic musical idea on which a composition is built or developed.
- **Melody** is a succession of musical tones, usually having a distinctive musical shape, or line, and a definite rhythm (the recurrent alternation of accented and unaccented beats).

Interpreting Art

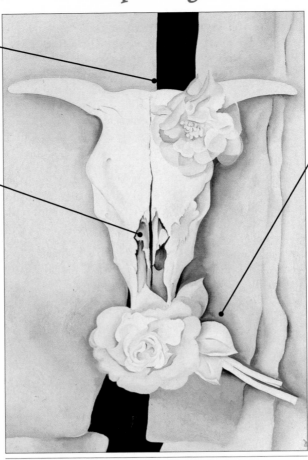

Form Verticality is the dominant form, as in the vertical line of the skull, the skull's vertical crack, and the band of black, running from top to bottom. The skull's horns form a horizontal line, thus adding a crosslike shape.

Color The colors are neutral-shades of black, gray, cream, and white. Inside the skull, darker hues-tan and ochre-cause it to stand out from the muted background.

Setting The cow's skull evokes the stark desert landscape of Taos, New Mexico, where the work was painted.

Religious Perspective Renaissance artists used human skulls to remind viewers of their mortality, and, here, the cow's skull suggests the unforgiving nature of the desert.

Psychological Perspective The overall feeling is one of contemplation: the pairing of incongruous objects-cow's skull and artificial flowers-reminds the viewer of the intimate relationships between life and death, beauty and ugliness, art and nature.

Depth Perception The work's surface is shallow and flat, a typical feature of modernist art. The skull appears to float in the foreground, and, at the same time, the black band seems to open into a mysterious space that recedes from the viewer.

GEORGIA O'KEEFFE. *Cow's Skull with Calico Roses.* Oil on canvas, 36 × 24". **1931.** Georgia O'Keeffe's passion for nature was inspired by a childhood on a Wisconsin farm. Her mature artistic style blended realism and abstraction. Her artistic trademark, as shown here: the abstraction of an object from nature, which she then painted according to her inner vision.

- **Harmony** is the simultaneous combination of two or more tones, producing a chord. More generally, harmony refers to the choral characteristics of a work and the way in which chords interact with one another.

With these basic categories in mind, let's consider a well-known musical work, *Rhapsody in Blue,* by George Gershwin (1898–1937). Even if you don't know this piece by name, it's very likely that you have heard it. It has been used in ads and in the sound tracks of many movies, including *Fantasia 2000;* it is also a standard accompaniment to images of New York City.

Imagine that you're seated in a concert hall and hearing this piece performed by a symphony orchestra (probably a "pops" orchestra, one that performs more popular classical music). When listening to a new piece of music or one you are not familiar with, it's a good idea to try to get a sense of its general mood and character—again, focusing on the creator's intent. What emotions or ideas is the composer trying to convey? What musical elements does the composer use to execute that intent?

You will notice, first of all, that the work is written for a small orchestra and a solo piano, the same instrumental configuration you would expect for a classical piano concerto (a concerto is a work for one or a few instruments and an orchestra, with much of its interest coming from the contrasts between the solo voice and the ensemble voice). But the opening notes of *Rhapsody in Blue* reveal something other than classical intentions: a solo clarinet begins low and sweeps up the scale in a seemingly endless "smear" of sound, finally reaching a high note, briefly holding it, and then plunging into the playful, zigzag melody that becomes one of the major themes of the work. Within moments, the orchestra enters and repeats the theme in the strings and brass, to be followed by the entry of the solo piano. Throughout the work, piano and orchestra alternate and combine to sing out beautiful melodies and create a varied and colorful texture. Variety also comes from different instrumentation of the themes and tunes, played first by a slinky muted trumpet, then by a sweet solo violin, later by a whole lush string section or a brash horn section.

You'll notice, too, the constant changes in tempo, now slower, now faster, almost as if the work is being improvised. Complex, syncopated, off-the-beat rhythms give the piece a jazzy feeling, and the combination of tones evokes the blues, a style of music in which certain notes are "bent," or lowered slightly in pitch, creating a particular sound and mood. The general feeling of the piece is upbeat, exciting, energetic, suggestive of a bustling city busy with people on the go. It may also make you think of Fred Astaire and Ginger Rogers movies you've seen on late-night TV—sophisticated, playful, casually elegant—and in fact, Gershwin wrote the music for some of their films.

What can we learn about this work from its title? Musical works often reveal their form in their titles (Fifth Symphony, Violin Concerto in D, and so on). A rhapsody is a composition of irregular form with an improvisatory character. Although you may have heard themes, repetitions, and echoes in *Rhapsody in Blue,* you probably were not able to discern a regular form such as might be apparent in a classical sonata or symphony. The word *rhapsody* also suggests rapture, elation, bliss, ecstasy—perhaps the feelings conveyed by that soaring first phrase on the clarinet. *Blue,* on the other hand, suggests the melancholy of the blues. The dissonance created by the combination of the two terms—like the combinations and contrasts in the music—creates an energetic tension that arouses our curiosity and heightens our interest.

In making these observations about *Rhapsody in Blue,* we've been noticing many of the formal elements of a musical work and answering questions that can be asked about any composition: What is the form of the work? What kind of instrumentation has the composer chosen? What is the primary melodic theme of the work? What tempos are used? How do the instruments or voices work together to create the texture? What is the overall mood of the piece—joyful, sad, calm, wild, a combination?

Now, at your imaginary concert, there may be notes in the program that will provide you with some context for the work. You will find that George Gershwin was a gifted and classically trained pianist who quit school at fifteen and went to work in Tin Pan Alley, a district in New York City where popular songs were written and published. His goal in writing *Rhapsody in Blue* (1924) was to blend classical and popular music, to put the energy and style of jazz into a symphonic format. Many listeners "see" and "hear" New York City in this piece. Gershwin created his own unique idiom, a fast-paced blend of rhythm, melody, and harmony that followed certain rules of composition but gave the impression of improvisation. He went on to write musicals, more serious compositions like the opera *Porgy and Bess,* and music for Hollywood films, all in his distinctive style. Information like this can help you begin to compare *Rhapsody in Blue* both with other works of the time and with other works by Gershwin. As in any analysis, integrating the formal and the contextual rounds out your interpretation and understanding of the work.

CONCLUSION

The foregoing materials should give you some ideas about how literature, art, and music can be approached in productive ways. By taking the time to look more closely, we gain access to the great works of our culture. This statement leads us to another issue: What makes a work "great"? Why do some works of art have relevance long beyond their time, while others are forgotten soon after their designated "fifteen minutes of fame"? These questions have been debated throughout history. One answer is that great art reflects some truth of human experience that speaks to us across the centuries. The voice of Shakespeare, the paintings of Georgia O'Keeffe, and the music of George Gershwin have a universal quality that doesn't depend on the styles of the time. Great art also enriches us and makes us feel that we share a little more of the human experience than we did before.

As both a student of the humanities and an audience member, you have the opportunity to appreciate and understand the arts. Despite the formal nature of academic inquiry, an aesthetic analysis is a personal endeavor. In looking closely at a creative work, seeking the creator's intent and evaluating its execution, you enrich your appreciation of the work with understanding; you bring the emotional reaction you first experienced to its intellectual completion. As twentieth-century composer Arnold Schoenberg once wrote, "You get from a work about as much as you are able to give to it yourself." This primer has been intended to help you learn how to bring more of yourself to works of art, to couple your subjective appreciation with intellectual understanding. With these tools in hand, you won't have to say you don't know much about art but you know what you like; you will be able to say you know *about* what you like.

Experience Humanities

The Great Sphinx. Ca. 2560 BCE. 65′ high × 240′ long. Giza, Egypt. Huge and majestic, the Great Sphinx, a lion with a man's face, stood silent sentinel before the Great Pyramid.

Prehistory and the Rise of Civilization in the Near East and Egypt

Preview Questions

1. *What* are the chief signs of the emergence of civilization in Mesopotamia and Egypt?

2. *How* did geography influence the development of government, society, and culture in Mesopotamia and Egypt?

3. *How* were the cultures of Mesopotamia and Egypt alike and different?

For some two hundred years, it has been customary to speak of "Western civilization" and, for a somewhat shorter time, to speak of the many cultures that have made up Western civilization. What do these terms mean? When people first spoke about "the West," they were referring to western Europe. But western Europe was the product of cultures and peoples who had lived around the Mediterranean Sea in antiquity, and eventually Europe exported its cultures to much of the rest of the globe. "West" is therefore as much an idea as a place. **Civilization** is in a way the largest unit within which any one person might feel comfortable. It is an organizing principle that implies common institutions, economic systems, social structures, and values that extend over space and time. **Culture** is a more restricted term. On one very general level, it means high culture: the fine arts and philosophy, for example. On another level, it means the totality of expressions and behaviors that characterize a readily identifiable group of people in a specific place and time. Every civilization enfolds many cultures, at any one time and across long periods of time. Mesopotamia and Egypt, like Greece and Rome, were cultures within ancient Western civilization, and they contributed powerfully to an enduring tradition.

The two structures to the left, the Great Sphinx and one of the Great Pyramids, are probably familiar to readers of this book. Why should that be so? After all, they are five thousand years old. The reasons are many, but among the most prominent are history and tradition. These monuments have a history and they have entered the Western tradition. They have become a part of who we are. Standing as they do at the beginning of Western civilization, they invite us to reflect on the people who erected them. What kinds of political power, social structure, and wealth permitted such monuments? What do they tell us about those people's tastes and sensibilities? Why did they choose to represent themselves in this way?

PREHISTORY AND EARLY CULTURES

Human beings long preceded culture and civilization. The remote ancestors of modern human beings emerged in Africa at least four million years ago. That is merely a moment in comparison to the roughly six billion years that planet Earth can boast. To put those huge numbers into perspective, let us imagine a calendar: if Earth appeared on January 1, then human ancestors showed up around the end of August, but civilization, and history, commenced a few minutes before midnight on December 31.

Perhaps two million years ago, the species *Homo,* or the *hominids,* made its appearance whereas *Homo sapiens,* the immediate ancestor of modern humans, emerged around two hundred thousand years ago. For a very long time, therefore, the key story was the development of the human species itself. Unfortunately, knowledge about these hominids is limited and fragmentary. They were hunters and gatherers, lived in natural shelters such as caves, and did not possess complex social structures. Hominids invented crude stone tools, used fire, and probably developed speech—a major breakthrough that enabled them to communicate in ways denied to animals. Their first stone tools were simple choppers and, later, hand axes, pointed tools, and scrapers, all chiseled with care. Hominids and *Homo sapiens* span the **Paleolithic** period, the Old Stone Age, a time roughly coterminous with the geological Pleistocene, the Ice Age, about 2,000,000 BCE to about 10,000 BCE.

Paleolithic Period

The latter millennia of the Paleolithic period are somewhat better known than earlier ones owing to discoveries in widely dispersed places. *Homo sapiens* had migrated across the Eastern Hemisphere and even the Western Hemisphere, reaching the latter by means of a land bridge that connected Siberia and Alaska. People had begun to use more sophisticated tools, such as fishhooks, bows and arrows, and needles (Figure 1.1). Most impressively, however, late Paleolithic peoples began to express themselves in art. Ice Age cave paintings of reindeer, bison, rhinoceroses, lions, and horses in Altamira, Spain, and in Lascaux and the Ardèche region of France date from the Upper Paleolithic (40,000–10,000 BCE) and are the earliest examples of human art (Figure 1.2). The purposes of the paintings in the Chauvet caves in the Ardèche region remain a mystery, but those at Altamira and Lascaux were probably elements in hunting rituals. By painting numerous wild animals pierced with arrows, the artists were attempting to ensure a successful hunt.

Another type of Upper Paleolithic art is seen in the carved female figurine found at Willendorf, Austria (Figure 1.3). Made of limestone, the statue is faceless and rotund. The distended stomach and full breasts suggest that the figure may have been a mother goddess used as a fertility symbol to represent the creative power of nature. As a mythological figure, the mother goddess appeared in many ancient cultures, beginning in Paleolithic times; approximately thirty thousand miniature sculptures in clay, marble, bone, copper, and gold have been uncovered at about three thousand sites in southeastern Europe alone. The supremacy of the mother goddess was expressed in the earliest myths of creation, which told of the lifegiving and nurturing powers of the female. The Willendorf figurine, with its emphasized breasts, navel, and vulva, symbolic of creativity, may have been used in religious ceremonies to ensure the propagation of the tribe or to guarantee a bountiful food supply. The statue also reveals the aesthetic interests of the sculptor, who took care to depict the goddess's hands resting on her breasts and her hair in tightly knit rows.

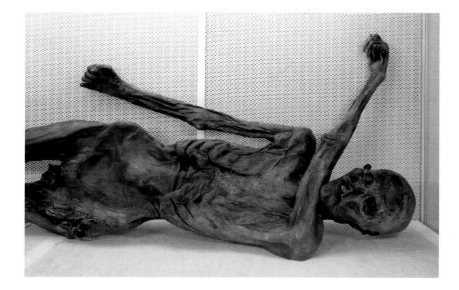

Figure 1.1   The Ice Man. South Tyrol Museum of Archaeology. In 1991 hikers in the Alps discovered the body of a man in melting ice. He turned out to be over five thousand years old. He died in a bloody fight after having eaten a last meal of bread and goat meat. He possessed a bow and arrows, a copper hatchet, and several pouches and containers. The Ice Man was about 5 feet 2 inches tall and had lived a very hard life.

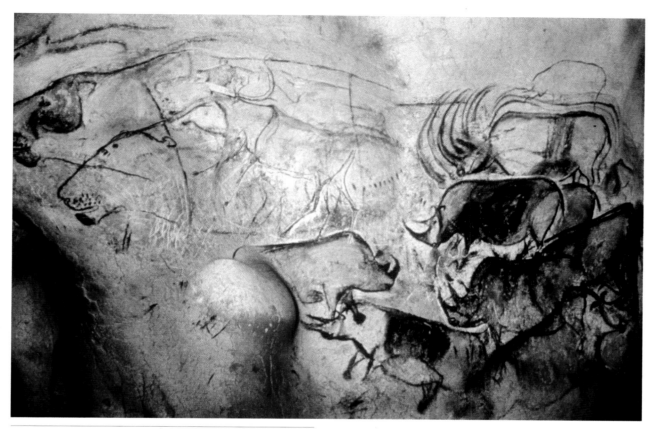

Figure 1.2   Herd of Rhinoceroses. Ca. 32,000–30,000 BCE. Chauvet Cave, Ardèche region, France. This naturalistic detail of a panel painting includes lions, bison, and a young mammoth (not visible here) moving across a vast expanse of the cave wall. The repeated black lines of the rhinoceroses' horns and backs create a sense of depth and give energy to the work.

The Neolithic Revolution

As the last glaciers retreated from Europe, during the Holocene (Recent) epoch of geological time, humans had to adapt to new living conditions. The brief Mesolithic period (Middle Stone Age) proved to be a decisive turning point. In the most important development in human history, hunters and gatherers became farmers and herders. Thus began, some ten thousand years ago, the **Neolithic** period, or New Stone Age. As *Homo sapiens* became farmers and herders, they gained knowledge about agriculture and developed wooden tools and other technologies for farming and herding. Their stone tools became more advanced than those in the Mesolithic period and included knives and hammers. Along with the domestication of animals, the animal-drawn plow was introduced to Mesopotamia, thus

Figure 1.3   Figurine from Willendorf. Ca. 25,000 BCE. Ht. 4³/₈″. Naturhistorisches Museum, Vienna. Discovered in about 1908 CE, this female statuette measures just under 5 inches high. Carved from limestone, it still shows evidence of having been painted red. Many other statues like it have been discovered, but this one remains the most famous because of the unusual balance it strikes between symbolism and realism.

Timeline 1.1   GEOLOGICAL TIME AND PREHISTORIC CULTURAL PERIODS   **All dates approximate and BCE**

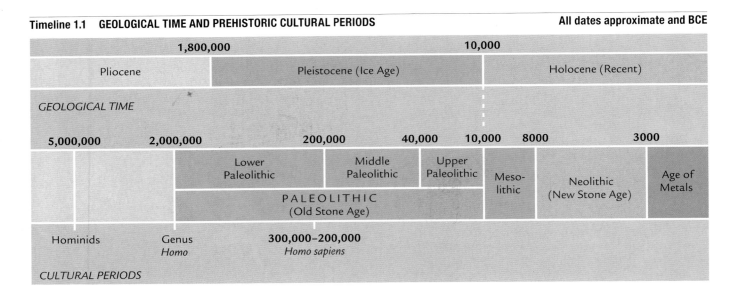

increasing the yield of crops. After 3500 BCE, the rise of the new technologies accelerated, making this one of the most fruitful eras for change that the world has ever known. In transportation the changes included two innovations: the boat (with and without sails) and the wheel—each with enormous potential for commerce, travel, and warfare. In construction and building, the discovery and use of kiln-fired bricks made houses, temples, and palaces possible. Five new technologies changed the domestic scene: weaving, dyeing (using animal and vegetable dyes), tanning, pottery making (both plain and kiln-fired), and lighting with oil lamps. Large-scale irrigation in dry lands expanded crop yields and brought new plants under cultivation, such as wheat, flax, millet, barley, and spices.

In Southeast Asia, Central America, parts of South America, and the Near East, humans ceased their nomadic existence and learned to domesticate wild animals. They learned to plow the earth and sow seeds, providing themselves with a more reliable, predictable food supply than in earlier times, which in turn permitted increased population, permanent settlements, and eventually urban centers. This agrarian pattern of life dominated the West until about 150 years ago.

The Age of Metals

The Neolithic Revolution expanded across the Near East and probably into Europe and Africa. Between 6000 and 3000 BCE, human beings also learned to mine and use copper, signifying the end of the Neolithic period and ushering in the Age of Metals. In about 3000 BCE, artisans combined copper and tin to produce bronze, a strong alloy, which they used in their tools, weapons, and jewelry.

The Bronze Age extended from about 3000 to about 1200 BCE. A herald of the Age of Metals was the mastery of gold and silver metalworking. Gold and silver were first reduced from their ores after 3500 BCE, but their scarcity made them too precious for general use. The shift from stone tools to bronze tools occurred at first in only a few areas in the Near East, China, and Southeast Asia. Elsewhere, especially in Europe, Mesoamerica, and the Andes of South America, stone continued as the dominant material for tools.

From Mesopotamia, where the earliest successful bronze was produced by anonymous artisans, this metalworking tradition was transmitted to Egypt, Greece, and elsewhere. It produced a host of new technologies. Writing is the hallmark of this period, with Egyptians putting words on papyrus, a flat writing surface made from pressed reeds, and Mesopotamians incising words on clay tablets. With the invention of writing, the silence of the prehistoric period gave way to the voice of the historic period.

Other technologies improved the lives of people during the Bronze Age. Construction methods moved along two different paths: in Egypt, stone building techniques arose, and in Mesopotamia, stepped temples, made of dried bricks, became the chief building style. Advances in transport were made, with sailboats plying their wares on Egypt's Nile and wooden ships maneuvering in the Mediterranean. Copper and tin were in short supply in Egypt and Mesopotamia. To ensure a continuous supply of these metals, complex trading ties and mining operations had to be established. Copper was found in neighboring Anatolia (modern Turkey), but tin was scarce, as it was mined in only a few places, in modern Serbia and Bulgaria at first, and in Cornwall, in modern England, after 2500 BCE. Domestic life made extraordinary advances in Mesopotamia, with many changes that are still part of life today, including baking bread in ovens, brewing beer, and distilling perfumes. In Egypt and

Learning Through Maps

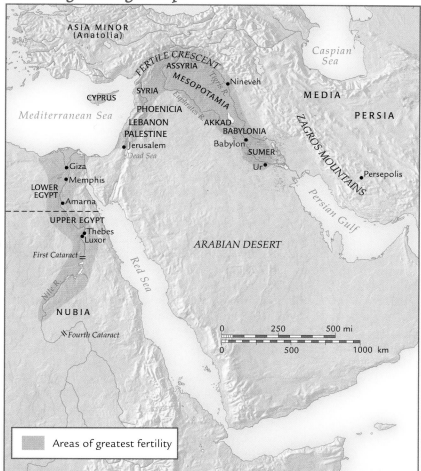

Areas of greatest fertility

Mesopotamia, making glass and wine became common, and, in Egypt, the invention of hand mirrors and the sundial lent new perspectives for people to experience. Urban culture also led to the widespread use of calendars, in both Egypt and Mesopotamia.

The Iron Age began in about 1200 BCE, but the making of iron has been dated to about 2000 BCE. Iron technology soon led to new devices, fashioned from either iron or steel, such as iron-tipped plows, weaponry, buckets, and locks and keys. Warriors quickly realized that sturdy iron defeats brittle bronze every time. Indeed, the outcome of some wars between 1200 and 1000 BCE was determined by which side wielded iron weapons.

THE RISE OF CIVILIZATION: MESOPOTAMIA

Civilization is based on a Latin word meaning "city" and "citizen." It was the Neolithic Revolution that made cities possible. That revolution depended on agriculture and the domestication of animals. Those

processes brought the division of labor, government, religion, priestly classes, arts and crafts, and sciences. Taken together, along with writing, these elements add up to civilization. Western civilization arose in Mesopotamia and Egypt (about 3500–3000 BCE). Both regions were ruled by kings who were supported by educated priestly classes and shared power with an economic and military elite. Their economies were slave based; their societies were hierarchical and stratified. Both had elaborate palaces and temples for governmental and ceremonial purposes.

Mesopotamia is a Greek word meaning "between the rivers." The valleys of the Rivers Tigris and Euphrates formed part of what is known as the Fertile Crescent, which starts at the Persian Gulf, runs slightly northwestward through the region between the rivers (roughly modern Iraq), and then turns westerly to the Mediterranean Sea and curves south along the shoreline toward Egypt (Map 1.1). This arc of land contained most of the fertile soil in the Near East, many heavily traveled trade routes, and early centers of civilization. The hill country and Zagros Mountains rise

Timeline 1.2   MESOPOTAMIAN CIVILIZATIONS   **All dates approximate and BCE**

3000		2350	2000	1600
	Sumerian		Akkadian	Babylonian

to the east of the Tigris-Euphrates valley, and the vast Arabian Desert stretches to the west. The rivers flow down to the Persian Gulf, draining an area approximately 600 miles long and 250 miles wide. Near the mouth of the gulf, in the river delta, human wanderers settled in about 6000 BCE.

The Sumerian, Akkadian, and Babylonian Kingdoms

Three successive cultures—Sumerian, Akkadian, and Babylonian—flourished in Mesopotamia for nearly fifteen hundred years (Timeline 1.2). As historian Samuel Kramer asserts, "History begins at Sumer."

The rulers of Sumer sought a just and stable society and fostered a rich cultural life. Sumer's most inspirational king, Gilgamesh [GILL-guh-mesh], ruled about 2700 BCE at Ur, one of the thirty or so cities of Sumer. His heroic adventures and exploits were later immortalized in the poem *The Epic of Gilgamesh.* A later ruler, Urukagina [Ur-oo-KA-gee-na], is known for reforming law codes and revitalizing the economy near the end of the Sumerian period (2350 BCE). But Urukagina's successors were unable to maintain Sumer's power, and the cities became easy prey for the Akkadians of northern Mesopotamia.

Akkadian rulers between about 2350 and 2000 BCE incorporated Sumerian culture into their own society and carried this hybrid culture far beyond the Tigris-Euphrates valley. According to legends—which are similar to the later story of the Hebrew leader Moses—Sargon (r. about 2334–2279 BCE), the first and greatest Akkadian ruler, was born of lowly origins and abandoned at birth in the reed marshes; yet Sargon survived and rose to prominence at the Sumerian court. Excavated inscriptions reveal that Sargon conquered the Sumerians and founded a far-flung empire to the east and northeast. At its height, Sargon's power was felt from Egypt to India, but his successors, lacking his leadership and skill, could not maintain the Akkadian Empire.

Babylonia was the third culture in Mesopotamia. From northern Mesopotamia, their power base, the Babylonians governed the entire valley from about 2000 to 1600 BCE. Under their most successful military leader and renowned lawgiver, Hammurabi [ham-uh-RAHB-e] (r. 1792–1750 BCE), the Babylonians reached their political and cultural ascendancy.

Agriculture dominated the economy of Mesopotamia. Harsh living conditions and unpredictable floods forced the inhabitants to learn to control the rivers through irrigation systems and cooperative tilling of the soil. Farmers eventually dug a complex canal system to irrigate cultivated plots at increasing distances from the river. As production increased, prosperity allowed larger populations to thrive. Villages soon grew into small cities—with populations ranging from ten thousand to fifty thousand—surrounded by hamlets and tilled fields. Trade developed with nearby areas, and wheeled vehicles—perfected by the Sumerians—and sailboats carried goods up and down the Tigris and Euphrates Rivers and eventually throughout the Fertile Crescent.

By the beginning of the Bronze Age, the family had replaced the tribe or clan as the basic unit in society. Families now owned their lands outright, and, under the general direction of the religious and secular authorities, they worked their fields and maintained irrigation ditches. Marriages were arranged by parents, with economics an essential consideration. According to the law codes, women possessed some rights, such as holding property; however, a wife was clearly under her husband's power. Divorce was easier for men than for women, and women were punished more severely than men for breaking moral and marital laws. As peoples fought and conquered each other, government became increasingly military in outlook and function and the roles and status of women declined. In sum, Mesopotamian women were originally able to participate actively in economic, religious, and political life as long as their dependence on and obligation to male kin and husbands was observed, but they progressively lost their relative independence because rulers extended the concept of patriarchy (rule by the fathers) from family practice into public law.

The political structure reflected the order and functions of the social system. At the top stood the ruler, who was supported by an army, a bureaucracy, a judicial system, and a priesthood. The ruler usually obtained advice from prominent leaders, meeting in council, who constituted the next layer of the social order: rich landowners, wealthy merchants, priests, and military chiefs. The next group consisted of artisans, craftspeople, and low-level businesspeople and traders. Below them were small landowners and tenant farmers. At the bottom of the social scale were slaves, who either had been captured in war or had fallen into debt.

The Cradle of Civilization

The three Mesopotamian cultures responded to the same geography, climate, and natural resources. The Sumerians were the most influential: from Sumer came writing, the lunar calendar, a mathematical computation system, medical and scientific discoveries, and architectural and technological innovations.

Writing   Thousands of clay tablets inscribed with the wedge-shaped symbols of Sumerian script have been uncovered in Mesopotamia, indicating that the Sumerians had developed a form of writing by 3000 BCE. With the invention of writing, people no longer had to rely on memory, speech, and person-to-person interactions to communicate and transmit information. Instead, they could accumulate a permanent body of knowledge and pass it on from one generation to the next.

At first, the Sumerians needed a simple way to record agricultural and business information and the deeds and sayings of their rulers. Their earliest symbols were **pictograms,** or pictures, carefully drawn to represent particular objects. To these they added **ideograms,** pictures drawn to represent ideas or concepts. A simple drawing of a bowl, for example, could be used to mean "food." As these pictures became stylized, meaning began to be transferred from the represented object to the sign itself; that is, the sign began to stand for a word rather than an object.

Later, Sumerian scribes and writers identified the syllabic sounds of spoken words and created **phonograms,** symbols for separate speech sounds, borrowing from and building on the earlier pictograms and ideograms. These simplified and standardized symbols eventually resulted in a phonetic writing system of syllable-based sounds that, when combined, produced words (Figure 1.4).

The Sumerian writing system is called **cuneiform** ("wedge shaped"), from the Latin word *cuneus* ("wedge"). Using wedge-shaped reeds or styluses, scribes pressed the symbols into wet clay tablets, and artists and craftspeople, wielding metal tools, incised the script into stone monuments or cylindrical pillars. Scholars have painstakingly deciphered thousands of clay tablets thus revealing the society and thought of the Sumerians and of their Akkadian and Babylonian successors.

Around 1050 BCE, the Phoenicians (fuh-NEE-shuns) improved on the syllabic writing they had inherited from their neighbors. They created the first alphabet, a system of writing in which one sign (we call them "letters") is assigned to each sound. Afterward, writing became more economical because it was not necessary to have a single symbol for every possible syllabic configuration (ba, ca, da, etc.). The original Phoenician alphabet had twenty-two letters, all consonants (Figure 1.5). The Phoenicians were great travelers and merchants, and from their homeland, in what is now Lebanon, they influenced the writing of many other peoples including, prominently, the Hebrews and the Greeks. The Greeks turned some Phoenician letters into vowels and created additional vowels too.

Religion   Sumerian, Akkadian, and Babylonian religions shared many basic attitudes and concepts that became the foundation for other Near Eastern belief systems. Fundamentally, Mesopotamian religion held that the gods had created human beings to serve them, that the gods were in complete control, and that powerless mortals had no choice but to obey and worship these deities. The hostile climate and unpredictable rivers (flooding that ranged from a torrent to a trickle) made life precarious, and the gods appeared

Figure 1.4   Sumerian Cuneiform Writing. Ca. 3000–1000 BCE. The columns illustrate the evolution of Sumerian writing from pictograms to script. Column 1 shows the pictogram: a man, an ox, and the verb "to eat" (represented by the mouth and a bowl). In column 2, the pictographic symbols have been turned 90 degrees, as the Sumerians did in their first writing. Columns 3 and 4 show how the script changed between 2500 and 1800 BCE. Column 5 is an Assyrian adaptation of the Sumerian cuneiform script.

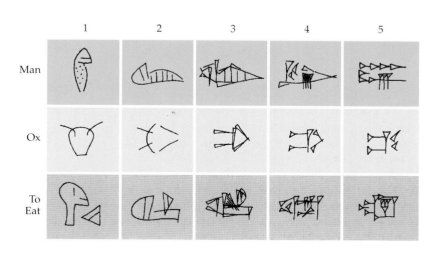

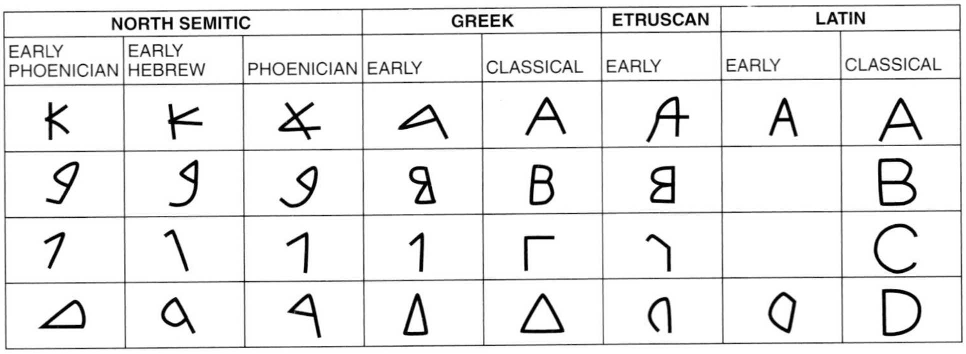

NORTH SEMITIC			GREEK		ETRUSCAN	LATIN	
EARLY PHOENICIAN	EARLY HEBREW	PHOENICIAN	EARLY	CLASSICAL	EARLY	EARLY	CLASSICAL
K	K	X	◁	A	A	A	A
9	9	9	8	B	8		B
7	\	1	1	Γ	ᒣ		C
△	◁	◁	△	△	⌂	⌂	D

Figure 1.5   First Four Letters of the Alphabet—a Comparison. This table presents, in comparative form, the opening four letters of the Phoenician, Greek, Hebrew, Etruscan, and Latin alphabets. The early Phoenician letters predated the rest, and other peoples adapted those letters into their writing styles.

Phoenician, Greek, Hebrew, Etruscan, and Roman letters.

capricious. The Mesopotamians held a vague notion of a shadowy netherworld where the dead rested, but they did not believe in an afterlife as such or any rewards or punishments upon death. Happiness seldom was an earthly goal; pessimism was a constant theme throughout their religion and literature.

Mesopotamian religion had three important characteristics: it was **polytheistic**—many gods and goddesses existed and often competed with one another; it was **anthropomorphic**—the deities were envisioned in human form and had their own personalities and unique traits; and it was **pantheistic**—everything, whether animate or inanimate, was suffused with divinity. Since Mesopotamians thought of their gods in human form with all the strengths and weaknesses of mortals, they believed their deities lived in the same way as people did, and they were pragmatic in approaching the supernatural powers. For example, they believed that their deities held council, made decisions, and ordered the forces of nature to wreak havoc or to bestow plenty on mortals.

Mesopotamians divided the deities into the sky gods and the earth gods. There were several major deities: Anu, the sky god; Enlil, the air god; Utu, the sun god; Enki, the god of earth and the freshwater god; Nanna, the moon goddess; Inanna (or Ishtar), the goddess of love and war; and Ninhursag, the mother goddess. Enlil emerged as the most powerful god for the Sumerians. He gave mortals the plow and the pickax, and he brought forth for humanity all the productive forces of the universe, such as trees, grains, and "whatever was needful."

Rituals, ceremonies, and the priesthood were essential to Mesopotamian religion. Although the average Mesopotamian might participate in worship services, the priests played the central role in all religious functions. They also controlled and administered large parcels of land, which enhanced their power in economic and political matters. Priests carefully formulated and consciously followed the procedures for rites and rituals, which were written on stone tablets and stored in their temples. This cultic literature not only told the Mesopotamians how to worship but also informed them about their deities' origins, characteristics, and deeds. Religious myths and instructions constituted a major part of Mesopotamian literature and made writing an essential part of the culture.

Literature   Of the surviving epics, tales, and legends that offer glimpses into the Mesopotamian mind, the most famous is *The Epic of Gilgamesh*. King Gilgamesh, whose reign in about 2700 BCE is well documented, became a larger-than-life hero in Sumerian folktales (Figure 1.6). In all probability, the Gilgamesh epic began as an oral poem and was not written on clay tablets for hundreds of years. The most complete surviving version, from 600 BCE, was based on a Babylonian copy written in Akkadian and dating from about 1600 BCE. Although this poem influenced other Near Eastern writings with its characters, plot, and themes, *The Epic of Gilgamesh* stands on its own as poetry worthy of being favorably compared with later Greek and Roman epics.

Through its royal hero, *The Epic of Gilgamesh* focuses on fundamental themes that concern warriors in an aristocratic society: the need to be brave in the face of danger, the choice of death before dishonor, the conflict between companionship and sexual pleasure, the power of the gods over weak mortals, and the finality of death. Above all, it deals with human beings' vain quest for immortality. As the tale begins, the extravagant and despotic policies of Gilgamesh have led his subjects to pray for relief. In response, a goddess creates from clay a "wild man" of tremendous physical strength and sends him to kill Gilgamesh. But Enkidu, as he is called, is instead tamed by a woman's love, loses his innocence, wrestles Gilgamesh to a draw, and becomes his boon companion.

As the epic unfolds, Gilgamesh chooses friendship with Enkidu rather than the love offered by the goddess Ishtar. Gilgamesh is punished for this choice by being made to watch helplessly as Enkidu dies from

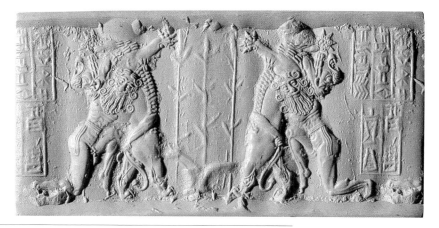

Figure 1.6   Gilgamesh Fighting a Lion. Ca. 2500–2000 BCE. Cylinder seal (left) and modern impression of a cylinder seal (right). British Museum, London. The separate scenes, rolled out on this impression from the seal, which is about 1 inch high, depict the Sumerian hero in one of his many battles against beasts. The artist heightens the intensity of the physical struggle by placing Gilgamesh, with his legs bent and arms locked around the lion, at a sharp angle under the animal to muster his brute strength against his foe.

an illness sent by the gods. Forced to confront the fate awaiting all mortals, a grieving Gilgamesh begins a search for immortality.

The next section of the epic, which details Gilgamesh's search, includes the Sumerian tale of the Great Flood, which parallels the later Hebrew story of Noah and the Ark. Although the Sumerian account of the flood was probably a later addition to the original story of Gilgamesh, the episode does fit into the narrative and reinforces one of the epic's major themes: the inescapable mortality of human beings. Gilgamesh hears the story of the flood from its sole survivor, an old man named Utnapishtim. Utnapishtim tells Gilgamesh how he built an ark and loaded it with animals and his family, how the waters rose, and how he released birds from the ark to discover if the waters were receding. The old man then explains how the gods, feeling sorry for the last remaining human, granted him immortality. Utnapishtim refuses to divulge the secret of eternal life to Gilgamesh, but the old man's wife blurts out where a plant may be found that will renew youth but not give immortality. Although Gilgamesh locates the plant, he loses it on his journey home. Gilgamesh, seeing the city of Uruk, which he had built, realizes that the deeds humans do on earth are the measure of their immortality and that death is inevitable.

The Epic of Gilgamesh is essentially a secular morality tale. Gilgamesh's triumphs and failures mirror the lives of all mortals, and the Sumerians saw themselves in Gilgamesh's change from an overly confident and powerful hero to a doubting and fearful human being. Those who, like Gilgamesh, ignore the power of the deities have to pay a heavy price for their pride.

Mesopotamia also gave the world the first known female literary figure, Enheduanna [en-hay-Doo-an-na] (fl. 2330 BCE), an Akkadian poet who wrote in the Sumerian language. Made priestess of temples in the Sumerian cities of Ur (see Figure 1.9) and Uruk by her father, King Sargon, she used her priestly offices and literary gifts to further his political goal of uniting the Sumerians and the Akkadians. In these posts, she composed hymns to both Sumerian and Akkadian deities, and these hymns became models for later poets. Enheduanna was especially devoted to Inanna, the Sumerian goddess of love, and she made this deity the subject of her best-known literary work, *The Exaltation of Inanna.* In this work, Enheduanna exalted, or raised, Inanna to supremacy in the Sumerian pantheon (all the gods and goddesses), her tribute for what she believed was Inanna's role in Sargon's triumph over a general uprising at the end of his reign.

Law   The central theme of Sumerian law, whose first existing records date from about 2050 BCE, was justice. From the earliest times, the Sumerian kings understood justice to mean "the straight thing"—that is, dealing fairly with all their subjects and prohibiting the exploitation of the weak by the strong. This concept of equity applied especially to economic matters, such as debts, contracts, and titles to land.

The most important set of laws from Mesopotamian civilization is that of the Babylonian king Hammurabi. Dating from about 1700 BCE, the Code of Hammurabi was found preserved on a seven-foot-high black stone **stele,** or pillar. At the top, Hammurabi is depicted standing in front of Shamash, the Babylonian and Sumerian god of justice. Like other ancient lawgivers

Figure 1.7   Code of Hammurabi. Ca. 1700 BCE. Basalt, ht. approx. 3′. Louvre. Hammurabi stands on the left, his hand raised before his mouth in the traditional Mesopotamian gesture of devotion, and Shamash, the sun god and protector of truth and justice, sits on the right. The cult of Shamash (in Sumeria, Utu) emerged from the earliest times, and this god's representation—flames shooting from the shoulders and hands holding symbols of power—was established in the Sumerian period. The relief, with its incised folds of cloth and ceremonial chair, is carved deep enough into the hard stone stele (7 feet 4 inches) to suggest a three-dimensional sculpture.

(Moses, for example), Hammurabi received the legal code from a deity. Below the two figures appear the prologue, the collection of laws, and an epilogue (Figure 1.7). The prologue lists Hammurabi's accomplishments and sings his praises while making it clear that the gods are the source of his power to establish "law and justice." The epilogue warns future rulers to carry out these laws or else be subject to defeat and ruin.

The laws concerning punishment for crimes are based on the judicial principle of *lex talionis,* or retaliation, which demands an "eye for an eye," although Hammurabi's code often substitutes payments in kind for damages done. The code constitutes decisions rendered in some three hundred actual cases. Accordingly, the code's provisions are not lofty and abstract but, instead, concrete and specific. Decisions deal with property rights, sales, contracts, inheritance, adoption, prices and wages, sexual relations (much more severely restricted for women than for men), medical

malpractice, and personal rights for women, children, and slaves. Hammurabi's code, like other Mesopotamian laws, was only one part of a complex judicial system that encompassed judges, courts, legal proceedings such as trials, and contracts.

Science, Mathematics, and Medicine   Mesopotamian science was strongly influenced by the region's polytheistic, anthropomorphic, and pantheistic religion. The Mesopotamians believed that a knowledge and understanding of the natural world was related to their deities' personalities and acts. Priests performed ceremonies and rituals not only to placate the gods and goddesses and to fend off their disruptive powers but also to deal with practical matters, such as land surveys, irrigation projects, sickness, and disease. Thus, Mesopotamia's priests were also astronomers, mathematicians, and purveyors of medicine.

Knowing that the deities were powerful and capricious, the priests were convinced that they could avert some of the divine wrath by observing, studying, and calculating the heavens—the abode of most of the gods. The priests assumed that, by understanding the movements of the stars, moon, and sun, they could forecast natural calamities, such as floods, pestilence, and crop failure. Around 3500 BCE, the priests in Sumer invented a calendar based on the movements of the moon. In this calendar, a "month" equaled twenty-eight days, but the year was divided into thirteen, not twelve, months. They then used this lunar calendar to make plans for the future. Once they were able to calculate the seasonal pattern of nature, they instituted a festival celebrating the New Year, which recognized the end of the growing season and the arrival of the next season.

Mathematics probably developed out of the need to measure and allocate land, build dams, remove dirt, pay workers, and regulate water. The Mesopotamian number system, likely influenced by their system of weights and coinage, used 60, not 100, as its base. Our calculation of degrees, minutes, and seconds evolved from this system. Later societies, like the Babylonian, built on this system to fashion complex formulas, theorems, and equations, which aided shopkeepers in managing their businesses and astronomers in mapping the heavens and plotting navigation charts. We differentiate religions and science today, so it is interesting to think that in Mesopotamia religious authorities took the first halting steps toward observational science by trying to make sense of the natural world.

Although the oldest surviving records of Mesopotamian medicine can be dated only to about 1600 BCE, these texts, preserved on stone tablets, represent earlier centuries of medical practice and tradition. In these texts, the authors connected disease with supernatural

SLICE OF LIFE

A Sumerian Father Lectures His Son

Anonymous
FOUND ON CLAY TABLETS

In this Sumerian text, dating from around 1700 BCE, a father rebukes his son for leading a wayward life and admonishes him to reform.

"Where did you go?"

"I did not go anywhere."

"If you did not go anywhere, why do you idle about? Go to school. Stand before your 'school-father,' recite your assignment, open your schoolbag, write your tablet, let your 'big brother' write your new tablet for you. After you have finished your assignment and reported to your monitor, come to me, and do not wander about in the street. . . .

"You who wander about in the public square, would you achieve success? Then seek out the first generations. Go to school, it will be of benefit to you. My son, seek out the first generations, inquire of them.

"Perverse one over whom I stand watch—I would not be a man did I not stand watch over my son—I spoke to my kin, compared its men, but found none like you among them. . . .

"I, never in all my life did I make you carry reeds in the canebrake. The reed rushes which the young and the little carry, you, never in your life did you carry them. I never said to you 'Follow my caravans.' I never sent you to work, to plow my field, I never sent you to work to dig up my field. I never sent you to work as a laborer. 'Go, work and support me,' I never in my life said to you.

"Others like you support their parents by working. . . .

"I, night and day I am tortured because of you. Night and day you waste in pleasures. You have accumulated much wealth, have expanded far and wide, have become fat, big, broad, powerful, and puffed. But your kin waits expectantly for your misfortune, and will rejoice at it because you looked not to your humanity."

Interpreting This Slice of Life

The key to interpreting this Slice of Life is to determine the tone of the father's speech to his son. *Tone* means "manner of speaking."

1. *What* tone does the speaker manifest here? *List* three words that assist you in identifying the tone of voice.

2. *How* does the father define *family,* and what expectations does the father have for his son?

3. To *which* class do the father and his son belong? *Explain.*

4. *What* are the father's values regarding education, worldly success, and family honor?

5. *Which* values in this Sumerian text are shared by families in American culture?

---

forces such as deities, ghosts, and spirits. Remedies involved the patient making sacrifices to the gods. At the same time, these texts counseled various treatments, such as administering potions made from herbs or plants. Mesopotamian diagnostic methods and curative practices, while outdated, followed a set of logical steps. First, the patient was examined to determine the nature of the disease and advised how to cure it. Then, the patient was sent to a healer, who prescribed certain medications or applied bandages or plasters. Additional evidence for Mesopotamian medicine comes from the Code of Hammurabi, in which doctors were held accountable for their mistakes and duly fined or punished. What contributions the Mesopotamians made to medicine tended to be lost over the centuries.

It was the Egyptians who came to be viewed as the most successful practitioners of medicine during ancient times and who influenced later societies, especially the Greeks.

Art and Architecture   The art of Mesopotamia also evolved from Sumerian styles to the Akkadian and Babylonian schools. Artisans worked in many forms—small seals, pottery, jewelry, vases, **reliefs** (figures and forms carved so that they project from the flat surface of a stone background), and statues—and in many media—clay, stone, precious gems, gold, silver, leather, and ivory. Artifacts and crafted works from all three civilizations recorded the changing techniques of the producers as well as the shifting

Figure 1.8   Sound Box from Sumerian Lyre, from Ur. Ca. 2685 BCE. Wood with inlaid gold, lapis lazuli, and shell, ht. of bull's head approx. 13″. University Museum, University of Pennsylvania, Philadelphia. The lyre's sound box, on which the bull's head is carved, is a hollow chamber that increases the resonance of the sound. Music played an important role in Mesopotamian life, and patrons often commissioned the construction of elegant instruments. Thus, even at this early stage of civilization, those with wealth influenced the arts.

tastes of the consumers, whether they were rich individuals decorating their homes or officials issuing commissions for statues to adorn their temples. The temples, usually the center of the city and set on high mounds above the other structures, were often splendidly ornamented and housed exquisitely carved statues of gods and goddesses.

A fine example of Sumerian artistry is a bull's head carved on the sound box of a lyre (Figure 1.8). Working in gold leaf and semiprecious gems, the unknown artist has captured the vigor and power of the animal in a bold and simple style. Such elegant musical instruments were played in homes and in palaces to accompany the poets and storytellers as they sang of the heroes' adventures and the deities' powers. The bull shape of the lyre reflects Sumerian religion, in which this animal was believed to possess supernatural powers.

Mesopotamian architecture often seems uninspired. Good building stone was not readily available in Mesopotamia—it had to be brought at great cost from the mountains to the east—so wood and clay bricks were the most common building materials. Even though the Mesopotamians knew about the arch, the vault, and the column, they did not employ them widely; they used primarily the basic **post-and-lintel construction** of two vertical posts capped by a horizontal lintel, or beam, for entryways. The clay bricks used in construction limited the builders in both styles and size. Domestic architecture was particularly unimpressive, partly by design and partly because of perishable materials. Private homes of clay bricks looked drab from the street; however, they were often attractive inside, with decorated rooms and built around an open courtyard. This is a common feature of ancient societies whereas, for many later peoples, power and status were communicated by impressive personal residences. The exteriors of temples and palaces were sometimes adorned with colored glazed bricks, mosaics, and painted cones arranged in patterns or, rarely, with imported stone and marble.

Although much remains to be discovered, it seems that Mesopotamian cities were surrounded by walls—with a circumference of up to five miles in early Sumer—and characterized by a broad central thoroughfare with a palace at one end and a temple complex at the other. Urban walls, with imposing and elaborately decorated gates, proclaimed the city's wealth and power. The most prominent structure in each Sumerian city was the **ziggurat,** a terraced brick and mudbrick pyramid that served as the center of worship. The ziggurat resembled a hill or a stairway to the sky from which the deities could descend; or perhaps the structure was conceived as the gods' cosmic mountain. A temple of welcome for the gods stood on the top of the ziggurat, approached by sets of steps. Shrines, storehouses,

Figure 1.9   Ziggurat of Ur. Ca. 2100 BCE. Ur (Muqaiyir, Iraq). A temple to Nanna, the moon god, stood on the top of the ziggurat, which was terraced on three levels. On the first level was an entryway approached by two sets of steps on each side and one in the front. The base, or lowest stage, which is all that remains of this "Hill of Heaven," measures 200 by 150 feet and stands 70 feet high. In comparison, Chartres cathedral in France is 157 feet wide, with each tower over 240 feet high.

and administrative offices were constructed around the base or on the several levels of the massive hill. In the low plain of the Tigris-Euphrates valley, the ziggurat dominated the landscape. The Tower of Babel, described in the Jewish scriptures as reaching to the sky, may have been suggested by the Sumerian ziggurats, some of which had towers.

Of the numerous ziggurats and temples that have survived, the best preserved is at Ur, in southern Mesopotamia, dedicated to the moon god, Nanna (Figure 1.9). Built in about 2100 BCE, this ziggurat was laid out to the four points of the compass. A central stairway led up to the highest platform, on which the major temple rested. Other cities constructed similar massive podiums in the hope that they would please the gods and goddesses, that the rivers would flood and thus irrigate their crops, and that life would continue. Thus, the central themes of Mesopotamian civilization manifested themselves in the ziggurats.

THE RISE OF CIVILIZATION: EGYPT

Egypt was said to be "the gift of the Nile." And so it was. The regular floods of the Nile made civilized life possible in Egypt. Red sandy deserts stretched east and west of the waterway. Beside the Nile's banks, however, the black alluvial soil of the narrow floodplain offered rich land for planting, although the river's gifts of water and arable land were limited. Irrigation canals and ditches plus patient, backbreaking labor were required to bring the life-giving liquid into the desert.

Because the survival and prosperity of the people depended on the Nile, the river dominated Egyptian experience. About 95 percent of the people lived on the less than 5 percent of Egyptian land that was arable and located along the Nile. People clustered in villages, the fundamental unit of Egyptian civilization. The reward for farm labor tended to be subsistence living, yet the perennial hope that next year's flood would bring a more bountiful harvest created an optimistic outlook that contrasted with the darker Mesopotamian view.

The Nile linked the "Two Lands," Upper and Lower Egypt, two regions whose differing geography made for two distinct ways of life. Since the Nile flows northward, Lower Egypt referred to the northern lands fed by the river's spreading delta, a region made wealthy by its fertile soil. In contrast, the harsh topography and poor farming conditions of the southern lands made Upper Egypt an area of near-subsistence living. In addition, Lower Egypt, because of its proximity to both Mediterranean and Near Eastern cultures, became more cosmopolitan than the provincial, isolated lands of Upper Egypt.

Whereas Mesopotamian kingdoms were subject to constant external pressures, Egypt was isolated by deserts on both sides and developed an introspective attitude that was little influenced by neighboring cultures. The Egyptians cultivated a sense of cultural superiority and achieved a unified character that lasted for three thousand years. Subjected to the annual flooding of the Nile and aware of the revolutions of the sun, Egypt saw itself as part of a cyclical pattern in a timeless world.

Timeline 1.3   EGYPTIAN CIVILIZATION   **All dates approximate and BCE**

6000	3100	2700	2185	2050	1800	1552	1079	525
Neolithic and Predynastic Periods	Early Dynastic Period	Old Kingdom	First Intermediate Period	Middle Kingdom	Second Intermediate Period	New Kingdom	Late Dynastic Period	Persian Conquest

The earliest Neolithic settlers in the Nile valley probably arrived in about 6000 BCE. These earliest Egyptians took up an agricultural life, working the surrounding lands, taming the river, and domesticating animals. In the rich alluvial soil, they cultivated barley, wheat, and vegetables for themselves and fodder for their animals. They hunted with bows and arrows and fished with nets, thereby supplementing their simple fare. They also planted flax, from which thread was woven into linen on primitive looms. Most tools and weapons were made of stone or flint, but copper, which had to be imported, became more important after 3500 BCE. The early Egyptians lived in simply furnished, flat-topped houses built of sun-dried bricks. These basic patterns characterized peasant life throughout much of Egypt's history.

Continuity and Change over Three Thousand Years

Manetho, a historian who wrote in the third century BCE, divided Egypt's rulers into twenty-six dynasties, or ruling families. Egypt stepped from the shadows of its preliterate past in about 3100 BCE, when Menes [MEE-neez] proclaimed himself king and united Upper and Lower Egypt. Modern historians lump Egypt's historical dynasties into three main periods, the Old, Middle, and New Kingdoms. These are preceded and followed by the early and late dynastic periods. Two intermediate periods separate the kingdoms from each other (Timeline 1.3).

In addition to unifying Egypt, the kings of the early dynastic period (about 3100–2700 BCE) brought prosperity through their control of the economy and fostered political harmony through diplomacy and dynastic marriages. These rulers, claiming to be gods on earth, adopted the trappings of divinity and built royal tombs to ensure their immortality.

With the Old Kingdom (about 2700–2185 BCE), Egypt entered a five-hundred-year period of peace and prosperity, as its political institutions matured and its language was adapted to literary uses. The most enduring accomplishment of the Old Kingdom became the pyramid—the royal tomb devised by the Fourth Dynasty kings (Figure 1.10). As the visible symbol of the kings' power, the massive pyramids served to link the rulers with the gods and the world around them. Yet, although the kings could impress their people with divine claims, they could neither subdue the forces of nature nor make their power last forever. For reasons not fully understood, these rulers lost their control over Egypt and thus ushered in an age of political fragmentation called the first intermediate period.

In the first intermediate period (about 2185–2050 BCE), civil war raged sporadically and starvation wiped out much of the populace. Eventually, a family from Thebes, in Upper Egypt, reunited Egypt and initiated the Middle Kingdom (about 2050–1800 BCE). The new dynasty, the twelfth, fortified the southern frontier with Nubia (roughly modern Sudan) and helped bring about a cultural renaissance, especially in literature, but unity was short-lived.

During the second intermediate period (about 1800–1552 BCE), the rulers at Thebes focused on Upper Egypt and on trade in the Red Sea region, which left Lower Egypt at the mercy of the Hyksos, Semitic-speaking people who immigrated from Palestine. Although based in the Nile delta, the Hyksos took advantage of horse-drawn chariots, bronze weapons, and composite bows to dominate most of Egypt. The Hyksos adopted Egyptian gods and intermarried with the local population thus opening Lower Egypt to outside influences just as Theban trade was doing the same thing in Upper Egypt. Inadvertently, Egypt entered the Bronze Age, adopted the horse, and assimilated cultural strains from Mesopotamia.

Ahmose I [AH-moh-suh], another Theban king, drove out the Hyksos and inaugurated the New Kingdom (1552–1079 BCE), the most cosmopolitan era in ancient Egyptian history. To the south, the pharaohs pushed Egypt's frontiers to the Nile's fourth cataract, conquering the Nubians long in residence there. To the northeast, Egypt's kings, now called pharaohs, pursued imperial ambitions against the cities in Palestine, Phoenicia, and Syria, a move that provoked deadly warfare with the Hittites of Anatolia.

The Hittites, the first Indo-European people of historical significance, emigrated from southern Russia to Anatolia around 3000 BCE. Gradually they built a

Figure 1.10   The Pyramids at Giza. Ground view from the south. Pyramid of Menkure (foreground), ca. 2525 BCE; Pyramid of Khafre (center), ca. 2544 BCE; Pyramid of Khufu (rear), ca. 2580 BCE. The Fourth Dynasty was the Age of Pyramids, when the pyramid's characteristic shape was standardized and became a symbol of Egyptian civilization. The Great Pyramid, in the rear, was the first structure at Giza; it originally stood 480 feet high but today is only 450 feet high. All three pyramids were originally surfaced with shiny, white limestone, but this covering was stripped in later centuries by builders in nearby Cairo; the only remnant of the limestone surface is the cap on the top of the Pyramid of Khafre, in the center.

powerful kingdom and defeated the kingdoms of Mesopotamia. They made skillful use of horses and chariots and also of iron weapons. At the height of their domination (about 1450–1180 BCE), they encountered the expanding Egyptians and warred with them continuously. After a great battle at Kadesh in 1274 BCE, itself essentially a draw, the Egyptians and Hittites concluded a treaty that divided Palestine and Syria between them. The treaty survives—the world's oldest international agreement—and its provisions are on display at the United Nations headquarters, in New York City. By about 1200 BCE, both the Egyptian and Hittite Empires were on the decline. Egypt's lack of iron ore probably contributed fatally to its military decline as its neighbors entered the Iron Age.

Just as they dominated the state, so the pharoahs controlled the predominantly agrarian economy, although departments of government or the priesthood of a temple often exploited the land and the king's laborers. In prosperous years, the pharaohs claimed up to half of the farm crops to support their building programs, especially funerary monuments. But in years of famine, dynasties fell and the state splintered into separate units. Politically, ancient Egypt alternated between central and local control.

Foreign trade was a royal monopoly. The government obtained cedar from Lebanon, olive oil from Palestine, myrrh from Punt, probably on the Somali coast, and lapis lazuli, a precious blue stone, from Afghanistan. Egypt never developed a coinage, so the pharaohs bartered for these imports with papyrus rolls (for writing), linen, weapons, and furniture. The pharaohs also exported gold from the eastern desert and copper from the Sinai peninsula. In addition, Egypt served as the carrier of tropical African goods—ebony, ivory, and animal skins—to the eastern Mediterranean.

Egyptian society was hierarchical, and at the top stood the pharaoh—the king and god incarnate. Because divine blood coursed through the ruler's veins, he could marry only within his own family. Tradition decreed that the chief queen, who was identified with the goddess Hathor, would produce the royal heir. If she failed to produce offspring, the successor pharaoh was selected from sons of the ruler's other wives or royal cousins. On rare occasions, when there was no suitable heir, the chief queen became the pharaoh, as did Hatshepsut [hat-SHEP-soot] in the New Kingdom.

Because there was no provision for a female king in Egyptian culture, the appearance of a female ruler is thought by scholars to signal a political crisis. Only four times in Egypt's three-thousand-year history was the king female; in contrast, there were more than two hundred male kings. Of the four female rulers, three appeared at the end of dynasties: Nitiqret [nee-tee-KRET] in the Sixth Dynasty, Nefrusobk [nef-RUU-sobek] in the Twelfth, and Tausret [touse-RET] in the Nineteenth. Hatshepsut's assumption of power was unique in that it occurred in the midst of a flourishing dynasty, though during the infancy of Thutmose III [thoot-MOH-suh], the heir apparent. Acting at first as regent to the young heir, Hatshepsut soon claimed the king-ship in her own right and reigned for about ten years. After her death, Thutmose III obliterated her name and image from her monuments, though the reason for their removal is unclear. He may have been expressing hatred of her, or he may have wanted to erase the memory of a woman who had seized power contrary to *maat*, the natural order of things.

Ranked below the ruling family were the royal officials, nobles, large landowners, and priests, all generally hereditary offices. The pharaoh's word was law, but these groups were delegated powers for executing his will. On a lower level, artists and artisans worked for the pharaonic court and the nobility. Peasants and a small number of slaves formed the bulk of Egypt's population. Personal liberty took second place to the general welfare, and peasants were pressed into forced labor during natural disasters, such as unexpected floods, and at harvest time.

A Quest for Eternal Cultural Values

Until the invasion of the Hyksos, Egypt, in its splendid isolation, forged a civilization whose serene values and timeless forms mirrored the religious beliefs of the rulers and the stability of the state. But as contact with other cultures and civilizations grew, Egyptian culture reflected new influences. Writers borrowed words from other languages, for example, and sculptors displayed the human figure in more natural settings and poses than in earlier times. Still, Egyptian culture retained its distinctive qualities, and innovations continued to express traditional ideals.

Religion   Mesopotamia's kings were **theocratic:** they believed that they ruled at the behest of the gods. Egypt's pharaohs were gods. Believing that the deities had planned their country's future from the beginning, the Egyptians thought of their society as sacred. From the time Menes first united Egypt, religious dogma taught that the king, as god on earth, embodied the state. Egyptian rulers also identified with various deities. For example, Menes claimed to be the "two ladies," the goddesses who stood for Upper and Lower Egypt. Other rulers identified themselves with Ra, the sun god, and with Ra's son, Horus, the sky god, who was always depicted as having the head of a falcon. Because of the king's divinity, the resources of the state were concentrated on giving the ruler proper homage, as in the Old Kingdom's massive tombs, designed on a superhuman scale to ensure his safe passage to the afterlife.

Egyptian subjects worshiped the pharaoh, but the pharaoh could venerate any deity he pleased. Hence, the shifting fortunes of Egypt's many cults depended on the ruler's preference. For example, early pharaohs favored Ptah (who, like the Hebrew God in Genesis, called things into being with words), whereas later ones preferred Ra, the sun god, and they honored this celestial deity by building him temples more impressive than their own royal tombs. Later still, pharaohs worshiped Amen ("hidden one"), and a series of rulers adopted his name, as in Amenemhat [AH-men-EM-hat]. Royal favor to a god generally increased the wealth and influence of the god's cult and priests. Consequently, by the time of the New Kingdom, society had become top-heavy with priests and their privileged religious properties.

Egypt came close to having a national deity during the New Kingdom when Akhenaten [ahk-NAHT-uhn] (r. about 1369–1353 BCE) reshaped the royal religion at his capital, Amarna. Elevating Aten, the god of the sun's disk, to supremacy above the other gods, Akhenaten systematically disavowed the older divinities—a heretical view in tolerant, polytheistic Egypt. This innovation, called **henotheism**—the worship of one god without denying the existence of other gods—aroused the opposition of conservative nobles who supported the powerful priests of the Theban god, Amen. Akhenaten ultimately failed to impose his innovation, and later pharaohs tried to erase his name and memory from history. The Amarna revolution, however, like the religious choices of the pharaohs generally, had little effect on the ordinary Egyptian, who continued to believe that the pharaoh could intervene with the other gods for the benefit of all.

The foremost distinguishing mark of Egyptian religion was its promise of immortality. Because the afterlife was imagined to be a carefree continuation of earthly existence, Egyptians had a more optimistic attitude toward human existence than that found in Mesopotamia. In the Old Kingdom, only the kings were accorded this reward. Eventually, nobles and royal officials were buried in the vicinity of the rulers' tombs, thereby ensuring their immortality as assistants to the risen god in the afterlife. By the first

Figure 1.11 Egyptian Writing. From the Old Kingdom onward, the hieroglyphs (in the top line) constituted the style of formal writing that appeared on tomb walls and in monuments. Religious and governmental scribes soon devised two distinct types of cursive script, a careful manuscript hand (in the middle line) and a more rapid hand (in the bottom line) for administrative documents and letters.

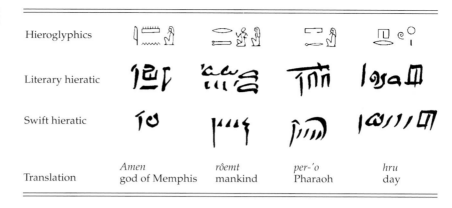

Hieroglyphics				
Literary hieratic				
Swift hieratic				
Translation	*Amen* god of Memphis	*rôemt* mankind	*per-'o* Pharaoh	*hru* day

intermediate period, the nobles had claimed their own right to immortality by erecting tombs on which the royal funerary texts were copied. Later, immortality was apparently opened to all Egyptians.

Writing and Literature Late predynastic Egypt (around 3100 BCE) borrowed the idea of writing from Mesopotamia. The Egyptians initially drew pictographs, called **hieroglyphs,** for such words as *hoe, arrowhead,* and *plow.* This early hieroglyphic script could also depict abstract words for which no adequate picture was available, but because such picture writing was time-consuming and difficult to execute, the scribes soon made the pictographs function as signs, or clusters of consonants, for other words (Figure 1.11).

Egyptian literature produced no single great work that rivals *Gilgamesh,* but the Egyptian experience was rich in its variety of literary **genres,** or types of literature. For example, pyramid texts, the writings inscribed in burial chambers (see the backgrounds in Figures 1.18 and 1.19), formed the chief literary genre in the Old Kingdom. As this era gave way to the first intermediate period, new prose genres, such as prophecies and pessimistic writings, arose that addressed the prevalent political disintegration and social upheaval. Such was the tenor of the times that writers expressed views contradicting Egypt's otherwise optimistic attitudes to death and life. *The Dispute of a Man with His Soul* describes a desperate mortal finally choosing the emptiness of death rather than life in a materialistic and violent world.

The prophecies, **hymns** (songs of praise to the gods), and prose narratives of the Middle Kingdom constitute the classical period of Egyptian letters. The most famous work of the Middle Kingdom, as well as of all Egyptian literature, is the *Story of Sinuhe,* a prose tale that celebrates the ruler Senusert I and his subject, the hero named in the title. Fleeing Egypt, Sinuhe earns fame and fortune in Lebanon yet yearns for his beloved homeland. Sinuhe's exploits smack of the folktale, for

in one episode he subdues a taunting giant of a man, much as David defeats Goliath in the Old Testament story. Eventually, a gracious Senusert writes to Sinuhe, forgiving his wandering subject's unnamed crime and inviting him to return home. The travel yarn concludes with a homecoming scene in which a joyful Sinuhe is reintegrated into Egyptian court society.

During the New Kingdom, in addition to songs praising the pharaoh, poets composed lyrics telling of the pain of parted lovers, and new genres included model letters, wisdom literature, and fairy tales. Akhenaten's revolution led to unique forms of literary expression, as in the *Hymn to Aten,* which praised this universal god. The hymn has similarities to Psalm 104 of the Old Testament, which suggests the relatively free flow of ideas during Egypt's imperial years.

Science and Medicine Natural philosophy, as a separate field of study, did not emerge in ancient Egypt. No term for either philosophy or science existed in the Egyptian language. The Egyptians put their efforts into what today would be called applied science. For example, they invented a convenient decimal number system rendered inconvenient by their cumbersome hieroglyphics. They devised problem-solving methods and related rules for measuring figures and calculating the volumes of solids. They kept accurate records of the annual floods of the Nile and built pyramids and other structures, which required knowledge of measurement and design.

Egyptians studied the movement of the stars, but Egyptian astronomy was not well advanced, being concerned primarily with casting horoscopes and the keeping of the civil calendar. Egypt's lasting contribution in this field was the calendar itself, which priests maintained for the celebration of religious rituals and festivals during the year. The Egyptians divided the year into twelve months of thirty days each, with five extra days at the end of the year. This calendar began each annual cycle on September 21, the autumnal equinox. Later, the Romans adopted the Egyptian calendar, with its twelve-month, 365-day cycle, and they in turn transmitted it to the modern world.

Medicine was another area of Egyptian scientific achievement, partly from a concern with the health of the living and partly from an acute interest in the physical remains of the dead. Mummies, the carefully prepared and preserve remains of dead persons, fascinate modern visitors to museums but also reveal the accumulated physical knowledge of the Egyptians. An ancient medical treatise, dating from about 1600 BCE (but possibly from as early as 3000 BCE), is the world's oldest surviving medical textbook. This surgical treatise offers a comprehensive survey of the human body, detailing the diagnosis, treatment, and outcome of various maladies that can afflict the human organs. A second medical treatise, dating from about 1550 BCE, lists hundreds of magical incantations and folk remedies for numerous illnesses and injuries, such as ingrown toenails and wounds inflicted by crocodiles, along with advice on ridding the house of vermin, insects, and scorpions.

Architecture   The classic Egyptian building was the pyramid, whose shape seemed to embody a constant and eternal order. During the Old Kingdom, the pyramid became the only building deemed suitable for a ruler-god's resting place preparatory to the afterlife. A modified version of the pyramid appeared first in about 2680 BCE in the step pyramid of King Djoser [ZHO-ser]

at Sakkareh, opposite Memphis (Figure 1.12). Later Egyptian rulers preferred the true pyramid form, and this design did not develop further.

The true pyramid appeared in the Old Kingdom when King Khufu [KOO-foo] erected the Great Pyramid at Giza, across the Nile from Cairo (see Figure 1.10). The anonymous architect executed this largest stone building in the world—6.25 million tons—with mathematical precision. Many of the tomb's two million stones were quarried on the site, although most were obtained farther upstream and ferried to Giza during the flooding of the Nile. The infinitesimally small deviation between the two sets of opposing base sides of the pyramid displays awesome technical capability. Later, two of Khufu's successors, Khafre [KAF-ray] and Menkure [men-KOO-ray], added their pyramids to make the complex at Giza the symbol of the Old Kingdom and one of the wonders of the ancient world.

The pyramids eventually gave way to funerary temples when the New Kingdom pharaohs began to construct splendid monuments for themselves that reflected Egypt's new imperial status. The temple of Queen Hatshepsut is perhaps the most beautiful example of this architectural development (Figure 1.13). Designed by the royal architect Senmut, the temple of Hatshepsut was carved into the face of a mountain across the Nile from Luxor. Senmut, adopting the post-and-lintel style of construction, gave the queen's temple two levels of pillared colonnades, each

Figure 1.12 Imhotep. **Step Pyramid of King Djoser. Ca. 2680 BCE. Sakkareh, Egypt.** Although the step pyramid at Sakkareh resembles the Mesopotamian ziggurat, the two structures have different origins. Sakkareh's step pyramid, with its terraced stages, evolved from an Egyptian prototype, which dated from the First Dynasty. Unlike ziggurats, which were made of dried-clay bricks, the step pyramid was made of cut stone, the first buildings to be so constructed in the world. The step pyramid has six levels on a 411-by-358-foot base and stands 204 feet high.

Figure 1.13 SENMUT. **Hatshepsut's Temple. Ca. 1490 BCE. Deir el Bahri, across from Luxor, Egypt.** Hatshepsut's temple was planned for the same purpose as the pyramids—to serve as a shrine for the royal remains. In actuality an ascending series of three colonnaded courtyards, this temple provided a spectacular approach to a hidden sanctuary carved in the steep cliffs.

accessible by long sloping ramps. The most arresting feature of Hatshepsut's temple is its round columns, which are used alongside rectangular pillars in the **porticoes,** or covered entrances. These columns—with their plain tops and grooved surfaces—suggest the graceful columns of later Greek architecture, although some scholars dismiss this similarity as coincidental. Be that as it may, this Egyptian monument, like the later Greek temples, shows a harmonious sense of proportion throughout its impressive colonnades.

Sculpture, Painting, and Minor Arts   The Egyptians did not understand art as it is defined today. Indeed, they had no word for art. Rather than being art for art's sake, Egyptian painting and sculpture served as a means to a religious end, specifically to house the *ka,* or spirit of a person or deity. Art was more than mere representation; images embodied all of the subjects' qualities.

In the royal graveyard at Giza, artisans of the Old Kingdom carved from the living rock a mythical creature that stirred the imagination of most peoples in the ancient world—a sphinx, a lion with a human head (Figure 1.14). Although this creature often inspired feelings of dread, in actuality there was little mystery to the sphinx, since its original purpose was to guard

Figure 1.14   The Great Sphinx. Ca. 2560 BCE. Sandstone, 65′ high × 240′ long. Giza, Egypt. Sphinxes, creatures part-lion and part-human, were often depicted in Egyptian art. The most famous sphinx is the one at Giza, carved from the rock on the site. The sphinx's colossal size prevented the anonymous sculptor from rendering it with any subtle facial expressions. More significant as a monument than as a great work of art, the Great Sphinx had a practical purpose—to guard the nearby pyramid tombs.

Interpreting Art

Subject *Nefertiti*, which means "The Beautiful One Has Come," was the wife and consort of Akhenaten. She is the only queen known to have shared rule with her husband.

Religious Perspective In Egyptian religion the rulers were gods. Hence this bust depicts Queen Nefertiti as a goddess, fit to be worshiped. However, the precise purpose for which this statue was carved is unknown. Archaeologists discovered the bust in 1912 in Amarna in the workshop of a sculptor named Thutmose.

Medium The statue is carved from limestone, painted with six colors ranging from the whites of the eyes to the reddish tint of the skin to the brilliant blue of the crown. The right eye has a quartz iris. The left eye was apparently left unfinished.

Symbolism Her surpassing beauty suggests that Nefertiti was, like a pharaoh, both divine and human. Her crown bears the *uraeus*, the image of a cobra ready to strike. This image signified power and protection and was a typical element of Egyptian regalia, the signs and symbols of royalty.

Style The face is thrust proudly forward, the elongated neck is elegant, and the long, slender nose is regal. The lips are lush and full. Cosmetics have been applied tastefully. Although the image is highly stylized, the sculptor has tried to capture a sense of *the* ideal woman.

Context The art of Amarna in Akhenaten's time abandoned the austerity of traditional Egyptian art. This bust achieves a naturalism and lifelike vitality that is unusual in Egyptian art of any period.

Possibly by Sculptor Thutmose, *Bust of Egyptian Queen Nefertiti.* **Ca. 1345 BCE. Limestone, ht. 20″. Neues Museum, Berlin.** This most exquisite example of Egyptian art has become an iconic figure of universal female beauty.

1. **Subject** Compare and contrast the face of Nefertiti with that of the chief queen in Figure 1.15.
2. **Religious** How does this bust of Nefertiti reflect its historical period?
3. **Style** Why has this statue become such an iconic image in Western culture?
4. **Symbolism** Why has the sculptor added paint to this limestone image?
5. **Context** What is the purpose of the regalia worn by Nefertiti?

the royal tombs, perhaps to frighten away grave robbers. Indeed, this first sphinx's face was that of Khafre, the Fourth Dynasty king whose pyramid stood nearby. Today, this crumbling relic stands as a reminder of the claims to immortality of the Old Kingdom rulers.

The sheer size and mythical character of the Great Sphinx set it apart from Old Kingdom sculptures in the round, which favored human-scale figures and realistic images. The life-size statue of King Menkure and his chief queen, found beneath the ruler's pyramid at Giza, shows this art's brilliant realism (Figure 1.15). The sculpture embodies the characteristics of what became the standard, or classical, Egyptian style: their left legs forward, the king's clenched fists, their headdresses (sacred **regalia** for him and wig for her), their rigid poses, their serene countenances, and the figures' angularity. Designed to be attached to a wall, the sculpture was intended to be viewed from the front, so the couple has a two-dimensional quality.

In contrast to practices in the Old Kingdom, the wives of rulers in the New Kingdom acquired claims to divinity in their own right. A statue of Hatshepsut (see p. 18) represents her in the clothing and with the sacred pose of pharaoh (Figure 1.16). Although more

Figure 1.15 *King Menkure and His Chief Queen.* Ca. 2525 BCE. Ht. 54¹/₂″.
Museum expedition. Museum of Fine Arts, Boston. This life-size slate sculpture
of Menkure, a Fourth Dynasty ruler, and his chief queen was removed from its resting
place beneath the king's pyramid at Giza (see Figure 1.10). In this sculpture, the figures
are represented as being of comparable size, unlike the usual depiction of husbands
as much larger than their wives, indicating their greater importance. The sizes here
probably reflect the royal status of the chief queen. The queen's subordination to the
king is subtly shown in her position on his left side, thought to be inferior to the right,
and her arm around his waist, an indication that her role was to encourage and support.

Figure 1.16 *Hatshepsut.* Ca. 1460 BCE. Marble, ht. 6′5″. Metropolitan
Museum of Art. Rogers Fund and contribution from Edward S.
Harkness, 1929 (29.3.2). This sculpture is one of more than two hundred
statues of Hatshepsut intended to adorn her massive and elegant funeral
temple at Deir el Bahri, across from Luxor, Egypt. The authoritative pose
and regalia convey her pharaonic status, and she is only subtly represented
as a woman.

than a thousand years separated this sculpture from that of Menkure (see Figure 1.15), in its expression of dignity and authority the statue of Hatshepsut bears a strong resemblance to the earlier work, thus demonstrating the continuity of the Egyptian style.

Figure 1.17 *Family Scene: Pharaoh Akhenaten, Queen Nefertiti, and Their Three Daughters.* Ca. 1350 BCE. Limestone, 13″ high × 15⁵/₁₂″ wide. **Ägyptisches Museum und Papyrussammlung, Berlin.** The religious ideas associated with Akhenaten's reforms are expressed in the lines streaming from the sun's disk above the royal couple. Each ray of the sun ends in a tiny hand that offers a blessing to the royal family.

A major challenge to Egypt's traditional, austere forms occurred in Akhenaten's revolutionary reign. A low-relief sculpture of the royal family exemplifies the naturalism and fluid lines that this artistic rebellion favored (Figure 1.17). Akhenaten nuzzles one of his daughters in an intimate pose while his wife, Nefertiti, dandles another daughter on her knees and allows a third to stand on her left arm. The domesticity of this scene is quite unlike the sacred gestures of traditional Egyptian sculpture, but the religious subject of this relief remains true to that tradition, as the rays streaming from the disk of Aten onto the royal family indicate.

Just as Egypt's sculpture in the round developed a rigid **canon,** or set of rules, so did two-dimensional representations acquire a fixed formula, whether in relief sculptures or in wall paintings. The Egyptians never discovered the principles of perspective. On a flat surface, the human figures were depicted in profile, with both feet pointing sideways, as in a painting from a New Kingdom funerary papyrus (Figure 1.18). However, the artistic canon required that the eye and the shoulders be shown frontally, and both arms had to be visible, along with all the fingers. The artist determined the human proportions exactly, by the use of a grid. The human figure was usually conceived as being eighteen squares high standing and fourteen squares high seated, with each unit equivalent to the width of one "fist"; anatomical parts were made accordingly proportional. The canon of proportions was established by the time of the Old Kingdom, and its continued use, with slight variations, helped Egyptian art retain its

Figure 1.18 **Opening of the Mouth Scene, Funerary Papyrus of Hunefer. Ca. 1305–1195 BCE. British Museum, London.** Egyptian painters and sculptors always depicted human subjects from the side, with the feet in profile, as in this painting on a papyrus manuscript deposited in a New Kingdom tomb. This painting's treatment of flesh tones of the human figures also typifies the Egyptian style. Egyptian men, represented here by the officiating priests, were consistently shown with red-brown, tanned skins at least partially reflective of their outdoor lives. Egyptian women, such as the mourners directly before the mummy, were usually painted with lighter complexions of yellow or pink or white. The Opening of the Mouth was a burial ritual, preparing the deceased to speak in the afterlife.

Figure 1.19 *Nebamun Hunting Birds.* Ca. 1400 BCE. From the Tomb of Nebamun, Thebes. Paint on gypsum plaster, ht. 32″. British Museum, London. For the nobleman Nebamun, hunting was a pastime not a necessity. Decorating his tomb with hunting scenes was Nebamun's way of ensuring that there would be plenty of birds to hunt in the afterlife. Note the faces in profile—typical in Egyptian art (see Figures 1.17 and 1.18).

unmistakable style. Wall paintings, in contrast to relief sculptures, permitted a greater sense of life and energy, as in the scene of Nebamun hunting birds, but the rules regarding the human figure still had to be observed (Figure 1.19). Given those stringent conventions, the Egyptian artists who worked in two dimensions were amazingly successful in creating the image of a carefree society bubbling with life.

Royal tombs have yielded incomparable examples of Egyptian sculpture, as in the burial chamber of the New Kingdom pharaoh Tutankhamen [too-tahn-KAHM-en]. Of the thirty-four excavated royal tombs,

only that of King Tut—as he is popularly known—escaped relatively free from ancient tomb robbers. A freestanding, life-size sculpture of the funerary goddess Selket was one of four goddess figures who watched over the gilded shrine that contained the king's internal organs (Figure 1.20). Her arms are outstretched in a protective fashion around her royal charge's shrine. The sculpture's style, with its naturalism and fluid lines, reflects the art of Amarna, the revolutionary style that flourished briefly in the fourteenth century BCE before being abandoned and replaced by Egypt's traditional formal style.

Timeline 1.4   HEIRS TO THE MESOPOTAMIAN AND EGYPTIAN CULTURES   **All dates approximate and BCE**

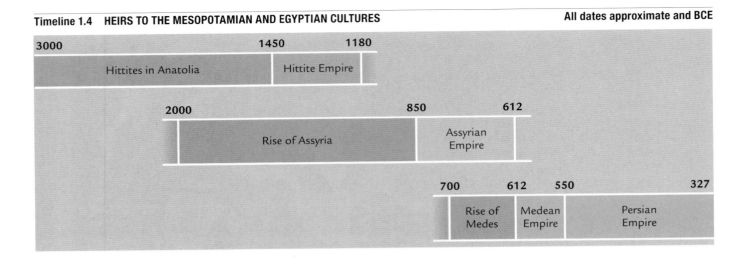

HEIRS TO THE MESOPOTAMIAN AND EGYPTIAN EMPIRES

With the decline of the Egyptian and Hittite Empires, the ancient Near East entered a confusing period. At first a number of small states emerged and enjoyed periods of independence. Israel (see Chapter 6) and Phoenicia were the most prominent. Then a series of ever-larger empires arose: the Assyrians, the Neo-Babylonians, and finally the Persians (Timeline 1.4).

The Assyrians

The earliest Assyrian tribes lived in the Upper Tigris region, in present-day Iraq. Their original state fell in the general collapse following the Egyptian-Hittite clash at Kadesh (1274 BCE). For some three centuries the Assyrians gathered their resources and then went on a series of lightning conquests that brought them to the Mediterranean coast. For a short time the Assyrians became the first people to rule both Egypt and Mesopotamia. Their successes were ideological and military. The Assyrians were relentless, cunning, and brutal. They also used iron weapons and swift-moving cavalry instead of chariots. After conquering an area, the Assyrians deported many of the people they did not kill or enslave. They waged utter destruction on anyone who dared to resist or rebel. Capable administrators and spies ensured significant human and material resources. Yet, just when it appeared the Assyrian Empire would continue for centuries, it was quickly defeated by the Medes and the Neo-Babylonians in 612 BCE, at Nineveh.

Cruelty and militarism manifested themselves in Assyrian culture and art. Their cities were built as fortresses. The temples to their gods were huge and adorned. Their rulers' palaces were constructed on a

Figure 1.20   *Selket*. Ca. 1325 BCE. Wood, overlaid with gesso and gilded, ht. 53⅝″. Cairo Museum, Egypt. This statue of the goddess Selket was found in King Tutankhamen's tomb in 1923, one of the great archaeological finds of the twentieth century. Discovered by Egyptologist Howard Carter, the tomb held thousands of royal artifacts and art objects, including the pharaoh's gold funerary mask, a solid gold coffin, a gold throne, chairs, couches, chariots, jewelry, figurines, drinking cups, clothing, weapons, and games. The fascinating story of the discovery is told in Carter's book, *The Tomb of Tutankhamen.*

magnificent and gigantic scale with open courtyards, terraces, and decorations. These royal residences expressed the empire's triumphs and sent a clear message of power to the Assyrian people and to subjected enemies. Among the ruins of the Assyrian palaces and sculpture, the portal carvings, or "guardians of the gates," and the wall reliefs remain as testaments to the glories and values of a fierce and proud people. The stone animals, placed as pairs at the entrances of palaces and temples, were there to impress visitors and to ward off evil forces. The human-headed winged bulls (Figure 1.21), found at several royal palaces, convey the power, aura, and mystery of the Assyrian kings—and the awe they sought to inspire.

The Neo-Babylonians

One beneficiary of the fall of the Assyrians was the Neo-Babylonian kingdom established in 626 BCE. Although militant and warlike, the Neo-Babylonians were also culturally sophisticated. In addition to helping to defeat the Assyrians, the Neo-Babylonians conquered Jerusalem and exiled the Hebrews of the kingdom of Judah (see Chapter 6). Under the direction of their greatest king, Nebuchadnezzar (605–562 BCE), the city of Babylon was largely rebuilt (Figure 1.22) and adorned with the famous "hanging gardens," a luxurious, terraced complex built for the queen. The Neo-Babylonians, like the Assyrians, were accomplished in astronomy. Their interests, however, were religious not scientific. That is, they observed the heavens closely to practice astrology. In the end, the Neo-Babylonians were no match for their erstwhile allies the Medes who, having merged with the Persians, conquered them in 539 BCE.

The Medes and the Persians

After their defeat of the Assyrians in 612 BCE, the Medes [Meeds], an Indo-European people from the southwest Iranian plateau, retained Nineveh, the Assyrian capital. From their homeland in the central Zagros Mountains, the Medes built an empire that eventually covered most of northern and western Mesopotamia and eastern Anatolia. The power of the Medes, however, proved to be short-lived. In about 550 BCE, their empire fell to the Persians, another Indo-European tribe led by the charismatic Cyrus the Great (559–530 BCE). The Persians, under a series of masterful rulers, forged the strongest and largest empire that the eastern Mediterranean had yet seen. At its height, Persian rule extended from Egypt in the south to central Russia in the north, and from Cyprus in the west to the Indus River in the east. Of its neighbors in the eastern Mediterranean basin, only mainland Greece eluded Persia's grasp. The Persians brought peace to a wide area; granted autonomy to most peoples; instituted common coinage, weights, and measures; and built good roads.

For two hundred years the Persian Empire and its culture had a brilliant run. The Persians created an eclectic style that derived from their own past as well as from the cultures of many of the peoples folded into the Persian Empire. For example, Persian arts had included distinctive vase painting and elegant

Figure 1.21 Human-Headed Winged Bull. Eighth century BCE. Gypseous alabaster, ht. 13′10″. Louvre. In Assyrian iconography, human-headed winged bulls—or lions—that guarded the entrances to royal residences and temples combined the characteristics of certain living beings. The head of a man represented intellectual power and the lord of creation; eagle wings were signs of speed and flight; the bull symbolized strength and fecundity, or, if the creature was a lion, then strength and the king of beasts. The carvings' five legs—an unnatural touch—gave each animal the appearance of either walking or standing still, depending on the perspective from which it was viewed. While their purposes are not fully understood, these guardian statues, with their imposing stance and symbolic meanings, made all who approached know that they were in the presence of a powerful ruler and forces.

Figure 1.22   The Ishtar Gate, Babylon. Ca. 575 BCE. Glazed brick, ht. 48′9″. Vorderasiatisches Museum, Berlin. Nebuchadnezzar dedicated this magnificent processional entryway to Ishtar, the goddess of love and war. It was one of eight gates into the city of Babylon. Excavated by German archaeologists between 1899 and 1914, the gate was reconstructed in Berlin. Dragons and aurochs (now-extinct oxen) are depicted on the gate. The hanging gardens have vanished, so only this gateway survives to convey a sense of Babylon's opulence.

Figure 1.23   Nobles Marching Up the Stairs. Ca. 512–494 BCE. Persepolis, Iran. This charming relief sculpture, carved on a wall facing a stairway at the Persian capital, Persepolis, depicts aristocrats mounting stairs to greet the king on New Year's Day, a sacred festival celebrated on the summer solstice and one of the major holidays in Mesopotamia. Each noble bears a flower offering as a tangible sign of his devotion to the monarch. The artist has humanized this courtly ritual by injecting an element of sly humor into the stately scene: one noble (the seventh from the right) sniffs his flower, and a second noble (the third from the right) turns to check on the progress of the procession behind him.

metalworking but no tradition of stone architecture. Now, under the empire, artists and craftspeople, many of whom were new subjects, built on that heritage and, at the same time, borrowed from their own building traditions. These borrowings included masonry techniques, the finished appearance of buildings, treatment of architectural and sculptural details as decorations, as on columns, and some new building types. In the end, Persian architecture became the first highly decorated style (between India in the east and Syria in the west) to use large dressed stone rather than brick.

Persian art was courtly and ceremonial and focused on heightening the dignity and authority of the king and his court. At the capital, Persepolis, lo-

cated in the Persian homeland of Parsa (modern Fars, in southern Iran), Cyrus the Great chose the site for a palace. His successor, King Darius I (duh-RYE-us) (r. 522–486 BCE), eventually built the first monumental palace there, and later rulers made splendid additions. Persepolis today is a ruin, having been looted during Alexander the Great's conquest in 330 BCE. Among the ruins, a magnificent decorative relief survives, depicting aristocrats as they offer tribute to the king on New Year's Day. Despite its battered condition, this relief attests to the stateliness of the Persian imperial style (Figure 1.23).

Persian visual arts also stressed contemplative themes with little action, as in the relief sculpture of King Darius (Figure 1.24). In this panel, King Darius

Figure 1.24   King Darius Giving Audience before Two Fire Altars. Found in the Treasury, Persepolis. Ca. 512–494 BCE. Limestone, length 20′. Archaeological Museum, Tehran. This relief sculpture, carved on the walls of the Treasury at Persepolis, shows King Darius seated before two fire altars. In front of him is the master of ceremonies, with his hand raised to his lips in a gesture of devotion. Two bodyguards, holding spears, stand to the right. The Persian sculptural style is shown by the stylized hair and beards, precise folds in the clothing, and formal poses of the figures.

is represented on a throne before two fire altars, as he receives a court official. Bending slightly from the waist, the official covers his mouth with the tips of his fingers—a gesture of devotion. These two sculptures illustrate the limited range of subjects, namely, the king and his court duties, employed in the art program of the Persian kings at Persepolis.

The fire altars depicted in the relief panel mentioned above are symbols of Zoroastrianism, the religion of the Persian prophet Zoroaster [ZOHR-uh-was-ter] (about 600 BCE), which became the official faith of the Persian court at the time of Darius I. Zoroastrianism is the most original and enduring of Persia's legacies. Rejecting polytheism, Zoroaster called for a dualistic religion in which the god of light, Ahura Mazda (Persian, "Wise Lord"), engaged in a universal struggle with the god of darkness, Ahriman. According to Zoroaster, not only did those who had led lives of purity gain favored treatment in the afterlife, but their actions also ensured the triumph of the forces of good in life on earth. These teachings later had a profound impact on Western philosophy and religion.

SUMMARY

By responding to the dramatic changes caused by the Neolithic Revolution, people in southern Mesopotamia and Egypt took the first steps along the path that led to civilization. They created governments, military and religious institutions, and increasingly sophisticated cultures characterized by complex technologies, alluring arts, and impressive architecture. The advent of writing permitted the rise of public record-keeping and also of literature. Geography played a key role in both areas. Mesopotamians, for example, lacked ready access to stone and built with mud bricks. Egyptians had plenty of nearby stone and used it imaginatively. Narrow fertile strips surrounded by forbidding deserts imposed very early a high degree of political and social regimentation. Above all, one people after another built on the work of their predecessors and created a platform, so to speak, running from North Africa to Central Asia, on which the foundations of the Western humanities were erected.

Legacies from Prehistory and Near Eastern and Egyptian Civilization

Today one cannot turn on the news without being deluged with stories about the Near East or the Middle East. There was no "news" in antiquity, but things would have been the same. This old, vast, rich, and complex region has been simultaneously at the root and at the forefront of the West. Greeks, Romans, Muslims, Crusaders, and modern European imperialists have continually warred, traded, and exchanged ideas with the lands of Gilgamesh and the pharaohs. Apart from the vast forces of history, we have inherited much else from these people. Students still go to school to lean their "a, b, c's." High school and college students study circles by means of *pi*. The ancients used lunar calendars and most people today use solar ones. But the ancients gave us sixty-second minutes and sixty-minute hours. The Egyptians remain perennially fascinating. If a museum has a display of mummies, there will be lines at the door. We no longer bury people in pyramids, but the distinguished architect I. M. Pei built a glass one to serve as an entrance to the Louvre Museum in Paris. And in 1986 a rather forgettable rock group, the Bangles, had a hit song called "Walk Like an Egyptian." For a while, lots of young people gallivanted around imitating poses from Egyptian art.

Louvre Pyramid, Paris. 115′ on each side, 70′ high. This glass and steel pyramid designed by I. M. Pei (1917–) opened in 1989 as the main entrance to the Louvre Museum. Pei's pyramid was in part a homage to the precise geometric designs of the great French landscape architect, André LeNotre. And, in part, the pyramid's geometric planes echoed the articulated planes of the Louvre's roof and surrounding buildings.

KEY CULTURAL TERMS

civilization

culture

Paleolithic

Neolithic

pictogram

ideogram

phonogram

cuneiform

polytheism

anthropomorphism

pantheism

stele

reliefs

post-and-lintel
   construction

ziggurat

theocracy

henotheism

hieroglyphs

genre

hymn

portico

regalia

canon

Temple of Hera, Paestum. Ca. 560–550 BCE. Limestone. Archaic temples set patterns long used by the Greeks. The buildings were aligned east-west, with the entrance in the east. A vast altar stood before the entrance, and people gathered around it to share a sacrificial meal. The enclosed space inside the temple's colonnade was off-limits except to the priests.

The Aegean

The Minoans, the Mycenaeans, and the Greeks of the Archaic Age

Preview Questions

1. *What* key aspects of the Minoan and Mycenaean cultures lived on among the later Greeks?

2. *What* were the principal political and social achievements of the Greek Archaic period?

3. *How* do epic and lyric poetry differ from each other?

4. In *what* ways do Greek religion and philosophy differ from each other, and how do both differ from the achievements of the Mesopotamians and Egyptians?

Three significant peoples thrived in the Aegean basin: the Minoans, the Mycenaeans, and then the Greeks. The former two were the first to achieve civilization in Europe from about 2000 to 1200 BCE. On the island of Crete and in southern Greece, these peoples built complex societies only to fall, the Minoans to the Mycenaeans and the Mycenaeans to the Dorians. For about three centuries after 1100 BCE the Greek world was poor, isolated, and a cultural backwater. Then, between about 800 and 500 BCE the Greek world entered the Archaic period. *Archaios* in Greek means "ancient," or "beginning," and this was indeed the beginning of Greek history and culture in the strict sense (Timeline 2.1, Map 2.1). On rocky coasts and rugged islands and peninsulas, the peoples of the Aegean basin coaxed a subsistence living from the thin, stony soil and turned to the sea for trade, conquest, and expansion. From the Bronze Age to the Iron Age, Minoans, Mycenaeans, and Greeks interacted with and learned from the cultures that surrounded them, chiefly those of the Hittites and the Egyptians, but whether it was in systems of writing or forms of sculpture, Aegean peoples were never content merely to borrow. They always adapted, blended, and, finally, superseded the contributions of other cultures. The Greek genius was partly a matter of stunning originality and partly a matter of creative synthesis.

The building to the left, a Greek temple in the Doric style, symbolizes many aspects of the Archaic period. It is balanced, ordered, and proportioned, but it does not yet achieve the harmony and beauty of the later classical period (see Chapter 3). This temple, now in ruins, is located in southern Italy, an area colonized by Greeks who left the mainland amid political and economic strife. Greeks not only learned from their neighbors, they also exported their own culture. Temples were usually the largest and most elegant buildings in a polis, the city-state form of political organization that was a key achievement of the Archaic period.

The peoples of Mesopotamia and Egypt seem at once remote and familiar, whereas the Greeks seem utterly familiar; they seem to be "like us."

Timeline 2.1   MINOAN AND MYCENAEAN CULTURES

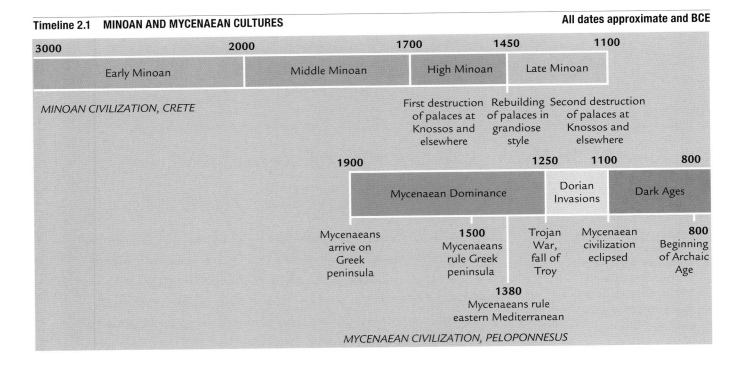

The most profound and recognizable features of the Western tradition derive from the Greeks. Whether one thinks of political institutions, literary forms, or aesthetic tastes, the Greeks were both original and influential. The Greeks shifted focus from gods and godlike rulers to men and women. Ordinary people were seen as having some control over their destinies and some moral responsibility for their actions. By the fifth century BCE the philosopher Protagoras could proclaim, "Man is the measure of all things."

PRELUDE: MINOAN CULTURE, 3000–1100 BCE

Civilization was already flourishing in Mesopotamia and Egypt when it first emerged in Europe, among the Neolithic settlements on the island of Crete. By about 2000 BCE, a prosperous and stable mercantile culture had emerged, and between 1700 and 1500 BCE, it reached its high point in wealth, power, and sophistication. This society, labeled Minoan after the legendary King Minos, had a complex class system that included nobles, merchants, artisans, bureaucrats, and laborers. Noble life centered on palaces, and twentieth-century archaeological excavations of several palace sites indicate that communities were linked in a loose political federation, with the major center at Knossos [NAH-sauce] on the north coast. Remarkably, Minoan palaces had no fortifications, suggesting that the cities

remained at peace with one another and that the island itself faced no threats from sea raiders. Crete's tranquil image is confirmed by the absence of weapons in excavated remains.

The palace of Minos, at Knossos, is the principal source of knowledge about Minoan Crete. The ruins, covering some three acres, though no longer paved or walled, provide a sense of the grandeur and expanse of this once-magnificent site (Figure 2.1). The palace included an impressive plumbing and drainage system and a complex layout of rooms and passageways on several levels. Belowground, a storage area contained huge earthenware pots that held grains, oils, and wines, probably collected as taxes from the populace and serving as the basis of trade and wealth. Beautiful **friezes** (bands of painted designs and sculptured figures) decorated the walls of rooms and hallways. **Frescoes,** wall paintings made by applying paint to wet plaster, of sea creatures (dolphins and octopuses), of beautiful women, and of intriguing bull-leaping rituals (Figure 2.2) enlivened the palace walls. These remains are highly revealing but, unfortunately, early Minoan writing, called **Linear A,** a syllabic system, cannot be read. No one knows the language of the Minoans, which adds to the mystery surrounding their origins.

Minoan religion appears to have been **matriarchal,** led or ruled by women, centering on the worship of a mother goddess, or great goddess, creator of the universe and source of all life. Statues of a bare-breasted earth goddess with snakes in her hands show how the

Learning Through Maps

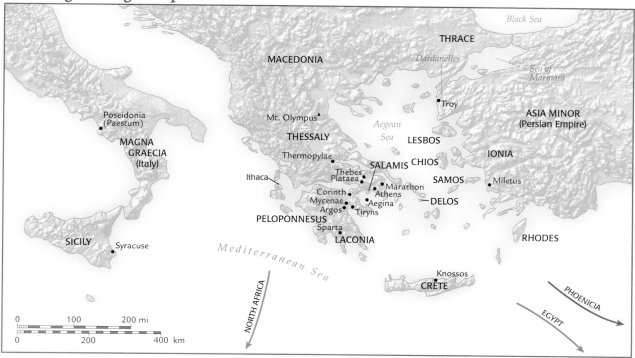

MAP 2.1   THE AEGEAN WORLD, 479 BCE

This map shows the location of the Minoan, Mycenaean, and Greek Archaic Age civilizations. *1. **Consider** the role of the Aegean and Mediterranean Seas in shaping these three civilizations. 2. **What** were the centers of Minoan and Mycenaean civilizations? 3. **Why** do you think the location of Troy helped to make it a wealthy and strategic city? 4. **Locate** the major city-states of the Greek Archaic Age. 5. **How** did geography influence the origins and strategies of the Persian War?*

Figure 2.1   North Entrance, Palace of Minos, Knossos, Crete. Ca. 1750–1650 BCE. The palace complex, with courtyards, staircases, and living areas, now partially restored, indicates that the royal family lived in comfort and security, surrounded by works of art. When British archaeologist Sir Arthur Evans uncovered these ruins in 1902, he became convinced that he had discovered the palace of the legendary King Minos and labeled the civilization *Minoan.*

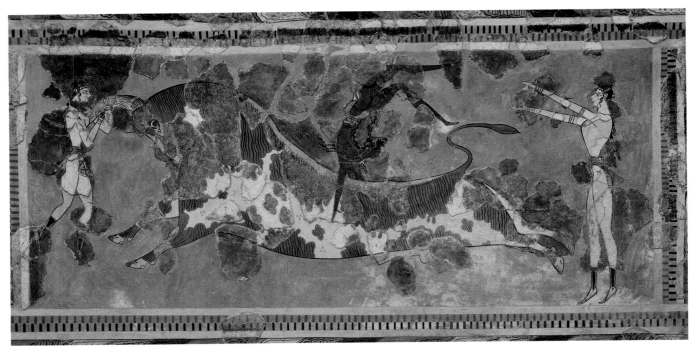

Figure 2.2 *Bull-Leaping.* **Ca. 1500 BCE. Archaeological Museum, Heraklion, Crete.** This fresco (approximately 32 inches high) from the east wing of the palace at Knossos is one of the largest paintings recovered from Crete. The association of young men and women with bulls in this scene brings to mind the legend of the Minotaur, in which seven youths and seven maidens were periodically sacrificed to a monster, half-man and half-bull, who lived in an underground labyrinth, supposedly on Crete. A bull cult may have been central to Minoan religion. Scholars have long debated whether the depiction of bull-leaping is real or fanciful. Prevailing opinion holds that skilled athletes could have performed the trick of vaulting over a bull's horns and back.

deity was portrayed by the Minoans, but the precise purpose of these statues is unknown (Figure 2.3). Minoans also honored numerous minor household goddesses and venerated trees and stone pillars, to which they probably attributed supernatural powers. Near the end of their era, the Minoans began to bury their dead in underground tombs and chambers, but neither the reason for the new burial practice nor its ritualistic meaning has been discovered.

Around 1600 BCE, Crete suffered when a nearby volcanic island erupted. About a century later, the mainland Mycenaeans conquered Crete but did not destroy Knossos. Around 1375 BCE, Knossos was devastated but it is not known how or why. The inhabitants of Crete had always relied heavily on trade, and this did not change under Mycenaean domination until about 1100 BCE.

The Greeks of the later Archaic Age had no direct knowledge of Minoan culture, but the Greek attitude toward the Minoans was shaped by mythology. **Myths** are traditional stories told about bygone eras by later peoples who are seeking to explain some of

Figure 2.3   Earth Goddess with Snakes. Ca. 1600–1580 BCE. Faience, ht. 13½″. Archaeological Museum, Heraklion, Crete. This cult figure was discovered in the Treasury of the Knossos Palace. Her triangular dress, with its apron and flounced skirt, is similar to those of Cretan youths in surviving frescoes.

their basic political, social, or religious practices and ideas. They are often communal and comforting in their explanations, and frequently provide insights into peoples' ways of thinking. As an example, Crete is traditionally the birthplace of the god Zeus. The Minoans worshiped a Zeus who was born in a cave, grew to manhood, and died. They venerated the site of his birth and honored him as a child. The later Greeks, however, believed Zeus to be the immortal father and ruler of the Olympian deities, and they were incensed by the Minoan belief that the god had died. The grain of truth in this story may be that, although the Greeks eventually dominated Crete in physical terms, elements of Minoan religion found their way into later Greek beliefs; thus, in a sense, the Olympian gods *were* born on Crete. Cretan influences on Greece may also be detected in language, social organization, and economic pursuits, although the Archaic Greeks did not regard the Minoan past as part of their heritage.

BEGINNINGS: MYCENAEAN CULTURE, 1900–1100 BCE

Mycenaean culture, named by archaeologists for Mycenae, a prominent fortress city, developed on the rugged lower Greek peninsula known as the Peloponnesus.

An aggressive warrior people, perhaps from the plains of southern Russia or from the upper Tigris-Euphrates valley, the Mycenaeans arrived on the peninsula in about 1900 BCE, and, by about 1500 BCE, they ruled the entire Peloponnesus. More is known about the Mycenaeans than about the Minoans. The archaeological record is more abundant, revealing several palace sites and numerous splendid artifacts. But writing is also critical in two distinct respects. First, the Mycenaeans adapted Cretan Linear A writing to their own language, a primitive form of Greek, and produced thousands of **Linear B** tablets. These tablets contain administrative and commercial documents that aid in understanding Mycenaean government. Second, the much later *Iliad* and *Odyssey* are set in the Mycenaean world and contain a good deal of authentic information about it.

Judging from the *Iliad*, Mycenaean society was aristocratic and hierarchical. A confederation of autonomous kings might occasionally accept the leadership of one of their number. For example, in the Trojan War, Agamemnon of Mycenae was the leader of all the Greeks. Excavations at Mycenae, especially its impressive Lion Gate (Figure 2.4), hint at the wealth and power of kings. Literary and artistic depictions suggest a society that prized military prowess. Linear B documents suggest a bureaucratic system that was

Figure 2.4   The Lion Gate at Mycenae. Ca. 1300 BCE. The Lion Gate is a massive structure of four gigantic blocks—two posts and a beam forming the entrance and a triangular block on which are carved the two 9-foot-high lions and the central column. So impressive were the megalithic Mycenaean fortresses to the later Greeks that they called them "cyclopean," convinced that only a race of giants, the Cyclopes, could have built them.

adept at raising taxes. There were certainly merchants in the Mycenaean world, the majority of whose people were farmers. Slavery existed but its exact significance is not clear.

Excavations show that the Mycenaeans appreciated fine objects and achieved a high level of technical skill. Within the citadel of Mycenae, six **shaft graves** (vertical burials) were discovered. One of them contained a spectacular gold burial mask (Figure 2.5) traditionally called the "Mask of Agamemnon." On discovering it, the famous German archaeologist Heinrich Schliemann telegraphed Berlin, "I have looked on the face of Agamemnon." Probably not—but it is a good story. The graves do reveal the care with which the Mycenaeans attended to the remains of their dead. It is tempting to think that they may have learned this from the Egyptians. Near Sparta, archaeologists unearthed a pair of gorgeous drinking cups, one of which is shown in Figure 2.6. The energy of the figures depicted on the cup is palpable, but no less noticeable is the technical mastery of the unknown artist.

After their conquest of the Minoans, the Mycenaeans extended their raiding and trading activities throughout the eastern Mediterranean. Between 1210 and 1180 BCE, they attacked the wealthy and strategic city of Troy, on the western coast of present-day Turkey (see Map 2.1). It is delightful to think that the face of the beautiful Helen launched a thousand ships, but the Trojan War was only the culmination of a bitter trade dispute. Although similar expeditions had brought spoils to the Mycenaeans on earlier occasions, this long, exhausting foray weakened them. The Myceaneans were no match for the Dorians, who invaded or migrated from the north in about 1100 BCE.

Technology in Minoan Crete and Mycenae

Early cultures in the Aegean—Minoan and Mycenaean—built on the bronze technology of earlier Near Eastern models (see Chapter 1). Bronze was the preferred metal of Mycenaean artisans, as it was for the Minoans before them, but copper, tin, silver, and gold were also used. All these metals were available from mines and deposits in the Mediterranean basin, except tin, which came from the British Isles. Crete and Mycenae used bronze for weapons and everyday objects until both societies collapsed before the onset of the Iron Age, in about 1200 BCE.

In military technology, the Minoans and the Mycenaeans followed the lead of Near Eastern neighbors but made some advances too:

- Bronze weapons: daggers, swords, spears, and javelins; and body armor, such as shields, helmets, and leg and arm coverings
- Introduction of the horse and of horse-drawn chariots by 2000 BCE
- Redesigned chariots by 1300 BCE, with six wheel spokes instead of four and axles under

Figure 2.5 *Mask of Agamemnon.* **Ca. 1500 BCE. Thinly beaten gold, c. 12″ across. National Archaeological Museum, Athens.** Although this is the only Mycenaean gold burial mask so far discovered, it is likely that high-status persons, especially kings, may have had such masks placed in their graves. This is reminiscent of the burial masks on the sarcophagi that held the mummies of prominent Egyptians.

Figure 2.6   Vapheio Cup. Ca. sixteenth century BCE. Gold, 3¹/₂″ high. National Archaeological Museum, Athens. This gold cup, one of two discovered in a tomb at Vapheio near Sparta, Greece, shows a man attempting to capture a bull. At the bottom of the image, the hunter tries to ensnare the bull by means of the net held in his outstretched arms. The curved line of the animal's arched back helps frame the scene, while the bull, with its size and muscular body, seems to be winning this ferocious struggle between man and beast. This cup is thought to be from the Mycenaean period, because its execution is less refined than the exquisite artistry of the other cup (not shown here), which is attributed to the Minoan style. However, both goldsmiths used the same technique: hammering out the scenes from the inside of the cup.

Figure 2.7 **Acropolis, Athens. View from the west.** The Acropolis dominates Athens in the twenty-first century just as it did in ancient times when it was the center of Athenian ceremonial and religious life. Today it is the towering symbol of Athens's cultural heritage as well as the center of the local tourist industry. A landmark in the history of town planning, the Acropolis is the ancestor of all carefully laid-out urban environments from ancient Rome to Renaissance Florence to modern Brasilia.

the rear platform, which enhanced stability and maneuverability

- Advances in shipbuilding: extending the height of the mast, enlarging the size of the sails, and redesigning the oar to increase rowing power

THE ARCHAIC AGE, 800–479 BCE

After the Mycenaeans, Greece entered a period known as the Dark Ages, "dark" because little is known about it. People lived in isolated farming communities and produced only essential tools and domestic objects. Commercial and social interchange among communities, already made hazardous by the mountainous terrain, became even more dangerous, and communication with the eastern Mediterranean kingdoms nearly ceased.

Yet some fundamental changes were slowly occurring. Political power was gradually shifting from kings to the heads of powerful families, laying the foundation for a new form of government, and iron gradually replaced bronze in tools and weapons, ushering in the Iron Age in Greece. Many Mycenaeans fled to the coast of Asia Minor, which later came to be called Ionia, thus paving the way for the formation of an extended Greek community around the Aegean and Mediterranean Seas.

In about 800 BCE, the Greeks emerged from years of stagnation and moved into an era of political innovation and cultural experimentation. Although scattered and isolated, they shared a sense of identity based on their common language, their heroic stories and folktales, their myths and religious practices, and

their commercial and trading interests. They claimed a common mythical parent, Hellen, who fathered three sons—the ancestors of the three major Greek tribes: the Ionians, the Aeolians, and the Dorians—and thus they called themselves Hellenes and their land Hellas. In the next three centuries, the Greeks reconstructed their political and social systems, developed new styles of art and architecture, invented new literary genres, and made the first formal philosophical inquiries into the nature of human behavior and the universe.

Political, Economic, and Social Structures

By the beginning of the Archaic Age, the isolated farming community was evolving into the *polis* (plural, *poleis*), a small city-state. Eventually some two hundred poleis lay scattered over the Greek mainland and abroad. Although each polis was unique, all shared some features:

- An *acropolis* (Figure 2.7): a high, fortified point, often the dwelling place of rulers and location of temples
- An *agora*: essentially a market area where the political, social, and economic life of the polis took place
- A *chora*: the agricultural hinterland that made a true polis a city-state

The polis was a remarkably flexible and creative institution that brought diverse people together into a real community. Poleis generated tremendous pride and loyalty among their citizens.

Simultaneous with the emergence of the polis, the Greek political system underwent a series of changes. As a result of these changes, more and more men were able to participate in the political life of the polis. The kings had been deposed by the leaders of noble families, who owned most of the land and possessed the weapons and horses. These wealthy warriors established **oligarchies,** or governments run by the few. Oligarchs looked out for their own interests but also provided exemplary leadership, fostered civic idealism, and supplied cultural and artistic patronage. However, most oligarchies eventually failed because of unforeseen and far-reaching military and economic changes. New military tactics now made obsolete the aristocratic warriors in their horse-drawn chariots. Foot soldiers—armed with long spears, protected by shields and body armor, and grouped in closed ranks called phalanxes—were proving more effective in battles. These foot soldiers, or hoplites, were recruited from among independent farmers, merchants, traders, and artisans, who were also profiting from an expanding economy. As their military value became evident, these commoners soon demanded a voice in political decisions.

Rising population and limited land generated acute tensions. Frustrated by the inability of reform efforts to solve deep-seated problems, in the sixth century BCE many poleis turned to rulers whom they entrusted with extraordinary powers to make sweeping economic and political changes. Many of these tyrants, as the Greeks called them, restructured their societies to allow more citizens to benefit from the growing economy, to move up the social scale, and to participate in the political process. However, some tyrants perpetuated their rule through heirs or political alliances and governed harshly for years, thus giving a simple word for ruler its modern negative meaning.

Increasing population and its attendant tensions generated another response: colonization. The Greeks sent citizens to join their earlier Ionian settlements and to establish new colonies along the coasts of Spain, North Africa, southern Russia (or the Black Sea), and Sicily and southern Italy, which became known as *Magna Graecia,* or Greater Greece. Colonies were expected to provide resources, especially food, for their *metropoleis* ("mother cities"). Foreign ventures and expanded trade increased the wealth of the new middle class and reinforced its desires for more economic opportunities and political influence, but the entrenched aristocracy and farmer-hoplites tried to deny the middle class access to power. Colonization solved some problems and generated others.

Politically, the Archaic period was important for three reasons. First, it saw the creation of the polis. Second, there was a dramatic expansion of political participation often accompanied by violent conflict between and within poleis. And third, the age of colonization spread Greek ideas, institutions, and artistic achievements throughout the Mediterranean world.

The Greek Polis: Sparta and Athens

Among the Greek poleis, Sparta and Athens stand out for their vividly contrasting styles of life and their roles in subsequent Greek history. Dorian Sparta chose to guarantee its integrity and future through stringent and uncompromising policies. Athens created an increasingly open system. Faced by land shortages and population pressures, the Spartans conquered and enslaved their neighbors, making them *Helots*—state slaves. To prevent rebellions and to control the Helots, who outnumbered the Spartans ten to one, a vigilant Sparta was forced to keep its military always on the alert. Spartan boys were trained through the *agoge* (the "upbringing") to be tough, brave, skilled, and self-reliant. All male Spartans over the age of thirty belonged to an assembly that could propose measures to a smaller council made up of Spartans over the age of sixty. There were also two kings and five annually elected officials who pronounced on the legality of legislation. The Spartan system had elements of monarchy, oligarchy, and democracy.

The history of Ionian Athens echoes the general pattern of change in the poleis during the Archaic Age (Timeline 2.2). Aristocrats initially ruled Athens through councils and assemblies. As long as farming and trading sustained an expanding population, the nobles ruled without challenge. But at the beginning of the sixth century BCE, many peasant farmers were burdened with debts and were threatened with prison or slavery. Having no voice in the government, the farmers began to protest what they perceived as unfair laws.

An aristocrat named Draco codified Athens's laws in about 625 BCE. His laws were harsh—"Draconian"— but by issuing them publicly, he made it clear that law (not arbitrary decisions) ruled the state. In about 590 BCE, the Athenians granted an aristocrat named Solon special powers to reform the laws. He abolished debt slavery, guaranteed a free peasantry, and overhauled the judicial system. Solon also restructured Athenian institutions by distributing political participation according to wealth, instead of restricting participation to the wealthy.

Solon's principal successor was Cleisthenes [KLICE-thu-neez], whose reforms established democracy in Athens beginning in 508 BCE. Cleisthenes realized that the great obstacle to civic-minded participation was

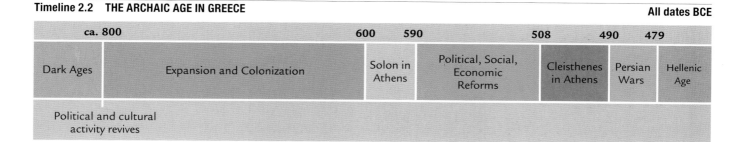

Timeline 2.2   THE ARCHAIC AGE IN GREECE

All dates BCE

ca. 800		600	590		508	490	479
Dark Ages	Expansion and Colonization	Solon in Athens	Political, Social, Economic Reforms		Cleisthenes in Athens	Persian Wars	Hellenic Age
Political and cultural activity revives							

formed by entrenched class interests. That is, he knew it would be hard to get small farmers, day laborers, merchants, and landed nobles to cooperate. So he created a new council in which he lumped together people from each of these groups in such a way as to force them to collaborate.

Cleisthenes' domestic reforms were one of the two major events that heralded the end of the Archaic Age and the coming of Greece's Hellenic (or classical) Age. The other event, the Persian Wars, was pivotal not only for Greece but also for Western civilization. If the autocratic and imperialistic Persians had won these wars, then the democratic institutions, the humanistic values, and the cultural landmarks that the Greeks were establishing would have been lost.

By the mid–sixth century BCE, the Persians ruled a huge empire in the Near East which had gradually incorporated the Greek poleis in Ionia. When Darius, king of the Persians in the late sixth century, demanded taxes from the Ionian Greeks, they revolted and looked to their homeland for support. A few poleis, including Athens, sent an expedition, which Darius defeated. To prevent future uprisings, Darius invaded the Greek peninsula and landed near Athens at Marathon in 490 BCE. The Athenian army defeated a vastly larger Persian force.

However, the Persians soon found a new and determined ruler in Xerxes [ZIRK-seez], son of Darius, who overran much of northern Greece. Under Spartan leadership, the Greeks attempted to trap the Persians at Thermopylae, a northern mountain pass, but they were annihilated by Xerxes' troops. Xerxes moved southward and sacked Athens, whose inhabitants escaped to the island of Salamis. The Athenians drew the Persian navy into narrow waters, where the swifter Greek ships outmaneuvered the more numerous but cumbersome Persian craft. After witnessing the destruction of his fleet, Xerxes returned to Persia. The remainder of the Persian army was routed at Plataea in 479 BCE. The Greeks' final victory over the mighty Persians created a euphoric mood in Athens and set the stage for the ensuing Hellenic Age.

The great service provided by Athens's seamen won them full participation in the political life of the city. After the war, the Athenians even introduced pay for public service so that such service would not be restricted to the idle rich. Athens had a weak executive and a powerful legislative system. Political thinkers in antiquity had very mixed feelings about Athens's government, admiring its massively inclusive character but criticizing its volatility and instability.

One of the most surprising contrasts between Sparta and Athens is the difference in the roles and status of women. In general, Spartan women, though expected to marry, spent their time outside the home and spoke freely to men; Athenian women were kept in seclusion and rarely talked with their husbands. What made Spartan women so independent was that, above all else, they were to be strong mothers of the vigorous males needed to maintain this warrior society. To that end, Spartan girls, alone among Greek females, were given public training, including choral singing and dancing, and athletics, in which they stripped just as Greek boys did. Spartan women were unique in being able to own land and to manage their own property.

Written sources suggest that the women of Athens pursued respectability as an ideal, which meant they were supposed to marry and stay indoors, overseeing their households and performing domestic chores. It is not clear how strictly this ideal was imposed on them in daily life. Athenian drama contains many instances of female characters complaining about their powerlessness, as when a wife is abandoned or a woman is left behind by her soldier-husband during wartime. But vase painting depicts women actively and positively participating in religious rituals, festivals, weddings, and funerals. Women's engagement in these events was deemed necessary to the smooth functioning of society.

Technology in Archaic Greece

The Archaic Greeks lived fully in the Iron Age although some artisans continued to work with bronze in limited fields, such as sculpture. As the Archaic period opened, the Greeks built on the technology of the earlier cultures of Crete and Mycenae, using mainly iron and steel (a refined form of iron) to build weaponry and body armor. Metalworkers learned to reduce iron from its ore in charcoal-fed furnaces, intensifying

Figure 2.8   Greek Trireme. This type of ship had emerged by 525 BCE and was used by the Ionian Greeks when they revolted against the Persians. It was large and fast but also maneuverable.

TABLE 2.1   THE NINE MUSES AND THEIR AREAS OF CREATIVITY

NAME	ART OR SCIENCE
Calliope	Epic poetry
Clio	History
Erato	Erotic poetry and mime
Euterpe	Lyric poetry and music
Melpomene	Tragedy
Polyhymnia	Sacred hymn
Terpsichore	Dance and song
Thalia	Comedy
Urania	Astronomy

the heat by means of a foot bellows. Harder and more readily available than copper and tin, iron drove out the general use of softer metals by 500 BCE.

Also important were the Greeks' improvements in sailing vessels. Between 800 and about 450 BCE, the Greeks developed several modifications of a basic oared ship. At first they used *uniremes* (Latin *remus* means "oar"), small, swift boats with a single row of oars on each side. Gradually the *trireme* developed, a decked ship with three rows of oars on each side (Figure 2.8). From about 700 BCE, the uniremes were outfitted with a beak or a battering ram, to be used in sea battles. This ramming device forever changed the nature of sea warfare. Prior to this time, ships had been designed to transport warriors to fight on land; now, they served as the site for the battles themselves. Greek ships became not only faster but larger as well. Size and speed had important implications for merchants, who could ship more goods farther and more quickly than before.

THE EMERGENCE OF GREEK GENIUS: THE MASTERY OF FORM

During the Archaic Age, the Greeks explored the natural world, probed human existence, and celebrated life by means of literature, philosophy, and art. These cultural accomplishments, like those of the older Near Eastern cultures, arose from religious beliefs and practices that played a central role in Greek life and history. In fact, the Greeks believed that creativity itself was a divine gift from the **muses,** the nine goddesses of artistic inspiration (Table 2.1). Guided by their muses, they created enduring works of art, literature, and theater, each with a universal appeal. Critical to the Greek experience, however, was a quest for understanding independent of religious explanations.

Religion

For the Greeks, religion was an essential part of private and public life. Indeed, the polis and religion could not be separated, for in the eyes of the Greeks the fate of each community depended on the civic deity. Public rituals and festivals forged community, infused civic pride, and recalled common heritage. Greek religion was always more civic than personal, more public than private. During the Archaic Age, Greek religion—an amalgam of deities derived from the original settlers as well as invaders and foreigners—evolved into two major categories: the Olympian and the chthonian. The **Olympian deities** dwelled in the sky or on mountaintops and were associated with the Homeric heroes and the aristocracy. The **chthonian** [K'THOE-nee-uhn] (from Greek *chthon,* "the earth") **deities** lived underground and were associated with peasant life, the seasons and cycles of nature, and fertility.

Olympian religion shared some traits with the polytheistic cults of the ancient Near East, including the notion that the deities intervene in daily affairs, the belief that they are like humans in many respects, and the idea of a pantheon of gods and goddesses. The Greeks endowed their deities with physical bodies and individual personalities, creating a fascinating blend of charm and cruelty, beauty and childishness, love of justice and caprice. These unruly and willful deities quarreled with one another and played favorites with their mortal worshipers. Faced with such favoritism among the deities, the Greeks themselves developed a strong moral sense. They came to believe that as long as they recognized the divinities' power and did not challenge them—and thus become victims of **hubris,** or pride—they would survive and often prosper.

Zeus, a sky god and first among the immortals, reigned as king on Mount Olympus, hurling thunderbolts and presiding over the divine councils. Sexually voracious, he sired both immortals and mortals. Hera, probably the great goddess of earlier cultures, was the sister and wife of Zeus. She watched over the women who appealed to her for help and kept a close eye on her wandering husband. Zeus's two brothers controlled the rest of the universe, Poseidon ruling the seas, all waters, and earthquakes, and Hades guarding the underworld where the dead reside. Zeus's sister Hestia protected the hearth and its sacred flame. Zeus's twin offspring, Apollo and Artemis, symbolized the sun and the moon, respectively. Apollo, Zeus's favorite son, personified the voice of reason. Artemis watched over childbirth and guarded wild creatures. Zeus's lying son Ares delighted in fierce battles and, as the war god, possessed a quick temper and few morals. He and Aphrodite—Zeus's daughter and the goddess of love and beauty—were adulterous lovers. Hephaestus, the ugly, lame son of Zeus who was married to Aphrodite in some tellings, was a master smith and the patron of artisans.

Two other children of Zeus rounded out the Olympic roster. Athena, the goddess of wisdom and patron goddess of Athens, was associated with warfare, the arts, and handicrafts. She was worshiped as a virgin goddess. Hermes, the god of trade and good fortune, was also the patron of thieves, although he was best known as a messenger for the other deities (Table 2.2).

The chthonian gods and goddesses were probably derived from ancient earth and harvest deities. At first they were worshiped only by the lower levels of society, but as ordinary people grew in influence, chthonian rituals spread and were integrated into civic rituals. Chthonian worship was open only to initiates, who were sworn to silence; hence, they were called mystery cults (from Greek *mystos*, "keeping silent"). Mystery cults constituted the personal element in Greek religion.

The chthonian practices originally invoked the powers of the earth to ensure a successful planting and a bountiful harvest. The "Mediterranean triad" of crops—olives, grapes, and cereal grains—led to two major cults emphasizing grains and grapes, the sources of bread and wine (olives lacked a cult). Demeter, a sister of Zeus, was a harvest goddess. She in turn had a daughter, Persephone, whom Hades abducted to his kingdom belowground. According to her cult legend, Demeter finally rescued Persephone, but not before Hades had tricked Persephone into eating a fruit that made her return to the underworld for part of each year. Thus, during the winter months, the earth is bare, but when Persephone and Demeter are together, the earth regains fertility. At Eleusis, a small village in Attica, Demeter was the focus of a mystery cult. Prospective initiates from all over Greece traveled there, apparently to receive her promise of immortal life.

Whereas Demeter's followers honored her in a dignified manner, Dionysus's worshipers, through wild dancing and wine drinking, hoped to be reinvigorated by their god and born again. Dionysus, the god of wine, came to represent the irrational, emotional, and uncontrolled aspects of human nature to the Greeks. In contrast, the rational, conscious, controlled aspects were associated with Apollo. The two aspects—Dionysian and Apollonian—were considered opposing but complementary. Eventually, a Dionysus cult arose in Athens, where Dionysus's followers annually held ceremonies honoring his power as god of the vine. Over the years these rituals became civic festivals, which in turn spawned the competitive performances of tragic drama in Athens in the sixth century BCE.

TABLE 2.2	THE OLYMPIAN DEITIES AND THE AREAS THEY RULED
GOD OR GODDESS	**DUTIES AND RESPONSIBILITIES**
Zeus	Chief deity and keeper of order on Olympus
Hera	Mother goddess, protector of women
Poseidon	Ruler of waters
Hades	Keeper of the underworld
Hestia	Protector of the hearth
Apollo	God of wisdom and moderation
Artemis	Virgin goddess who aided women
Ares	Amoral god of violence and warfare
Aphrodite	Goddess of passion, love, and beauty
Hephaestus	Patron of craftspeople
Athena	Goddess of wisdom and warfare
Hermes	God of merchants and thieves; messenger for the gods

Figure 2.9   The Delphic Sanctuary. Aerial view. Late sixth to fourth century BCE. The ruins of Apollo's temple—this is an earthquake zone—reveal a rectangular foundation and a few standing columns. A sacred way, or road, zigzagged up the mountain to the shrine. During the fourth century, a gymnasium (boy's school), theater, and stadium were built on the site.

Chthonian and Olympian religion fused at Delphi, about 100 miles northwest of Athens and the most important shrine in the Greek world (Figure 2.9). In the second millennium BCE a sanctuary was dedicated there to Gaia, the earth goddess. Mythology says the shrine was founded by Zeus. Mythology also says that around 750 BCE Apollo killed a python and took its place in giving oracles—divine answers to questions put by ordinary people—through a priestess, the Pythia. Pythians were always women over fifty years of age and of blameless life. Most Greek poleis founded treasuries at Delphi where they offered everything from statues and valuables to arms captured in war. Whereas cities had their own gods, Delphi belonged to all the Greeks.

Literature

During the Archaic Age, the Greeks produced some of the greatest literature of the Western heritage, with stories as adventurous, amusing, and heartfelt as they are sophisticated, structured, and rich with many of the values we still hold dear today.

Epic Poetry   The originator of the major conventions of **epic poetry** is traditionally believed to be Homer, a **bard,** or poet who sang his verses while accompanying himself on a stringed instrument. In the *Iliad* (ca. 750 BCE) and the *Odyssey* (ca. 725 BCE), Homer sang of the events before, during, and after the Trojan War, stories that had circulated among the Greeks since the fall of Mycenae. He entertained an aristocratic audience eager to identify with the Mycenaean past. For many years, his poems were transmitted orally by other bards and probably did not exist in written versions until the sixth century BCE. Homer's authorship and, indeed, even his very existence are established solely by tradition. Nevertheless, by the end of the Archaic Age, the appeal of Homer's poetry had embraced all social levels, and his authority and influence approached that of a modern combination of television, Shakespeare, and the Bible.

The epic genre displays certain features. Always in verse, an epic's language is elevated and its tone is serious. Epic possesses a universalizing quality—what is said is held to be true for all times and places, not for a specific moment. The characters in an epic are deeply human and yet, in their prowess or wisdom or cunning, are greater than most humans. Homer's epics have some distinctive characteristics that recur in Greek culture. Homer delights in verbal play. He revels in competition, sometimes verbal, sometimes physical. And in Homer we can begin to see the characteristic Greek interest in balance, order, harmony, and proportion.

The basic appeal of Homer's epics lies in their well-crafted plots, filled with dramatic episodes and finely drawn characters. Set against the backdrop of the Trojan War, the *Iliad* describes the battle for Ilium, another name for Troy, and the *Odyssey* recounts events after the Greeks defeat the Trojans. The *Iliad* focuses on Achilles, the epitome and paradox of heroic Greek manhood. Achilles was angry and refused for a long time to fight because Agamemnon, the Greeks' leader, had taken away his prize slave girl. Just as the polis was taking shape, Homer invited reflection on participation and allegiance: Where does one draw the line between self-interest and the common good? In contrast to the battlefield heroics of the *Iliad,* the *Odyssey* narrates the wanderings of the Greek warrior Odysseus after the fall of Troy. Moreover, the *Odyssey* celebrates marriage, for Odysseus, despite some amorous adventures, remains fixed on thoughts of his wife, Penelope, who waits for him in Ithaca.

In both poems, the deities merrily intrude into the lives of mortals, changing and postponing the fate of friend and enemy alike. For example, Homer presented Zeus, the nominal protector of the moral order, as forever under siege by other gods seeking help for their favorite mortals. Homer's roguish portraits of the deities remained indelibly imprinted in the minds of the general populace of Greece. So great was Homer's authority that his works made him the theologian of Greek religion. His stories of the gods and goddesses, although not completely replacing other versions of their lives, became the standard that circulated wherever Greek was spoken.

In addition to poetic forms and themes, Homer gave texture to the Greek language. Similes, figures of speech in which two unlike things are compared, help make the dramatic, exotic events understandable to all. For example, Homer creates a vivid image of Odysseus as a ferocious killer when he compares him to a lion "covered with blood, all his chest and his flanks on either side bloody." In a less violent simile, Homer has Achilles compare his fellow Greeks to "unwinged" baby birds and himself to their nurturing mother. Homer's images also provide a rich repertoire of ready phrases and metaphors, known as **Homeric epithets,** such as "the wily Odysseus," "the swift-footed Achilles," and the "rosy-fingered dawn." These phrases constitute ready-made metrical units (think of the beat in music) that permitted the bard to "compose" his poem orally.

Homer also served as a guide to behavior for the Archaic Greeks. Because they became part of the Greek educational curriculum, his poems acquired an ethical function. *Pais* in Greek means a young man and *paideia* means bringing up the young. A young man who, having learned his Homer, took Achilles or Odysseus for a model would learn to maintain his well-being, to speak eloquently in the company of other men, to give and receive hospitality, to shed tears in public over the death of his closest friend, to admire the beauty of women, to esteem the material wealth of other nobles, to appreciate songs of bravery, and, above all, to protect his reputation as a man and warrior. On the other hand, a young wife who imitated Penelope, the patient and faithful wife of Odysseus, would inhabit a constricted world as she learned to weave at the loom, to manage a household, to cultivate her physical beauty, and to resist the advances of other men.

Lyric Poetry   Verses sung to the music of the **lyre** (a handheld stringed instrument), or **lyric poetry,** became the dominant literary expression in the late Archaic Age, and **lyric** verses have dominated Western poetry ever since. Lyric poetry, which originated later than the epic, expressed an author's personal, private thoughts, though the muse Euterpe was credited with the inspiration. The shift from epic to lyric poetry in the sixth century BCE coincided with changes in the polis, where the rising democratic spirit encouraged a variety of voices to be heard.

Of the several types of lyric poetry, *monody,* or the solo lyric, became the most influential in Archaic Greece. Poets of monody achieved relative simplicity by using a single line of verse or by repeating a short stanza pattern. Whereas the Homeric epics survive relatively intact, the solo lyrics exist in fragments. For example, of Sappho's [SAF-oh] nine books of verse, only one complete poem and several dozen fragments survive. And all the music has been lost. The ancients, however, regarded Sappho (about 600 BCE) as the greatest of lyric poets. The philosopher Plato hailed her as the tenth muse in a short lyric he dedicated to her. A truly original writer, Sappho apparently owed no debt to Homer or any other poet. Her work is addressed to a small circle of aristocratic women friends on her native island of Lesbos in the Aegean. She was deeply personal in her interests, writing chiefly about herself, her friends, and their feelings for one another. In her elegant but restrained verses, Sappho sang mostly about moods of romantic passion: of longing, unrequited love, absence, regret, jealousy, and fulfillment. Sappho's willing vulnerability and her love of truth made the solo lyric the perfect vehicle for confessional writing.

Philosophy and Science

The mental attitudes that exemplified the democratic challenge to established authority in the Archaic Age also brought forth thinkers who questioned the power and, ultimately, the existence of the gods. Just as the democrats constructed a human-centered state, so did the philosophers conceive of a world where natural processes operated and human minds could grasp

SLICE OF LIFE

The Worlds of Women and Men in Ancient Greece

By pairing these two very different perspectives, it is possible to see the chasm that lay between the worldviews of women and those of men in ancient Greece. Because there are no records of ordinary people from the Archaic Age, human reactions to Archaic life come almost exclusively from famous individuals, such as Sappho and Alcaeus [al-KAY-us]. In the following poems, they express human emotions across time and class, but their subjects are rather different. Sappho (about 600 BCE) describes her intensely personal feelings, as in this ode to a lost love. In contrast, Alcaeus (about 620–about 580 BCE) sings of his anguish when he was banished for political activities in the polis of Mytilene on the island of Lesbos—Sappho's hometown too.

Sappho
HE SEEMS TO BE A GOD

Sappho's lyrical poems reflect the constricted world of Greek women. In this ode, she describes the pangs of jealousy and grief she feels on seeing someone she loves respond to another.

He seems to be a god, that man
Facing you, who leans to be close,
Smiles, and, alert and glad, listens
To your mellow voice

And quickens in love at your laughter
That stings my breasts, jolts my heart
If I dare the shock of a glance.
I cannot speak,

My tongue sticks to my dry mouth,
Thin fire spreads beneath my skin,
My eyes cannot see and my aching ears
Roar in their labyrinths.

Chill sweat slides down my body,
I shake, I turn greener than grass.
I am neither living nor dead and cry
From the narrow between.
But endure, even this grief of love.

Alcaeus
LONGING FOR HOME

Unlike Sappho, Alcaeus wrote about the world of men. His works were collected into ten books in antiquity, but only a few fragments survive today.

Plunged in the wild chaste-woods I live
a rustic life, unhappy me,
longing to hear Assembly called
and Council, Agesilaidas!

From lands my grandfather grew old
possessing, and my father too,
among these citizens who wrong
each other, I've been driven away.

An outland exile: here I dwell
like Onomacles, the Athenian
spear-wolf, out of the fray. To make
peace with . . . is no wise.
So to the precinct of the gods,
treading the dark earth . . .
. . . I live
keeping well out of trouble's reach.

Now Lesbos' long-robed girls are here for the beauty
    contest. All around,
the women's wondrous annual cry,
the holy alleluia, rings.
When will the gods from all my trials
deliver. . . .

Interpreting This Slice of Life

1. *What* emotions does Sappho express in her poem?

2. *How* does Sappho describe her body's reaction to jealousy?

3. *What* does Alcaeus long for while he is away from his homeland?

4. *Why* is Alcaeus away from home?

5. *How* does the mood of these poems by Sappho and Alcaeus differ from the mood of Homer's poetry?

TABLE 2.3 PHILOSOPHERS OF THE ARCHAIC AGE

PHILOSOPHER	TIME	ACHIEVEMENT
Thales	About 585 BCE	First philosopher and founder of philosophic materialism
Pythagoras	About 580–about 507 BCE	Founder of philosophic idealism
Heraclitus	About 545–about 485 BCE	First dialectical reasoning; belief in continual flux

them. These Greek thinkers invented **natural philosophy,** a term that encompasses the fields we now call "philosophy" and "science." The close connection between philosophy and science persisted until the Newtonian revolution of the seventeenth century CE. From that point on, science simply demonstrated what happened in nature without speculating about its purpose. The Greeks asked both "how" and "why."

Natural Philosophy   The origins of natural philosophy, like those of lyric poetry, are hidden in the fragmentary historical record, but we can nevertheless say that formal Western philosophy began on the Ionian coast of Asia Minor in the sixth century BCE. There, in the polis of Miletus, thinkers known as the Milesian school speculated that beneath the ever-changing natural world was an unchanging matter (Table 2.3).

Thales [THAY-leez] (fl. 585 BCE), the founder of the Milesian school, reasoned that the fundamental substance of the universe was water—an outlook that made him a materialist, because he thought that everything was made of matter. From the standpoint of modern science, Thales was wrong and so were the rest of his circle, who proposed other elements—earth, air, fire, and "the infinite"—as the underlying essence. But more important than their conclusions regarding matter were their convictions that there is regularity in the universe and that human reason can ultimately understand the natural order. Their belief in rationality not only determined the direction of speculative thought but also initiated the steps that led to physics, chemistry, botany, and other sciences. Proposing that the universe is governed by natural laws, these first philosophers questioned divine explanations for natural events, a development deplored by those who found satisfactory explanations in religion.

When the Persians conquered Asia Minor near the end of the sixth century BCE, the center of intellectual thought shifted to Athens and to southern Italy and Sicily, where a tradition emerged that challenged the Milesian school. Pythagoras [puh-THAG-uh-ruhs] (about 580–about 507 BCE), the leader of the Italian school, rejected the concept of an underlying substance. Instead, he proclaimed, "Everything is made of numbers," by which he meant that mathematical

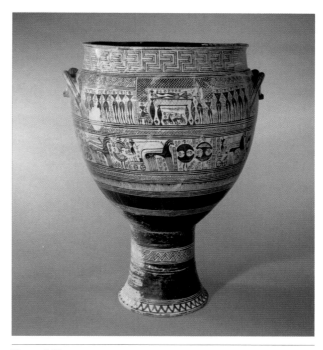

Figure 2.10   By The "Dipylon Master." The Dipylon Krater. Ca. 750 BCE. Painted terra cotta funerary vessel, ht. 42″. The Metropolitan Museum of Art, New York. Found in the Dipylon cemetary at Athens, this Krater is executed in the geometric style. Grace, order, and harmony mark every aspect of its beautiful design. Strips of color and geometric designs alternate with two bands of figural designs, themselves in geometric patterns; note how chests become triangles. The upper one shows mourners in highly abstract representation while the lower one centers on a prosthesis panel showing the deceased person with, to the left, two small figures that may be a wife and child. This is how Pythagoras "saw" the world.

relationships explained the basic order in nature—an outlook that made him an idealist, because he thought that an immaterial principle was the root cause of things. His musical studies probably led him to this conclusion. He may have observed that a plucked string vibrated, making a certain sound; if the string were cut in half and plucked again, then a new note an octave higher than the first, with twice as many vibrations per second, would be heard. Hence, mathematical ratios determined musical sounds. Pythagoras then concluded that "numbers" explain everything in the "cosmos," his term for the orderly system embracing the earth and the heavens (Figure 2.10).

Interpreting Art

Composition Two figures are captured in dynamic action. Achilles is shown mainly in profile thereby drawing the viewer's attention to the frontally depicted Pehthesilea. Each figure is identified by name.

Subject Matter Following an unknown source—this episiode from the Trojan War is not in Homer—Exekias depicts the moment when Achilles, his arm poised to strike, is moved by the beauty of the Amazon queen Penthesilea and falls in love. He killed her nonetheless but later grieved over her.

Artist's Intent Exekias is only one of many sixth-century vase painters who signed their works, probably to win fame and increase sales.

Style Executed in the black-figure style, the figures are painted in black and details are incised with a stylus. The red background of plain baked clay might be glazed.

Form Despite its modest size, this amphora was probably owned by a prosperous family. Ordinary people would have used ceramic ware without figured decorations or with geometric designs.

Context Vase paintings, such as this, were central to the culture of Archaic Greece, along with the kouros and korē statues (see Figures 2.15–2.18); the popularity of Homeric themes, in general; and the winning of greater roles by ordinary men in the life of the polis.

SIGNED BY EXEKIAS. *Achilles Killing the Amazon Queen Penthesilea.* **Ca. 530 BCE. Clay, ht. of jar 16″. British Museum, London (B 210).** Almost the only painting surviving from ancient Greece is found on ceramic vessels. By the sixth century BCE, black-figure ware emerged as a major art form. Exekias painted this scene on an Athenian amphora, a vase with an oval body, cylindrical neck, and two handles, used for wine or oil.

1. **Composition** Who are the figures depicted on this amphora?
2. **Subject** What are the basic details of the story depicted here?
3. **Intent** What were the artist's intentions in creating a work such as this?
4. **Style** Identify the chief characteristics of the black-figure style.
5. **Form** Why is it likely that a prosperous family owned this amphora?
6. **Context** What does this amphora reveal about Archaic Greece?

A third philosopher, Heraclitus [hair-uh-KLITE-uhs] (about 545–about 485 BCE), appeals more to the modern age than does any other thinker in Archaic Greece. Heraclitus pioneered a philosophic tradition that found truth in constant change, as in his well-known idea that a person cannot step twice into the same flowing river. In addition, he devised the earliest dialectical form of reasoning when he speculated that growth arises out of opposites, a fundamental tenet of dialectic thought. This original idea led him to argue that "strife is justice" and that struggle is necessary for progress.

Further thinkers began to ask what it means to *know,* how it is possible to know. For example, some questioned whether the five senses—sight, smell, touch, taste, hearing—are actually capable of securing accurate information about the world. Others began to wonder about language: What are the limits of words' ability to articulate and communicate understanding? These philosophers laid the foundations for **epistemology,** the branch of philosophy concerned with the nature of knowledge.

Architecture

The supreme architectural achievement of the Greeks, the temple, became the fountainhead of the building components, decorative details, and aesthetic principles that together have largely shaped Western architecture until today. In its origins during the Archaic Age, the temple, probably made of wood, was a sacred structure designed to house the cult statues of the civic deities. As the Archaic Age gathered economic momentum, each polis rebuilt its wooden sanctuaries in stone.

A diagram of a typical temple illustrates how much the building has influenced Western architecture (Figure 2.11). Generic Greek architecture is called **post-beam-triangle construction** (also known as post-and-lintel construction). *Post* refers to the columns; *beam* (or lintel) indicates the horizontal members, or **architraves,** resting on the columns; and *triangle* denotes the triangular area, called a **pediment,** at either end of the upper building. Other common features include

- The **entablature**—all of the building between the columns and the pediment,

- The **cornice**—the horizontal piece that crowns the entablature, and
- The **stylobate**—the upper step of the **stereobate,** the base on which the columns stand.

A typical temple had columns on four sides, which in turn enclosed a walled room, called a **cella,** that housed the cult image. Each temple faced east, with the doors to the cella placed so that, when opened, the sunrise illuminated the statue of the deity.

The earliest temple style in Greece was called **Doric,** because it originated in the Dorian poleis and adopted the simplicity of design and scarcity of decorative detail characteristic of the austere Dorian taste (Figure 2.12). The Doric columns have plain tops, or **capitals,** and the columns rest directly on the stylobate without an intervening footing. On the entablature of each Doric temple is a sculptural band, called a *frieze,* which alternates three-grooved panels, called **triglyphs,** with blank panels, called **metopes** [MET-uh-peez], that could be left plain or filled with relief sculptures. The triglyphs are reminders of the temple's origin as a wooden building when logs, faced with bronze, served as overhead beams.

An excellent example of the Doric style in the Archaic Age is the Temple of Hera in Paestum, in southern Italy (Figure 2.13). The Temple of Hera (about 550 BCE) was constructed from coarse local limestone. This large temple has a somewhat ungainly appearance, due in part to the massive architrave and the small spaces between the columns. The builders attempted to remedy this defect (without total success)

Figure 2.11   Elements of Greek architecture.

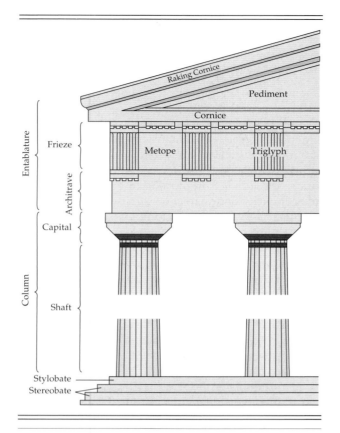

Figure 2.12   Greek architecture of the Doric Order.

Figure 2.13   Temple of Hera, Paestum. Ca. 560–550 BCE. Limestone. This temple, with its heavy, squat columns, stands not only as a model of Archaic Greek architecture but also as a reminder of Greek wealth and expansion. Colonists from mainland Greece settled in southern Italy, the land they thought of as "Greater Greece," in the seventh and sixth centuries BCE, bringing with them the Olympian gods and goddesses and ideas of how to build temples in their honor.

Figure 2.14   Temple of Aphaia, Aegina. 510 BCE. The Temple of Aphaia in Aegina became the standard for the Doric temple style from its creation until it was superseded by the Athenian Parthenon in the 440s. Built of local limestone, covered in stucco, and painted, the Temple of Aphaia gleamed like a jewel in its carefully planned site overlooking the sea. Constructed and decorated with strict attention to artistic refinements, such as the slender columns and the lifelike sculptures, this temple represents the climax of Archaic architecture.

by introducing refinements into the temple's design. The columns were made to appear strong and solid enough to support the entablature by enlarging the middles of the shafts, a technique known as **entasis.** The artisans also carved vertical grooves, called **flutes,** along the shafts to give the columns a graceful, delicate surface and enhance their visual three-dimensionality.

After much experimentation, Greek architects overcame the awkwardness of the early Doric style by deciding that a temple's beauty was a function of mathematical proportions. The Temple of Aphaia—erected in 510 BCE by the citizens of Aegina, Athens's neighbor and perennial enemy—seems to embody this principle (Figure 2.14). The architect of this temple achieved its pleasing dimensions by using the ratio 1:2, placing six columns on the ends and twelve columns on the sides. The Temple of Aphaia, with its harmonious proportions and graceful columns, became the widely imitated standard for the Doric style over the next half century.

Sculpture

Like the art of Mesopotamia and Egypt, Greek sculpture was rooted in religious practices and beliefs. The Greek sculptors fashioned images of the gods and goddesses to be used in temples either as objects of worship or as decorations for the pediments and friezes. Of greater importance for the development of Greek sculpture were the **kouros** (plural, kouroi) and the **korē** (plural, korai), freestanding statues of youths and maidens, respectively. Before 600 BCE, these sculptures had evolved from images of gods, into statues of dead heroes, and finally into memorials of ordinary people, like civic notables or victorious athletes.

What made the **Archaic** statues of youths and maidens so different from Egyptian and Mesopotamian art was the Greek delight in the splendor of the human body. In their representations of the human form, the Greeks rejected the sacred approach of the Egyptians and the Mesopotamians, which stressed conventional, static poses and formal gestures. Instead, Greek sculptors created athletic, muscular males and lively, robust maidens. Health and beauty were as important as religious purpose.

The first Archaic statues of youths owed much to the Egyptian tradition, but gradually Greek sculpture broke free of its origins. An early example of the kouros type of sculpture is the New York Kouros (Figure 2.15), now in New York City's Metropolitan Museum of Art. Artistically, this marble statue of a youth with the left foot forward, the clenched fists, the arms held rigidly at the sides, the stylized hair, and the frontality—the quality of being designed for viewing from the front—shows the Egyptian influence (see Figure 1.15). The Greek sculptor has moved beyond Egyptian techniques, however, by incorporating

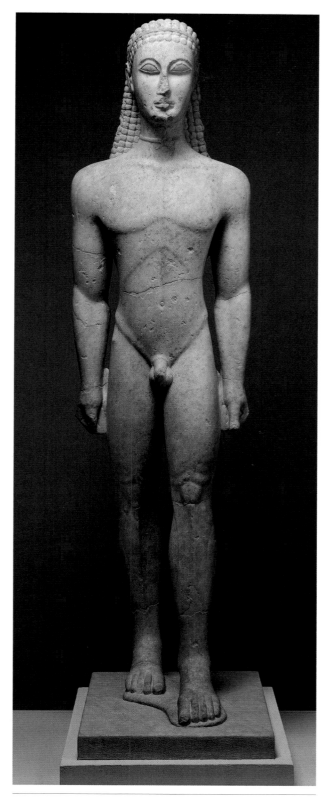

Figure 2.15 New York Kouros. Ca. 615–590 BCE. Marble, ht. without plinth 76⅝". Metropolitan Museum of Art. Fletcher Fund, 1932 (32.11.1). The New York Kouros is one of many similar statues dating from about the beginning of the sixth century BCE. During that century, the male and female statues evolved from rigid and stereotyped models to natural and anatomically correct forms.

changes that make the figure more lifelike, such as by attempting to show the correct shape of the knees and suggesting an actual person's mouth. That the result is not a realistic or idealized human figure is less important than that the sculptor studied the human body with fresh eyes and endeavored to represent it accurately. With such groundbreaking works as the New York Kouros, the Greeks launched a dynamic tradition that later artists continually reshaped.

A generation after the New York Kouros, new sculptors expressed their changed notion of a beautiful living male body in such works as the Anavysos Kouros (Figure 2.16). This sculpture, which was probably a dedicatory offering to a god or a goddess, still shows a powerful Egyptian influence, but it takes a giant step forward to a greater sense of life. The taut body and muscled torso convincingly reproduce the athletic qualities of an Olympic competitor. The legs are flexed and the right arm and shoulder are slightly in advance of the left, suggesting motion. The curious facial expression, known as the "Archaic smile," gives an enigmatic quality to the marble figure.

The korai sculptures, like the statues of youths, evolved from a frozen, lifeless style toward a greater realism, although women were never depicted in the nude at this stage in Greek sculpture. The earliest draped korai sculptures mixed Mesopotamian and Egyptian traditions with Greek ideas, sometimes producing an interesting but awkward effect. Such an early work is the Auxerre Korē (Figure 2.17)—named for the museum in Auxerre, France—whose cylindrical shape is copied from Mesopotamian models and whose rigid pose, wiglike hair, and thin waist are borrowed from Egypt. The Greek sculptor added the broad mouth and the Greek peplos (a loose-fitting outer robe) decorated with a meander pattern, but the Auxerre Korē, despite its charming details, is rigid and inert.

The Peplos Korē (Figure 2.18), dating from about a century later, expresses beautifully the exciting changes that were taking place in late Archaic sculpture. The statue wears a chiton, or tunic, over her upper torso, and a belted peplos. The sculptor has replaced the rigidity of the Egyptian pose with a more graceful one, as shown, for example, by the way the figure holds her right arm. Traces of a painted necklace may be seen, for the Peplos Korē, like all Greek sculpture, was painted to make the figure as true to life as possible. The often-awkward Archaic smile is here rendered to perfection, giving this lovely maiden an aristocratic demeanor.

The Greek tradition of representing males nude and females clothed persisted throughout the Archaic Age and well into the succeeding Hellenic Age. The Greeks readily accepted male nudity, witnessing it in the army on campaigns, in the gymnasium during exercises, and in the games at Olympia and elsewhere, and this

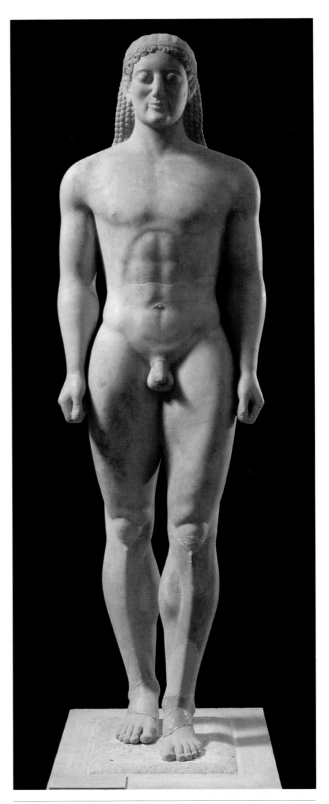

Figure 2.16   Anavysos Kouros. Ca. 540–520 BCE. Marble, ht. 76˝. National Archaeological Museum, Athens. The Anavysos Kouros possesses the distinguishing characteristics of all kouroi: frontality, attention to bodily details, and a general formality. However, its subtle innovations—more precise musculature and more liveliness than the New York Kouros in Figure 2.15—foreshadow the Hellenic sculpture style.

Figure 2.17 Auxerre Korē. Ca. 675–600 BCE. Limestone. Louvre. The Auxerre Korē represents a fairly early stage in the development of this female form. The small size of the sculpture (about 29½ inches high) suggests that it may have been part of a burial rite. Traces of red pigment on the bust indicate that this korē was once painted to make it appear more lifelike.

Figure 2.18 Peplos Korē. Ca. 535–530 BCE. Marble, ht. 48″. Acropolis Museum, Athens. The korē, a statue of a young draped female, was highly popular during the Archaic Age, which set the standard for later Greek art. The Peplos Korē depicted here—with her beautiful face, elegant dress, and expectant countenance—represents the highest expression of this early style. Like the Anavysos Kouros, this statue conveys a vivid sense of life.

acceptance is reflected in their art. But they were much less comfortable with female nudity (except in Sparta, where women exercised in the nude), so women were usually depicted draped or robed.

This discussion of Archaic sculpture may conclude with two figures that pull together the themes already encountered. Figure 2.19 shows a reconstruction of the east pediment of the Temple of Aphaia (see Figure 2.14) depicting Athena presiding over a battle between Greeks and Trojans. Aphaia's sculptures are now in a museum in Munich—virtually no Greek pedimental sculptures are still in place. This reconstruction conveys a wonderful sense of what those many pediments

would have looked like. In Figure 2.20, a statue from the east pediment depicts a dying warrior. On the eve of the Persian Wars, the Greeks reminded themselves of an earlier war against an enemy from the East. Notice the beautiful balance, order, and symmetry of the figures as a group in the reconstruction drawing. In looking at the singular dying warrior, notice his nobility and his humanity. Here dies a man carrying out his duty. Of course, his body is superbly crafted—better even than those of the kouroi. In sculpture, as in almost every aspect of life, advances are coming at an accelerating pace.

Figure 2.19   Reconstruction Drawing of the East Pediment of the Temple of Aphaia at Aegina. Staatliche Antikensammlung und Glyptothek, Munich, after Janson after Fürtwangler. Marble, ht. ca. 40′. This drawing displays what pedimental sculpture would have looked like. Notice especially how the sculptor had to fit his figures into a complex triangular space by making each one proportionately larger as they approach the summit of the triangle.

Figure 2.20   *Fallen Warrior.* East pediment, Temple of Aphaia at Aegina. Ca. 510 BCE. Marble, ht. 72″. Staatliche Antikensammlung und Glyptothek, Munich. This dying soldier commands respect more than pity. Indeed, do we see him falling down or struggling to get up?

SUMMARY

Civilization arose in Europe in the Aegean world in the second millennium BCE, first on the island of Crete and then on the adjacent Greek mainland. The Minoans, peaceful folk and avid traders, built a complex society, erected majestic palaces, and created beautiful artworks. Influenced themselves by the Hittites and Egyptians, they in turn influenced the Myceneans. At several sites in the Peloponnesus the Myceneans, led by kings and warriors—the people we meet in Homer's *Iliad*—also built palaces and created works of art that still dazzle the eye. The identity of the Myceneans is still a little mysterious, but they did speak Greek and bequeathed to the later Greeks religious, mythical, and political ideas. After about 1100 the Greek world plunged into darkness. Around 800 BCE the Archaic period opened and, over the next several generations, the Greek polis took shape and political power, no longer confined to kings and mounted warriors, came to be shared with farmers and merchants. Intercity rivalries and a rising population led many Greeks to leave home and settle in colonies around the Mediterranean shores. The polis was dynamic not only in political life but also in literature and the arts. Epic and lyric poetry flourished. Philosophy, as a rational way of understanding the world, appeared in several places. Sculptors began to capture the human form and to invest it with motion, with life. Builders created flexible, adaptable models.

The Legacy of the Aegean World

The Archaic Age in Greece marked a decisive moment in history. The new way of life devised by the Archaic Greeks gave rise to what we call, in retrospect, the **humanities**—those original artistic and literary forms that made the Greeks unique by turning the focus of human striving away from the divine and toward humanity. Homeric heroes and the figures in sculpture reveal a turn to the individual, to the flesh-and-blood human. The attempt by Greek philosophers to understand the world in purely rational terms inaugurated a tension still felt today between reason and revelation, between religion and science. We still read the literature of the Archaic period and admire its arts and crafts. Nowadays movies, rock concerts, and football games are called "epic." We do not have to look far to see geometric designs on everything from clothing to building facades. Readers of this book have probably studied geometry and have thereby contended with the Pythagorean Theorem: $C^2 = a^2 + b^2$. There are Doric buildings all around us. In the nineteenth century some intellectuals said, "You were born in Greece." They had a point.

Second Bank of the United States, Philadelphia, 1824. Designed by William Strickland (1788–1854), one of the founders of the Greek Revival movement in the United States.

KEY CULTURAL TERMS

frieze	chthonian deities	post-beam-triangle construction	capital
fresco	hubris	architrave	triglyph
Linear A	epic poetry	pediment	metope
matriarchy	bard	entablature	entasis
myth	Homeric epithet	cornice	fluting
Linear B	lyre	stylobate	kouros
shaft grave	lyric poetry	stereobate	korē
oligarchy	lyric	cella	Archaic
muse	natural philosophy	Doric	humanities
Olympian deities	epistemology		

**LYSIPPOS. Bust of Aristotle. Ca. 330 BCE. Marble Roman copy of Greek bronze, ht. 12.5".
Louvre.** Aristotle was born in Stagira, in the far north of Greece. His father was a doctor, who
became the court physician to the Macedonian kings. Aristotle studied in Plato's Academy
in Athens. He was a handsome man, but the artist has not idealized him.

3

Classical Greece
The Hellenic Age

Preview Questions

1. *How* did the Peloponnesian War impact Athens and the other Greek poleis in the Hellenic Age?

2. *Define* tragedy and comedy and *explain* what the popularity of Athenian theater teaches us about the city, its people, and their interests.

3. *What* intellectual attitudes and assumptions are shared by these Hellenic cultural achievements: history, medicine, and philosophy?

4. *What* is classicism and *how* is it manifested in architecture, sculpture, and painting of the Hellenic Age?

*The **Hellenic** Age, extending from* the Greek defeat of the Persians in 479 BCE to the death of Alexander the Great in 323 BCE, was the golden age of ancient Greece. Indeed, it was one of the most brilliant, creative, and dynamic periods in all of human history. It has become "classic." **Classic,** or **classical,** has a rich array of meanings. It can simply mean "best." It can mean "of enduring significance." Or it can mean a standard by which all other things are judged. In all these respects the Hellenic Age was classical.

The figure at the left represents Aristotle, one of the greatest philosophers of the Hellenic Age. His influence extends to our own time. If specialization is valued today, it is precisely Aristotle's astonishing range of intellectual interests that attracts us to him. He wrote on literary theory and political philosophy; on logic and ethics; on biology and botany. Look at his portrait sculpture. With its receding hairline, furrowed brow, and wrinkled face, this is a real human being. Humanity was the highest ideal of the Hellenic Age. The bust is a copy of the original fourth-century work by Lysippos [LY-sipp-us] (370–310 BCE), the second greatest Hellenic sculptor. The Hellenic Age has left us a gallery of famous figures: Sophocles and Thucydides, Pericles and Alexander, Socrates and Plato.

Not only was the Hellenic Age marked by exceptional versatility across the fields of human endeavor, but significant strides were also made within each one. In philosophy, for example, the work of the Archaic philosophers was deepened and expanded. Above all, however, philosophers tried to understand human beings more than to understand the natural world around them. Nevertheless, much of our understanding of the natural world today still depends on the empirical observations of Hellenic philosophers. Medicine became an empirical discipline with the causes of illness divorced from divine intervention or moral failings. History emerged as a distinct discipline dedicated to understanding the relevance of past human action to present reality and future possibility.

Figure 3.1 *Apollo.* **West pediment, Temple at Olympia. Ca. 460 BCE. Marble, ht. 10'2". Archaeological Museum, Olympia, Greece.** Apollo's serene countenance in this splendidly crafted head reflects his image as the god of moderation. As the deity who counseled "Nothing in excess," Apollo was a potent force in combating the destructive urges that assailed the Greeks. This sculpture is executed in the Severe style, or the first stage of the Hellenic classical style, which is evident by the turn of the head to the right. However, its wiglike hair indicates the lingering influence of the Archaic style.

Various archaic rituals and celebrations coalesced into drama in its classic tragic and comedic forms. The epic and lyric poetry of the Archaic Age was little in evidence in the Hellenic era, but the plays written for the stage were in beautiful and expressive verse. Artists in several media overcame every obstacle in capturing and interpreting the human form. Architecture saw the perfection of the Archaic Doric style and the elaboration of a new Ionic style. In virtually every area of the humanities, the Greeks of the Hellenic era not only achieved high standards but also set standards that people would seek to emulate for the next 2,500 years.

Balance, order, harmony—what the Greeks called *sophrosyne*—were central tenets of the age, even as they appreciated the human inclination toward the opposite. Playwrights balanced competing moral positions. Artists avoided excess. Aristotle was THE philosopher of moderation. Greek life always stood in a tense field bounded by Apollo (Figure 3.1), the god of rational thought, ethical standards, and aesthetic balance, and Dionysius, the god of wine, drunken revelry, sexual excess, and madness (Figure 3.2).

The polis may have been the most creative achievement of Archaic Greece, but it did not have a happy experience in the Hellenic Age. Although the Greeks could not imagine living in any other kind of community, they could not make the polis work over the long term. Individual cities were unstable, racked by internal violence, and frequently at war with one another. It is worth reflecting on the fact that the cultural achievements of the Hellenic era all took place amid war and strife.

Figure 3.2 *Dionysus and His Followers.* **Ca. 430 BCE. Staatliche Museen, Berlin.** Scrolling around a perfume vase, this painting depicts a bearded Dionysus seated on the right with his followers. Of his twelve devotees, eleven are maenads, young female revelers; the last is the bearded Silenus, the foster father and former schoolmaster of Dionysus. Silenus is depicted on the lower left in his usual drunken, disorderly state.

Learning Through Maps

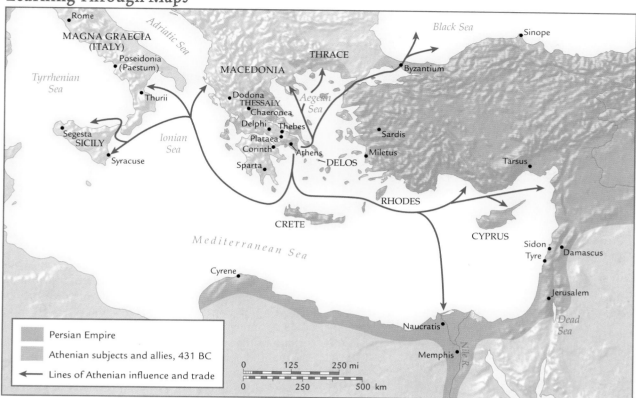

MAP 3.1 THE ATHENIAN EMPIRE, 431 BCE

This map shows the Athenian and Persian Empires on the eve of the Peloponnesian War. *1. **Compare** the Athenian and Persian Empires, with respect to size and sea and land configuration. 2. **Notice** the difference between Athenian and Spartan influence in the eastern Mediterranean. 3. **How** did the locations of Athens and Sparta influence their respective naval and military policies? 4. **In what way** did the distance between Sicily and Athens affect the course of the Peloponnesian War? 5. **Observe** that Macedonia's proximity to Greece helped in its conquest of the late fourth century BCE.*

DOMESTIC AND FOREIGN AFFAIRS: WAR, PEACE, AND THE TRIUMPH OF MACEDONIA

On the eve of the Hellenic Age, the Greeks, having defeated the Persians, were united only in their continuing opposition to Persia and in their hostility to any polis that tried to control the others. Although they cooperated on short-term goals that served their common interests, goodwill among the poleis usually evaporated once specific ends were met. If the period was marked by division, rivalry, and conflict, it was also generally prosperous. Wealth made possible some aspects of a brilliant culture that sometimes reflected on but that was never deflected by strife.

Political Phases of the Hellenic Age

The Hellenic Age is divided into four distinct phases:

- The Delian League
- Wars in Greece and with Persia and the ensuing Thirty Years' Peace
- The Peloponnesian War
- Spartan and Theban hegemony and the triumph of Macedonia (Timeline 3.1)

After defeating the Persians, the Greeks realized that a mutual defense organization was the key to preventing further Persian attack. In 478 BCE, a number of poleis formed the Delian League, a defensive alliance, with Athens at its head. But Athens soon began to transform the voluntary league into an Athenian Empire. As the oppressive nature of Athenian policies emerged, Athens's independent neighbors became alarmed.

Athenian power, however, was restricted by strained relations with Sparta, by the continuing menace of Persia, and by the highly unstable Delian alliance. When a negotiated settlement finally resolved Persian claims, the Delian League fell apart, leaving Athens vulnerable to its enemies on the Greek mainland. First Thebes and then Sparta led attacks on Athens. The war dragged on, but in 445 BCE, when Sparta unexpectedly withdrew, Athens won a quick victory that forced its enemies to negotiate.

The ensuing Thirty Years' Peace (which lasted only fourteen years) brought the Hellenic Age of Athens to its zenith. Athenian democracy expanded so that even the poorest citizens were empowered with full rights (though women continued to be excluded). Artists and sculptors beautified the Acropolis, and the three great Athenian tragedians—Aeschylus, Sophocles, and Euripides—were active in the drama festivals. Drawing

Timeline 3.1   PHASES OF HELLENIC HISTORY   **All dates BCE**

478	460		431	404		323
Delian League	Wars in Greece and with Persia	Thirty Years' Peace	Peloponnesian War	Spartan and Theban Hegemony		Triumph of Macedonia

Figure 3.3   *Pericles*. Ca. 440 BCE. Marble, ht. 19³/₄″. Vatican Museum. Pericles possessed a vision of Athens as the political, economic, and cultural center of the Greek world. Even though this portrait bust is a Roman copy of the Greek original, it conveys Pericles' strong sense of leadership and determination.

on the Delian treasury, Pericles [PER-uh-kleez], the popular leader and general, launched a glorious building program that was essentially a huge public works project (Figure 3.3). In a speech over Athens's war dead, Pericles offered an eloquent summation of Athenian democracy, praising its use of public debate in reaching decisions, tolerance of diverse beliefs, and ability to appreciate beauty without sacrificing military strength. His conclusion boasted that Athens was the model for Greece.

However, those poleis that were not enamored of Athenian aggression became convinced that war was the only way to protect themselves. Athens's foreign policy and its expansionism had given rise to an alliance so delicately balanced that neither side could allow the other to gain the slightest advantage. When Athens's neighbor Corinth went to war with Corcyra (present-day Corfu) in western Greece, Corcyra appealed to Athens for aid. Athens's initial victories frightened Corinth, whose leaders persuaded the Spartans to join with them in the Peloponnesian League. The Peloponnesian War (431–404 BCE) had begun.

Pericles knew the league was superior on land but thought the Athenians could hold out indefinitely within their own walls and win a war of attrition. However, a plague broke out in Athens in 430 BCE, killing many citizens, including Pericles. The first phase of the war ended in 421 BCE, when a demoralized and defeated Athens sued for peace.

The second half of the Peloponnesian War shifted from Greece to distant Sicily and the West—a move that sealed Athens's fate. In 416 BCE, a Sicilian polis begged Athens for military assistance. In trying to conduct a war so far from home, the Athenians lost their fleet and never recovered their military and economic power.

In the early decades of the fourth century BCE, first Sparta and then Thebes emerged as the preeminent city-state, but these power struggles only further weakened the poleis and made them easy prey for an invader. At the northern edge of the civilized Greek world, that invader was gathering its forces. Macedonia was a primitive Greek state, governed by a king and whose people spoke a rough dialect of the Greek language. Its king, Philip II, having been a hostage in Thebes when young, had become a *philhellene*—a lover of Greek culture. A brilliant soldier, Philip expanded Macedonia to the east as far as the Black Sea. He then moved southward, conquering the poleis of central Greece. The poleis hastily raised an army, but Philip's well-disciplined troops crushed it at Chaeronea in 338 BCE. After establishing a league between Macedonia and the poleis, Philip granted the Greeks autonomy in everything except military affairs. He then announced an all-out war against Persia but was assassinated before he could launch his first campaign.

Philip's nineteen-year-old son, Alexander, succeeded to the throne. Tutored in philosophy by the renowned Aristotle, Alexander nevertheless had the heart of a warrior. When Thebes and other poleis attempted to take control at Philip's death, Alexander burned Thebes to the ground, sparing only the house of the poet Pindar. Placing a general in command of

**Figure 3.4　*Alexander the Great.* Ca. 200 BCE. Marble, ht. 16⅛".
Istanbul Museum.** Alexander's youth and fine features, idealized perhaps
in this portrait bust, add to the legends that have accumulated around
one of the most famous conquerors in history. Later rulers measured
themselves against Alexander, whose dream of a united world was cut
short by his early death.

Greece, Alexander turned his sights to the East (Figure 3.4).

Alexander dreamed of a world united under his name and of a culture fused from Hellenic and Persian roots. His armies marched into Asia Minor, Egypt, and Mesopotamia, absorbing the great Persian Empire; then they swept east through Asia to the Indus River in India. As he conquered, Alexander destroyed and looted the great centers of Eastern civilization, but he also founded new cities and spread Greek culture.

Alexander's dream ended abruptly with his death in 323 BCE at the age of thirty-two. Seizing the opportunity presented by his sudden death, the Greeks revolted against the Macedonian oppressors, but they were quickly overwhelmed. The Macedonians then occupied Athens and installed an aristocratic government. Thus ended democracy and the Hellenic phase of Greek history.

THE ARTS OF HELLENIC GREECE: THE QUEST FOR PERFECTION

Throughout this era of shifting political fortunes, artistic and intellectual life flourished. The polis continued to be a fertile and dynamic institution. Athens—bursting with energy—was the jewel of the Greek world. Atop its Acropolis, perfectly proportioned mar-

ble temples gleamed in the brilliant Aegean sun (Figure 3.5). Below, in the agora (market area), philosophers debated the most profound questions of human nature. Hundreds of citizens congregated outdoors to serve in the assembly, where they passed laws or sat on juries that made legal rulings. Citizens who were at leisure cheered on the athletes exercising in the open-air gymnasium (Figure 3.6). During drama festivals, all of Athens's citizens turned out to share a gripping tragedy or to laugh uproariously at the latest comedy.

Theater

The theater, in which the dramatic form known as **tragedy** reached a state of perfection, was one of the most prominent civic institutions in Greece. Greek theater originally arose in connection with the worship of Dionysus. The word *tragedy* in Greek means "goat song," and this word may refer to a prehistoric religious ceremony in which competing male **choruses**—groups of singers—sang and danced, while intoxicated, in homage to the god of wine; the victory prize may have been a sacrificial goat. Whatever its precise origins, during the Archaic Age theater in Athens had taken the form of a series of competitive performances presented annually during the Great **Dionysia,** celebrated in March. Although the names of numerous tragedians are known to us, the plays of only three survive—and we have only a handful of their plays. Eventually comedy took its place alongside tragedy as a public spectacle and as another component of the Dionysiac festival. Only one comedian's plays are extant. All the while, music grew in prominence, in connection with tragedy and independently.

At first, the chorus served as both the collective actor and the commentator on the events of the drama. Then, in the late sixth century BCE, according to tradition, the poet Thespis—from whose name comes the word *thespian,* or "actor"—introduced an actor with whom the chorus could interact. The theater was born. Initially, the main function of the actor was simply to ask questions of the chorus. During the Hellenic Age, the number of actors was increased to three, and, occasionally, late in the fifth century BCE, a fourth was added. Any number of actors who did not speak might be on the stage, but only the three leading actors engaged in dialogue. In the fifth century BCE, the chorus achieved its classic function as mediator between actors and audience. As time went on, however, the role of the chorus declined and the importance of the actors increased. By the fourth century BCE, the actor had become the focus of the drama.

Because the focus of tragedy was originally the chorus, the need for a space to accommodate their dancing and singing determined the theater's shape. The chorus performed in a circular area called an

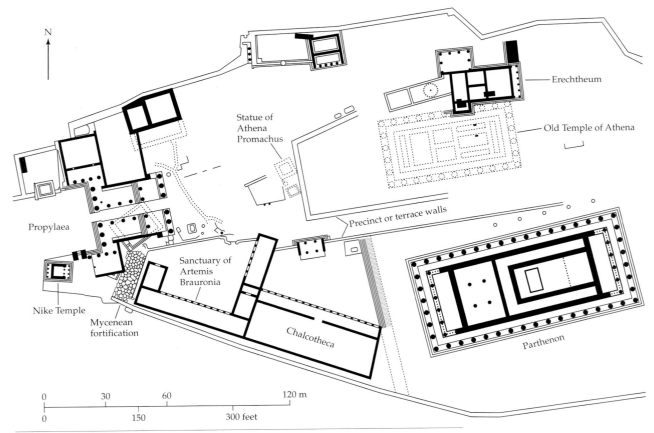

Figure 3.5   Plan of the Acropolis. This plan shows the sites of the major temples: the Parthenon (Figure 3.13), Athena Nike (Figure 3.14), and the Erechtheum (Figure 3.15). For an overall view, compare Figure 2.7.

Figure 3.6   *Athletes in the Palaestra.* Second quarter of the fifth century BCE. Marble, ht. 12¹/₂″. National Archaeological Museum, Athens, Greece. This low-relief sculpture depicts athletes warming up in the open-air exercise area (gymnasium) where spectators would congregate to urge on their favorites. The youth on the left is preparing for a footrace, and the one on the right tests his javelin. The pair in the center have just begun to wrestle. This relief was originally part of a sculptured base built into a wall that the Athenians constructed after the Persian Wars.

Figure 3.7 Theater at Epidaurus. Ca. 300 BCE. The best-preserved theater in Greece is the one at Epidaurus. Although tragedy was created only in Athens, the popularity of the art form led to the construction of theaters all over Greece—a telling index of Athens's cultural imperialism. The acoustics in this ancient auditorium were remarkable. Performers' voices could be heard clearly throughout the theater even though it is in the open with fifty-four rows of seats accommodating fourteen thousand spectators.

orchestra, or "dancing place," in the center of which was a functioning altar, serving as a reminder that tragedy was a religious rite. The audience sat around two-thirds of the orchestra on wooden bleachers or stone seats under the open sky. The other third of the orchestra was backed by a wooden or stone building called the *skene* [SKEE-nee], which could be painted to suggest a scene and through which entrances and exits could be made (Figure 3.7).

Such simple set decorations may have provided a slight bit of realism, but Greek theater was not concerned with either realism or the expressiveness of individual actors. Instead, ideas and language were crucial. The actors—all men, even in the female roles—wore elaborate masks designed to project their voices, platform shoes, and long robes, which helped give the dramas a timeless, otherworldly quality.

Plays were performed in tetralogies (sets of four) on successive days of the Great Dionysia. Each competing playwright offered three tragedies (a trilogy), not necessarily related in theme or subject, that were performed during the day, and a satyr-play that was performed later. A **satyr-play** usually featured the indecent behavior and ribald speech of the satyrs—sexually insatiable half-men, half-goats—who followed Dionysus. That the Greeks liked to watch three deeply serious dramas followed by a play full of obscene high jinks demonstrates the breadth of their sensibility.

Tragedy The essence of Greek tragedy is the deeply felt belief that mortals cannot escape pain and sorrow. The dramatists shared with Homer the insight that "we men are wretched things, and the gods . . . have woven sorrow into the very pattern of our lives." Although terrible things happened in the tragedies—murder,

incest, suicide, rape, mutilation—the attitude of the play toward these events was deeply moral. And violence was never depicted onstage.

The tragedies were primarily based on the legends of royal families—usually the dynasties of Thebes, Sparta, and Argos—dating from the Age of Heroes of which Homer sang in his epics. Since the audience already knew these stories, their interest focused on the playwright's treatment of a familiar tale, his ideas about its moral significance, and how his language shaped those ideas. The plots dealt with fundamental human issues with no easy solutions, such as the decrees of the state versus the conscience of the individual or divine law versus human law. Humans were forced to make hard choices without being able to foresee the consequences of their decisions. Nonetheless, the dramatists affirmed that a basic moral order existed underneath the shifting tide of human affairs. The political leaders of Athens recognized and accepted tragedy's ethical significance and educative function and thus made the plays into civic spectacles. For example, the audience was composed of citizens seated according to voting precincts, and Athenian warriors' orphans, who were wards of the polis, were honored at the performances.

According to the Greek philosopher Aristotle, whose immensely influential theory of tragedy, the *Poetics,* was based on his study of the dramas of the Hellenic Age, the purpose of tragedy was to work a cathartic, or purging, effect on the audience, to "arouse pity and terror" so that these negative emotions could be drained from the soul. The tragic heroes were warnings, not models; the spectators were instructed to seek modest lives and not aim too high.

Aeschylus Aeschylus [ES-kuh-luhs] (about 525–about 456 BCE), the earliest of the three dramatists whose plays survive, won first prize in the Great Dionysia thirteen times. He composed about ninety plays of which only seven are extant. He is believed to have added a second actor. His masterpiece, the *Oresteia,* is the only trilogy that has survived, and even here the satyr-play is missing. The framing plot is the homecoming from Troy of the Greek king Agamemnon, who had sinned by sacrificing his daughter to gain military success; his murder by his vengeful and adulterous wife, Clytemnestra; and the dire consequences of this killing.

Aeschylus's treatment of these terrible events in the *Oresteia* embodies some of the principles of classicism. In the first place, Aeschylus shows great simplicity by avoiding distracting subplots: The first play, *Agamemnon*, tells the story of the king's death and Clytemnestra's triumph; the second, the *Libation Bearers*, relates the vengeance murder of Clytemnestra by her son, Orestes; and the third, *Eumenides*, halts—with the help of the Olympians Athena and Apollo—the cycle of revenge by instituting an Athenian court to try such cases. The trilogy is symmetrical in that Agamemnon's murder in the first play serves as punishment for the sacrifice of his daughter, Clytemnestra's death in the second avenges her slaying of Agamemnon, and the courtroom drama of the third absolves Orestes of the crime of matricide.

Finally, Aeschylus shows great restraint inasmuch as all deaths occur offstage, and the chorus or messengers only describe them. However, for the Athenian audience, the *Oresteia* had moral significance as well as stylistic power. By transforming the Furies, the blind champions of vengeance killing, into the "Kindly Ones" (*Eumenides*), Aeschylus, in effect, affirmed the ethical superiority of the rational Olympians over the earthbound chthonian divinities (see Chapter 2). The *Eumenides* was topical, too, since the Athenians were reorganizing their courts of law at the time of its first presentation. In the *Oresteia*, Aeschylus confronts and resolves the opposition between several seemingly irreconcilable polarities—Olympian and chthonian gods, divine and human justice, religious cult and civic ritual, and fate and free will (Figure 3.8).

Sophocles   Sophocles [SOF-uh-kleez] (about 496–406 BCE), the most prolific of the great tragedians, wrote about 125 plays (only 7 survive) and he added a third actor. Popular among the Athenians, he won first prize in the Great Dionysia twenty-four times. Sophocles' *Antigone* (442 BCE) expresses beautifully the principles of classical tragedy. The simple plot treats the conflicts between King Creon and his niece Antigone. The principal, although not the sole, philosophical issue explored by the play is whether human or divine law should take precedence. Antigone's two brothers have killed each other in a dispute over the Theban crown.

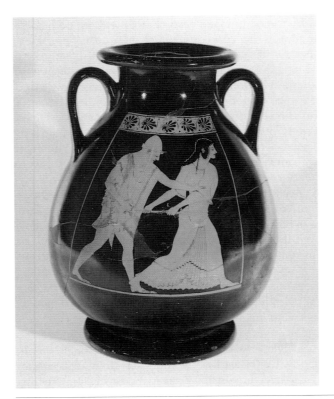 

Figure 3.8   *Orestes Slaying Aegisthus.* Ca. late sixth century BCE. Kunsthistorisches Museum, Vienna.
This red-figure vase painting presents a different version of events in Argos from that given by Aeschylus in the *Libation Bearers*, the second play of the *Oresteia*. The vase painter portrays Clytemnestra bearing an ax (left), a detail Aeschylus omitted, and the sister between Orestes and his mother is not named Electra as she is in the *Oresteia*. However, painter and playwright agree that Orestes killed Aegisthus, his mother's lover.

Creon decrees that Eteocles, who died defending the city, be buried with honor but that the body of the rebel Polyneices be left as carrion for wild beasts. Antigone, whose name in Greek means "born to oppose," defies his order and buries her brother in compliance with religious teachings. Arrested and imprisoned, Antigone hangs herself, and Creon's son and wife kill themselves. Too late, King Creon sees the light; he gives up his throne, saying, "There is no man can bear this guilt but I."

Several tensions are at issue here. Creon represents the typical tyrant, concerned only with law and order. His son, Haemon, is the voice of democracy, opposing the tyrannical will of his father. Creon believes in the superiority of public power over domestic life, in the necessity of the state to seek power for its own sake, in the priority of war over the commands of love, and in the right of men to control women. When the king tries to persuade his son to renounce his love for the disobedient Antigone, they argue about all four of these issues. Whether the Athenian citizens sided with Creon or Haemon is unknown, but *Antigone* has become the classic example of a tragic dilemma wherein two rights confront each other. In his desire for balance, Sophocles gives equally powerful arguments to the play's opposing characters.

Sophocles returned to the history of the Theban dynasty in later plays about Antigone's ill-fated father, Oedipus. In *Oedipus the King,* he tells how the Theban ruler unwittingly kills his father and marries his mother and later blinds himself to atone for his guilt. Though fate has a pivotal role in Oedipus's story, the playwright also emphasizes the part the hero's weakness plays in his downfall. Aristotle's *Poetics* held up this work as a model of Greek tragedy. In *Oedpius at Colonnus,* his last play, Sophocles portrays the former king at peace with himself and his destiny.

Euripides   By the time Euripides [yu-RIP-uh-deez] (about 480–406 BCE) was writing for the stage, Athens was fighting for its existence in the Peloponnesian War. Euripides was in tune with the skeptical mood of the later years of this struggle, and, by presenting unorthodox versions of myths and legends, he exposed the foolishness of some popular beliefs and, sometimes, the emptiness of contemporary values. When he staged *The Trojan Women* in 415 BCE, the Athenians could not have missed the parallel between the cruel enslavement of the women of Troy after the Greeks destroyed their city and the fate of the women on the island of Melos, which Athens had just subjugated.

For his ninety or more tragedies (eighteen survive), the Athenians awarded the first prize to Euripides only five times, perhaps because his unorthodox plays angered the audience. But later ages, far removed from the stresses of Hellenic times, found his dramas more

to their liking. Among the extant works, *The Bacchae* [BACK-kye] is his masterpiece, a gruesome tale about the introduction of the worship of Dionysus into Thebes. In this play, the bacchae (another name for the drunken followers of Dionysius), blinded by religious frenzy, kill the king of Thebes under the delusion that he is a wild animal. Euripides' dark tragedy may have been a warning to the citizens of Athens about the dangers of both excess and repression in religion and politics.

Euripides followed classical principles in *The Bacchae,* using a single plot, offstage violence, and well-defined conflict, but he also extended the range of classical drama with his unorthodox, even romantic, language and his skeptical treatment of familiar themes. Whereas Aeschylus and Sophocles presented clear but difficult moral dilemmas, Euripides' stance was morally vague and ambiguous. Moreover, Euripides pointed the way toward a different sort of theater by having the severed head of the hero brought onstage at the end of the tragedy. With Euripides, the creative phase of classical theater came to an end.

Comedy   Comedies were performed in the Great Dionysia just as the tragedies were, and they were also entered in contests in another festival, known as the Lesser Dionysia, celebrated in late winter. Comedies refused to take anyone or anything seriously, and they blended exquisite poetry with coarse language. They featured burlesque actions, buffoonery, slapstick, obscenity, and horseplay, and actors wore grotesque costumes with padded bellies or rumps to give a ridiculous effect (Figure 3.9). Comic playwrights invented their own plots and focused on contemporary matters: politics, philosophies, the new social classes, and well-known personalities. Even the deities were ridiculed and portrayed in embarrassing situations.

The freedom of the comic playwrights could exist only in a democracy. And yet the freedom was limited to a highly ritualized setting—the drama festivals—which allowed, even encouraged, the overturning of rules and the burlesquing of traditions. This controlled expression of the unspeakable provided a catharsis that strengthened communal bonds in the polis. At the same time, the comic playwrights demonstrated their faith in the basic good sense of the average citizen.

The comedies of Aristophanes [air-uh-STOF-uh-neez] (about 445–about 388 BCE) are the primary source for what is known as **Old Comedy,** comic Greek plays with a strong element of political criticism. Aristophanes composed forty-four works (eleven survive). Like Euripides, he wrote his plays for war-torn Athens, and he satirized famous contemporaries such as the thinker Socrates, depicting him as a hopeless dreamer. Aristophanes must have offended many Athenians, for they awarded him first prize only four times.

Figure 3.9   Detail, Scene from a Comedy. Mid–fourth century BCE. Ht. of vase 15²/₃″. British Museum, London. This scene, painted on a mixing bowl, portrays a situation from a Greek comedy. The actors on the right and left are outfitted in the grotesque costume of comedy with padded rumps and genitals. That these characters are onstage is indicated by the decorations at the bottom of the frame.

In *Lysistrata,* Aristophanes transcended the limitations of the comedic form and approached the timeless quality of the tragedies. A sexually explicit and hilarious comedy, *Lysistrata* points out the absurdity of the prolonged Peloponnesian War and, by implication, all war. In the play, *Lysistrata,* an Athenian matron, persuades the women of Athens and Sparta to withhold sex from their husbands until the men sign a peace treaty. Filled with sexual innuendos, obscenities, and ridiculous allusions to tragic dramas, the play ends with stirring reminders to the Greeks of their common ancestry, their joint victory over the Persians earlier in the century, and their reverence for the same gods. First staged in 411 BCE, seven years before Sparta won the Peloponnesian War, this play commented on but failed to derail Athens's headlong rush to disaster.

After the Peloponnesian War and the restoration of a restricted democracy in 403 BCE, free speech was severely repressed in Athens. Comedies still relied on burlesque and slapstick, but their political edge was blunted. The great creative age of Greek theater was now over.

Music

Like other peoples of the ancient Near East, the Greeks used music both in civic and religious events and in private entertainment. But the Greeks also gave music a new importance, making it one of the humanities along with art, literature, theater, and philosophy. Music became a form of expression subject to rules, styles, and rational analysis. One reason for this was that the Greeks believed music fulfilled an ethical function in the training of young citizens. They also believed that music had divine origins and was inspired by Euterpe, one of the nine muses (thus the word *music*).

The vast repertoire of Greek music has vanished. Greek music apparently followed the diatonic system, which had been invented by Pythagoras (fl. 530 BCE), using a scale of eight notes, each of which was determined by its numerical ratio to the lowest tone. The Greek composers also devised a series of scales, called **modes,** which functioned roughly like major and minor keys in later Western music. The modes, however, were not interchangeable the way keys are, because the Greeks believed that each mode produced a different emotional and ethical effect on the listener. Thus, the Dorian mode, martial and grave in its emotional impact, was thought by the Greeks to make hearers brave and dignified; the tender and sorrowing Lydian mode, to make them sentimental and weak; and the passionate and wild Phrygian mode, to make them excited and headstrong. Believing that such emotional manipulation made free citizens difficult to govern, Plato banished virtually all music from his ideal republic. Modern research has been able to reproduce all the Greek modes, but otherwise this music remains a mystery.

Despite music's high ethical status in Greece, it had no independent role in Hellenic culture. Instead, music was integrated with verse, notably in epic and lyric poetry and in tragedy and comedy, with either the lyre (a handheld stringed instrument) or the aulos (a wind instrument) providing accompaniment.

HISTORY, PHILOSOPHY, SCIENCE, AND MEDICINE

The finest poetry of the Hellenic period is to be found in plays. However, new literary forms, especially in prose, became the hallmarks of the age. Historical writing emerged and writers achieved a high level of skill. Philosophy soared far above the achievements of the Archaic period and began to differentiate itself from natural science. Medical writers produced works that would be influential for nearly two millennia.

History

The study of history began in the fifth century BCE, when Greeks started to analyze the meaning of their immediate past and to write down in prose the results of their research, or *historia*—the Greek word for "inquiry." The Greeks before the classical period had only a dim sense of their past; what they knew came from Homer, local traditions, and mysterious

Mycenaean ruins. Herodotus [he-ROD-uh-tuhs] (about 484 BCE–about 430 BCE) was the first to approach history as a distinct subject and to practice historical writing in anything like the modern sense. He was motivated by the belief that the present has its causes in the past and could be a guide for the future. His *Histories* recorded and analyzed the Persian Wars, which he interpreted as Europe versus Asia, or West versus East. In his desire to be fair to both sides, Herodotus traveled to Persia and recorded what he learned there.

The *Histories* have been criticized for implausible and inaccurate information, but Herodotus's clear prose style, masterful storytelling skills, concern for research, impartiality, belief in cause and effect, and desire to leave a record of the past as a legacy to future generations have justly earned him the title "father of history."

Yet, for all his excellence, Herodotus pales in comparison with Thucydides [thew-SID-uh-deez] (died about 401 BCE), whose subject was the Peloponnesian War, in which he fought. Thucydides was much more skeptical and analytical than Herodotus, and although he had reservations about democracy, he admired Pericles and strove to be completely fair in his account of Periclean Athens. He saw the weaknesses of his beloved polis and realized the baleful effects of imperialism. In his *History of the Peloponnesian War,* he even wrote objectively of his own role as the losing admiral in a naval battle.

Thucydides also used ordinary events to illuminate human motives and fundamental causes and effects in history. Like the Greek dramatists, he showed that human weaknesses and flaws created the real-life tragedies he observed around him. His insight into human nature was penetrating as he chronicled how individuals shift loyalties and redefine their values to justify their actions. Like a medical writer, he explored the health of the body politic. He rose above his narrative to give lessons to future generations. He argued that events that happened in the past would recur in some way—he did not say they would simply repeat themselves—and thus history, carefully studied, can teach the future.

Philosophy, Science, and Medicine

During the Hellenic Age, philosophy and science experienced a radical transformation. Both types of learning came to focus on the place of humans in society, rather than concentrating on the composition of the natural world. Increasing attention was dedicated to ethics, right conduct, and **epistemology,** the branch of philosophy that deals with knowledge and cognition.

When the Hellenic Age opened, natural philosophy remained divided into two major camps: the materialists and the idealists (see Chapter 2). The materialists,

who continued the inquiries of Thales and the Milesian school, believed that the world is made of some basic physical thing. The idealists, in contrast, whose thought stemmed from Pythagoras and the Sicilian school, were nonmaterialists, reasoning that the physical world is illusory and that behind it lies a realm accessible only by contemplation.

By the mid–fifth century BCE, this simple pattern was being challenged by new philosophies, and by 400 BCE, a revolution in thought had occurred that overshadowed everything that had gone before. The first assault came from Sicily, where a new school of thinkers proposed to reconcile materialism and idealism. Then, in Athens, a group of teachers called the Sophists questioned philosophical inquiry itself and the notion of absolute truth. The corrosive ideas of these figures provoked Socrates, the most revolutionary thinker of the entire ancient world, to respond to their claims. Socrates' life marked a watershed in Greek thought. All Greek thinkers before him are now known as Pre-Socratics, and those who came after him—chiefly Plato and Aristotle in Hellenic Greece—followed his lead in studying the human experience (Table 3.1).

The Pre-Socratics   The major Pre-Socratic thinkers tried to determine the nature of the physical world. For Parmenides [par-MEN-uh-deez] (fl. after 515 BCE) and his followers in the polis Elea, for example, the world was a single, unchanging, unmoving object whose order could be known through human reason. This attempt to reconcile materialism and idealism was modified by Parmenides' student Empedocles [em-PED-uh-kleez] (about 484–about 424 BCE), who claimed that everything, animate or inanimate,

TABLE 3.1 PHILOSOPHY IN THE HELLENIC AGE

PHILOSOPHY	EMPHASIS
Pre-Socratic	The physical world; nature; debate over materialism and idealism
Sophist	Humanistic values; practical skills, such as public speaking and logic
Socratic	Enduring moral and intellectual order of the universe; the psyche (mind/soul); "Virtue is Knowledge"
Platonist	Ideas (Forms) are the basis of every thing; dualism, the split between the world of Ideas and the everyday world; rationalism; severe moderation in ethics
Aristotelian	Natural world is the only world; empiricism, using observation, classification, and comparison; "golden mean" in ethics

originated in the four elements of earth, water, fire, and air. These elements were unchanging, but the opposing forces of love and strife could combine them in different ways, to the detriment or benefit of humans. This explanation of change is **metaphysical,** which means that it is based on abstract and speculative reasoning, not on empirical observation.

The atomists, another school of Pre-Socratic thinkers, believed that everything is composed of atoms—eternal, invisible bodies of varying size that, by definition, cannot be divided into smaller units—and the void, the empty space between the atoms. Atomic theory was developed most fully by Democritus [de-MOK-ruht-us] of Thrace (fl. after 460 BCE). The movement and shape of the atoms were sufficient to explain not only physical objects but also feelings, tastes, sight, ideas—in short, every aspect of the physical world.

The Sophists   The Sophists—from the Greek word *sophia,* or "wisdom"—scorned Pre-Socratic speculation about atoms and elements as irrelevant and useless. These traveling teachers claimed to offer their students (for a fee) knowledge that guaranteed success in life. Their emphasis on the development of practical skills, such as effective public speaking, led their critics to accuse them of cynicism and a lack of interest in higher ethical values, but the Sophists were deeply serious and committed to humanistic values. Protagoras [pro-TAG-uh-ruhs] (481–411 BCE), the most renowned of the Sophists, proclaimed that "man is the measure of all things." This summed up the Sophists' argument that human beings, as the center of the universe, have the power to make judgments about themselves and their world—that they naturally see everything in relation to themselves. The Sophists helped free the human spirit to be critical and creative. If there was a danger in their teaching, it was a tendency toward unrestrained skepticism. By stressing that human beings have the power to shape the world, the Sophists opened themselves to charges of impiety and undermining traditional values, because the traditional Greek view was that the gods controlled everything. The Sophists' denial of norms, standards, and absolutes registered with the populace because the dramatists responded to them. Sophocles condemned the Sophists while Euripides embraced many of their ideas.

The Socratic Revolution   Socrates [SAH-kruh-teez] (about 470–399 BCE) launched a new era in philosophy. Given his passionate conviction that an enduring moral and intellectual order existed in the universe, he opposed almost everything the Sophists stood for. But Socrates shared certain traits with them, such as his rejection of philosophizing about nature, his focus on human problems, and his desire to empower individuals to make their own moral choices.

Socrates' method for arriving at true moral and intellectual values was deceptively simple yet maddeningly elusive. At the heart of his thinking was the *psyche* (mind, or soul); being immortal, the psyche was deemed more important than the mortal and doomed body. Those who want wisdom must protect, nourish, and expand their psyches by giving their minds the maximum amount of knowledge. The knowledge the psyche acquired had to be won through stimulating conversations and debates as well as by contemplation of abstract virtues and moral values. Only then could the psyche approach its highest potential.

"Virtue is Knowledge," claimed Socrates; he meant that a person who knows the truth, acquired through personal struggle for self-enlightenment, will not commit evil deeds. And this moral dictum may be reversed: those who do wrong do so out of ignorance. If people used their psyches to think more deeply and clearly, they would lead virtuous lives. Socrates' belief in the essential goodness of human nature and the necessity of well-defined knowledge became central tenets of Western thought.

After having pointed out the proper path to wisdom, Socrates left the rest up to his students. Bombarding inquiring youths with questions on such topics as the meaning of justice, he used rigorous logic to refute all the squirming students' attempts at precise definition. Then—as shown by Plato's dialogues, the principal source for what we know about Socrates—the students, collapsing into confusion, admitted the serious gaps in their knowledge. Socrates' step-by-step questions, interspersed with gentle humor and ironic jabs, honed his students' logical skills and compelled them to begin a quest for knowledge in light of their self-confessed ignorance. Many teachers in Greece and Rome adopted the Socratic method, and it remains an honored pedagogical device.

The Athenians of this era began to perceive Socrates as a threat to their way of life. This short, homely, and rather insignificant-looking man—as surviving statues reveal—aroused suspicion in the polis with his public arguments (Figure 3.10). When Athens fell to the Spartans in 404 BCE, opposition to Socrates swelled. Many citizens now found subversion or even blasphemy in his words and in the behavior of his followers. Five years after the end of the Peloponnesian War, Socrates was accused of impiety and of corrupting the Athenian youth; a jury declared him guilty and sentenced him to die. Plato, a former student, was so moved by Socrates' eloquent, though ineffective, defense and by the injustice of his death sentence that the younger man dedicated the remainder of his life to righting the wrong and explaining the Socratic philosophy. Indeed, Plato devoted four works to the last days of Socrates including the *Phaedo,* which is a deathbed scene with an argument in support of immortality.

Figure 3.11   Roman Copy of a Bust of Plato. Ht. 13³/₄″. Staatliche Antikensammlung und Glyptothek, Munich. A copy of the original portrait bust of Plato by the famous portrait sculptor Silanon. Supposedly, King Mithridates of Persia commissioned the image for the Academy, but it was not installed until after Plato's death in 348. Plato means "the broad." Note the broad forehead, the broad, flat nose, and the austere, far-gazing countenance. Compare this image with those of Socrates (p. 69) and Aristotle (p. 56).

Figure 3.10   _Socrates._ Ca. 200 BCE–100 CE. Ht. 10¹/₂″. British Museum, London. This Roman marble copy of the original Greek statue supports the unflattering descriptions of Socrates by his contemporaries. By portraying the philosopher with a receding hairline and a dumpy body, the anonymous sculptor has made one of the world's most extraordinary human beings look very ordinary.

Plato   The spirit of Socrates hovers over the rest of Greek philosophy, especially in the accomplishments of his most famous student, Plato (about 427–347 BCE) (Figure 3.11). Plato's philosophy is the fountainhead of Western **idealism,** a thought system that emphasizes spiritual values and makes ideas, rather than matter, the basis of everything that exists. **Platonism** arose out of certain premises that were Socratic in origin— the concept of the psyche and the theory of remembrance. Like Socrates, Plato emphasized the immortal and immutable psyche over the mortal and changeful body. But Plato advanced a new polarity, favoring the invisible world of the Forms, or Ideas, in opposition to the physical world. The psyche's true home was the world of the Forms, which it inhabited before birth and after death—the time when the psyche was lost in wonder among the eternal Ideas. In contrast, the body lived exclusively in the material world, completely absorbed by the life of the senses. Once trapped inside the body, the psyche could glimpse the higher reality, or Forms, only through remembrance.

Nonetheless, Plato thought that through a set of mental exercises the psyche would be able to recall the Ideas to which it had once been exposed. The best training for the psyche, provided in Plato's school, the Academy, was the study of mathematics, since mathematics required signs and symbols to represent other things. After the mastery of mathematics, the student proceeded, with the help of logic, to higher stages of abstract learning, such as defining the Forms of Justice, Beauty, and Love. By showing that wisdom came only after an intellectual progression that culminated in an understanding of the absolute Ideas, Plato refuted the Sophists, who claimed that knowledge was relative.

A major implication of Plato's idealism was that the psyche and the body were constantly at war. The psyche's attempts to remember the lost Ideas met resistance from the body's pursuit of power, fame, and physical comforts. This dualism especially plagued the philosopher, the lover of wisdom; but the true philosopher took comfort in recognizing that at death the psyche would return freely to the world of the Forms.

Plato identified the Form of the Good, the ultimate Idea, with God, yet the Platonic deity was neither the creator of the world nor the absolute and final power. Instead, Plato's deity was necessary for his idealism to function; in his thought, God was the source from which descended the imperfect objects of the natural world. In a related theological notion, he, like Socrates, attributed the presence of evil to ignorance; but Plato added the psyche's misdirected judgment and insatiable bodily appetites as other causes of evil.

Socrates' death provoked Plato to envision a perfect state where justice flourished. The book that resulted from Plato's speculations—the *Republic*—sets forth his model state and, incidentally, launched the study of political philosophy in the West. Plato thought that a just state could be realized only when all social classes worked together for the good of the whole, each class performing its assigned tasks. Because of the importance of the psyche, social status was determined by the ability to reason, not by wealth or inheritance. A tiny elite of philosopher-kings and philosopher-queens, who were the best qualified to run the state, reigned. Possessing wisdom as a result of their education in the Platonic system, they lived simply, shunning the creature comforts that corrupted weaker rulers.

The two lower ranks were similarly equipped for their roles in society by their intellects and their training: a middle group provided police and military protection, and the third and largest segment operated the economy. In Plato's dream world, both the individual and the society aimed for virtue, and the laws and the institutions ensured that the ideal would be achieved.

Aristotle   Socrates may have been revolutionary; Plato was certainly poetic; but Aristotle [AIR-us-tah-tuhl] (384–322 BCE) had the most comprehensive mind of the ancient world. His curiosity and vast intellect led him into every major field of inquiry of his time except mathematics and music. Born in Macedonia, he was connected to some of the most brilliant personalities of his day. He first studied philosophy under Plato in Athens and then tutored the future Alexander the Great. After Philip's conquest of Greece, Aristotle settled in Athens and opened a school, the Lyceum, that quickly rivaled the Academy, Plato's school.

Although his philosophy owed much to Platonism, Aristotle emphasized the role of the human senses. To Aristotle, the natural world was the only world; no separate, invisible realm of Ideas existed. Nature could be studied and understood by observation, classification, and comparison of data from the physical world—that is, through the empirical method.

Aristotle rejected the world of the Forms because he believed that Form and Matter were inseparable, both rooted in nature. Each material object contained a predetermined Form that, with proper training or nourishment, would evolve into its final Form and ultimate purpose. This growth process, in his view, was potentiality evolving into actuality, as when an embryo becomes a human or a seed matures into a plant. Thus, the philosopher could conclude that everything has a purpose, or end.

Aristotle's thought rested on the concept of God, which he equated with the First Cause. Aristotle's God was a logical necessity not a supernatural figure. Rejecting Platonic dualism and its exclusive regard for the psyche, Aristotle devised a down-to-earth ethical goal—a sound mind in a healthy body—that he called happiness. To achieve happiness, he advised, in his *Nicomachean Ethics*, striking a mean, or a balance, between extremes of behavior. For example, courage is the mean between the excess of foolhardiness and the deficiency of cowardice. Noting that actions like murder and adultery are vicious by their very nature, he condemned them as being unable to be moderated. Although Aristotle disavowed many of Plato's ideas, he agreed with his former mentor that the cultivation of the higher intellect is more important than that of the body.

Aristotle's ethics were related to his politics, for he taught that happiness finally depended on the type of government under which an individual lived. Unlike Plato, who based his politics on speculative thinking, Aristotle reached his political views after careful research. After collecting 158 state constitutions, Aristotle, in his *Politics*, classified and compared them, concluding that the best form of government was a constitutional regime ruled by the middle class. His preference for the middle class stemmed from his belief that they, exciting neither envy from the poor nor contempt from the wealthy, would honor and work for the good of all.

Aristotle's influence on Western civilization is immeasurable. In the Middle Ages, Christian, Muslim, and Jewish scholars studied his writings, regarding them as containing authoritative teachings on the natural world. Today, Aristotelianism is embedded in the official theology of the Roman Catholic Church (see Chapter 10), and Aristotle's logic continues to be taught in college philosophy courses.

Medicine   Little is known of the life of Hippocrates [hip-OCK-re-teez] (about 460–377 BCE), the major figure in classical Greek medicine. In his own lifetime, he was highly regarded and apparently traveled extensively through Greece and Asia Minor, healing the sick and teaching aspiring physicians.

SLICE OF LIFE

Secrets of a Successful Marriage in Ancient Greece

Xenophon
FROM *OECONOMICUS*

It is not surprising that the Greeks were concerned with how to have a good marriage. Xenophon (about 445–355 BCE), a famous military commander, historian, essayist, and student of Socrates, discussed marriage in his essay on domestic economy, or home life. It is a fairly accurate depiction of the marital ideal among well-to-do Greeks of the time. The dialogue form was common in works like this.

I [Socrates] said, "I should very much like you to tell me, Ischomachus, whether you yourself trained your wife to become the sort of woman that she ought to be, or whether she already knew how to carry out her duties when you took her as your wife from her father and mother."

[Ischomachus replied,] "What could she have known when I took her as my wife, Socrates? She was not yet fifteen when she came to me, and had spent her previous years under careful supervision so that she might see and hear and speak as little as possible. . . .

"[A]s soon as she was sufficiently tamed and domesticated so as to be able to carry on a conversation, I questioned her more or less as follows: 'Tell me, wife, have you ever thought about why I married you and why your parents gave you to me? It must be quite obvious to you, I am sure, that there was no shortage of partners with whom we might sleep. I, on my part, and your parents, on your behalf, considered who was the best partner we could choose for managing an estate and for children. And I chose you, and your parents, apparently, chose me, out of those who were eligible. Now if some day the god grants us children, then we shall consider how to train them in the best way possible. For this will be a blessing to us both, to obtain the best allies and support in old age. But at present we two share this estate. I go on paying everything I have into the common fund; and you deposited into it everything you brought with you. There is no need to calculate precisely which of us has contributed more,

but to be well aware of this: that the better partner is the one who makes the more valuable contribution. . . .

"'Because both the indoor and the outdoor tasks require work and concern, I think the god, from the very beginning, designed the nature of woman for the indoor work and concerns and the nature of man for the outdoor work. For he prepared man's body and mind to be more capable of enduring cold and heat and travelling and military campaigns, and so he assigned the outdoor work to him. Because the woman was physically less capable of endurance, I think the god has evidently assigned the indoor work to her. . . .

"'Because it is necessary for both of them to give and to take, he gave both of them equal powers of memory and concern. So you would not be able to distinguish whether the female or male sex has the larger share of these. And he gave them both equally the ability to practise self-control too, when it is needed. . . .

"[B]ecause they are not equally well endowed with all the same natural aptitudes, they are consequently more in need of each other, and the bond is more beneficial to the couple, since one is capable where the other is deficient.'"

Interpreting This Slice of Life

1. Based on this selection, *what* was the role of women in marriage in Hellenic Greece?

2. At *what* age was the wife in the selection married?

3. *What* impact would the wife's youth have on the dynamics of the marriage?

4. *Discuss* the role of material matters (money, property, and other forms of wealth) in Greek marriage, as depicted here.

5. *What* attitude does the speaker, Ischomachus, have toward male and female intellectual abilities?

6. *Compare and contrast* modern attitudes toward marriage with those represented in this selection.

Hippocrates was born on the island of Cos in the Aegean Sea and probably taught at the medical school located there. In the second and third centuries CE, scholars collected about seventy works attributed to him, the Hippocratic Collection, which ensured his future reputation. Today, Hippocrates is still the "father of medicine" and identified with the Hippocratic oath, which most medical students take at the

commencement of their medical careers. This oath, which he certainly did not compose, spells out the duties and responsibilities of a physician and sets ethical standards and personal behavior practices.

Regardless of how little is known of Hippocrates, he is still recognized as one of the first physicians to reject supernatural explanations as causes of illness. Instead, he observed and studied the body and its parts from a scientific and clinical point of view. Most specifically, Hippocrates believed that diseases were caused by imbalances of the four "humors," which he identified as the four fluids—blood, phlegm, black bile, and yellow bile—within the physical body. He asserted that disease was not the invasion of evil spirits or controlling deities. If these humors were kept in balance—such as by administering drugs, prescribing diets, or removing excess blood or other humors—then the body would heal itself and the patient would recover.

In one of the works attributed to him, Hippocrates discusses the "sacred" disease, now known as epilepsy. At the time, conventional wisdom explained epilepsy as a "divine affliction," a sign that the patient was favored by the gods. In contrast, Hippocrates argues that epilepsy has natural causes that can be identified and treated. He also comments on the brain, terming it the source of all emotions and senses and the "most powerful organ in the human body."

THE VISUAL ARTS

In architecture, sculpture, and painting, Greeks of the Hellenic Age outstripped their Archaic forebears. Doric architecture was brought to a peak of perfection and then surpassed by a new order, the Ionic. The emerging humanism of the kouroi and korai yielded to classical sculpture of almost inexpressible beauty and naturalism. Finally, the gorgeous black-figure and red-figure ware of the Archaic period was complemented by exquisite white-ground ware.

Architecture

The temple was the supreme expression of Hellenic architecture. By Hellenic times, the Greek world was polarized between eastern (the mainland and the Aegean Islands) and western (Magna Graecia) styles of temple design, although in both styles the temples were rectilinear and of post-beam-triangle construction. Influenced by the Pythagorean quest for harmony through mathematical rules, the eastern builders had standardized six as the perfect number of columns for the ends of temples and thirteen, or twice the number of end columns plus one, as the perfect number of columns for the sides. These balanced proportions, along with simple designs and restrained decorative schemes, made the eastern temples majestically expressive of classical ideals.

Architects in western Greece, somewhat removed from the centers of classical culture, were more experimental than those in the Greek mainland. Their buildings deviated from the eastern ideals, as can be seen in the Second Temple of Hera at Paestum, built

Figure 3.12   Second Temple of Hera at Paestum. Ca. 450 BCE. Limestone. This temple of Hera is among the best-preserved structures from the ancient world. Since Hera may have been a chthonian goddess before becoming consort to Olympian Zeus, it is appropriate that this Doric temple, with its ground-hugging appearance, be her monument.

of limestone in about 450 BCE (Figure 3.12). The best preserved of all Greek temples, this Doric structure does not have the harmonious proportions of the eastern version of this style. Although the Second Temple of Hera owed much to eastern influences, including the six columns at the ends and the porches, it had too many (fourteen) columns on the sides, its columns were too thick, and the low-pitched roof made the building seem squat.

Between 447 and 438 BCE, the architects Ictinus [ik-TIE-nuhs] and Callicrates [kuh-LICK-ruh-teez] perfected the eastern-style Doric temple in the Parthenon, a temple on Athens's Acropolis dedicated to Athena (Figure 3.13). When completed, this temple established a new standard of classicism, with eight columns on the ends and seventeen on the sides and with the numeric ratio 9:4 used throughout, expressed, for example, in the relation of a column's height to its diameter. Inside, the builders designed two chambers, an east room for a forty-foot-high statue of Athena and a smaller room housing the Delian League treasury. The rest of the Acropolis project, finally finished in 405 BCE, included the Propylaea, the gate leading to the sanctuary; the temple of Athena Nike, a gift to Athens's patron goddess thanking her for a military

Figure 3.13 ICTINUS AND CALLICRATES. **The Parthenon, Athens. Third quarter of the fifth century BCE. Pentelic marble.** A great humanistic icon, the Parthenon has had a long history since its days as a Greek temple. It served successively as a Christian church, a mosque, and an ammunitions depot, until it was accidentally blown up at the end of the seventeenth century CE. Today, concerned nations are cooperating with the Greek government through UNESCO to preserve this noble ruin.

victory (Figure 3.14); and the Erechtheum, a temple dedicated to three deities.

Ictinus and Callicrates introduced many subtle variations, called refinements, into their designs so that no line is exactly straight, horizontal, or perpendicular. For example, the stepped base of the temple forms a gentle arc so that the ends are lower than the middle; the floor slopes slightly to the edges; and the columns tilt inward away from the ends. These and other refinements were no accidents but, instead, were intended to be corrections for real and imaginary optical illusions. The Parthenon's fame exerted such authority in later times that these refinements, along with harmonious proportions, became standardized as the essence of Greek architecture.

The second order of Greek architecture, the Ionic, originated in the late Archaic Age and, like the Doric, came to flourish in Hellenic times. The **Ionic** style, freer than the Doric and more graceful, reflected its origins in the Ionian world; traditionally, the Ionians contrasted their opulence with the simplicity of the Dorians. In place of the alternating metopes and triglyphs of Doric buildings, the Ionic temple had a running frieze to which sculptured figures might be added. More decorated than the plain Doric, the Ionic columns had elegant bases, and their tops were

Figure 3.14 CALLICRATES. **Temple of Athena Nike, Athens. Late fifth century BCE. Marble.** Designed by Callicrates, one of the Parthenon's architects, this miniature temple was begun after 427 BCE and probably completed before 420 BCE. Like the Parthenon, it was dedicated to the city's patron goddess, Athena, though here she was honored as Nike, goddess of victory. This temple's simple plan includes a square cella with four Ionic columns at the front and back and a sculptural frieze, devoted to scenes of mythic and contemporary battles, encircling the upper exterior walls.

73

Figure 3.15   MNESICLES. The Erechtheum, Athens. View from the west. Ca. 410 BCE. Marble. The Erechtheum was probably built to quiet conservatives who rejected Athena's new temple, the Parthenon, as a symbol of Athenian imperialism. Reflecting its ties with the past, the Erechtheum housed the ancient wooden cult statue of Athena, which pious Athenians believed had fallen from the sky. Its Ionic porches set the standard for the graceful Ionic order. The Porch of the Maidens (above), which was inaccessible from the outside, fronted the southern wall.

crowned with capitals that suggested either a scroll's ends or a ram's horns. What solidified the Ionic temple's impression of elegance were its slender and delicate columns.

The Athenians chose the Ionic style for the exquisite, though eccentric, Erechtheum, the last of the great buildings erected on the Acropolis (Figure 3.15). The artistic freedom associated with the Ionic style may have led the architect, Mnesicles [NES-uh-kleez], to make the floor plan asymmetrical and to introduce so

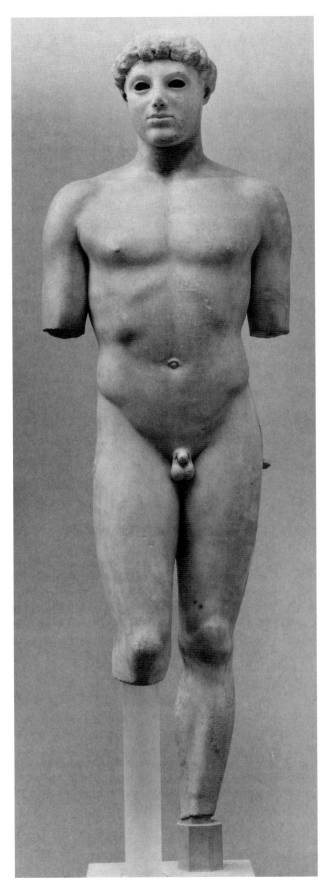

Figure 3.16   *Kritios Boy.* Ca. 480 BCE. Ht. 3′10″. Acropolis Museum, Athens. This statue is carved from marble probably mined at Mount Pentelicus in Attica. Two features—the treatment of the eyes, which were originally set with semiprecious stones, and the roll of hair—show that the Kritios sculptor was accustomed to working in bronze. The figure's beautifully rendered muscles and sense of inner life announce the arrival of the Hellenic style; the contrapposto, used sparingly here, foreshadows later developments in Greek sculpture.

many design variations, but a more likely explanation was Mnesicles' need to integrate three existing shrines into a single building—those of the Olympians Athena and Poseidon and the mythical king Erechtheus [eh-RECK-thee-us], who introduced the horse to Athens. Mnesicles took the unusual step of stressing the site's unbalanced nature by adding two Ionic porches and the temple's crowning feature, the Porch of the Maidens. With his bold design, Mnesicles created a marvelous illusion of harmony that was in keeping with the Hellenic Age's classical ideals.

Sculpture

Equally impressive is the Greek achievement in sculpture. Believing that the task of sculpture is to imitate nature, the Greeks created images of gods and goddesses as well as of men and women that have haunted the Western imagination ever since. They not only forged a canon of idealized human proportions that later sculptors followed but also developed a repertoire of postures, gestures, and subjects that have become embedded in Western art.

During the Hellenic Age, classical sculpture moved through three separate phases: the **Severe style,** which ushered in the period and lasted until 450 BCE; the **high classical style,** which coincided with the zenith of Athenian imperial greatness; and the **fourth-century style,** which concluded with the death of Alexander the Great in 323 BCE.

Sculpture in the Severe style, inspired perhaps by its association with funeral customs, was characterized by a feeling of dignified nobility. The *Kritios Boy*—showing a figure fully at rest—is an elegant expression of this first phase of classicism (Figure 3.16). Kritios [KRIT-ee-uhs], the supposed sculptor, fixed the

mouth severely and altered the frontality, a feature of the Archaic style, by tilting the head subtly to the right and slightly twisting the upper torso. The flat-footed stance of the Archaic kouros has given way to a posture that places the body's weight on one leg and uses the other leg as a support. This stance is called **contrapposto** (counterpoise), and its invention, along with the mastery of the representation of musculature, helped to make the classical revolution. Thereafter, sculptors were able to render the human figure in freer, more relaxed poses.

The central panel of the so-called Ludovisi Throne, another sculpture from the same period, conveys an air of quiet gravity (Figure 3.17). The subject is probably the birth of Aphrodite as she rises from the sea, indicated by pebbles under the feet of her attendants, the stooping figures on either side. This relief reflects a perfect blending of late Archaic grace (Aphrodite's stylized hair and the hint of Archaic smile) with the dignity of the Severe style (the delicate transparent draperies and the convincing realism produced by foreshortening the arms of the three figures).

In contrast to the Severe style, which accepted repose as normal, the high classical style was fascinated with the aesthetic problem of showing motion in a static medium. The sculptors' solution, which became central to high classicism, was to freeze the action, resisting the impulse to depict agitated movement, in much the same way that the tragic playwrights banished violence from the stage. In effect, the high classical sculptors stopped time, allowing an ideal world to emerge in which serene gods and mortals showed grace under pressure. A striking representation of this aspect of high classicism is the bronze statue of Poseidon, or Zeus, found in the Aegean Sea off Cape

Figure 3.17 *The Birth of Aphrodite.* **Ca. 460 BCE. Ht. 2′9″. National Museum of the Terme, Rome.** The Ludovisi Throne, with its three relief panels, is a controversial work, because scholars disagree about its original function, the interpretation of its panels, and even its date. Discovered in Rome in the late nineteenth century, it probably was carved in Magna Graecia, perhaps for an altar, and brought to Rome in antiquity. The figure of Aphrodite was one of the first nude women depicted in large-scale Greek sculpture. The goddess is rendered in softly curving lines— a marked deviation from the Severe style and a forecast of the sensuous tendency of later Greek art.

Figure 3.18 *Poseidon* (or *Zeus*). Ca. 460–450 BCE. Bronze, ht. 6′10″. National Museum, Athens. The Greek conception of the nobility of their gods is nowhere better revealed than in this magnificent bronze sculpture of Poseidon (or Zeus). Grace, strength, and intellect are united in this majestic image of a mature deity. Poseidon's eyes originally would have been semiprecious stones, and the statue would have been painted to create a more realistic effect. If Poseidon, he hurls a trident; if Zeus, a thunderbolt.

Artemision. It captures to perfection high classicism's ideal of virile grace (Figure 3.18). The god (whose maturity is signified by the beard and fully developed body) is shown poised, ready to hurl some object. In such sculptures as this, the Greeks found visual metaphors for their notion that deities and mortals are kin.

High classical sculptors wanted to do more than portray figures in motion; some, especially Polykleitos [pol-e-KLITE-uhs] of Argos, continued to be obsessed with presenting the ideal human form at rest. In his search for perfection, Polykleitos executed a bronze male figure of such strength and beauty—the *Doryphoros* ("Spearbearer")—that its proportions came to be regarded as a canon, or set of rules, to be imitated by other artists (Figure 3.19). In the *Doryphoros* canon, each of the limbs bears a numeric relation to the body's overall measurements; for example, the length of the foot is one-tenth of the figure's height. Other principles of high classicism embodied in the *Doryphoros* include the slightly brutal facial features, typical of this style's masculine ideal; the relaxed contrapposto; and the controlled muscles.

Greek architecture reached its zenith in the Parthenon, and, similarly, classical Greek sculpture attained its height in the reliefs and sculptures of this celebrated temple. Under the disciplined eye of the sculptor

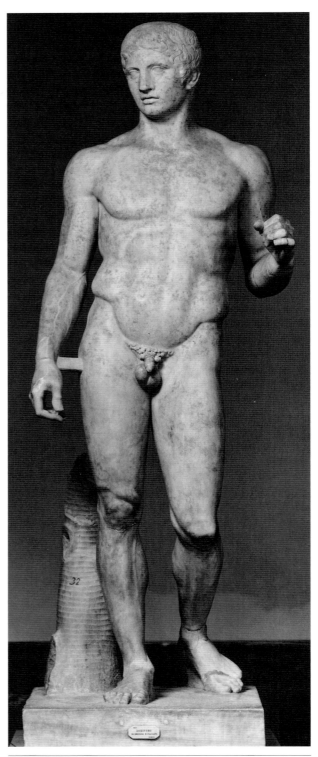

Figure 3.19 *Doryphoros*. Ca. 440 BCE. Marble copy of a bronze original by Polykleitos, ht. 6′6″. Museo Nazionale Archeologico, Naples. The *Doryphoros* expresses the classical ideal of balanced repose. The nude figure rests his weight upon the right leg. The left arm, extended to hold the now-missing spear, balances with the right leg. The left foot, barely touching the ground, balances with the relaxed right arm. Besides representing idealized repose, the *Doryphoros* was also recognized as the embodiment of human beauty with its ordered proportions, well-toned musculature, and rugged features.

Interpreting Art

Influence Supposedly the most famous statue in antiquity, more than a dozen copies survive today. Later painters imitated the statue as well, for example, the Italian master Sandro Botticelli (Figure 12.5).

Composition The first known full-sized female nude executed in Greece, the figure stands in contrapposto and exhibits the "Praxitelean curve." Showing no rigidity, the body works exactly as it should. The statue was carved so as to be viewed from all sides—as it was in a temple.

Female Body Previously, women had been depicted in revealing garments but never nude. People were allegedly shocked by this statue but came from all over Greece to see it. Its ancient nickname was *Venus Pudica* ("Modest Venus") because she shields her genitalia with her right hand. In later copies she raises her left hand to cover her breasts. The figure is true to life, graceful, and sensuous. In one Greek poem, the poet portrays Aphrodite asking "When did Praxiteles see me naked?"

Religious Perspective Aphrodite presides over sexuality and reproduction. Young women about to be married sacrificed to Aphrodite so that their first sexual experience would be pleasant and productive. She was also associated with fertility of the earth. Men worshiped her as the goddess of seafaring.

Political Perspective In Athens especially, Aphrodite was called *pandemos* ("the whole people"), meaning that she was worshiped as the protectress of all the people who were seafarers and farmers and who hoped to reproduce.

Subject *Aphrodite* drops her clothes on a hydria (a Greek vessel for carrying water) before stepping into her bath. The model may have been the sculptor's lover Phyrne.

PRAXITELES. *Aphrodite of Knidos.* Ca. 350 BCE. Roman copy. Marble, ht. 6′8″. Vatican Museum. Created for a temple on the island of Knidos, this statue became a kind of tourist attraction as people came from all over Greece to see it. To appreciate the sculptor's exquisite style, compare this statue with the *Hermes* on page 79.

1. **Subject** What characteristics does this statue share with other Greek statues and with Praxiteles' Hermes?

2. **Composition** Compare this statue with the other representations of females in Chapters 1, 2, and 3.

3. **Female Body Perspective** Given that male nudes appeared very early and apparently elicited no criticism, why do you think the female nude was so slow to appear?

4. **Religious Perspective** How does this statue both reveal and hint at the power of Aphrodite?

5. **Political Perspective** Why was Aphrodite suitable for worship by "all the people"?

6. **Influence** Why do you suppose this was the most famous statue in antiquity?

Figure 3.20 *Centaur Versus Lapith.* **Metope XXX, south face of the Parthenon. Ca. 448–442 BCE. Marble, ht. 56″. British Museum, London.** This struggling pair was designed to fit comfortably into the metope frame, and thus the proportions of the figures in relation to each other and to the small space were worked out with precision. The intertwined limbs of the warrior and the centaur visibly demonstrate the new freedom of high classicism. The anguished countenance of the lapith, however, is almost unique in high classicism and is a portent of the more emotional faces of the Hellenistic style, the next major artistic development.

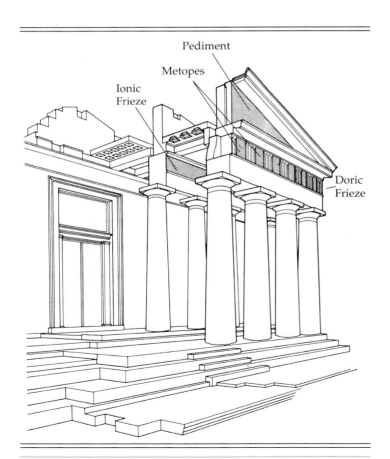

Figure 3.21   The Location of the Sculptures on the Parthenon. This cutaway view shows the metopes on the Doric frieze, the Ionic frieze, and the pediments of the Parthenon, which were covered with sculptures celebrating the glory of Athens.

Figure 3.22   Grave Stele of Hegeso. Ca. 410–400 BCE. Ht. 5′9″. National Archaeological Museum, Athens. Grave markers like this one were produced in profusion in Athens and probably helped to disseminate the Phidian style. Hegeso was a noble lady and this tomb marker was probably erected by her husband. As Figure 3.20 shows a lapith in agony, so this stele reveals tenderness, attentiveness, and intimacy. Here is Greek humanism at its most humane.

Phidias [FIHD-e-uhs], craftspeople carved patriotic and mythological subjects destined for various parts of the building. Taken as a whole, the sculptures revealed the Parthenon to be a tribute to Athenian imperialism as much as to the goddess Athena.

On the Parthenon's metopes—the rectangular spaces on the Doric frieze—sculptors portrayed scenes in the prevailing high classical style. In panel after panel, the metope sculptors depicted perfect human forms showing restraint in the midst of struggle, such as Amazons against men, Greeks against Trojans, and gods against giants. The south metopes portrayed the battle between the legendary lapiths and the half-men, half-horse centaurs (Figure 3.20). For the Greeks, the struggle between the human lapiths and the bestial centaurs symbolized the contest between civilization and barbarism or, possibly, between the Greeks and the Persians.

Inside the columns, running around the perimeter of the upper cella walls in a continuous band, was a low-relief frieze (Figure 3.21). Borrowed from the Ionic order, this running frieze introduced greater liveliness into high classicism. The 525-foot-long band depicts the Panathenaea festival, Athens's most important civic and religious ritual, which was held every four years. This panoramic view of the procession concluded with a stunning group portrait of the twelve gods and goddesses, seated in casual majesty, awaiting their human worshipers. The entire Parthenon frieze was the most ambitious work of sculpture in the Greek tradition.

The beautiful grave stele of Hegeso (Figure 3.22) is in the Phidian style, the presumed style of Phidias. The deceased lady has selected a necklace from a jewel box held by her attendant. The billowing garments reveal arms, legs, and breasts. These are real people. The figures themselves merge into the background as if it were empty space. Sculptors had by now mastered form and could concentrate on interpretation.

The transition to fourth-century style coincided with the end of the creative phase of tragedy and the disintegration of the Greek world as it passed into the Macedonian political orbit. Sculpture remained innovative, since each generation seemed to produce a master who challenged the prevailing aesthetic rules, and free expression continued as a leading principle of fourth-century style. But sculptors now expressed such new ideas as beauty for its own sake and a delight in sensuality. Earlier classicism had stressed the notion that humans could become godlike, but the last phase concluded that gods and mortals alike reveled in human joys.

This new focus is apparent in Praxiteles' [prax-SIT-uh-eez] *Hermes with the Infant Dionysus.* This sculpture, perhaps the only original work by a known sculptor that survives from Hellenic Greece, portrays two gods blissfully at play (Figure 3.23). Hermes, lounging in

Figure 3.23 PRAXITELES. *Hermes with the Infant Dionysus.* **Ca. 350–340 BCE. Marble, ht. 85″. Archaeological Museum, Olympia, Greece.** In this statue of Hermes, Praxiteles changed the look of classical art with his rendering of the god's body. For example, Hermes' small head and long legs contributed to the Praxitelean canon for the male figure. The sculptor has also created a dramatic contrast between Hermes' well-muscled body and his soft face. As a direct result of Praxiteles' new vision, sculptors in the Hellenistic Age would become interested in more frankly sensual portrayals of the human figure, both male and female.

a casual yet dignified pose, probably dangled grapes before the attentive baby god. The contrapposto posture, beautifully defined in Hermes' stance, became widely imitated as the **Praxitelean curve.** Praxiteles' treatment of the male figure had superseded the more rugged *Doryphoros* canon. Hermes' sensuous body, his intent gaze, and his delicate features are hallmarks of fourth-century classicism.

Painting

In the Hellenic period, red-figure ware was more popular than black-figure ware, but both styles continued to be produced (see Figures 3.8 and 3.9). New toward the end of the fifth century was white-ground ware. Surviving examples are almost all painted on lekynthoi (oil jugs, for funeral offerings). Two features of this new style are striking. First, the white-ground ware style shares traits with the period's sculpture, but it is unclear which came first. A look at the Hegeso stele (see Figure 3.22) and the *Mistress and Maid* by the so-called Achilles Painter (Figure 3.24) shows the same melancholy scene interpreted in almost the same way. Second, the white background in the white-ground ware gave the painter the opportunity to draw and color freely, allowing the figures to emerge from seemingly empty space. The painter's command of spatial effects creates a powerful three-dimensionality. In painting, this command of space is corollary to the sense of movement in sculpture.

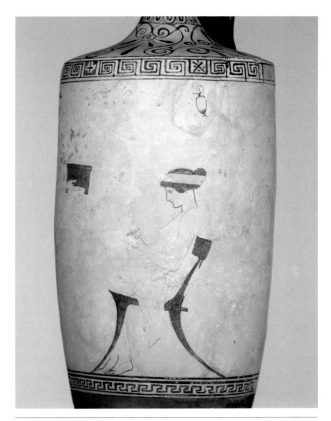

Figure 3.24 THE SO-CALLED ACHILLES PAINTER. *Mistress and Maid.* Ca. 440–430 BCE. Ht. 16″. Staatliche Antikensammlungen und Glyptothek, Munich. Probably made in Athens, this white-ground vessel has perhaps the most refined, delicate surviving painting from ancient Greece. Compare the Hegeso stele (Figure 3.22).

SUMMARY

After leading the Greeks to victory over Persia, Athens tried but failed to dominate the Greek world. For the next two centuries, no other polis achieved a dominant position although several tried. Domination finally came from the barbarian north, from Macedon.

Political and military failures notwithstanding, Greece, and especially Athens, soared to new cultural heights. Aeschylus, Sophocles, and Euripides improved the form and refined the content of Greek theater. They established tragedy as an art form. Their contemporary Aristophanes brought comedy to a new peak of perfection. Herodotus invented historical writing as a distinct intellectual exercise, and Thucydides added to it rigorous analysis and interpretation. Hippocrates set medicine on a scientific path. Philosophers turned from the natural world to humanity itself. Sophists denied all eternal, immutable standards. They did not teach people how to discern right and wrong but, instead, how to prevail. Socrates was shocked by the Sophists' teachings. He believed deeply in truth, and in people's ability to know and to communicate what was true. But his relentless questioning of everything brought his downfall. His most famous pupil, Plato, looked for truth in the realm of Ideas beyond the illusory world of daily life. Plato's pupil Aristotle sought reality in daily life and experience and called for careful observation and serious attention to language. In architecture, experimentation with the Doric form eventually resulted in the Parthenon in Athens, one of the greatest buildings ever erected. Sculpture passed through three phases: Severe, high classical, and fourth century. Sculpture decorated buildings in friezes and graced many settings as freestanding figures. In sculpture, as in all the arts and letters of the Hellenic Age, the hallmark was greater and greater **humanism**—a sensitivity to and celebration of human beings.

The Legacy of Classical Greece

Modern debts to Hellenic Greece are too numerous to count here. Athenian *demokratia*—rule by the people—has been a constant ideal and inspiration. In the "Arab Spring" of 2011, people all over the Middle East and North Africa rose up to defend their right to participate in public life. Students of politics and political science may not realize that the very subjects they are studying and the language they use to do so are Greek inventions. Classical "revivals" several times preceded the modern architecture that was in many ways a rejection of classical norms, but postmodern buildings often artfully combine the austerities of modernism with decorative details drawn from the classical repertoire. Hellenic classicism continues to shape the way we perceive beauty. Greek literature remains an integral part of school and college curriculums; its form and messages retain their attraction. Like some Greek thinkers we prize empirical study of the world around us, but like others we ask whether what we perceive constitutes all there is.

Sometimes the influence of classical Greece is seen in American popular culture. People speak of "Platonic" relationships when they want to characterize close relationships that are not romantic. Sigmund Freud taught us to think about "Oedipus complexes." Law students everywhere are taught by the Socratic method. In late 2011 "Lysistrata Jones" opened on Broadway. In this retelling of Aristophanes's tale, the girlfriends of some really bad college basketball players withhold sex until the guys start winning. Aristophanes comedy and the Broadway play both have their goofy side while dealing with important and sensitive subjects, ending a foolish war in one case and getting rid of a losing mentality in the other. The long-running show *Saturday Night Live* mocks our contemporary world the way Aristophanes mocked his. Every four years the world's athletes assemble in Olympic games. In the Halls of Congress Greek-inspired sculpture and themes instruct and inspire tourists and our "solons."

CARLO FRANZONI (1789-1819). *The Car of History.* **Marble, 1819. National Statuary Hall, Washington, D.C.** Clio, the Muse of History, stands in a winged chariot representing the passage of time and records events as they occur. The car rests on a marble globe around which the signs of the zodiac are carved. The clock, whose works were executed by Simon Willard (1753–1848), forms the wheel of the chariot. The *Car of History* is in the neoclassical style—the preferred style of the founders of the American republic who saw it as representing democracy and freedom.

KEY CULTURAL TERMS

Hellenic	*skene*	idealism	contrapposto
classic (classical)	satyr-play	Platonism	Praxitelean curve
tragedy	Old Comedy	Ionic	humanism
chorus	modes	Severe style	
Dionysia	epistemology	high classical style	
orchestra	metaphysical	fourth-century style	

Old Market Woman. **Third or second century BCE. Marble copy of bronze original, ht. 49".** **Metropolitan Museum of Art, New York.** Whether she was a poor peddler or an affluent shopper, this old woman would never have appeared in Hellenic art. She would have violated the quest for "the good, true, and beautiful." Yet, in Hellenistic times, ordinary people and everyday scenes had their value and beauty.

The Hellenistic World

Preview Questions

1. *How* were the Hellenistic monarchies alike, and *how* did they differ from the Hellenic poleis?

2. *What* evidence do you find for the cosmopolitan character of Hellenistic life?

3. *What* values do Hellenistic literature, philosophy, and art share, and *how* do they differ from Hellenic achievements in these areas?

The Hellenistic Age extended from the death of Alexander the Great in 323 BCE to the definitive triumph of Rome in the Mediterranean world in 31 BCE. The period is called **Hellenistic** to signal that it was different from the Hellenic Age yet very much its heir and beneficiary. Instead of being purely Greek in culture, the period might be described as "Greekish." The chief dynamic of the Hellenistic world was a remarkable blend of Greek and local cultures from Persia to the western Mediterranean. Hellenic Greeks could not imagine life outside a polis. Hellenistic "Greeks" were citizens of the world and did not even have to be Greek. While the Greek element was everywhere dominant, and gave coherence and unity to the age, Hellenistic culture was **cosmopolitan,** a word that imagines the world (*cosmos*) as a city (*polis*) and the city as a world. The Hellenistic Age was multicultural, open, and tolerant in ways that no preceding cultures had been and that no future ones would be until late in the twentieth century. The Hellenistic world also created the framework within which Roman and then Islamic empires and cultures would spread and take root. Indeed, the end of the Hellenistic period corresponds with the ascendancy of Rome (see Chapter 5).

The statue of an old woman to the left symbolizes many aspects of the Hellenistic world. First, there was a greater acceptance of all kinds of people—young and old, rich and poor, powerful and peasant. Second, the artistic skills attained in the Hellenic period had by no means deteriorated. The old woman is not beautiful but her statue is beautifully done. Third, there is a certain ambiguity. Some think the statue represents a poor woman who peddled her wares—she is holding chickens and fruit—in the market square. Others think she is a respectable old lady who is on her way to a Dionysiac festival. She wears an elegant chiton (a kind of draped tunic), a himation (a cloak), and dainty sandals, and she has an ivy wreath in her hair. Status was not so clear and sharply defined as in Hellenic Greece. Statues like this were offered to the gods, in this case

Figure 4.1   Black Youth. Third to second century BCE. Bronze. Metropolitan Museum of Art, New York. Beginning in the Archaic Age, Greek artists occasionally depicted black Africans in their works. During the Hellenistic Age, with the migration of peoples and the increased use of slaves, sculptors frequently chose black figures as subjects. This small bronze statue of a young African is an illustration of the racial diversity of the Hellenistic world. Despite the figure's exaggerated half-crouch, the statuette is probably not meant to represent an athlete, as he is not depicted fully nude. Note the sash around the waist, with the end draped down the upper thighs. The figure more likely was intended to represent a worker engaged in some task, as reflected in the object or objects (now lost) that he was holding in his hands.

probably to Dionysius. Personal and participatory cults were more prominent in Hellenistic times than in the Hellenic era.

The Hellenistic world extended over a vast geography from the western Mediterranean world to central Asia. The cultural tone was still set in cities but now Antioch and Alexandria, not Athens and Sparta, were the key centers. Work in mathematics and science took several leaps forward. Philosophy continued to develop in the classical Greek tradition, but new philosophies put greater emphasis on ethical problems than ever before and on providing guidance for daily living. Literature was not as rich, on the whole, as in the Hellenic period. The arts remained faithful to the technical standards of the classical world but added new aesthetic sensibilities (Figure 4.1).

THE CHANGING FRAMEWORK OF POLITICS

Alexander the Great died suddenly in 323 BCE without having made any provision for his succession. Within a few decades, three of his chief generals carved up the vast realm that had been conquered, but never really governed, by Alexander. They built large, reasonably successful kingdoms that eventually fragmented and then succumbed to Rome's legions (Timeline 4.1). Several smaller kingdoms emerged too in the Hellenistic world and they also fell to Rome.

The Major Hellenistic Monarchies

Following a civil war, three resourceful military commanders—Antigonus, Seleucus, and Ptolemy—eventually divided Alexander's empire among themselves. Antigonus and his successors took many years to secure control of Macedon and Greece. Even then they had to share rule with the Greek cities that had banded together in two confederations. Seleucus took southern Anatolia, Palestine and Syria, Mesopotamia, and the former Persian Empire. Ptolemy took Egypt and the adjoining coast of North Africa.

The **Antigonid** rulers of Macedon and Greece aimed at absolute rule but always had to share power with the Aetolian League in northern Greece and the Achaean League in southern Greece. Technically their rule lasted from 272 BCE to 146 BCE, when they and their allies were defeated for the third time by Rome. These leagues managed to attain a stability in Greece, albeit under the watchful eye of Macedon, that eluded the classical Greeks. Athens retained a functioning democracy until almost 200 BCE. Sparta collapsed at the end of the classical period and then revived somewhat in Hellenistic times as people were won over to a revived form of the ancient Spartan system.

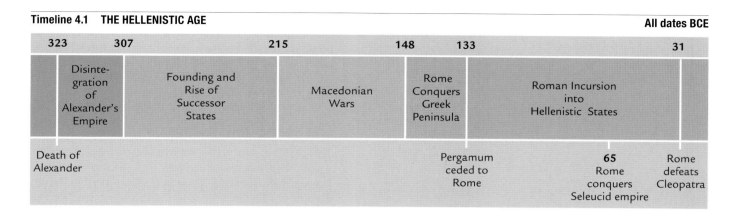

Timeline 4.1   **THE HELLENISTIC AGE**

All dates BCE

323	307	215	148	133	31
Disintegration of Alexander's Empire	Founding and Rise of Successor States	Macedonian Wars	Rome Conquers Greek Peninsula	Roman Incursion into Hellenistic States	

Death of Alexander

Pergamum ceded to Rome

65 Rome conquers Seleucid empire

Rome defeats Cleopatra

Learning Through Maps

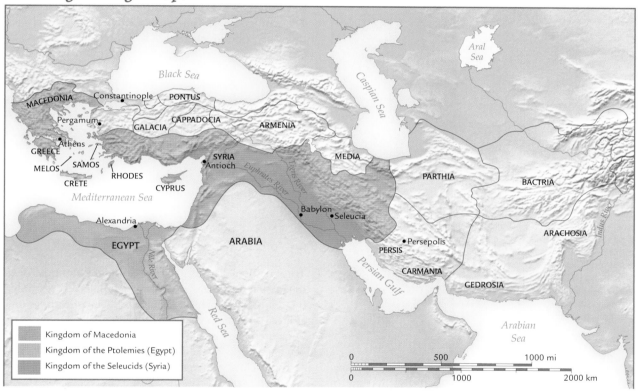

MAP 4.1   THE SUCCESSOR STATES AND THE HELLENISTIC WORLD

This map shows the Hellenistic world and the successor states, which emerged after the breakup of Alexander the Great's empire. *1. **Notice** the differing sizes of the successor states and the respective region controlled by each. 2. **Consider** the impact of geography and regional cultural traditions on the three kingdoms. 3. **Locate** the major cities of these kingdoms. 4. **How** did Alexandria's location in Egypt help to make it the dominant city of the Hellenistic world?*

Seleucid rule extended from 312 BCE, when they wrested Babylon from the Antigonids, to 64 BCE, when Syria became a Roman province. The Seleucids warred often on their eastern frontier and gradually lost control of Parthia and Bactria (Map 4.1). They ruled from Sardis in Asia Minor, Antioch in Syria, and Seleucia in Mesopotamia. The Seleucids created dozens of colonies mainly made up of Greeks and Macedonians, thus spreading Greek culture into what is now Afghanistan and Pakistan.

Ptolemy I seized Egypt almost immediately after Alexander's death and his successors ruled until the last of them, Cleopatra, became embroiled with Rome and committed suicide in 31 BCE. The **Ptolemies** established by far the richest, most powerful, and most stable of the main Hellenistic kingdoms. They

Figure 4.2 Rosetta Stone. Ca. 197–196 BCE. British Museum, London. Scholars were unable to decipher hieroglyphics until the nineteenth century. Napoleon's soldiers found this inscribed stone in the Rosetta branch of the Nile—hence its name—when they invaded Egypt in 1799. The text at the bottom is in Greek, which scholars could read. Guessing that all three texts recorded the same event, scholars first solved the hieratic (priestly) cursive in the middle and then moved on to the hieroglyphic at the top. Modern Egyptology began with this discovery. The stone bears a decree issued by priests at Memphis in 196 BCE establishing the divine cult of King Ptolemy V.

harnessed the immense wealth of Egypt and generally treated the local population well. By the time of Ptolemy V (r. 210–180 BCE) these Macedonian kings had become Egyptianized, representing themselves as pharaohs (Figure 4.2).

The large kingdoms could not prevent the emergence of some smaller ones. The most prominent of these were Epirus in western Greece and Pergamum in western Asia Minor. Epirus was first a kingdom allied to Philip II of Macedon. Under kings and then as a federal league, the Epirots led an uncertain life until the Romans conquered them in 167 BCE. The Attalids, the ruling dynasty of Pergamum, achieved freedom from the Seleucids in 263 BCE. In 133 BCE King Attalus III died, willing his kingdom to Rome. Reflective of Attalus's scholarly interests, Pergamum's acropolis

boasted a splendid palace, a library second only to Alexandria's, and a marble temple to Athena. Scattered on the hillside beneath the acropolis were shrines, markets, and private dwellings of prosperous citizens. At the base of the hill, the merchants, artisans, and slaves lived crowded together (Figure 4.3).

The Nature of Government

The primary form of government in the Hellenistic world was theocratic kingship. This institution ranged from a mild form in Macedon, where neither Macedonian nor Hellenic sensibilities were sympathetic to divine rulers, to an extreme form in Ptolemaic Egypt where the kings gradually came to be seen as gods, as the pharaohs had before them. The Seleucids were heirs to the semi-divinized monarchy of the Persians. Theocratic kings either were regarded as gods or were thought to be answerable only to the gods. Philosophers equated the happiness and stability of realms and peoples with the fortunes of the kings.

In the major Hellenistic kingdoms, government and military posts were initially reserved to Macedonians and Greeks. As time passed and the newcomers assimilated to the natives, the resulting cultural blend opened opportunities for at least local elites to secure prime positions. Because the monarchies frequently fought against each other and then against Rome, native peoples also obtained significant places in the military.

THE TENOR OF LIFE

This creation of large-scale states under kings destroyed the Hellenic political order in which poleis were guided by their citizens. Throughout the Hellenistic kingdoms, citizens became subjects. The Hellenistic economic order rested on specialized luxury crafts and professional occupations, international trade and banking, and an abundant and cheap supply of slaves. Large ports such as Carthage, Syracuse, Alexandria, Tyre, and Athens exported and imported basic agricultural commodities such as grain, olive oil, wine, and timber, exchanging them for expensive goods like pottery, silks, jewelry, and spices.

Class divisions in Hellenistic society were pronounced. For the rich, urban life was often luxurious and cosmopolitan, but most of society remained provincial. Those in the middle social ranks, primarily merchants and skilled artisans, struggled to keep ahead and hoped to prosper. However, for the poorest free classes—laborers, unskilled workers, and small landowners—life offered little. Slaves, whose numbers grew during the wars of this period, were expected to bear the brunt of all backbreaking labor.

Figure 4.3 Acropolis at Pergamum. Second century BCE. Reconstruction by H. Schlief. Antikensammlung, Staatliche Museen, Berlin. Pergamum architecture was in the Hellenic style, but the city's mixed population and economy made it the commercial and political hub of a Hellenistic kingdom. Under Eumenes II, the capital and the country reached their height of power around 160 BCE.

The Experiences of Women

Hellenistic women were affected by the period's growing cosmopolitanism. Women, along with men, moved to the newly conquered lands and created new lives for themselves in frontier towns. In Alexandria and other large cities, some restrictions of Hellenic Greece were maintained, but others were relaxed or discarded. For example, royal and non-Greek women were able to conduct their own legal and economic affairs, though non-royal Greek women were still forced to use a male guardian in such cases. Dowries remained the custom among Greek families, but unmarried respectable women now had the option of working in the liberal arts, as poets and philosophers, and in the professions, as artists and physicians. Alexander's mother, Olympias, was a powerful, influential woman, and several times women of the Ptolemaic family ruled Egypt. Unmarried women who were unconcerned about their reputations served as courtesans and prostitutes, living outside the norms of respectable society. Hellenistic literature reflects changed mores, portraying women in carefree situations apart from the gaze of their husbands or fathers. In economic matters, some women became prosperous in their own right, and, just as

men did, they made charitable bequests and erected impressive gravestones. Despite these changes, Hellenistic society was dominated by men. The surest sign of women's subordinate role was that the Greek practice of infanticide, which was as old as Greek civilization, continued as a way for families to rid themselves of unwanted females.

Urban Life

Alexander's most enduring legacy to the Hellenistic world was his new image of the city. The city is as old as civilization, since urban life is by definition a component of civilized existence. For Alexander, cities were keystones holding together his diverse and vast empire—serving as centers of government, trade, and culture and radiating Greco-Oriental civilization into the hinterland. Alexander is reputed to have founded more than seventy cities during his conquests, many of which were named for him.

The burgeoning cities of the Hellenistic world accentuated the period's growing class divisions. As rural folk flocked to the cities seeking jobs and trying to better their economic condition, some succeeded while others slipped into poverty and despair. Their failures divided the rich from the poor, thus intensifying class conflicts. As rural migrants adjusted to urban ways, they affected the values and beliefs of the times, in particular, the various philosophies and religions (see the section "Philosophy and Religion"). And, in everyday life, a new survival strategy arose among upwardly mobile city folk as a way to avoid class conflict. These people chose to shed their provincial ways and ethnic identities and to adopt the ideal of the *cosmopolitan*—the Greek term for a person with a universal or worldwide view.

Greek migrants constituted a special challenge to Hellenistic culture. Greeks who left their home city-states to seek their fortunes in the successor states of Alexander's empire impacted every phase of life. Drawn to cities and ports across the eastern Mediterranean, Greek would-be traders, bankers, and seamen arrived, spreading their way of life and influencing the local culture—thus further blending the societies of the period. Many became government officials—bureaucrats, advisers, diplomats—or soldiers and sailors. Most, however, pursued business and professional careers or found work in the visual and performing arts. Their numbers and high-profile presence ensured that Greek culture and values would play a preeminent role in Hellenistic thought and art.

The expansion of trade within this diverse culture benefited Greek and non-Greek alike. The period's kings, seizing the opportunity to enrich themselves and their states, lengthened and improved existing overland trade routes and linked up with routes to India and into parts of Africa. After Egypt's king learned about the monsoon season in the Indian Ocean, regular sea trade with India began during periods of good

weather, thus ensuring the importance of Coptos, a city on the upper Nile, as the western terminal for this overseas trade.

The premier Hellenistic city was Alexandria at the mouth of the Nile in Egypt, founded by Alexander in 331 BCE (Figure 4.4). Under the Ptolemies, Alexandria grew to be a world city that attracted both the ambitious who sought opportunities and the apathetic who wanted to be left alone. Every desired attraction is said to have existed here, just as in the teeming cities of the twenty-first century. By the end of the first century BCE, Alexandria's population rose to perhaps one million and the city was divided into five sections, including one reserved for royalty and separate residential quarters for the Egyptians and the Jews, the latter of whom were attracted by the city's opportunities and tolerant atmosphere. Whereas the polis of the Hellenic Age was self-contained, with a relatively homogeneous population, Alexandria's racially and ethnically diverse groups were held together by economic interests. With busy harbors, bustling markets, and international banks, Alexandria became a hub of commercial and financial enterprises, similar to modern port cities.

Alexandria's economic vitality was matched by the splendor of its cultural achievements. The world's first research institute—a museum, the house of the muses (see Table 2.1)—was built here as a place for scholars to study and to exchange ideas (Figure 4.5). Nearby was the famed library, whose staff of poets and scholars aimed to collect one copy of every book ever written. At the time of the Roman conquest in the late first century BCE, the library contained nearly seven hundred thousand volumes, the largest collection in the ancient

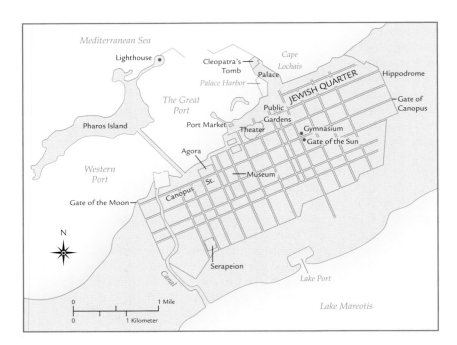

Figure 4.4 Plan of Ancient Alexandria. Third century BCE. Designed by Deinocrates of Rhodes, Alexander's personal architect, Alexandria was laid out in a grid formed by intersecting avenues and streets. The entire city was enclosed by a wall, accessible by four massive gates at the ends of the major avenues. To the north lay two harbors that made the city the most vital port in the Mediterranean. The harbors were protected by an outer island, at the point of which stood the lighthouse of Pharos—now lost. Remarkable for its colossal size, the lighthouse was considered one of the wonders of the ancient world.

Figure 4.5 *Muse Melpomene* (or *Polyhymnia* [?]). Roman copy, probably of a mid–second century BCE original by Philiskos of Rhodes. Ht. 4′11″ without plinth. Capitoline Museum, Rome. The sculptor has portrayed the muse in a simple but dignified pose—leaning forward on a support, left foot upturned, chin resting on a curved right hand—and swathed in a thin mantle of fabric that falls into rhythmic folds. The contrast between the serenely meditative face and the dynamic drapery pattern is characteristic of Hellenistic art (see pp. 96–100).

world. By then, Alexandria had become a beacon for great minds, attracted by the city's rich intellectual life and cosmopolitan atmosphere.

HELLENISTIC CULTURES

Hellenistic culture reflected the tastes and needs of the period's diverse states. Greek tragedy lost its vitality when separated from its roots in the independent polis, but comedy appealed to sophisticated urban audiences who were seeking diversion. Nondramatic literature, chiefly poetry and romance, was competent and entertaining but more artificial than profound. New philosophies and religions arose in response to the urban isolation and loneliness that many people experienced. And, finally, grandiose architecture addressed the propaganda needs of autocratic rulers, and realistic sculpture reflected the tastes of an increasingly cosmopolitan, secular culture.

Nevertheless, the values of Hellenistic culture did not so much replace the standards of Hellenic classicism as they enriched and elaborated the older ideals. Hellenistic artists and authors agreed with their Hellenic forebears that art must serve moral purposes, revealed through content and formal order. Greek became the major language across a vast expanse of lands and peoples. Scholars speak of the *Koinè* ("common") Greek language of the time. The Koinè was a somewhat simplified version of the Attic (i.e., Athenian) Greek that had become dominant in the Hellenic period.

Drama and Literature

In the Hellenistic Age, Greek comedy began to resemble modern productions. The grotesque padding worn by the actors gave way to realistic costumes; masks were redesigned to be representative of the characters portrayed; and the actors assumed a dominant status over the chorus. Comedies became a form of popular amusement, and Hellenistic playwrights developed a genre known as **New Comedy** to appeal to the pleasure-seeking audiences who were flocking to the theaters. Avoiding political criticism and casual obscenity, New Comedy presented gently satirical scenes from middle-class life.

The plays were generally comic romances on such themes as frustrated first love or marital misunderstandings, and although the endings were inevitably happy and there was much formula writing—somewhat like today's situation comedies on television—the plays reflected the comprehensive range of the Hellenistic style. The characters, for example, were familiar types drawn from the rich diversity of Hellenistic society—the courtesan, the grumpy old man, the slave, the fawning parasite. New Comedy remained steadfastly middle class, however, for the traditional social order always prevailed in the end. For example, a favorite plot device of New Comedy hinged on discovering that a seemingly lowborn character was actually from a respected—and often wealthy—family.

Both ancient and modern critics tend to regard Menander [muh-NAN-duhr] (about 343–291 BCE) as the leading author of New Comedy. He wrote more than one hundred plays for the Dionysia festival in Athens, winning first prize for comedy eight times, and is credited with perfecting the **comedy of manners,** a humorous play that focuses on the way people interact in a particular social group or class. The play reminds us of the Hellenistic focus on ordinary scenes from daily life (Figure 4.6).

The Woman from Samos is a robust example of Menander's work. Dating from about 321 BCE, this comedy concerns the identity of an orphaned baby and features stock characters: a courtesan, a young lover, an

Figure 4.6 *The Street Musicians.* Ca. 100 BCE. 16⁷/₈ × 16¹/₈″. **Museo Archeologico Nazionale, Naples.**
This mosaic may portray a scene from a comic play. Two masked figures dance and play the tambourine and the finger cymbals while a masked female figure plays the tibia, or double oboe. This mosaic was found in the so-called Villa of Cicero at Pompeii.

old lover, a humorous neighbor, and two comic slaves. Menander first presents a household in which the father believes that he and his son are wooing the same woman, when, in actuality, the son is involved with the girl next door. Then, when a foundling appears, absurd misunderstandings arise and false accusations are made. The play ends happily with all characters reconciled, the son wed to his true love, and the father and mistress married in a joyous ceremony—a typical New Comedy resolution. Western comedy would be inconceivable without Menander. His style was assimilated into Roman comedy, which passed the spirit of his work into the dramas of the Italian Renaissance and from there into the comedies of Shakespeare and Molière and in situation comedies on television.

Two Alexandrian writers stand out: the poets Theocritus [the-OCK-ruht-us] (about 310–250 BCE) and Apollonius [ah-po-LOW-nee-us] (third century). Theocritus created a new poetic form, the **pastoral,** which would influence later classical and modern European literature. Pastoral poems describe the lives of shepherds and farmers in a somewhat artificial, idealized

way. Theocritus drew his images from the memory of his earlier years in rural Sicily, and his charming, nostalgic verses appealed to many country folk who had also left the quiet rustic life for the excitement of the Hellenistic cities even though pastoral poetry often deprecated urban life. Theocritus also wrote what he called **idylls** (from the Greek word meaning "little picture"), which offered small portraits, or vignettes, of Hellenistic life. Some of these poems reveal much about everyday affairs, noting the common concerns and aspirations of all generations—love, family, religion, and wealth. Theocritus created especially sympathetic portraits of a woman's love for a man.

Apollonius's most famous work is the verse romance *The Argonautica,* a tale of Jason and the argonauts' quest for the golden fleece. The story is rich with fantasy, adventure, battles, and love. Jason's lover Medea is in many ways the most compelling character in the story, and Apollonius sets off her brains against Jason's brawn. Apollonius in effect created the romance as a literary genre. *The Argonautica* was immensely popular in Rome.

SLICE OF LIFE

Street Scene in Hellenistic Egypt

Theocritus
FROM *IDYLLS*, THIRD CENTURY BCE

In Hellenistic Egypt, two society matrons, Gorgo and Praxinoa, each with her maid in tow (Eutychis and Eunoa, respectively), make their way through the crowded streets of Alexandria, on their way to the palace of Ptolemy II to hear a singer perform at the festival of Adonis.

[GORGO:] [C]ome, get your dress and cloak on, and
   let's go to King Ptolemy's palace and take a look
   at this Adonis. The Queen, I hear, is doing things
   in style.
PRAXINOA: Oh, nothing but the best. Well, they can
   keep it.
GORGO: But when you've seen it, just think, you can
   tell those who haven't all about it. Come on, it's
   time we were off.
PRAXINOA: Every day's a holiday for the idle.

• • •

[Out in the street.]
   Ye Gods, what a crowd! The crush!
   How on earth are we going to get through it?
   They're like ants! Swarms of them, beyond
      counting!
   Well, you've done us many favours, Ptolemy,
   since your father went to heaven.
   We don't get those no-goods now, sliding up to us
   in the street and playing their Egyptian tricks.
   What they used to get up to, those rogues!
   A bunch of villains, each as bad
   as the next, and all utterly cursed!
   Gorgo dear, what will become of us?
   Here are the king's horses! Take care,

my good man, don't tread on me.
   That brown one's reared right up!
   Look how wild he is! He'll kill his groom!
   Eunoa, you fool, get back!
   Thank God I left that child at home.
GORGO: Don't worry, Praxinoa.
   We've got behind them now.
   They're back in their places.
PRAXINOA: I'm all right now.
   Ever since I was a girl, two things
   have always terrified me—horses,
   and long, cold snakes. Let's hurry.
   This great crowd will drown us.

• • •

GORGO: Look, Praxinoa! What a crowd at the door!
PRAXINOA: Fantastic! Gorgo, give me your hand.
   And you, Eunoa, hold on to Eutychis.
   Take care you don't lose each other.
   We must all go in together. Stay close by us.
   Oh no! Gorgo! My coat! It's been ripped
   clean in two! My God, sir, as you hope
   for heaven, mind my coat!

Interpreting This Slice of Life

1. *What* is the "plot" in this story of life in the big city?
2. *What* is the mood of the women in the story?
3. Based on this vignette, *what* appears to be the position of women in Alexandrian society?
4. *Who* was the audience for this poem?

Philosophy and Religion

As life in Hellenistic cities became more multicultural, the sense of belonging that had characterized life in the Hellenic poleis was replaced by feelings of isolation, of loneliness, even of helplessness. As a consequence, two seemingly contradictory points of view emerged: individualism and internationalism. Those who held these attitudes were searching for continuity in a rapidly changing world; were seeking identity for the individual through common interests, values, and hopes; and were striving to understand events that seemed unpredictable and beyond human control.

Philosophies and religions offered answers that seemed as contradictory as the problems themselves. One philosophy urged a universal brotherhood of all human beings, united regardless of race, status, or birth; another, despairing of the world, excluded most people and appealed to a chosen few. Religions, similarly, provided varying answers. One faith preached salvation in a life after death, and another turned to magic to escape Fate—that blind force that controlled human life. The most enduring of this period's philosophies were Cynicism, Skepticism, Epicureanism, and Stoicism (Table 4.1).

Figure 4.7 *Diogenes and Alexander the Great.* **First century CE. Villa Albani, Rome.** This Roman relief shows that Diogenes and Alexander the Great, two figures of the Hellenistic Age, were living presences for the Romans. The philosopher Diogenes is carved sitting in his famous tub, a symbol of his contempt for creature comforts. The world conqueror Alexander is on the right, pointing his finger at the Greek thinker. The dog portrayed on top of the tub is a reference to Cynicism (the word cynic is from the Greek word for "dog"). Diogenes asserted that humans should live simply—like dogs.

TABLE 4.1 PHILOSOPHY IN THE HELLENISTIC AGE

PHILOSOPHY	EMPHASIS
Cynicism	True freedom arises from realizing that if one wants nothing, then one will never lack anything; *autarky* (self-sufficiency) is the goal.
Skepticism	Nothing can be known for certain; question all ideas; *autarky* is the goal.
Epicureanism	Only the atoms and void exist; pleasure is the highest good; death is final in its extinction of consciousness; the gods play no active role in human affairs.
Stoicism	The world is governed by the divine *logos,* or reason, or nature; wisdom and freedom consist of living in harmony with the *logos*; all humans share in the divine *logos*; *autarky* is the goal.

Cynicism Of the four schools, **Cynicism** had the least impact on Hellenistic civilization. The Cynics, believing that society diverted the individual from the more important goals of personal independence and freedom, denounced all religions and governments, shunned physical comfort, and advocated the avoidance of personal pleasure. In the Cynics' logic, true freedom came with the realization that if one wanted nothing, one could not lack anything. By isolating themselves from society, they sought a type of self-sufficiency the Greeks called *autarky* [AW-tar-kee].

The most prominent Cynic, Diogenes [die-AHJ-uh-neez] (about 412–323 BCE), openly scorned the ordinary values and crass materialism of his society. His contrary personality so fascinated Alexander the Great that the ruler, upon being insulted by the Cynic, is reported to have said that if he were not Alexander, he would prefer to be Diogenes (Figure 4.7)! The principles of Cynicism offended the educated, and its pessimism offered no hope to the masses.

Skepticism The proponents of **Skepticism** argued that nothing could be known for certain, an extreme conclusion they were led to by their belief that the senses were unreliable sources of knowledge. Thinking that everything was relative, the Skeptics maintained that all ideas must be questioned and that no single philosophy was true. When their critics pointed out that such unrelenting questioning was clearly not a practical answer to life's uncertainties, the Skeptics replied that certainty could be achieved only by admitting that truth was unknowable—a circular response. The Skeptics thought that if they recognized that intellectual inquiry was fruitless, then they too could avoid frustration and achieve *autarky*. The Skeptics, even though they attracted a smaller audience than the Cynics, had a greater impact on Western reasoning.

Epicureanism   The strict and quiet way of life advocated by **Epicureanism** appealed to aristocrats who were more interested in learning than in politics. It began as the philosophy of the Greek thinker Epicurus [ep-uh-KYUR-uhs] (about 342–270 BCE), who founded a school in Athens where pupils, including slaves and women, gathered to discuss ideas (Figure 4.8). For Epicurus, the best way to keep one's wants simple, and thus to achieve happiness, was to abstain from sex and focus instead on friendship. Friendship was a mystic communion, based on shared need, in which men and men, men and women, rich and poor, old and young, of all nationalities and any class supported each other in trusting relationships. This vision guided Epicurus's school, where life became a daily exercise in friendship. It was an ideal that appealed to women since, in making them men's equals, it showed that there was more to their lives than bearing children and raising families.

Epicurus based his ethical philosophy on the atomic theory of those Greek thinkers who saw the universe as completely determined by the behavior of atoms moving in empty space (see Chapter 3). Epicurus accepted this picture, but with one significant modification: he argued that because atoms on occasion swerved from their set paths and made unpredictable deviations, it was possible, even in a deterministic universe, for humans to make free choices. Like the atomists, Epicurus also believed that the senses presented an accurate view of the physical world. Thus, by using the mind as a storehouse for sense impressions and by exercising free will in their choices, individuals could reach moral judgments and ultimately live by an ethical code.

For Epicurus, the correct ethical code led to happiness, which was realized in a life of quiet—separated and withdrawn from the trying cares of the world. Furthermore, those who would be happy should keep their wants simple, not indulge excessive desires, and resist fame, power, and wealth, which only brought misery and disappointment.

Figure 4.8   *Epicurus.* Ca. 290–280 BCE. The Metropolitan Museum of Art, New York. This marble bust of Epicurus, discovered in southern Italy and inscribed with his name, is a copy of the original bronze sculpture. Many busts and likenesses of Epicurus have been found, indicating the popularity of his philosophy in Hellenistic times, especially during the Roman era.

Another characteristic of Epicurean happiness was freedom from fear—fear of the gods, of death, and of the hereafter. Although Epicurus believed that the gods existed, he also believed that they cared nothing about human beings, and therefore no one needed to be afraid of what the gods might or might not do. As for death, there was, again, nothing to agonize over because when it did occur, the atoms that made up the soul simply separated from the body's atoms and united with other particles to create new forms. With death came the end of the human capacity to feel pleasure or pain and thus the end of suffering. Consequently, death, rather than being feared, should be welcomed as a release from misfortune and trouble. Pleasure, in the Epicurean view, was the absence of pain. The happy Epicurean, standing above the cares of the world, had reached *ataraxia,* the desire-less state that the Hellenistic Age deemed so precious.

Stoicism   Both Epicureanism and **Stoicism** claimed that happiness was a final goal of the individual, and both philosophies were essentially materialistic, stressing the importance of sense impressions and the natural world. The Stoics, however, identified the supreme deity with nature, thus making the natural world divine and inseparable from the deity. The supreme being was also another name for reason, or *logos,* and hence nature was also rational. The Stoics' God was law and the author of law, which led to the notion that the workings of nature were expressed in divine laws.

The Stoics likewise discovered God in humanity. The Stoics' God, being identical with reason, gave a spark to each mortal's soul, conferring the twin gifts of rationality and kinship with divinity. The Stoics thus believed that reason and the senses could be used jointly to uncover the underlying moral law as well as God's design in the world, proving God's wisdom and power over human life and nature.

There was in Stoicism a tendency to leave everything up to God. Stoics came to accept their roles in life, whether rich or poor, master or slave, healthy or afflicted, and such a resigned and deterministic outlook could (and did) lead to apathy, or unconcern. However, the ideal Stoic, the sage, never became apathetic. The sage escaped Stoicism's fatalistic tendency by stressing a sense of and dedication to duty. Doing one's duty was part of following the deity's plan, and Stoics willingly performed their tasks, no matter how onerous or laborious. The reward for living a life of duty was virtue. Having achieved virtue, the Stoics were freed from their emotions, which they thought only corrupted them. The Stoics had thus achieved *autarky,* the state of self-sufficiency sought by many Hellenistic philosophers.

Stoicism was unique among the Hellenistic philosophies in holding out the promise of membership in a worldwide brotherhood. Perhaps inspired by Alexander the Great's dream, the Stoics advocated an ideal state, guided by God and law, that encompassed all of humanity of whatever race, sex, social status, or nationality in a common bond of reason. As humans carried out their duties in this larger community, they would rise above local and national limitations and create a better world.

Religion had a firmer hold on most people than philosophy. The belief in Fate, a concept borrowed from Babylonia, gripped the lives of many people in the Hellenistic world. To them, Fate ruled the universe, controlled the heavens, and determined the course of life. Although no one could change the path of this nonmoral, predestined force, individuals could try to avoid the cruel consequences of Fate by various methods. The pseudoscience of astrology, also from Babylonia, offered one alternative. Magic was now revived, and many people tried to conjure up good spirits or to ward off evil ones. Nevertheless, it was the mystery cults—springing from the primitive chthonian religions of Greece (see Chapters 2 and 3) and elsewhere—that eventually emerged as the most popular and effective response to Fate.

Numerous chthonian cults spread from the Seleucid kingdom and Egypt to the Greek mainland, where they were combined with local beliefs and rituals to create religions that fused different beliefs and practices. By the second century BCE, converts were being attracted from all over the Hellenistic world to the well-established mystery cults of Orpheus and Dionysus in Greece and to the new religions from Egypt and the old Persian lands. The growth of these cults in turn sparked an increase in religious zeal after about 100 BCE, resulting in more ceremonies and public festivals and the revival of older faiths.

The Egyptian mystery cults grew, becoming popular across the Hellenistic world. The goddess Isis, long known to the Egyptians, became especially prominent. The Egyptians worshiped Isis as the "great lady" who watched over the Two Lands of Egypt and the home. In legend, Isis brought her murdered husband-brother, Osiris, back to life with her unwavering love. Osiris's resurrection symbolized to the faithful the new life awaiting them at death. Isis herself was identified with the annual flooding of the Nile, thus assuring the Egyptians of another year of survival. Like the pharaohs, the Ptolemies claimed to be the incarnation of Isis's son, Horus (Harpocrates) (Figure 4.9).

The secret rites of the mystery cults, which communicated the thrill of initiation and the satisfaction of belonging, answered deep psychological needs in their Hellenistic converts. This universal appeal cut across class and racial lines and attracted an ever-widening segment of the populace. With their promise of immortality, these rituals contributed to the atmosphere of the Roman world in which Christianity would later be born.

Science and Technology

While Hellenistic scientists owed much to their Hellenic predecessors, they were more practical and less theoretical than the followers of Plato and Aristotle. They were interested in methodologies more than in speculation, and they tended to question, observe, and experiment rather than to offer explanations and quarrel over abstract issues. They focused on day-to-day matters, such as measuring distances, calculating navigation routes, designing war machines, and solving mathematical problems. And, finally, scientists and philosophers worked in isolation, having little contact either as individuals or in groups. They were nonetheless able to make scientific advances and discoveries unequaled in any other age—until Europe's Scientific Revolution in the 1600s (see Chapter 16).

The astronomer Aristarchus of Samos [air-uh-STAR-kus] (fl. about 270 BCE) maintained that the sun was the center of the universe and that the earth rotated on its own axis. His conclusions, though considered correct today, were rejected by other ancient astronomers, who thought his views contradicted common sense. Another astronomer, Eratosthenes [er-uh-TAS-thuh-neez] (about 276–194 BCE) of Cyrene, who at one time headed the library in Alexandria, measured the circumference of the earth by creating a mathematical formula based on the differing angles cast by the sun's rays on the earth, when observed from two sites, separated by a known distance. He also devised a grid for measuring the circumference of the earth, using lines running from north to south and east to west—a system implying that the earth was round.

Euclid [YU-klehd] (fl. about 300 BCE), the most influential mathematician of his time, gave the classic formulations of both plane and solid geometry. His writings laid out mathematical theorems, axioms, propositions, and definitions. He was known as the father of geometry, and Euclidean geometry became the basis of mathematical studies until the nineteenth century.

The best-known Hellenistic scientist, Archimedes [are-kuh-MEED-eez] (about 287–212 BCE) was a mathematician, astronomer, and inventor. He made signal contributions in geometry, but he is best remembered for his studies in gravity, mechanics, hydrostatics, the principle of buoyancy, and for his many inventions. Among his inventions were the Archimedean screw for raising water; improved compound pulleys; and engines of war, including catapults and ramming towers. Many legends accrued to Archimedes' life, including the famous story, undoubtedly apocryphal, in which he discovered the principle of buoyancy—the relation of fluid loss to weight displacement—while seated in his bath. Excited by the discovery, he leaped from his tub and ran naked down the street, shouting *"Eureka!"*—Greek for "I have found it."

Architecture

As in Hellenic times, architecture in the Hellenistic Age reflected the central role that religion played in people's lives. Public buildings served religious, ceremonial, and governmental purposes, but the temple continued as the leading type of structure. Hellenistic architects modified the basic temple and altar forms inherited from Hellenic models to express the grandeur demanded by the age's rulers. The altar, which had originated in Archaic Greece as a simple structure where holy sacrifices or offerings were made, now became a major structural form, second in importance only to the temple, because of its use in state rituals.

The **Corinthian** temple embodied Hellenistic splendor. The Corinthian column had first appeared in the Hellenic period, when it was probably used as a decorative feature. Because it was taller, more slender,

Figure 4.9   Isis with Her Son Harpocrates (left) and God Anubis (right). First century CE. Terra-cotta, ht. approx. 7″. British Museum, London. This small terra-cotta figurine—probably used as a votive—blends Greek sculptural style with Egyptian symbolism. The goddess is portrayed wearing an Egyptian headdress and is flanked by her son and the jackal-headed Anubis, the god of the dead. Greek features include the goddess's tightly curled hair, her slightly contrapposto pose, and the graceful drapery of her dress. The statue, fired on the Italian peninsula in the first century CE, testifies to the goddess's popularity throughout ancient times and across the Mediterranean world.

and more ornamented, with its lush acanthus-leafed capital, than either the Doric or the Ionic column, the Corinthian column was now used on the exterior of temples erected by Hellenistic builders for their kings. In time, Hellenistic taste decreed that the Corinthian column was appropriate for massive buildings. The Corinthian order later became the favorite of the Roman emperors, and it was revived in the Renaissance and diffused throughout the Western world, where it survives today as the most visible sign of Hellenistic influence.

The most outstanding Corinthian temples combined grandeur with grace, as in the Olympieum in Athens, now a ruin (Figure 4.10). Commissioned by the Seleucid king Antiochus IV [an-TIE-uh-kuhs], the Olympieum expressed his notion of a diverse, international culture united under Zeus, his divine counterpart and the lord of Mount Olympus. The temple, the first to use Corinthian columns, was constructed during three different and distinct historical eras. The stylobate, or base, was laid in the late Archaic Age but then abandoned; the Corinthian columns were raised by Antiochus IV in about 175 BCE, after which work was suspended indefinitely; it was finally completed in 130 CE under the Roman emperor Hadrian, a great admirer of Greek culture. The temple is stylistically unified, however, because it was finished according to the surviving plans of its second-century BCE architect. Despite its massive size and lack of mathematical refinements, the Olympieum presented an extremely graceful appearance with its forest of delicate Corinthian columns, consisting of double rows of twenty columns each on the sides and triple rows of eight on the ends.

Figure 4.10 The Olympieum, Athens. Various dates: late sixth century BCE; second quarter of second century BCE; completed, second quarter of second century CE. The thirteen standing Corinthian columns were part of the original plan of the Olympieum's architect. After the temporary cessation of building in 164 BCE, some of this temple's unfinished columns were transported to Rome and reused in a building there. Their use in Rome helped to popularize the Corinthian style among political leaders and wealthy tastemakers.

Before there were temples, there were altars, the oldest religious structure in the Greek world. The earliest altars were simple slabs, made wide enough to allow sacrificial animals to be slaughtered. During the Hellenistic Age, the altars were substantially enlarged. The biggest appears to have been the 650-foot-long altar, permitting the sacrifice of more than one hundred cattle at one time, funded by the ruler of Syracuse in the third century BCE.

The magnificent altar of Zeus at Pergamum has been reassembled in Berlin. It is easy to see why ancient travelers called it one of the wonders of the world (Figure 4.11). The actual altar, not visible in the photograph, stands lengthwise in a magnificent Ionic colonnaded courtyard. The courtyard itself is raised on a **podium,** or platform; below the courtyard, the sides of the structure are decorated with a sculptured frieze depicting the deities at war. The overall design—with the frieze below the columns—appears to be an inversion of the usual temple plan. This altar was but one part of a concerted effort to transform Pergamum into another Athens. Thus, the idea of a "new" Athens—a recurrent motif in the humanistic tradition—had already been formulated by the Hellenistic Age.

Sculpture

Like Hellenistic architects, Hellenistic sculptors adapted many of the basic forms and ideas of the Hellenic style to meet the tastes of their day. The Hellenistic sculptors retained such Hellenic principles as contrapposto

Figure 4.11   Altar of Zeus at Pergamum. (Reconstruction.) 170s BCE. Pergamon Museum, Berlin. This masterpiece of Hellenistic architecture was erected in the 170s BCE by Eumenes II, the king of Pergamum, to commemorate his victories over various barbarian states in Asia Minor. Eumenes believed himself to be the savior and disseminator of Greek culture, and this altar with its giant frieze was meant to suggest Hellenic monuments, such as the Athenian Parthenon.

and proportion as well as the Hellenic emphasis on religious and moral themes. But Hellenistic art increasingly expressed a secular, urban viewpoint, and Hellenic restraint often gave way to realism, eroticism, theatricality, and violence, expressed and enjoyed for their own sake. Some of these Hellenistic qualities are apparent in two refreshingly naturalistic sculptures *Boy Struggling with a Goose* (Figure 4.12) and *Sleeping Eros* (Figure 4.13). These images show an interest in children, a rare subject in Hellenic art. The figures are **genre subjects,** artistic renderings of subjects from daily life. But the boy struggling with the goose also represents a mock-heroic battle and its playfulness masks a sense of violence. The earth-bound, innocent, and sleeping Eros contrasts with his normal flying and capricious nature.

A taste for the theatrical is also evident in one of the most famous images of the age: *The Nike of Samothrace,* sometimes called the "Winged Victory" because Nike was the Greek goddess of victory; Niké in Greek means "victory" (Figure 4.14). Nike appears to be sailing into the wind. Her clothing is beautifully rendered but clings so tightly to her body as to evoke sensuality.

Between 230 and 220 BCE, King Attalus I of Pergamum dedicated in Athens a group of bronze sculptures that celebrated his recent victory over the barbarian Gauls. By donating these bronzes to Athens, which was outside of Pergamum's political orbit, the Attalid ruler hoped to establish his cultural credentials as a

Figure 4.12   *Boy Struggling with a Goose.* Roman copy of a Greek original, dating from second half of second century BCE. Marble, ht. 33¹/₂". Staatliche Antikensammlung und Glyptothek, Munich. When Hellenistic sculptors freed themselves from the ideals of Hellenic art, one of the results was the production of works on unhackneyed themes, as in *Boy Struggling with a Goose.* So popular was this genre scene that several versions of it are known from antiquity. Its popularity reflects the age's delight in childhood and its joys—perhaps an outgrowth of the rising status of women in Hellenistic times.

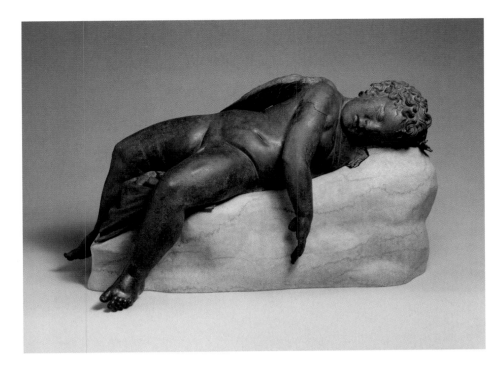

Figure 4.13   Bronze statue of Eros sleeping. 3rd century B.C.–early 1st century A.D. Greek or Roman; Hellenistic or Augustan period. Bronze, length 33⁹/₁₆″. The Metropolitan Museum of Art, New York. This plump, sleeping baby with tousled hair is not only supremely naturalistic but also a good example of the power of bronze to capture life. The stature seems to be based on close observation. Only the tiny wings differentiate this god from a human baby. Archaic depictions of Eros made him a handsome youth. Images like this one show the brave experimentation of the Hellenistic period.

Figure 4.14   *Nike of Samothrace.* Ca. 190 BCE. Marble, ht. 8′. Louvre. The wildly agitated draperies and soaring wings embody exuberant action, a defining characteristic of this turbulent age. The statue was part of a group that included a war galley. Victory was indeed a constant quest of the Hellenistic Age.

Figure 4.15   *Dying Gaul.* Ca. 230–220 BCE. Roman marble copy of a bronze original, ht. 3′. Capitoline Museum, Rome. The rulers of the Hellenistic kingdom of Pergamum preferred art that was showy and overwrought, a taste that perhaps stemmed from their insecurity at being a new dynasty. A Pergamene style of sculpture developed under these kings, in which gestures were theatrical and anatomical features were portrayed in exaggerated depth. The *Dying Gaul* is a superb example of this style.

defender of Greek culture and thus further his claims to rule over the entire Hellenistic world.

One of these pieces, *Dying Gaul* (which survives only in a Roman marble copy), shows a mortally wounded barbarian warrior (Figure 4.15). The torque, or twisted necklace, he wears identifies him as a Gaul. Lying close by are his sword and trumpet. The sculptor

Interpreting Art

Literary Source In Virgil's *Aeneid,* Laocöon (lay-OK-ooahn) warns the Trojans not to bring the wooden horse inside Troy, even though he did not know it was full of Greek soldiers, hence the famous line "Beware Greeks bearing gifts." Two serpents emerged from the sea and killed Laocöon and his sons.

Form The sculptural group brims with energy, as may be seen in the tormented faces of the victims, in their twisted, muscular bodies, in the serpent's coils that frame the scene, and in the deep folds of the draperies.

Composition Laocöon and his sons—depicted larger than life—are being crushed and perhaps devoured by two huge serpents. The sculptors have made an extraordinarily close study of human anatomy.

Moral Perspective Virgil's story of Laocöon had two different morals: (a) Apollo, whose cult demanded priestly chastity, sent the serpents to punish the priest and his sons; and (b) Athena, who favored the Greeks in the Trojan War, sent the serpents to silence Laocöon's warnings about the horse.

Context The dynamic, agitated, theatrical figures in this group reveal the ways in which the arts of the Hellenistic era jettisoned the stately grace and reserve of the Hellenic period.

Influences This sculptural group vanished in antiquity and was rediscovered in 1506, when it profoundly influenced Michelangelo and the subsequent rise of baroque art (see Chapters 13 and 15).

HAGESANDROS, POLYDOROS, AND ATHANADOROS. *The Laocöon Group.* Ca. 50 CE. Roman copy (?) of a Hellenistic work. Marble, ht. 8′. Vatican Museum. This statue is probably a Roman copy of the original executed on the island of Rhodes.

1. **Literary Source** What is the literary source for the subject of this sculpture and what does this tell us about Hellenistic culture?
2. **Composition** What are the dominant visual characteristics of this sculptural group?
3. **Religious Perspective** What are two different ways in which this image can be given a religious interpretation?
4. **Context** How does the Laocöon Group conform to the tastes and styles of the Hellenistic world?
5. **Audience** What inferences can you draw about the tastes and interests of the audience for art like this?

---

demonstrates his keen eye for realistic details in the open wound oozing blood from the warrior's rib cage and by the blank stare as he faces death. The Hellenistic style's appreciation of the melodramatic is evident in the tension between the warrior's sagging body and his efforts to prop himself up. But by treating a foreign enemy with such nobility, the anonymous sculptor perpetuated the deep moral sense that was central to Hellenic art. Like the *Nike of Samothrace* and the *Dying Gaul,* the *Bronze Boxer* exhibits a certain theatricality but, again like the Gaul, this probably professional

fighter possesses a kind of nobility (Figure 4.16). After 146 BCE, an outstanding sculptural school flourished on the Island of Rhodes for more than two hundred years. Probably the most stunning sculpture of Rhodian and Hellenistic art is *The Laocöon Group* (see Interpreting Art).

If Hellenistic artists took delight in old ladies (p. 82), children, warriors, and athletes, then there was no less appreciation of female beauty, a famous example of which is the *Aphrodite of Melos,* perhaps better known as the *Venus de Milo* (Figure 4.17). This

Figure 4.16 *Bronze Boxer.* **First century BCE. Bronze, 4′2″. National Museum of the Terme, Rome.** The artist spares the viewer no ugly detail: battered face, broken nose, cauliflower ears, missing teeth, scars. Ancient boxers did not bob and weave but instead stood fairly still and exchanged blows until one of them succumbed. Did this man win or lose? Either way, he is not a "loser." He retains a certain dignity.

Figure 4.17 *Aphrodite of Melos (Venus de Milo).* **Ca. 160–150 BCE. Marble, ht. 6′10″. Louvre.** This celebrated statue represents the classicizing tendency, derived from Greek tradition, in Hellenistic art. The head is executed in the pure Hellenic style, as seen in the serene countenance, the exquisitely detailed hair, and the finely chiseled features. However, the body, with its frank sensuality and its rumpled draperies, is clearly in the Hellenistic style.

original sculpture, carved from Parian marble, shows many borrowings from the tradition of Praxiteles (see Figure 3.23). Both Aphrodite and Hermes exhibit exaggerated contrapposto; a sensuous, even erotic, modeling of the body; and a serene countenance with an unmistakable gaze. However, the Hellenistic sculptor, demonstrating a playful flair with the rolled-down draperies, calls attention to Aphrodite's exposed lower torso. The *Aphrodite of Melos* was part of the growing influence of **neoclassicism,** which swept the disintegrating Hellenistic world in the wake of Rome's rise to greatness. Neoclassicism, developing first in Athens in the late third century BCE and later in Pergamum and other cities, was a kind of nostalgia for the Athenian Golden Age of the fifth and fourth centuries BCE.

SUMMARY

Hellenistic is the name for the period that followed the death of Alexander the Great. The term suggests that the culture of this world was everywhere deeply influenced by the Greeks (the Hellenes) but that it was not a purely Greek culture. As in Hellenic times, cities were the great cultural and economic centers, but now many of the greatest cities, Alexandria and Antioch, for example, were far from Greece. Instead of numerous autonomous poleis, as in the Hellenic period, the Hellenistic era was marked by several huge kingdoms and a number of smaller ones. The major kingdoms were created by some of Alexander's generals: the Antigonids in Macedon, the Seleucids in Mesopotamia and Syria, and the Ptolemies in Egypt. The culture of the Hellenistic era was cosmopolitan, multicultural, tolerant, and experimental. Successful in many ways, the Hellenistic monarchies ultimately succumbed to a resourceful, determined foe: Rome.

The arts in the Hellenistic world both continued and departed from Hellenic norms. In philosophy, ethics and the problems of daily existence took precedence over the nature of matter and the locus of reality. Religion was more personal, less civic than in Hellenic times. Practical science took several leaps forward. Architecture tended toward the opulent and ostentatious. Sculpture maintained the superb skills of the Hellenic period but sometimes abandoned the calm and restraint of that earlier time to add more human, expressive, diverse touches.

The Legacy of the Hellenistic World

Our world is certainly full of skeptics and cynics. We call people who are courageous in the face of disaster "stoic." Divine-right kingship in the West can be traced to Hellenistic roots, and it lasted in some areas until quite recently. Hellenistic science was both innovative and foundational. A recent book claims that the rediscovery of Lucretius in the fifteenth century launched the modern world. Hellenistic art and architecture were flourishing when Rome's legions marched into the Mediterranean world. Romans copied and transmitted what they saw. As in Hellenistic times, today's art is not confined to representations of the rich and the mighty. Our call for multicultural tolerance and understanding would have made sense in Alexandria. Globalism today provokes anxieties similar to those of the cosmopolitan Hellenisitc world.

Students go to college to get their "parchment." Parchment is actually a French rendering of Latin *pergamenum* which was the writing material used in and thus named after Pergamum. Ptolemaic support for Alexandria's Museum set a precedent for state support of cultural and intellectual activity. Most college students have done honorable battle with Euclid's geometry. Even high school physics replicates the experiments of Archimedes. The insouciant youthful "Whatever!" would delight the cynic Diogenes.

DUANE HANSON, *Young Shopper*. 1973. Polyester and fiberglass, polychromed in oil, with accessories. Life size. The Saatchi Gallery, London. Hanson (1925–1996) was an American master of "pop" art or of what some called hyperrealism. He produced countless images that are eerily true to life. Of this one, he said, "I like the physical burdens this woman carries. She is weighted down by all of her shopping bags and purchases, and she has become almost a bag herself. She carries physical burdens—the burdens of life, of everyday living. But initially, it's quite a funny sculpture." Compare the market woman on page 82.

KEY CULTURAL TERMS

Hellenistic	New Comedy	Skepticism	podium
cosmopolitan	comedy of manners	Epicureanism	genre subject
Antigonids	pastoral	*ataraxia*	neoclassicism
Seleucids	idyll	Stoicism	
Ptolemies	Cynicism	*logos*	
Koinè	*autarky*	Corinthian	

A scene along the Appian Way south of Rome. Named for the statesman Appius Claudius, the road was begun in 312 BCE. It consisted of a level earthen surface, over which were laid small stones and mortar, heavier gravel, and then interlocking paving stones. The road was slightly crowned to facilitate drainage.

5

Classical Rome
From Republic to Empire

Preview Questions

1. *What* were the major stages in the political and military development of the Roman Republic?

2. *What* were the essential characteristics of the Augustan Principate?

3. *What* were the most important aspects of the Roman ethos?

4. *How* did Golden Age and Silver Age literature differ?

5. *What* were the domestic, civic, and propagandistic aspects of Roman art?

There is an old saying: "All roads lead to Rome." The Romans conquered their neighbors in Italy, then achieved domination in the western Mediterranean, and finally created an empire that extended from Scotland to Mesopotamia. Eventually, indeed, all roads led to Rome. And for two millennia people in the West have had the sense that their culture traced a path back to Rome.

One of those roads, the Appian Way, is pictured to the left. Begun in 312 BCE, the Appian Way originally extended about 130 miles from Rome to Cumae and was finally stretched to Brindisi, a major port on Italy's east coast, a total distance of almost 350 miles from Rome. As Rome extended its conquests, the Romans built roads and bridges. They also built cities or added typical Roman amenities—baths, theaters, forums—in the lands they conquered, and also built vast aqueducts to bring water to cities. The poet Virgil, whom we will meet again later in this chapter, said to his countrymen, "Remember, Romans, these will be your arts: To rule the people under law, to teach the ways of peace to those you conquer, to spare defeated people, to battle down the proud." Virgil explicitly admitted that "others"—he meant Greeks—were more skilled than Romans in the arts and in science. But he put his finger on precisely what people have always recognized as Rome's great talents and great gifts to posterity. No legal system has been more influential than the Roman. Roman government has been adopted and adapted for centuries. Roman imperialism—for good or ill—has captured the fancy of countless would-be Caesars. Moreover, as this simple picture of a haunting stretch of road suggests, the Romans were intensely practical. War, law, and government were indeed their arts. But the Romans were also among the greatest civil engineers of history.

Rome arose in the Hellenistic world and, for a very long time, Roman arts and letters were Hellenistic in form and substance. The Romans were great imitators: most great works of "Greek" art adorning museums the

Timeline 5.1   THE ROMAN REPUBLIC, 509–31 BCE

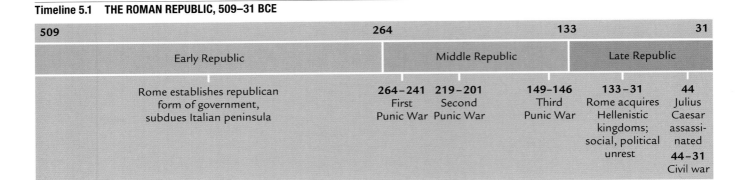

509		264		133		31
Early Republic		Middle Republic		Late Republic		
Rome establishes republican form of government, subdues Italian peninsula	264–241 First Punic War	219–201 Second Punic War	149–146 Third Punic War	133–31 Rome acquires Hellenistic kingdoms; social, political unrest	44 Julius Caesar assassinated 44–31 Civil war	

world over are in fact Roman copies, and Roman poets and playwrights adapted Hellenistic models. But before the Romans could imitate Hellenistic artists and writers, they had to encounter them. The Romans did this first in Italy and then, battle by battle, across the Mediterranean world. In one of those battles the Romans captured the Greek historian Polybius, who wondered "how a people so recently barbarian" had managed to conquer the known world.

THE RISE OF ROME

The ancients told a complex story about Rome's foundation. Aeneas [uh-NEE-us], whose mother was the goddess Aphrodite and whose father was related to the Trojan royal family, escaped after the Mycenaeans captured Troy. He wandered for many years and finally landed on the shore of Latium [LAY-shum], the plain in central Italy where Rome would rise. King Latinus gave his daughter Lavinia to Aeneas in marriage. Several generations later Aeneas's descendant King Numitor was overthrown by his brother who, to eliminate rivals, exposed Numitor's grandsons Romulus and Remus on the bank of the Tiber. Legend holds that they were rescued by a she-wolf who suckled them until a shepherd found and raised them. The boys displayed great leadership qualities but quarreled and Romulus killed Remus. The legend goes on to say that Romulus founded Rome. The Romans always believed that their city had been founded in the year we call 753 BCE.

Etruscans and Greeks

The earliest influences on Rome were exerted by the **Etruscans.** These fascinating people are of mysterious origins. More than 13,000 scraps of their writing survive but cannot be read because their language has not been deciphered. Some ancient writers believed the Etruscans migrated to the west coast of central Italy from Lydia in Asia Minor, but others believed they were native to Italy. They lived in ten or so cities located in a triangular area bounded by the rivers Arno and Tiber and the sea (Map 5.1). Etruscan art and

artifacts demonstrate intense connections with southern Italy, Greece, Asia Minor, and Egypt. The Etruscans occasionally fought with the Greeks of southern Italy and by the seventh century BCE they dominated Latium. A series of early Roman kings were actually Etruscans.

The Etruscans built temples but none has survived. Apparently they modified the Doric order by putting columns on bases and omitting flutes. They created elaborate tombs of which a number survive. Some tombs have rectangular chambers hewn into solid rock—albeit the rock is tufa, a soft stone that hardens when exposed to air. Others are round, half sunken into the ground, and then walled, and then covered with soil. Both kinds of tombs were elaborately decorated with sculpture and fresco (Figure 5.1). Etruscan sculpture has a pleasing, lifelike quality reminiscent of Greek Archaic sculpture (Figure 5.2). Tomb paintings are vivid, colorful, and expressive; Egyptian influences are easy to see. Etruscan art provides keen insights into the visual environment as Rome was taking shape.

Magna Graecia—southern Italy and Sicily—was colonized by Greeks beginning in the eighth century BCE. The Romans traded, and eventually fought, with these Greeks. But from Greek language, art, and architecture, the Romans learned a great deal too.

The Roman Republic

According to tradition the Romans rose up in 509 BCE, overthrew the last of the seven Etruscan kings who had ruled them, and created a republic. The Latin *res publica* means simply a "public thing"—something that was the concern of the people, not merely of the ruler. For about two centuries after the overthrow of the monarchy, Rome was violent and volatile. A small number of **patricians** (from Latin *patres,* "fathers") dominated a much larger number of **plebeians.** The origins of these two groups are obscure. The patricians were large landowners, whereas the plebeians were small farmers, laborers, artisans, and perhaps merchants. A small number of patricians controlled the **senate** (from Latin *senex,* "old man"), and all patricians

Learning Through Maps

MAP 5.1 ITALY BEFORE THE ROMANS

This map shows the major cities of both Etruria—the land of the Etruscans—and of Magna Graecia. Some modern Italian cities are shown to provide a frame of reference. *1. **Note** the position of the major Greek sites and their openness to the Mediterranean. 2. **Observe** the relatively dense concentration of Etruscan sites. 3. **Consider** how early Rome's neighbors exerted influence—by land and sea.*

Figure 5.1 *Tomb of the Leopards.* **Tarquinia. 480–470 BCE. Fresco.** This scene from an Etruscan tomb depicts a banquet. Reclining on couches, male and female diners talk and share food and drink, as two male waiters serve the party. Because of such joyous scenes, the Etruscans are thought to have been optimistic in the face of death. The scenes in the tombs and the objects placed in them suggest a happy continuation of earthly existence—an attitude similar to that of the Egyptians. Egyptian artistic influences are evident in the contrasting skin tones of the figures, with women paler than men. Greek influence can be seen in the dining arrangement and in the modeling of the bodies.

Figure 5.2 *Sarcophagus.* **Cerveteri. Ca. 520 BCE. Terra-cotta. Length 6'7". Museo Nazionale di Villa Giulia, Rome.** This husband and wife are portrayed as if reclining at dinner (compare Figure 5.1), but they also display intimacy in touching each other. The scene is opulent and optimistic: eternity will be a wonderful banquet. The bodies are similar to those in Archaic Greek sculptures but are perhaps more supple, graceful. The Archaic smile is, however, unmistakable.

participated in an assembly that could pass laws binding on the whole population. The plebeians had an assembly too, but its laws were binding only on them.

The patricians needed plebeian manpower to fight their wars. The plebeians realized that this put them in a strong bargaining position, and three times they seceded from the state—in effect, went on strike—to demand political concessions. By 287 BCE all formal, political distinctions between the patricians and the plebeians were gone. All Romans could vote for officials and all Romans (with insignificant exceptions) could be elected to any office. Rome was governed by two annually elected consuls who had both executive and military power. Other annually elected officers included praetors [PREE-tors], who were judicial officers, and various financial and public works officers. Ten tribunes continued to look out for the interests of the plebeians. All Romans belonged automatically to two assemblies. The senate, once a body reserved for patricians, became instead a body of former office-holders. The senate, interestingly, could issue opinions but could not pass laws. Membership in one assembly was regulated by wealth and, in the other, by residence. In the early third century BCE, therefore, Rome was technically a democracy.

The Rise of the Roman Empire

Warlike and ambitious, the Romans campaigned for two centuries against their neighbors in Italy, including the Greeks of Magna Graecia. When the Romans began to fight with the Greeks, the latter called in outside reinforcements. The first of these came from the Kingdom of Epirus, whose King Pyrrhus [PEER-us]

(319-272 BCE) invaded Italy and battled with the Romans twice. Though he was victorious, his victories cost him so dearly that he said if he kept winning like that he was bound to lose. Thus we still speak of a "Pyrrhic victory." Having become embroiled with the Greeks of southern Italy, the Romans also got involved with the Greeks of Sicily and, more importantly, with the mighty Carthaginians, who claimed a kind of protectorate over the island. Carthage was originally a Phoenician colony, and the Carthaginians were the dominant commercial and military power in the western Mediterranean. The Romans fought three "Punic" (the Roman name for the Carthaginians; it means the "purple people" because of the purple dye for which Phoenicians were famous) Wars (261–241, 218–201, and 149–146 BCE). These wars were long, brutal, costly—and full of famous characters and incidents as well. For example, the Carthaginian general Hannibal decided in the Second Punic War that Rome might be more effectively attacked by land than by sea. Accordingly he marched an army from Spain over the Alps into Italy and brought along elephants, partly to transport his *matériel* and partly to terrify the Romans. In the end, determination carried the Romans to victory and hence to hegemony in the western Mediterranean.

While the Second Punic War was still raging, a Macedonian king lent Pyrrhus some aid. The Romans considered this a cause for war and began a series of wars that eventually brought them control of the eastern Mediterranean. The future of the whole Mediterranean basin became clear when in 133 BCE King Attalus III of Pergamum died without heirs and willed his kingdom to Rome. At the battle of Actium in 31 BCE

Timeline 5.2 PRINCIPATE AND PAX ROMANA

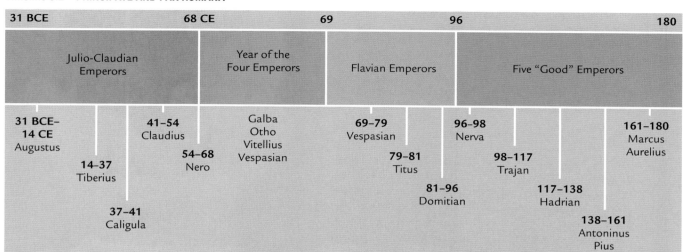

the Romans defeated the forces of Cleopatra, the last of the Ptolemies, and secured definitive control of the Hellenistic world. In the meantime, various Roman generals undertook the conquest of Spain and Gaul, the latter triumph being the work of Julius Caesar (100–44 BCE). In five centuries a tiny city-state won an empire that stretched from the Atlantic to Mesopotamia.

The Decline of the Roman Republic

Polybius [PUH-libb-ee-us] (about 200–118 BCE) believed the secret to Rome's success was to be found in its "balanced" political system: the consuls bore aspects of monarchy, the senate of oligarchy, and the assemblies of democracy. As a Greek, Polybius was struck by the apparent stability of the Roman system. But that stability was more apparent than real, and in the later decades of the second century it came unraveled.

The Roman system depended on social and political deference. A handful of families dominated all the elective offices for some 350 years. The senate, as noted, could only issue opinions, but its opinions were deeply influential. In the senate itself, the oldest member always spoke first. In the voting assemblies, young and old caucused—a good Roman word still used!—together, but the old voted first. Roman speeches often began with a recitation of the *mos maiorum*—the "customs of our ancestors"—which inevitably set a conservative tone. In the Roman household, the **paterfamilias** (the "father of the family") had virtual life and death authority over the entire household. Roman historians tended to write serial biographies of great and virtuous leaders.

Rome's incessant warfare brought huge territorial gains but serious problems as well. Simultaneous wars on several fronts put too many men in charge of armies. Victorious commanders secured wealth and fame that they turned into political power in Rome. Sometimes, army veterans supported their upstart commanders, while lesser generals became faction leaders. Viewed a little differently, many "New Men," as the Romans called them, rose to prominence. They came from obscure families with no experience of Roman politics. New Men, old soldiers, and numerous immigrants from all over the Hellenistic world had neither an understanding of nor a loyalty to the old-fashioned Roman way of doing things. Between 133 and 31 BCE, the Roman Republic collapsed amid frequently violent political strife in which politicians murdered each other and their followers. Men stood for office repeatedly whereas, traditionally, offices were held for only one year. Faction leaders got laws passed in the assemblies to reward their followers and strengthen their groups. So-called popular leaders battled "Optimates," who insisted they alone stood for the good, traditional Roman values. The cycle of violence finally left only one man in charge: Gaius Julius Caesar Octavianus, who was Julius Caesar's adopted nephew.

The Augustan Principate

The reign of Octavian (r. 31 BCE–14 CE) inaugurated a new phase of Roman history. Wearied by decades of unrelenting strife, what was left of the senate conferred almost complete power on Octavian in 27 BCE and called him "Augustus." The regime he inaugurated, called the **principate** [PRIN-chuh-pate] (from Latin *princeps*, "first citizen"), lasted until the death of Marcus Aurelius in 180 CE. These two centuries were marked by institutional stability, imperial expansion and then consolidation, and widespread prosperity.

After a century of civil war, the genius of Augustus brought order out of chaos. He used his power with discretion and was content to be hailed as princeps,

 Figure 5.3   *Head of Augustus.* **Bronze, ht. 18.2″ (46.2 cm). British Museum, London.** This head is all that remains of a complete statue erected on the frontier between Egypt and Nubia (modern Sudan) in about 27 BCE, shortly after Augustus assumed power. Portrayed with short, curly hair, the statue conveys youth and authority, beauty and power. In about 25 BCE the ferocious, one-eyed Queen Candace of Meroë raided the Roman frontier and hauled away the statue. She placed it under the steps to her royal palace so that those who entered would trample on Caesar. Rome never avenged this affront.

first citizen. He sometimes held one of the republican magistracies (consul, praetor), but usually let others hold them, thereby satisfying ambitious individuals and creating the impression that power was shared. Augustus permitted the senate to control many provinces, but he retained control of the militarily threatened and economically prosperous ones (especially Egypt) (Figure 5.3). Above all, he controlled the military; he was the *imperator,* the commander, hence the emperor. In truth, the principate was a thinly disguised military dictatorship, but Augustus made it look like a largely civilian regime with military backing (see Map 5.2).

Learning Through Maps

MAP 5.2   THE ROMAN EMPIRE IN THE TIME OF HADRIAN (117–138)

This map presents the Roman Empire at its greatest territorial extent. Compare this map to Map 5.1.   *1. **Where** had the Roman Empire expanded after Augustus? 2. **What** major cultural zones can you identify within this empire? 3. **What** major strategic problems did this empire present?*

Figure 5.4 Timgad, Algeria. Ca. 100 CE. Timgad, strategically located at the intersection of six Roman roads in North Africa, was typical of the towns built by the Romans during the Pax Romana and populated by ex-soldiers and their families. The town was planned as a square with two main avenues crossing in the middle where the forum stood and all other streets intersecting at right angles. The so-called Arch of Trajan in the foreground marked one of the main thoroughfares, which was lined with columns. Temples, baths, fountains, markets, a theater, and private homes made the city a pleasant place to live.

For two centuries the principate worked remarkably well. Some emperors were gifted while others were feckless and foolish. The senate was at once prestigious and powerless. The emperors effected a working compromise with the urban elites of the empire. The Herods of Judea (see Chapter 6) are a good example: they "went Roman" not because of coercion but because it was in their interest to do so. Rome propped them up and they served Roman interests. The entire empire was governed by a few hundred aristocratic amateurs who served brief tenures as provincial governors. Rome required little from its citizens: peace, good order, and taxes.

Augustus and his successors down to Trajan [TRAY-jun] (r. 98–117) basically rounded off the conquests of the late republic and ushered in the **Pax Romana,** the Roman Peace, an age of public order and military stability. They added Britain while establishing the Rhine and Danube Rivers as the frontiers in the west, the northern edge of the Sahara Desert in the south, and Mesopotamia in the east. Rome briefly pushed north of the Danube into Dacia. It is important to remember that "Roman Peace" is how the Romans looked at things. Those millions of people did not ask to be conquered. The wily historian Tacitus (discussed later in the chapter) said the Romans "made a vast desert and called it peace."

The world-historical significance of the Pax Romana may be grasped by thinking of it as the Hellenistic world with several key differences. Geographically, Rome's empire extended vastly farther to the west but somewhat less far to the east. The Hellenistic world was, however, a collection of political entities whereas the Roman Empire was one. The Hellenistic world was prosperous but unevenly so. All evidence suggests that the Roman Empire was more prosperous and more widely so. Hellenistic culture was fundamentally Greek; indeed, even Roman Republican culture was Greek at its roots. Imperial culture added Latin as an essential component. The Romans added urban amenities—aqueducts, baths, theaters—wherever they went (Figure 5.4). The ease with which Christianity spread is one excellent gauge of the effectiveness of the Pax Romana.

Figure 5.5   *Patrician with Busts of Ancestors (Barberini Togatus).* **Early first century CE. Marble, ht. 5'5". Palazzo dei Conservatori, Rome.** The stern and wrinkled faces of the anonymous patrician and his ancestors convey the quiet dignity and authority of the typical paterfamilias. Some scholars think that these portrait busts, with their unflattering realism, were modeled on death masks.

THE ROMAN ETHOS

The Romans thought of themselves as simple, practical people. The ideal Roman was the citizen farmer who, when necessary, took up arms to defend himself, his household, or his state. Romans professed to dislike everything foreign although they owed immense debts to the peoples and cultures of the Hellenistic world as well as to the Greeks of Magna Graecia and the Etruscans.

Roman Values

By Athenian standards, the Romans were a dull lot who lacked intellectual brilliance, were too self-controlled, and were fearful of the imagination. Like the Spartans, they cultivated a virile moral sense that prized self-reliance. The great Roman statesman Cato the Elder (234–149 BCE) taught his son agriculture, law, and the history of Rome and of his family. A closely related set of values describes the ideal Roman citizen:

- *Pietas,* piety, but actually loyalty, dependability
- *Gravitas,* or gravity, meaning "a deep-seated seriousness"
- *Constantia,* constancy, perseverance, dedication
- *Magnitudo animi,* or magnanimity, "greatness of soul," a lack of concern for wealth and status

To sum up: Duty, discipline, and sacrifice characterized the ideal Roman. Unfortunately, these values no longer guided public or private conduct in the last decades of Rome's republic.

The Roman Family

Latin *familia* means more than our word *family.* The Roman *familia* was not just a closely related group of people living together but, rather, included the entire household and other living relatives as well. The oldest living male was the *paterfamilias* (Figure 5.5), the father of the family, but really more than that for he had virtual life and death authority over his household. Patrician families were especially aware and proud of their descent. As a rule, Romans had three names. Take Gaius Julius Caesar, for example. Gaius was the name his family would have called him, as one of us today might be called John or Robert. There were only about a dozen male names in Rome. Julius was his *gens* name, that is, the name of his tribe, the Julians. Caesar was the name of the particular clan within a tribe. Daughters generally were named after their father's tribes. The first daughter of Julius Caesar would have been called Julia, the second daughter, Julia Secunda. Roman families tended to have just a few sons and rarely more than one daughter. Women at Rome enjoyed considerable autonomy in law and Roman literature is full of influential women (Figure 5.6).

Perhaps because women already enjoyed a measure of equality in Etruscan times, Roman women were not secluded and invisible the way Athenian women tended to be.

Patronage, another word that derives from *pater* ("father") means "protector." Patrons and clients constituted another kind of Roman family. Generals were patrons to their soldiers, as we have seen. Wealthy landowners were often patrons to their peasant neighbors.

Figure 5.6 *Eumachia.* **Mid–first century CE. Marble. Museo Archeologico Nazionale, Naples.** This statue of Eumachia, which was found at Pompeii, shows that Roman matrons were involved in public life. The inscription on the statue's base praises Eumachia for having donated a building in the town's forum for the use of the fullers—workers involved in making woolen cloth. Her statue was paid for by the fullers' association in gratitude for her gift. Her idealized face reflects the Hellenic ideal preferred during the reign of Augustus in the first century CE.

Powerful men always had many clients. Patrons might look out for the legal, economic, or political interests of their clients, who could be expected to support their patrons politically, for example, by voting their preferences in the assemblies. Patron-client bonds were another aspect of the culture of deference that characterized Roman society.

Roman Religion

Roman religion began in the household, in the *familia.* Janus was the god of the doorway and became the god of the gates of the city. Vesta was the goddess of the domestic hearth and became the goddess of the civic hearth. Early Roman religion probably owed a lot to the Etruscans but is almost completely obscure to us. By the time we have abundant source material, the Romans themselves had encountered the Greeks of Magna Graecia and of the Hellenistic world. Hence the familiar Roman gods and goddesses are the Greek Olympians with Roman names and sometimes with slightly adjusted areas of responsibility (Table 5.1). As they fought and traded, the Romans met other religions too and brought them home. From Egypt they imported the cult of Isis and from Asia Minor, Cybele. In other words, and as elsewhere in the Hellenistic world, mystery cults (see Chapter 4) supplemented civic religion in the daily experience of most people.

For Romans, religion was fundamentally civic. *Religio,* whence our word *religion,* basically means "to bind." Roman religious rites were intended to bind the gods and goddesses, to get them to deliver abundant crops, healthy childbirths, or victory in war. In order to bind the gods, the Roman had countless rituals throughout the annual calendar. One group of Roman

TABLE 5.1   THE CHIEF ROMAN GODS AND GODDESSES AND THEIR GREEK COUNTERPARTS

ROMAN	GREEK
Jupiter	Zeus
Juno	Hera
Neptune	Poseidon
Pluto	Hades
Vesta	Hestia
Apollo	Apollo
Diana	Artemis
Mars	Ares
Venus	Aphrodite
Vulcan	Hephaestus
Minerva	Athena
Mercury	Hermes

Interpreting Art

Composition A rare double portrait of a man and his wife, small in size but rich in meaning.

Subject A scene of a married couple as revealed by their joining right hands, the key symbolic act in a Roman marriage ceremony.

Style Hellenistic, or Roman, realism contrasts sharply with Hellenic idealism. These are fully realized figures. The quality of the work is very high; note the deep folds in the clothing, the lines in the man's face, and his "pinkie ring."

Social Perspective Marriage was central to the Roman ethos. Note how the wife lays her hand on her husband's shoulder, a touching gesture of support and care.

Moral Perspective The figures communicate a strong bond, fidelity, and the harmony of an old married couple. The husband's impassive countenance suggests experience and maturity. The wife's gaze is serene.

Context Images like this one, which communicates intimacy and domesticity, would have adorned the homes of prosperous Romans.

Double Portrait of Marcus Gratidius Libanus and Gratidia. Late first century BCE. Marble with traces of color, ht. 23¼". Museo Pio Clementino, Vatican City.

1. **Subject** What features of this sculpture tell you that this is a married couple?

2. **Style** Compare and contrast this figure's style with Figure 5.2 and with the *Old Market Woman* on page 82.

3. **Social Perspective** Identify and explain the gestures in this sculpture.

4. **Moral Perspective** How do you read the faces in this sculpture?

5. **Context** What might a sculpture like this have meant to a Roman family?

---

priests, the pontiffs, held responsibility for rites dealing with war and peace, agriculture, and domestic life. The chief priest, the *Pontifex Maximus,* was an elected official. *Pontifex* [PON-tee-feks] means "bridge builder." Rome's first civic priest supposedly built the very first bridge over the Tiber. Another group of priests, the *augurs* [AWE-gurs], observed the flight of birds or the entrails of sacrificed beasts to see if the gods were favorable to a particular course of action—say, starting or ending a war or passing a law. As the hearth fire in a home was never to die out, so too Rome's civic hearth was kept burning by the Vestal Virgins.

Imperial Rome added a feature to Roman religion, the cult of the emperor. Republican officials had never been viewed as divine. As the emperors differentiated themselves more and more from the rest of the

Romans and as Rome conquered lands that had long experienced theocratic kingship, the divinization of the emperors was irresistible. Across the empire, the cult of the emperor provided a bond of focus and unity. How seriously did the Romans take the divinity of their emperors? When the rather austere emperor Claudius was on his deathbed (54 CE), he is reported to have said, "I think I am becoming a god."

ROMAN LITERATURE AND PHILOSOPHY

Except for some scraps of legal material and a few inscriptions, the earliest Roman writing was in Greek because Latin was as yet too poor for high art. Gradually the Romans encountered, assimilated, and then contributed to Hellenistic literature in their own increasingly polished language. Latin literature began to flourish in the middle years of the republic with history, lyric and epic poetry, comedy, and tragedy, initially in the Greek style but gradually in a distinctive Roman style. This period also saw the rise of a Roman theatrical tradition influenced both by roots in boisterous Etruscan religious celebrations and by contact with the Greek theater.

The Literature of the Republic

The oldest Latin text is a treatise on agriculture by Cato the Elder but Plautus [PLAW-tuhs] (about 254–184 BCE), a plebeian, launched Rome's great age of comic theater, indeed of literature, with his almost 130 plays. His genius lay in breathing fresh life into the stale plots and stock characters borrowed from Menander and other Hellenistic, New Comedy playwrights. In Plautus's hands, the mistaken identities, verbal misunderstandings, and bungled schemes seemed brand new. Rome's other significant comic playwright was Terence [TAIR-ents] (about 195–159 BCE), a Carthaginian slave who was brought to Rome, educated, and set free. Although he wrote only six plays, Terence won the acclaim of Rome's educated elite, perhaps because of the pure Greek tone and themes of his works. Rome's stodgy aristocrats decreed that the earliest theaters have no seats. If people were going to enjoy *that* sort of thing, they would have to do it standing up.

Plautus and Terence had no real successors as playwrights, but in the first century BCE Roman poetry began to flourish. Two major poets with distinctively different personalities and talents appeared: Lucretius and Catullus. Both were heavily influenced by Greek literature. Lucretius [lew-KREE-shuhs] (about 94–55 BCE) stands in the long line of didactic literary figures dating from Homer. A gifted poet, with his well-turned Latin phrases and imaginative and vivid language, Lucretius wrote *De Rerum Natura (On the Nature of Things)* to persuade the reader of the truth of Epicureanism, the philosophy based on scientific atomism that denied divine intervention in human affairs (see Chapter 4).

In contrast to Lucretius's lengthy poem, the verses of Catullus [kuh-TUHL-uhs] (about 84–54 BCE) are characterized by brevity, one of the hallmarks of the Alexandrian school of the Hellenistic Age. Catullus is best remembered for his love poems, which draw on the lives of his highborn, free-spirited circle in Rome and express his innermost feelings of desire, disappointment, and jealousy. As a typical Hellenistic author, Catullus wrote poems whose language ranged from sublime to coarse and whose themes extended from the sensual to the frankly erotic.

The efforts of Lucretius and Catullus pale, however, when placed beside those of their contemporary Cicero (106–43 BCE), who dominated Roman letters in his own day so much that his era is often labeled the Age of Cicero (Figure 5.7). By translating Greek treatises into Latin, Cicero created a philosophical vocabulary for the Latin language where none had existed before. For centuries, his collected speeches served as models of both public oratory and written argument. Today's readers rank Cicero's collection of letters, most by him, some addressed to him (a few written by his son), as his masterpiece. These nearly nine hundred letters, frank in style and language, offer a unique self-portrait of a major public figure in ancient times. Cicero also wrote extensively on law and politics. As a public figure he attained high office but failed in his effort to achieve the *concordia ordinum,* the "concord of the orders," that is, peace and understanding among Rome's warring factions.

Figure 5.7   *Cicero.* **First century BCE. Capitoline Museum, Rome.** The anonymous sculptor of this bust of Cicero has caught the character of the man as recalled in literary sources. Honored as one of Rome's finest intellectuals and a patriot devoted to rescuing the state from chaos, he is depicted deep in thought with stern and resolute features. This idealized portrait contributed to the mystique of Cicero as a hero of the Roman Republic.

SLICE OF LIFE

A College Student's Letter Home

MARCUS, SON OF CICERO

Cicero's son Marcus, having spent all his money, wrote in 44 BCE to his father's secretary Tiro. Because of the press of public life, Cicero often relied on Tiro to handle his correspondence. Knowing that Tiro will relay a message to his father, Marcus offers assurances that he has mended his ways and describes his schoolwork.

That the rumors, which reach you about me, are gratifying and welcome to you, I have no doubt at all, my dearest Tiro; and I shall make every effort to guarantee that this opinion of me which is springing up more distinctly every day becomes twice as good. For that reason you may with unshaken confidence fulfill your promise of being the trumpeter of my reputation. For the errors of my youth have caused me such grief and agony that not only do my thoughts shrink from what I have done, but my very ears shrink from hearing it talked about.

I must tell you that my close attachment to Cratippus is not so much that of a pupil as that of a son. For not only do I attend his lectures with enjoyment, but I am greatly fascinated also by the charm of his personality. I spend whole days with him, and often a part of the night. Indeed, I implore him to dine with me as often as possible. Now that we have become so intimate,

he often strolls in upon us when we least expect him and are at dinner, and throwing to the wind all austerity as a philosopher, he bandies jokes with us in the most genial manner possible.

As to Bruttius, why should I mention him at all? There is never a moment when I allow him to leave my side. He leads a simple and austere life, but that the same time he is a most delightful man to live with. For there is no ban upon merry talk in our literary discussions and our daily joint researches. I have hired lodgings for him next door, and, as far as I can, alleviate his penury out of my own narrow means.

Besides all this I have begun to practice declaiming in Greek with Cassius; but I like practicing in Latin with Bruttius.

I beg of you to see that a secretary is sent to me as quickly as possible—best of all a Greek; for that will relieve me of a lot of trouble in writing out lecture notes.

Interpreting This Slice of Life

1. *How* was education conducted in Greece and Rome?
2. *How* credible does Marcus's letter to his father strike you?
3. *Compare and contrast* the life of a typical student today with that of Marcus.

The Golden Age

The reign of Augustus marked the Golden Age of Roman letters. This period's three greatest poets, Virgil, Horace, and Ovid, captured the age's euphoric mood as peace and stability once more returned to Rome. Of these three writers, Virgil best represented the times through his vision of Rome and his stirring verses. In prose, Livy captured the spirit of the age with his inspiring tales of Rome's greatness.

The works of Virgil [VUR-jill] (70–19 BCE), a modestly born Italian from Mantua, were inspired by Greek literary forms—idylls (or vignettes), didactic (instructive) poems, and epics—yet his use of native themes and his focus on the best traits in the Roman people give an authentic Roman voice to his work. Deeply moved by Augustus's reforms, he put his art in the service of the state. Virgil's pastoral poetry, the *Eclogues* and *Georgics,* celebrated rural life and urged readers to seek harmony with nature in order to find peace—advice that became a significant moral theme of the

Western heritage. But Virgil is best known for the *Aeneid,* an epic poem in twelve books that he wrote in imitation of Homer. In this work, infused with Roman values and ideals, Virgil gave full voice to his love of country, his respect for Augustus, and his faith in Rome's destiny.

The *Aeneid* tells of Aeneas, the legendary Trojan hero who wandered the Mediterranean before founding Rome. In the first six books, Virgil models his tale on the *Odyssey,* writing of travel and love. The second half is modeled on the *Iliad,* stressing fighting and intrigue. The *Aeneid* became Rome's bible and its literary masterpiece. Children were often required to memorize passages from the poem to instill in them the values that had made Rome great. Aeneas served as the prototype of the faithful leader who would not be diverted from his destined path. The work's rich language led later poets to mine the *Aeneid* for expressions and images. As Homer inspired Virgil, so Virgil became the model for Western poets.

The second major poet of the Golden Age was Horace (65–8 BCE), another humble Italian who welcomed Augustus as Rome's savior and offered patriotic sentiments in his verses. His poems, which were written to be read aloud, use Alexandrian forms such as odes and letters in verse. A master and even innovator with poetic forms, Horace was playful and creative with language. He helped to create a new literary genre, the **satire,** which rebuked the manners of the age. Horace was at his best in addressing the heartbreaking brevity of life: "what has been, has been, and I have had my hour."

Ovid [AHV-uhd] (43 BCE–about 17 CE), the third voice of the Golden Age, was a wealthy Italian who did not devote his verses to patriotic themes or pay lip service to conventional morality. Ovid's love poems speak of the purely sensual and fleeting quality of sex and ignore the enduring value of committed love. His *Art of Love* offers advice, in a manner bordering on the scientific, on how to seduce women. Such advice contrasted with Virgil's and Horace's attempts to raise the moral level of the Romans. The austere Augustus exiled Ovid.

Ovid's masterpiece was the *Metamorphoses,* or *Transformations.* Somewhat irreverently, Ovid breathed new life into more than two hundred Greek and Roman myths and legends that centered on the transformation of people into other forms. This work is the source of our knowledge of many classical myths, and medieval and Renaissance poets turned to it continually for inspiration.

A fourth writer, the historian Livy (59 BCE–17 CE), also embodied the spirit of the times. He wrote a massive history of Rome in 142 books of which only 35 survive, basically telling in prose the story Virgil told in verse. But where Virgil ended with the age of Aeneas, Livy came down to his own times; albeit all the contemporary material has disappeared. An accomplished Latin stylist, Livy tells stories about Rome's real or legendary heroes to instruct his contemporaries about proper beliefs and conduct.

The Silver Age

The literary period from the death of Augustus to the end of the second century is called the Silver Age. In this period, the patriotic style of the previous era was replaced by the critical views of writers who often satirized Roman society and the state. Lacking the originality of the Golden Age, the writers of this era looked to their predecessors for models while they polished their phrases and reworked earlier themes. This shift in literary taste reflected a new educational ideal, which stressed skills in debate and oratory. As a result, moral considerations became secondary to aesthetic effects, with writers using rhetorical flourishes and exaggerated literary conceits.

An outstanding Silver Age talent was Seneca [SEN-e-kuh] (4 BCE–65 CE). Born into a wealthy family in Spain, Seneca became a powerful senator and the age's chief Stoic thinker. He is best remembered as a dramatist, though his works failed to measure up to the Greek heritage. His ten extant plays relied on emotionalism, rhetorical excess, and stage violence—the perennial traits of Roman tragedy. After his day, the staging of tragedies ceased, not to be revived for more than fifteen hundred years.

The Silver Age produced several Latin poets, chief among them Juvenal [JOO-vuh-nall] (about 60–140 CE), who trained his censorious gaze on the follies of the empire. Juvenal expressed his outraged observations in sixteen satires, the literary form originated by Horace and others. The voice that speaks in Juvenal's satires is embittered, perhaps a reflection of his obscure social origins. But the carefully crafted language—obscene, bilious, funny, and evocative but always just right—made him the master of this genre in Rome, if not in world letters.

The leading historian of the Silver Age was Tacitus [TASS-uh-tus] (about 55–117 CE), famed also as an orator and politician. Like the greatest of Greek historians, Tacitus was a superb stylist, wrote about his own times, and stressed human responsibility. But the values he stressed, and often found lacking, were wholly Roman. Tacitus acquired his knowledge of statecraft as the governor of the province of Asia (present-day southwestern Turkey). Among his works are two that have earned him the front rank among Roman historians. The *Annals* focus on the rulers after the death of Augustus in 14 CE until the murder of Nero in 68. The *Histories* then pick up the story of Rome and carry it through 96, when the tyrannical Domitian was assassinated. A master of the Latin language, Tacitus had a flair for dramatic narrative. Like other Roman historians, he wrote history with a moral purpose, but his critical spirit set him apart from those who had nothing but glowing praise for Rome. Tacitus's perspective was that of a proud senator who could not conceal his distaste for Rome's loss of political freedom. He concluded that tyranny was an innate flaw in the imperial system.

Philosophy

The major Hellenistic philosophies came to Rome in the second century BCE. Chief among these was Stoicism but its greatest influence was achieved later, through the teaching of Seneca, Epictetus, and the emperor Marcus Aurelius. Seneca's fame as a philosopher rests on his *Moral Letters.* These letters, usually written in response to pressing ethical problems, are filled with good advice, even though they break no new philosophical ground. In one letter, for example, Seneca counseled a grieving acquaintance to maintain dignity and inner strength in the face of a loved one's death.

Epictetus [ep-ik-TEET-uhs] (about 55–115 CE) not only preached but also lived his Stoic creed. According to tradition, Epictetus, though a slave in Rome, won his freedom because of his teachings. He subsequently founded a school in Asia Minor and attracted enthusiastic converts. He did not write anything, but Arrian, a pupil, composed the *Discourses* and the *Handbook,* both in Greek, which together preserved the essence of his master's ideas. Epictetus's philosophy reflected his own victory over personal misfortune. He advised patience in the face of trouble, indifference to material things, and acceptance of one's destiny. Although these ideas represented a rehash of basic Stoic beliefs, his moral wholeness gave them a special appeal.

Stoicism's finest hour arrived in 161 CE when Marcus Aurelius became emperor. Converted to Stoicism in his youth, the emperor wrote an account (in Greek) of his daily musings—called *Meditations*—while he was engaged in almost continuous warfare against barbarian invaders. His journal came to light after his death and was soon recognized as a masterpiece of Stoicism. Like all Stoics, Marcus Aurelius admonished himself to play with dignity the role that providence had assigned: if a divine plan guides the universe, then he must accept it; if, however, the world is ruled by chance, then a well-regulated mind is the best defense. Such reasoning enabled him to avoid moral confusion. His death in 180 signaled the end of ancient Stoicism.

MUSIC

The Greek tradition in music was so powerful that for a long time Roman music simply perpetuated Greek forms and ideas. And yet the Romans originally used music only for practical purposes and rejected the Greek notion that music performed an ethical role in educating the soul or mind.

Not until imperial times did music come to play an important role in Roman life. Under the emperors, music became wildly popular, as all classes succumbed to its seductive charms. **Pantomimes**—dramatic productions with instrumental music and dances—became the spectacle favored by the Roman masses. In the long run, the pantomimes became a symbol of music's decadent trend under the empire. The largest of these productions featured three thousand instrumentalists and three thousand dancers, but the more common size was three hundred performers in each category. A more serious sort of music was kept alive by the wealthy classes, who maintained household orchestras and choruses for their private amusement. An even more cultivated audience encouraged poets such as Horace to set their verses to music, thus continuing the Greek tradition of lyric poetry.

Although what Roman music actually sounded like remains a subject of conjecture, Roman musical instruments, borrowed from across the Mediterranean world, can be identified with some certainty. From Greece came the stringed instruments, the lyre and the kithara, along with such woodwinds as the single aulos, or oboe, and the double aulos—which the Romans called the tibia. From the Etruscans came the brasses. The Romans delighted in the harsh sounds made by these instruments, incorporating them into their military music just as the Etruscans had done. The hydraulic organ, or water organ, was probably perfected in Hellenistic Alexandria, but in imperial Rome it became a crowd-pleaser, adding deep, voluminous sounds to the pantomimes. The taste of the imperial Roman audience is evident in the water organ, impressive not for its musical qualities but as a feat of engineering expertise.

THE VISUAL ARTS

Architecture and sculpture dominated Rome's visual arts, but they were pressed into the service of practical needs. The Romans commissioned buildings and statues to serve the state, religion, or society, but they recognized that the practical did not exclude the beautiful and that the functional did not rule out the elegant. The wealth generated by the empire made possible building on a scale never before matched. Augustus is said to have found a city of brick and left a city of marble.

Architecture

Over the years, the Romans used many types of materials in their public and private buildings. The architects of the early republic built with sun-dried bricks and used terra-cotta, a fired clay, for roofs and decorations. As Rome's wealth grew and new materials were imported, the bricks retained an important though less visible role in buildings, chiefly in foundations and walls. By the late republic, two new products had been adapted from the Greeks, mortar and **ashlars** (massive stones hewn into rectilinear shapes with even surfaces and square corners), which, in time, revolutionized the face of Rome.

Much of the impetus for the building revolution sprang from the Romans' improvement of mortar. They produced a moldable concrete by mixing lime, sand, small rocks, and rubble, but because the concrete was visually unappealing, the builders began to cover it either with slabs of expensive and highly polished marble and granite or with the off-white, marble-like travertine easily available around Rome.

The Romans' most significant innovations in architecture were made with the rounded arch, which already had a long history by the time they began to experiment with it. The Mesopotamians probably invented this arch, the Greeks knew about it, and the Etruscans used it in their drainage systems. The arch's

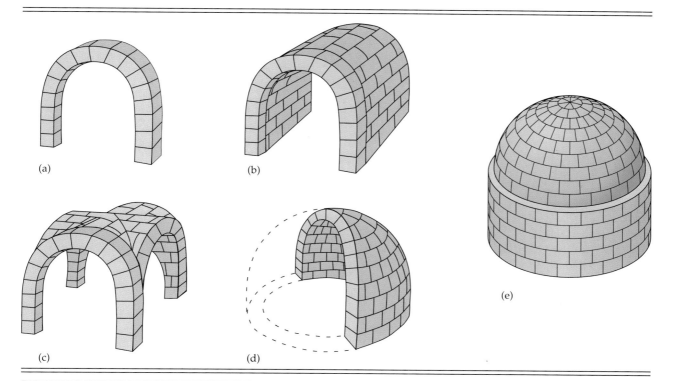

(a)

(b)

(c)

(d)

(e)

Figure 5.8   Structures Used in Roman Architecture. Beginning with the basic arch (a), the Romans created the barrel vault (b) and the cross vault (c). These structural elements, along with the dome (d), which they formed by rotating a series of arches around a central axis, and the dome on a drum (e), gave the Romans the architectural elements they needed to construct their innovative temples and monuments.

basic round form is created with wedge-shaped stones called **voussoirs.** A **keystone** at the center of the semi-circle locks the arch in place. The installed arch is amazingly strong, diverting the weight of the upper walls both outward and downward onto columns or other supports (Figure 5.8).

The Romans demonstrated their inventive genius by creating ceilings, or **vaults,** from arches—by transforming the simple rounded arch into barrel vaults, groined vaults, and domes. They created the **barrel vault**—named because it looks like a barrel divided lengthwise—by building a series of contiguous arches. They intersected two barrel vaults at right angles to produce a **groined,** or **cross, vault.** Finally, the dome, the crown jewel of Rome's architectural vocabulary, was constructed essentially by rotating an arch in a full circle. It was then placed on a drum or enclosed cylinder. The Romans were also able to build arches more safely after they discovered the correct mathematical ratio (1:2) between the height of an arch and the width of its base.

The prototype of imperial temples is the well-preserved Maison Carrée in Nîmes, France, a major provincial city. Built in about 16 BCE, the Maison Carrée

incorporated Etruscan and Greek ideas (Figure 5.9). Raised on a platform in the Etruscan manner, this temple shows other Etruscan borrowings in the central stairway, the deep porch, and the engaged columns— that is, the columns built into the walls of the cella, the inner sanctum housing the cult statue. Greek influences are visible in the low gable—the triangular end of the building's roof—and the Corinthian columns. The Greek notion that beauty lies in mathematical harmony is also expressed in the predetermined ratio of the area of the cella to the area of the temple's porch.

Besides perfecting their version of the rectilinear temple, the Romans invented the round temple, as seen in the Pantheon, a sanctuary dedicated to all their deities. The Pantheon consists of three different units: the entrance porch, or portico, with its supporting columns; the huge drum, housing the sanctuary proper, which is attached to the porch; and the dome, set on top of the drum (Figure 5.10). This design showed the Romans' reliance on a native heritage, because the rounded shape was probably inspired by the circular religious shrines of the pre-Romans, as modern archaeology has shown. The Pantheon also combined a religious with a secular image: the dome symbolized both the heaven of the deities and the vastness of the empire.

But the Pantheon did more than reflect the deep longings of the Roman people; its rich interior illustrated the Roman genius for decoration (Figure 5.11). A polychrome marble floor and a dome with recessed panels created a dazzling interior, and statues, decorative columns, triangular pediments, niches, and other

Figure 5.9 Maison Carrée. Ca. 16 BCE. Base 104′4″ × 48′10″. Nîmes, France. This temple was probably modeled on temples in Rome, since buildings with Corinthian columns and similar overall designs were being constructed in the capital at this time. Reproducing architecture in the provincial cities was another way in which the Romans spread civilization throughout their conquered lands.

Figure 5.10 Pantheon Exterior. 126 CE. Rome. In modern Rome, the Pantheon is crowded into a piazza where it faces a monument topped by an Egyptian obelisk. However, when built under the emperor Hadrian, the Pantheon was part of a complex of structures that complemented one another, and the temple's facade faced a set of columns in an open forecourt. Its original setting reflected the Roman sense that urban space should be organized harmoniously.

Figure 5.11 Pantheon Interior. 126 CE. Rome. The inner diameter of the dome is 144 feet. The height of the dome is 72 feet, or one-half of the total height (144 feet) of the building. The sunlight sweeps around the interior and plays on the dome's decorations as the earth turns, creating constantly changing patterns of light and design.

architectural details alternated around the circular room. The most unusual effect of all was the round hole, thirty feet in diameter, called the **oculus,** or eye, which opened the dome to the sunlight and the elements. The Pantheon is the oldest standing domed structure in the world.

Rome's architecture consisted of more than beautiful temples. The city of Rome was the center of government for the Mediterranean world, the nucleus of the state's religious system, and the hub of an international economy. And at the heart of the city was its **forum,** which functioned like the agora of Greek city-states. In the forum, citizens conducted business, ran the government, and socialized among the complex of public buildings, temples, sacred sites, and monuments. As part of his reforms, Augustus rebuilt and beautified much of the republican forum.

In addition to forums, columns, and arches, the emperors commissioned amphitheaters as monuments to themselves and as gifts to the citizens. The amphitheaters were the sites of the gladiatorial contests and other blood sports that were the cornerstone of popular culture in the empire. The most famous of these structures was called the Colosseum, actually the Flavian amphitheater, named in honor of the dynasty that built it (Figure 5.12). The name Colosseum, dating from a later time, referred to a large (i.e., colossal) statue of the emperor Nero that stood nearby.

The exterior of the Colosseum was formed by stacking three tiers of rounded arches on top of one another; Greek columns were then inserted between the arches as decorations—Doric columns on the first level, Ionic on the second, and Corinthian on the third. A concrete and marble block foundation supported this immense amphitheater. The playing area, or arena (Latin for "sand"), was made of wood and usually covered with sand. A honeycomb of rooms, corridors, and cages ran underneath the wooden floor. The Colosseum's vast size—it could seat eighty thousand people—and unusual features, such as its retractable overhead awning, made it one of the triumphs of Roman engineering, but the spectacular and brutal contests between men, and sometimes women, and wild beasts, in varied combinations, that took place there symbolized the sordid side of Rome.

Like modern urban centers, Roman towns needed a continuous supply of water. In meeting the water demands of the cities, the Romans displayed their talent for organization and their preference for the practical by creating an elaborate network of aqueducts, sluices, and siphons that ran by gravity from a water source in nearby hills and culminated in a town's reservoirs and fountains.

The Romans started building underground aqueducts in about 300 BCE and constructed the first elevated aqueduct in 144 BCE. Under Augustus, they

Figure 5.12 Colosseum. Ca. 72–80 CE. Ht. 166'6". Rome. Although the Flavians were a short-lived dynasty, starting with Vespasian in 69 CE and ending with Domitian in 96, they left Rome this structure, one of its most enduring landmarks. The Romans created the oval amphitheater (literally, "theater on both sides") by joining two semicircular Greek theaters, another example of their ingenuity and practicality.

completed an aqueduct to serve the city of Nîmes that crossed the Gardon River in southern France (Figure 5.13). Known as the Pont du Gard, this section of the aqueduct has a beautiful and functional design. Six large arches form the base, and above them are eleven smaller ones supporting a third tier of thirty-five even smaller arches. Atop the third tier is the sluice through which the water flowed, by gravity, to Nîmes. This graceful structure is a reminder of how the Romans transformed an ordinary object into a work of art.

Sculpture

The reign of Augustus was important in the development of Roman sculpture. Under his rule, imperial portraiture reverted to the idealism of Hellenic Greece, displacing the realistic art of the Hellenistic era, or late republic in Roman terms. But Augustus's pure idealism did not prevail for long, for under his successors sculpture became more propagandistic—that is, more

Figure 5.13 Pont du Gard. Ca. late first century CE. Ht. 161'. Gardon River, near Nîmes, France.
This aqueduct spanning the river was only one segment of the 50-mile system that supplied water to Nîmes. Between 8,000 and 12,000 gallons of water were delivered daily, or about 100 gallons per inhabitant.

Figure 5.14 *Augustus,* **from Prima Porta. Ca. 14 CE. Marble, ht. 6′7¹/₂″. Braccio Nuovo, Museo Chiaramonti, Vatican Museums.** This statue of Caesar Augustus (r. 31 BCE–14 CE), the founder of the Roman Empire, was uncovered at Prima Porta, the villa of his wife, Livia. The statue closely resembled the ruler yet presented him as godlike. Augustus's imperial successors commissioned similar sculptures to convey a sense of their dignity and power.

symbolic of imperial power. This move to symbolic idealism reflected the later emperors' need to find a highly visible way in which to overawe, and thus draw together, Rome's increasingly diversified masses.

Two major sculptural works associated with Augustus, the Prima Porta portrait and the Ara Pacis, or the Altar of Peace, helped to popularize the idealistic style. Augustus's statue, commissioned after his death, stood in a garden on his widow's estate, Prima Porta, just outside Rome (Figure 5.14). The pure Hellenic style is evident in Augustus's relaxed stance and idealized face, both of which were modeled on the *Doryphoros* by Polykleitos (see Figure 3.19). However, the accompanying symbols reveal the propagandistic intent of the sculpture and were portents of the path that imperial portraits would take. For example, the cupid represents Venus, the mother of Aeneas, and thus Augustus is symbolically connected to the legendary origins of Rome.

The second idealistic sculpture, the marble Ara Pacis, was funded by the senate as an offering of thanks to Augustus for his peacekeeping missions. The entire structure was set on a platform and enclosed by three walls. On the fourth side, an entrance with steps led to the altar (Figure 5.15). Relief sculptures decorated the

Figure 5.15   Ara Pacis. 9 BCE. Marble, width 35′. Rome. Like the Prima Porta statue, the Ara Pacis became a model for later emperors, who emulated its decorations, symbols, and size. The altar was rediscovered in the sixteenth century, excavated in the nineteenth and early twentieth centuries, and restored in 1938.

Figure 5.16 *Family of Augustus,* **Ara Pacis relief. 9 BCE. Marble, ht. 63″. Rome.** The figures in low relief, moving from right to left, are separated yet linked by their placement and clothing. The child to the right of center is given great prominence: he faces right while all the adults in the foreground are looking left and a man places his hand on the child's head. This singling out of the child may be an act of endearment or of recognition that he is to be the emperor.

Figure 5.17 *March of the Legions,* **from the Arch of Titus. Ca. 81 CE. Marble relief, approx. 6 × 12½′. Rome.** This rectangular marble relief occupies the south side of the Arch of Titus. It commemorates the Roman victory in the Jewish War of 66–70 CE, when the Romans put down a rebellion by the Jews in Judea and subsequently dispersed them across the Roman world. In the relief, the Roman soldiers hold aloft the Jewish holy relics from the Temple as they seem to press forward and pass under the arch on the right.

interior and exterior walls, some in an idealized style and others in a realistic style (Figure 5.16). The resulting tension between realism and idealism marked this altar as an early work in the imperial style.

This type of sculpture reached its highest potential as a propaganda tool on triumphal arches and victory columns, such as the Arch of Titus and Trajan's Column. One of the reliefs from the Arch of Titus, the *March of the Legions,* portrays the army's victory march into Rome after the destruction of the Temple in Jerusalem in 70 CE (Figure 5.17). Trajan's column portrays his campaigns in Dacia (roughly modern Romania) (Figures 5.18 and 5.19). The equestrian statue of Marcus Aurelius (Figure 5.20) represented a new departure in Roman sculpture and propaganda that would have many imitators from later antiquity to the recent past.

Painting and Mosaics

Murals, or wall paintings, the most popular type of painting in Rome, have been found in private dwellings, public buildings, and temples. Surviving works hint at a highly decorative, brightly colored art. Originally the Romans applied **tempera,** or paint set in a binding solution, directly onto a dry wall. However, this quick and easy method produced a painting that soon faded and peeled. Later they adopted fresco painting (see Chapter 2) as the most practical and lasting technique. The Romans were drawn to many subjects: Greek and Roman myths, architectural vistas, religious stories, ritual performances, genre scenes (everyday events), and landscapes.

**Figure 5.18   Trajan's Victory Column. 106–113 CE. Ht. 125',
including base. Rome.** Borrowing the idea of a victory column from Mesopotamia, the pragmatic Trajan used art to enhance his power in the eyes of the citizens. This work commemorated his conquest of Dacia—present-day Romania. The marble column, set on a foundation, enclosed a winding stairway that led to an observation platform and a statue of Trajan. Spiraling around the column's shaft was a stone relief sculpture that told the story of Trajan's victory in lively and painstaking detail.

**Figure 5.19   Detail of Trajan's Victory Column. Ht. of relief band
approx. 36".** Wrapped around the column is the 645-foot relief carving with 2,500 figures. Color was applied to heighten the realistic effect. Trajan placed this column in a massive new forum he erected, and the column itself was readily visible from the first and second stories of the forum's library.

Figure 5.20 *Marcus Aurelius.* **Ca. 173 CE. Bronze, ht. 16′8″. Piazza del Campidoglio, Rome.** The unknown artist has represented Marcus Aurelius as a warrior-emperor, but the militaristic image is offset somewhat by the Stoic ruler's face. Here we see a human being lost in thought and far removed from pomp and power.

Among the many landscapes painted by Roman artists are the splendid garden frescoes from the Villa of Livia at Prima Porta (Figure 5.21). This fresco, depicting a distant garden, is framed by twin horizontal walls at its bottom and a jagged border at the top. Roman artists never mastered mathematical perspective; instead, they used the placement of objects, animals, and human figures to create a sense of space, as in this fresco. The patterned fence (foreground) and the stone wall (in the rear), with a walkway in between and a tree in the center, create the illusion of depth. The placement of the bushes, smaller trees, shrubs, fruits, and flowers behind the walls further augments the fresco's perspective. The vast array of identifiable plants and birds typifies two themes of Augustan art, as the art of the reign of Augustus is called. Those themes are prosperity and peace, thus suggestive of the propagandistic nature of the art of the period.

A more vital art form was the mosaic. The Romans learned to make **mosaics,** assemblages of tiny bits of stone, glass, or metal, from the Hellenistic Greeks in the third century BCE, but by the third century CE, several local Roman mosaic styles had sprung up across the empire. Although subjects varied, certain ones seemed always to be in vogue, such as still lifes, landscapes, Greek and Roman myths, philosophers and orators, and scenes from the circus and amphitheaters. A mosaic from Tunisia (North Africa) shows the intricacy of design and variety of color that artisans achieved even in the Roman provinces (Figure 5.22).

LAW AND WAR: ROME'S "ARTS"

As Virgil said, it was Rome's task to rule the world under law. Fundamentally, Roman law aimed to give every man his due. From Hellenistic philosophy, especially Stoicism, Roman law inherited the idea of **natural law,** that is, the idea that there is somehow a law woven into the fabric of the universe that is independent of any rules proposed by human agents. Roman

Figure 5.21 *Garden Scene.* **Villa of Livia, Prima Porta. Ca. 20 BCE. Fresco. Museo di Palazzo, Massimo, Rome.** This garden scene represents a particular style of Roman fresco painting that began in the first century BCE and was still popular in the Age of Augustus. Labeled *architectural*, these paintings were often divided into three horizontal planes and framed by columns to give the sense of a wall opening or looking through a window onto a bucolic view of the world beyond the villa or house.

law developed over many centuries. The first written code, the Twelve Tables, dates from about 450 BCE. During the course of the Roman Republic, the assemblies passed many laws that became part of the Roman tradition. Every year, the praetors issued an edict that specified what they would address in their year of service. Together these sources built up a body of law that, eventually, came to be interpreted and explained by jurisconsults, men learned in the law.

Rome's army was second to none in antiquity. It never lost a battle in which it faced an enemy on even terms. Rome's weapons included swords, daggers, pikes, spears, maces, and bows. Defensively, Roman soldiers sported shields, helmets, and body armor consisting of woven iron mail. The Romans used two types of artillery: one hurled huge spears and the other stones.

Rome's greatest advantage, however, came from its deployment of manpower. The Greek phalanx met the enemy as one massed unit. Roman legions were divided into thirty maniples ("handfuls") that were subdivided into sixty centuries. The Roman army was adaptable and maneuverable regardless of the terrain or the disposition of the enemy.

Figure 5.22 Calendar Mosaic. Late second to early third century CE. From the Maison des Mois at El Djem. Detail of 5 × 4′ mosaic. Sousse Museum, Sousse, Tunisia. The El Djem Calendar comprises twelve small scenes, each representing a month, the name of which is inscribed in Latin. The Roman year began with March (top middle) and ended with February (top left corner). The months are symbolized by either religious or rural activities, such as in the September panel, which shows two figures standing in a vat crushing grapes.

SUMMARY

The Romans conquered Italy, next the western Mediterranean region, and then the Hellenistic East. Their progress was slow and steady and not without setbacks. While building a vast empire, the Romans also developed a democratic, republican constitution. For more than three centuries that constitution proved stable and workable, but eventually war, New Men, and foreign ideas weakened the traditional Roman system and, amid civil wars, the republic collapsed. Into the breach stepped Augustus Caesar, who inaugurated a new regime, the principate, that gave the Roman world two centuries of peace, good government, and prosperity. Augustus's genius was cloaking a military dictatorship in a mantle of republican institutions and values.

Roman culture grew slowly from native roots and Hellenistic fertilization. The earliest Roman drama and poetry was decidedly Hellenistic, but by the time of Augustus the Roman voice was increasingly heard. The Roman ethos fancied itself stern, austere, serious, and purposeful. All of this was true to a degree, but the Romans knew how to enjoy themselves and their taste for satire proves that they liked a good joke. Cities, roads, and aqueducts put Roman skill and practicality on display. The Romans did, however, have a fine aesthetic sense as their eager imitation of the best in Greek art readily demonstrates. For centuries all roads did indeed lead to Rome, although one Roman comic complained that the world's scum washed up in the Tiber!

The Legacy of Classical Rome

The Greeks gave us the words *politics* and *political*, but most of the rest of our political vocabulary is Roman: senate, caucus, committee, and quorum, for example. Russian czar is simply Caesar. What Polybius called a balanced or mixed constitution, we call the separation of powers. Where the Declaration of Independence says "we hold these truths to be self evident," that is natural law, Roman style. Fascists took their name from the *fasces*, the bundle of rods surmounted by an ax carried in front of Roman politicians in public processions. Modern states, for example Hitler's Germany at the Nuremberg rallies, imitated Roman triumphal processions. Thomas Jefferson's love for all things Roman can be seen to this day on the Grounds of his University of Virginia and in Virginia's state capitol. St. Peter's basilica in Rome and St. Paul's in London are based on the Pantheon. Virtually all the *autoroutes* or *autostrade*— what we call interstates—in modern Europe sit on top of Roman roads. The sublime poet Dante took Virgil as his guide and Tennyson, who knew a thing or two about poetry, called him "wielder of the stateliest measure ever molded by the lips of man." Seneca influenced Shakespeare. Rome's satires inspired, to name just a few authors, Erasmus, Cervantes, Molière, Swift, Voltaire, Poe, and Twain. Classic films, such as *Three Coins in the Fountain* and *Roman Holiday*, take the eternal city as their background. But ancient Rome inspired *Cleopatra* in the 1960s and in *Gladiator* and *Spartacus* recently. PBS ran a popular series on Rome in 2005. Patronage retains its place in both arts and politics.

The Rotunda, University of Virginia, 1822–1826. Designed by Thomas Jefferson, the Rotunda was the last building constructed in the original "Academical Village." It is a one-half scale model of the Pantheon in Rome, 72 feet in diameter. It even has a 14-foot oculus.

KEY CULTURAL TERMS

Etruscans	principate	keystone	mural
res publica	Pax Romana	vault	tempera
patricians	satire	barrel vault	mosaic
plebeians	pantomime	groined vault (cross vault)	natural law
senate	ashlar	oculus	
paterfamilias	voussoir	forum	

Christian Good Shepherd. Second century CE. Marble, ht. 39″. Vatican Museum.

Judaism and the Rise of Christianity

Preview Questions

1. *What* were the major stages in the historical development of ancient Israel?

2. *How* do written and material evidence combine to reveal the history of Israel?

3. *What* were the central teachings of Christianity?

4. *How* do written and material evidence reveal Christianity's relationship to classical culture?

The Egyptians, Mesopotamians, Greeks, and Romans made significant and enduring contributions to the unfolding Western tradition. At the height of their power, they were often identified by their political and governmental structures—kingdoms, city-states, or empires—and historians have described them in terms of their states. However, the Western tradition has also been shaped and enriched by peoples who did not establish kingdoms or empires, but whose ideas and beliefs have survived to the present day. The first of these people were the Hebrews, the second, early Christians. Henceforth, *the Western humanities* constitutes a blend of the Greco-Roman and of the Judeo-Christian traditions.

In comparison to their surrounding neighbors, the Hebrews were, indeed, small in number and exerted little political or economic dominance. Yet they formulated and preserved a unique religious experience and tradition that has been active and influential for nearly three thousand years. The early Christians emerged in a Jewish milieu, spread across the Roman world, and came to be the single official faith of the empire in the fourth century CE.

Judaism, the religion of the Hebrews, was affected by nearby tribes and kingdoms while Christianity, original in many ways, owed much to Judaism and to its surrounding classical world. Their similarities and differences regarding depictions of God can be seen in the image of the Good Shepherd. Hebrews were absolutely forbidden to depict their God. Early Christians inherited this Jewish prohibition, but soon began to circumvent this aversion by adopting symbolic images. The Good Shepherd clearly represented Christ but certainly was not meant to *be* him. The image is a metaphorical, not a physical, representation. The Hebrew scriptures often refer to God as a shepherd, and the Christians, who retained those scriptures as the Old Testament, frequently referred to Jesus Christ as a shepherd in their scriptures, the New Testament. The statue is of high quality. Its patron is unknown but must have been a person of some standing and

Timeline 6.1   JEWISH CIVILIZATION

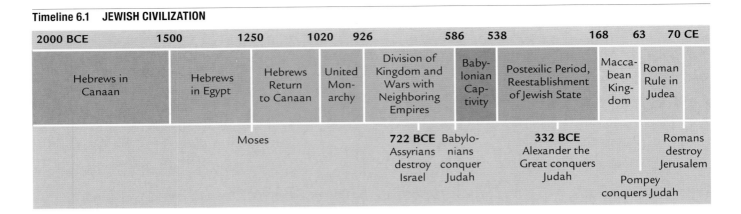

substance to commission the work. The image is reminiscent of the works of Praxiteles, the renowned Greek sculptor—in sum, a biblical image in classical form.

The Jews and the early Christians were also connected in their use of a common language—Greek. The Jews adopted the Greek of the Hellenistic world to communicate with one another after being scattered by their political foes. Early Christians used Greek from the start to disseminate their message across the Roman Empire. Jewish and Christian writings reveal evident borrowings of both words and ideas from their surrounding world. Like the statue as a connection of the two faiths, Judaism and Christianity speak old words in a new world and new words in an old world.

JUDAISM

Judaism is one of the oldest religions in the world. It originated in the third millennium BCE among a tribal Middle Eastern people who placed themselves at the center of world history and created sacred texts for passing on their heritage. Unlike the history and religion of other ancient peoples, the history and religion of the Jews are so inextricably connected that they cannot be separated.

The People and Their Religion

Around 2000 BCE, Akkadian rule collapsed and Babylonian power slowly emerged. Among many displaced tribes the Hebrews were the most significant historically. Under their patriarch Abraham, the oldest and most respected male leader, they migrated from Sumer to the land of Canaan, which included parts of what are now Israel and Lebanon. Abraham and his people were primarily pastoralists but also engaged in some trade (Timeline 6.1). The Hebrews considered themselves unique, a belief based on the relationship between Abraham and a supernatural being who spoke to him and whom he obeyed. This deity made a **covenant,** or solemn agreement (the outward sign of which was the circumcision of all male children), with

Abraham to protect his family and bring prosperity to his offspring if they agreed to obey his divine commands. Although this Hebrew deity was associated with nature, he differed from other Mesopotamian deities in his commitment to justice and righteousness. He was an ethical god and sought to impose ethical principles on humans (Map 6.1).

Egypt, Exodus, and Moses   The Hebrews prospered for decades in Canaan, but around 1500 BCE, in a time of famine, a group migrated south into the more prosperous Egypt, which had recently been overrun by the Hyksos, a Semitic people with whom the Hebrews shared language and cultural traits. The Hebrews thrived over the next few centuries, until the Egyptians overthrew the Hyksos and enslaved the Hebrews. In about 1250 BCE, the extraordinary leader Moses rallied the Hebrews and led them on the Exodus from Egypt—one of the most significant events in Jewish history. As the Hebrews wandered in the desert on the Sinai peninsula, Moses molded his followers into a unified people under a set of ethical and societal laws, which they believed were received from God. After forty years of wandering, followed by Moses's death, the Hebrews finally returned to Canaan, the Promised Land pledged by Yahweh to their forefathers.

The laws of Moses were unique among ancient peoples because they were grounded in the covenant between the Hebrews and God and because no distinction was made between religious and secular offenses. All crimes were seen as sins and all sins as crimes. Those who committed crimes could not simply make reparation to their victims; they also had to seek forgiveness from God. There were some crimes, such as murder, that were so offensive to God that they could not be forgiven by human beings alone. Furthermore, human life was seen as sacred because it was given by God, who created and owned all things; individual humans were precious because they were made in God's image.

The core of Mosaic law was the Ten Commandments, which set forth the proper behavior of human

Learning Through Maps

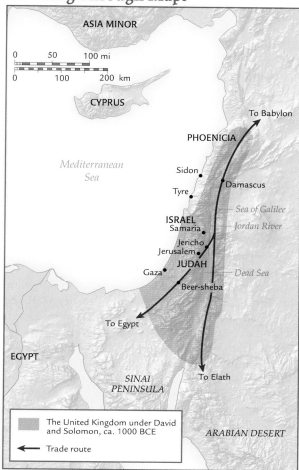

ASIA MINOR

0   50   100 mi

0   100   200 km

CYPRUS

Mediterranean Sea

PHOENICIA

To Babylon

Sidon

Tyre

Damascus

Sea of Galilee

ISRAEL
Samaria

Jordan River

Jericho
Jerusalem

JUDAH

Gaza

Dead Sea

Beer-sheba

To Egypt

EGYPT

SINAI PENINSULA

To Elath

ARABIAN DESERT

The United Kingdom under David and Solomon, ca. 1000 BCE

Trade route

MAP 6.1   ANCIENT ISRAEL

This map shows the Hebrews' ancient kingdom, known as the United Monarchy, forged by the rulers David and his son Solomon. The map also shows the kingdoms of Israel and Judah, the two Hebrew states that emerged when the United Monarchy split on the death of Solomon, in 926 BCE.   *1. Locate* the capitals of these two kingdoms. *2. How* was the cultural life and religious faith of the nation of Israel influenced by foreign neighbors? *3. What* impact did Israel's size and location have on its history and religious faith? *4. Notice* the scale of the map and compare it to the scale of Map 5.2, The Roman Empire under Hadrian.

TABLE 6.1   THE TEN COMMANDMENTS

1. You shall have no other gods before me.
2. You shall not make for yourself a graven image, or any likeness of any thing that is in heaven above, or that is on the earth beneath, or that is in the water under the earth. . . .
3. You shall not take the name of the Lord your God in vain. . . .
4. Observe the sabbath day, to keep it holy, as the Lord your God commanded you. . . .
5. Honor your father and your mother. . . .
6. You shall not kill.
7. Neither shall you commit adultery.
8. Neither shall you steal.
9. Neither shall you bear false witness against your neighbor.
10. Neither shall you covet your neighbor's wife . . . or anything that is your neighbor's.

Source: The Bible, Revised Standard Version, Deuteronomy 5:6–21.

Figure 6.1   Stone Menorah. Second century CE. Ht. 18″. Israel Museum, Jerusalem. Although this particular menorah dates from the second century CE, the seven-branched candelabrum had been in use as a religious symbol for centuries. According to Jewish beliefs, God gave Moses explicit instructions on how to craft the menorah, which was made for the tabernacle, or house of prayer. Later the menorah came to symbolize knowledge and understanding as well as the light of God protecting the Jews.

beings (Table 6.1). The commandments became the basis of a renewed covenant. The Hebrew God tolerated no rivals; he was seen as the sole, omnipotent creator and ruler of the universe. If individuals followed his laws and worshiped him alone, they would be rewarded, and if they strayed, they would be punished. Likewise, if the people followed the divine commands, they would prosper, and if they disobeyed, they would meet with adversity. As the mediator of the covenant between God and the Hebrew people, Moses played a crucial role in shaping Judaism into a comprehensive system of ethical **monotheism,** the belief that there is only one God and that God demands a high standard of personal and societal behavior.

As they wandered through the Sinai desert, the Hebrews carried with them a sacred decorated box called the Ark of the Covenant. Within it were the stone tablets on which the Ten Commandments were carved. Details of how to craft the Ark and all the other sacred objects used in worship were dictated to Moses by God (Figure 6.1). In the desert, the deity also revealed a new name for himself—YHWH, a name so sacred that pious Jews never speak or write it. In the Middle Ages, European scholars rendered YHWH as Jehovah, but today

TABLE 6.2 HISTORICAL STAGES OF THE TEMPLE IN JERUSALEM

NAME	CONSTRUCTION DETAILS	DATE DESTROYED
Solomon's Temple. Also called First Temple.	Completed under King Solomon, 957 BCE.	587/586 BCE, by the Babylonians.
Second Temple. Also called Herod's Temple after being rebuilt in 26 CE.	Completed 515 BCE. Rebuilt at order of King Herod (d. 4 BCE) between 20 BCE and 26 CE.	70 CE, by the Romans. A section of the Western Wall (also called the Wailing Wall) survived; it was incorporated into the wall around the Muslim Dome of the Rock and al-Aqsa mosque in 691 CE.

this term is generally considered a false reading of the sacred letters. In modern English, YHWH is usually rendered as Yahweh. In biblical times, Jewish priests called the deity Adonai, the Semitic term for Lord.

The Kingdom of Israel   In about 1000 BCE, the Hebrews established a monarchy, and from the late eleventh century to the end of the tenth century BCE, the nation flourished under a series of kings—Saul, David, and Solomon. The people called themselves Hebrews to distinguish themselves from others while others called them Israelites. The popular king David centralized the government and shifted the economy away from herding and toward commerce, trade, and farming.

Solomon, David's son, brought the Hebrew, or Israelite, kingdom to its pinnacle of power and prestige. He signed treaties with other states, expanded Israel's trade across the Middle East, and raised the standard of living for many of his subjects. He completed the building of Jerusalem begun by David, which, with its magnificent public structures and great temple, rivaled the glory of other Middle Eastern cities. The Temple of Solomon, also known as the First Temple, housed Israel's holy relics, including the Ark of the Covenant, and became the focal point of the nation's religion, which required pilgrimages and rituals, based on the religious calendar (Table 6.2; Figure 6.2). The Hebrew religion required ritual offerings (sacrifices of animals on large altars and wine, incense, and grain mixed with oil on small altars) twice daily. These offerings were conducted by priests in the Temple in Jerusalem as a community ritual for the entire Hebrew nation; individuals could also arrange for sacrifices to be made on their own behalf.

Figure 6.2   Horned Altar. Tenth century BCE. Carved limestone, ht. 26½″. The Oriental Institute of The University of Chicago. Middle Eastern peoples made sacrifices to their deities on altars, but the small horned altar, as pictured here, was unique to the Hebrews. Horned altars are described in the Bible, especially as a ritual object in the Temple in Jerusalem, built in the tenth century BCE. However, this horned altar was discovered at Megiddo, one of the cities of the Hebrew kingdom. Originally, then, sacrifices could be performed away from the Temple in Jerusalem.

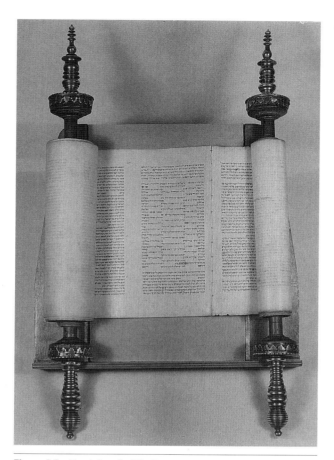

Figure 6.3 Torah Scroll of the Pentateuch. Nuremberg, 1700–1751. Johann Conrad Weiss. Ink on vellum, staves, wood with silver, cast and engraved. The Jewish Museum, New York. The ancient Hebrews recorded their scriptures on parchment scrolls. The scroll of the Pentateuch was wound on two staves. The scrolls were not decorated or illuminated with designs, animals, or humans because the Bible forbade any likeness of Yahweh and artistic expressions were not encouraged. However, some sacred books were illustrated and ornamented at various stages of Hebrew history. The carved staves on which the Pentateuch was wound were often embellished. Evidence exists that by the fifth century CE, the scrolls might have been encased in a container of precious metal, and by the fifteenth century, they were enclosed in containers adorned with reliefs and Hebrew lettering.

King Solomon was a patron of literature and the arts, and under his rule Hebrew culture expanded, notably in law, writing, music, and dance. As the Hebrews' oral traditions gave way to written records, Hebrew authors wrote down their laws and their earliest histories, which are preserved in the first books of the Bible (Figure 6.3). These Hebrew works predate by five centuries the writings of the great Greek historians Herodotus and Thucydides, but, unlike the Greek writers, the Hebrew historians made God the central force in human history and thus transformed the unfolding of earthly events into a moral drama portraying God's relationship with his chosen people.

Solomon's achievements came at a heavy price, for they undermined his people's religious foundations, intensified class divisions, and tended to divide the northern and southern tribes. When Solomon died in 926 BCE, the tensions between the regions intensified and the United Monarchy separated into two states: Israel in the north, with its capital at Samaria, and Judah in the south, with its capital at Jerusalem.

During the period of the two Hebrew kingdoms, a new type of religious leader, known as a prophet, appeared. The prophets warned of the fatal consequences of breaking Yahweh's commandments. They also demanded social justice for the helpless and the downtrodden. In the face of a widening gulf between rich and poor, the prophets predicted that if the well-off did not aid the less fortunate, Yahweh would bring down the evil rulers and, in the future, punish the selfish and reward the sufferers. But the words of the prophets, such as Hosea and Amos in Israel and Isaiah and Jeremiah in Judah, seemed to go unheeded.

The Babylonian Captivity and the Postexilic Period In 722 BCE, the tiny nation of Israel was destroyed by the Assyrians. Judah, to the south, endured for another one hundred fifty years, but in 586 BCE, the Babylonians conquered Judah, destroying Solomon's Temple in Jerusalem and deporting most of the Hebrews to Babylonia. The approximately forty years of exile, known as the Babylonian Captivity, became one of the major turning points in Jewish history.

At the end of the sixth century, the Jews (Jew comes from Hebrew *yehudi* [yeh-HU-dee] meaning "Judaean" via the Greek *iudaios* and Latin *Judaeus;* after the exile, Jew tended to displace both Israelite and Hebrew) were freed by the triumphant Persians, who were sweeping across the ancient world under Cyrus (see Chapter 2). Returning to Judah, the Jews rebuilt Jerusalem including their Temple, now known as the Second Temple. Believing that God had rescued them, they established a theocratic state—a government ruled by those who are recognized as having special divine guidance and approval—and dedicated themselves to the correct formulation and observation of their religious beliefs. Many exiles remained outside the homeland and became known as Jews of the **Diaspora,** or the Dispersion.

After their return from Babylon, the Jews expanded their views of Yahweh. Some of them at least came to view their faith as universal and not restricted to the Jews. The Hebrews' earlier perception of themselves as a chosen people under a universal deity was reinforced as they concluded that Yahweh had used the Persians to free them. Furthermore, the Jews started to incorporate two new features into their religion: **eschatology,** or the concern with the end of the world, and an interest in **apocalypse,** prophecies about the coming of God and a day of judgment. This future world would be led by a **Messiah,** or Anointed One, who would bring peace and justice to all. Perhaps

Figure 6.4   Model of the Reconstructed Second Temple (Herod's Temple) in Jerusalem. This model of the Second Temple shows the strong influence of Hellenistic-style architecture, particularly in the colonnaded arcades, the decorative frieze, and the tall, slender Corinthian columns flanking the main entryway. The Second Temple was destroyed by Roman legions in 70 CE, but one wall was left standing.

influenced by the dualism of Persian Zoroastrianism, Jews began to differentiate heaven and hell as places of reward and punishment.

The Hellenistic and Roman Periods   Alexander the Great conquered Judah in 332 BCE, and after his death the area became part of the Seleucid kingdom, centered in Syria. Hellenistic culture and ideas proliferated and deeply affected Jewish life. Growing tensions between the Jews and the Hellenistic leaders erupted in 168 BCE when the Seleucid king Antiochus IV tried to impose the worship of Greek gods on the Jews, placing a statue of Zeus in the Second Temple in Jerusalem. Antiochus's violation of the sacred place enraged the Maccabean clan, whose inspired leadership and bravery led to a successful revolt and the recapture of the Second Temple. The Maccabean family ruled Judah as an independent commonwealth for approximately one hundred years. Then, in 63 BCE, the Romans conquered most of the Middle East. They subsequently incorporated Judah (in what was now called Palestine) into their empire as Judea and placed the Jewish lands under client kings (loyal, pliable dependents).

The Romans ruled through the Jewish Herodian dynasty. Herod the Great, who ruled from 37 to 4 BCE, rebuilt Jerusalem, including the Second Temple, and promoted Hellenistic culture (Figure 6.4). But conditions under the Romans became unbearable to the Jews, and in 66 CE a rebellion broke out. After the First Jewish War (66–70), the Romans captured Jerusalem and destroyed the Second Temple. The Western Wall, or Wailing Wall, of the Second Temple in Jerusalem remained standing and came to symbolize the plight of the Jewish people (Figure 6.5). A revolutionary group known as Zealots held out until 73 at Masada, a sheer-sided mesa on the shores of the Dead Sea (Figure 6.6).

Figure 6.5   The Western Wall today. The Western Wall, sometimes called the Wailing Wall, is the sole remaining structure of the temple erected by Herod the Great. When Muslims conquered Jerusalem in the seventh century, the Western Wall became the buttress of the former temple mount, the *Haram es-Sherif* (the "Noble Sanctuary"), on which two important mosques—Muslim houses of worship—were constructed. Jews from all over the world come to pray at the Western Wall.

SLICE OF LIFE

A Jewish Eyewitness to the Destruction of the Second Temple

Flavius Josephus
A JEWISH SOLDIER IN THE ROMAN ARMY

The Jewish historian Josephus (about 37–100 CE) was an eyewitness to one of the darkest days in Jewish history: the destruction of the Second Temple in Jerusalem on September 8, 70 CE. He became an admiring, though sometimes reluctant, soldier in the Roman cause. Assigned to General Titus, he was among the troops that sacked and burned the temple on that fateful day. The following account is taken from Josephus's History of the Jewish War *(75–79 CE).*

At this moment one of the [Roman] soldiers, not waiting for orders and without any dread of such an act but driven on by some frenzy, snatched a brand from the blazing fire and, lifted up by a comrade, hurled the torch through the golden door which gave access to the buildings of the Temple Precinct from the north side. As the flames surged up, a great cry to match their feelings arose from the Jews, and they rushed to the defence, reckless of their lives and prodigal of their strength once they saw that the purpose of their previous watch was gone. . . .

As the fire gained strength, Titus found that he could not restrain the surge of his enthusiastic soldiers. . . .

Most were driven on by the hope of loot, for they thought that the inside of the building must be full of money if the outside, which they could see, was made of gold. One of those who had got in forestalled the attempts of Titus, who had rushed in to check them, and hurled a brand against the hinges of the door. Suddenly flames appeared from within, which forced back Titus and his officers, leaving those outside to kindle the blaze unhindered. In this way, though much against Titus's will, the Temple was burnt. . . .

Interpreting This Slice of Life

1. *What* was the source of conflict between the Romans and the Jews?
2. *Do* you find Josephus's account credible, given that he was both a Jew and a Roman soldier?
3. *What* role does General Titus play in the assault?
4. *How* are the Roman soldiers depicted?
5. *How* does Josephus depict the Jewish rebels?

Figure 6.6   Masada, Israel. This outcropping of rock in the forbidding terrain outside Jerusalem was a natural fortress. King Herod had built one of his palace-fortresses here in the years just before the birth of Christ. For three years the Zealots occupied its ruins, holding out against the Romans after the end of the First Jewish War in 70 CE.

When their cause became hopeless, they committed suicide rather than surrender to the Romans.

To make sure the Jews would no longer be a problem for the Romans, the Roman government in the late first century CE ordered the dispersal of the Jews throughout the empire. However, this second Diaspora did not end the Jews' cultural, intellectual, and religious existence. On the contrary, the Jewish way of life continued, though it changed. With the fall of the Temple in Jerusalem, Jews worshiped in synagogues, or congregations, which eventually were headed by rabbis, or teachers. Over the centuries, the rabbis' teachings evolved into Rabbinic Judaism, based on the Torah and the Talmud (from Hebrew, "learning"), a collection of legal rulings and commentaries. Rabbinic Judaism established a mode of worship and moral code that Jews worldwide have followed down to modern times.

Societal and Family Relationships   To be a Jew one had to be born of a Jewish mother, yet Hebrew society was patriarchal. Of 1,426 people named in the Hebrew Bible, 1,315 are male. Only males could bear the sign of God's covenant—circumcision. Women could not own or inherit property, sue in court, or initiate a divorce. Women could not enter the temple; they worshiped in a courtyard outside. The Hebrew religion had no goddesses. Nevertheless, the Bible recounts stories of numerous brave, clever, and wise women. Men were in principle equals but there is plenty of evidence for wide divisions in wealth, status, and power. Generally, Hebrew society had much in common with that of its neighbors. It was in religion where the Hebrews were different.

The Bible

The Jews enshrined their cultural developments in the Bible, their collection of sacred writings, or **scriptures.** Known as the Old Testament to Christians, the Hebrew Bible (from the Greek word for "book") contains history, law, poetry, songs, stories, prayers, and philosophical works. Evolving out of a rich and long oral tradition, parts of the Bible probably began to assume written form during the United Monarchy in the tenth century BCE. By then the Hebrews had an alphabet, which, like that of the Greeks, was probably derived from the Phoenicians. Having acquired a written language and a unified political state, the Hebrews shared a consciousness of their past and desired to preserve it. They assembled and recorded various historical accounts, songs, and stories, plus the sayings of the prophets. Sometime in the fifth century BCE, Jewish scholars and religious leaders canonized (declared official) parts of these writings as divinely inspired. They became the first five books of the Bible, known as the Torah or the Pentateuch. The Hebrew Bible's ultimate form was reached in 90 CE when a council of Jewish rabbis added a last set of writings to the **canon.**

Another important development in the transmission of the Hebrew scriptures was their translation into other languages. In the third century BCE, after many Jews had been influenced by Hellenistic culture, a group of Alexandrian scholars collected all the authenticated Jewish writings and translated them into Greek. This Hebrew Greek Bible was called the Septuagint, from the Latin word for "seventy," so named because of the legend that it was translated by seventy scholars.

The final version of the Hebrew Bible is divided into three parts: the Law, the Prophets, and the Writings (Table 6.3). (Christians divide the Old Testament into four parts.) The Law, also called the Torah (from Hebrew, "instruction"), recounts the story of God's creation of the world and the early history of the Hebrews. More important, it details the establishment of the covenant and the foundation of the moral and ritualistic codes of personal and societal behavior that underlie Judaism.

The Prophets recount a good deal of historical material but above all are full of moral and spiritual instruction. They reflect constantly on the Torah and reminded the Hebrews when they failed to keep their covenant with God and where they treated each other poorly. Disasters, the Prophets say, are divine rebukes. The Writings reflect diverse viewpoints and contain many types of literature, including poetry, wise sayings, stories, and apocalyptic visions of the end of time. Some of these books, such as Job, Ecclesiastes, and Proverbs, reflect in both style and content the influence of other cultures on Jewish beliefs.

There is also a body of Jewish literature outside the canon. The Apocrypha are books written between 200 BCE and 100 CE that include wisdom, literature, stories, and history, including the history of the Maccabees. Though not part of the Jewish canon, these books were included in the Septuagint, the Greek translation of the Hebrew Bible, and accepted by the Roman Catholic Church as part of the Christian Old Testament.

Early Jewish Architecture and Art

The description of the Temple in 1 Kings makes it sound similar to the "long-house" temples found in other civilizations of that time and probably indicated the influence of foreign neighbors. According to the Bible, Solomon's Temple was a rectangular building comprising a porch; a sanctuary, or main hall; and an inner sanctum that housed the Ark of the Covenant. Artists and craftspeople decorated the interior with carvings of floral designs and cherubs, highlighting these with gold. The building was made of ashlars, and two large freestanding columns were placed at the entryway. The Temple may have been raised on a platform. A court surrounded the Temple, and a large altar stood inside the court.

TABLE 6.3 BOOKS OF THE HEBREW BIBLE AND THE CHRISTIAN BIBLE OLD TESTAMENT

HEBREW BIBLE		CHRISTIAN BIBLE OLD TESTAMENT	
The Law (Torah)		*The Pentateuch*	
Genesis	Numbers	Genesis	Numbers
Exodus	Deuteronomy	Exodus	Deuteronomy
Leviticus		Leviticus	
The Prophets		*The Historical Books*	
(Early Prophets)		Joshua	2 Chronicles
Joshua	2 Samuel	Judges	Ezra
Judges	1 Kings	Ruth	Nehemiah
1 Samuel	2 Kings	1 Samuel	Tobit*
(Later Prophets)		2 Samuel	Judith*
Isaiah	Micah	1 Kings	Esther
Jeremiah	Nahum	2 Kings	1 Maccabees*
Ezekiel	Habakkuk	1 Chronicles	2 Maccabees*
Hosea	Zephaniah		
Joel	Haggai	*The Poetical or Wisdom Books*	
Amos	Zechariah	Job	
Obadiah	Malachi	Psalms	
Jonah		Proverbs	
		Ecclesiastes	
The Writings		Song of Solomon (Songs)	
Psalms	Esther	Wisdom*	
Proverbs	Daniel	Sirach*	
Job	Ezra		
Song of Songs	Nehemiah	*The Prophetical Books*	
Ruth	1 Chronicles	Isaiah	Obadiah
Lamentations	2 Chronicles	Jeremiah	Jonah
Ecclesiastes		Lamentations	Micah
		Baruch*	Nahum
		Ezekiel	Habakkuk
		Daniel	Zephaniah
		Hosea	Haggai
		Joel	Zechariah
		Amos	Malachi

*Roman Catholics include these books in the canon and refer to them as deutero-canonical ("secondary canon"); Protestants sometimes place them in an appendix with other Apocrypha.

When the Jews were released from the Babylonian Captivity by the Persians, they returned to their homeland and built the Second Temple in the late sixth century BCE. It exhibited a simpler design and decoration scheme than did Solomon's Temple. Meanwhile, the Jews of the Diaspora gathered in Hellenistic cities to read the Torah and to pray in buildings that became synagogues, or houses of worship. No record survives of how these synagogues looked or how they might have been decorated until the third century CE.

Greek influences became apparent in Jewish architecture during Hellenistic times. One Maccabean ruler, John Hyrcanus [hear-KAY-nuhs] (135–106 BCE),

constructed a fortress-palace at present-day Araq el Emir in Jordan that shows this influence clearly. The facade of the palace blended Greek columns and oriental carvings, typical of the Alexandrian architectural and decorative style. The edifice and its carvings were probably similar to the Second Temple in Jerusalem. One of the few decorations remaining from this palace is a lion fountain (Figure 6.7). Carved in high relief, the lion is well proportioned and conveys a sense of power with its raised front paw and open mouth.

The lingering influence of late Greek architecture on Jewish structures is also seen in a set of tombs dug out of the soft limestone rocks east of Jerusalem in the

Figure 6.7   Lion Fountain at the Palace of John Hyrcanus. Second century BCE. Araq el Emir, Jordan. This lion, Greco-Oriental in style, was carved deeply into the stone's surface to create a high-relief work. The lion's tail, wrapped around its right rear leg, is balanced by the raised left front leg, creating a feeling of strength and agility.

Figure 6.8   Tomb of Bene Hezir. Early first century BCE. Kidron Valley, Israel. The tomb of Bene Hezir (on the left) shows the influence of Greek architecture in its post-and-lintel construction and its Doric columns. Even though the area was subject to Roman impact at this time, Roman influence is not apparent in the architecture. Priests from the Hezir family, as recorded in 1 Chronicles 24, were buried in what has been determined to be the oldest tomb in Israel's Kidron Valley. Scholars disagree over whether the structure in the center with the pyramidal roof belonged to the tomb of Bene Hezir.

Kidron Valley. According to the inscription on them, these tombs contain the remains of priests from the Hezir family (Figure 6.8). The tomb on the left displays Doric columns, and the one in the center fuses Greek Ionic columns and an Egyptian pyramidal roof. Several other tombs in the vicinity reveal a similar melding of styles.

During the reign of King Herod the Great (r. 37–4 BCE), architecture in Judea exhibited a further mix of Greek styles with Jewish motifs. King Herod's magnificent fortress-palace at Masada may have been a conscious blending of the two cultures in an effort to bridge the gap between the Roman and Jewish worlds (see Figure 6.6). The various buildings in Herod's complex contained many representative Greco-Roman features, including fluted Corinthian columns and marble facings (Figure 6.9).

The Second Commandment forbade graven images, which meant cult images that could be worshiped. Jews always observed this prohibition strictly. The commandment also forbade "likenesses"—a prohibition that has been understood in different ways from antiquity to the present. Clearly, no cult images were permitted in any circumstances. But as noted there were images in the Temple and, in several places in the Hebrew Bible, God commanded images to be made. The surviving lion from John Hyrcanus's palace cannot have been the only likeness in that place. Whatever else there may have been has vanished along with everything else from earlier centuries. The palace of Herod at Masada had beautiful geometric designs

Figure 6.9   Hall of Herod's North Palace. Late first century BCE. Masada, Israel. These Corinthian columns were originally plastered over and painted. Carved directly out of the hill's rock, they formed a natural corridor around the banqueting hall. Herod built this and other splendid palaces to impress the Jews and win their political sympathy, but he failed to do either.

(Figure 6.10), but no likenesses of humans or animals survive. From the middle of the third century, however, at Dura Europos in upper Mesopotamia, there survive the ruins of a magnificent synagogue that had beautiful figural images depicting many scenes from the scriptures (Figures 6.11 and 6.12). A Jewish catacomb in Rome has images from the same period. By the end of the fifth century CE, a floor mosaic from the synagogue Hammam Lif in Tunisia shows in another medium the capacity of Jewish artists to create images that were beautiful, inspiring, and related to the scriptures (Figure 6.13). The so-called "Exodus Prohibition" may have put a damper on Jewish figural art but did not completely prevent it.

Figure 6.10   Mosaic from Herod's Palace. Late first century BCE. Masada, Israel. The Greek practice of mosaic making was adopted by both the Romans and the Jews. The patterned designs around the borders of this mosaic from Herod's Palace are typically Greek, and the organic image in the center is typically Jewish.

Figure 6.11 *Moses Giving Water to the Twelve Tribes of Israel.* **Fresco. Synagogue. 240s CE. Dura Europos, Syria. Reconstructed in the National Museum, Damascus, Syria.** This fresco is from a house-synagogue (a place of worship set up within a private residence) that was discovered in the early twentieth century, after having been filled with rubble in 256 CE, as part of a defense plan for the city of Dura Europos. Only sections of the walls survive. The room featured benches running around the walls and a niche for the Torah scrolls in the western wall. The paintings depict various events from the Hebrew Bible, most having to do with national salvation, such as Samuel Anointing David, the Ark Brought to Jerusalem, and the Exodus from Egypt. Painted by anonymous artists, these works were executed in tempera, a medium made of pigments blended with egg yolks and water, applied to dry plaster. This fresco was part of the Exodus group and was based on Numbers 2:2–12. It portrays Moses seated and holding a staff, as he delivers life-giving water (via "tubes") to the tribes, symbolized by twelve huts, each with a single figure. A menorah stands in the center rear.

Figure 6.12   Scenes from the Western Wall, Synagogue of Dura Europos, Syria. 240s CE. National Museum, Damascus. In the center of the wall is the Torah shrine, the place where the Torah rolls were kept, above which is a representation of the Temple—long since destroyed—and of a menorah (left) and the sacrifice of Isaac (right). Spreading across the whole wall is a beautiful, and exceedingly well accomplished, set of images representing key scenes from the Hebrew Bible.

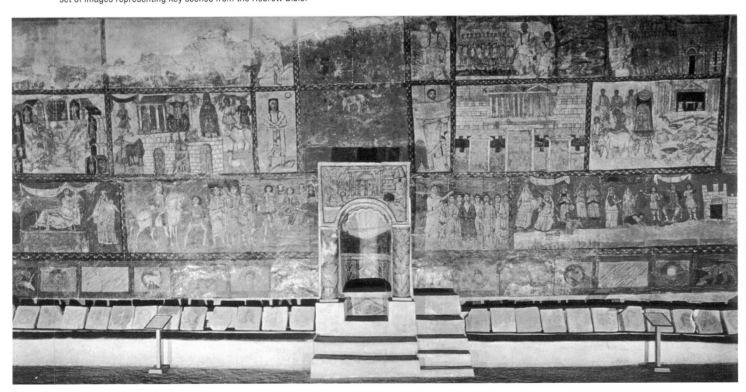

Figure 6.13   Mosaic of a Duck Enclosed in a Vine Scroll. Fourth to fifth century CE. 34^1/$_2$ × 33^1/$_{16}$″. From the Floor of a Synagogue at Hammam Lif, Tunisia. Brooklyn Museum. Ducks could symbolize wealth, good fortune, or a clever person. This image represents one panel from a floor mosaic that had numerous images of plants, birds, other animals, and Jewish symbols, such as a menorah.

CHRISTIANITY

The rise of Christianity was as surprising in the short term as it was important in the long term. The wandering teacher Jesus Christ was neither rich nor powerful, but he attracted followers who eventually took his teachings throughout the Roman world and beyond. Originally a sect within Judaism, Christianity gradually emerged as a distinct religion. One measure of the historical impact of Christianity lies in the way dates have been marked in the Western world.

The period before Jesus's birth is known as BC, or "before Christ," and the era after his birth is termed AD, or *anno Domini,* Latin words meaning "in the year of the Lord," the title of respect given to Jesus by Christians. Although Christianity and the church have declined from their zenith in the Middle Ages, the Christian calendar remains in effect throughout the West as well as in many other parts of the world—a symbol of the continuing power of this creed. In this textbook, reflecting today's multicultural world, the term BCE, "before common era," replaces BC, and the term CE, "common era," replaces AD.

The Life of Jesus Christ and the New Testament

The surviving primary sources for the origin of Christianity are writings in Greek by early believers who were openly partisan. According to them, Christianity began within the Jewish faith among the followers of Jesus, a deeply pious and charismatic Jew who ended up founding a dynamic new religion instead of renewing Judaism.

Jesus was born to Mary and Joseph in Judea in about 4 BCE (a date that reflects errors in early Christian time-reckoning). After narrating the events surrounding his birth, the accounts of Jesus's life are almost silent until he reaches the age of about thirty, when he commenced a teaching mission that placed him squarely in conflict with prevailing Jewish beliefs and authorities. Jews of various social classes heard Jesus's message, and he soon had a small group of followers who believed that he was the Messiah, the Anointed One who would deliver the Jews, promised by God to the prophets. He was also termed the Christ, taken from the Greek for "the anointed one." Performing miracles and healing the sick, he preached that the Kingdom of God was at hand. Neither then nor now has it been easy to say just what Jesus meant by "Kingdom of God," but to prepare for it he urged his followers to practice a demanding and loving ethic.

Growing discord between the Jewish establishment and this messianic band caused Roman leaders to classify Jesus as a political rebel. In about 33 CE, he was crucified by the Romans (Timeline 6.2). Three days later, some of his followers reported that Jesus had risen from the dead and reappeared among them. His resurrection became the ultimate miracle associated with his teachings, the sign that immortal life awaited those who believed in him as the son of God and as the Messiah. After forty days, Jesus ascended into heaven, though not before pledging to return when the world came to an end.

The outline of Jesus's life is set forth in the first three books, called **Gospels,** of the Christian scriptures. The early Christian community believed that the writers, known as Matthew, Mark, and Luke, were witnesses to Jesus's message; hence they were called **evangelists** after the Greek word *evangelion*—for those who preached the gospel, or the good news. The Gospels, although providing evidence for the historical Jesus, were not intended as histories in the Greco-Roman sense because they were addressed to Christian converts. Mark's Gospel was the earliest, dating from about 70; the Gospels of Matthew and Luke are dated a little later. They made use of Mark's narrative and added the *logoi,* the "sayings" of Jesus. These three works are known as the synoptic Gospels (from the Greek words *syn,* for "together," and *opsis,* for "view") because they take essentially the same point of view toward their subject. Between 90 and 100, a fourth, and somewhat different, Gospel appeared—that of John—which treats Jesus as a wisdom teacher, a revealer of cosmic truths. The author of the Fourth Gospel has Jesus teach the possibility of being born again to eternal life.

Timeline 6.2   CHRISTIANITY TO 284 CE

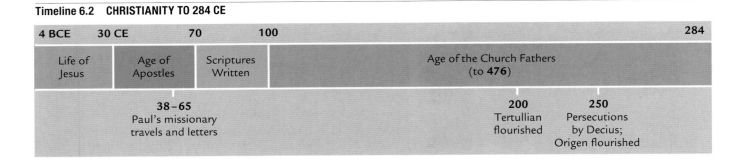

Despite their similarities, the synoptic Gospels reflect a schism, or split, in the early Christian church. Peter, one of Jesus's original disciples, headed a Judaizing group that stressed the necessity of first becoming a Jew before becoming a Christian. Paul, a Jew who converted to Christianity after the death of Jesus, led a group that welcomed gentile, or non-Jewish, members. Mark's Gospel was written in part to support Paul's gentile faction and therefore takes a negative tone toward Jews. Matthew was written in part as a corrective to Mark and made Peter, according to Roman Catholic doctrine, the "rock" on which the church was founded—the biblical source for the belief that Peter was the first pope.

Luke's Gospel was an effort by the early Roman church to deny, after the fact, that a schism had ever existed. Luke also wrote the Acts of the Apostles, the earliest account of the fledgling Christian community. This work records the activities of Jesus's followers immediately after his resurrection and defines some of the church's first rituals and beliefs, including a rejection of Jewish dietary laws and the practice of circumcision. The Acts also affirmed the opening of Christianity to gentiles, a policy that in the future would aid in the spread of Christianity. At the time the Acts was written, however, Paul and other missionaries were preaching mainly to Greek-speaking Jews and Jewish converts scattered across the Roman Empire. Paul's Roman citizenship enabled him to move about freely.

The meaning of Jesus's life and teachings was further clarified by Paul, who had persecuted the Christians of Judea before joining the new faith. Between 50 and 62, Paul, who was familiar with Greek philosophy, addressed both local issues and broader theological concerns in epistles, or letters, the earliest writings among the Christian scriptures, although only seven of the fourteen so-called Pauline epistles are generally recognized as having been written by him. These epistles constitute Christianity's first **theology,** or presentation of religious teachings in a reasonably organized fashion. Paul directed his letters to communities he either founded or visited across the Roman Empire: Ephesus and Colossae (Galatia), Philippi and Thessalonica (Macedonia), Corinth (Greece), and Rome (Map 6.2).

Paul's interpretation of the life of Jesus was based on the "Suffering Servant" section of the book of Isaiah in the Old Testament. The Suffering Servant was described as noble and guiltless, but misunderstood and suffering on behalf of others. Paul set forth the doctrine of the Atonement, whereby a blameless Christ suffered on the cross to pay for the sins of humankind. Christ's life and death initiated a new moral order by offering salvation to sinful human beings who otherwise were doomed to eternal death and punishment by Adam's first sin. But, according to Paul, human redemption was not automatically given, for a sinner must have faith in Jesus Christ and his sacrifice.

Paul's teachings also stressed that Christ's resurrection, which guaranteed everlasting life for others, was the heart of Christian beliefs, an argument echoed in the synoptic Gospels. Pauline Christianity made a radical break with Judaism by nullifying the old law's authority and claiming that the true heirs of Abraham were not the Jews but the followers of Christ. Paul also affirmed that obedience to Christ led to righteousness, which demanded ascetic living, with particular stress on sexual chastity.

The final section of the Christian scriptures was the book of Revelation, dating from about 95. This apocalyptic scripture projected the end of the world and the institution of a new moral order on the occasion of Jesus's return and final judgment. Revelation's picture of Rome as a corrupt Babylon destined for destruction reflected the early church's hatred of the existing political and social order. But the book, filled with enigmatic sayings and symbols, proved controversial, and not all ancient church communities accepted its authority.

By the mid–second century, the four Gospels, the Acts of the Apostles, the fourteen Pauline epistles, the seven non-Pauline epistles, and Revelation were accepted as the canon of Christian scriptures, or the New Testament (Table 6.4). Believing themselves to be the new Israel, the early Christians also retained the Hebrew scriptures, called the Old Testament. Although the spoken language of the Jews in Palestine was Aramaic,

MAP 6.2 THE EARLY CHRISTIAN WORLD

This map shows the spread of Christianity after the death of Jesus.
1. **Identify** the major churches in existence by the end of Paul's ministry.
2. **Which** of these churches did Paul found or visit? 3. **Which** church was best positioned to become the mother church of Christianity? **Why?**
4. **Consider** the impact of geography on the location of these churches.
5. **Is** there a connection between the major cities on Map 5.2, the Roman Empire under Hadrian, and the location of the Christian churches on this map?

a Semitic tongue, the Christian canon was composed in Koiné Greek, like the Hebrew Septuagint. The use of Greek reflected the triumph of Paul and the gentiles as well as the pervasive Hellenistic culture.

Christians and Jews

Despite the distinctive features of early Christianity, many Jewish ideas and rituals contributed to the new religion. The Christian vision of Yahweh was rooted in Judaism: a single, creating, universal God who spoke through sacred texts (the canon) and who demanded moral behavior from all humans. Both Jewish and Christian ethical standards required social justice for individuals and for the community. Likewise, the Christian image of Jesus as Messiah was framed within the context of Jewish prophetic literature. Christian

TABLE 6.4 BOOKS OF THE NEW TESTAMENT

Gospels	
Matthew	Luke
Mark	John

Acts of the Apostles	
Acts	

Epistles	
Romans	Titus
1 Corinthians	Philemon
2 Corinthians	Hebrews
Galatians	James
Ephesians	1 Peter
Philippians	2 Peter
Colossians	1 John
1 Thessalonians	2 John
2 Thessalonians	3 John
1 Timothy	Jude
2 Timothy	

Apocalypse	
Revelation	

apocalyptic writing, such as Revelation, also shared a common literary form with Jewish models such as the book of Daniel.

Even when Christians rejected specific Jewish ideas, such as the sanctity of the Mosaic law, the early church continued discussions on human righteousness and sin in terms familiar to Jews. The Christians probably adapted their rite of baptism from a ceremony similar to that of the Jews of the Diaspora. Christians also kept the idea of the Sabbath but changed it from Saturday to Sunday, and they transformed the festival of Passover (a celebration of the Hebrews' escape from Egypt) to Easter (a festival celebrating Jesus's resurrection). The church sanctuary as a focal point for prayer and learning evolved out of the Jewish synagogue, as did Christian priests from the Jewish elders. And the Christian **liturgy,** or the service of public worship, borrowed heavily from the Jewish service with its hymns, prayers, and Bible reading.

Judaism also influenced Christian thought by transmitting certain ideas from Zoroastrianism, including such dualistic concepts as Satan as the personification of evil, heaven and hell as the two destinies of humankind, and a divine savior who would appear at the end of time.

Despite the common heritage of Christians and Jews, relations between them were stormy. After the Council at Jamnia in Judea in 90, when the Jews established the final version of their sacred canon, there was no place in Judaism for the Christian message. As revealed in Paul's letters, the Jews viewed the followers of Jesus Christ as apostates, people who had abandoned or renounced their true religion. Accordingly, the Jews tried to deny the Christians the protection that Jewish leaders had negotiated with Roman authorities regarding their distinctive religious beliefs. For example, Jews were not required to worship the emperor as a god. Until the end of the second century, Jews and Christians occasionally engaged in violent clashes.

Christianity and Greco-Roman Religions and Philosophies

Christianity also benefited from its contacts with Greco-Roman mystery cults and philosophies. Whether or not the rituals of the cults of Cybele, Isis, or Mithra directly influenced Christianity, they did share religious ideas—for example, salvation through the sacrifice of a savior, sacred meals, and hymns. Christianity, as a monotheistic religion, paralleled movements within the cults of the second and third centuries that were blending all deities into the worship of a single divinity. Among the Greco-Roman philosophies, both Stoicism and Neoplatonism influenced Christianity as the church shifted from its Jewish roots and became hellenized; the Stoics taught the kinship of humanity, and the Neoplatonists praised the spiritual realm at the expense of the physical world.

Christians in the Roman Empire

The Romans initially regarded the Christians as a Jewish sect, but during the First Jewish War, the Christians evidently held themselves aloof. The Christian attitude seemed to be that the Jews had brought calamity upon themselves through their rejection of Christ. Similarly, Christians remained untouched during later persecutions of Jews by Romans in 115–117 and in 132–135. As their faith expanded during the first century, individual Christians encountered sporadic persecution, though there was no state policy of persecuting Christianity.

As the empire descended into chaos in the third century, Christians were sometimes blamed for its troubles. The emperor Decius [DEE-see-us] (r. 249–251) mounted a wide-ranging political test that required all citizens (men, women, and children) to make a token sacrifice to him. When the Christians refused to honor the emperor in this manner, hundreds of them were killed, including several of their local leaders, or bishops. Decius's sudden death ended this assault, but in 257 Valerian (r. 253–260) renewed it, which resulted in the martyrdom of the bishop of Rome and the leading intellectual, Cyprian. The killings eventually ceased, but for the rest of the century the survival of the Christian church was uncertain and depended on a muted existence.

Despite persecutions by the authorities, the Christian church drew much sustenance from Roman culture. The language of the church in the western provinces became Latin, and in the eastern provinces the religious leaders adopted Greek. The canon law that governed the church was based on the Roman civil law. Most important, the church modeled itself on the Roman state: bishops, the chief Christian officers in cities, had jurisdiction over territories called dioceses just as the secular governors controlled administrative dioceses.

In addition, the church was moving toward a monarchical form of government. Because the authority of the officeholders was believed to descend from Jesus's faithful supporters, those bishoprics (territories ruled by bishops) established by apostles—such as the one in Rome that tradition claimed was founded by both Peter and Paul—emerged as the most powerful.

From an insignificant number of followers at the end of the first century, the church had attained a membership of perhaps five million, or about a tenth of the population of the empire, by the end of the third century. The smallest communities were scattered along the frontiers, and the largest congregations were in Rome and the older eastern cities. Social composition of the church came to include progressively higher classes. By the late second century, the middle classes, especially merchants and traders, were joining the church. Aristocratic women sought membership, but men of the highest classes tended to remain unconverted.

Christianity's appeal to women was complex, though all seemed to respond to its promise of salvation and the apostle Paul's egalitarian vision (Galatians 3:28): "There is neither Jew nor Greek, there is neither bond nor free, there is neither male nor female: for ye are all one in Christ Jesus." Female converts also found the Christian community to be a refuge from the anonymity and cruelty of Roman society; the church formed a secret underworld of close relationships among people drawn together by an ascetic but loving way of life. Christianity offered power by allowing them to influence others by their faith; it widened their horizons through intimate contacts with spiritual leaders; it gave them new identities through foreign travel and involvement in a cause that was life sustaining; and, for those who chose lives of chastity, it could serve as a means of birth control and freedom from the constraints of marriage and family life.

Early Christian Literature

By the late second century, the status of the church had attracted the attention of leading Roman intellectuals, such as the philosopher Celsus [KEL-suhs] and the physician Galen [GAY-len]. Celsus ridiculed the Christian notion of the resurrection of the body and the new religion's appeal to women and slaves. On the other hand, Galen found merit in Christianity because of its philosophical approach to life and its emphasis on strict self-discipline (see Chapter 7).

In the second century, postbiblical Christian literature, generally unremarked by the secular world, took two forms. **Apologists,** vigorous, principled defenders of Christianity, offered arguments that Christians were loyal, dependable subjects of Rome; that Christianity and Judaism were different; and that living a Christian life in a pagan world was difficult, but possible. Theologians—for example, Tertullian [tehr-TULL-ee-un] (about 160–230) and Origen [OHR-uh-juhn] of Alexandria (about 185–254)—began to define basic Christian teachings, to create a distinctive Christian vocabulary, and to relate Christian thought to classical learning.

Tertullian's life and writings showed the uncompromising nature of Christianity. Trained in Stoic philosophy in Roman Carthage, Tertullian later converted to the new faith after he witnessed the serenity of Christians dying for their religion. The strength of his beliefs made him a spokesperson for North Africa, where a cult of martyrs made the area the "Bible belt" of the Roman world. Writing in Latin, he helped to shape the western church's voice in that language. His

diatribes against the pleasures of the theaters and arenas and his intense denunciation of women as sexual temptresses became legendary. In the severest terms, Tertullian rejected the Greco-Roman humanistic heritage, preferring the culture of Christianity.

Origen of Alexandria shared Tertullian's puritanical zeal, but he did not repudiate humanistic learning. In his mature writings, composed in Greek, Origen brought Christian thought into harmony with Platonism and Stoicism. Origen's Jesus was not the redeemer of the Gospels but, rather, the *logos* of Stoicism (see Chapter 4). The *logos,* or reason, liberated the human soul so that it might move through different levels of reality to reach God. Origen's Platonism led him to reject the notion of the resurrection of the body as described in the Gospels and Paul's letters and to assert instead that the soul is eternal. Although some of Origen's ideas were later condemned, his philosophic writings, which were read secretly, helped free Christianity from its Jewish framework and appealed to intellectuals. Origen also initiated the allegorical method of reading the scriptures. Behind the plain words on the page, Origen taught, there were layers upon layers of deeper meaning.

Christian women writers in this earliest period were very rare, because intellectual discourse was dominated by men. Women did play important roles in the new faith—such as Mary Magdalene, who waited at Jesus's empty tomb, and Lydia and Priscilla, whom Paul met on his travels—but their voices are almost always heard indirectly. In their theoretical writings, men often addressed women's issues, such as Tertullian's "The Apparel of Women." Nevertheless, the voice of one Christian woman from this period has come down to us: that of Vibia Perpetua (about 181–203 CE) of Carthage in North Africa, one of the first female saints. An anonymous account of the Christian martyrs' struggles includes a verbatim reproduction of Perpetua's writings in prison. Filled with heartbreaking detail, the account describes her prison ordeal as she awaited death while nursing her child. The sentence was imposed because she refused to renounce her faith (see Slice of Life).

Early Christian Art

Although some early Christian writers, including Tertullian and Origen, condemned the depiction of religious subjects as blasphemous, pious Christians, attracted by the pull of humanism, commissioned frescoes for underground burial chambers and sculptures for their sarcophagi, or marble tombs. Christian painters and sculptors slowly fused their religious vision with the Greco-Roman tradition, a style that would dominate the art of the late empire. Religious values and themes were central to Western art for more than a thousand years, until the Italian Renaissance.

SLICE OF LIFE

A Christian Mother Faces Death from Roman Authorities

Vibia Perpetua
A MARTYR IN THE EARLY CHRISTIAN CHURCH

Vibia Perpetua, an educated young woman from a wealthy Carthaginian family and a convert to Christianity, defied an edict against proselytizing issued by the non-Christian emperor in 202. She was jailed and died in the arena of Carthage in 203. This excerpt is part of her personal account of her last days before martyrdom.

A few days later we were moved to a prison [in Carthage]. I was frightened, because I had never been in such a dark place. A sad day! The large number of prisoners made the place stifling. The soldiers tried to extort money from us. I was also tormented by worry for my child. Finally, Tertius and Pomponius, the blessed deacons responsible for taking care of us, bribed the guards to allow us a few hours in a better part of the prison to regain our strength. All the prisoners were released from the dungeon and allowed to do as they wished. I gave suck to my starving child. . . . I was permitted to keep my child with me in prison. His strength came back quickly, which alleviated my pain and anguish. The prison was suddenly like a palace; I felt more comfortable there than anywhere else.

Interpreting This Slice of Life

1. *Why* was Vibia Perpetua being held captive by the Romans?

2. Since the Roman guards were eager for bribes, *what* does this reveal about their attitude toward Christians?

3. *How* does Vibia Perpetua's faith sustain her in prison?

4. *Compare and contrast* the religious conflict depicted here with religious conflicts in modern times.

In imperial Rome, citizens had the legal right to bury their dead in **catacombs** (underground passageways and chambers) alongside the roads leading out of Rome (Figure 6.14). Many catacombs had **arcosoliums,** square or rectangular arched rooms cut into the rock to serve as chapels or burial vaults. By the late second century, some of the tombs displayed Christian symbols and subjects. Some images were purely symbolic, for example, crosses, chi-rho's, evangelist symbols, and fish (*ichthus,* the Greek word for fish, makes an anagram interpreted as "Jesus Christ, Son of God, Savior") (Figure 6.15). In the catacomb of Priscilla, a third-century fresco depicts a shepherd as a symbol of Jesus (see Interpreting Art). This depiction, one of the most popular figural image in early Christian art, is based on the idea of Jesus as the shepherd of his flock of followers.

Even though the shepherd and sheep convey a Christian message, the image adapts a familiar Greco-Roman

Figure 6.14   The Roman Catacombs: A Narrow Corridor with Niches for Burials. Because of their belief in a bodily resurrection, proper burial loomed large in the minds of early Christians. Roman Christians joined with other citizens in burying their dead along subterranean passages underneath the city. In 400, when Christianity triumphed in Rome, the custom of catacomb burial ceased. Knowledge of the catacombs passed into oblivion until 1578, when they were rediscovered and became subjects of study and veneration.

Interpreting Art

Literary Source The Bible refers to shepherds many times, but Luke 15: 4–5 is almost certainly the source here: "Who among you, if he has a hundred sheep and loses one of them, does not leave the ninety-nine in the wasteland and follow the lost one until he finds it? And when he finds it, he puts it on his shoulders in jubilation."

Composition A very simple image comprising a shepherd, two sheep, two trees or bushes, and two birds.

Style A limited color scheme, and faint, almost fuzzy, illusionistic figures float in space. This style was common in late Hellenistic times.

Context Priscilla was a Roman woman of senatorial rank who donated the land where the catacomb that bears her name is located. She may have been Christian.

Religious Perspective Shepherds are mentioned often in both the Jewish and Christian Bibles and stand for the loving care of God for his people. It is a metaphor that spawned not only art but also poetry and song.

Cultural Perspective The shepherd image was originally secular and symbolized either a king and his people or a teacher and his pupils. Christianity took over the image. Tombs in antiquity had often been decorated, but in Egypt the images were intended to delight the dead person in the next life whereas Christian images were meant to inspire and comfort the living.

Christ as the Good Shepherd. Third century CE. Fresco. Catacomb of Priscilla, Rome. This fresco was painted on the ceiling of an *arcosolium* in the catacomb beside the Via Salaria.

1. **Literary Source** What is the source for the Good Shepherd image?
2. **Composition** Where is this image located and why is it there?
3. **Style** What are the chief stylistic features of this image?
4. **Context** Define catacomb and arcosolium.
5. **Religious Perspective** What is the significance of a shepherd's image?

---

theme—known in both art and literature—that identified such diverse figures as the philosopher Pythagoras and the Orphic cult leader Orpheus with shepherds. The pose of the youth carrying an animal on his shoulders appeared in Archaic Greek sculpture as early as the sixth century BCE (Figure 6.16). The painter of the Good Shepherd ceiling fresco portrays the shepherd as a beardless youth without distinctive, godlike traits. The second-century statue of a shepherd depicted as

Figure 6.15 Symbolism and Early Christian Art. Christ monogram in a wreath. Central panel of a sarcophagus, marble bas relief, Early Christian, 4th century CE. Museo Pio Cristiano, Vatican Museums. Early Christians had some aversion to figural representations and used symbols, such as chi-rho and alpha-omega. Chi and rho are the first two letters of "Christ" in Greek. Alpha and omega are the first and last letters of the Greek alphabet, signifying God as the beginning and the end. The evangelist symbols—man, lion, bull, and eagle—were derived from the book of Revelation; however, the four symbols have numerous antecedents, for example, in Assyrian iconography.

Figure 6.16 *Calf Bearer.* Ca. 570 BCE. Marble, ht. 65″. Acropolis Museum, Athens. This sixth-century BCE Greek statue shows a young man carrying a calf probably intended for a ritual sacrifice. The statue is executed in the kouros style, popular in the Archaic Age, as indicated by the frontality, stiffness, and stylized beard. The shepherd image later became associated with Jesus in the early Christian period.

Figure 6.17   Scenes from Chamber (Arcosolium) of the Velata, Catacomb of Priscilla, Rome. Ca. 250–300. The deceased woman is depicted in the center in an *orans* ("praying") position. Presumably she is ascending to heaven. This would be a standard image in Christian art until modern times. At the figure's right (the viewer's left), a bishop is blessing the woman's wedding. The bride holds a scroll, the Roman *tabula nuptialis*, a document that spelled out the wife's duties. A youth presents the wedding veil. To the figure's left (the viewer's right), the woman is depicted with an infant child. Such depictions of mother and child would soon be appropriated by Christian artists for the standard depiction of Mary and Jesus. In fact, the oldest surviving image of Mary and the baby Jesus stands on another wall of this same arcosolium.

the chapter-opening image (see page 128) attests to the widespread use of this image. By such representations as these, the artists in effect declared the limits of their art in penetrating the mystery of Jesus as both God and man. That is, they confined themselves to symbolic images.

In the catacomb of Priscilla, in the same arcosolium whose ceiling is graced by the Good Shepherd, a late third-century image reveals scenes from the life of a dead woman buried there (Figure 6.17). Christian art was beginning to gain some narrative sophistication and its production values were getting higher and higher. This may point to greater wealth in the Christian community.

SUMMARY

The historical experience of the Hebrews was relentlessly difficult. They were always surrounded by more powerful peoples who attacked and conquered them. They lived in a tiny land from which it was hard to scratch a bare existence. However challenging their lives may have been, the Hebrews clung tenaciously to their covenant with Yahweh that obliged them to believe in only one God, to worship him in specifically defined ways, and to promote justice among themselves. Viewing God as just and righteous, the Hebrews believed that their calamities resulted from

their own failures. The Hebrews wrote down a vast library of religious literature, some of which was essentially historical and spelled out the formulation of the covenant and God's ongoing relationship with his people. Some of it was prophetic and constantly called people to believe and to behave. Some of it was beautiful literature, such as the Psalms. And some of it was homey, practical advice for daily living.

During Augustus's reign over the Roman world, a young Jew, Jesus, arose and began calling on people to repent and hear the good news, the gospel, that he was professing. Jesus attracted a band of loyal followers and taught them by means of inspiring stories. His message was simple, and in a Jewish context, ancient: love God and love your neighbor. But Jesus, who called himself the son of God, also relaxed the requirements of the countless rules under which Jews had always lived. The Romans saw Jesus as a troublemaker and executed him. His dispirited followers rallied and a Jewish convert, Paul, joined their number. Gradually, they spelled out the Christian message in a body of writings that they called the New Testament, to differentiate those writings from the Hebrew Scriptures, thereafter called by Christians the Old Testament. Christianity spread throughout the Roman world despite occasional persecution. Christians began to develop a church with regular officials and to write works of theology, books that sought to interpret and explain the Christian message. And, finally, Christianity began to adapt the arts of antiquity to its own purposes.

The Legacy of Judaism and Early Christianity

Not a day goes by when Israel is not in the news. Surrounded by hostile people, the Jews in that country maintain confidence in their right to the land God promised Abraham. In antiquity, Jews were disparaged because they got in the way of imperialists or because they were a small minority practicing what seemed to others strange religious rituals. Eventually, anti-Jewish prejudices turned into malevolent anti-Semitism, the hatred of Jews as a people. In Hitler's Germany an attempt was made to eliminate the Jews as a people. But alongside prejudice and persecution, there are other stories. To be inclusive, people today speak of the "Abrahamic faiths": Judaism, Christianity, and Islam. It is crucial to remember that Judaism was the source for the other two. From both Judaism and Christianity, the West has inherited a moral and an ethical code. Pick up an American coin and see stamped on it "In God we trust." The prodigious learning of the ancient rabbis has been retained and revived down through the centuries. Since the eighteenth century, Jews have made fundamental contributions to the western humanities in almost every area of life. The modern world would be inconceivable without Itzhak Perlman or George Gershwin, Albert Einstein or Betty Friedan. Readers of this book probably grew up reading books by Judy Blume and Shel Silverstein.

For centuries Christianity had a privileged place in the West. The Romans made Christianity the state religion of the empire, and during the Middle Ages the culture was fundamentally Christian. The church was the great patron of builders, artists, and musicians into the modern world. The Protestant Reformation sundered Christendom but hardly diminished Christianity's cultural influence. Modern secularization has indeed weakened Christianity's influence but has by no means eradicated it. The "Religious Right" and the Catholic Church remain major players in American politics, although religious influences in European society are increasingly weak; for example, topics like abortion and evolution are prominent in America. But religious schools continue to educate numerous pupils, and the Vienna Boys' Choir still attracts packed houses eager to listen to stirring renditions of Latin chants from the Middle Ages. The bishop of Rome—the pope—remains the most visible and in many ways the most respected religious leader in the world. And a recent pope, John Paul II (1978–2005), initiated a long-overdue process of healing relations between Jews and Christians.

Pope John Paul II visiting the chief rabbi of Rome, Elio Toaff, on April 13, 1986. This marked the first time a pope had ever visited a synagogue or embraced a rabbi. John Paul would go on to visit synagogues in Poland and Israel.

KEY CULTURAL TERMS

covenant	apocalypse	Gospels	apologists
monotheism	Messiah	evangelists	catacomb
Diaspora	scripture	theology	arcosolium
eschatology	canon	liturgy	

The Basilica of Santa Sabina on the Aventine Hill in Rome. The church was consecrated by Pope Celestine (422–432). Sabina was an obscure Roman martyr who allegedly suffered death in 126.

7

Late Antiquity

The Transformation of the Roman Empire and the Triumph of Christianity

Preview Questions

1. *What* were the most important changes in the structure and organization of the Roman Empire from the reign of Augustus to that of Justinian?

2. *What* were the most important aspects of the growth of the Catholic Church as an institution in the Roman world?

3. *What* did the church fathers have in common with each other? *What* did they have in common with the secular writers who preceded them?

4. *What* did the Christian visual arts owe to pagan art? In *what* ways did Christian and pagan art differ?

A historian once said that the mystery of Rome's empire is not that it fell, but that it lasted so long. Indeed, Rome acquired its first provinces in 241 BCE and the empire continued expanding until 117 CE. The western empire disappeared in 476 but an eastern empire lasted until 1453. It is important to realize that scholars no longer talk about a catastrophic "fall" of the Roman Empire but, instead, speak of a "transformation" of the Roman world. This transformation took a long time and manifested itself in numerous ways. It is more usual now to speak of "late antiquity," a period from about 200 to about 600, and to see that period as having its own characteristics and integrity. The Roman Empire itself nearly collapsed in the third century, was reformed in the fourth, and divided forever in the fifth (Timeline 7.1). The western empire vanished as barbarian kingdoms replaced it but the eastern empire continued in various forms for another millennium. The truly dynamic development in late antiquity was the rise of the Catholic Church as an institution and the elaboration of a rich and widespread Christian culture as the last stage of ancient civilization.

The image to the left is a view down the nave of the **basilica**—a rectangular structure that dated back to the second century BCE and, by the early empire, was often built to house marketplaces or public assembly halls—of Santa Sabina in Rome that reveals much about late antiquity and the transformation of the Roman Empire. Previously, basilicas served as assembly halls, law courts, and markets. Santa Sabina, however, is a Christian church. Under the empire new basilicas were usually named for emperors; this one is named for a Roman Christian martyr. The building was built just twenty years after the Visigoths sacked Rome, which shows that even in a time of crisis the ancient world still had the resolve and resources to build major buildings. The twenty-four beautiful Corinthian columns that flank the nave of the church were appropriated from a temple of the Roman goddess Juno showing that Christianity had superceded Rome's pagan religion. Rome's first great Christian buildings were patronized by

Timeline 7.1   THE WORLD OF LATE ANTIQUITY

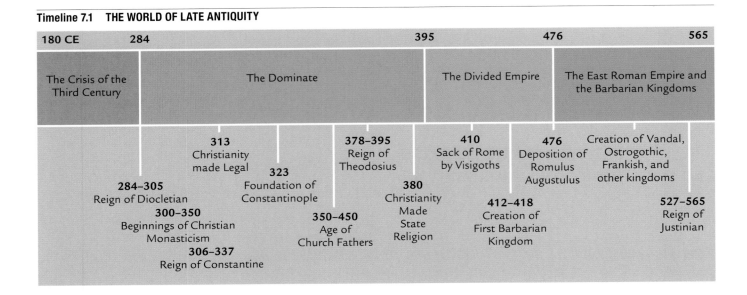

emperors but this one was built by Rome's bishop—a symbol of the church's growing power. The fascination and enigma of late antiquity is that everything changed while much remained the same.

THE TRANSFORMATION OF THE ROMAN EMPIRE

After two centuries of effective rule, Rome's vast empire plunged into a continuing state of crisis in the third century that had political, military, and economic dimensions. The emperors Diocletian and Constantine addressed each challenge. While they braked Rome's slide into chaos, they also transformed the Roman regime in basic respects. Ultimately, their reforms proved more durable in the East than in the West.

The Crisis of the Third Century

Between 235 and 284, Rome had twenty-two emperors. Many reigns lasted only a year or two, and few emperors died a natural death. The military side of the principate had completely trumped the civilian side. Civil war was endemic, with one military commander after another trying to get his troops to back his claim on the imperial office.

Institutional chaos could not have come at a worse moment. For the first time, Rome faced threats along multiple frontiers simultaneously. A revived Persian Empire threatened Mesopotamia, Germanic peoples pressed hard against the Rhine and Danube, and Berber tribesmen raided the North African frontier.

The economy was in shambles. Inflation was rampant and the government's usual response was to debase the currency—to reduce the amount of pure silver

and gold in coins. Debasement of the coinage merely worsened the inflationary spiral: prices went up and money bought less. Disparities between rich and poor were growing greater by the year. The uncertainty of the military situation led farmers to leave exposed, but fertile, territories for cities where there was no work for them.

There was a spiritual and cultural crisis too. The government lashed out against Christians as never before, casting about for scapegoats. The literature of the age, and there is not much of it, is grim and pessimistic. Almost no major buildings were built but cities everywhere were enclosed in massive walls (Figure 7.1). Despair reigned.

The Reforms of Diocletian and Constantine

During more than fifty years of rule, Diocletian (284–305) and Constantine (306–337) completely transformed the Roman state. They responded to the central issues in the third-century crisis and laid the foundation on which the late Roman Empire stood.

To address the irregularity in the imperial succession, Diocletian instituted the **tetrarchy,** or the rule by four (Figure 7.2). The empire was divided into two halves, East and West, each half to be ruled by an Augustus with a subordinate Caesar. The senior Augustus was to have ultimate authority, and the Caesars were to gain experience and then succeed the Augustuses. Constantine, however, shared rule with three of his sons, and for the rest of Roman history the tetrarchal and dynastic systems coexisted. Diocletian and Constantine also created an elaborate administrative hierarchy in the empire with four prefectures, fourteen dioceses, and more than one hundred provinces. The number of imperial officials rose from a few hundred

Figure 7.1 The Aurelian Walls, Rome. 271–275. Fearing a barbarian attack, the emperor Aurelian constructed a huge fortification for the city of Rome. The original Aurelian Wall was 21 feet high to its battlements and extended for 11.5 miles. The wall sported 381 rectangular projecting towers and, originally, seventeen gates through which passed the major roads to and from Rome. The emperor Maxentius (306–312) doubled the height of the walls. Long stretches of the Aurelian Walls and some of the original gates survive today.

to tens of thousands. Both emperors substantially increased the size of the Roman army. Constantine developed flexible mobile field armies stationed near cities behind the frontiers to meet threats more effectively. Both emperors also took steps to get control of spiraling prices and to stabilize the currency. Constantine, finally, created a new capital for the East. He chose the old Greek colony of Byzantium, which he renamed for himself, Constantinople ("Constantine's polis"). Across the fourth century, emperors built Constantinople into the greatest city in the empire, more important even than Rome, although Rome kept much of its historical and psychological significance (Map 7.1).

Diocletian and Constantine, and their successors, abandoned the idea of the principate in favor of a regime called the **dominate,** from *dominus* ("lord and master"). They increasingly adopted Persian and Hellenistic customs such as sprinkling gold dust in their hair, appearing infrequently in public, and requiring people to bow before them. These rulers unquestionably enhanced the power and prestige of the imperial office, but they did so at a cost: there was no longer any pretense that the emperor was a magistrate who ruled with the consent of the people and senate.

The two reformers treated Christianity very differently. In 303, Diocletian launched the last and greatest persecution of Christianity. At Milan in 313, Constantine issued an edict that made Christianity a legal faith, on a par with all other faiths. Near the end of his life, Constantine openly embraced the new faith. During his reign, however, he conferred privileges on the church, for example, freeing the clergy from military service and some taxes. In addition, he facilitated the construction of major Christian churches in Rome: the Lateran Basilica and St. Paul's Outside the Walls along with, aided by his mother Helena, the Church of the Holy Sepulcher in Jerusalem.

Figure 7.2 *Diocletian's Tetrarchy.* Ca. 300. Porphyry, approx. 51″. St. Mark's cathedral, Venice. In this group portrait of the tetrarchs, the four rulers—two Augustuses, or leaders, joined by their two Caesars, or successors—stand clasping shoulders to signify their unity and loyalty. By this time, the political leaders were no longer wearing imperial togas, as seen in the figures' cloaks, tunics, and hats; but the eagle-headed swords and decorated scabbards show that fine workmanship in armor was still practiced in late Rome. Despite the solidarity suggested by the sculpture, the tetrarchy was not a successful reform of the imperial administration.

Learning Through Maps

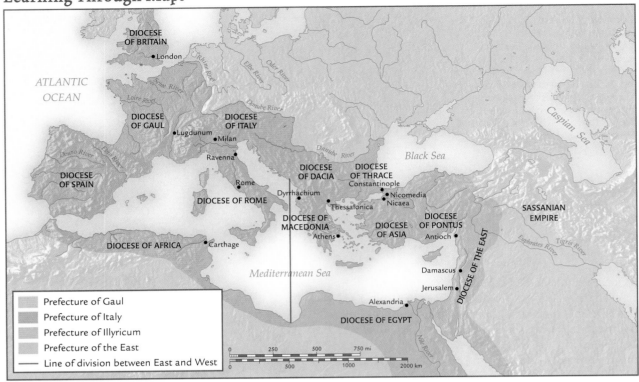

MAP 7.1 THE ROMAN EMPIRE IN THE FOURTH CENTURY

This map shows the Roman Empire after the reforms of Diocletian and Constantine. *1. **Notice** the role of rivers and bodies of water in determining the empire's frontiers. 2. **What** was the impact of geography on establishing the pattern of governmental dioceses? 3. **Notice** also the dividing line between the eastern and western halves of the empire. 4. **Compare** the location of the Hellenistic kingdoms in Map 4.1, The Hellenistic World, with the location of the same regions in this map.*

The Later Roman Empire in West and East

The western empire eventually vanished while the eastern empire reformed once again. Except for a few years in the 390s, the Roman Empire was never again ruled by a single emperor. The western court was occasionally at Rome but more often at Milan, Arles, Trier, or Ravenna. The eastern court was always at Constantinople. And the courts were often fierce rivals.

Although the western empire in late antiquity generally had less effective leadership than the eastern empire, the West's great challenge came from the barbarians. Who were these people and how did Rome try to deal with them?

Barbarians is a catch-all term for a host of Germanic peoples—so called because they spoke Germanic languages—who lived beyond the Rhine and Danube frontiers. The barbarian peoples were not coherent ethnic groups but, instead, loose confederations. Through diplomacy, war, and commerce, the Romans had dealt with these peoples for centuries. Contemporaries called them Franks, Lombards, Goths, Vandals,

and other names, but each group was a loose band of different peoples organized under a leader usually called a king. In 300 CE all of these peoples were outside Rome's frontiers, but by 500 several of them had secured kingdoms inside the former western provinces. There was never a single, coordinated movement that can be called "the barbarian invasions." Some people did indeed invade the empire, but most were settled by the Romans themselves inside the empire. One historian spoke of "an imaginative experiment that got a little out of hand."

Beginning with Constantine, emperors often made treaties with barbarian groups. Usually the aim was to have these federates (from *foedus*, "treaty") defend a section of the frontier. Building on this model, the Romans allotted some barbarians lands inside the empire and assigned them specific tasks—policing brigands, defending frontiers, guarding coastlines, administering territory. The Visigoths, as an example, crossed the Danube in 376, defeated a Roman army in 378, and threatened Italy for a generation in a complex game aimed at

Learning Through Maps

MAP 7.2   THE ROMAN WEST CA. 500

This map represents the former western provinces of the Roman Empire after the end of direct imperial authority. Compare this map to Map 7.1.
*1. **What** had changed? 2. Had anything remained the same?*

securing them official recognition. They sacked Rome in 410 and, in the end, received most of southern Gaul. Later, the Ostrogoths held Italy under nominal Roman authority. The Vandals, on the contrary, forcibly seized North Africa. The system worked reasonably well for a time. A coalition of barbarians in Gaul serving under a Roman general defeated the invading Huns in 451. By the middle of the fifth century, however, the western government lost virtually all of its territory and tax revenues. By 476, the traditional date for Rome's "fall," the western empire had no meaningful authority and a barbarian general sent the imperial insignia to Constantinople, saying that there was no longer any need for an emperor in the West. The key point is that the western empire gradually shifted from provinces to kingdoms in a process which, for a long time, the Romans thought they controlled (Map 7.2).

Ruling from Constantinople, the eastern emperors had two fundamental objectives: to defend the empire's Balkan and Mesopotamian frontiers; and to ensure tax revenues and food supplies. The Balkans were threatened by Germanic peoples and by Slavs, whereas Mesopotamia stood face-to-face with a revived Persia.

Constantinople was primarily provisioned by Egypt, so controlling that province was critical. A stunning symbol of the East's resolve and resources is the vast set of landward walls built by Theodosius II (r. 408–450) to protect Constantinople (Figure 7.3).

Most of Rome's eastern rulers were hardened military men. In Justinian (r. 527–565) the greatest of them took the throne. Called "the emperor who never sleeps," Justinian launched a series of wars to recover Rome's former western provinces. His generals recaptured North Africa and Italy and took a strip of land on Spain's Mediterranean coast. Justinian substantially revised the imperial administration, jettisoning the traditional split between military and civilian control in favor of a system that placed most authority in military hands. He also issued the definitive codification of Roman law, the *Corpus Iuris Civilis* (529–532), and built the vast and magnificent church of Hagia Sophia (Figure 7.4).

By the middle of the sixth century, the western half of the Roman Empire was gone forever but the eastern half appeared to be a going concern. As the Byzantine Empire, the Roman East survived for a millennium,

Figure 7.3 **The Theodosian Walls.** During the reign of Theodosius II (408–450), massive brick and masonry walls were erected across the landward side of the peninsula at whose end Constantinople is sited. Outside the walls there was a complex network of moats and ditches. The city withstood all attacks until western crusaders took it in 1204.

although it would experience several major transformations. The slowly transforming western empire provided a stable framework for the emergence of the successor kingdoms, and the eastern empire remained a bulwark of Hellenistic and of Greco-Roman civilization for centuries. East or West, however, the Roman Empire of late antiquity knit together the peoples and cultures of the ancient world, gave definitive shape to a new late antique culture, and transmitted that culture to the Middle Ages.

Figure 7.4 ISIDORE OF MILETUS AND ANTHEMIUS OF TRALLES. **Hagia Sophia, Exterior. 532–537. 270′ long × 240′ wide, ht. of dome 180′. Istanbul.** The Byzantine emperors transformed their capital into a glittering metropolis that easily outshone ravaged Rome. The most magnificent building in the city was Hagia Sophia ("Holy Wisdom"), originally built by Justinian as a church. The building's 101-foot-diameter dome makes it the largest domical structure in the world. Two half-domes at either end double the interior length to more than 200 feet. The beauty of Hagia Sophia made the domed church the ideal of Byzantine architecture.

SLICE OF LIFE

A Roman Delegate at a Barbarian Banquet

Priscus

In the fifth century, the Roman world was ravaged by Attila the Hun, the barbarian king who ruled a vast state in central and southeastern Europe (r. 434–453). Demanding tribute and holding prisoners for ransom, Attila and his fierce army invaded the Balkans and Greece in the east, and Italy and Gaul in the west. In 448, Theodosius II (r. 408–450), emperor of Rome's eastern empire, sent ambassadors to Attila's court to address certain issues, such as subsidies. The Greek historian Priscus (fl. 450–475), who was part of the Roman delegation, gives an eyewitness account of a banquet meeting.

When [three o'clock] arrived [Maximin, the head ambassador and I] went to the palace. . . . [A]ll the chairs were ranged along the walls of the room. . . . Attila sat in the middle on a couch; a second couch was set behind him, and from it steps led up to his bed, which was covered with linen sheets and wrought coverlets for ornament. . . . The places on the right of Attila were held chief in honour, those on the left, where we sat, were only second. . . . [A] cup-bearer . . . handed Attila a wooden cup of wine. He took it, and saluted the first in precedence, who . . . stood up, and might not sit down until the king, having tasted or drained the wine, returned the cup to the attendant. All the guests then honoured Attila in the same way. . . . [T]ables, large enough for three or four . . . were [then] placed next [to] the table of Attila. . . . A luxurious meal, served [by attendants] on silver plates, had been made ready

for us . . . but Attila ate nothing but meat on a wooden trencher. In everything else, too, he showed himself temperate; his cup was of wood, while to the guests were given goblets of gold and silver. His dress, too, was quite simple, affecting only to be clean. The sword he carried at his side, the latchets of his . . . shoes, the bridle of his horse were not adorned, like those of the other[s] . . . with gold or gems or anything costly. . . . When evening fell torches were lit, and two barbarians coming forward in front of Attila sang songs they had composed, celebrating his victories and deeds of valour in war. When the night had advanced we retired . . . , not wishing to assist further at the potations [drinks].

Interpreting This Slice of Life

1. *Why* was Priscus able to observe Attila the Hun in such an intimate setting?

2. *Describe* the seating arrangement at the banquet.

3. *Why* do Attila's personal dress and accessories differ from those of the other barbarians?

4. *Is* there any evidence in this account of Attila's taste for personal luxury?

5. Contemporaries of Priscus greatly feared Attila the Hun, giving him the nickname "the Scourge of God," because of the savagery of his military campaigns. *Why* does Priscus portray him differently?

THE TRIUMPH OF CHRISTIANITY

The Roman administration persecuted, then tolerated, and finally supported both the Christian faith and the church. The most influential bequest of the Roman Empire to the subsequent history of western civilization was Christianity and the Catholic Church.

The Growth of the Catholic Church

After Constantine granted toleration to Christianity in 313, the church could function as a legal, public institution with visible leaders and structures. As an institution, the church developed an empire-wide structure that no pagan religion had ever possessed. In virtually every significant city of the empire, the Christian bishop became a prominent local figure,

partly a function of his growing social prominence. For a long time bishops were men of obscure or middling status, but by the fifth century it was common for them to have aristocratic backgrounds. As Christians gradually became the majority of the population in all towns and increasingly in the countryside too, bishops came to have influence over and responsibility for more and more people. They looked out for the poor, and for widows and orphans, and in some cities they had thousands of people on their charity rolls. Bishops intervened in legal disputes between citizens and interceded with the state for Christians caught in the web of judicial conflict. Especially in the West, where the imperial regime was slowly disappearing, they looked after urban amenities and tended to the food supply. On numerous occasions, bishops assembled from throughout the empire in councils to debate points of theology and to settle matters of daily religious practice.

Among all the bishops, the bishops of Rome gradually achieved a leading position. In Rome, the bishops, called popes, based their claims to authority on two key ideas. First, they believed, Christ has uniquely assigned leadership among the apostles to Peter. Second, Christian communities everywhere tried to trace their origins to one of the apostles in order to claim an authentic tradition of teaching and authority. **Apostolic succession,** the idea that the authority of bishops descended from the authority of the apostles, was in Rome coupled with the **Petrine Idea,** the doctrine that special authority fell to Peter's successor. Peter died as bishop of Rome, so it was believed that Peter's successors continued to possess his authority over the church. Leo I (pope, 440–461) was the greatest exponent of the idea of Roman leadership in the church.

The root meaning of *catholic* is "universal." In 325 the bishops gathered at Nicaea to define a creed, an authoritative and uniform statement of belief. With minor modifications that creed is still recited in many Christian churches to this day. The need for a creedal statement arose because of the teaching of an Alexandrian priest, Arius (about 250–336), who taught that Jesus Christ was not "consubstantial with the Father" as the creed still has it and, to preserve strict monotheism, that "there was when he [Christ] was not." The larger problem was that Christians were arguing over how God could be a Trinity, three persons—Father, Son, and Holy Spirit—in one. Arius's teachings were accepted by many people, including a Gothic priest, Ulfilas (311–383), who converted many barbarians to Arian Christianity.

In the fifth century, another ferocious quarrel arose over how to explain that Jesus Christ was true God and true man, as Catholic Christianity taught. Miaphysites (literally, "one-nature-ites") held that Christ was fundamentally divine. Arianism and Miaphysitism were the most significant **heresies** of antiquity, beliefs chosen by large numbers of people despite official condemnation.

Christian Monasticism

A fascinating and durable achievement of late antique Christianity was monasticism. There was always a tension in Christianity between those who wished to flee the world and those who wished to change it. Some Christians after 313 felt life had become too pleasurable. Whatever their motivations, in the fourth century, first in Egypt and then everywhere, thousands of men and women abandoned city, family, jobs, sex, food—indeed, all life's pleasures—to join monasteries.

Anthony of Egypt (251–356) came from a wealthy, Christian family. Around 270 he gave up all he had and went into the desert to live as a solitary, to pray, and to discipline his bodily desires. Gradually he attracted followers who wanted to learn from his austere way of life. Somewhat later, Pachomius (292–348) also went into the desert. A convert to Christianity and a former soldier, he too attracted followers. Unlike Anthony, however, Pachomius organized his followers into communities that ate, worked, and prayed together. Such communities were called monasteries where, ironically, groups of men or women lived alone together. The leaders of such communities were called abbots or abbesses.

Christianity and the Roman State

Relations between the Roman state and the Catholic Church were complex. Roman officials executed Jesus but Constantine made Christianity legal. Theodosius I (378–395) passed laws that effectively made Christianity in the Roman form the state religion of the empire. But emperors meddled in the selection of bishops and intervened in the increasingly bitter doctrinal quarrels that cropped up among rival Christian groups. At the end of the fifth century, Emperor Anastasius I (r. 491–518) issued a decree to settle a doctrinal quarrel. Gelasius I [juh-LAY-zee-us] (pope, 492–496) wrote him a letter saying that emperors had *power* whereas priests had *authority*. These words had powerful resonance in Latin language and Roman culture. Gelasius argued that the authority of priests was superior to the power of emperors because priests were concerned with immortal souls but emperors only with mortal bodies. Whatever his authority, Gelasius did not have the power to coerce the emperor. But Leo I within the church and Gelasius within the Roman Empire had made claims that would echo down through the centuries.

Varieties of Christian Experience

Christianity spread through a Roman world that was astonishingly diverse in languages and cultures. One reason for Christianity's success was its ability to adapt to and assimilate the local cultures it encountered. In the Roman East, centering on Constantinople, Christians used the Greek language and the Septuagint version (see Chapter 6) of the Old Testament. From Antioch to the east into Mesopotamia and beyond a Christian community used the Syriac language for worship and scholarship (Figure 7.5). In Egypt Christians used the local Coptic language. Syriac and Coptic Christians quarreled with both Rome and Constantinople on theological issues. In the West, Latin was the dominant language. Each of these Christian communities believed itself to be the heir to and representative of the authentic catholic—universal—tradition.

Figure 7.5 *The Rabbula Gospels.* **586. Laurentian Library, Florence. Cod. Plut. I, 56, folio 4v.** Written in a monastery in northern Mesopotamia, this famous gospel book, named after its scribe, has beautiful images in vibrant colors and energetic lines. It is written in Syriac, the major language of Eastern Christianity. The folio reproduced here shows the Syriac script between the columns of the canon table. Canon tables were often included in Christian gospel books to display the chapters of the individual gospels side-by-side for easy reference.

The Romans never gave much thought to the peoples living beyond their frontiers as long as they did not have to fight with them. Christians were different. They had been told by Christ to "go and teach all nations." Missionaries such as Ulfilas, a Gothic convert, spread the faith among the barbarians living along the Danube. In the fourth century two young Christians, Edesius and Frumentius, who were merchants from Tyre, were captured on a trading venture to Nubia, today's Ethiopia. They were taken to the royal palace, eventually entered the king's service, and began preaching Christianity. Frumentius later traveled to Alexandria, where he was made a bishop. More missionaries followed in later years and by the sixth century northern Ethiopia was a major Christian power, the only one in sub-Saharan Africa. Also in the sixth century, Cosmas *Indicopleustes* ("the India-explorer") traveled to the subcontinent and, to his considerable surprise, found large communities of both Greek- and Syrian-speaking Christians already living there.

THE SECULAR CULTURE OF LATE ANTIQUITY

The rich and diverse culture of the Golden and Silver Ages (see Chapter 5) ended amid the difficulties of the third century. Not much poetry or history survives. The brief efflorescence of pagan culture in the late fourth century had no lasting influence. There were only a few significant philosophers but their reinterpretation of Platonism would be influential for centuries. Ancient medicine reached its high point in late antiquity, and both of Rome's greatest legal codifications date from this period. The key cultural development of the era began in the background and then burst into full view: the rise of a rich and diverse Christian culture.

Philosophy

Some late antique thinkers adopted the Stoicism that had been dominant in the principate in either its Greek or Latin manifestations; others were interested in blending the various Greek schools—Platonic, Aristotelian, and Stoic, among others—into a philosophic synthesis. The outstanding example of this latter trend was **Neoplatonism,** a school of thought founded primarily by Plotinus [plo-TIE-nuhs] (205–270). Neoplatonism was the last major school of philosophy in the ancient world. The movement began as an attempt to correct the problem at the heart of Plato's system—the seemingly irreconcilable split between the absolute world of Ideas and the perishable material world. This Platonic dualism could and did lead to the notion that the everyday world has little purpose in the overall scheme of things. Plotinus now succeeded in bridging the two worlds with his theories, and his writings later influenced Christian thinkers in the Middle Ages and the Italian humanists of the Renaissance.

Plotinus resolved Platonic dualism not with logical analysis but with mystical insight, claiming that the union of the physical and spiritual worlds could be grasped only through an ecstatic vision. His retreat from philosophy into mysticism occurred during the crisis of the third century, when many people fled from urban violence to the relative peace of their villas and estates in the countryside.

Science and Medicine

Unlike the Greeks, the Romans made few original contributions to science. However, in medicine the Romans made some original contributions. The scientific aspect of Roman medicine went through three stages. The first stage grew out of Rome's agricultural heritage: remedies for sick farm animals, such as applying salves soaked in wool, had been widely used on humans for generations. The powerful *paterfamilias* acted as a physician, using ancestral expertise and home remedies. Roman medicine entered its second stage when Greek doctors finally gained acceptance among the Romans, many of whom harbored suspicions of all things Greek. By the start of the empire, in 31 BCE, Roman medicine had entered a third stage, as Greek and Roman medicine merged into a hybrid form—ranging from diagnostic procedures to pharmacology. The Roman army, with its hospitals and surgeons, carried Roman medicine throughout the empire.

Based on their lasting influence, the two most important doctors from this period are Celsus and Galen. The reputation of Celsus (fl. first century CE) as a knowledgeable philosopher was enhanced by the encyclopedia he compiled, which included articles on philosophy, agriculture, and the military, as well as medicine. Much of what is known about early medical history and Roman medicine, such as surgical procedures, hygienic practices, and treatment of various diseases, is found in this work. It was rediscovered in the early Renaissance (see Chapter 12) and was influential for several centuries, but only the section *On Medicine* has survived into modern times.

Galen of Pergamum (129–about 216 CE) was Rome's most famous medical authority. After studying medicine in Pergamum, Smyrna (modern Izmir, Turkey), and Alexandria, Galen settled in Rome. He soon became a fashionable physician, catering to Rome's elite. Several emperors, including Marcus Aurelius and Commodus, made Galen their court physician. Galen wrote more than five hundred medical treatises, covering such topics as anatomy, physiology, hygiene, exercise and diet, and pharmacology. In general, he followed scientific guidelines: collecting data, relying on experience and observation, and keeping to a set of general principles. His vast erudition and imperious writing style made him the West's chief authority on medicine, until about 1650. Later, his commanding status became a burden, when some of his findings on human anatomy, based on his dissection of dogs rather than humans, impeded the progress of medical knowledge.

Law

Under the empire, there were three important developments in the history of Roman law. First, the emperors themselves could make law; that is, law no longer had to be made in assemblies. "What pleases the prince has the force of law" was a favorite motto of imperial supporters. Second, building on republican precedents,

the *jurisconsults,* or *jurisprudentes,* became more prominent. These were specialists in the theory and science of the law—which is what jurisprudence means. Third, Theodosius II (in 438) and then Justinian (from 529 to 532) codified Roman law by gathering and systematizing the writings of the jurisconsults and the legislation of earlier emperors.

The Theodosian Code, intended to be a collection of all Roman law down to his reign, appeared just as Rome's western provinces were being carved up into kingdoms. By means of that code, the barbarian peoples learned Roman law and incorporated it into their own legal traditions. But it was Justinian's *Corpus Iuris Civilis* that proved to be the most influential law book in human history. Its three major parts are the *Codex,* a collection of all laws issued since Theodosius; the *Digest,* a systematic collection of the writings of the jurisconsults, which made their opinions easy to reference; and the *Institutes,* basically a textbook for law schools.

FROM THE SECULAR TO THE SPIRITUAL: CHRISTIAN LITERATURE

Christian writers looked to the future and a new world to come. With their eyes firmly fixed on heaven, they were indifferent to Rome or to any worldly state. They believed in eternal life but not, like Virgil and his readers, in Rome's eternity. After Constantine decreed toleration for Christians in 313, these authors moved into the mainstream and slowly began to overshadow their pagan rivals. The bitter differences of opinion between them and the pagans, which characterized the late fourth century, faded in the early fifth century. By then Christian literature had triumphed, though it remained deeply indebted to Greco-Roman thought and letters. Christian literature represented the last great achievement of ancient literature.

The Fathers of the Church

By about 300, Christian writers began to find a large audience as their religion continued to win converts among the educated. Although they extolled the virtues and benefits of the new faith, they did not necessarily abandon classical philosophy and literature; they believed that some of these writings conveyed God's veiled truth prior to the coming of Christ, and thus they combined classical with biblical learning. Revered later for their personal lives and public deeds, superior talents, resolute convictions, and commanding personalities, the fathers, as these Christian writers were known, not only were powerful figures within the church but also often intervened in secular matters, instructing the

local authorities and even the emperors. Moreover, their writings laid the foundation of medieval Christian doctrine and philosophy. The three most renowned were Ambrose, Jerome, and Augustine.

Ambrose (about 339–397), the son of a high Roman official, embarked on what would doubtless have been a distinguished public career. Unexpectedly, however, the citizens of Milan elected him bishop. Ambrose vigorously opposed the Arian heresy, and as bishop of Milan he aided the urban poor and the victims of barbarian assaults. In scholarly sermons, he condemned the emperors for the social injustices of their reigns. His letters shed light on problems of church government, and his treatises analyzed controversies dividing the church. His biblical commentaries brought Origen's allegorical method to the West and to Latin (see Chapter 6). Ambrose's hymns, perhaps his most memorable contribution, introduced to the Western church another way for Christians to praise their God and enrich their ceremonies (Figure 7.6).

Ambrose's involvement in two controversies underscores the tensions of the age as a secular classical world gave way to a Christian one. The first controversy arose when the troops of Emperor Theodosius I slaughtered a great many people in Thessalonica (Greece). In response, Ambrose compelled the emperor to do public penance for this horrific act. Ambrose's position was that the emperor was a member of the church, not its master. The second controversy was over the altar to the goddess Victory housed in Rome's senate house. It was removed and replaced several times in the fourth century, and when Symmachus (about 345–402), the leader of Rome's remaining pagans, restored it once again, claiming that it was an essential symbol of Rome's identity, Ambrose prevailed upon the emperor to remove it—this time for good.

The second major church father, Jerome (about 345–420), wrote extensively on religious issues, but his most enduring work was his preparation of the **Vulgate** (from *vulgus,* "common people") Bible. Jerome used his knowledge of Greek and Hebrew to revise the existing Latin texts and to translate anew many biblical books. The mark of his Bible's success is that, with some revisions, it remains the standard of the Roman Catholic Church today. Like Ambrose, Jerome received a classical education. Later, after settling in Bethlehem,

Figure 7.6   *Ambrose.* Ca. 470. Church of Sant'Ambrogio, Chapel of San Vittore in Ciel d'Oro, Milan. This portrait of Ambrose conveys some of the spiritual intensity of the powerful fourth-century bishop of Milan. The work is one of few mosaics that survived the destruction brought by Germanic assaults in northern Italy. Although the artist shows some feeling for the shape and movement of the body, the mosaic strongly reflects the artistic ideals developing in the eastern provinces: frontality, flatness, enlarged eyes, and stylized pose.

he founded a monastery, where he devoted most of his days to his biblical studies. His reclusive habits and his harshly critical opinions of Roman society made him controversial.

Of all the church fathers, Augustine (354–430) exercised the greatest influence on Christianity. In his youth in North Africa, he studied classical literature and thought, including Neoplatonism. Augustine then journeyed, via Rome, to Milan, where he met Ambrose, whose persuasive sermons assisted in his conversion. Augustine, convinced of Christianity's intellectual integrity and spiritual vitality, retired to North Africa and dedicated himself to spreading his new faith. However, his commanding personality and administrative skills soon propelled him into church politics.

Augustine joined the debates raging in the church. During his lifetime, his writing came to represent the voice of orthodox beliefs. He opposed the Donatists, who claimed that a priest's sin would make the sacraments invalid. Augustine's position—that each sacrament worked in and of itself and depended on the grace of God, not the worthiness of the priest—became the church's official stance. But his greatest fury was against Pelagianism, which asserted that good works alone could earn salvation for a sinner and that people had it within themselves to do good. Augustine's argument—that salvation can be achieved only by God's grace—rested on his rejection of free will and his insistence on original sin, the belief that all humans are tainted by a sin inherited from Adam.

During a long, active life, Augustine wrote many kinds of religious works, but his two major achievements are *The Confessions* and *The City of God. The Confessions,* written at the end of the fourth century, traces his search for intellectual and spiritual solace and details his dramatic conversion. In this spiritual autobiography, Augustine castigates himself for living a sinful, sensual life. Although he was remorseful and guilt-ridden for not having found God sooner, he came to believe that his efforts to understand the world by studying Greco-Roman philosophy, literature, and religion affirmed his desire to search for life's ultimate truths.

Augustine's conversion occurred in a garden in Milan, where a child's voice commanded him to read the scripture. Opening the Bible at random, he read from a letter of Paul, which directed him to arm himself with Jesus Christ as a way of combating the sins of the flesh. Upon reading this passage, Augustine wrote: "The light of confidence flooded into my heart and all the darkness of doubt was dispelled." Now certain of his faith, he dedicated himself to his new mission, adopted an ascetic style of life, and, ultimately, accepted church leadership as the bishop of Hippo, in North Africa.

Shortly after the Visigoths' sack of Rome in 410, Augustine began *The City of God,* a theological interpretation of human history. In this work Augustine addresses the central question confronting the Romans of that generation: Why was their empire subjected to so many catastrophes? To those who blamed the Christians, he replied that the decline of Rome was part of God's plan to prepare the world for the coming of a divine kingdom on earth. If the city fell, it was best for the human race. Augustine expounded and reinforced this argument in the first ten books of *The City of God* as he attacked Greco-Roman philosophies and religions.

In the concluding twelve books of the work, Augustine elaborated his view of world history, which relied on the Hebrew experience and Christian sources. At the heart of his argument lay what he called the two cities in history, the City of God and the City of Man. The City of God was the realm of the redeemed. The course of history traced the slow redemption of the City of Man, the realm of sinful humans, by the City of God. History would end when the City of God triumphed. In the City of God, the saved would enjoy an eternal happiness that paganism had promised but could not deliver. Augustine also abandoned the cyclical view of history in favor of a linear, providential version: history had a purpose, it was going somewhere—namely, to God's final judgment.

Church History

In addition to theology, early Christian writing included a new literary genre—church history. Eusebius [you-SEE-be-uhs] (about 260–340), bishop of Caesarea in Palestine from 314 until his death, made no claims to impartiality in his *Ecclesiastical History.* It makes the bishops the heroes, for Eusebius believed that they ensured the truth of Christianity. His story is organized church by church and bishop by bishop, revealing the importance then attached to apostolic succession. He also charted the church's spiritual, intellectual, and institutional life in its martyrs, thinkers, and leaders from its earliest days until 324. When his account can be corroborated, Eusebius has been found to be reliable. Written in Greek, and soon translated into Latin, Eusebius's influential history was inspired by the secular Greco-Roman historians, and he followed them in quoting from written sources. He consulted both the Old and the New Testaments, Christian scholars, and the Greek classics, including Homer and Plato.

Christian writers also developed two other kinds of historical writing. In the passion narrative, authors provided accounts of the final torments and death of the martyrs. These texts were both inspiring and comforting in the age of persecution and then instructive thereafter. In the other, hagiography, authors wrote biographies of especially holy men and women as guides to Christian living for later generations.

Poetry

During the fourth and fifth centuries, a number of Christian poets showed how this most typical of ancient literary arts could be adapted to Christian purposes. The Roman senator turned monk, Paulinus of Nola (342–431), was born in Gaul but lived much of his life in southern Italy. He was taught by Rome's last great pagan poet, Ausonius (310–395), who became Christian at the end of his life. Paulinus is best known for a series of poems on the life of St. Felix of Nola and on the monastic life. Prudentius (348–about 413), a Spaniard who wrote theological works, hymns, and many poems, was a master of the poet's art. His *Psychomachia* is an allegory in which Christian virtues and human vices wage a cosmic battle for souls. Caelius Sedulius (fl. early fifth century), a third Christian poet, had learned his Virgil at school and took it to heart. His *Paschal Song* is a retelling in epic verse of the story of Christ's life and crucifixion.

MUSIC

While the pagan music of late Rome was in decline, Christian music was just beginning to take shape. The Christians took the principles of Greco-Roman music and integrated them into the Jewish tradition of singing the psalms and the liturgy to make music a dynamic part of their worship. In later times, this Christian practice gave birth to a rich body of sacred music that utilized both singers and instrumentalists.

In late antiquity, however, evidence for instruments is scarce and sacred music seems to have been limited to chanting and unaccompanied singing. Perhaps inspired by the congregational singing in Jewish synagogues, Christians everywhere developed a new musical genre, the hymn, a song of praise to God. Ephrem the Syrian (306–373) wrote verses that, as hymns, were set to complex melodies. He composed verses consisting of four to ten half-lines sung by a soloist. A choir or the congregation then responded with a single, simple verse called an **antiphon.** Much the same kind of singing was also done in Coptic Egypt and beyond in Ethiopia, and Romanos the Melode (c. 540) developed antiphonal singing in Constantinople. The hymns of Ephrem and Romanos remain influential in Syriac and Greek Christianity to today. The hymn tradition in the West begins with Ambrose, who wrote elegant verses set to melodies. An Ambrosian hymn, consisting of eight stanzas of four verses each, was sung antiphonally, with half the congregation singing one stanza and the other half singing the next one.

THE VISUAL ARTS

Architecture and sculpture dominated Rome's visual arts, but they were pressed into the service of practical needs. The Romans commissioned buildings and statues to serve the state, religion, or society, but they recognized that the practical did not exclude the beautiful, and the functional did not rule out the elegant. When Christianity became free and public, the church adapted basic Roman styles and techniques for its churches and for its sculpture. Through the church, therefore, Roman architecture and sculpture were transmitted to succeeding centuries.

Architecture

After the third-century crisis, Diocletian revitalized architecture. To help restore centralized rule, he used art, specifically architecture, as a sign of his new power. He constructed the last great public baths in Rome, large enough for thousands of people to use at one time. As part of his imperial reforms—indeed, as a propaganda statement that all was well again—Diocletian built a palace on the Dalmatian coast (modern Croatia), where he spent his last twelve years. Strategically located halfway between the western and eastern centers of power, his residence resembled a Roman camp in its symmetrical layout. The palace serves as a fitting monument for this soldier who restored law and order to a world racked by civil war and incompetent rulers.

Visitors entered the palace by the main gate on the north side and walked along a path lined with columns across the central intersection and into the **peristyle,** or colonnaded courtyard (Figure 7.7). Those who traveled this far would be reminded of Diocletian's presence by such architectural features as the long entryway, the domed vestibule, and the grandiose courtyard. Beyond the vestibule, on the south side bordering the sea, were the imperial apartments, the guards' barracks, rooms for private audiences, and banquet halls. This residence incorporated nearly all the major designs and techniques, including the arch and mortar mixtures, known to Roman builders. More important, its impressive splendor symbolized divine authority combined with secular political power.

Just as Diocletian's palace was one of the last pagan edifices, the Arch of Constantine was the last pagan triumphal arch (Figure 7.8), erected to celebrate the emperor's victory in 312, which led to the issuing of the Edict of Milan. The Romans had built triumphal arches since republican times, but they usually had

Figure 7.7   Diocletian's Palace. Ca. 300. Split, Croatia. The peristyle, or colonnaded courtyard, screened off the buildings on the left and right, enhanced the enclosed atmosphere, and focused attention on the vestibule. Behind the peristyle, on the left, stood Diocletian's tomb (now a church) and, on the right, the Temple to Jupiter (now the Baptistery of St. John).

single openings whereas Constantine's arch has three. The circular **medallions** set between the detached columns on the side arches help to balance these smaller arches with the central arch. The decorated **attic,** or crown of the arch, with its statues of barbarian peoples, blends well with the lower sections. The senate and the Roman people, according to the inscription, gratefully dedicated this arch to Constantine for his deeds as their liberator from civil war and as their new emperor.

Much of the arch's decoration was borrowed from other monuments; for example, some of the reliefs and carvings came from works honoring the victories of Trajan, Hadrian, and Marcus Aurelius; and where a likeness of the emperor is intended, the original has been remodeled to resemble Constantine. Despite Constantine's celebrated conversion to Christianity, however, the arch clearly reflects a strong pagan influence. The symbols and figures stress human action, and only one small frieze hints at divine intervention.

Figure 7.8   Arch of Constantine. 312–315. Ht. 68′10″. Rome. The frieze that encircles the monument narrates the emperor's preparations for war, his victory, and his triumphant entry into Rome. The scenes depicted on the Arch of Constantine, like those on Trajan's Column (Figure 5.18), memorialized the Roman ruler's presence at every stage of a military campaign.

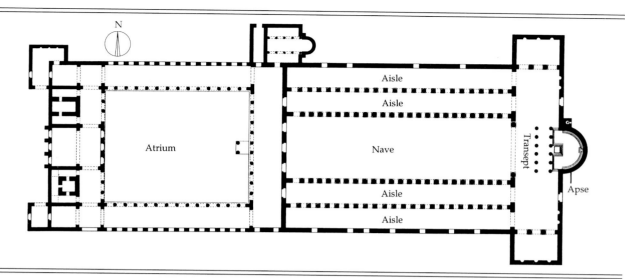

Figure 7.9   Floor Plan of Old St. Peter's Basilica. Ca. 330s–340s. Rome. Old St. Peter's Basilica was the most important structure in Christian Europe until it was demolished in the sixteenth century to make way for the present St. Peter's. Constantine, or perhaps his son Constantius II, dedicated Old St. Peter's on the spot that was believed to be the burial site of Peter, to whom Jesus had given authority over the church. Of the original basilica nothing remains, but sixteenth-century drawings show that it was cruciform (cross shaped), had a wide central nave with two aisles on either side, and was fronted by an atrium, where worshipers washed their hands and faces before entering the sanctuary.

A shift from pagan to Christian architecture began after 313 under Constantine's inspiration and patronage. He ordered the building of churches as places of worship for congregations and as memorials at holy places in Rome, Palestine, and other parts of the empire. Financed and supported by the state, this ambitious enterprise resulted not only in the spread of Christianity but also in the founding of new artistic values and architectural forms. The basic design of the churches that Constantine had constructed was derived from the basilica.

Although basilicas varied in detail, the basic floor plan used for churches was simple: a rectangular hall with an **apse,** or curved projection at the eastern end. Two or four rows of parallel columns usually divided the hall into a central area, or **nave,** and side **aisles.** The roof was taller over the nave section with a **clerestory**— windows were set high in the outside nave walls to let in light. The apse, where ceremonies were performed or where holy relics—physical remains of martyrs and saints—were placed, was often screened off from the worshipers, who stood in the nave. In some structures there was an **atrium,** or open courtyard, in front of the main hall.

No fourth-century Roman basilica churches remain, but drawings, such as that of the floor plan of the basilica of Old St. Peter's, suggest their appearance (Figure 7.9). The spacious atrium was surrounded by a colonnaded **porticus.** It is further possible to form a sense of Old St. Peter's by comparing an artist's reconstruction of the Basilica Ulpia in the forum of Trajan (Figure 7.10) with a much later drawing of the interior of St. Peter's (Figure 7.11). St. Peter's Basilica, traditionally ascribed to Constantine but more likely erected under his successor, built to mark the grave of the apostle who, by tradition, founded the church in Rome, included a **transept,** or crossing arm, that intersected the nave at the apse end of the building, making it **cruciform** (cross shaped). This first St. Peter's Basilica attracted pilgrims for centuries.

Sculpture

During Diocletian's reign and before Christianity's assimilation of the Roman arts, the late empire produced some unique and monumental works, such as the group portrait of Diocletian's tetrarchy, carved in porphyry (see Figure 7.2), Constantine's triumphal arch (see Figure 7.8), and the colossal statue of Constantine, a composite of marble and metal (Figure 7.12). The generalized features of these figures show the trend to symbolic representation characteristic of the art of the late empire and the movement away from the idealized or realistic faces of classical sculpture.

Christian sculpture was undergoing aesthetic changes similar to those taking place in secular art. By the end of the third century, Christian art was symbolic in content and impressionistic in style (see Chapter 6).

Figure 7.10   Basilica Ulpia, Forum of Trajan, Rome. Artist's reconstruction. This huge basilica, the largest in Rome, became a center of political life and the site of law courts upon its construction by the emperor Trajan (98–117). Unlike later Christian basilicas, this one had no religious significance.

Figure 7.11   Interior of Old St. Peter's, Rome (engraving), English School, (18th century). Private Collection. This drawing was done before Pope Paul V (1605–1621) ordered the destruction of the interior of Old St. Peter's whose atrium and facade had already been torn down. Comparing this image with that of the Basilica Ulpia and the floor plan of Old St. Peter's makes the major architectural features clear to see and understand.

Figure 7.12   Colossal Statue of Constantine. Ca. 313. Marble and metal. Palazzo dei Conservatori, Rome. Like Diocletian, Constantine consciously nurtured the image of the emperor as a larger-than-life figure. The head, itself about 8 feet high, was of white marble whereas the body was a brick core with a wooden framework and a gold exterior. The whole enthroned figure stood about 40 feet high. Constantine placed the statue in the basilica recently constructed by his rival Maxentius whom he defeated at the Milvian Bridge in 312. The emperor meets no one's gaze. If he is not depicted as a god, then he surely is no mere man either. The statue symbolizes the simultaneously aloof and authoritarian ideology of the regime called the dominate.

Simple representations of Jesus and the apostles had become common in the underground church. After 313, artists began to receive the patronage of the Roman state and also of bishops and wealthy Christians.

Christian Rome's reshaping of the humanistic tradition can be seen in the carvings on **sarcophagi.** The growing acceptance of burial rather than cremation and the resultant increased demand for sarcophagi afforded many artists new opportunities to express themselves. After the second century, rich Roman families commissioned artists to decorate the sides of these marble coffins and tombs with images of classical heroes and heroines, gods and goddesses, military and political leaders, and scenes of famous events and battles. Christians adapted existing funerary styles to new subject matter with Christian themes (see Interpreting Art). The sculptor's art could be employed in wood as well. The doors of the church of Santa Sabina in Rome have numerous panels depicting scenes from the life of Christ, including the oldest known representation of the Crucifixion (Figure 7.13).

Painting and Mosaics

In the fourth century, Christian frescoes flourished in the Roman catacombs and continued the symbolic, impressionist style of the previous era (see Chapter 6). Non-Christian paintings are extremely scarce from the fifth century, except for a few works such as a collection of **miniatures**—small illustrations—for Virgil's *Aeneid,* probably painted for a wealthy patron. This extensive picture cycle (Figure 7.14), more than 225 scenes, recalls the style of earlier paintings, but it is also an early example of a new medium, the illustrated book. Books

Figure 7.13   *Crucifixion Scene.* Main door, Santa Sabina, Rome. Ca. 430. Cyprus wood. Reigning opinion maintains that the doors of the church are contemporary with its construction which makes this image the oldest known depiction of the Crucifixion. For a very long time, Christians were reluctant to depict the execution of the Son of God on a cross; this image must therefore be considered experimental. Note that Christ is larger than the figures to his left and right—a perspective that is theological, not geometric. Christ is more important so he is portrayed bigger. The three figures are awkwardly posed in orant position and there are no crosses, albeit there are nails visible in the hands. Whereas Christ is depicted as youthful and beardless on the sarcophagus of Junius Bassus, he is here portrayed bearded and older. In mosaics (Figures 7.17 and 7.18) it will be seen that this would become the standard iconography—a term meaning a systematic, replicable mode of presentation.

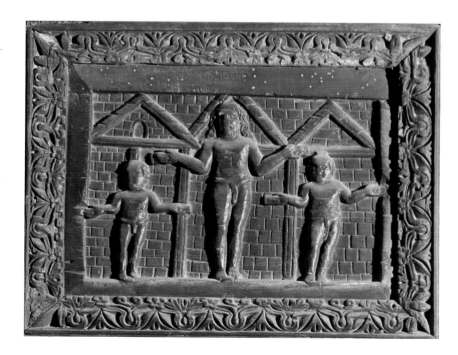

Interpreting Art

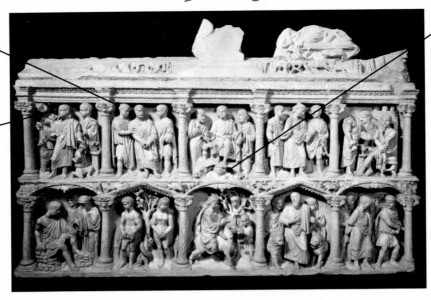

Style The sculpture is in late classical style, with ideas of harmony and balance. Some of the deeply carved figures give the impression of sculpture in the round.

Subject The biblical scenes depict (top, left to right) Abraham and the sacrifice of Isaac, the arrest of Peter, Christ enthroned between Peter and Paul, Christ as a prisoner, and Christ before Pontius Pilate; (bottom, left to right) the patience of Job, Adam and Eve, Christ's entry into Jerusalem, Daniel in the lion's den, and Paul being led to martyrdom.

Theological Perspective The Old Testament scenes are prophetic of the New Testament events and all scenes point to Christ. Christian writers viewed the entire Old Testament as foreshadowing the New Testament. Scenes of sacrifice dominate, but Christ's sacrifice on the cross is not depicted.

Pagan Elements Amid the Christian symbols, pagan remnants remain. In the top center, Christ appears above and with his feet resting on a personification of a pagan sky god, implying that Christ is now the ruler of the universe. He is depicted as a philosopher.

Setting The sarcophagus was created in that dynamic moment when Christianity was coming to dominate the Roman world. The wealthy could afford the finest artists who adapted classical modes to Christian subjects.

Symbolism The sarcophagus shows Christian beliefs in (on its front) scenes from the Old and New Testaments—the two parts of the Christian Bible; (on its ends) *putti* (small children) harvesting grapes (left end) and grain (right end)—symbols of bread and wine, elements in the Christian Eucharist, or Holy Communion.

The Sarcophagus of Junius Bassus. After 359. Marble, 4′ × 4′ × 8′. St. Peter's Treasury, Vatican City. Junius Bassus (d. 359), a Roman aristocrat, served as prefect of the city of Rome. His sarcophagus was discovered in 1595 under the floor of St. Peter's near the tomb of the apostle.

1. **Stylistic Influence** In what respects are classical ideals evident in the sculpture on the sarcophagus?

2. **Biblical Influence** What relationship can be seen between the Old and New Testament scenes?

3. **Cultural Influence** How does the sarcophagus reveal the blending of classical and Christian ideals?

4. **Symbolism** Identify key aspects of the symbolism in the sculptures.

5. **Context** Why did Christians decorate the sarcophagi of their dead?

Figure 7.14   Illumination from Virgil's *Aeneid*. Ca. 400. 6 × 6″. Vatican Library, the Vatican. This page from an illustrated manuscript of Virgil's *Aeneid* shows Dido, the Queen of Carthage (center), flanked by Aeneas (left) and a guest. The scene depicts the banquet, described at the end of Book I, that Dido gave in honor of the newly arrived Trojans. After the meal, Aeneas recounted his escape from Troy and seven subsequent years of wandering. Faithful to the *Aeneid*'s description, the painting represents Aeneas speaking to Dido while she appears to be calling for the attendant, in the lower right corner, to wash the hands of the diners. Such works derive from pagan circles in late fourth century Rome that were trying rather ostentatiously to assert Rome's classical identity in an increasingly Christian world.

were now written on parchment and bound in pages rather than written on scrolls. In the Middle Ages, this type of decorated, or illuminated, book would become a major art form.

In **mosaics,** subjects varied, although certain ones seemed always to be in vogue, such as still lifes, landscapes, Greek and Roman myths, philosophers and orators, and scenes from the circus and amphitheaters. In late antique mosaics, the subject matter for pagan and Christian works stands in sharp contrast. Among the many pagan mosaics that survive are those at the Villa Romana del Casale, a Roman estate near the town of Piazza Armerina in central Sicily. The villa, built in the early fourth century on the ruins of a second-century structure, was the residence of either a rich Roman aristocrat or a high-ranking Roman official. The estate operated for more than one hundred fifty years until the buildings fell into disuse when the Vandals invaded Sicily. This partially restored villa contains the largest, most valuable collection of late Roman mosaics in the world.

Over thirty-five thousand square feet of mosaic flooring covers a complex of rooms, including baths, a gymnasium, guest quarters, peristyles or open courts, and long hallways. One of the hallways, the Corridor of the Great Hunt, over two hundred feet long, depicts the hunting, capturing, and transporting of wild animals, which were typically found in the five provinces of the empire's diocese (administrative division) of Africa. These animals—antelopes, kids, lions, boars, and wild horses—were destined for Rome's Colosseum or arenas in other cities. Composed of two hunts, the narrative scene begins at either end of the corridor, with scenes of the hunters trapping or caging their prey. Then there are scenes at the ports where soldiers and slaves load the animals onto a ship, which is laden with crates, and, in the center of the hallway, the same ship is depicted as having arrived in Rome, where slaves unload the boxes and lead the animals away (Figure 7.15). The soldiers, slaves, and officials can be clearly identified by their dress and armor and their roles in the narrative. Their diverse facial features and multicolored skin tones indicate the diversity of the Roman Empire in the fourth century.

Among the many examples of life in the late Roman Empire recorded in the pagan mosaics at the Villa

Figure 7.15 *Loading the Wild Animals.* **Detail from mosaic. Early fourth century. Villa Romana del Casale near Piazza Armerina, Sicily.** This detail from the Corridor of the Great Hunt expresses the energy and activity found in nearly every mosaic on this site. Two workers struggle with the antelope on the gangplank, as sailors on deck prepare for the sailing. These mosaics were probably created by North African artists whose skills were well known during the late Roman period. Many motifs and scenes, in particular those of the Great Hunt, were standard design elements employed in North Africa and across the Roman Empire. Given the repetition of some of the decorations and motifs, and the uniform quality of the mosaics, the entire project was likely done over a five- to ten-year period by the same design crew and skilled workers. Some stones were quarried locally, but the colored ones were imported from Africa.

Figure 7.16   Putti *Harvesting Grapes*. Mosaic. Fourth century. Church of Santa Costanza, Rome. Besides alluding to communion, this scene illustrates the Christian scripture John 15:1, in which Jesus says, "I am the true vine, and my Father is the vinedresser." *Putti* are depicted trampling grapes and loading grapes into carts pulled by oxen; the rest of the scene is a labyrinth of vines, making up an arbor, amid which other *putti* are gathering grapes. This scene hearkens back to representations of the cult of Dionysus; we know it is Christian only because it is in a Christian church.

Figure 7.17   *Christ in Glory*. Mid to late fifth century. Mosaic. Church of Saints Cosmas and Damian, Rome. The scene depicts Christ's Second Coming wreathed in clouds of fire. The biblical text depicted here is from the book of Revelation. Compare the representation of Christ here with the one on the sarcophagus of Junius Bassus (see Interpreting Art figure). There, Christ is shown as an ancient philosopher. Here, he takes on the "Jewish" features that would be common for a millennium: long dark hair, heavy beard, olive skin.

Figure 7.18   *The Good Shepherd.* **Ca. 450. Mausoleum of Galla Placidia, Ravenna, Italy.** The young, beardless Christ—still the accepted image of the Christian savior in the fifth century—supports himself with the cross and feeds the sheep, the symbol of the church, with his right hand. Foliage and plants in the background tie in with similar decorations on the mausoleum's ceilings and walls. Upon entering the small tomb, worshipers would immediately be confronted with this large figure of Christ.

Romana del Casale were various scenes of children, including young boys hunting animals and young girls gathering roses. These scenes, found in a floor decoration in the bedroom of the son of the owner, confirm that the pagans liked pictures of young children, or *putti,* in the role of adults at work or play or even in religious scenes. In the very first Christian art, some artists adopted this playful genre for scenes of grape harvesting, as in a mosaic from the Church of Santa Costanza, Rome (Figure 7.16). In Christian art, however, the scene was a disguised representation of the Christian communion, in which wine made from grapes became the blood of Christ (see Interpreting Art figure). In effect, pagan art could be enjoyed and reinterpreted at the same time.

In the fifth and sixth centuries, the apses of almost all Christian basilicas acquired majestic mosaics, most of them depicting Christ. In Rome's pagan basilicas the apse was often the site of a cult statue, so Christians effectively repurposed this space in their churches. In Rome's church dedicated to Saints Cosmas and Damian, there is a particularly good example from the fifth century (Figure 7.17). After Justinian's reconquest of Italy, Ravenna became a showplace for patrons and mosaicists. In the small, cruciform mausoleum of Galla Placidia, a daughter of Emperor Theodosius I (r. 378–395), there is an especially attractive Good Shepherd in the space above the entry door (Figure 7.18). The nearby church of San Vitale has numerous mosaics. Flanking the altar are two, one depicting Justinian and his courtiers and the other depicting the emperor's wife, Theodora, and her courtiers (Figure 7.19). These fifth- and sixth-century styles would have a long life in medieval Rome and in the Byzantine Empire.

Figure 7.19   *Theodora and Her Attendants.* **Ca. 547. Church of San Vitale, Ravenna, Italy.** This mosaic featuring the empress Theodora faces a panel of her husband, Justinian, with his courtiers. Together, these mosaics communicate the pageantry and luxury of this age. The man on Theodora's right draws back a curtain, inviting the imperial party into some unseen interior. Note that Theodora offers a chalice. Opposite, Justinian offers bread. They seem to be depicted in an offertory procession bringing the elements for communion.

SUMMARY

After a century of severe political, military, economic, and spiritual crises two Roman emperors, Diocletian and Constantine, reformed the state and brought it to another period of greatness. Their reforms militarized the Roman Empire, thereby abandoning all pretense that the emperor was a magistrate. The Romans recruited barbarians to fight other barbarians and, especially in the West, parceled out their imperial provinces into Germanic kingdoms. In the East, a Roman regime survived, albeit much reduced in size. Constantine granted toleration to Christianity and later emperors patronized the church and churchmen, even going so far as to make Christianity the only legal faith—alongside Judaism. Having gained its freedom, the church developed sturdy institutional structures and a flourishing culture. Some Christians fled the world and joined monasteries in order to pursue God more purely. Others, the church fathers, assimilated the classical message and reinterpreted it in terms appropriate to Christianity. Late antiquity's innovative musical form was the Christian hymn. Secular buildings were no longer built but magnificent Christian basilicas grew up everywhere. In sculpture, fresco, and mosaic, classical styles and techniques were employed to create a vibrant Christian art. Late antiquity was a world of interlocking and reinforcing continuities and changes.

The Legacy of Late Antiquity

The Hellenistic world, and then the Roman Empire, provided a stable framework for historical development across a huge geography for more than eight centuries. This stability and longevity helps to explain why there are discernible similarities in art and architecture in places ranging from Britain to Afghanistan. Across that same span, boys once learned Greek and Latin epics and later learned the Psalms. The laws and institutions of every state that emerged within lands that had once been Rome's betray their origins in Roman ideas and practices.

The impact of late antiquity has been both direct and indirect. In law, for example, the deep imprint of Rome can be discerned today in places as different as France, Scotland, Quebec, and Louisiana. The papacy is the world's oldest continuously functioning institution. In late antiquity, popes and emperors had a hard time defining their respective spheres of authority. People today still struggle to define the proper roles of the church and the state. The church fathers remain influential and the Catholic Mass, the form of worship that took shape in late antiquity, continues to inspire great music such as the *Requiems* by Ralph Vaughan Williams (1936) and Maurice Duruflé (1947). Modern dictators learned from Roman emperors how to put huge statues of themselves in prominent places for propaganda purposes. One of the most famous monuments in Paris, the Arc de Triomphe, was consciously modeled on the triumphal arches of Roman emperors. In depicting hearty but naked French youths fighting Germanic warriors in chain mail, the Arc even borrowed iconographic themes from Rome.

Arc de Triomphe (Triumphal Arch). Ht. 164', w. 148'. Paris. Begun by Napoleon in 1806, the Arc was not finished until 1836. It celebrated the victories of France's revolutionary and Napoleonic armies. The tomb of France's unknown soldier lies beneath the Arc. For a detail of the sculptures on the Arc, see Figure 19.1. When Hitler's Nazi army captured Paris, in 1940, it deliberately humiliated the French by marching under their treasured emblem.

KEY CULTURAL TERMS

basilica	Neoplatonism	apse	transept
tetrarchy	Vulgate	nave	cruciform
dominate	antiphon	aisles	sarcophagus
apostolic succession	peristyle	clerestory	miniatures
Petrine Idea	medallions	atrium	mosaics
heresy	attic	porticus	

Silver Denarius of Charlemagne. Munzkabinett Staatliche Museen zu Berlin. This coin was struck at Mainz about 812. The image is thought to depict Charlemagne reasonably accurately. The legend reads KAROLUS IMP(erator) AUG(ustus): Charles Emperor Augustus.

The Heirs to the Roman Empire
Byzantium and the West in the Early Middle Ages

Preview Questions

1. *What* principal factors contributed to the development of a Byzantine culture?

2. *By what means* did the Carolingians attempt to ensure uniformity across their vast realm?

3. *What* similarities and differences do you observe in the literary interests of the Byzantines and western Europeans during the early Middle Ages?

4. In regard to the figural arts of the early Middle Ages, *what* carried over from late antiquity and *what* was new?

If the late Roman world were envisioned as a long evening, the early Middle Ages might be seen as a long morning. The years between 600 and 1000 saw the eastern Roman Empire evolve into a Byzantine Empire that would last until Constantinople was conquered by the Ottoman Turks in 1453. In the West, small kingdoms gave way to the huge empire of Charlemagne, which, in turn, dissolved into the realms of France and Germany. The surprising development in the early Middle Ages was the emergence of the Islamic Caliphate, the subject of Chapter 9.

The small silver coin—gold coins then being scarce—depicts the emperor Charlemagne in profile, crowned with a laurel wreath and wearing Roman garb. Its diminutive size reveals a characteristic of the early Middle Ages—everything happened on a smaller scale than in Roman times. Regardless of the coin's size, Charlemagne is portrayed as a powerful ruler; indeed, he had been crowned emperor in Rome in 800. Such coins reminded Charlemagne's contemporaries who he was and what he had accomplished. He had given Europe a sense of unity and purpose for the first time in more than three hundred years. His court attempted to recapture the Roman and Christian heritages of late antiquity. He supported scholars who gave a distinctive identity to this new Europe; one contemporary poet called Charlemagne "the father of Europe." During his reign artists and architects created and built *more Romano* ("in the Roman style"), which would last to our days.

Governments employed fewer people, controlled smaller territories, and provided fewer services. Population was contracting everywhere until the ninth century, and cities were shrinking in both size and importance. Rome, for example, probably had fifty thousand people in 600, a dramatic drop from the roughly half-million in the time of Constantine. Government was less bureaucratic and depended more on personal relationships, but the economy remained overwhelmingly rural and agricultural.

Timeline 8.1   THE BYZANTINE EMPIRE

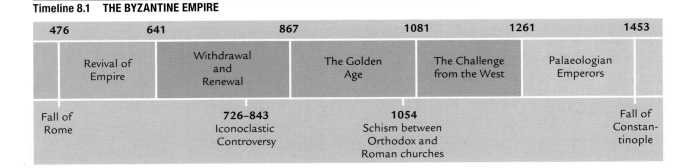

476	641	867	1081	1261	1453
	Revival of Empire	Withdrawal and Renewal	The Golden Age	The Challenge from the West	Palaeologian Emperors
Fall of Rome		726–843 Iconoclastic Controversy	1054 Schism between Orthodox and Roman churches		Fall of Constantinople

There was trade, but absent the command presence of the Roman Empire, commerce was restricted to local exchange and to a modest scale of trade in luxury goods.

Religion was a decisive feature of both East and West in the early medieval world. The church helped to stabilize political, social, and economic life. Church schools provided for the preservation of ancient learning and the training of the clergy. The church continued to function as a key patron for art and architecture, and Christian subject matter dominated the pictorial arts. During this period, moreover, East and West began to develop ever more distinctive patterns of religious life. By 1000 it is possible to speak of Orthodox Christianity and Roman Catholic Christianity. In addition, warriors, merchants, and missionaries carried Christianity far beyond the boundaries of the old Roman world, especially to those areas that constitute Europe today.

Having moved from its classical to its late antique phase, the West now entered the Middle Ages. In the seventeenth century, a Dutch scholar used the Latin phrase *medii aevi*, the "Middle Ages," to define the period between the end of antiquity and the Renaissance. Western civilization is still divided into three periods: ancient, medieval, and modern. The term was once exclusively pejorative; medieval implied backward, ignorant, superstitious. Today the term is only a scholarly and academic label.

THE BYZANTINE WORLD

Between the sixth and eighth centuries, the eastern Roman Empire evolved into a distinctive regime that modern scholars call *Byzantine* (Timeline 8.1). The name derives from Byzantium, the Greek colony on which Constantine erected his new city, Constantinople. Byzantines, however, always called themselves Romans, albeit they did so in Greek. Three themes dominated the history of Byzantium: foreign threats, institutional reforms, and religious change.

The Birth of Byzantium: War and Government

After the death of Justinian in 565, the eastern Roman world faced severe challenges. Persians threatened the east, while Slavs, Bulgars, and Avars pressed against the Danube frontier. The Lombards conquered most of Italy. Berber tribesmen rendered the reconquest of North Africa almost meaningless. Until Heraclius [her-ah-KLI-us] came to the throne in 610, most emperors were poor leaders.

Heraclius (r. 610–641) restored the treasury and fought with Persia. In brilliant campaigns, he defeated Rome's old foe but suddenly faced a new threat from the Arabs (see Chapter 9). Exhausted from Rome's wars with Persia, Byzantium had no answer for the Arabs and lost Syria, Palestine, and most of North Africa. Heraclius's successors in the eighth century created a shaky frontier with the Arabs in Anatolia (modern Turkey), which held until the lightning campaigns of the Seljuk Turks in the eleventh century. But Byzantium could not prevent Avar raiding along the Danube, Slavic settlement in the Balkans, and the creation of a Bulgarian kingdom. Northern Italy was abandoned; no resources could be spared to hold it. After years of gains and losses along the frontier with Bulgaria, Basil II "the Bulgar Slayer" (r. 976–1025) eliminated the first Bulgarian kingdom. Nevertheless, the basic geographic outline of the Byzantine Empire had taken shape by 800 (Map 8.1).

Because of these wars, Byzantium's institutions were reformed several times. Rome's wars had been fought by professional standing armies financed by tax revenues. With the exception of some troops in immediate attendance on the emperor, Byzantium gradually developed armies that were settled on the land, in lieu of pay, under the leadership of local officers. The zones within which these armies were settled were called **themes** (see Map 8.1). The theme system provided troops that could be mobilized locally to face threats and did not constitute a continuous draw on the treasury. Local military commanders combined

Learning Through Maps

MAP 8.1   EARLY MEDIEVAL BYZANTIUM

This map shows the Byzantine Empire as it existed from the eighth century until western crusaders captured Constantinople in 1204. In Anatolia the frontier often moved back and forth slightly according to the politics and diplomacy of the day. In the eleventh century, the Seljuk Turks conquered vast stretches of eastern and central Anatolia. *1. Based on this map,* **why** *did Byzantium have little interest in the West?*

civil and military authority in their hands. Justinian had begun the process of joining civil and military authority, and by the middle of the ninth century the process was complete.

The large and intrusive late Romans government was simplified. There were more branches of government, but they employed fewer men and the great officials were less powerful and prestigious than their predecessors had been. The emperors lived in a magnificent palace complex in Constantinople and rarely left the city. In the 720s Leo III issued a new law code, the *Ekloga,* which, as an abbreviation of Justinian's code, testifies to the empire's contraction.

The Birth of Byzantium: Culture and Religion

A reduced geography and transformed institutions were not the only changes experienced by the eastern Roman regime as it became Byzantine. At the most basic level, Greek replaced Latin as the underlying basis for culture. This happened notwithstanding the

fact that only about one-third of Byzantium's population were native speakers of Greek. Leo's *Ekloga,* for example, was issued in Greek whereas Justinian's code had been published in Latin. The emperors called themselves "emperor of the Roman" but did so in Greek, *Basileus tōn Romaiōn.*

From a territorial point of view, the Byzantine Church was smaller than the church of late Roman times. The great cities of Alexandria, Jerusalem, and Antioch were in Muslim hands and thus were isolated from Christian Constantinople. The patriarch of Constantinople often had trouble gaining assent from the bishops in the lands that remained to the empire. The emperor was literally the patriarch's next-door neighbor and frequently involved himself in church affairs.

Monasticism was important in both East and West, but in the East monks were often seen as counterweights to the imperial regime. Monasteries had acquired great wealth and immense prestige. Numerous patriarchs came from the monastic order. Many bright

Figure 8.1   Mount Athos. In 963 Athanasius the Athonite founded a monastery on the Athos peninsula of Chalcidice in the Greek part of Macedonia. Eventually, twenty monasteries clustered on the peninsula. The buildings shown here date from various periods but reveal the isolated setting.

and capable young men were drawn to the monastic life instead of to the imperial service. From its Egyptian origins, monasticism had two prominent forms, eremitic and cenobitic. The former, from *heremos,* Greek for "desert," was austere and solitary; think of hermits. The latter, from *koinos bios,* Greek for "common life," was communal. Byzantine monasticism was primarily cenobitic with eremitic aspects. Monasteries could be found throughout the empire. In 963 a major monastic complex arose on Mount Athos, eventually comprising numerous monasteries and more than eight thousand monks (Figure 8.1).

The manifestation of the Christian faith that can be called Orthodoxy emerged over several centuries. It was rooted in the Greek scriptures, the Septuagint (see Chapter 6), and the writings of the Greek church fathers (whereas the Vulgate and Latin fathers were predominant in the West). There were differences in basic practices. For instance, Latin clergy were generally celibate whereas Eastern clergy could marry. The two communities celebrated Easter, the feast commemorating Christ's resurrection from the dead, on different days. There were theological differences too; East and West recited the Nicene Creed slightly differently, for example. In 1054 the pope and the patriarch excommunicated each other inaugurating a schism— a split—that lasted a thousand years.

A famous incident in Byzantine religious history reveals some of the tensions and characteristics of the age. In 726 Emperor Leo III began agitating against icons. As small, detached, frontal, and timeless images, icons had a history reaching back to at least the fifth century. As images that were believed by some to have miraculous powers, icons were of much more recent vintage, no older than the seventh century. Leo, a rugged military man, not an urban sophisticate, believed that icons violated the biblical prohibition of graven images and that their growing prominence explained why God was punishing the empire. Leo's son Constantine V (741–775) was a knowledgeable theologian himself and persuaded a number of bishops to write against icons. Irene, serving as regent for her son Constantine VI, convoked a council at Nicaea in 787 and restored the veneration of icons. What did this mean? It meant that people could kiss icons or approach them with candles and incense—and carry them around as protection against demons or illness. In 815 the emperor instituted a milder form of opposition to icons, but in 842 this was also overcome.

This struggle over icons is called the Iconoclastic Controversy. Iconoclasts were those who broke, effaced, or destroyed icons. Iconodules were those who venerated icons. Almost all surviving evidence on the controversy comes from iconodules who had no

Timeline 8.2   THE EARLY MEDIEVAL WEST

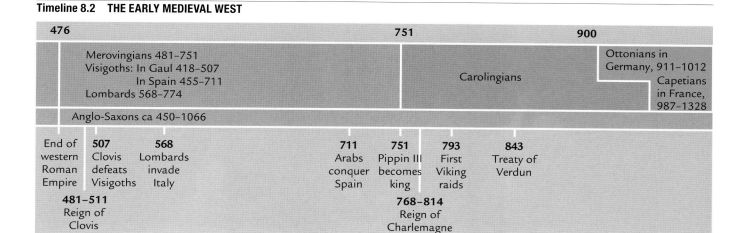

interest in representing their opponents' views fully or accurately. Even art was mobilized by the iconodules. The Khludov [CLUE-doff] Psalter, for example, has an image depicting a Roman centurion piercing Christ's side with a lance while, below, a figure is portrayed whitewashing an image of Christ. The message is clear: harming an image of Christ is like harming Christ himself (Figure 8.2). In reality, little art was destroyed and few people suffered physically although many were exiled. The controversy was a battle over how to read the Bible and how to understand the traditions of the church. The popes resolutely opposed Byzantine iconoclasm as did everyone else in the West. Both the existence of icons and the controversy over them illustrate some of the ways in which Orthodoxy was tracing its own path.

THE EARLY MEDIEVAL WEST

Most of the earliest kingdoms established within Rome's former western provinces had relatively brief runs on history's stage. Justinian conquered the Vandal kingdom in Africa and the Ostrogothic kingdom in Italy as part of his effort to recapture Rome's glorious imperial past (see Chapter 7).

The Visigoths' story is different. Settled in Gaul by the Romans, the Visigoths created a successful kingdom despite their Arianism. After the collapse of Roman authority in the West, they found themselves face-to-face with the Franks, who defeated them decisively in 507 and confined them to Spain, where they had been expanding their influence for decades. The Visigoths built an impressive kingdom in Spain and in 589 embraced Catholicism. Unfortunately, the defeat of 507 so damaged the prestige of the Visigothic monarchy that it was never able to create strong central institutions. As a result, between 711 and 716, Visigothic Spain fell to a Muslim army from North Africa.

The future of the West fell into the hands of the Anglo-Saxons and Franks (Timeline 8.2). The Anglo-Saxons were a conglomeration of peoples from what is today southern Denmark and northern Germany. By 410 the Romans had withdrawn their troops from

Figure 8.2   Khludov Psalter, folio 51 verso. Ca. 843. Constantinople. 7.67 × 5.9″. Moscow State Historical Museum. Most of the images in this book of psalms pertain to standard theological issues, but some, like this one, are polemical. The key verse here is (Septuagint or Vulgate 51.9 or RSV 52.7): "See the man who would have none of God's help but relied on his store of riches and found his strength in his folly." A psalter like this would have been a book for private devotions, so this one gives a sense of the depth of feeling surrounding the image debates.

Learning Through Maps

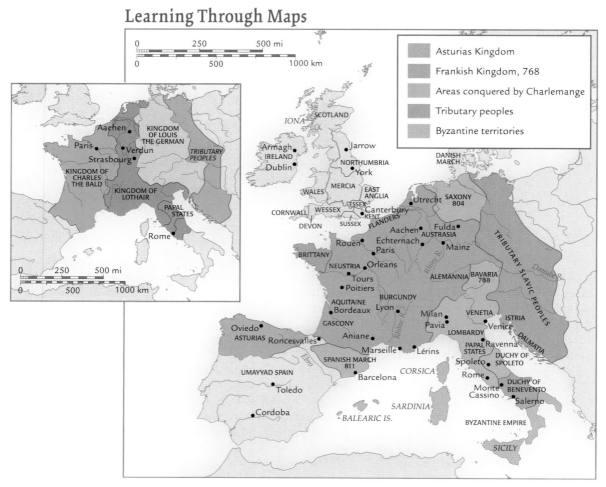

MAP 8.2   THE CAROLINGIAN EMPIRE, THE BRITISH ISLES, AND THE TREATY OF VERDUN

This map shows three areas: (a) small kingdoms in the British Isles; (b) the vast extent of the Carolingian Empire, including old Frankish territories and the new lands added by Charlemagne; and (c) the division of Charlemagne's empire by his grandsons in 843. In comparing this map to Map 5.2:   *1.* **What** *lands did the Carolingians rule that the Romans did not?* *2.* **How** *does this map aid in understanding the Carolingian foundations of European civilization?* *3.* **What** *is the significance of the location of Charlemagne's capital in Aachen rather than in Rome?*

Britain to deploy them elsewhere. Within a generation, bands of Angles and Saxons began settling in Britain. They settled slowly and, for the most part, peacefully across most of eastern and southern Britain. By 600 there were several small independent Anglo-Saxon kingdoms (Map 8.2). For two or three centuries, leadership within Britain passed from one kingdom to another as aggressive kings expanded at the expense of their neighbors. Anglo-Saxon kings issued law codes, held court in impressive wooden halls (Figure 8.3), and adopted some of the symbolic trappings of rulership such as wielding scepters. The greatest of the early kings, Offa of Mercia (757–796), issued laws, presided at church councils, and negotiated with the pope and with Charlemagne. In the latter endeavor he revealed his aspirations when he tried—unsuccessfully—to

arrange a marriage between his son and Charlemagne's daughter.

While political consolidation was slowly taking shape, ecclesiastical organization proceeded at a quicker pace. The British had been nominally Christian when the Romans departed, but their fate is difficult to grasp. The Anglo-Saxons were pagan. England's conversion to Catholicism had two roots. Irish missionaries from the Isle of Iona began working in the north, in what is now lowland Scotland. In 597 Gregory I (pope, 590–604) sent Augustine (d. 604/09) and a group of monks to evangelize the southern kingdom of Kent. The king of Kent had a Catholic Frankish wife, so Christianity must have made some inroads. Augustine and his successors established a base at Canterbury and began pressing their missionary work to the

Figure 8.3 Yeavering Hall. Ca. 600. Reconstruction. Kirknewton Parish, Northumberland, England. Yeavering is the modern name for Gefrin, a British word meaning "hill of the goats." Archaeological excavations beginning in 1953 and continuing to today have identified several buildings and numerous burials on the site. The hall pictured here was in use around the year 600. From this site, kings ruled the surrounding territory. The site overall reveals British, Anglo-Saxon, Frankish, and Roman influences. Yeavering Hall is one of four nearly contemporary halls discovered in Northumbria. Readers of the Old English epic Beowulf (discussed later) will be reminded of Heorot, the great hall of King Hrothgar, where powerful men drank and deliberated while Queen Waltheow passed out mead.

north. All the while, Irish missions had been pressing south. In 664, at Whitby, a council decided in favor of Roman over Irish practices. The archbishops of Canterbury became the leaders of England's church although another archbishopric was set up at York in the eighth century. England had a small number of rather large bishoprics, so monks played a key role in evangelizing the countryside.

The Franks were a confederation of peoples first visible in the historical record around 250 and, by about 400, living along the Rhine in what is now the Netherlands. For two or three generations, they expanded south across what is now Belgium and northern France. Under their king Clovis (r. 481–511), the Franks consolidated their power in the Paris region and defeated the Visigoths. Clovis, the most powerful and famous member of the Merovingian family (named for

a legendary ancestor, Merovech), embraced Catholicism and collaborated with the influential bishops of Gaul. On his death, he treated the kingdom as if it were a personal patrimony and divided it among his sons. For more than two centuries, there was rarely a unified Frankish kingdom. Nevertheless, the idea of a single kingdom of the Franks persisted. All the Franks identified common enemies in the Saxons and Bavarians, and common laws were observed. Royal courts were centers of political action and intrigue. Kings ruled, supported by aristocrats, whose privileges were guaranteed in return. Factional squabbles among the aristocrats finally led to a weakening of the effective power of the Merovingian kings and the rise to prominence of the Carolingian family. The name Carolingian derives from *Carolus,* Charles, the name of several members of the dynasty but especially of *Carolus Magnus,* Charles the Great, or Charlemagne.

THE WORLD OF CHARLEMAGNE

The Carolingians rose to prominence by varied means. Some members of the family were clever and ruthless. Others had vast landholdings—land was wealth in that world—and they made strategic marriage alliances with other key families. And several members of the family were great warriors. Charles Martel (the Hammer) (about 684–741) defeated near Poitiers in 733 a Muslim raiding party that had originated in Spain. The victory vastly enhanced the Carolingians' reputation. For almost a century the Carolingians dominated the office of Mayor of the Palace, a sort of prime minister to the Merovingian kings.

In 749 Pippin III, son of Charles Martel and father of Charlemagne, asked the pope if it were right that in the land of the Franks the one who had the royal title had no power while the one who lacked the royal title had real power. The pope said that this situation contravened the divinely instituted order, and in 751 the Franks made Pippin their king. In 754 the pope visited the Franks to enlist their help against the Lombards. Pippin defeated the Lombards and forced them to give the pope all the lands they had, technically, conquered from Byzantium. In these actions lay the origins of the Papal States, then about one-third of Italy, but today only the 108 acres of Vatican City. The pope crowned and anointed Pippin, his wife, and their sons. Royal anointing, based on the anointing of Saul by Samuel in the Old Testament (1 Samuel 10:1), was new here, although it had been widely practiced in the ancient Near East. The rite of anointing added divine approval to that of the pope and the Franks. When Pippin died in 768, his two sons divided his kingdom. One of them died in 771 leaving the older brother, Charles, who would be known to history as Charlemagne.

The Reign of Charlemagne

The greatness of Charlemagne (r. 768–814) is legendary. In the forty-six years of his reign, commanders acting in his name fought fifty-three campaigns. Yet Charles did not always accompany his armies and is not remembered as a brilliant strategist or charismatic leader. He was deeply pious but sired a dozen children out of wedlock and slaughtered 4,500 Saxons in a fit of rage. He could read and speak several languages but never learned to write. Nevertheless, Charles, who had a tidy, almost fastidious mind, fostered a massive program of educational renewal. He reformed secular and ecclesiastical institutions, took a keen interest in theological controversies, and raised the intellectual level of his clergy.

The most famous event in Charlemagne's reign was his coronation as emperor by Leo III (pope, 795–816) on Christmas day in 800 at St. Peter's Basilica in Rome. The pope had been attacked by a Roman mob and fled to the Franks for protection. Charles traveled to Rome to investigate. For more than a decade, men around Charles had been calling him emperor or insisting that he deserved to be emperor. Some said that the imperial throne was vacant because Irene, a woman, was ruling in Constantinople. The coronation was Leo's own idea and upset Charlemagne. Charlemagne never called himself a Roman emperor, and in 813 he crowned his son Louis (r. 814–840) as his successor in the chapel at Aachen, his capital, before the assembled Franks. After a lapse of more than three centuries, there was again an emperor in the West (see Map 8.2).

Pippin, Charlemagne, and Louis enjoyed almost a century (751–840) of unified rule over most of western Europe. They laid the foundation on which European civilization would be built. Once or twice per year they gathered the several hundred counts, the key local officials appointed by the ruler, in a great assembly where issues were debated and decisions made. The decisions took the form of **capitularies,** edicts issued in chapters (*capitula*). Each year, officials—*missi dominici,* "envoys of the lord king"—were sent two by two, one layman and one cleric, through specified territories to investigate whether the capitularies were being applied. Sons of powerful aristocrats regularly spent some time at the royal court to learn the ways of the regime, and great churchmen frequently gathered in councils that legislated for the Frankish church as a whole. Charlemagne and Louis sought to impose uniformity in canon law, monastic practices, and church worship on all their lands.

The Carolingian Renaissance

As long ago as 1839, a scholar spoke of the "Carolingian Renaissance." The phrase was intended to capture the spirit of rebirth, renewal, and reform that characterized the age. The Renaissance was born in the hearts and minds of the Carolingian rulers. Charlemagne had both the vision and the resources to promote a mighty movement, and he saw himself in some ways as an Old Testament king. People around him compared him to David, the simple yet learned warrior, and to Solomon, the wisest of kings. Charles compared himself to Josiah in his duty to visit, to admonish, and to correct, and also saw himself as something like a bishop. He was deeply influenced by a book, *The Pastoral Rule,* written by Pope Gregory I. Although Gregory had written it as a guide to bishops' behavior, Charles took to heart the idea that rule was not a privilege or a benefit to the ruler but, instead, a massive responsibility conferred on some by God for the benefit of everyone else.

As for resources, Charlemagne's wars brought plunder and tribute and also created peace and prosperity in his lands. Charles did not hesitate to use his vast wealth to promote the church, which, in turn, became the great patron of scholarship and the arts. In the Carolingian period, several dozen cathedral churches and more than three hundred monasteries were built or rebuilt. Charles also used his resources to attract the best minds from all over Europe. About one of them, Alcuin, who came from England, a scholar said, "He landed on the Continent with a bag of books and died the lord of twenty thousand men."

Charlemagne was concerned about the low level of education that prevailed and the lack of teachers, schools, and libraries. In capitularies, therefore, he commanded that cathedrals and monasteries should establish schools (even sons of laymen not destined for clergy were permitted to attend). Only well-trained men—the schools were restricted to boys and men—should be permitted to teach. Copies of important books were to be secured and then multiple copies made for dissemination. To avoid mistakes, only the most experienced scribes were to be employed. By the middle years of Charlemagne's reign, a new script, **Carolingian minuscule** (Figure 8.4), began to spread from one church or monastery to another. This was an extremely clear and legible script characterized by simple letter forms. So comprehensive and systematic were the efforts of Carolingian scholars that the oldest surviving manuscript of over 90 percent of all Latin classical works is Carolingian. Ironically, Renaissance humanists of the fourteenth and fifteenth centuries emulated this handwriting because they mistakenly believed the manuscripts they kept finding were Roman.

The curriculum in Carolingian schools was the same as in the schools of antiquity: **the seven liberal arts.** The arts were grammar, rhetoric, dialectic, arithmetic, geometry, astronomy, and music. Grammar involved the acquisition of basic skills in Latin. Rhetoric had for a long time been less focused on speaking well

Figure 8.4   Carolingian Minuscule. Ninth century. Bibliothèque Nationale de France, Paris. This text, a capitulary of Louis the Pious now in the Stiftbiliothek of St. Gall in Switzerland, exemplifies the key features of the new script that dates from the reign of Charlemagne. Earlier scripts had deteriorated badly and both Charlemagne and Louis wanted legible texts copied by experienced scribes. They were concerned that poorly written texts might lead to abuses in prayer, worship, and government. In the example pictured here you can see capital ("majuscule") and small ("minuscule") letters, and spaces between words. The lines of text are straight and well spaced. The various little marks about the letters in some words are abbreviations that saved space—and thus expensive parchment.

than on a kind of literary criticism, the ability to identify and also to write figures of speech. Dialectic meant formal logic. Arithmetic and geometry were practical, useful for doing sums, building, and measuring property. Astronomy was useful for navigation but also included elements of astrology. Music was more like musicology, the science of music, than the skill of performance.

Overall the Carolingian program was limited, practical, and functional. It was also intelligently designed and remarkably effective across Charlemagne's empire. While the program was designed to achieve basic literacy among the religious and secular leaders of society, it also produced a number of astonishingly learned and gifted scholars.

The Post-Carolingian World

The Carolingian Empire began breaking up in the middle of the ninth century. One man ruled the realm from 751 to 840, but thereafter there were always rival claimants. In 843 Charlemagne's grandsons divided the empire with the Treaty of Verdun. Although no one could have seen it at the time, that treaty established the foundations for the later kingdoms of France and Germany. In addition to familial strife, the sheer size and complexity of the Carolingian realm militated against its long-term cohesion. Finally, the ninth century saw a return of external attacks unseen since the fifth century. Vikings, Magyars, and Muslims ravaged Europe's coasts and frontiers. These raids were psychologically damaging, economically disruptive, and politically destabilizing.

In what was becoming France, the Carolingian family finally succumbed to a rival, Hugh Capet (r. 987–996), who secured the throne definitively for his family. The Capetians would rule France until 1328. From one point of view, government was failing and anarchy was ascendant. From another point of view, however, small territorial principalities—Normandy, Anjou, Champagne, for example—were emerging on the local level with extremely effective government. Ironically, these counties and duchies looked like miniaturized versions of the former Carolingian state. They preserved both memory and practices that later French kings would draw upon to rebuild the monarchy.

In what was becoming Germany, the dukes of Saxony worked hard to create an effective state. They controlled their own lands in Saxony with an iron fist and led successful military campaigns against the Slavs and the Magyars. The three greatest Saxon kings, all named Otto, supported the church and drew it into their government. They were also great patrons of culture. And in 962, Otto I was crowned emperor in Rome, which added great prestige to the dynasty.

In England, the Vikings first appeared in 793 and they were a real menace for a century after that. Effective government whether secular or ecclesiastical virtually ceased, and intellectual life ground to a halt. In 871 Alfred (r. 871–899) became king of Wessex (see Map 8.2). Although at that time he was confined to a swamp in the south of England, little by little he rallied his forces and then went on the offensive. He faced a major threat: a Viking army was trying to conquer England. Alfred won several victories in the south and

Learning Through Maps

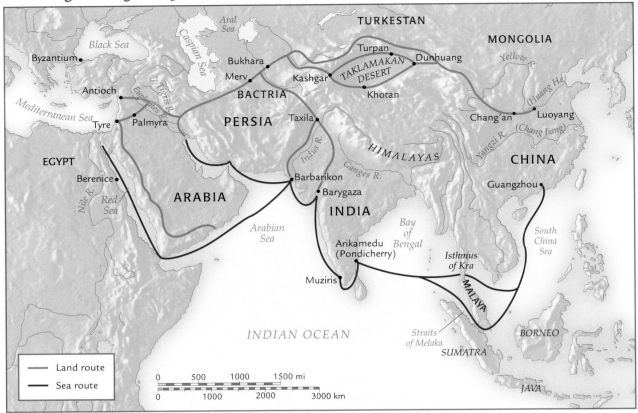

MAP 8.3 THE SILK ROAD

This map represents the complex network of land and sea routes that connected the Mediterranean with China, Central Asia, and India. *1. **Note** the complexity of the road system that made up the Silk Road: one overland route and one via water, with various alternative paths along each way. 2. **Note** also the Silk Road's end points. 3. **Discuss** the value of silk cloth and spices to the people in and beyond the Mediterranean. 4. **Compare and contrast** China's presence in the Silk Road economy with China's presence in today's global economy.*

then marched north, rolling back the Viking forces as he did so. When he died in 899, the south of England was entirely free of Viking threats and the tide had turned. Alfred, who shared Charlemagne's interest in education and culture, attracted scholars and patronized churches and schools. He lamented the fact that Charlemagne had turned to England for scholars while he had to go to the Continent to find them. Alfred personally translated various works from Latin into Old English so that their contents would be available in a devastated England.

The Greek East and Latin West were not isolated from each other. They traded with each other and with the Muslims who controlled the eastern and southern shores of the Mediterranean (see Chapter 9). What is more, the Silk Road connected the Mediterranean basin with the lands stretching across central Asia to India and China (Map 8.3). Raw silk and silk cloth became prized luxuries, and eastern spices—black pepper and cinnamon to name but two—enlivened the palates of people well beyond the Mediterranean. The Silk Road hinted at the vast international commercial and cultural connections that would mark later centuries.

THE LITERARY ARTS IN THE EARLY MIDDLE AGES

Some early medieval writers were prodigiously learned, and a few were capable of achieving real originality. Most writers, whether from the East or West, devoted prime energy to preserving and explicating the ancient heritage in both its secular and Christian forms. The culture of Byzantium was almost exclusively Greek and looked back to the Greek classics and the writings of the Greek church fathers. Similarly, in the West, the culture was Latin and drew inspiration from the Latin classics and Latin church fathers.

Byzantine Writers

Throughout the early Middle Ages, Byzantine writers sought to preserve a fragile heritage. For example, John Moschus (550–619) wrote *The Spiritual Meadow* as a collection of brief lives of famous eastern ascetics. He tried to transmit a sense of their habits and customs to later ages. The work was widely read both as a historical guide and as spiritual instruction. In the ninth century, Photius [FOH-shus] (810–893) compiled his

Library, a collection of 280 extracts from a wide array of classical authors. In many cases, the extracts found in the *Library* are all that survive of some ancient works. Photius, who was one of the great figures of his age and twice patriarch of Constantinople, seems to have felt that a tradition was slipping away.

Two works had more practical aims. The *Strategikon* [struh-TEE-juh-kon], a manual of military science, appeared around 600. It was either written or commissioned by the emperor Maurice (r. 581–602). In twelve books, mainly on cavalry warfare, the book provides strategic, tactical, and logistical details. In the tenth century, the emperor Constantine VII Porphyrogenitus [PORE-fear-oh-gen-uh-tus] (905–959) wrote two treatises, *On the Administration of the Empire* and *On Ceremonies.* Designed as handbooks to guide governmental and court procedures, the books contain a great deal of information—for example, on officials and rituals—that is invaluable to modern historians.

Other writers produced works that were both original and influential. Maximus the Confessor (580–662) was a profound theologian who wrote during the Christological controversies over Christ's divine and human natures in the seventh century. He was the greatest Neoplatonist among Byzantine theologians. John of Damascus (about 676–749) is best known today for *Three Orations Against Those Who Attack Holy Images,* which he wrote after Emperor Leo III began campaigning against icons. In the Byzantine tradition, however, John's most important work was *Fountain of Knowledge,* a compendium of theology organized by means of acute dialectical reasoning drawn mainly from Aristotle. John laid down in this work a great deal of the technical terminology that was subsequently used in Orthodox theology and philosophy. And, as Maximus was the great Neoplatonist, so John was the great Aristotelian.

Byzantium produced two historians of note. Michael Psellos [SELL-us] (1018–about 1081) was a prolific author who wrote on law, philosophy, theology, and history. His *Chronography* is a history of the period 976 to 1078. Michael was an eyewitness to much of the story he told and, as an adviser to several emperors, he was unusually well informed. His account brims with fascinating details, but its most memorable feature is its credible character sketches of powerful Byzantines.

The other Byzantine historian of note was Anna Comnena [kawm-NEE-nuh] (1083–about 1153), daughter of Emperor Alexius I Comnenus. Anna's *Alexiad* was one of the first known works of history by a woman. Joining Christian and classical knowledge and following the rigorous method pioneered by the Greek historian Thucydides (see Chapter 3), the *Alexiad* is a scholarly study of the reign of Anna's father, Alexius. Despite the author's obvious bias toward her father and confused chronology, the work is the best source for this period in Byzantine history. Especially valuable for Western readers is its portrait of the soldiers, saints, and hangers-on of the First Crusade (1096) passing through Constantinople on the way to Jerusalem. To Anna Comnena's non-Western eyes, the European Crusaders were a crude, violent bunch, more greedy for loot than concerned about salvation.

The Latin West

Several figures stand out as preservers of the old Roman ways and ideas. In Italy there were four. Boethius [BOW-ee-thee-us] (480–525) hailed from an ancient Roman family and served the Ostrogothic king Theodoric until he was suspected of treason, imprisoned, and executed. Versatile, Boethius wrote a treatise on music and planned to translate all of Aristotle's works into Latin. He managed only to finish some of Aristotle's logic treatises, and for the next several centuries the logic taught in schools was based on these Boethian translations. While he was in prison awaiting death, Boethius wrote a work that was extremely popular and influential for centuries, *The Consolation of Philosophy.* Cast in dialogue form, this **prosimetric**—sections alternate between verse and prose—treatise probes the questions of why fortune seems so fickle, why good people are afflicted with misfortune, what consolation there may be for poor mortals. Boethius and Lady Philosophy go back and forth, she saying to him at one point, "No man can ever be truly secure until he has been forsaken by Fortune." Happiness, in other words, is a fleeting thing. Although deeply imbued with Christian values, the text makes no explicit appeal to Christian teachings. Happiness, the work suggests, can be found only in philosophical contemplation.

Cassiodorus [CASS-ee-oh-DOR-us] (about 490–585) was, like Boethius, a servant of Theodoric. Unlike the philosopher, however, Cassiodorus was loyal to the end. He held high office three different times and, for some years, kept the court's official records. These letters, the *Variae,* are written in an elegant Latin and provide crucial information for modern scholars. Cassiodorus had longed for a durable reconciliation between Goths and Romans, and, when that proved impossible, he retreated to his family estates at Squillace in southern Italy and established a school of Christian studies. There, Cassiodorus wrote biblical commentaries and the work for which he is best known, *Institutes of Divine and Human Readings.* The divine institutes is arranged according to the books of the Bible and lists the best commentators on each book. The human institutes is arranged according to the seven liberal arts and lists the best manuals and commentaries on each art. This work of stupendous learning was in every medieval library.

Pope Gregory I—one of two popes called "the Great"—came from a senatorial family and served as prefect of Rome. Later he retired from public life, endowed several monasteries, and joined one. To his distress, he was elected pope in 590. In elegant, classical Latin he wrote a manual for bishops, the *Pastoral Care*, which was one of the most frequently copied books in the Middle Ages. He wrote a long moral treatise based on the biblical book of Job and voluminous biblical commentaries. In his more than 860 surviving letters he showed himself to be an exceptional administrator. Gregory I truly was the ideal pastor.

Contemporary with Boethius and Cassiodorus was the great monastic father, Benedict of Nursia (480–ca. 545). Born into a family of modest means in Rome, Benedict withdrew from the secular world and went out into the wilderness to live an ascetic life. Around 520, he established his own community about eighty miles from Rome at Monte Cassino. There he wrote a *Rule* for his monks. In seventy-three chapters, based largely on the Bible, Benedict set forth a comprehensive guide to life with three guiding principles: obedience, stability, and conversion. The first involved absolute obedience to the abbot, to the father figure in the monastery, a renunciation of the willfulness of the individual monk. Stability meant a pledge to remain in a monastery after one had entered; Benedict despised wandering holy men. Finally, monks were to undertake a complete change of their way of life—a conversion. Benedict wrote his *Rule* for Monte Cassino alone, but Pope Gregory I admired it and wrote approvingly about it. The Anglo-Saxons had a special fondness for Benedict's *Rule*, and Charlemagne considered it the ideal expression of monasticism. He issued capitularies demanding that all monasteries adopt the *Rule*. Ironically, Benedictine monasticism, although based on Benedict's *Rule*, was actually created by men who came long after him.

In Spain, the Bishop of Seville Isidore (560–636) was a commanding figure. Highly educated, Isidore wrote histories, biblical commentaries, a book on offices and duties within the church, and his *Etymologies* in twenty books. In this latter work, Isidore's aim was to create an encyclopedia of all knowledge organized according to the principle that the origins and meanings of words reveal a tremendous amount of practical information. Throughout the Middle Ages, Isidore's book was copied and studied.

At the court of Charlemagne, Alcuin [AL-kwin] (about 730–804) was the architect of the academic and intellectual revival. Charlemagne attracted him to court with a promise of support for a broad program of reform. He had been trained in the excellent schools in the north of England and was one of the most learned men of his time. Alcuin was a good poet, a sound theologian, and a solid biblical scholar, but he is best remembered as a teacher who wrote elementary texts and taught Charlemagne's children, including his daughters. Although Alcuin did not leave behind a body of original scholarship or beautiful literary works, he was supremely influential. Some two dozen of his pupils founded schools in the ninth century.

One individual above all others exemplifies the best of the Carolingian Renaissance: Theodulf of Orléans (about 750–821), a Visigoth. Charlemagne called Theodulf to court in about 790. His first task was to write *The Book of King Charles Against the Synod*, which constituted Charlemagne's official rejection of the Second Council of Nicaea in 787. The work, a brilliant dismantling of every argument raised both for and against images at Nicaea, argued the basic Carolingian position on sacred art: it was legitimate to possess such art for commemoration or decoration and heretical to worship or destroy sacred art. His learning, particularly his command of the Bible and the church fathers, was impressive, and he knew Hebrew, which was unusual in his age. Theodulf also wrote a treatise on baptism, a set of guidelines for priests in his diocese, and an angry work deploring the corruption of officials. He was also the finest poet of his age, a craftsman with both form and language. Moreover, he was a gifted architect and designed a beautiful chapel at Germigny-des-Prés (Figure 8.5).

In a period when new states were being created and new peoples were being brought into the church, historical writing flourished. Writers tried their best to get a sense of where they themselves, or their peoples, or their age, fit in the grand sweep of time. The idea of history in Augustine's *City of God* had made such questions urgent: if history had begun when God created the world and would continue until God returned to judge the world, people wondered where they stood at the moment.

Gregory (538–594), the bishop of Tours, who came from an old, distinguished family, was a prolific author. In addition to voluminous writings about the lives of the saints, he wrote *Ten Books of Histories*. Gregory began at the beginning—with the Creation—and quickly brought his account up to the Roman conquest of Gaul and then to the rise of the Franks. He portrays long-term historical continuities, not ruptures. The largest part, more than eight books, of Gregory's *Histories* treats the sixth century, but it would be a mistake to say that Gregory was preoccupied with the Franks. In fact, Gregory sketches out an implicit comparison between his own world and the world of the biblical kings. His overall intention is moral and didactic: he aims to teach lessons about good and bad behavior and the consequences of each. His Latin is not elegant and, by classical standards, is often clumsy, but Gregory is a wonderful storyteller with a sharp eye for detail.

Bede [BEED] (672/3–735) was a product of the cultural crosscurrents of northern England. That is, he was heir to the Irish, English, and Roman traditions. From the age of five, he lived in the monasteries of

Figure 8.5   Oratory, Germigny-des-Prés, France. 806. Theodulf designed this oratory as part of a palace complex. Everything except this building was later destroyed by Vikings. Internally the building is a Greek cross. Externally the building is almost square with single apses on the north, south, and west sides, and a triple apse on the east side. A high tower covers the central bay while barrel vaults cover the N, S, E, and W side bays. The corners have shallow domes supported by **squinches** (projecting arches placed diagonally at the internal angles of towers to support round superstructures; compare pendentives—see Figure 8.13). Centrally planned churches were rare in the Carolingian world. Theodulf adopted a style that would become normative later in Byzantium but that had never previously appeared in the West.

Monkwearmouth and Jarrow. Bede was a prolific author who wrote on time reckoning, for example, and popularized the use of AD (*anno Domini,* "in the year of the Lord") dating. He wrote many biblical commentaries and was the first to use a system of references that anticipates the modern footnote. Bede is best known for his *Ecclesiastical History of the English People,* a work modeled on Eusebius's *Ecclesiastical History* (see Chapter 7), which he knew in Latin translation. For the "English People," Bede imagines a common history long before they had a common polity—that history was religious. Instead of beginning his history with the creation of the world, he starts with Christianity's first stirrings in Britain. Here again was an homage to Augustine. Bede

was trying to show how the City of God, at least in Britain, was being built apart from the City of Man. Bede's Latin is clear, graceful, and correct.

Bede lived in a world where no one spoke Latin—it had to be acquired in school. Consequently, Latin was learned in Britain more precisely than it was in Gregory of Tours' Gaul, where the Latin people spoke every day was close to the written language. As the spoken language was evolving into French, so too the written language looked less like old-fashioned Latin. It was Alcuin, from Bede's England, who urged the reform of language that Charlemagne implemented. Ironically, by correcting Latin, the Carolingians killed it; they began turning it into a dead language. The Romance

SLICE OF LIFE

Marriage Diplomacy Nets a Diplomatic Insult

Liudprand of Cremona

Bishop Liudprand (about 920–972) of Cremona, emissary of the German ruler Otto I (the Great), traveled (968) to Constantinople to arrange a marriage between Otto's son and a Byzantine princess. Here, he describes his strained meeting with the emperor to King Otto.

On the fourth of June we arrived at Constantinople, and after a miserable reception, meant as an insult to yourselves, we were given the most miserable and disgusting quarters. . . .

On the sixth of June, which was the Saturday before Pentecost, I was brought before the emperor's brother Leo, marshal of the court and chancellor; and there we tired ourselves with a fierce argument over your imperial title. He called you not emperor, which is Basileus in his tongue, but insultingly Rex, which is king in yours. I told him that the thing meant was the same though the word was different, and he then said that I had come not to make peace but to stir up strife. Finally he got up in a rage, and really wishing to insult us received your letter not in his own hand but through an interpreter. . . .

On the seventh of June, the sacred day of Pentecost, I was brought before Nicephorus himself in the palace called Stephana, that is, the Crown Palace. He is a monstrosity of a man. . . . He began his speech as follows:—

It was our duty and our desire to give you a courteous and magnificent reception. That, however, has been rendered impossible by the impiety of your master, who in the guise of an hostile invader has laid claim to Rome; . . . has tried to subdue to himself by massacre and conflagration cities belonging to our empire. . . .

To him I made this reply: "My master did not invade the city of Rome by force nor as a tyrant; he freed her from a tyrant's yoke, or rather from the yoke of many tyrants. . . . Your power, methinks, was fast asleep then; and the power of your predecessors, who in name alone are called emperors of the Romans, while the reality is far different. . . .

Interpreting This Slice of Life

1. *What* was the purpose of the mission of Bishop Liudprand to the Byzantine court?

2. *Why* was a churchman entrusted with this mission?

3. *Discuss* church-state relations in both Byzantine and early medieval culture, based on the evidence of this Slice of Life.

4. *Why* was Liudprand insulted by being addressed as the ambassador of a king?

5. *What* were the issues at stake in this argument between Liudprand and the emperor's brother Leo?

6. *Speculate* on the reaction of Otto to this report from his ambassador Liudprand.

---

languages—French, Italian, Spanish—continued to evolve while Latin did not. It remained the language of learning, church, and government for a long time, but it was no longer the language in daily use.

Another highly regarded historian was Einhard (about 770–840), who came from a noble family in the Main River region of what is now western Germany. His family sent him to a monastery for his education but the abbot, recognizing his talent, sent him to court. Although a generation younger than Charlemagne, Einhard became his good friend. Einhard wrote a good deal but is best known for the most successful and popular of all medieval biographies, *The Life of the Emperor Charles.* Einhard wrote this work about 828, fourteen years after Charlemagne died, in a beautiful, classicizing Latin. Near the beginning, he professed his admiration for Cicero (see Chapter 5) and

said that Ciceronian eloquence was necessary to the subject at hand. He used Stoic virtues—self-restraint and magnanimity, for example—to craft his portrait of Charlemagne and took his basic structure from Suetonius, the Roman historian who wrote *The Lives of the Twelve Caesars.* In consequence, Einhard's portrayal is not chronological but instead thematic—wars, private affairs, public affairs, personal qualities, and so forth. Several things are striking about Einhard's *Life.* First, its author was a layman. Second, learning was not exclusive to the clergy. And third, the book was the first secular biography; for the past five hundred years, all biographies had been about saints. Einhard's learning and his literary aspirations reveal the achievements of the Carolingian Renaissance.

In the tenth century, one historian towered over all the others—and there were a good many. Liudprand

[LOOD-prand] of Cremona (922–972) traveled widely and observed much. He spent time in Constantinople, where he learned Greek along with a sharp dislike for all things Byzantine. Liudprand wrote accounts of his journeys to Constantinople and the *Deeds of Otto I.* Although an Italian, Liudprand admired Otto. Primarily, however, he intensely disliked the petty squabbling among the Italian princes of his day. A shrewd judge of character despite a penchant for caricature, Liudprand created memorable portraits of the characters who crossed his path.

The one original philosopher in the early Middle Ages was an Irishman, John Scottus Eriugena [air-ee-oo-GAY-nuh] (815–877), who accepted the invitation of Charles the Bald, one of Charlemagne's grandsons, to come to his court and pursue his studies. An excellent Greek scholar, Eriugena translated works by Greek church fathers into Latin. His most important work, the *Periphyseon,* was an attempt to reconcile Platonic philosophy and Christianity. He argued that nature could be divided into four categories:

- Nature which is not created, but creates (God)
- Nature which is created and creates (the Platonic Forms or Ideas—see Chapter 3)
- Nature which is created and does not create (things perceived by the senses)
- Nature which neither creates nor is created (God, to whom all must return)

In the thirteenth century, Eriugena's work was declared heretical because he had not drawn sufficient distinction between the Creator and his creation. His philosophical achievement was nevertheless considerable.

Two women writers, working against overwhelming odds, left their mark on this virile age: Dhuoda [DOO-oh-duh] (fl . 840s), a laywoman, and Hrotsvitha [RAWTS-vee-tuh] (935–about 975), a nun. About Dhuoda herself little is known. A noblewoman from the Rhineland, she married a Frankish count from the south of France. In the early 840s she wrote a manual of advice for his son William, whom his father had taken to the Frankish court. While not particularly original, the work urges William to attend to religious duties, honor family members, and learn the ways of the court. Of perhaps greater interest, the book shows Dhuoda in command of a fine Latin style in her prose and verse. She knew the Bible, and also several texts by church fathers, extremely well. Surely, Dhuoda's learning and writing ability were not unique among laywomen in her era, but only her book has been recovered.

A century later, Hrotsvitha, who came from a noble Saxon family and lived in a convent in Gandersheim, made an even greater impression than Dhuoda. She was an exceptionally skilled poet, well versed in the Bible, and familiar with Horace, Virgil, Ovid, Plautus, and Terence (see Chapters 5 and 7). Taking Terence as her model, Hrotsvitha wrote six plays, which survive. In these plays, she held up Christian women—virgins, ascetics, and martyrs—as exemplary figures in opposition to Terence's fickle and immoral women. Hrotsvitha is hailed as Germany's first woman poet.

The Vernacular Achievement

Vernacular writings are those written in a language other than Latin. The earliest vernacular writings appeared in lands outside the boundaries of the former Roman Empire. In Wales around 600, Aneirin [un-NEE-run] wrote the *Gododdin* [guh-DOTH-un], which is about a fierce battle between the advancing Saxons and the British. In Ireland, a great many legal, religious, and literary works were written in Old Irish. One remarkable tale, the *Tain* [toyne], centering on the epic-scale cattle raid of Cooley, was set down in its extant form in the eighth century. In this tale, Queen Maeve of Connaught [kuh-NOTT] raids Cooley to capture the brown bull, but the hero Cuchulian [KOO-hull-un] defeats her. *Tain* is a rich and intriguing tale full of universal themes and Irish peculiarities.

The Anglo-Saxons too were precocious in developing an impressive literature in Old English. In addition to legal, historical, and religious material, there survive thousands of lines of verse. Some of the lyric and elegiac poetry of Anglo-Saxon England is beautiful and moving. Best known, however, is the extraordinary anonymous epic *Beowulf.* Probably a work of the tenth century, this poem of 3,182 lines features a series of verbal and physical combats. Men fight monsters and one another, and loyalties are pledged and strained. The work is set in a remote past but clearly deals with contemporary issues. Although *Beowulf* makes no reference to Christianity or the church, some scholars see in it an implicit struggle between Christian and heroic values. The poem is dominated by a sense of gloom and foreboding—perhaps a poignant comment on human life itself.

On the Continent the German lands of the Carolingian world produced some interesting material in Old Saxon and Old High German. The most important work in Saxon is the *Heliand* [HAY-lee-ahnd] (*Savior*), an imaginative recasting of the Gospels. Almost certainly this ninth-century work was intended as an aid in evangelizing the militant Saxons. In this version, Jesus and the twelve apostles form a war band and Jerusalem becomes a hill fort.

THE VISUAL ARTS IN THE EARLY MIDDLE AGES

Brilliant visual display was a constant feature of the early medieval environment. Royal and imperial courts were major centers of patronage, but the church was the most generous patron. Accordingly, most art had religious themes and subject matter. If significant secular art existed, little has survived. Freestanding sculpture became very rare, although relief sculpture sometimes appeared in churches and some very fine ivory carvings survive. Large-scale mosaics were less common than in late Roman times, but in a few places, works of great beauty and high technical proficiency did appear. Painting regularly occupied two sites: the walls of churches and the pages of books.

East and West, a blending of cultural traditions is in evidence. In Byzantium, the late antique heritage mixed with the visual culture of frontier regions. In the West, late antique, barbarian, and Celtic traditions fused in a new art of beauty, energy, and originality.

Figure 8.6   Icon of Christ. Sixth century. Constantinople. Encaustic on wood, 33 × 18". This icon, preserved in the extremely remote monastery of St. Catherine on the Sinai peninsula, is an early example of what became a traditional way of representing the mature Christ in medieval art. Most icons were executed in an abstract, illusionistic style, but this one has a high degree of naturalism. The unknown artist uses naturalism to convey the religious message: this is both the son of God (signaled by the golden halo) and the son of man (indicated by the precise rendition of hand gestures and facial hair and features). The use of gold, an artificial touch, is a defining feature of Byzantine style.

Byzantine Art

Byzantine styles became relatively fixed in the age of Justinian. The Ravenna mosaics (see Chapter 7) are illustrative of the dominant style. Far off in the Sinai peninsula, however, monks at the monastery of St. Catherine painted or imported stunning icons. The

Figure 8.7   Icon of the Crucifixion. Ca. 700. Monastery of St. Catherine, Sinai. Tempera, 18.25 × 10". The Virgin (left) and St. John (right, the beloved disciple) stand on either side of the crucified Christ and in front of the two crucified thieves (the painting in its current state shows only the thief in the left rear). Beneath the cross, two Roman soldiers, oblivious to the meaning of the Crucifixion, cast lots for Christ's garments upon his death. The diminished size of the soldiers in relation to the central figures is typical of Byzantine style. This icon, based on John 19:18–26, represents a biblical narrative, unlike other icons that focus on a single, isolated figure (see Figure 8.6).

majestic icon of Christ (Figure 8.6), perhaps painted in the sixth century in Constantinople, makes Christ present to the viewer both immediately and timelessly. The naturalistic style evokes a sense of reality: this is not a picture of Christ; this *is* Christ. The picture attracts the reverence and awe of the viewer. Perhaps painted in the early eighth century, the crucifixion scene from St. Catherine's is quite different (Figure 8.7). Here, Christ is erect and garbed like a royal figure. His head is slightly tilted, he bears the crown of thorns, and his eyes are closed. He has suffered and died. This picture both evokes reverence and teaches a central truth of Christianity.

The iconoclastic era was probably less damaging to art than heretofore thought. Some images were removed, painted over, or replaced with simple crosses.

But on the whole, the early Byzantine environment was not as richly decorated as the post-iconoclastic world would be. In Hagia Sophia, for example, there is very little evidence of pre-iconoclastic images. In 867, however, the patriarch Photius installed a large mosaic of Mary and Jesus in the apse (Figure 8.8). There are earlier examples of this particular image—for example, the one commissioned by Pope Paschal I in Santa Maria in Domnica in Rome in the 820s (Figure 8.9). Subsequently this became one of the two dominant ways of depicting Mary with the baby Jesus. The Virgin of Vladimir, painted in Constantinople around 1100 (Figure 8.10), is the second. The former is called a *hodegetria* [hoe-duh-GEE-tree-uh], from Greek, "one who points the way," which means Mary essentially presents Jesus to the viewer. The latter is an *eleousa*

Figure 8.8 *Virgin and Child.* **Mosaic, Apse, Hagia Sophia, Constantinople, 867.** Between the ninth and twelfth centuries, Hagia Sophia received a vast program of figural mosaics. It appears that the church had mainly floral or geometric designs before that. The final victory of the iconodules in 842 may have encouraged them to begin putting images everywhere. As Figure 8.9 indicates, Rome and Constantinople may have been in some competition over claiming Mary's patronage.

Figure 8.9 *Virgin and Child.* **Mosaic, Apse, Santa Maria in Domnica, Rome, 817–824.** During his reign, Pope Paschal I donated several large mosaics to Roman churches as one way of registering his disapproval of Byzantine policies. This one has a special resonance. Since the seventh century, both Constantinople and Rome had claimed Mary as their special patroness. Here, Paschal presents himself as Mary's humble attendant, and he looks out to the assembly as if to remind them that he alone intercedes for them with Mary. His square nimbus (or halo) signifies a living person, and his face may reflect what he actually looked like.

Figure 8.10 *Icon of the Virgin and Child.* **Ca. 1100. Constantinople. 30.7 × 21.65″. Tretyakov Gallery, Moscow.** This icon depicts a loving moment between Mary and Jesus: their faces are pressed together, his face tilted upward and his gaze fixed upon her eyes. Painted in Constantinople, this icon was sent to Kiev as a gift to the new Russian church. Later it was moved to Vladimir and eventually to Moscow. The faces are original, but the rest of the work has been refurbished several times. Legend attributed this painting to St. Luke, and the faithful believed it to be miraculous.

Figure 8.11 *David Composing His Psalms,* **from Paris Psalter. Ca. 950. Constantinople. 14.75 × 10.4″. Bibliothèque Nationale de France, Paris. (Ms. Gr. 139 fol 1 v.)** This most richly decorated of all Byzantine psalters puts Byzantine classicism on vivid display. The scene is portrayed in receding three-dimensionality. David sits with his harp, but Melodia—the personification of song—and the nymph Echo attend him. In the lower right, Bethlehem is personified as a classical river god. David's presence in this painting has a dual purpose. First, in religious terms, he points to the coming of Christ (Matthew traces Christ's lineage from David). Second, David is the symbol of perfect rulership—a just and learned ruler (his learning based on his supposed authorship of the Psalms).

[ELL-ay-oo-sah], from Greek, "a tenderness," which means that the viewer sees Mary and Jesus in intimate relation with each other.

In the middle of the tenth century, amid other historicizing and classicizing efforts, an anonymous painter in Constantinople produced the magnificent Paris Psalter. This book has fourteen full-page images (Figure 8. 11) that exude a classicizing style which contrasts with the polemical messages and conventional style of the Khludov Psalter (see Figure 8.2).

Byzantine Architecture

Justinian's Hagia Sophia had a profound impact on all that would follow in Byzantium. Scholars now know that placing a dome on a square or elongated nave was not so much started as perfected in Hagia Sophia; there were earlier examples in Asia Minor. It is the sheer scale of Hagia Sophia that is novel. The Byzantines developed the **pendentive** (Figure 8.12), an inverted concave triangle that permitted the placement of a round dome over straight walls (Figure 8.13). Another critical feature of Hagia Sophia and of churches influenced by it is that it is centrally planned. In other words, it abandoned the traditional Roman basilican plan.

With Hagia Sophia showing the way, the success of the octagonal, or eight-sided, church of San Vitale in Ravenna helped to make the centrally planned church the signature Byzantine style (Figures 8.14 and 8.15). Although quite different in feel and effect, both San Vitale and Hagia Sophia add a vertical dimension that further escapes the horizontality of the basilican form preferred in Rome and generally in the Catholic

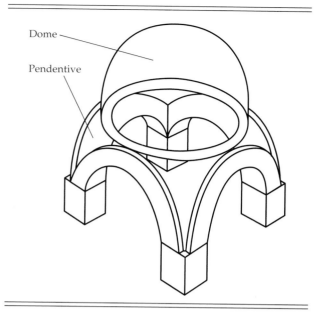

Figure 8.12   Pendentives. A pendentive is a triangular structure that permits the placement of a dome over a square space. The triangular arrangement receives the weight of the dome and transfers the thrust of the dome's weight to pier below the triangle.

Figure 8.13 Isidore of Miletus and Anthemius of Tralles. **Hagia Sophia, Interior. 532–537. Istanbul.** Hagia Sophia was the mother church of the Orthodox faith. After the Ottoman conquest, the church became an Islamic mosque, and some of the trappings, such as the calligraphic writings, survive from this stage of the building's life. Today, Hagia Sophia is a museum, and its striking mixture of Byzantine and Islamic elements makes it a vivid symbol of the meeting of West and East. The pendentive is clearly to be seen in the center of the picture.

West. The impact of this new style can be seen in the eleventh century monastic church of Hosios Loukas (St. Luke) (Figure 8.16).

Western Art

In the British Isles, images which artists saw in old books or perhaps during their travels combined with native tradition to produce a style that was playful and pleasing. The Ardagh [ARR-daw] Chalice—the cup used for the consecration of wine in Holy Communion—is a splendid example of Irish metalwork (Figure 8.17). The plain surfaces show a restraint appropriate to a liturgical vessel, but handles, rim, edges, and medallions provided the artist with an opportunity to give full vent to his flair for decoration. The extraordinarily intricate interlace designs fashioned from thin gold wire are thoroughly Irish in inspiration and exceptionally beautiful.

Manuscript illumination is another artistic realm in which the Irish excelled. The astonishing Book of Kells, probably made at Iona around 800, has been called "the chief relic of the Western world." In the page displayed in Figure 8.18, a Mary and Jesus scene, decoration and color are prominent. The elaborate interlace border is full of animal heads. Within the image, there are interlaces, gemlike sections, and complex geometric designs. While the reds and greens are vivid, blues are noteworthy too, along with gold. The figures are delightfully abstract yet recognizable.

The scene has an overall balance and harmony that is pleasing to the eye.

In England, in many manuscript paintings, the Irish influence may be seen in decorative patterns, along with other artistic and scholarly conceits, as in, for example, the Ezra Portrait from the Codex Amiatinus (Figure 8.19). Painted at the monasteries of Monkwearmouth and Jarrow in northern England, this painting is framed much in the manner of the Irish style. And its illusionistic appearance—modeled in light and dark and with naturalistic colors—is reminiscent of late antique art. The subject matter is biblical: Ezra, a Jewish prophet, copying the law after the exile. The setting, a library with books in a cabinet, perhaps suggests the quest in early medieval Europe to recapture the classical heritage.

Figure 8.14 San Vitale. 526–547. Ravenna, Italy. The centrally planned, octagonal church has antecedents in both East and West but, apart from Hagia Sophia, San Vitale is considerably larger than any predecessors. The exterior creates visual interest and complexity. The cupola is octagonal on the outside but domed on the inside. Construction was completed under Bishop Maximian (546–557), and the building was financed by Julianus Argentarius, a local financier. The church was built over the presumed grave of St. Vitalis as a thank-offering for the defeat of the heretical (Arian) Ostrogoths and the restoration of Justinian's authority.

Figure 8.15 Plan of San Vitale. Ravenna, Italy. This ground plan brings out the distinctive design elements of the church. The external octagon envelops a series of internal semicircular bays. The aisle is circular instead of horizontal. Above the aisle is a gallery, originally reserved to women for worship. The mosaics portraying Justinian and Theodora were on the sides of the apsidal sanctuary at the center right (for the one depicting Theodora, see Figure 7.19).

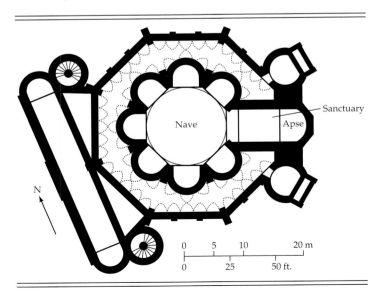

Figure 8.16 Hosios Loukas. Ca. 1020. Phokis, Greece. The Katholikon Church (the principal church in a monastery) was built on the site of the tomb of a local, wonder-working saint, Blessed Luke of Stiris. The use of pendentives and squinches creates a dome-over-square internal space of elegance and fine proportions. The interior has a rich array of mosaics and of decorative marble fittings.

Figure 8.17   Ardagh Chalice. Ca. 800. 7″ high × 7.67″ wide × 4″ deep. National Museum of Ireland. This chalice was found by two boys digging in a potato field in 1868 in the village of Ardagh in County Limerick. Assembled from 254 separate pieces of silver, gold, bronze, brass, pewter, glass, and enamel, this chalice is the supreme example of early Irish metalwork. The artist combined several different techniques including engraving, casting, filigree, cloisonné, and enameling. There are more than forty separate designs on the chalice with motifs ranging from prehistoric European, to Roman, Byzantine, and Celtic.

Figure 8.18   *Virgin and Child,* from Book of Kells. Ca. 800. 13 × 9.5″. Trinity College, Dublin. (Ms. 58 fol 34 r.) A mother holding an infant was a common scene in classical art and one early adopted by Christian artists. But here classical values have been left behind. The immobile faces and the modeling of the figures are so stylized that it is difficult to see what space they occupy. The painter took real delight in bright, arresting colors and in amazingly complex geometric and animal designs. Pictures like this one represent something new in medieval art. It is instructive to compare this image with Figures 8.8, 8.9, and 8.10.

Figure 8.19   *Prophet Ezra,* from Codex Amiatinus. Before 716. Monkwearmouth-Jarrow. 19.8 × 13.6″. Biblioteca Medicea Laurenziana, Florence. (Ms. Amiatinus 1 fol 5 r.) Bede's monasteries produced three complete (that is, both Old and New Testaments) Bibles, of which the Codex Amiatinus (so named because in the Middle Ages it was kept at the monastery of Monte Amiata in Italy) alone survives. It is the oldest surviving witness to Jerome's Vulgate. The portrait of Ezra copying out the Law after the Jews returned from exile (see Chapter 6) was placed at the front of the book—perhaps to symbolize the copying out of the Law in far-off England.

Figure 8.20 *Christ in Majesty*, **from Godescalc Evangelistary. 781–783. 12.63 × 8.25″. Bibliothèque Nationale de France, Paris. (Ms. nouv. acq. Lat. 1203, fol 3 r.)** Commissioned by Charlemagne as a gift for Pope Hadrian I, this book of gospel readings is written in Carolingian minuscule—one of the earliest surviving examples of this new script. The image of Christ in majesty portrays a youthful Christ, much as had been done in early Christian art but unlike the mature, bearded Christ that was emerging in Byzantine art.

Figure 8.21 *Presentation Miniature*, **from First Bible of Charles the Bald (Count Vivian Bible). 845. Paris, Tours. 19.5 × 14.75″. Bibliothèque Nationale de France, Paris. (Ms. Lat. 1 fol 423 r.)** This presentation scene, depicting the Carolingian ruler, comes from one of four complete Bibles produced by the monastery of Tours in the time of Charles the Bald (r. 838–877). While Charlemagne, the dynasty's greatest figure, left no contemporary portraits (except maybe on the silver denarius), his heirs fared much better, as can be seen in this splendid likeness. This vivid scene, with its natural colors, has a sense of depth, created by the modeling in light and dark. The painter stresses the ruler's status by enhancing his size at the expense of his officials. Thus, the seated Charles is as tall as Count Vivian of Tours, standing on the left.

On the Continent, in the Carolingian era, many traditions flowed together not least because the kings could attract the best scholars and artists to the royal court from all over Europe. Book painting began under Charlemagne with the Godescalc Evangelistary, an illuminated manuscript containing the Gospel readings for the Mass. Made between 781 and 783 by the court scribe and painter Godescalc, it contained five decorated figures, including *Christ in Majesty* (Figure 8.20). This figure, which became common in medieval art, shows Christ enthroned as the ruler of the world. In such figures as this one, local, Celtic, late antique, and Byzantine styles merge to make the Carolingian style. Despite the otherworldly subject, the artist has given the scene a natural feel with his use of natural colors and the sense of depth, which is conveyed by his use of light and dark. A significant advance in artistic technique and style appeared about twenty years later in the Lorsch Gospels, an illuminated manuscript of the Gospels produced at the scriptorium of Lorsch (in modern Germany) around 800. The unknown artist produced a series of arresting images, such as *Christ in Majesty* (see Interpreting Art).

Carolingian painting reached a glorious climax with the images in the spectacular Count Vivian Bible, produced by the monks at Tours (in modern France) and presented to Charles the Bald at Christmas, 845. The last image (Figure 8.21) in this Bible depicts the book's presentation to Charles—one of the first portrayals of an actual event in the Middle Ages. One of the arresting aspects of this image is its political and theological message: the right hand of God (above the enthroned Charles) is a clear signal of the source of the king's authority to rule. The figures are arrayed in a circle suggesting a procession (the artist had to work within his space!). The faces in the picture have

Interpreting Art

Composition An enthroned Christ, floating in space signifying that he is eternal—not bound to any place or time—is encircled by a circular band with eight angels and symbols of the four evangelists.

Context Few frescoes or mosaics survive from the early Middle Ages, so the majority of extant paintings are in books. Such paintings are called *illuminations*. The Carolingian court had the resources to summon skilled artists to produce at least a dozen books like this one. This kind of art was private and devotional, not public.

Aesthetic Perspective The Christ figure is painted in a classicizing style. The ground is purple, the imperial color. The page was underlaid with gold, signifying the richness of the offering. The circular and rectangular bands imitate the patterns of fine metalwork with designs adapted from Celtic and Germanic art. Along each band are cameos meant to look like jewels.

Iconographic Perspective Christ's left hand touches a gospel book while his right is extended in blessing. Surrounding Christ are the four evangelist symbols (see Chapter 6): Matthew, the man; Mark, the lion; Luke, the bull; and John, the eagle. Christ's right foot extends slightly into the picture space signifying that he shares heaven and earth.

Religious Perspective This image is called a *maiestas*, a "majesty." Christ is depicted as the all-ruling king. The image was taken over from late antique and Byzantine representations of Christ as *pantocrator*, "all ruler."

Ideological Perspective Although Carolingian kings, especially Charlemagne, saw themselves as the embodiment of Old Testament kings, they believed that the ultimate source of their kingship was Christ the King.

Christ in Majesty, from Lorsch Gospels. Ca. 810. Middle Rhine. 14.625 × 10.625". Batthyaneum Library, Alba Julia, Romania. (Ms. R II 1 fol 18 v.) This magnificent Gospel Book, prepared under the patronage of Charlemagne's court as a gift for the monastery of Lorsch, contains this figure and a series of four, full-page evangelist portraits. The manuscript was divided in the Middle Ages. The Gospels of Matthew and Mark are now in Romania while Luke and John are in the Vatican.

1. **Context** Why is book art more likely to survive than wall art?
2. **Aesthetic Perspective** Identify both classical and medieval elements in this image.
3. **Iconographic Perspective** Why did artists develop certain stylized, repeatable ways of representing certain images?
4. **Religious Perspective** What does Christ depicted "in majesty" suggest?
5. **Ideological Perspective** How might Carolingian kings have based their authority on that of Christ?

---

a certain sameness about them but are nevertheless lifelike. The king is flanked by two of his officials and then by two soldiers in Roman military gear. The references may be Roman or imperial or both. Charles, although enthroned, seems to float in space. The whole scene is bounded by an architectural frame.

Another grand era in the history of book painting happened during the reign of Otto III (r. 982–1002). A fine example of Ottonian art, taken from his tenth-century Gospel Book, produced at the monastery of Reichenau (in modern Germany), is the image that depicts Otto enthroned (Figure 8.22). In the manuscript, this image is one of two facing images. In the other one, Otto is depicted receiving homage from the provinces that comprised his realm—Slavinia, Germania, Gallia, and Roma. In contrast to the naturalism of Carolingian art, Otto is represented in a stiff, erect pose that suggests eminence and power. Staring without

Figure 8.22 *Emperor Enthroned*, from Gospels of Otto III, perhaps Reichenau. 997–1000. 13 × 9.375″. Bayerische Staatsbibliothek, Munich. (Ms. Clm. 4453 fol 24 r.) The drawing and modeling of the figures in this image are simple. The painter attains sophistication by the use of brilliant colors and plentiful gold. The scale (as in Figure 8.21) is hieratic, not natural; that is, figures are scaled according to their importance.

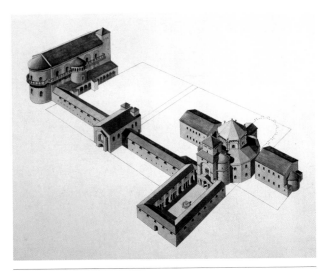

Figure 8.23 **Model of Charlemagne's Imperial Complex at Aachen. By Leon Hugot. Cathedral Museum, Aachen.** This model makes clear the basic components of the palace complex. The basilican royal hall and octagonal chapel align north-south with the hall to the north. The porticus—basically a covered passageway—joins the two main structures.

seeing, he meets no one's gaze. Flanking Otto are secular and ecclesiastical officials, the former holding swords and the latter Bibles, symbolizing the dual nature of Otto's imperial rule. That Otto's mother was a Byzantine princess may account for the presence of Byzantine features in these paintings.

Western Architecture

For two hundred years, nothing was built in the Christian West on anything like the scale of Hagia Sophia or San Vitale. Then, in the eighth century, the return of peace and prosperity awakened aspirations. In the south of Italy at the monastery of San Vincenzo al Volturno and in England at Winchester, huge—about 300-foot-long—basilicas were built. In Rome, Pope Hadrian I (772–795) built and rebuilt one church after another, and his successor, Leo III (795–816), erected two large **triclinia**—rectangular, multi-apsed banqueting and reception halls—for the papal court. At Aachen, Charlemagne began building his palace complex in about 788. He took up residence there in 794, and the structures were largely completed by 806.

The essential components of the original palace complex were a basilican hall, a long porticus, and a chapel (Figure 8.23). The hall, nearly 175 feet in length, was two stories high and contained official and residential quarters. The building was a **triconch**, that is, with an apse at one end and **conches** (apse-like

extrusions) on each long side. Triconch buildings had become very prestigious in late antiquity. The **porticus,** or covered gallery, ran more than 350 feet from the hall to the chapel. The chapel was modeled somewhat on San Vitale, or perhaps on the Lateran baptistery in Rome (Figure 8.24). The exterior is sixteen sided and the interior core is an octagon (Figure 8.25). The massive piers and powerful arches create alternating triangular and rectangular bays in the ambulatory at ground level. The piers then rise to create a gallery twice as high as the main floor. The gallery is surrounded by slender columns brought from Rome and Ravenna and by exquisite bronze **balustrades,** vertical posts connected by metal grillwork, apparently cast on the site. The piers reach to the base of the cupola, which is octagonal like the central core of the building. The overall effect of the chapel is stunning: the chapel is both massive and powerful, but, at the same time, it appears to spring from the ground and soar vertically to the heavens.

Aachen was spectacular, but its centrally planned design was not influential. The longitudinal basilica triumphed in the Carolingian world and after. To the traditional rectangular Roman basilica, Carolingian builders added two new features. At the monastery of Fulda (in modern Germany) and at some other places, for example, Cologne cathedral, basilicas were double apsed—they had an apse at each end (Figure 8.26). The Carolingian innovation with the brightest future however was the **westwork,** a tall, multistoried structure on the western end of a church. Divided into multiple interior chambers, westworks had both ceremonial and practical uses. Only one example of Carolingian westwork survives, at the monastery of Corvey in Saxony (in modern Germany) (Figure 8.27).

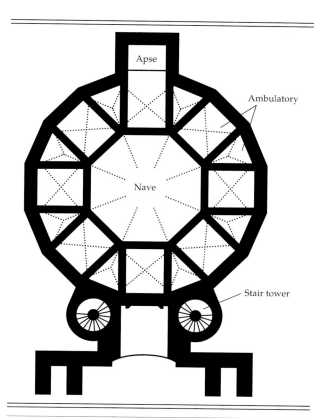

Figure 8.24   Palace Chapel. Aachen. Ca. 788–806. This chapel is the chief work of Carolingian architecture. The work is impressively complex in its mathematical proportions. For instance, each of the octagonal bays (vertical divisions of the interior or exterior of a building marked not by walls but by architectural features such as windows, columns, or vaulting) measures 18 feet across for a total of 144 feet, which is almost exactly the width of the building. The building may imitate San Vitale, but it is a significant reinterpretation. One late source says that the "master" responsible for the building was the otherwise completely unknown Odo of Metz. Most scholars think Einhard played a major role in its design and construction.

Figure 8.25   Ground Plan, Aachen Chapel. This plan illustrates the architectural complexity of the building. Comparing this plan with that of San Vitale in Ravenna (see Figure 8.15) reveals San Vitale's influence and shows how the Carolingian builders innovated.

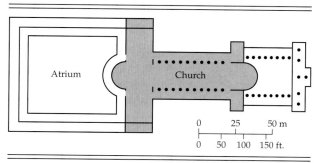

Figure 8.26   Plan of the Monastic Basilica of Fulda. 791–802. The double apses are clearly visible in the plan.

Figure 8.27   The Westwork of the Monastic Basilica of Corvey. Saxony. 883–885. This massive, yet flat, simple, and elegant western entry to the monastic church of Corvey is the largest standing example of Carolingian architecture. The rounded windows at the top with columns were added in the twelfth century during restorations.

TECHNOLOGY

The early Middle Ages saw some playful developments. For example, Liudprand, the envoy of Otto I to Constantinople, tells of Byzantine thrones that rose hydraulically and of magical golden trees in which artificial birds sang pretty tunes. But practical advances were more important in the military and agricultural fields.

Military Technology: Byzantine

- The Byzantine navy improved on Roman models with the *dromon,* a warship manned by a crew of up to three hundred men and capable of carrying bowmen, catapults, and the metal tubes for Greek fire (see below).
- By 700 the lateen sail was in use, allowing ships to be more responsive to the winds.
- Greek fire, probably a mixture of crude oil, sulfur, and resin, which would burn on water and stick to a surface, was first employed in 678 against the Arabs at the siege of Constantinople. Heated and then pushed through a metal tube, by means of a pump, or thrown from catapults in breakable containers, Greek fire became a very effective weapon in naval battles.

Military Technology: Western European

- The war saddle was adapted from contacts with invading peoples and provided greater stability for the rider.
- The curb bit, inserted in the horse's mouth, gave the rider greater control of his mount.
- The stirrup, probably borrowed from the Avars, further enhanced the rider's stability and control.
- The larger, more powerful warhorse was imported from the Arab world, through Spain.
- Mounted infantry, drawing on the technologies just listed, gave the Carolingians the capacity to move larger forces to more distant battlefields.

Agriculture

- The bipartite estate (later called the manor) divided lands in such a way that 25 to 40 percent of the land was reserved to a lord while the remainder of the estate was worked by the peasants for themselves. This type of estate permitted lords to remunerate vassals, and vassals to support themselves profitably.
- Vastly more land was brought under cultivation by clearing forests and draining marshes.
- Many areas switched from two- to three-field systems: two thirds of an estate were planted each year, usually one in spring and one in winter crops, with one third lying fallow. Previously it had been common to farm only half an estate per year.
- Heavy iron plows, with a mould board that turned the soil dug up by the plowshare, were used on large estates (but may not have spread to ordinary peasants).

MUSIC

Einhard reports that Charlemagne loved the "old barbarian songs." Unfortunately, neither he nor anyone else wrote them down. All the music that survives from East or West is religious and, at that, connected with the liturgy. Moreover, almost everything known pertains to vocal music.

Music became integral to the church's liturgy during the early Middle Ages and kept alive the Greek heritage of music as an art form. From this religious foundation ultimately arose all of the sacred and secular music of the modern West. The name of Pope Gregory the Great is preserved in the early medieval musical form the **Gregorian chant,** which became the official liturgical music of the early church—used in the Mass (the celebration of the Eucharist) and other services of the yearly cycle of public worship. The chants consisted of a single melodic line sung by male voices in unison—called **monophony**—without instrumental accompaniment. They had an impersonal, nonemotional quality and served religious rather than aesthetic or emotional purposes. Notwithstanding this aim, the chants cast a spell over their listeners, evoking in them feelings of otherworldliness, peace, and purity.

The ninth century saw two of the most important advances in music history: the rise of **polyphony**—two lines of melody sounded at the same time—and musical notation. Polyphony, unlike the monophonic Gregorian chants, gave music a richer, more textured quality. Musical notation owed much to Charlemagne's desire for uniformity in worship. He sought to impose Gregorian chant, but how might this be possible? The transmission of melodies required a face-to-face encounter between a trained singer and his pupils. Only by developing a system of written musical notation could anything approaching uniformity be achieved. First, at the monastery of Saint Amand in northern France, **neumes**—a pattern of dots and squiggles—began to be placed above the lines of text, to help singers follow the contour (up or down) the melody. Two later composers, Hucbald (d. 930) and Guido of Arezzo (d. 1050), created the staff, parallel lines running across a page and signaling pitch.

SUMMARY

Rome had two heirs. One, Byzantium, the eastern Roman Empire, gradually evolved into a new medieval regime. Faced with severe military threats, this new Byzantine Empire reformed its military and political institutions. Its Christian community developed a distinctive religious tradition that we know as Orthodoxy. In the West, small kingdoms on the Continent coalesced into the Carolingian Empire, the largest western regime between Rome and Napoleon. That regime put a decisive stamp on European culture with its blend of Roman, Germanic, and Christian elements. In Britain, Roman collapse was followed in turn by small Anglo-Saxon kingdoms, a unified kingdom, assaults by Vikings, and a renewed England. In intellectual life, Byzantines and Europeans struggled to revive an ancient Christian and classical heritage while also making contributions of their own. In art and architecture, local and ancient traditions were synthesized in new ways.

The Legacy of Byzantium and the West in the Early Middle Ages

Istanbul, since the Ottoman conquest of 1453 the name for Constantinople, remains the spiritual center of Orthodox Christianity as Rome remains the home of Catholicism. Byzantium evangelized the Slavs and eventually Moscow would be regarded as the "Third Rome." The popes once ruled much of Italy but today preside over only a small enclave surrounded by modern Rome. The empire of Charlemagne constitutes the foundation on which modern Europe was built. The original European Economic Community of 1957 included Germany, France, Belgium, Italy, Luxembourg, and the Netherlands—exactly Charlemagne's "Europe." Today's "Eurozone" encompasses seventeen members. Every year since 1950, the city of Aachen has awarded the "International Charlemagne Prize" to a person who has made an outstanding contribution to European unity. Caroline minuscule forms the basis for most modern typefaces, including the one in this book. There are still communities of Benedictine monks all over the world. Today's musical scores are but modifications of the system created in the early Middle Ages. Today's churches no longer always point their most prominent facade to the west, but to the extent that they are vertical and prominent, they are Carolingian. The Carolingians anchored the seven liberal arts at the core of an educational system that has not yet vanished. Students of the humanities owe a debt to Alcuin and Charlemagne.

Figure 8.28 Charlemagne Prize Medallion. Awarded every year by the Aachen city government on Ascension Thursday—the Christian feast is a deliberate attempt to evoke Europe's increasingly faint Christian past—the Karlspreis, or Prix de Charlemagne, is meant to honor a distinguished person in the name of the ruler deemed the "founder of European culture." The gold medallion is reminiscent of gold medallions issued from time to time by Charlemagne himself but is actually an exact copy of Aachen's early-twelfth-century town seal. Its legend reads "Charles the Great Emperor of the Romans." Charlemagne would have rejected that title!

KEY CULTURAL TERMS

themes	squinch	conch	monophony
capitularies	vernacular	porticus	polyphony
Carolingian minuscule	pendentive	balustrade	neumes
the seven liberal arts	triclinia	westwork	
prosimetric	triconch	Gregorian chant	

The Great Mosque of Mecca. The original mosque was built in the seventh century, but the present one is essentially the Ottoman mosque of 1570. The mosque covers some 3,840,563 square feet. Its central courtyard, with the *kaaba* shrine, is the site of pilgrimage for Muslims from all over the world.

The Rise of Islam

622–1520

Preview Questions

1. *What* forces contributed to the cohesion and to the disunity of the Islamic Empire?

2. *How* can Islam be been called a religion of "orthopraxy" (right conduct) more than of "orthodoxy" (right belief)?

3. *To what extent* do Western concepts such as realism, illusionism, and naturalism apply to the Islamic arts?

4. *Describe* the two main kinds of mosques. How are mosques like and unlike churches?

The Islamic faith with its new political regimes constituted a third heir to the Roman Empire. The word *Islam* is Arabic for "submission" (to God); a *Muslim* is "one who has surrendered," or accepted the beliefs and practices of Islam. At its largest, the Islamic Caliphate, or Empire, stretched from Spain to the frontiers of China (Map 9.1). The Islamic world built on the culture of the Arabs, the teachings of the prophet Muhammad, and the traditions of many of the peoples folded into the caliphate. Creative and international, Islamic culture was the source of both scholarly advances and artistic achievements.

The photograph shows thousands of pilgrims assembled in the courtyard of the Great Mosque in Mecca, the most hallowed shrine in the Islamic world. The Great Mosque brackets this chapter: founded in the 630s and in its present form rebuilt by the Ottomans in 1570. Since the time of Muhammad, every Muslim male is expected to make a pilgrimage to this mosque at least once in his lifetime. The Muslim community, the *umma Muslima,* includes all those who have made the "surrender." Although it arose among the Arabs, Islam is no longer identified with a particular country or region or with any one ethnic or racial group. The mosque is not only a place of worship but also a school. Its architecture bears the distinctive characteristics of Islamic architecture all over the world.

The pre-Islamic Arabs inhabited the Arabian peninsula, a dry land wedged between the Red Sea and the Persian Gulf. Bedouin sheep and goat herders and small farmers occupied the land while urban merchants lived in the towns along the Red Sea coast. Neither the Romans nor the Persians ever conquered the Arabian peninsula. By the early seventh century, the Arabic language had spread throughout the peninsula, binding the inhabitants with a common tongue and oral literary tradition. Jews and Christians, lured by the prospects of wealth and trade, migrated into southern Arabia. From them the Arabs acquired additional knowledge of

Learning Through Maps

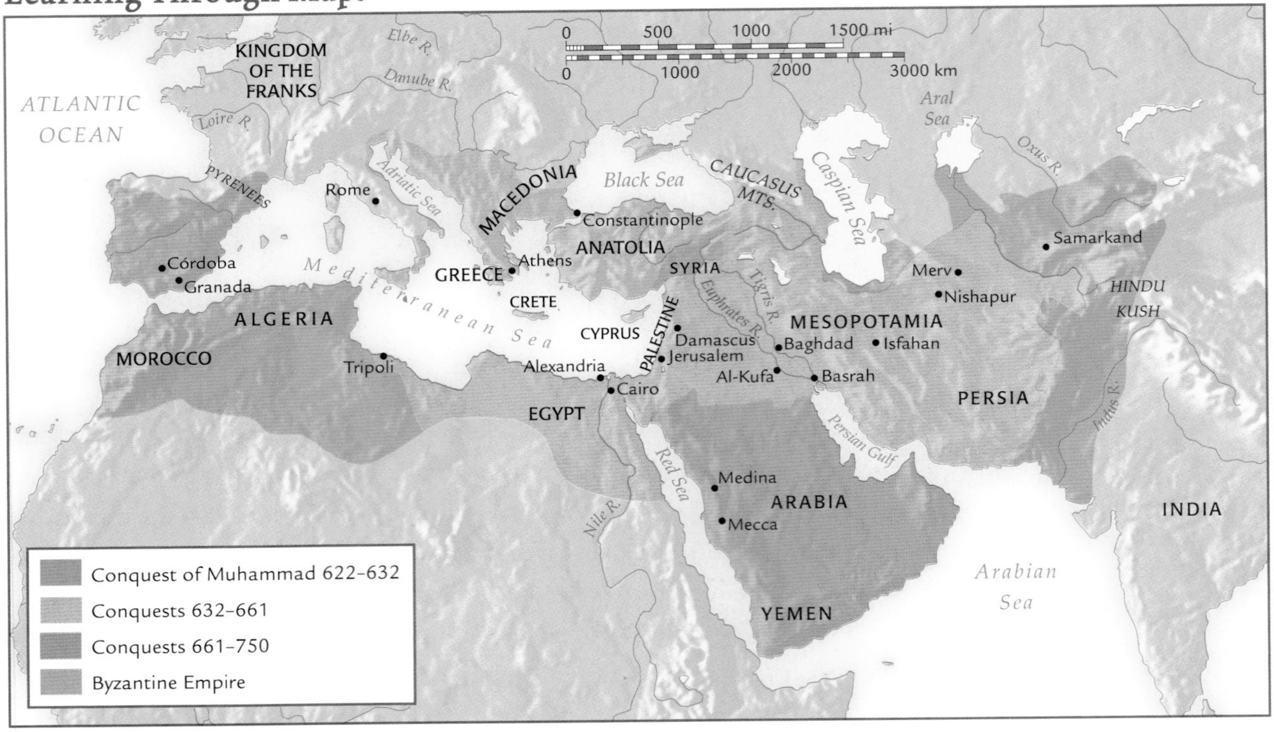

MAP 9.1 THE WORLD OF ISLAM, 622–750

This map shows the successive expansion of the Islamic world between 622 and 750. *1. **Notice** the three phases of expansion. 2. **Consider** how the expansion of Islam threatened the Byzantine Empire and the Kingdom of the Franks. 3. **Identify** the three successive capitals of the Islamic Empire. 4. **What** problems would the Muslims face in conquering so much land so quickly and ruling such diverse peoples? 5. **Compare** the size of the Islamic holdings in 750 with the size of the Roman Empire under Augustus in Map 5.2, The Roman Empire in the Time of Hadrian.*

weaponry, textiles, food and wine, and writing. In Mecca, the leading commercial city on the southern trade route, Jews, Christians, and Arabs not only exchanged products and wares but also shared ideas and values.

MUHAMMAD, THE PROPHET

Muhammad, the founder of Islam and one of the most commanding figures in history, was born in the city of Mecca in 570. His father was from a minor but respected clan within the city's most powerful tribe, the Quraysh. Orphaned when quite young, Muhammad was reared by grandparents and an uncle. He entered the caravan trade, acquired a reputation for honesty, and became financial adviser to a wealthy Quraysh widow, Khadija [kah-DEE yah], whom he married. Their only surviving child, Fatima [FAT-uh-mah], was to become a revered religious figure (Figure 9.1).

In 610 Muhammad began to receive revelations from the archangel Gabriel that convinced him Allah had called him to be his prophet to the Arab people. Muhammad slowly gathered a small band of converts.

As his fame grew, he became known simply as "the Prophet."

At first, Mecca's leaders paid scant attention to Muhammad. However, he became a controversial figure when, in the name of Allah, he declared that there was only one God, attacked the polytheistic beliefs of his fellow Arabs, and condemned as idolatrous the *Kaaba* ("cube"), a local pagan shrine that housed a sacred black rock. Since the Kaaba was not only a holy place but also a source of revenue generated by the thousands of pilgrims who visited it each year, Mecca's leaders feared that they were in danger of losing one of their most profitable attractions. They also considered Muhammad to be socially inferior and uneducated. Soon hostility turned to persecution. Fearing for his life, Muhammad and a few followers fled, in 622, to Yathrib, a neighboring city. This historic flight, or Hegira (*hijra*), transformed Muhammad's message of reform into a call for a new religion. And the date, 622 CE, marks the year 1 for Muslims.

According to tradition, Muhammad was welcomed into Yathrib and quickly made a name for himself by settling several disputes that had divided its citizens.

Figure 9.1 *Fatima.* **Chester Beatty Library, Dublin.** Fatima, veiled and dressed in white, kneels beside two of Muhammad's wives. Although Fatima is not mentioned in the Qur'an, her reputation grew over the years among the Shiite Muslims. She became the ideal woman, possessing extraordinary powers similar to those of the Virgin Mary in Roman Catholicism. Devout Shiite women appeal to her for guidance and protection, and worship at her shrines.

He emerged as a judge and lawgiver as well as a military leader. In Yathrib, Muhammad was able to found his ideal community, where religion and the state were one. Yathrib became known as Medina, or "the City," a name that denoted its position as Islam's model city.

Before the Hegira, Muhammad had formulated the basic doctrines of Islam. In Medina, he put them into practice to solve social and legal problems and to offer guidelines for everyday life and social interactions. Muhammad, it is believed, also drew up a charter defining relations among the Medinese people, his own followers, and the Jews, who were influential in the city. Most important, this charter established several fundamental principles. Faith, not blood or tribe, unified the believers; Muhammad, as the voice of Allah, was a ruler and not a consensus builder; and Islam was the only source of spiritual and secular authority. Medina became a theocratic state as political and religious objectives blurred into one. Eventually, tensions between the Jews and the followers of Muhammad reached the point where Muhammad exiled the Jews. At the same time, he expunged any rituals that might have had Jewish associations. Specifically, he changed the direction for praying from Jerusalem to Mecca, he called for pilgrimages to the Kaaba, and he moved the day of collective prayer from Saturday to Friday.

While Muhammad held sway in his newly adopted home, conflicts between Medina and Mecca grew as Medinese raiders attacked the caravans traveling over the trade routes from Mecca. Desert warfare soon erupted. From 624 to 628, the two cities fought three major battles, the last one resulting in a victory for Muhammad's forces. Now in full control of Medina and having repelled the Meccan army, Muhammad was ready to return to Mecca.

Muhammad and about one thousand of his followers set out as pilgrims to the Kaaba shrine. Mecca's Quraysh leaders faced a dilemma: If they attacked or tried to prevent the pilgrims from worshiping, they would be violating their role as protectors of the shrine. But if they did nothing, they risked turning their city over to Muhammad and his supporters. As a way out of this impasse, a Quraysh delegation negotiated a treaty that allowed Muhammad to visit Mecca the next year as a pilgrim in exchange for his returning to Medina. This peaceful solution convinced many Arab tribes that Muhammad's new faith and tactics were legitimate, and they soon converted to Islam.

In 629 Muhammad made his pilgrimage, winning new converts during a three-day visit. The next year, when the Quraysh attacked one of Muhammad's allied tribes, he raised an army of ten thousand to march on Mecca. Faced with these odds, the Quraysh opened the city, their leaders accepted the new faith, and the Prophet entered triumphantly. He destroyed the pagan idols at the Kaaba, and he forgave his enemies who became Muslims. Nearby tribes sent delegations to Mecca, from which contacts Muhammad constructed a network of personal and political alliances across the Arabian peninsula based on recognition of Mecca's power and agreement not to attack Muslims and their allies. On the eve of his death in 632, Muhammad had achieved what no Arab leader before him had done: he had brought peace to Arabia and united its inhabitants; and, at the same time, he had given the Arabs a new faith based on revelation, an ethical code of conduct, and a monotheistic deity.

IMPERIAL ISLAM

Islam evolved through a series of dynasties in the first nine hundred years of its history. The dynasties can be divided into five major periods, which sometimes overlapped (Timeline 9.1).

The Post-Muhammad Years

A leadership crisis followed Muhammad's death until the Meccan elite chose Abu Bakr [AH-bu BAK-er] (573–643) as *caliph* ("representative" or "successor"). Abu Bakr and his three successors were Meccans, early converts to Islam, and relatives of the Prophet by marriage. Islamic tradition calls them the *rashidun* ("rightly guided") to distinguish them from the caliphs of later dynasties. The first three rashidun caliphs were great warriors; the last three were murdered. Ali, killed in 661, was Muhammad's cousin and son-in-law, having married the Prophet's daughter, Fatima. Centuries later the *Shia,* the party of Ali, looked back to Ali as the divinely appointed. To this day, that Islamic world is divided between the Shiites and Sunnis.

During his brief rule, Abu Bakr suppressed a revolt of Arab tribes and launched numerous raiding parties beyond the Arabian peninsula—a step that inaugurated Islam's imperial period. Although the Arabs took their share of loot, they neither destroyed towns or villages—indeed, they tended to build new ones—nor tried to convert their new subjects to Islam. "People of the book" (*dhimmis*)—initially, Christians and Jews but later Buddhists too—were allowed to keep their religion as long as they paid taxes and obeyed the local Muslim authorities.

The Umayyad Dynasty

Muawiyah [mu-A-we-ya] (about 602–680) founded the Umayyad dynasty in 661, which lasted until 750. Muawiyah moved the capital of his new empire from Medina to Damascus—a cosmopolitan trade center located more centrally in the Middle East—signifying an important shift in Arab politics and worldviews.

Timeline 9.1   THE WORLD OF ISLAM, 630–1517

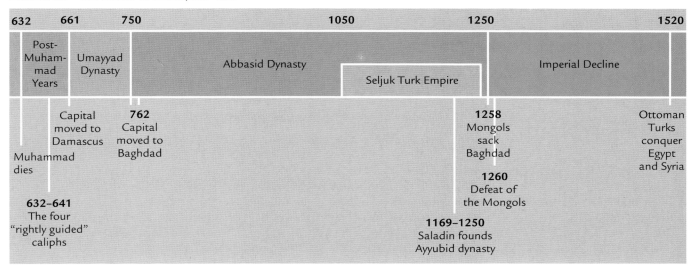

Under this dynasty, territorial expansion continued. As more people came under Arab control and converted to Islam, intense social and political conflicts arose in the caliphate. Old converts looked down on new ones, and Meccan elites lorded it over everybody.

The Abbasid Dynasty

During the 740s, a series of uprisings by frontier peoples and recent converts undermined the Umayyad regime. In 750 an army led by a member of the Abbasid clan defeated the last Umayyad ruler. The Abbasids, who claimed to be descendants of Abbas, the uncle of Muhammad, moved the capital from Damascus to Baghdad in modern Iraq—an old trading city that now became Islam's cultural center and the home of the caliphs. During the Abbasid period, Islamic peoples from other traditions began to play prominent roles in government, society, and culture. The Persians, a people with a centuries-old civilization, now exerted a strong influence in the arts and learning and set the tone and atmosphere at the Abbasid court. Persians also staffed the state bureaucracy and ran the government. Persian prime ministers, who ruled in the name of the caliph, made day-to-day decisions. Turks, Kurds, and other hired mercenaries gradually replaced Arabs in the imperial armies.

The Fragmentation of the Caliphate

The rulers in Baghdad proved incapable of holding the vast caliphate together. By the late ninth century, the Abbasids controlled a glittering court but had little effective power elsewhere. They had gradually handed military authority to Turkish mercenaries, and, when marauding Seljuk Turks invaded the caliphate in the eleventh century, Abbasid rule ended, even though there were caliphs until 1258. The Seljuks also dealt the Byzantines a crushing defeat in 1071 that resulted in the emperor's eventual request for Western assistance; that assistance took the form of the Crusades.

In their empire, the Seljuks generally ruled through local sultans, and, as the central power weakened, some of the sultans became especially influential. One was the charismatic Saladin (1137–1193), a Kurd and the founder of the Ayyubid dynasty that ruled Egypt as well as much of Palestine, Syria, and Iraq from 1169 to 1250. Saladin is best known for defeating the largest crusading army ever assembled in 1187, but he is more important for his governmental acumen and his elevation of Cairo into a center of learning. By the 1250s the fearsome Mongols, who had been conquering Muslim lands in central Asia since the 1220s, reached Mesopotamia and seized Baghdad—thus putting an end to the Abbasids and to what was left of Seljuk power.

The idea of a caliphate, embracing the Muslim world, reflected a central teaching of Islam: the *umma Muslima*—the belief in a single community of believers. Until the 750s, the Umayyad Caliphate did realize that dream. Fragmentation began with the Abbasids. Spain was never part of the Abbasid Caliphate but stayed loyal to its Umayyad conquerors. Then, in 956, Spain emerged as the Western Caliphate of Córdoba, a period of great intellectual achievement. Córdoba maintained unified rule only until 1031 after which date Spain broke down into numerous independent principalities. At the same time, North Africa was falling prey to a series of rival Muslim dynasties. And Egypt was ruled by no fewer than three dynasties in this period: the Shiite Fatimids, the Ayyubids (just discussed), and the Turkish Mamelukes. The Mamelukes, in turn, defeated the Mongols in 1260, causing further splintering of the Islamic lands.

The Rise of the Ottomans

Anatolia (Turkey) fragmented into numerous small states. The leader of one of them, Osman (1258–1326), whose name means "Bone Breaker," proved to be ambitious and capable. By 1300 he dominated Anatolia and in 1302 he defeated a Byzantine army. He founded a dynasty—Ottoman derives from his name—that would rule until the early twentieth century. In the fourteenth and early fifteenth centuries, the Ottoman sultans expanded their conquests in the Balkans. Mehmet the Conqueror (r. 1451–1481) conquered Constantinople and made it his capital. Sultan Selim (r. 1512–1520) expanded into central Asia as well as conquering Iran and Egypt. The Ottoman Empire became the premier state in the eastern Mediterranean. Its dominations depended on the control of vast trade routes (Figure 9.2), a huge and well-trained army, and the *millet* system which accorded considerable religious autonomy to subject regions.

Islam as Religion

Islam's confession of faith—the *shahadah*—is simple: "There is no God but Allah and Muhammad is His prophet." Muslims worship the same God as Jews and Christians, but Muslims believe Muhammad to be the final prophet in a tradition that dates from Abraham and Moses in Judaism, and that recognizes Jesus Christ, not as the son of God, but as the giver of the Christian prophecy.

Figure 9.2   Courtyard and Mosque. Sultan Han Caravanserai. Aksaray, Turkey. 1229. Heavily restored.
This *caravanserai*, or way station for merchants, pilgrims, and other travelers, was built by the Seljuk sultan Alaad-Din Kayqubad. *Han* is Turkish for "caravanserai." Located along well-traveled caravan routes, at distances about a day's travel apart (about twenty-five miles), caravanserais were usually heavily fortified and offered amenities, such as food and lodging for travelers, fodder and stables for the animals, and protection to all. The courtyard of the Sultan Han caravanserai is surrounded by an arcade that opens to a series of rooms on one side and covered places on the other. A small mosque stands in the center of the courtyard.

Figure 9.3   Fragment from a Qu'ran with Kufic script, North African (vellum). African School (10th century). Chester Beatty Library, Dublin. Kufic calligraphy, which originated in the city of al-Kufa in Iraq, was used in mosque decoration and the writing of early copies of the Qur'an. Because Islam opposed the representation of figures in most art, calligraphy was one of the major forms available to Muslim artists.

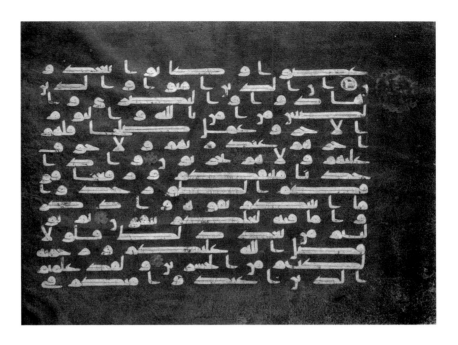

Muhammad's prophecies make up the text of the *Qur'an,* a word that literally means "recitation" (Figure 9.3). These prophecies were assembled in final form in the generation after the Prophet's death. Nevertheless, for pious Muslims, the Qur'an is the eternal word of God revealed through the archangel Gabriel to the Prophet. In the historical context, however, the Qur'an was compiled by Muslim scholars between 640 and 650 on the orders of the caliph. Again on a caliph's orders, all other collections of sayings were gathered in Mecca and destroyed. From the middle of the seventh century, there has been a single authoritative text. Finally, the caliphs insisted that the language of the Qur'an be the Arabic dialect of the Quraysh tribe.

The text of the Qur'an consists of 114 *suras* (chapters) arranged from the longest to the shortest. Each chapter is divided into *ayas* (verses). The whole collection is about two-thirds as long as the New Testament. The style resembles a type of rhymed prose. Muhammad's utterances reveal him to be a master of literary expression and rhetoric. Many converts came to Islam because they were swayed as much by the Qur'an's evocative language as by its message. Its elevated tone and poetic qualities appeal to the faithful's soul, or inner being.

Within a century of Muhammad's death, a collection of the Prophet's sayings, proclamations, and instructions appeared in the Hadith, or "the report (or narrative)" of the prophet's actions and sayings. Likewise, there emerged written collections of the Sunnah, the religious customs and practices of the Prophet. Muslims use the Hadith and Sunnah as a supplement to the Qur'an and regard it as a source to explain their laws, rituals, and dogma. Today, the Hadith, Sunnah,

Qur'an, commentaries on the Qur'an, and the Arabic language make up the core curriculum taught in Islamic religious schools.

In early Islam, two types of schools soon emerged. The elementary school, maintained by a mosque (house of worship), offered boys basic religious education, along with training in how to read and interpret the Qur'an. Advanced learning took place in a *madrasa,* the first of which was established in the ninth century in Fez, in modern Morocco. By the twelfth century, these schools had spread to most major cities in the Islamic world. At first, their curriculum included only law, literature, philosophy, and theology, but, over time, mathematics, astronomy, and medicine were added (Figure 9.4). Some *madrasas* became famous for particular areas of study, and local rulers often supported these schools in order to attract scholars and heighten their own prestige.

The Qur'an and the Hadith offer truth and guidance to the faithful. However, the core of Muslim religious life rests on the Five Pillars, or Supports, of the Faith—which include the *shahadah* and four required devotional practices. The four acts of devotion are to pray (*salat*) five times a day facing Mecca (Figure 9.5), to fast (*sawm*) from dawn to sunset during the month of Ramadan, to give alms (*zakat*) to the poor, and to make a pilgrimage (*hajj*) to Mecca at least once in one's life.

Not one of the Five Pillars but central to the faith is the idea of *jihad,* which basically means "to strive" or "to struggle." Muslims "struggle" against sinning, or doing evil, and strive to follow the demands of the Qur'an and the Five Pillars of the Faith. Thus, *jihad* is a moral or spiritual striving or fight within the individual to do the right thing. However, *jihad* has other

Figure 9.4   Scene from a *Madrasa*. Bibliothèque Nationale de France, Paris. (Ms. Arabe 5847 fol 5v.) This manuscript page, with Arabic writing at the top and bottom, shows a Muslim scholar, the second person to the right holding an open book, explaining a particular text to his students. Behind the students and teacher are stacks of books set on open shelves, suggesting a library setting for the classroom. All students are male and have beards—as required by Islamic law. Adorning the room's upper level are typical decorative motifs of Islamic art, such as intricate foliage patterns and designs.

meanings, such as "holy war," a definition often found in the Western media. Many modern Muslims reject the linkage between *jihad* and holy war, but certain groups within Islam consider *jihad* to be a Sixth Pillar of the Faith. The belief that *jihad* means holy war can lead, and has led, to military action on the part of individuals, of groups, or of states to protect the community, to defend the faith, or to promote Islam.

In the eighth century, Muslim orthodoxy, also known as Sunni Islam, was challenged by the rise of Sufism, a mystical movement. Sufism emerged as both a reaction to the worldliness of the Umayyad dynasty rulers and a desire, on the part of some especially dedicated Muslims, to return to what they perceived to be the simpler faith that Muhammad had taught and practiced. Sufis rejected the legalism and formalism that had crept into Islam, and they challenged the power and influence of the *ulama,* or the learned elite who interpreted the Qur'an and guarded the tradition

of the faith. A majority rejected the Sunni position that all revelations from Allah were now complete, for they felt that religious truths were to be found in many places, even in other faiths. The word *Sufi* derives either from Arabic *safa,* meaning "pure," or from *suf,* meaning "wool." So pure Muslims wore coarse woolen garments as a symbol of their ascetic life and in memory of the simple garb worn by Muhammad. In some ways, Sufism resembled Christian monasticism.

Like most societies where codes of law are rooted in religious practice and tradition, the Muslim world established the holy law of Islam—the *Sharia*—on their faith. For Muslims, this body of sacred laws was derived, in its earliest forms, from the Qur'an, Sunnah, and Hadith. Although Muslim jurists, intellectuals, and scholars have added to the Islamic law over the centuries, the basic purpose remains the same: to tell the faithful what to believe and how to live their daily lives.

Figure 9.5 Kutubiyya *Minbar*. Ca. 1137–1145. Bone and colored woods, ht. 12′10″, width 2′10¼″, depth 11′4¼″. Kutubiyya Mosque, Marrakech, Morocco. Islamic. Three-quarter view from the right. Richly decorated *minbars*, or portable pulpits, were used by local prayer leaders to address worshipers during Friday services. A *minbar* is basically a wooden staircase on wheels, with a seat at the top of the stairs for the prayer leader. This intricately detailed example was assembled from perhaps a million pieces of bone and fine African woods.

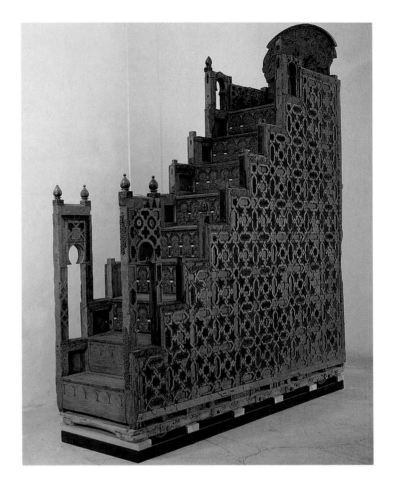

MEDIEVAL ISLAMIC CULTURE

From the ninth to the twelfth century, Islamic scholars, intellectuals, and inventors made significant advances in medicine; in the humanities, including mathematics, philosophy, and history; and in technology. Muslim scholars tended to be highly versatile, often making contributions in more than one field of study.

Medicine

Muslim doctors, whose skills were superior to those of their Western contemporaries, obtained their knowledge from Greek texts that were translated into Arabic about the middle of the ninth century. In addition, Islamic medicine had a practical approach to the curing of disease, namely, through the use of observation and experimentation. Islamic medicine also made advances in ophthalmology, formulated new drugs, stressed the role of diet in the treatment of various maladies, and made the first clinical distinction between measles and smallpox. Surgeries, such as amputations, trepanning (opening the skull), and cesarean sections, were occasionally performed (Figure 9.6).

Figure 9.6 A Doctor Performing an Operation. Edinburgh University Library. Muslim physicians normally did not operate on patients, preferring to use medicines and noninvasive procedures. Sometimes operations were necessary, as in this illustration of a woman having a cesarean section. The surgeon is helped by several attendants: the one on the right holds the patient's head, while the one on the left hands instruments to the doctor.

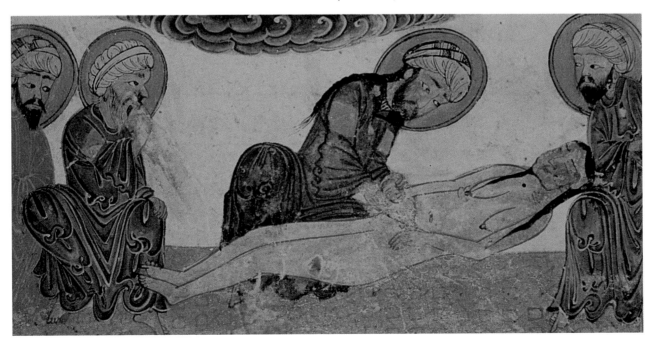

Muhammad al-Razi [al-RAY-zee] (about 865 to between 923 and 935) set the standard for medicine, both as a practicing doctor and as a scholar. A prolific writer, he compiled a twenty-volume medical encyclopedia in which he noted his own findings and took issue with the ancient Greeks and their medical tradition. Al-Razi also treated childhood diseases and wrote a treatise on them, earning the title "Father of Pediatrics." Most of his writings were translated into Latin and became part of the curriculum in Western medical schools until the nineteenth century.

Mathematics and Astronomy

Al-Khwarizmi [al-KWAHR-iz-me] (780–850) advanced the field of algebra; he also introduced Hindu numerals, which became known as Arabic numerals, and used them to make calculations. His near-contemporary al-Battani [al-ba-TAN-e] (about 858–929) corrected errors in the Ptolemaic planetary system and constructed an elaborate astronomical table. His writings on equinoxes and eclipses, in which he showed the possibility of solar eclipses, were translated by European scholars into Latin, making him the best-known Arab astronomer in medieval Europe (Figure 9.7). Both al-Khwarizmi and al-Battani were associated with the "House of Wisdom" in Baghdad, the capital of the Abbasid dynasty. Another scholar, Ibn al-Haytham [IB-en al-hi-THAM] (965–1039), who spent his life in Cairo, studied the Ptolemaic system of planetary motions, expanded on the mathematical work of Euclid, and developed new ideas about optics and light rays. Through points of contact in Sicily and Spain, Muslim mathematics and astronomy were influential in the West until the seventeenth century.

Philosophy and History

The two most creative early Muslim thinkers were Ibn Sina [IB-en SEE-nah] (980–1037), known in the West as Avicenna [av-ah-SEN-ah], and Ibn Rushd [IB-en RUSHT] (1126–1198), known in the West as Averroës

Figure 9.7 *Shahanshahnama (Book of the King of Kings).* **1581–1582. From historian Lokman bin Seyyid Huseyin. Topkapi Palace Museum, Istanbul.** In the 1570s, Arab astronomers, under the guidance of Taqi al-Din, the head astronomer of the Ottoman Empire, studied the heavens with various instruments at an observatory in Istanbul. To make their observations and calculations, they used astrolabes, hourglasses, globes, and a mechanical clock built by Taqi al-Din. Many of their instruments were similar to those later used by Western astronomers in the explorations of the universe.

[uh-VER-uh-weez]. Both were well educated in the liberal arts, and although both were trained in medicine and became highly respected physicians, they wrote extensively not only in medicine but also in metaphysics, theology, and religion.

Philosophy   Avicenna and Averroës served at the courts of Islamic rulers, where they engaged in heated controversies with other Muslim scholars. Avicenna, a Persian, spent most of his life in present-day Iran. By the age of twenty-one, he had mastered logic, metaphysics, and Islamic law and religion as well as medicine. Appointed court physician, he advised and served numerous Persian rulers. Over the years he wrote nearly two hundred works on medicine and other sciences, languages, philosophy, and religion. His *Canon of Medicine,* one of the most important books in the history of medicine, surveyed the achievements of Greek and Roman physicians, Arab doctors, and his own findings. As Avicenna's reputation grew, Arab and Western medical schools used his encyclopedia of classical and Arab medicine as their authoritative source for centuries. His philosophical works addressed Aristotelian philosophy and Neoplatonism and attempted to reconcile both to Islam, including the Qur'an and other holy writings. Through these works, Avicenna strived to understand the essence of God in the physical and metaphysical worlds. His writings on the nature of God later influenced Western medieval thought, especially Scholasticism (see Chapter 10).

Averroës, Islam's foremost thinker and one of the world's greatest minds, had even more of an impact on the West than did Avicenna. Born and reared in Córdoba, Spain, in a distinguished family, Averroës held important government positions, including chief judge of the judiciary system and personal physician to the caliph. Among his vast works, which he wrote while performing judicial duties, were comprehensive commentaries on Aristotle's writings, effectively reconciling the Greek thinker's ideas with Islamic thought. Western scholars used his Arabic versions of Aristotle, translated into Latin, to help reconcile Aristotelian and Christian thought. Averroës' writings were studied in Western schools and universities until modern times.

History   The study of history first played a role in Islamic thought because of the supreme significance of Muhammad's life to Islam. Biographies of the Prophet and histories of his time appeared soon after his death. Later generations developed a taste for diverse historical genres, including accounts of territorial conquests, family genealogies, and town histories. However, Islamic history—and, indeed, the study of history—took a giant step forward in the works of Ibn Khaldun [IB-en kal-DOON] (1332–1406).

Ibn Khaldun's fame rests on a multivolume history of the world, especially the *Muqaddima* or *Prolegomena,* which serves as the introduction to his lengthy study. Ibn Khaldun examined ancient societies with an eye to identifying their characteristics and the stages of their evolution. He was one of the first thinkers to deal with supply and demand, the role and value of currency, and stages of economic development as a society evolves from an agricultural to an urban economy. In Ibn Khaldun's view, which echoes that of the Greek writer Thucydides, the best historical studies downplay the role of religion or divine forces and focus on the role of human activity. Historians, by probing beneath the surface explanations of human behavior, would discover that humans are governed not by religion or idealism but rather by status concerns and the desire to identify with certain groups. Ibn Khaldun also offered a theory explaining the rise and fall of civilizations: As a civilization decays, its social bonds weaken, and it falls victim to a more vigorous people from outside its frontiers. The outsiders overthrow the weakened civilization, become powerful, and then cycle into a state of decay, to be invaded by more powerful intruders—an outlook that reflected Ibn Khaldun's knowledge of the dramatic impact of Seljuk Turk, Mongol, and other nomadic forces on Muslim life.

Technology

Islamic technology, like Islamic science and philosophy, continued and expanded the Greco-Roman heritage. As Islamic culture spread from its Middle Eastern home, its technology borrowed new features from the Far East, Iran, and India. While making no dramatic breakthroughs, Muslim artisans were skilled at perfecting the achievements of others. And, over time, Muslim technology served as a bridge to Western technology. Muslims made noteworthy technological advances in three areas: papermaking, hydraulics, and mechanical engineering.

Papermaking   The art of papermaking originated in China, perhaps in the second century CE.

- The first paper was made from old rags and organic fibers, softened by soaking in water, dried, pressed, and cut into sheets.
- China kept papermaking a royal monopoly and largely secret until the eighth century, when supposedly, a Chinese prisoner of war revealed the secret of making paper to his Islamic captors.
- Paper mills began to be built on rivers.
- In 793, Baghdad became the site of the first paper mill in the Islamic world.
- In 1151, papermaking reached Muslim Spain. From Spain, European cities learned the art of papermaking.

Hydraulics   From the Greek word meaning "water organ" or "water hollow tube," hydraulics is the branch of engineering concerned with water flow and the use of liquids to power machines. It has been at the forefront of Muslim technology since the eighth century.

- Hydraulics was important for irrigation, powering mills (for grinding grain into flour, crushing sugarcane, and sawing wood), and raising water from a lower to a higher level.
- Hydraulics enhanced prosperity; for example, Baghdad had a system of dams, canals, and mills that tapped the waters of the Tigris River.
- A huge dam, 1,400 feet wide, at Córdoba, in Spain, served an irrigation system and mills.
- Valencia, Spain, had an elaborate desilting process for purifying water.
- The water clock—powered by water moving through interlocking hollow tubes, which activated cams, shafts, pulleys, wheels, and wheels within wheels—became a hallmark of Muslim technology (erected in Toledo, Spain; Damascus; Baghdad; and Fez, Morocco) in the eleventh through fourteenth centuries.

Mechanical Engineering   Muslim artisans worked in two distinctly different areas of mechanical engineering:

- Development of utilitarian devices employed in daily life, such as pumps (to remove water from mines) and the astrolabe (for telling time and navigation—it permitted determination of the position of the sun or stars relative to the horizon).
- Development of automata, self-regulating machines, designed to entertain courtly audiences by controlling fountains and clocks.

Literature

In pre-Islamic Arabia, Arabic was basically a spoken language, developed by desert Bedouins and spread into urban areas by traders, who adapted it to their needs. Within this tribal culture, poets played a critical role, because they were thought to be wizards inspired by a *jinn*, or spirit. They eventually created a body of works that were transmitted orally by *rawis*, professional reciters of poetry. The preferred poetic form was the **qasida** ("ode"), composed in varied meters with a single rhyme. These poems, celebrating tribal life, personal glory, and love and wine, helped create a community identity and became the preferred model for poetic expression. Between 800 and 1300, Arabic became standardized as a written language. Called literary Arabic, or classical Arabic, it took the basic form of the language of the Qur'an, though modified to suit changing needs.

Critical to understanding Islam's literary culture is the concept of **adab,** an Arabic word initially meaning "rules of conduct," "manners," or "good habits." *Adab* first appeared in the eighth century as a literary genre, with the translation into Arabic of a Persian work on statesmanship. Among the elite, *adab* came to mean "refinement," which included having certain skills, such as the ability to swim and to ride horses, and, especially, having deep knowledge of Islamic poetry, prose, and history and of the Arabic language. In modern Arabic, *adab* simply refers to the whole of literature.

Poetry   Pre-Islamic poetry did not disappear with the advent of Islam. The most famous surviving works are *al-Mu'allaqat* ("The Hanged Poems," or "The Seven Odes"), which, according to tradition, were suspended on the walls of the Kaaba while it was still a pagan shrine. The Prophet, though rejecting the pagan themes, recognized the poetry's power and called for poets to adapt the ode for religious ends.

Another genre that survived from pre-Islamic times was the elegy, or lament, especially for the dead. Usually composed by a woman, most often the dead hero's sister, the elegy became a favorite of Islamic poets. The best of these pieces were those by the female poet al-Khansa [al-kan-SAH] (d. after 630), who lived into the early Islamic period.

A new literary genre, the **ghazal,** a short lyric usually dealing with love, emerged in early Islamic Arabia. Composed in rhyming couplets, the *ghazal* often drew on the poet's personal life. Of these early poets, Jamil (d. 701) set the standard for later writers. His usual theme was impossible love: star-crossed lovers devoted to each other unto death. Persian, Turkish, and Urdu poets, adapting the *ghazal* into their languages, made it a popular genre in the Islamic world.

Two centuries later in Islamic Spain, Ibn Hazm [IB-en KAZ-um] (994–1064) produced the highly influential *The Ring of the Dove*, which blends poetry with prose and focuses on the art of love. In this work, he argues that the "true" lover finds happiness in pursuit of rather than in union with the beloved—a central idea of Arabic poetry that may have influenced Provençal poetry (see Chapter 10).

The Persian-speaking region of the Islamic world produced the gifted poet Rumi (1207–1273), active in Afghanistan, Persia, and Anatolia (modern Turkey). A Sufi mystic, Rumi greatly influenced Muslim ascetic thought and writing and, most important, Turkish religious life. As part of prayer ritual, the Sufi order of Whirling Dervishes created a whirling dance. Rumi's literary legacy is twofold: the *Diwan-e Shams,* a collection of poems addressed to a Sufi holy man and the poet's master; and the *Masnavi-ye Ma'navi* ("Spiritual Couplets"), a complex work, part Sufi handbook, part anthology of proverbs and folktales. The theme of the *Diwan-e Shams* is the poet's deep love for his master, a metaphor for the Sufi idea of an all-consuming love for

God. The *Masnavi,* written in rhyming couplets, a Persian genre, presents the Sufi "way" through pointed stories and anecdotes.

Prose   Literary prose in Arabic originated at the Abbasid court in Baghdad, mainly as the creation of clerks and translators. A vast literature gradually emerged, but the genres were limited because of Islam's moral objection to drama and pure fiction—drama because it "represented" reality and was thus not real, and fiction because it made no claim to truth. Early writings from the Abbasid court were collections of proverbs; tales of tribal warfare known as *ayyam al-'Arab,* or "The Days of the Arabs"; and, especially, "night conversations," or *musamarah,* which evoked lively communal evenings around desert campfires. Organized loosely about a well-worn theme, filled with puns, literary allusions, and colorful vignettes of tribal life, and, above all, animated by love of the Arabic language, the "night conversations" reminded urban Arabs of their past and inspired the *maqamah* genre, a major prose achievement.

The *maqamah* ("assembly") genre was created by al-Hamadhani [al-HAM-uh-tha-NE] (969–1008). Blurring the line between fact and fiction, his *maqamahs* are entertaining works, focusing on rogues, dreamers, and lowlifes, written in rhymed prose to display his learning and literary art.

The foremost writer in the *maqamah* genre was al-Hariri [al-ka-RE-re] (1054–1122), a government official in Basra and a scholar of Arabic language and literature. Al-Hariri's poems are noted for verbal fireworks, humor, and exquisite usage of Arabic language and grammar. In the *Maqamat,* or *The Assemblies of al-Hariri,* he focuses on the adventures of the learned rogue and vagabond Abu Zayd, as reported by a narrator, al-Harith. Abu Zayd, who resembles the author in his poetic powers and lively intelligence, repeatedly uses his skills as a storyteller to charm presents from wealthy victims.

During this time, the collection of stories known as *The Thousand and One Nights,* first translated into Arabic from Persian, was circulating in the Muslim world. It is perhaps the most famous example of the "tale within a framing tale" literary genre in all of literature. The framing tale, probably from an Indian source, tells of the woman Shahrazad (Scheherazade), who devises a storytelling plan to keep the vengeful king Shahryar from his mad scheme of murdering a wife a day because an earlier wife had betrayed him. The tales come from many lands, including India, Iran, Iraq, Egypt, Turkey, and possibly Greece, and represent various genres—fairy tales, romances, legends, fables, parables, anecdotes, and realistic adventures. Originally, fewer than a thousand tales existed, but as the stories grew in popularity, new ones were added to make the number exact. This collection

has supplied the West with many legendary figures, such as Aladdin, Ali Baba, and Sinbad the Sailor. In the Arab world, however, Islamic scholars have not accepted *The Thousand and One Nights* as classical literature, criticizing it for colloquial language and grammatical errors.

Art and Architecture

Islamic art and architecture developed within a cultural setting dominated by the Qur'anic ideal that religion should govern all aspects of living. In an effort to sanctify human life, this ideal made no distinction between the artistic and the practical, the private and the public, the secular and the divine. Thus, art and architecture, like the rest of Islamic culture, had no purpose beyond serving religious faith.

The Qur'an forbade the worship of idols. In time, this ban was extended to mean that artists were supposed to be prohibited from representing all living things. Nevertheless, figural images did appear all over the Islamic world at different times. Artists did become abundantly inventive in the use of nonrepresentational forms. The **arabesque**—a complex figure made of intertwined floral, foliate (leaf shaped), or geometric forms—emerged as a highly visible sign of Islamic culture (Figure 9.8). Geometric shapes, floral forms, and **calligraphy,** or beautiful writing, decorated walls, books, and mosaics (see Figure 9.3).

Islamic tenets allowed borrowing from other cultures, so long as what was borrowed was adapted to the teachings of the Qur'an. From Greco-Roman architecture came the column and the capital, the rib and the vault, and the arcade. From Byzantine architecture came the dome, the most prominent feature of the Islamic style, and the pendentive, the support feature that made the dome possible. From Persian art and architecture came miniature painting, the vaulted hall, the teaching mosque, the pointed arch, and floral and geometric ornamentation. And from Turkish art and architecture came a grand artistic synthesis, which raised Persian influence to a dominant role in Islamic art and architecture, in the zone stretching from Egypt eastward, after 1200.

Architecture   The oldest extant Islamic monument is the Dome of the Rock in Jerusalem, a shrine for pilgrims dating from between 687 and about 691 (Figure 9.9). Located in a city already sacred to Jews and Christians, and built over a rock considered holy by Muslims and Jews, the shrine proclaimed by its presence that Islam was now a world religion. For Muslims, the shrine's rock marked the spot from which the founder of their faith, Muhammad, made his "night journey" to heaven. For Jews, it was where Abraham intended to sacrifice his son Isaac. Because Muslims also claim Abraham as their ancestor, the site was thus given added meaning. Today, the Dome

Figure 9.8   The "Ardebil" Carpet. Formerly in the Mosque of Ardebil, Iran. 1539–1540. Woolen knotted carpet, 37'9½" × 17'6". Victoria and Albert Museum, London. Arabesque leaves fill the yellow medallion at the center of this exquisite carpet. The medallion is surrounded by sixteen ogees (pointed ovals), which also contain arabesques. A section of this design is repeated in the corners of the interior rectangle. Praised as "the greatest example of carpet weaving in the world," this carpet of silk and wool was woven for a Persian mosque. At least thirty-two million knots were needed to complete it.

domes of Byzantine churches, this dome is made of wood covered with gold. The dome's splendor reflected the opulent aesthetic emerging in the Muslim world, as well as the ambitions of the Umayyad caliph who commissioned it.

The architectural aesthetic of the Dome of the Rock is echoed in its art program. Unlike Byzantine churches, whose plain exteriors contrasted with brilliant interiors, the Dome of the Rock is a feast for the eyes throughout. Everywhere there are mosaics, tiles, and marble, much of which was added later. In obedience to the Qur'anic ban, there is no figural art. Arabesques, foliate shapes, scrolls, and mosaics of purple and gold, inspired by Byzantine and Persian designs, animate the surfaces, and more than seven hundred feet of Arabic script—repeating passages from the Qur'an—are written on both interior and exterior surfaces. Sixteen stained-glass windows allow muted daylight to play across the interior surfaces.

The Dome of the Rock did not set the standard for Islam's dominant building type, the **mosque,** or, in Arabic, *masjid,* "place for bowing down." The Prophet himself established the basic plan with the house of worship he constructed in Medina. This first mosque, now lost, reflected the simple values of early Islam. It consisted of a rectangular courtyard, covered by a roof resting on palm trunks and enclosed by walls made of raw bricks. The wall facing Mecca, the direction for prayer, was designated the *qiblah* wall, and a pulpit was erected from which Muhammad led prayers, preached, decreed new laws, and settled disputes. The courtyard also functioned much as the Greek *agora* and the Roman forum, providing a public meeting space. With its varied activities—judicial, political, social, and religious—this first mosque expressed the Islamic ideal of the unity of life.

Later mosque builders followed the example set by the Prophet. Plain in exterior ornament and rectangular in shape, mosques were distinguished from secular buildings by their interior features and spaces— basins and fountains for ritual hand washing, porticoes for instruction, a screened enclosure to shield the prayer leader, and an open area for group prayers (Figure 9.10). Sometimes the mosque was crowned with a dome, as in Byzantine churches, but the Islamic dome's high melon shape distinguished it from the spherical

of the Rock remains one of Islam's holiest places, after Medina and Mecca.

The architecture of the Dome of the Rock draws mainly on Roman and Byzantine sources, but the aesthetic spirit reflects the new Islamic style. Its basic plan—an octagon covered by a dome—was rooted in Roman and Byzantine tradition, and the dome's support system—a tall **drum** or wall, resting on an **arcade,** or a series of arches supported by columns—was derived from Byzantine models. But, unlike the stone

Figure 9.9 The Dome of the Rock. Ca. 687–691. Diameter of dome approx. 60′; each outer wall 60′ wide × 36′ high. Jerusalem. This Islamic shrine is filled with theological symbolism. The dome itself is a symbol of the heavens, and the dome's thrusting shape represents the correct path for the faithful to follow. The eight-sided figure on which the interior drum rests is an image of the earth, and the rock enclosed within this sacred space is the center of the world—a traditional Islamic belief. This belief arises, in part, because the Dome of the Rock stands on the Temple Mount—the location of Solomon's Temple and its successors. Thus, this building symbolizes Islam's claim to be the successor to and fulfillment of the Judaic and Christian faiths.

Figure 9.10 The Great Mosque of Kairouan, Tunisia. Ninth century. Stone, approx. 395 × 230′; ht. of minaret without finial 103′. As in the other civilizations of this period, the dominant building type in Islam was the house of worship. This mosque, with its plain walls and square tower for calling the faithful to prayer, reflects the simple style of early Islam. Inside the walls, a large unadorned courtyard serves as a praying area.

SLICE OF LIFE

Fears of Assimilation in a Multicultural Society

Paul Alvar

In early-ninth-century Spain, the Umayyad rulers in Córdoba extended certain religious, legal, and civic rights to Christians, known as Mozarabs, and to Jews, who as dhimmis, or "people of the book," shared some religious beliefs with the Muslim community. However, in the 850s, peaceful relations between Muslims and Christians broke down after the Umayyad government executed about fifty Christians for disrespecting Islam. In a contemporary account, the Christian layman Paul Alvar laments how some young people in the Christian community were reacting to the government's crackdown. His account reveals the fear of assimilation to another culture and faith, and the subsequent loss of cultural and religious identity—a timeless issue in our multicultural society today.

All the handsome young Christians, skilled in language, conspicuous in manner and action, distinguished in gentile learning, accomplished in Arabic eloquence, study most eagerly the books of the Arabs, read them most intently, talk about them most earnestly, and come together with immense eagerness, after having joyfully shut down their own language and, being ignorant of ecclesiastical beauty, condemn as most vile the rivers of the church flowing from paradise. For pity's sake, Christians are ignorant of their own language . . . But countless men can learnedly explain the ostentatious works of the Arabs . . . and they are more learned in the poems of that people and more appreciative of their subtle beauty . . . .

Interpreting This Slice of Life

1. *Why* were the Spanish Muslims tolerant of Jews and Christians?

2. *What* was the background to the conflict between the Muslims and the Mozarabs?

3. *Why* should we be careful in accepting Paul Alvar's views on the Arabization of young Christians?

4. *Why* were these young Christians attracted to Islamic culture?

Byzantine form. A tall, slender tower, or **minaret,** from whose pointed top a Muslim official, the *muezzin,* called the faithful to prayer five times a day, also identified the mosque. Inside the mosque, from the earliest times, rich decorations reminded worshipers of the beauty of paradise: brilliant mosaics and oriental carpets emblazoned the floors, facings and calligraphic friezes beautified the walls, metal or ceramic lamps cast a twilight glow onto the faithful at night, and richly decorated *minbars,* or pulpits (see Figure 9.5), elevated the prayer leader above the worshipers. The type of mosque inspired by Muhammad's example is called the **congregational mosque,** or **Friday mosque,** a horizontal structure that houses the Friday worshipers in a central courtyard with a domed fountain for ablutions. With the Arab conquests, mosques of this type were built across the Islamic world, from southern Spain and Morocco to China.

Early in the history of Islam, Abd al-Rahman (731–788), a member of the Umayyad dynasty who survived the Abbasid revolt, made his way to southern Spain, where he founded a new kingdom. In 786 he began to build the Great Mosque—an awe-inspiring example of the congregational mosque style. Constructed on the site of a Roman temple and a Christian church, the mosque was laid out in the traditional rectangular plan. During the next century, local rulers enlarged the Great Mosque four times to make it the largest sacred building in the Islamic world. The second expansion added an elaborately decorated *qiblah* and three domed chambers of Byzantine-inspired mosaics and gold ornamentation. But the most striking feature of the Great Mosque is the row after row of double-tiered horseshoe arches (Figure 9.11). The slender lower columns were salvaged from Roman buildings and Christian churches, and double-height arches were then placed on them. These rounded arches of red brick and yellow stone produce alternating patterns of light and color down the seemingly endless aisles.

The ninth-century Ibn Tulun mosque in Cairo is an imposing example of the congregational mosque (Figure 9.12). Four rows of arcades stand between the faithful and the east wall (the direction of Mecca), and portals of pointed arches open into the arcaded area. A minaret with a winding staircase rises just beyond the mosque, which is built of brick faced with

Figure 9.11 Arches of the Great Mosque. Stone and brick columns, ht. 9'9", exterior 590 × 425'. Eighth to tenth centuries. Córdoba, Spain. The Great Mosque, nearly as large as St. Peter's Basilica in the Vatican, contains 850 pillars with 19 aisles running north to south and 29 going east to west. Although Spanish Christians, in 1236, converted it into a cathedral and constructed a high altar in the interior and, in the sixteenth century, added chapels around the quadrangle, the Great Mosque still stands as a monument to the Umayyad kingdom in southern Spain and a crowning achievement of Islamic architecture and decorative art.

Figure 9.12 Ibn Tulun Mosque, Cairo. 876–879. Red brick covered with white stucco, exterior 531 × 532½'. The finest surviving example of the congregational style, the Ibn Tulun mosque was imitated throughout the Islamic world. This view, from inside the courtyard, shows a domed fountain used for ritual washing. Outside the walls rises the spire of a four-story minaret, set on a square base with a cylindrical second story and an exterior staircase.

stucco. In later Islamic mosques, the pointed arches and decorated stucco work became basic features of this style. During the Christian Middle Ages, Western architects borrowed the pointed arch and adapted it to their own needs, using it to perfect the Gothic style of architecture.

In the twelfth century in the eastern Islamic lands ruled by the Seljuk Turks, a new type of mosque, inspired by Persian architecture but retaining the basic rectangular plan of the Friday mosque, emerged. The new mosque type was called a teaching mosque, because it provided distinctive areas for the *madrasa*, the religious school for advanced study. The teaching mosque proved to be a popular innovation, and, between the twelfth and eighteenth centuries, architects built similar structures in Egypt, central Asia, and India.

Figure 9.13   Masjid-i Jami (Great Mosque). Eleventh and twelfth centuries. Isfahan. The view of the central courtyard and *iwan* (vaulted hall) of this teaching mosque is framed by the arched opening of the facing *iwan*. Various mosque facilities, including living quarters for teachers and students, are located in the areas around the *iwans*.

The most famous example of a teaching mosque is the Masjid-i Jami, or Great Mosque, in Isfahan (in modern Iran), the capital of the Seljuk dynasty in the eleventh and twelfth centuries (Figure 9.13). Four huge vaulted halls, or *iwans*, open into a central courtyard. Prayers are said in the *iwan* that opens toward Mecca, and the other three serve as areas for study, school, and rest. Viewed from the courtyard, the opening in each *iwan* constitutes a huge arch set into a rectangular facade, faced with blue tiles—a specialty of Persian artisans and the signature color of the Seljuk rulers. At once conservative and adaptable, Islamic architecture penetrated sub-Saharan Africa. In Djenne (JENN-eh) in Mali, a major African kingdom that had converted to Islam by the ninth century, a Great Friday mosque was built in adobe in the thirteenth century (Figure 9.14).

Painting   Notwithstanding the Qur'anic prohibition, one branch of Islamic art—book painting, or the art of the book—usually depicted realistic scenes. A few surviving examples show that the art of the book was practiced in the early days of Islam. However, after 1100, in rapid succession, two brilliant schools of book painting emerged, each devoted to representational scenes. Little known in the West, the first school flowered in Syria and Iraq, and its artists were probably Arab, strongly influenced by Persian tradition. The second was the world-famous school of **Persian miniatures,** which flourished in Persia from the thirteenth to the seventeenth century.

Of the Arab painters whose works survive, Yahya ibn Mahmud al-Wasiti [YAK-yah IB-en mak-MOOD al-WAH-see-tee] (fl. 1230s) is generally recognized as the best. Working in Baghdad, he illustrated al-Hariri's *maqamat,* a twelfth-century work. Each picture depicts a colorful episode in the life of the con artist Abu Zayd, rendered with an eye to detail (Figure 9.15). The typical format of the page includes arranging the scene's focus into the frontal plane, keeping the background neutral in color, and creating a setting with the barest of details, such as a small hill or a single tree. Near Eastern tradition is apparent in the very large eyes, the dark outline of the figures, and the bunched drapery folds.

The Persian miniatures were produced under the patronage of the Mongol sultans, who had replaced the caliphs as rulers. Although the Mongols brought Chinese influences to the Persian miniatures, the Muslim artists rejected the openness of Chinese space and created their own ordered reality, as shown in a superb example from the early sixteenth century (see Interpreting Art). Like all Persian miniatures, this exquisite work is characterized by fine detail, naturalistic figures and landscape, and subtle colors.

Figure 9.14   Great Friday Mosque of Djenne, Mali. Thirteenth century. Adobe covered with mud plaster. By the ninth century, a string of prominent Muslim states in West Africa had commercial relationships with the Mediterranean world along the trade routes built up over millennia by the Berber tribesmen of North Africa. Merchants brought salt, dates, copper, and gold, the latter in profusion, to cities in North Africa and to Cairo in Egypt. Muslim traditions also passed back to the south. This mosque with its three minarets was the center of a major school that disseminated Islamic teaching in Africa.

Music

Music has historically been a controversial topic in Muslim culture. Only a few musical genres have gained universal approval, such as the call to prayer (*adhan*), the chanting of the Qur'an, and the chanting of poems and prayers during certain religious events, including the Prophet's birthday, pilgrimages, and Ramadan. Clerics often question other musical forms, especially instrumental music, claiming such music undermines faith. And yet, music traditionally has thrived in the Muslim world.

Music was a constant presence in Muslim life, as heard in the five daily calls to prayer, echoing loudly from minarets in towns and cities across the Muslim world. A single male voice chants the call to worship, according to fixed rules, in which each phrase is followed by a longer pause. As the prayer unfolds, each phrase grows progressively longer and more ornamented in style. In each day's first prayer, the phrase "Prayer is better than sleep" is inserted into the

sequence, before the last two statements. The Islamic call to prayer, in English translation, is

> "God is great" (repeated four times)
> "I bear witness that there is no god except God" (twice)
> "I bear witness that Muhammad is the Messenger of God" (twice)
> "Hasten to the prayer" (twice)
> "Hasten to real success" (twice)
> "Allah is the Greatest" (twice)
> "There is none worthy of worship but Allah"

Early Islamic music employs a microtonal system, in which the intervals, or distances between sounds (pitches) on a scale, are **microtones,** or intervals smaller than a semitone—the smallest interval in mainstream Western music before jazz.

Vocal music initially was dominant in Muslim culture, with instrumental music used only to support singing. Instrumental music later won its freedom

Figure 9.15 YAHYA IBN MAHMUD AL-WASITI. *Abu Zayd Preaching.* **Book painting. 1237. Bibliothèque Nationale de France, Paris.** Abu Zayd, here disguised as a religious official, preaches to a group of pilgrims. Islamic touches include the beards of male pilgrims and head coverings of both men and women. The artist creates a lively scene, in the manner of street theater, in the way he shows the pilgrims' varied eye and facial movements, including an exchange of glances, stares into the distance, heads lifted upward, and a head looking down.

under Spain's Umayyad rulers, who were great patrons of musicians and, most notably, of secular music. Meanwhile, religious music was given a new direction by the Sufi sect, who, in their pursuit of religious emotion, encouraged singing, chanting, and **recitative,** or vocal passages delivered in a speechlike manner. A major change arose in Turkey, where the Sufi order of Whirling Dervishes introduced music into their mosques.

Musicians across the Muslim world played many instruments, representing three groups of instruments and drawn from varied traditions. These included, from the string group, the *ud* (lute), the pandore (a bass lute), the psaltery (a trapezoidal-shaped zither), the harp, the *qithara* (guitar), and the *rabab* (rebec, a lute-shaped fiddle); from the wind group, the flute, the reed pipe, and the horn; and from the percussion group, tambourines (square and round), castanets, and various drums, such as *naqqara* (nakers, or small kettledrums) and *tabla* (a pair of wooden drums). Most of these instruments were adopted into Western music, especially as a result of cultural encounters during the Crusades.

Interpreting Art

Subject Qur'an 1:17 may be paraphrased: A journey of a single night was made by a servant of God from the "sacred place of worship" to the "further place of worship."

Theological Perspective Traditionally, the "servant of God" was Muhammad and the "sacred place of worship" was Mecca. The early commentators interpreted the "further place of worship" as heaven (*miraj*) and believed that the ascension of the Prophet took place from Mecca. Under the Umayyads, the "further place of worship" was interpreted as Jerusalem. The versions were later reconciled such that the *Isra* was taken to be a night journey to Jerusalem with the ascension to heaven occurring from there.

Content Muhammad is portrayed riding the *buraq,* a mythical winged horse, and being accompanied by the archangel Gabriel amid a host of angels.

Cross-Cultural Influences The *buraq* has parallels in the winged beasts of ancient Mesopotamia and later central Asian art. The biblical story of Elijah riding into the sky on a fiery chariot (2 Kings 2:7–12) is also a source.

Style The image blends Christian, Persian, central Asian, and Chinese motifs. The faces in particular betray Buddhist features, and the fiery halos around Muhammad and Gabriel are Chinese. The image reveals superbly the extraordinary melting pot of Islamic culture.

Composition The surface is virtually flat, the picture two-dimensional. The absolute centrality of Muhammad to the scene creates a sense of perspective that is not geometric but is still effective. By ringing Muhammad and Gabriel with angelic figures, the artist achieves an effect of great energy and movement. The artist took sheer delight in rich colors of many hues.

The Night Journey of Muhammad. **Persia. Sixteenth century. British Library, London.** This Persian miniature represents a key Muslim belief: Muhammad made a night journey (*Isra*) from Mecca to Jerusalem before his ascension to heaven. His face was left blank because it was deemed blasphemous to depict his visage. This painting was executed during the Mongol period, as the Asian invaders, though converts to Islam, did not share the Arabs' abhorrence of figural art.

1. **Theological Perspective** Why might different traditions have developed about the Prophet's ascension to heaven?
2. **Content** What are the essential elements in this picture?
3. **Cross-Cultural Influences** Identify shared cultural traditions represented in this picture.

4. **Style** Identify Mesopotamian, central Asian, and Jewish traditions represented in this image.
5. **Composition** Discuss the sense of perspective conveyed by this picture.

SUMMARY

Whereas the Roman Empire took four centuries to reach its zenith, the Islamic Caliphate reached a vast extent in merely a century. The caliphate itself proved unable to maintain unity but the Ottoman Turks rejuvenated the caliphate, which lasted until the twentieth century. Although political, social, and military factors contributed to the emergence of the caliphate, the key factor was the religion of Islam itself. Muhammad taught an uncompromising monotheism that blended peoples and cultures in a community of believers—the *umma Muslima*—who recognized one holy book, the Qur'an, and a simple set of practices, the "Pillars of Islam." Having enveloped diverse peoples and cultures, Islamic culture was always open to many influences. Muslims adapted the cultures of Greece and Rome, of Arabia and Persia, of India and central Asia. Islamic science made breakthroughs in mathematics and hydraulic engineering. Islamic philosophy synthesized and reconciled Aristotelian and Platonic ideas. Islamic literature drew on classical, Arabic, and Persian traditions. Islamic architecture adapted classical and Byzantine forms and structures. In key respects the Islamic world was a bridge between the classical, the Asian, and the medieval worlds.

The Legacy of Medieval Islam

One of every five people on earth today is a Muslim. Of all the lands ever conquered by Islam, only Iberia was ever reconquered by Christians. Only Arabic can be used for Muslim worship, a powerful unifying force for more than a billion people, but only a minority of Muslims are Arabs or are fluent in Arabic. Today's *jihadists,* radical Muslims bent on expanding their faith and diminishing the impact of the West, are a constant source of tension in the world. In western Europe, some governments seeking to protect their own identities pass laws denying Muslim women the right to wear veils that cover their hair and neck, or the *chador,* the garment that covers the entire body with only a slit for the eyes. In 2011 parts of the Arab world exploded in the so-called Arab Spring, when people rose up against oppressive regimes from Tunisia to Yemen to Syria. It remains to be seen whether those lands will obtain Western-style democracies or strict Islamic regimes. Most Westerners are not aware that countless Arabic words have entered into common English usage: algebra, almanac, cotton, elixir, saffron, and syrup to name just a few. Were it not for the Arabs, we would be computing with cumbersome Roman numerals instead of the elegant Arabic numerals to which we have become accustomed. There are also more subtle reminders of our inheritance from medieval Islam. In 1888 the Russian composer Nikolai Rimsky-Korsakov based his lyrical, allusive symphonic work *Scheherazade* on the storyteller from the *Arabian Nights.* And in the postmodern world, the poet Rumi has an international fan base because of the continuing appeal of his spiritual and love-struck lyrics.

Muslim Women Demonstrate in Favor of the Islamic Headscarf. In 2003 French Muslim women protested in Strasbourg against a series of laws passed in France intended to maintain the strict secularity of the state. The law specifically banned public wearing of the *hijab*, the veil worn by pious Muslim women to cover their hair and neck. The sign the women are carrying reads "Law Against the Veil or Law Against Islam."

KEY CULTURAL TERMS

madrasa

jihad

qasida

adab

ghazal

maqamah

arabesque

calligraphy

drum

arcade

mosque

qiblah

minaret

minbar

congregational mosque
(Friday mosque)

iwan

Persian miniature

microtone

recitative

Nave, Amiens Cathedral. View from the west. Ca. 1220–1236. France. Maximum height 139'. The morning sun exploded through the choir windows to make the end of the building dissolve in light. In the Bible, there are many images and metaphors based on light.

The High Middle Ages

1000–1300

Preview Questions

1. *What* are some of the chief signs that Europe was expanding in the High Middle Ages?

2. *What* roles did faith and reason play in the intellectual life of the High Middle Ages?

3. *What* traditions combined to form courtly love and *why* is this important?

4. *Discuss* the relationship of the Romanesque style to the Gothic style, showing how the latter developed from the former.

Europe recovered slowly from the crises of the late Carolingian period to begin one of the most dynamic, creative periods in its history. If in the post-Roman world everything had shrunk, now everything expanded. Europe's population doubled between 1000 and 1300, reaching about seventy million. New states emerged in the Slavic world and in Scandinavia. Governments grew in scope, gaining greater competence and authority. Cities grew larger and became increasingly important in economic, political, and intellectual life. Latin literature flourished and vernacular literature appeared in French, German, Italian, and Spanish. Schools grew in size and sophistication, and a new kind of school, the university, assumed leadership in intellectual life. Romanesque and then Gothic art, in painting, sculpture, and architecture, soared—literally and figuratively—to new heights.

The nave of Amiens cathedral, one of the dozens of Gothic cathedrals built in this era, is a testament in stone and glass to the age's spiritual and substantive qualities. Carolingian exterior verticality has been brought inside. The ribbed vaults, pointed arches, and numerous windows are a tribute to the rediscovery of ancient geometry. But there is also a calm logic here—and the twelfth- and thirteenth-century schools were dominated by logic. A building like this was very expensive, which reflected the economic prosperity of the time. But after money, geometry, and logic, there is also something mysterious, uplifting, spiritual about Amiens cathedral. In a world of bureaucrats, merchants, and logicians, there were also mystics who, in almost Platonic terms, imagined realities beyond those the eye could see.

POLITICS AND SOCIETY

King Alfred the Great of England (r. 871–899) said that a kingdom needed "men of war, men of prayer, and men of work," and two French bishops spoke in the same terms. This tripartite scheme is helpful as a way of thinking about how medieval society and politics functioned—and it is contemporary. Nevertheless, this view is too narrow. Those who work, for example, were, in this aristocratic way of looking at things, the peasants, but not the townspeople, who were increasingly numerous and prominent. In addition, the scheme did not include women and minorities, such as Jews.

Lords and Vassals: Those Who Fight

The term **feudalism** is almost synonymous with medieval social and political practices, although the term itself never appeared in the Middle Ages. Like all modern words that end in *ism*, feudalism has been used in different ways. Feudalism can mean a kind of government with shared, segmented power and authority; a set of relationships between free men bound to each other in both personal and material ways; or the exploitation of the peasantry by the nobility. While each of these definitions grasps a part of the truth, none grasps it whole, and it is impossible to speak about a feudal "system." People from Iceland, through Britain and France, to Russia, over many centuries, had numerous ways of organizing politics and government that can be called feudal.

The best way to understand feudalism is to examine the mutual, honorable relationships between lords and vassals. Lords were those who held both public and private power in their hands. They could be kings, or the powerful local officers of kings, or self-serving regional leaders who profited from the breakup of the Carolingian Empire. The great problem of government in the Middle Ages was harnessing the numerous lords to peaceful and productive purposes. Vassals, who were the retainers of lords, swore homage and fealty to a lord, and promised aid and counsel. Homage involved a public, ceremonial acknowledgment of allegiance, and fealty implied loyalty. Aid usually took the form of military service, and counsel meant giving advice, whether privately and intimately or publicly in hall or court. Lords agreed to protect their vassals in judicial disputes or against the attacks of others and usually provided them with something of material value, such as clothing and weapons, housing, money, or land. When land was involved, it was called a fief (*feudum* in Latin, whence feudalism). A fief was an estate—typically of the bipartite kind (see Chapter 8)—that was already developed and inhabited. The fief was supposed to support the vassal and

free him—almost without exception, only men were involved—to perform his service (Figure 10.1).

This was a violent society whose leaders were men trained to fight, ideally their lord's enemies but sometimes each other. These warrior-aristocrats shared a guiding ethos: **chivalry,** from the French *cheval,* horse; so chivalry—*chevalerie*—means "horsiness," the way of life for men who fought on horseback

The word also meant "knighthood." The essential values of the chivalric knight were prowess (a knight who cannot fight is a contradiction in terms); courage; loyalty, an ideal that was often violated; and generosity, openhanded giving.

Originally, chivalric values were male and martial and did not pertain to relations between the sexes. Later, in the twelfth century, female influences began turning rough-and-ready warriors into gentlemen.

Figure 10.1   A Vassal Paying Homage, from the Westminster Psalter. Ca. 1250. British Library, London. (MS Royal 2 A XXII, fol 220.) The image shows a decked-out warrior: sword, chain mail, banner and lance, and horse. He also bears crosses on his cloak—he is *crucesignatus*, "signed by the cross," that is, a crusader. Is he offering his hands in homage to his feudal lord or extending them in prayer to God? One cannot say. He seems the perfect knight in secular or spiritual terms.

But as early as the tenth century, the church began to try to ameliorate and redirect the worst excesses of the warriors' behavior. In the Peace and Truce of God, a movement that began in France and then spread widely, the church tried to civilize violence. Fighting was forbidden on religious feasts (more than 150 days per year) or near churches, and noncombatants and their property were to be protected. Framed more positively, knights were to protect the weak and the poor, women, widows, and children. Instead of fighting other Christians, knights were to direct their violence against pagans and infidels. Ironically, though, church teachings against violence served as one spur to crusading.

Peasants: Those Who Work

The routine of the serfs and the free peasants—rural slaves were comparatively rare—was dictated by custom and regulated by daily and seasonal events (Figure 10.2). Men and women worked together in the fields, eking out a bare subsistence from their tiny plots of land; they lived in wooden huts, reared their children, and found relief in the church's frequent holy days (the source of the modern term *holiday*). Some of the farming innovations (such as three-field crop rotation, which allowed the land to replenish itself, and improved plows) introduced in the Carolingian period began to be more widely used, and the plight of the peasants improved. Increasing the productivity of the soil brought economic benefits to the lord, who could then, if he wished, pay the peasants in coin and sell them tracts of land. Moreover, the expanding commercial economy led many lords to desire more money to buy luxuries. To acquire such money, they often permitted peasants to exchange labor services for money payments. In general, the lot of the peasant in France and England improved while, in some areas of central and eastern Europe, serfs continued to be exploited for centuries.

The Rise of Towns (and the Rest of Those Who Work)

Towns grew larger and assumed greater roles in medieval life (Figure 10.3). Urban life became more competitive and the residents formed associations, called guilds, to protect their special interests. The artisan and craft guilds, for example, regulated working conditions, created apprenticeship programs, and set wages; merchant and banking guilds developed new businesses and supervised trade contracts. These guilds often quarreled over issues inside the town walls, but they joined hands against the intrusions of the church and the local nobility.

Because urban economic life often conflicted with the interests of popes, bishops, kings, counts, and others who dominated the towns, urban dwellers, led by the guilds, founded self-governing regimes, called communes, often with written charters that specified their rights in relation to their various lords. Italy led the way but, by about 1200, many towns in northern and western Europe had charters, and their political independence spurred economic growth.

Artisans and merchants needed buyers, secure trade routes, and markets for their products. The earliest trade routes were the rivers and the old Roman roads, but as demand increased in the West for luxury

Figure 10.2 Agricultural Laborers at Work. Aelfric writings, Canterbury. Eleventh century. British Library, London, Cott Claud, B IV f.79v. In the top panel, four men harvest grain with various handheld tools, and, in the lower panel, five men carry bundles of grain. The scribe who painted these panels, as part of his copying duties, must have witnessed such scenes often in the harvest season. The laborers' costume—a loose-fitting tunic or gown, reaching below the knee, belted at the waist, and with long sleeves and a round neck—was typically worn by both sexes in Europe, from the fall of Rome until fitted garments emerged, after 1340.

Figure 10.3   AMBROGIO LORENZETTI **(active ca. 1319–1347).** *Street Scene in Medieval Siena.* **Detail from** *Allegory of Good Government in the City.* **1338–1339. Fresco in the Sala della Pace, Palazzo Pubblico, Siena.** Although an idealized image, this painting is nevertheless an accurate representation of medieval Siena as a bustling country town built on a hill. Signs of prosperity abound. In the middle right and center, farmers, perhaps from the nearby countryside, lead pack animals loaded with sacks of wool and other goods. Nearby, three weavers are making textiles. On the lower right, a goatherd coaxes his flock, probably to the city market. In the middle left foreground, a shopkeeper arranges his wares. Through the large opening on the left may be glimpsed a classroom, where a seated teacher addresses his students. On the extreme right, two women, perhaps servants, carry objects, one woman with a large bundle balanced on her head.

items from the East, new trade routes opened. Italian cities led this international commerce, trading the luxurious woolen cloth of Flanders for the silks of China and the spices of the Middle East (Map 10.1). Along the overland routes in Europe, local lords guaranteed traders safe passage through their territory for a fee. In the twelfth and thirteenth centuries, the fairs of the Champagne region in France brought virtually all of Europe's commerce together.

As on the estate, the position of women in the medieval urban world was subordinate to that of men, even though urban women often worked closely with their husbands in trade or crafts. In this hierarchical society, gender roles became increasingly differentiated through custom and legislation. The few women with economic power, such as those directly involved in manufacturing and trade or the occasional rich widow who kept her husband's business afloat, were exceptions to this general exclusionary rule. Some aspects of the cloth and brewing industries were such exceptions.

In Europe's growing towns, Jewish communities became more numerous and important. Often forbidden to own land, Jews specialized in commerce, banking, and moneylending. Jewish scholars were sometimes confidentially consulted by Christian schoolmen. The growth of Jewish communities led to an increase in anti-Semitism. In the twelfth century, mobs attacked Jews and governments sometimes confiscated their wealth. Atrocities were perpetrated on Jewish communities by crusading armies on their march to the East (see Interpreting Art).

Medieval Government

During the High Middle Ages, four impressive governments emerged in western Europe: France, England, Germany, and the papacy. However, their political fortunes varied. Germany was the most powerful state in tenth-century Europe and the weakest in the thirteenth. The papacy rose steadily in power and influence to about 1200 and then declined. France and England

Learning Through Maps

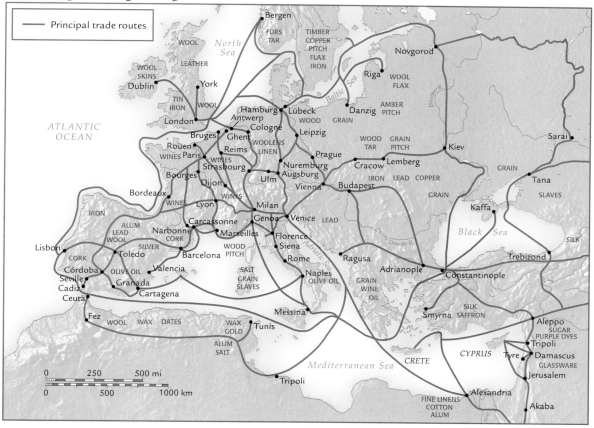

MAP 10.1   PRINCIPAL TRADING ROUTES AND TOWNS OF EUROPE, 1300

This map shows the major towns and trading routes in Europe at the end of the High Middle Ages. *1.* **Note** *the important role played by sea trade.*
2. **Identify** *some key crossroads of trade. 3.* **How** *did the location of the north Italian cities help to make them leaders in trade? 4.* **Consider** *the extensive nature of the long-distance trade between Europe and its neighbors. 5.* **Consider** *also the impact of climate on the products made and produced in various regions.*

both developed strong, effective central governments but took very different paths to that destination (Timeline 10.1).

The French Monarchy   Patience, luck, fame, feudalism, and faith all contributed to the development of the French monarchy. When Hugh Capet came to the throne in 987, he established a dynasty that ruled until 1328. The Capetians followed similar policies, patiently wearing down and overcoming one rival after another, first in northern France and then toward the south. They saw two-thirds of their land fall into English hands and then got almost all of it back. They scrupulously insisted on feudal rights when it suited their purposes—seizing lands from recalcitrant vassals, for example, then retaining them. They also built up effective institutions. By the end of the thirteenth century, King Philip IV "the Fair" (r. 1285–1314) could issue laws for all of France.

During this time, the French established themselves as the cultural leaders of Europe. France had the best university and the most famous scholars. Its architecture was dominant, and its literature was emulated. The Capetians, alone among all their contemporaries, produced a saint: King Louis IX (r. 1226–1270), or Saint Louis, revered for his crusading zeal and personal piety. France and its monarchy were going to face severe challenges in the late Middle Ages, but in 1300 France was a formidable force in Europe and vastly stronger than it had been in 1000.

The English Monarchy   Unlike the French, the English suffered several invasions, their ruling families were short-lived, and their monarchs were forced to relinquish some of their power. In the tenth century the Vikings savaged England; in 1016 the country was overrun by Cnut of Denmark and, in 1066, conquered by William of Normandy (Figure 10.4). In 1135 and

Interpreting Art

Subject *Ecclesia* (church) lords it over *Synagoga* (synagogue). Sculptures with this theme appeared on the facades of several cathedrals between 1225 and 1250.

Composition *Ecclesia* stands erect, crowned, and holding a battle lance and a chalice—a symbol of the Eucharist. Synagoga droops, wears a blindfold, bears a broken staff, and appears to be dropping the tablets of the Jewish law. Both personifications are lovely, but Ecclesia wears a gorgeous gown while Synagoga wears a plain shift that flops gracelessly over her feet.

Context The figures flank the double doors of the south transept of Strasbourg cathedral. The square in front of the south doors was a major public space in the city and the Jewish district was nearby. The sculptures proclaimed very publicly an anti-Jewish message.

Style and Influence The sculptures, just over life-size, are credible human beings. They conform to Romanesque "historicist" norms, deriving from ancient Roman buildings where actual people were portrayed. Later, on Gothic buildings, facade sculptures became elongated and column-like.

Religious Perspective Ecclesia and Synagoga flank a sculpture of wise King Solomon surmounted by a figure of Christ. Together the sculptures proclaim "supercession": Grace has triumphed over law; the Old Testament has value only insofar as it foretells Christ. Christianity has triumphed over Judaism.

Historical Perspective These dramatic figures reflect this period's growing anxiety about Jewish wealth and influence and about Jewish refusals to accept Christian teaching. Their placement near Strasbourg's Jewish quarter would have made them constantly visible, and their meaning would have been immediately grasped by anyone—Jew or Christian.

Figures of Ecclesia and Synagoga on the Facade of the South Transept of Strasbourg Cathedral. Ca. 1225. Both Ecclesia and Synagoga ht. approx. 6′4″.

1. **Comparison** Identify and compare the similarities and differences between the two sculptures.
2. **Context** What is significant about the placement of these figures?
3. **Style and Influence** Relate these images to those on Roman monuments and buildings (Figures 5.15, 5.16, 5.17, 7.2).
4. **Symbolism** Name various ways in which these figures communicate supercession.
5. **Historical Perspective** What cultural impact would these figures have had in thirteenth-century Strasbourg?

1154 the crown changed hands, and in the thirteenth century the English experienced one domestic crisis after another. Yet, in spite of the turmoil, England's kings managed to construct an effective kingdom.

As conquerors, Cnut and William the Conqueror in the eleventh century, and later Henry II of Anjou (r. 1154–1189), possessed some political advantages: they had opportunities to redraw the political map. Each of these kings was politically astute, however, and managed to expand royal power while keeping the barons quiescent. Each had vast overseas interests that were sometimes distracting but that also provided wealth for the rulers and outlets for restless nobles.

Henry II, especially after his marriage to Eleanor of Aquitaine (1122–1204), controlled directly or indirectly some two-thirds of France. Nominally he was a vassal of the French king, but the reality was not in French favor. King John (r. 1199–1215), a weak ruler, managed to lose most of England's French holdings. With his prestige fatally damaged, John's key vassals forced him to sign the Magna Carta in 1215. The king was compelled to admit that he was not above the law, had to observe due process of law, and had to take baronial advice.

One thing the English barons wanted to advise about was the stunning growth of royal institutions across the twelfth century. England's financial ministry

Timeline 10.1   THE MONARCHIES IN THE HIGH MIDDLE AGES

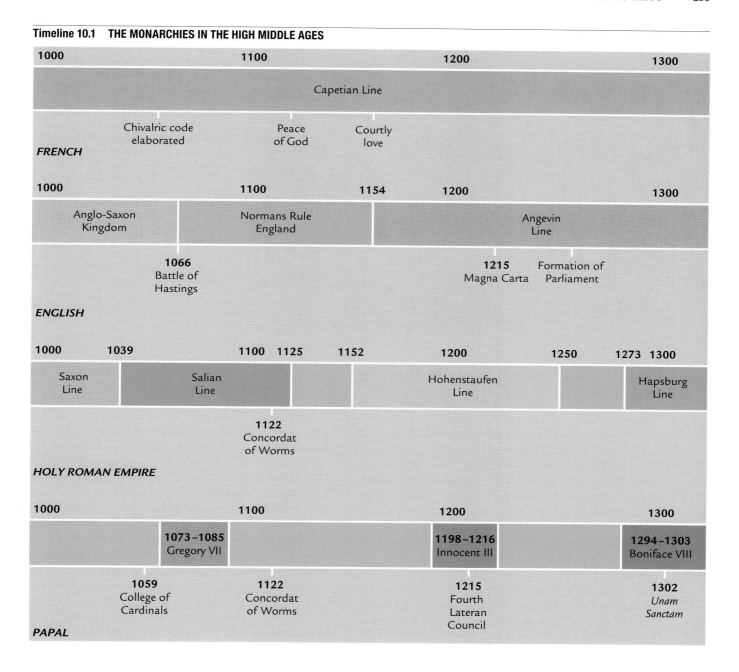

FRENCH

1000	1100	1200	1300

Capetian Line

Chivalric code elaborated — Peace of God — Courtly love

ENGLISH

1000	1100	1154	1200	1300

Anglo-Saxon Kingdom — Normans Rule England — Angevin Line

1066 Battle of Hastings

1215 Magna Carta   Formation of Parliament

HOLY ROMAN EMPIRE

1000	1039	1100	1125	1152	1200	1250	1273	1300

Saxon Line — Salian Line — Hohenstaufen Line — Hapsburg Line

1122 Concordat of Worms

PAPAL

1000	1100	1200	1300

1073–1085 Gregory VII — **1198–1216** Innocent III — **1294–1303** Boniface VIII

1059 College of Cardinals — **1122** Concordat of Worms — **1215** Fourth Lateran Council — **1302** *Unam Sanctam*

was efficient and incorruptible and its judicial system, effective and fair. Through a system of well-ordered courts, England began operating with a common law—a single law applicable to all. During the thirteenth century, the barons and townsmen challenged the crown over how to institutionalize criticism and dissent. The crisis was resolved with the founding of Parliament (a "talking together," from the French *parler,* "to speak"), a venue for the king and the elite to meet, negotiate, and make decisions.

The German Empire   In contrast to France and England, the German Empire did not become unified but slowly disintegrated because of frequent dynastic changes and conflicts with the church. In the tenth century, the Ottonian kings built Europe's strongest realm. These fierce warriors, the conquerors of the Magyars and of neighboring Slavs, were, after 962, once again emperors. They controlled the church, with its substantial wealth and educated personnel, and were heirs to the Carolingian ideology that they ruled by the grace of God and were answerable to God alone.

In the eleventh century, under more peaceful conditions in the east, Germany's rulers no longer won prestige and plunder, and could not distract the nobles with profitable wars. There were also repeated changes of dynasty. In 1056 a powerful king died and left a child as his heir—always a dangerous situation in a dynastic

Figure 10.4 *These Men Wonder at the Star. Harold.* **Panel from the Bayeux Tapestry. Third quarter of the eleventh century. Wool embroidery on linen, ht. 20″. Bayeux, France.** Today housed in the cathedral of Bayeux, this famous embroidery provides an important historic record of the events leading up to the Battle of Hastings in 1066 and presents a justification for the Norman conquest of England. Harold is cast as a villain who breaks his oath of allegiance to William and loses the English crown as a result of this treachery. Halley's comet, interpreted as an evil omen, appeared over England in February 1066. The comet is shown in the center of the upper border. On the left, men point to the comet, and on the right Harold also seems upset by the comet. Beneath Harold and his adviser are outlines of boats, implying a possible invasion by the Normans.

state. Unexpectedly, a major crisis in relations with the church broke out.

The **Investiture Controversy,** ostensibly a struggle over the right to invest—appoint and install—churchmen by laymen, was one of the most significant events of the Middle Ages. For centuries, powerful lords had been investing bishops and abbots with their offices; this was a way to extend their authority through the church, and sometimes they received payments for making appointments. Where kings were concerned, however, the matter was more complicated. Insofar as they considered themselves God's chosen agents on earth, they imagined the clergy, even the popes, to be their natural helpers and subordinates. The clergy came to regard its freedom from lay control as crucial and also to view the buying and selling of church offices as a serious sin, called simony. And, finally, the papacy, which had reformed its worldliness, emerged under a series of resolute popes who saw themselves as the chief earthly representatives of heavenly power, and considered kings and other rulers to be their helpers and subordinates. The Investiture Controversy raged for more than fifty years. In the end, secular rulers lost the right to invest clerics with the symbols of their religious offices although they could still draw them into their governments.

Germany suffered a damaging blow to its prestige and power during the Investiture Controversy because several emperors who confronted the papacy had to make humiliating concessions. Simultaneously, the rulers faced a restless nobility that took advantage of the situation to strengthen its political power. Finally, the emperors, attempting to resurrect a new Roman Empire, became embroiled in Italy. By the thirteenth

century—when France and England were achieving unity—German rulers were more interested in Italy than in Germany. And, when they invaded Italy, they found themselves facing the formidable Papal States, which generated new struggles with the papacy. By 1300 Germany's once-powerful monarchy was shattered.

The Papal Monarchy The medieval church was a hierarchical institution, and in the High Middle Ages the popes reached the high point of their power and influence. Consequently, historians speak about "the papal monarchy." Papal power rested on several foundations. In 910 at Cluny in Burgundy, William of Aquitaine founded a monastery, declared it free of all lay control, and placed it under the protection of the pope (Figure 10.5). Over the next two centuries, Cluny became a powerful force for reform in the church as its monks insisted on the moral and intellectual reform of the clergy, and on freedom for the church. Eventually, Cluny's zeal for reform penetrated Rome and the papacy placed itself at the head of a broad reform movement—the Investiture Controversy was but one aspect of this movement. In the curia—the papal government—the papacy built complex institutions and, during the High Middle Ages, the judicial and financial branches of the papal government expanded. By 1200 the popes had the most complex government in Europe. The legal system, the canon law, of the church was unrivaled. The popes had disciplinary tools that gave them influence all over Europe. They could excommunicate an individual—declare him outside the community of the faithful. They could impose an interdict on a region—a suspension of religious services. They could send legates, in effect ambassadors,

Figure 10.5 Pope Urban II Consecrates the Great Abbey Church of Cluny (III). **Book of Offices. Late twelfth century. Bibliothèque Nationale de France, Paris.** In this small manuscript painting, Pope Urban II (r. 1088–1099) consecrates the third version of the Great Abbey Church at Cluny. In the consecration service, the church is transformed into sacred ground and thus dedicated to the service of God. Framed by architectural features suggestive of the church's interior, the pope (the large standing figure on the left) offers a papal blessing before the high altar (under the domed center section). The artist has skillfully suggested a crowded church of worshipers, including Cluniac monks and nuns and various church officials. Pope Urban II, a member of the Cluniac order, preached the First Crusade in 1095.

to conduct inquiries or to represent them. And they could institute courts of Inquisition, strict judicial forums that operated on the basis of Roman law. Finally, popes could call councils. In the Fourth Lateran Council of 1215, the largest council since antiquity, Innocent III (pope 1198–1216) presided like the uncrowned king of Europe.

By 1300 secular forces were gaining strength in Europe and many rulers thought the popes had claimed too much. Both French and English kings defied the pope's refusal to let them tax the clergy. The king of France summoned a French bishop before his court, much to the pope's chagrin. Boniface VIII (pope, 1294–1303) issued a papal bull (from Latin *bullum,* "seal"), *Unam Sanctam,* with a powerful affirmation of papal primacy in both church and state. However, very few rulers honored the bull and some reacted by force. For example, the king of France sent his lawyers and a military force to arrest the pope. Boniface fled but died soon thereafter.

MEDIEVAL CHRISTIANITY AND THE CHURCH

Christianity and the church touched every aspect of life in medieval Europe. Important moments of life—birth, marriage, death—were attended by Christian rituals, and the Christian calendar regulated life from farming to government. Rulers imagined themselves to be divinely appointed and inspired. Literature and

art had Christian themes, and music lifted praises to God. Neither before nor since the High Middle Ages have Christianity and the Catholic Church exercised so profound and pervasive an influence.

Christian Beliefs and Practices

The immense authority of the church sprang from the belief shared by the overwhelming majority of medieval people that the church held the keys to the kingdom of heaven and provided the only way to salvation. By attempting to adhere to the Christian moral code and by participating in the rituals and ceremonies prescribed by the church and established by tradition, Christians hoped for redemption and eternal life after death.

These rituals and ceremonies were inseparable from the religious doctrines. They derived from the teachings of Jesus and Paul, the church fathers, particularly Augustine, and were further defined by medieval theologians. Finally, the Fourth Lateran Council of 1215, under Pope Innocent III, officially proclaimed the sacraments as the outward signs of God's grace and the only way to heaven.

As established by the council, the sacraments numbered seven: baptism, confirmation, the Eucharist (Holy Communion), penance, marriage, last rites, and ordination for the priesthood. Baptism, the Eucharist, and penance were deemed of primary importance. In baptism, the parents were assured that the infant had been rescued from original sin. In the Eucharist, the central part of the Mass, the church taught that a miracle occurred whereby God, through the priest, turned the bread and wine into the body and blood of Jesus. That the outer appearance of the bread and wine remained the same while their inner substance changed was explained by medieval theologians in the doctrine of transubstantiation.

Penance evolved into a rather complicated practice. First, sinners felt contrition—sorrow—and then they confessed their sins individually to a priest; the priest conveyed God's forgiveness for the mortal penalties of sin so that hell could be avoided; the priest then directed that an earthly punishment—the penance—be carried out in an effort to erase the effects of the sin. Depending on the severity of the sin, penance could range from a few prayers to a pilgrimage or a crusade. This sacrament was made even more complex by its association with purgatory.

With the groundwork laid by Augustine in the fifth century and Pope Gregory the Great in the sixth century, the doctrine of purgatory was given more explicit form by thinkers of the High Middle Ages. Neither hell nor heaven, purgatory was a third place, where those who had died in a state of grace could avoid damnation by being purged, or purified, from all stain of sin. All souls in purgatory were ultimately destined for heaven; penance was a means of reducing time in purgatory. Thus the living could do penance on earth in hope of spending less time in purgatory.

Religious Orders and Lay Piety

The clergy were the most visible signs of the church's presence in everyday life. The "secular" clergy (from Latin *saeculum,* "world") moved freely in society, and the "regular" clergy lived apart from the world in monasteries under a special rule (*regula,* in Latin). The monasteries served as refuges from the world, where men and women could seek salvation by daily rounds of prayer.

As noted earlier, the Cluniac monks originated the reform movement that helped to establish the moral and political authority of the medieval church. Other waves of reform followed, the most important of which was represented by the founding of the Cistercian order in the twelfth century. Bernard of Clairvaux [klair-VOH] (1090–1153), a saint, a mystic, and one of the most forceful personalities of the period, founded over 160 Cistercian abbeys. The Cistercians believed that the Cluniacs were too rich and powerful and that they failed to observe the Rule of St. Benedict strictly. They adopted an austere life and often lived in isolated monasteries where the brothers worked with the local peasants. Whereas the Cluniacs understood the Benedictine motto "To Labor Is To Pray" in such a way that they turned prayer into work and accordingly

had elaborate and lengthy worship, the Cistercians understood work as manual labor and simplified their worship.

In convents, women could devote themselves to Christ and follow ascetic lives filled with prayer, contemplation, and service. And they could live in community with other women, under the authority of women. In some houses, they had opportunities for education. Convents had existed since late antiquity, although seldom with the large endowments monasteries enjoyed or with as much influence in local affairs.

Convent life nurtured several gifted women who influenced this age, most notably Hildegard of Bingen (1098–1179), founder and abbess of the Benedictine house of Rupertsberg near Bingen (modern Germany). Her writing and preaching attracted scores of supporters in Germany, France, and Switzerland, including most of her male superiors. She was highly influential with major figures of the time, as evidenced by her correspondence with Eleanor of Aquitaine, the emperor Frederick Barbarossa, and various popes. Hildegard wrote on the medical arts, music, theology, and the history of science, but her visionary tracts had the most impact on her contemporaries. Her first book, titled *Scivias (Know the Ways of the Lord),* included descriptions of her visions, the texts of liturgical songs, and a sung morality play, *Ordo Virtutum (The Company of the Virtues),* the first of its kind. She also illuminated manuscripts (Figure 10.6) and composed sacred poetry, which has survived in monophonic musical settings and has found new audiences today. Hildegard was a bold talent and left a superb legacy, especially given the belief of the time that it was dangerous to teach a woman to read and write, because it could lead to independent-mindedness and thus upset the social order.

Another type of religious order appeared in the thirteenth century with the rise of two major mendicant, or begging, orders, the Franciscans and the Dominicans, whose members were called **friars** (from Latin *fratres,* "brothers"). The Franciscans had an urban ministry, working among the poor and sick, and the Dominicans were preachers, working among heretics. Although both orders made important contributions, the Franciscans had a greater impact on medieval society, largely because of the attractive nature of the order's sainted founder, Francis (1182–1226), and their urban work. Francis's piety, selflessness, and legendary humility remain inspiring (Figure 10.7).

Alongside monastic reform, in the thirteenth century a wave of lay piety swelled up from all ranks of society, triggered by a mixture of religious fervor and social protest. Typical of these novel movements were the beguines, independent communities of laywomen dedicated to good works, poverty, chastity, and religious devotion. Unlike nuns, who isolated themselves

Figure 10.6 Hildegard's Awakening: A Self-Portrait from *Scivias*. Ca. 1150. Hildegard's description of the moment when she received the word of God is effectively captured in this illumination: a "burning light coming from heaven poured into my mind." The Holy Spirit inflames her mind as she etches the word of God on a tablet; Volmar, the priest of the abbey and her loyal secretary, gazes at the event. The simplistic sketch of the towers and building is typical of twelfth-century illuminated manuscripts.

from the world, the beguines had regular contact with society—caring for the sick at home and in hospitals, teaching in both girls' and boys' schools, and working in the textile industry. The beguines first established themselves in northern France and then, along with male lay brethren called beghards, spread to Germany and the Netherlands, usually in proximity to Dominican houses. Some members of these communities became influential spiritual guides. For example, Mechthild of Magdeburg (about 1207–1282) wrote *The Flowing Light of the Godhead,* a mystical account of her religious odyssey. The beguine and beghard communities also provided the audience for medieval Germany's finest devotional writer and a great mystic of the Christian tradition, Meister Eckhart (about 1260–1328).

Figure 10.7 ATTRIBUTED TO GIOTTO. *St. Francis of Assisi's Trial by Fire Before the Sultan.* Before 1300. Fresco. Basilica of St. Francis, Assisi, Upper Church, nave. This painting, from a cycle of twenty-eight frescoes detailing the life and miracles of St. Francis of Assisi, shows the saint (center, with a halo around his head) preaching before the enthroned sultan al-Malik Kamil (r. 1218–1238), the last of the Ayyubid dynasty (right). The setting is Egypt, the center of the sultan's holdings, which included Syria and Palestine. Trying to convert the sultan to Christianity, St. Francis, backed by a second Franciscan friar, challenges the sultan's Islamic clergy to join in a walk through the blazing fire on the bottom left, as a test of their respective religious faiths. The sultan gestures toward the fire with his right hand, as four Muslim clergy prepare to leave on the far left. This fresco, completed perhaps seventy years after the saint's death, was painted during a time when Franciscan missionaries were active in Egypt and other Middle Eastern lands.

Beguines, beghards, and mendicants won approval from religious authorities, but other lay groups were condemned as heretics because they refused to submit to ecclesiastical authority. The most prominent of these heretical sects was the Albigensian, which was centered at Albi in southern France. The Albigensians were also known as Cathars (from the Greek for "pure"). Their unorthodox beliefs were derived partly from Zoroastrianism (see Chapter 1), the source of their concept of a universal struggle between a good God and an evil deity, and partly from Manichaeism, the source of their notion that the flesh is evil. The Albigensians stressed that Jesus was divine and not human, that the wealth of the church was a sign of its depravity, and that the goal of Christian living was to achieve the status of Cathari, or perfection.

These unorthodox beliefs spread rapidly across much of southern France, permeating the church and the secular society. After they murdered his legate in 1208, Pope Innocent III called for a crusade against the Albigensians. His call appealed to the nobles eager to seize the heretics' land, kings eager to extend their authority in the south, and persons of faith who were offended by heresy. It took decades to root out the Albigensians. The heretics were treated with cruelty, and, as the thirteenth century proceeded, many of them were summoned before courts of Inquisition—ecclesiastical tribunals charged with identifying heresy. The crusade against the Albigensians reflected a shared medieval belief: those who rejected Catholic beliefs were traitors.

There were also groups that were less obviously unorthodox. The Waldensians—for example, followers of Valdes (or Peter Waldo; about 1180–1210), from Lyons in France—wished to follow what they believed to be the apostolic life: they wanted to embrace poverty and preaching. The church grudgingly accepted the former but refused the latter. Some Waldensians were reconciled but others were declared heretics.

The Crusades

The **Crusades** were a defining event of the High Middle Ages—and like all defining events the Crusades are and have remained controversial. To free the Holy Land, or Palestine, from the Muslims, whom Christians then regarded as unbelievers, the Christian church preached nine Crusades between 1095 and 1272 but many motives propelled the crusading movement. Modern scholars call these campaigns the "Crusades" because their soldiers were *crucesignati*, "signed by the cross" (crusaders wore crosses on their clothing). Scholars also enumerate the Crusades, "First," "Second," and so forth.

After their defeat by the Seljuk Turks at Manzikert in 1171, the Byzantines appealed to the pope for merce-

naries to help them recover their lost lands. After about 1000, Italian merchants began expanding their commercial enterprises in the Mediterranean at the expense of the Muslims. The Peace and Truce of God may have diverted violence outside European society. Already in the tenth century a series of wars launched in Spain by Christian rulers against Muslim authorities—called the *Reconquista*, "the reconquest"—served as a precedent for campaigns in the eastern Mediterranean. In 1095, with a powerful speech at Clermont in France, Pope Urban II tapped these forces to launch the movement we now know as the Crusades.

The First Crusade did recapture Jerusalem and established several small, vulnerable crusader principalities in the eastern Mediterranean. Subsequent Crusades were less successful. The Fourth Crusade in 1204 went terribly wrong for the papacy and the crusading movement when the Venetians, who were to transport the crusaders, hijacked it to attack enemies in the Adriatic before a would-be Byzantine ruler persuaded the crusaders to attack Constantinople. From 1204 to 1261 the Byzantine Empire was in the hands of western knights, a fatal blow to the empire. Later Crusades, even one led by Saint Louis, failed because the crusaders had no secure footing in the Muslim East. In 1291 Muslim forces captured the last crusader stronghold, Acre, and the movement effectively ended.

The Byzantines had wanted soldiers to help them recapture Anatolia and watched helplessly as religiously inspired Westerners sought to liberate the Holy Land. Italian merchants gained valuable trade concessions all over the eastern Mediterranean, which they maintained until modern times. Large numbers of landless young warriors sought their fortunes in the East, but Europe did not become noticeably less violent. Women sometimes gained authority as they managed the lands of their absent husbands. While the Crusades stand as a symbol of the expansive energy and religious zeal of high medieval Europe, their long-term impact was a heightening of the already tense relations between Christians and Muslims (Figure 10.8).

Beyond the Boundaries

The Crusades were not the only incidents of Europe's expansion beyond its traditional boundaries. A number of intrepid mendicant missionaries set out to convert the fearsome Mongols (see Chapter 9), who had obliterated the remnants of the caliphate. Among them was William of Rubruck (1220–1293), a Flemish Franciscan. He had accompanied Saint Louis on the Seventh Crusade (1248) but then set out from Constantinople to try to win the Mongols for Christianity. He traveled more than six thousand miles and failed in his mission because the Mongols eventually converted to Islam. William's *Itinerary*, an account of his

Figure 10.8   Crusaders Attacking a Muslim Fortress. Twelfth century. Bibliothèque Nationale de France, Paris. Crusaders, dressed in chain mail, catapult severed enemy heads into a Muslim fortress. Note the identifying cross on the banner at the top. Mutual atrocities, such as depicted here, fueled horror stories of the Crusades and helped engender a legacy of mistrust that still complicates Western and Muslim relations today.

remarkable travels, circulated widely in Europe and heightened interest in exotic lands and peoples. William sparked a correspondence between the Mongol khans and the papacy.

More famous than William was the Venetian merchant and traveler Marco Polo (1254–1324), whose father and uncle set out into Asia and apparently met Kublai Khan in 1269. A little later the three of them began an epic journey that lasted twenty-four years and ended at the imperial court in China. Marco's *Memoires*—interestingly, published in French, then the international language—provided Europeans with an exciting and informative account—how much of it is strictly accurate will never be known—that inspired people for centuries to explore the Orient on their own. Not least among them was Christopher Columbus.

William and Marco opened the eyes of Europeans to worlds they had scarcely imagined but with which they would have increasing relations until the present day.

THE AGE OF SYNTHESIS: EQUILIBRIUM BETWEEN THE SPIRITUAL AND THE SECULAR

Between 1000 and 1300, Christian values permeated European cultural life. The Christian faith was a unifying agent that reconciled the opposing realms of the spiritual and the secular, the immaterial and the material—as symbolized in many cities and towns by the soaring spires of the local **cathedral**—a bishop's church, named after his *cathedra,* or chair, the seat of his authority (Figure 10.9). Medieval culture drew from the humanities of the classical world, the heritage of the various European peoples, and, to a lesser extent, the traditions of Byzantium and Islam. Because of these diverse influences, the culture of the High Middle Ages was never uniform. What many writers, thinkers, and artists shared was a set of common sources, concerns, and interests.

Theology and Learning

From about 1000 onward, scholars revived the school system that had flourished under the Carolingians. These monastic schools—along with many new cathedral schools—appealed to an age that was hungry for learning and set Europe's intellectual tone until about 1200. During these two centuries, the only serious rival to the schools was a handful of independent scholars who drew crowds of students to their lectures in Paris and elsewhere. By 1200 new educational institutions had arisen—the universities—that soon surpassed both the monastic and cathedral schools and the independent masters. Since then, universities have dominated intellectual life in the West.

The Development of Scholasticism   **Scholasticism** is a term applied to the style and substance of learning in the High Middle Ages. The arts curriculum remained dominant in this period, but whereas grammar had been the focus in the Carolingian period, logic came to dominate after about 1100. During the eleventh century, several thorny theological problems had arisen and scholars began to approach them in a new way. Instead of appealing to authorities—the Bible, the church fathers, decisions of church councils, papal decrees—theologians began to apply logical analysis, human reasoning, to the solution of problems.

Across the High Middle Ages, more of the work of Aristotle became available to scholars. Some of Aristotle's logical tracts had been available for a long time in the translations of Boethius (see Chapter 8), but now more of his logical work plus a host of his other writings were accessible. Most of this work entered Europe via Latin translations from medieval Arabic translations of the Greek originals. Aristotle was a pagan, so

SLICE OF LIFE

When Love Knows No Boundaries

Heloise

THE ABBESS OF LE PARACLETE, FOUNDED BY ABELARD

The letters of Abelard, a monk, and his student Heloise (about 1101–1164), who later became a nun, are still read because they offer glimpses into the hearts of lovers whose devotion transcends any historical period or social context. In this letter, Heloise writes to Abelard after they have been forced to separate. His scholarly reputation has been tainted, and, for his transgression, Abelard has been castrated by men in the hire of Fulbert, Heloise's uncle and protector.

You know, beloved, as the whole world knows, how much I have lost in you, how at one wretched stroke of fortune that supreme act of flagrant treachery robbed me of my very self in robbing me of you; and how my sorrow for my loss is nothing compared with what I feel for the manner in which I lost you. Surely the greater the cause for grief the greater the need for the help of consolation, and this no one can bring but you; you are the sole cause of my sorrow, and you alone can grant me the grace of consolation. . . . God knows I never sought anything in you except yourself; I wanted simply you, nothing of yours. I looked for no marriage-bond, no marriage portion, and it was not my own pleasures and wishes I sought to gratify, as you well know, but yours. The name of wife may seem more sacred or more binding, but sweeter for me will always be the word mistress, or, if you will permit me, that of concubine or whore. I believed that the more I humbled myself on your account, the more gratitude I would win from you, and also the less damage I should do to the brightness of your reputation.

Interpreting This Slice of Life

1. *What* are the relationships among Abelard, Heloise, and Fulbert?

2. *What* is the treachery to which Heloise refers in her letter?

3. *In what ways* does Heloise think Abelard can console her?

4. *How* does Heloise describe her love and relationship to Abelard?

5. *Why* do we still read their correspondence and love letters?

6. *Does* this letter have a modern tone and message? *Why or why not?*

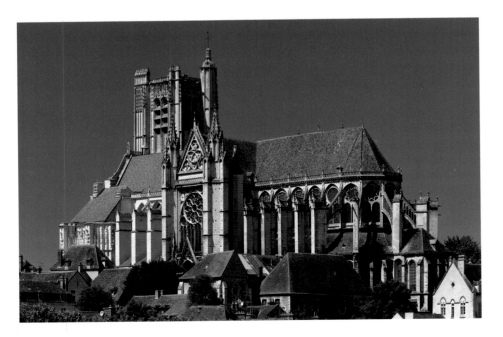

Figure 10.9   Auxerre Cathedral. Begun ca. 1225. Auxerre, France. Looming over the town and dominating the countryside for miles around, the Gothic cathedral symbolized the preeminent role of the Christian church in medieval life. No other building could soar past its spires, either literally or figuratively. People worshiped inside it, built their houses right up to its walls, and conducted their business affairs within the shadows of its towers. Thus, the cathedral also symbolized the integration of the secular and the sacred in medieval life.

his immense learning posed an acute problem: How could the potentially competing claims of faith and reason, of natural and of divine truth, be reconciled?

The Scholastic method used deductive logic to clarify existing issues and to explore the intellectual ramifications of a topic. A Scholastic thinker would pose a problem, argue for and against various possible solutions to the problem, and then draw a conclusion, which itself led to a new problem. The arguments deployed might come from Christian or pagan sources, but the aim was to achieve synthesis and reconciliation, not to prove that one kind of learning was superior to another. Anselm (1033–1109), the most accomplished logician since Aristotle and the formulator of an ingenious proof for the existence of God, expressed the early Scholastic view this way: "Faith Seeking Understanding."

Peter Abelard

Among the daring independent masters who challenged the standing of the great cathedral schools, the greatest, and most controversial, was Peter Abelard [AB-uh-lard] (1079–1142). Intellectually gifted and instinctively argumentative, Abelard quarreled with his own teachers and with other influential scholars. He quickly became the sensation of Paris and his words found eager listeners.

What divided Abelard and his teachers was the problem of universals, an intellectual issue that arose between 1050 and 1150 and attracted attention for centuries. This controversy revolved around the question of whether or not universals, or general concepts, such as "human being" and "church," exist in reality or only in the mind. At stake in this dispute between the two schools of thought, known as **realism** and **nominalism,** were basic Christian ideas, such as whether Jesus's sacrifice had removed the stain of original sin from each individual. The realists, following Plato, reasoned that universals do exist independently of physical objects and the human mind. Hence, "humanity," for example, is present, albeit imperfectly perceived, in every individual. In opposition, the nominalists said that universals are merely names (from Latin *nomen,* name) and claimed that only particular objects are real. Hence, "church" and "human being" exist only in particular instances.

In these debates, Abelard showed that extreme realism denied human individuality and was thus inconsistent with church teachings. For his part, Abelard taught a moderate realism that held that the universals existed, but only as mental concepts and as mental devices to sharpen and focus thinking. When new translations of Aristotle became available, thinkers discovered that Abelard and the Greek genius agreed in part about universals, a discovery that further enhanced Abelard's fame.

The Rise of the Universities

The university—called a *studium generale* because it was a place where almost everything could be studied—emerged around 1200 in the towns where numerous masters and pupils converged. Imitating the practices of secular guilds, the masters organized, in the north, and the students, in the south, especially in Italy. Irrespective of who organized the university, the central issues were faculty appointments, curricula, examinations, and fees. The universities secured charters from both royal and ecclesiastical authorities. Universities typically had an arts faculty and then one or more higher faculties in law, medicine, and theology. Paris was especially famous for theology, Bologna for law, Montpellier for medicine. Students came from all over Europe to attend universities and, as foreigners, life was often hard for them; they were overcharged for food and housing and were mistreated by the local townspeople. The baccalaureate degree was earned after four to six years of intense engagement with the liberal arts. Higher degrees in specialized subjects could take years and followed upon the production of a serious piece of scholarship and a rigorous public examination.

Intellectual Controversy and Thomas Aquinas

The Scholasticism of the thirteenth century differed in degree, not in kind, from that of the twelfth. Resting on systematization and controversy, it culminated in the magisterial works of Thomas Aquinas.

Already in the twelfth century, some scholars had begun to organize learning across whole fields. Gratian (d. by 1160), a monk from Bologna, produced the *Decretum,* a systematic manual of canon law containing more than four thousand entries drawn from the Bible, church fathers, and conciliar and papal decrees. It became the standard reference and textbook for canon law. Peter Lombard (1100–1160) wrote *Four Books of Sentences* (a "sentence" is a conclusion in a Scholastic disputation) treating in thorough and orderly fashion virtually the whole of the Christian faith under the headings the Trinity, the Creation and Sin, the Incarnation and the Virtues, and the Sacraments. For centuries the *Sentences* was the standard text in theology.

Islamic thinkers, among them Ibn Rushd [IB-en RUSHT], known in the West as Averroës [uh-VER-uh-weez] (see Chapter 9), contributed to the development of Scholastic thought. Averroës was a major Aristotelian scholar who wrote vast commentaries—detailed explanations and interpretations—on the master's writings. He took from Aristotle certain ideas such as the eternity of matter and the denial of individual immortality. As more of Aristotle's works became available, and as Averroës' commentaries circulated, some scholars at the University of Paris, called Latin Averroists, believed they could reconcile those writings with Christian doctrines. Differences of opinion became more acute when in 1255 the Parisian masters assigned the teaching of Aristotle's *Metaphysics* and writings on natural science. The Latin Averroists wished to keep philosophy and theology distinct, and they were accused of teaching a double truth. When those in charge of the curriculum realized the challenges posed by Averroës and his disciples, they condemned many Averroist propositions.

Parisian theologians devised two ways to relate the new learning to orthodox beliefs. The more traditional view was set forth by the Franciscan Bonaventure [bahn-uh-VEN-chur] (1221–1274). Denying that knowledge was possible apart from God's grace, Bonaventure, following Augustine's mode of reasoning, argued that truth had to begin in the supernatural world and thus could not arise in the senses, as Aristotle had argued. A new and brilliant theological view, and the one that prevailed, was set forth by Thomas Aquinas [uh-KWI-nus] (1226–1274), a Dominican friar who taught at the University of Paris for many years. Avoiding the pure rationalism of the Latin Averroists and the Augustinianism of Bonaventure, Thomas Aquinas steered a middle path, or *via media*, which gave Aristotle a central role in his theology while honoring traditional Christian beliefs. This theological system—called Thomism—in its complex design and sheer elegance remains one of the outstanding achievements of the High Middle Ages.

Of Thomas Aquinas's two monumental *summas*—comprehensive summaries of human thought—the *Summa Theologica* is his masterpiece. In this work, he showed that God had given human beings two divine paths to truth: reason and faith. Following Aristotle, he made the senses a legitimate source for human knowledge—a bold step that sharpened the difference between reason and faith. At the same time, Thomism escaped the strict rationalism of the Latin Averroists by denying that philosophy, or reason, could answer all theological questions. Aquinas claimed that natural reason, based on sensory knowledge, could prove certain truths—that God and the soul exist—but that spiritual reason (or revealed truth) alone could prove that the soul was immortal, that Jesus had been born of a virgin, and that God was Triune, or had three aspects.

Thomas Aquinas's contributions to medieval thought extended beyond theology into political and economic matters. He followed Aristotle in seeing the secular state as natural and necessary. For Aquinas, politics and society had "natural" ethical roots, which allowed him to write about, for example, law, marriage, and economic issues such as usury (the practice of charging exorbitant interest) and setting a just price for consumer goods.

Science and Medicine

Medieval science inherited classical works and interpreted them within the framework of Christian theology. As noted above, by 1200, many Latin translations of Arabic versions of Greek scientific and philosophical works, as well as original writings by Muslim scientists and thinkers, were available in the West. Their arrival coincided with the birth of the universities. The spread of these writings encouraged scientific-minded scholars to explore the natural world. Once again, conflicts and differences arose as natural truths confronted Christian teachings.

Science   Scholastic thinkers faced the daunting challenge of reconciling Aristotelian science and its Muslim commentaries with Christian thought. For Thomas Aquinas, the study of nature was not an end in itself but a means to understand God and his creation. Thus, any question about the natural world, such as motion, light, cosmology, or matter, would include Aristotle's and other thinkers' explanations, but the reason to explore these topics was to discover God's purposes, such as for creating the universe (cosmology) or living things (matter). Often the pursuits of medieval science were in direct relationship to their theological importance, such as studying light in order to account for a particular characteristic of God ("God is Light") or trying to understand the process of creation found in the biblical book of Genesis. Even though the role of reason was carefully circumscribed within the context of Christian thought and often had to give way to revelation, a genuine rational tradition persisted throughout this period—one that originated in ancient Greece and passed through medieval Islam, then would be transmitted into Renaissance thought, and, finally, would help bring about the Scientific Revolution, which would inaugurate modern times.

Medicine   Medieval medicine also inherited beliefs and practices from the past while making significant advances. The preservation of ancient medical texts and the teaching of these works in the newly founded universities and hospitals paved the way for modern medicine.

Included in the vast number of Greek and Roman texts now made available to the learned were the writings of Hippocrates and Galen (see Chapters 3 and 7). Their works, along with *The Canon of Medicine*, by the Muslim scholar Avicenna (see Chapter 9), became the basis of the curricula in the new medical schools. The first prestigious medical schools were in Salerno, Italy, dating from the ninth century, and Montpellier, France, founded in about 1200; they were eclipsed in the late Middle Ages by new medical schools in Paris, and in Bologna and Padua, in Italy.

In these schools, aspiring doctors read medical works, attended lectures by scholars and practicing physicians, dissected human bodies (after the mid–thirteenth century), and learned to identify and treat certain disorders and diseases. Students were taught that the body is composed of four humors—black bile, phlegm, blood, and yellow bile—a belief of the ancient Greeks. Patients who suffered from certain maladies would be treated to correct the imbalance of humors by means of herbs, diet, or bleeding. Of the many teachers in these schools, perhaps the most influential was William of Saliceto [sah-le-CHAY-toe] (1210–1277), an Italian who taught at the University of Bologna and, later, was city physician (appointed medical officer) in Verona, Italy. In his book, *Cyrurgia*, or *Surgery*, the most advanced study on this subject in his day, he discussed surgical anatomy and advocated a union between medicine and surgery—a view that ran contrary to the prevailing medical wisdom that relegated surgery to the status of a craft. In the twelfth century, an anonymous author compiled three lengthy medical texts that came to be called the *Trotula*. The second of these treatises, *On the Cures of Women*, was probably written by a woman named Trota.

The physicians formed guilds to set standards and regulate the profession; many became rich. Cities also built the first hospitals in the West, often founded by religious orders or by secular guilds. These hospitals were one of the few places women could be involved in medicine as nurses, since they were barred from medical school. Poorer city dwellers relied on untrained doctors or barbers who performed simple operations. Apothecaries sold drugs that were usually herbal or derived from animals or from minerals believed to possess healing powers.

Literature

Latin remained the language of learning, but not all Latin writings were confined to law, philosophy, and theology. There were numerous histories treating the ancient world or the age of King Arthur but more often chronicling the contemporary period. Latin poetry—especially Latin lyric poetry—flourished as well, rich in metric subtleties, extremely learned in content, and filled with classical and Christian allusions. Some of the poets, the **goliards,** or roaming scholars, were probably young clerics who addressed both church intellectual and secular audiences with poems ranging from sophisticated intellectual topics to lighthearted themes of love.

The most surprising development of the High Middle Ages was the explosion of writing in the vernacular, or popular, spoken language. Lay poets at the courts of northern France developed a new liter-ary genre, the ***chansons de geste,*** or "songs of brave deeds," the majority of which were composed in Old French. The *chansons de geste* honored the heroic adventures of warriors who had lived in the time of Charlemagne and often memorialized a minor battle or, more rarely, even a defeat. These epics were based on Christian values, but supernatural and magical elements were commonly a part of their plots. Of the many *chansons de geste*, the masterpiece is the *Song of Roland*, which became the standard for the genre (Figure 10.10).

Figure 10.10 Charlemagne Panels. Ca. 1220–1225. Stained-glass window, Chartres cathedral. Chartres, France. The *Song of Roland* was so well known and well loved that scenes from the poem were depicted in the stained-glass windows of Chartres cathedral, constructed in the thirteenth century. Even though the Charlemagne panels were inspired by a secular poem, they were situated in the ambulatory behind the main altar, one of the cathedral's most sacred areas. In one scene, Charlemagne is shown arriving too late to save Roland's life. Other panels depict him donating a church and traveling to Constantinople.

Figure 10.11   Konrad von Altstetten Embracing His Beloved in the Springtime. Manesse Codex, Zurich. Ca. 1300. Heidelberg University Library. (Codex pal. Germ. 848 fol 249 v.) 14 × 9⅞". This manuscript contains the largest collection of Middle High German love songs. The charming and vivid scene shown here reveals love emerging in the springtime. Konrad von Altstetten may have been the mayor of St. Gallen in the early fourteenth century.

The basis for the *Song of Roland* was passed down orally for three hundred years and did not reach its final written form until about 1100. The narrative is based on a historical event, the destruction of a troop of Frankish warriors, led by Count Roland (a vassal of Charlemagne) and of Charlemagne's revenge for this massacre. Superimposed on this supposedly Carolingian tale are later chivalric values, militant Christianity, and primitive nationalism. For example, Roland and his men are brave, loyal, pious, and honorable—exaggerating the ideals of Charlemagne's day. Charlemagne never fought Muslims in Spain, and Roland was killed by Basques in the Pyrenees, but the *Song of Roland* breathes the spirit of the First Crusade. Finally, this poem portrayed the Franks as ready to die for "sweet France," a notion unthinkable in Charlemagne's time but emerging in the twelfth century.

Courtly Writing   Inspired by Latin lyric verse, and perhaps by the love poetry of Islamic Spain (see Chapter 9), vernacular lyric poetry began to appear in the eleventh century in the Provençal dialect of southern France. Its supreme expression was the **canzone,** or love poem, the ancestor of all later Western love poetry. At the cultured courts of southern France, professional **minstrels,** or entertainers, sang the songs before the assembled court; the poems' composers, called **troubadors** (from Provençal *trobar*; compare French *trouver,* "to find"—thus troubadors were "finders," "inventors") came from various social classes, including nobles. Addressed to court ladies whose identities were thinly disguised in the poems, troubadors made devotion to a highborn, probably unattainable, woman the passionate ideal of the chivalrous knight. In the mature Provençal lyrics, adulterous passion was the central theme, and women were idolized and made the masters over men. Where previously adoration had been reserved for God, the troubadour lyrics now celebrated the worship of women (Figure 10.11).

After 1150, courtly **romances** replaced the *chansons de geste* in popularity. The romances were long narratives, usually in verse, of the chivalric and sentimental adventures of knights and ladies. The name *romance* arose from *mettre en romanz,* Old French for "to put into the vernacular." Their subjects derived from stories of ancient Troy and Celtic legends from the British Isles, the most enduring of which proved to be the stories of King Arthur and his knights of the Round Table.

The first poet to make Arthur and his court his subject was Chrétien de Troyes [KRAY-tyan duh TRWAH], who set the standard for later romances. Chrétien (fl. 1165–1180) was the court poet of Marie de Champagne, the countess of Champagne. His treatment of the adulterous love of the knight Lancelot and Arthur's queen, Guinevere, is characteristic of the way romances combined aristocratic, courtly, and religious themes. In this version, Lancelot rescues Queen Guinevere after experiencing many adventures and personal humiliations for her sake; this humbling of Lancelot is necessary to teach him to love Guinevere with unquestioning obedience. But Lancelot has to cope with his loyalty to Arthur, his lord and Guinevere's husband.

Another literary genre that flourished simultaneously with the romance was the **lay** (French, *lai*), a short lyric or narrative poem meant to be sung to the accompaniment of an instrument such as a harp. The oldest lays are the twelve surviving by Marie de France (fl. about 1170), a poet from Brittany who lived most of her life in England. Based on Arthurian stories, Marie de France's lays were stories of courtly love, often adulterous (for instance, a young wife kept under close watch by a jealous old husband), usually faced with conflict, always with a moral lesson. Writing in

Old French, Marie addressed the French-speaking nobility of post–Norman Conquest England, an audience that may have included King Henry II and Queen Eleanor of Aquitaine. Marie's lays were part of the outpouring of writing that made Old French literature the most influential in Europe until the rise of Italian literature in the age of Dante Alighieri.

This **vernacular literature** gave rise to a new ethos called **courtly love.** The product of courts, this ethos envisioned "fine love" as the love of an unattainable lady and male refinement in manners and behavior. It is difficult to know how seriously to take the conventions of courtly love. Perhaps it was ironic or even satirical: men became love vassals. Certainly, this ethos flew in the face of Christian morality. It is not clear that hearty lords and vassals became gentlemen. But courtly love marked medieval and later literature deeply.

Dante   Vernacular writing appeared in Italy in the thirteenth century, later than it had in France. But by 1300 Italy had produced the greatest literary figure of the High Middle Ages, Dante Alighieri [DAHN-tay ah-legg-ee-AIR-ree] (1265–1321). A native of Florence, in Tuscany, Dante was the first of a proud tradition that soon made the Tuscan dialect the standard literary speech of Italy (his impact is comparable to Luther's Bible in German and the King James Bible in English).

Born into a minor aristocratic family, Dante gained a broad education in both Greco-Roman and Christian classics but little is known about his schooling. Attracted to the values of ancient Rome, he combined a career in public office with the life of an intellectual—a tradition of civic duty inherited from the ancient Roman republic. When Dante's political allies fell from office in 1301, he was exiled from Florence for the rest of his life. During these years, poor and wandering about Italy, he composed the *Commedia,* or *Comedy,* which stands as the culmination of the literature of the Middle Ages. As in antiquity, comedy means a story with a happy ending. The *Comedy*'s sublime qualities were immediately recognized, and soon its admirers attached the epithet "Divine" to Dante's masterpiece.

Divided into three book-length parts, the *Divine Comedy* narrates Dante's fictional travels through three realms of the Christian afterlife. Led first by the ghost of Virgil, the ancient Roman poet, Dante descends into hell, where he hears from the damned the nature of their various crimes against God and the moral law. Virgil next leads Dante into purgatory, where the lesser sinners expiate their guilt while awaiting the joys of heaven. At a fixed spot in purgatory, Virgil is forced to relinquish his role to Beatrice, a young Florentine woman and Dante's symbol of the eternal female. With Beatrice's guidance, Dante enters paradise and rises to a vision of God, for him "the love that moves the sun and all the stars."

The majestic complexity of Dante's monumental poem, however, can scarcely be conveyed by this simple synopsis. Written as an allegory, the *Divine Comedy* was meant to be understood on several levels. Read literally, the poem bears witness to the author's personal fears as a mortal sinner yet affirms his hope for eternal salvation. Read allegorically, the poem represents a comprehensive synthesis of the opposing tendencies that characterized medieval culture, such as balancing the classical with the Christian, Aristotle with Aquinas, the ancient with the new, the proud with the humble, the profane with the sacred, and the secular with the spiritual.

Of the great cultural symbols that abound in the *Divine Comedy,* the richest in meaning are the central figures of Virgil and Beatrice, who represent human reason and divine revelation, respectively. In the poem, Virgil is made inferior to Beatrice, thus revealing Dante's acceptance of a basic idea of Thomas Aquinas—reason can lead only to awareness of sin; revelation is necessary to reach God's ultimate truth. Besides this fundamental Christian belief, the two figures convey other meanings: Virgil stands for classical civilization and the secular literary life; Beatrice (Italian for "blessing") symbolizes spiritualized love and Christianized culture. By turning Beatrice into an image of God's grace and love, Dante revealed that the High Middle Ages were open to new paths to Christian truth. Alongside faith and reason, pure love might lead to God.

Dante's vision of the afterlife underscored his belief that humans have free will. Predestination had no place in his system, as his picture of hell shows. With one exception, all of the damned earned their fate by their deeds on earth. Excepted were the people consigned to limbo—the virtuous pagans who lived before Jesus and thus were denied his message of hope. Moreover, those in limbo, such as Aristotle and Plato, were not subjected to any punishment other than being denied God's presence.

The intricate structure of Dante's massive poem owes much to numerology, a pseudoscience of numbers that absorbed the medieval mind. The numbers three and nine, for example, occur prominently in the *Divine Comedy.* Three is a common symbol of the Christian Trinity (the union of the Father, the Son, and the Holy Spirit in one God), and the poem is written in a three-line verse form called *terza rima* (a three-line stanza with an interlocking rhyme scheme, as *aba, bcb, cdc, ded,* and so on, ending in a rhyming couplet), which was Dante's invention. Dante identified the number nine with the dead Beatrice, whose soul lived on in the ninth heaven, the one nearest to God. He also divided hell, purgatory, and paradise into nine sections each.

Despite its allegorical and theological features, the *Divine Comedy* is a deeply personal poem. Dante rewards and punishes his Florentine friends and foes by the location that he assigns each in the afterlife. He also reveals his private feelings as he enters into discussions with various saints and sinners along the way. Above all, he sought harmony between the church and the secular state on earth and peace in his beloved Florence.

Architecture and Art

Just as scholars and writers devoted their efforts to exploring religious concerns and Christian values, artists, artisans, and architects channeled their talents into glorifying the Christian house of worship. Because the dominating physical presence of the church made it a ubiquitous symbol in both the countryside and the towns, architecture ranked higher than the other arts in medieval life. Indeed, the arts lacked an independent status, for they were regarded as mere auxiliary sources of church decoration—wall paintings, statues, and **stained-glass** windows, most of which portrayed saints and biblical heroes (Figure 10.12). In this respect, these art forms conformed to the church's teaching that the purpose of art was to represent Christian truth.

In about 1000, an international style called the **Romanesque** emerged. The first in a succession of uniform styles to sweep over Europe, the Romanesque was carried along by the monastic revival until about 1200. But by 1150, the **Gothic style** was developing in Paris; it was to become the reigning style of the towns for the remainder of the Middle Ages, succumbing finally to Renaissance fashion in about 1500.

Romanesque Churches and Related Arts   *Romanesque* is a term invented in the nineteenth century to describe the dominant architectural style after the Carolingian and before the Gothic. Although based on the architectural language of ancient Rome, Romanesque was not a pure Roman style but rather embraced elements inspired by Christianity, along with innovations beginning in the Carolingian period and continuing for some two centuries. Romanesque builders adapted the Roman basilica plan, rounded arches, vaulted ceilings, and columns for both support and decoration. Inspired by Christian beliefs, they pointed the basilicas toward Jerusalem in the east and curved each building's eastern end into an apse to house the altar. A transept, or crossing arm, was added at the church's eastern end to achieve a cross shape (Figure 10.13). Other Christian beliefs dictated such practices as having three doorways in the western facade—to symbolize the Trinity. To Roman and Christian elements, Romanesque builders added innovative design features, such as the **narthex**

Figure 10.12   Scenes from the Life of Christ. Detail. Ca. 1150–1170. Stained-glass windows, each panel 40$\frac{1}{6}$" wide × 41$\frac{1}{3}$" high. West facade, Chartres cathedral. The stained-glass windows of Chartres cathedral are renowned as the most beautiful examples of this craft to survive from the Gothic period. Of Chartres' windows, those in the west facade have been much praised for the brilliant effects created by their jewel tones of red, blue, and gold, as well as white, with small areas of green and lemon yellow. Taken from the central window of the west facade, this detail shows eighteen of its twenty-four panels, treating the life of Christ. Visible in the detail are panels depicting the annunciation (bottom left row), the visit of the three wise men (left and right, third row from bottom), and the flight into Egypt (left and right, sixth row from bottom). In the design, square panels alternate with roundel forms to frame each scene; red is the ground color for the squares and blue for the roundels. The windows can be awe inspiring, as in the reaction of the scholar Henry Adams, who described the cathedral's interior as a "delirium of coloured light."

(a porch or vestibule, usually enclosed, leading into the nave), vaulting techniques, and a wealth of ornamental detail, to create the most expressive and disciplined architectural style since the fall of Rome. Romanesque had many points of origin and spread through the international order of Cluny; along pilgrimage routes; and in imitation of Roman and German imperial churches. Comparatively few Romanesque churches can be viewed today in anything like their original condition. Some were torn down and replaced by later styles, but most have been substantially modified. Romanesque appears to have moved through two phases.

The **First Romanesque style** originated in Germany and along the Mediterranean, in the zone ranging from Dalmatia (modern Croatia), across northern Italy and Provence (southern France), to Catalonia (northeastern Spain). Simple in design, the First Romanesque churches were built of stone rubble, a Roman technique, and covered with flat, wooden roofs. With high walls and few windows, they resembled fortresses, a trait that came to characterize both Romanesque styles. The defining exterior features of the First Romanesque churches were a web of vertical bands or buttresses along the sides and a sequence of small arcades below the eaves (Figure 10.14). Because these features may have originated in Lombardy (north central Italy), they are usually called **Lombard bands** and **Lombard arcades.** Later builders experimented with the Lombard bands and arcades, creating spectacular churches, such as the Speyer cathedral in Germany (Figure 10.15). At Speyer, Lombard bands establish a rhythmic, vertical sequence on the walls of the apse. Variations on the Lombard arcade form include, on the lower part of the apse, the elongated, relatively windowless arcade attached to the wall; on the top part of the apse, the open, or "dwarf," arcaded gallery; and, on the wall above the apse, the arched

Figure 10.13   Floor Plan of a Typical Romanesque Church. This floor plan identifies the characteristic features of a Romanesque church with its cruciform floor plan: (1) narthex, (2) towers, (3) nave, (4) side aisles, (5) transept, and (6) apse.

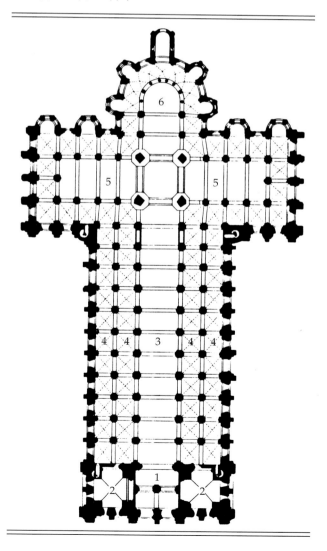

Figure 10.14   Santa Cruz de la Seros (Aragon), Church of San Caprasio, Spain. View from the north. Last quarter of the eleventh century. This church, though simple in the extreme, embodies the basic elements of the First Romanesque style. These elements include stone rubble walls, which have not been faced; a small number of windows; a flat, wooden roof; and both Lombard bands and Lombard arcades.

Figure 10.15   **Speyer Cathedral. View from the east. Speyer, Germany. Begun about 1030, completed before 1150.** Speyer cathedral, whose massive size rivals that of the great mother church at Cluny, the home of the Cluniac order of monks, represents the climax of the First Romanesque style.

niches arranged in stairstep fashion and the line of Lombard arches below the roofline.

The **Second Romanesque style** derived from Cluny III, founded 1088 and the third church built on this site (see Figure 10.5). Cluny III (destroyed in the 1800s) was greatly admired in its day for its vast scale, including double transepts and crossing towers, towers at the ends of the transepts, a double-aisled nave covered with a barrel vault, and a rich decorative program of religious art, both inside and out. The spectacular success of the Cluniac movement in the eleventh and twelfth centuries led to the spread of the Second Romanesque style throughout Europe (Figure 10.16). These churches were richly decorated and

earth hugging, with massive walls and few windows, though more and larger windows than in the First Romanesque. Their castle-like exteriors made them spiritual fortresses. Many Second Romanesque churches were pilgrimage churches—destinations for pilgrims traveling vast distances to see and venerate holy relics, the supposed bones of saints.

A celebrated pilgrimage church in the Second Romanesque style is Sainte-Marie-Madeleine in Vézelay, France. Attached to a Cluniac convent, this church attracted penitents eager to view the bones of Mary Magdalene. Vézelay's builders followed a basilica design with a cruciform floor plan. Inside, the most striking feature is the nearly 200-foot-long nave, which could

Figure 10.16   **Basilica of Sacre-Coeur, formerly Abbey Church of the Virgin and St. John the Baptist, Paray-le-Monial, France. View of nave, looking east. Begun 1110s–1120s, completed mid–twelfth century. Nave height approx. 147'7½"; length approx. 72'2⅛".** The monastery at Paray-le-Monial became part of the Cluniac system in 999. Tradition links St. Hugh, abbot of Cluny (1049–1109), with the building of the Paray-le-Monial basilica. As head of the Cluniac order, Hugh commissioned Paray to be a scaled-down version of the great mother church, Cluny III. It replicates Cluny III's vaulting techniques, using barrel vaults in the nave and groin vaults in the aisles, combined with pointed arches—derived from Muslim architecture. (The pointed arches used at Cluny III and Paray-le-Monial were not related to the development of Gothic-style architecture.) As in Cluny III, the east end culminates in a semicircular arcade resting on slender columns. The nave, consisting of only three vaulted sections, is markedly shorter than Cluny III's nave, reflecting the lack of pageantry associated with the small monastic community at Paray-le-Monial.

Figure 10.17   View of Nave, Looking East. Church of Sainte-Marie-Madeleine, Vézelay, France. Ca. 1089–1206. Vézelay's nave was made unusually long so that religious pilgrims might make solemn processions along its length. A reliquary, or an area for displaying holy relics, was later set aside in the choir. Within the choir, the design of the ambulatory provided ample space for masses of pilgrims to view all the relics at one time.

hold a large number of pilgrims and accommodate religious processions (Figure 10.17). Typical of Romanesque architecture, the nave is divided into bays, each framed by a pair of rounded arches constructed from blocks of local pink and gray stones. These colors alternate in the overhead arches and create a dazzling effect for which this church is famous. The ceiling of each bay is a groin vault—a Roman building technique. The support system for the tall nave walls—an arcade, or series of arches resting on clusters of columns—was also taken from Roman architecture. Vézelay's builders used sculpture to provide "sermons in stone" to remind illiterate visitors of the stories they heard in sermons. Instead of copying Greco-Roman columns, the artisans created their own style of decorated column. The capitals, or tops, of the interior columns are sculptured with religious scenes and motifs, such as one that shows Jacob, one of the Hebrew patriarchs (on the left), wrestling with the angel (Figure 10.18). The angel, clutching his robe in his left hand, raises his right hand to bless Jacob. The simple figures with their dramatic gestures and expressive faces accurately convey the message in Genesis (32:24–30) that Jacob has been chosen by God to lead the Hebrew people. The art is typically Romanesque: the feet point downward, the limbs are placed in angular positions, and the drapery folds are depicted in a stylized manner.

A more mature Romanesque style appears in the carvings on the **tympanum**—the triangular area—over the south portal of the tower porch at Moissac, one of the two extant elements of the twelfth-century abbey church. The other surviving element is a **cloister,** a covered arcade (where the monks walked to say their daily prayers) surrounding a quadrangle, which originally connected the church to the monastic community. The tympanum carvings probably depict a vision of the Christian apocalypse, much of which is based on the book of Revelation (Figure 10.19). Jesus is portrayed in glory, indicated by the cross-shaped symbol behind his head and the oval in which he sits enthroned, and he wears a crown. Surrounding him are the four evangelist symbols, namely, man (Matthew), winged lion (Mark), winged bull (Luke), and eagle (John) (see Chapter 6). Jesus and the four symbols are, in turn, encircled by ten of the twenty-four elders listed in Revelation 4, while fourteen other elders sit in a line below, gazing up at the Savior. The elders hold cups and musical instruments as described in Revelation 5. This tympanum sculpture

Figure 10.18   *Jacob Wrestling with the Angel.* Decorated column capital. Church of Sainte-Marie-Madeleine, Vézelay, France. Ca. 1089–1206. The Vézelay capitals survive in near-immaculate condition. Late medieval moralists considered their vivacity and gaiety inappropriate in God's house, and the offending sculptures were plastered over. When they were uncovered during a nineteenth-century restoration of the church's interior, the capitals were revealed in their charming originality.

Figure 10.19 *Christ in Glory with Four Evangelist Symbols and the Twenty-four Elders.* **Tympanum over south portal. Church of St. Pierre, Moissac, France. Ca. 1125.** The jam-packed imagery in this tympanum and surrounding space is typical of the allover patterns used in the Romanesque style. Nevertheless, there is artistic order here. Stylized floral forms are aligned rhythmically along the lintel and around the tympanum frame, and human and animal shapes encircle the seated Jesus, who is rendered four times larger than the elders. The tympanum itself is divided into three zones by the horizontal lines of clouds below Jesus's feet and above the second row of elders.

served as a warning about life's ultimate end to those who passed through the south portal.

Besides church building and church decoration, the Romanesque style was used in manuscript illumination, which had originated in late Rome and flourished in the early Middle Ages. During the High Middle Ages, new local styles arose, inspired by regional tastes and by a knowledge of Byzantine painting brought from the East by crusaders. English monks probably developed the finest of these local styles.

The Bury Bible, painted at Bury St. Edmunds monastery, reflects an English taste that is calmer and less exuberant than Continental styles. Two panels from the Bury manuscript, set off by a border of highly colored foliage, show an episode in Moses's life (Figure 10.20). Borrowings from Byzantine art may be detected in the elongated figures, the large eyes, the flowing hair, and the hanging draperies. The naturalness of these scenes presents a vivid contrast to the spirited agitation of French Romanesque art.

Gothic Churches and Related Arts   The word *Gothic* was a critical term invented by later Renaissance scholars who preferred Greco-Roman styles and imagined that Gothic architecture was so ugly that only the ferocious Goths could have been responsible for it. In fact, the Gothic grew out of the Romanesque and was not a barbarian art. Today the term *Gothic* has no negative connotations.

Gothic architecture sprang from multiple impulses. Dawning Scholasticism, the recovery of Euclid's geometry, and faintly emerging Platonism induced builders to adopt extravagant geometrical designs and to incorporate light symbolism. Prosperous townsmen

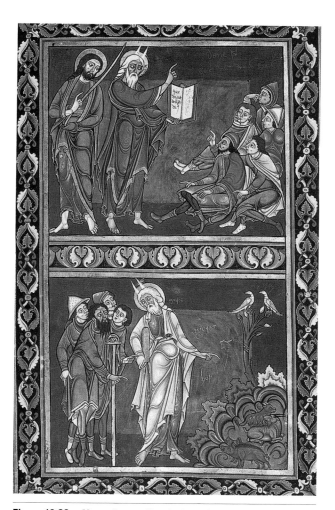

Figure 10.20 *Moses Expounding the Law of the Unclean Beasts.* **The Bury Bible. 1130–1140. Approx. 20 × 14″. Bury St. Edmunds, England. Corpus Christi College, Cambridge.** These panels depict Moses delivering the dietary laws to the ancient Hebrews. The responses of his audience reveal the sure hand of the artist, known only as Master Hugo. For example, in the upper panel one figure pulls at his nose, while a nearby companion looks skeptical. Moses's head is depicted with horns, which reflected a biblical mistranslation of the term for the radiance that surrounded Moses after receiving God's law.

joining of two arches of identical height but different widths, which, in turn, permits complex shapes and sizes. Second, the **ribbed vault** is lighter and more graceful than the barrel and groin vaults characteristic of Romanesque architecture; it also exerts less stress and facilitates experimentation with shapes. Third, point support—basically, the support of structural elements at only certain points—permits the replacement of heavy, stress-bearing walls with curtains of stained glass. The points of support might be massive internal piers or intricate skeletal frameworks, called **buttresses,** on the outside of the church; elongated and delicate buttresses are sometimes called "flying buttresses." These three elements—pointed arch, ribbed vault, and point support—produce a building that is characterized by verticality and translucency (Figure 10.21). The desired effect is one of harmony, order, and mathematical precision—Scholasticism in stone.

The glory of the Gothic church—the **choir**—was all that remained to be built. The plan and inspiration for the choir (the part of the church reserved to the clergy) were the pilgrimage churches, such as Vézelay, that had enlarged their apses by creating ambulatories, zones where people could mill about without disrupting the services, to accommodate pilgrims. In Suger's skillful hands, the east end of St. Denis was now elaborated into an oval-shaped area—the choir—ringed with several small chapels (Figure 10.22). At the heart of the choir was the apse, now arcaded; a spacious ambulatory area divided the apse from the chapels (Figure 10.23).

Between 1145 and 1500, the Gothic style presented an overwhelming image of God's majesty and the power of the church. A Gothic exterior carried the eye heavenward by impressive vertical spires. A Gothic interior surrounded the daytime worshiper with colored, celestial light; the soaring nave ceiling, sometimes rising to more than 150 feet, was calculated to stir the soul. In its total physicality, the Gothic church stood as a towering symbol of the medieval obsession with the divine.

During the High Middle Ages, the Gothic style went through two stages, the Early and the High. The Early Gothic style lasted until 1194 and was best represented by Notre Dame cathedral in Paris. The High Gothic style flourished until 1300 and reached perfection in the cathedral at Amiens, France.

Early Gothic Style, 1145–1194 The cathedral of Notre Dame ("Our Lady," the Virgin Mary) in Paris made popular the Early Gothic style, making it a fashion for other cities and towns. Begun in 1163, the cathedral was the most monumental work erected in the West to that time. Its floor plan was cruciform, but the length of the transept barely exceeded the width of the aisle walls

demanded larger, more magnificent churches. Increasing wealth made larger projects possible.

Two problems with the Romanesque stood in the way: the groin vaults were so heavy that the nearly windowless walls had to be extremely thick to support their great weight, and the rounded arches limited the building's height. Between 1137 and 1144, the Gothic style was created by Suger [sue-ZHAY] (about 1081–1151), the abbot of the royal Abbey Church of St. Denis, near Paris. Suger's startling originality resulted from his combining a number of elements that had long been in use—three in particular: First, a **pointed arch** (adapted from the Muslim world) is more elegant than a round one; it also permits the

(Figure 10.24). Part of Notre Dame's beauty stems from the rational principles applied by the builders, notably the ideal of harmony, best expressed in the integration of sculpture and decorative details with building units. For instance, the west facade is divided into three equal horizontal bands: the three doorways, the **rose window** and **blind arcades** (walled-in windows), and the two towers (Figure 10.25). Within each subdivision of this facade, figurative sculpture or architectural details play a harmonizing role, from the rows of saints flanking each of the portals to the **gargoyles,** or grotesque animals or humans carved in stone peering down from the towers.

Figure 10.21   Principal Features of a Typical Gothic Church. In this schematic drawing, the features are numbered from the nave outward: (1) nave arcade, (2) pointed arch, (3) vault, (4) clerestory, (5) flying buttress, (6) buttress, and (7) gargoyle.

Figure 10.22   Ambulatory. Church of St. Denis, Paris. Ca. 1145. This view of the choir of St. Denis shows a portion of the ambulatory that allowed pilgrims to view the chapels in the apse. The evenly spaced support columns and the pointed arches create this flowing, curved space. The ribbed arches in the ceiling are also central to the Gothic skeletal construction.

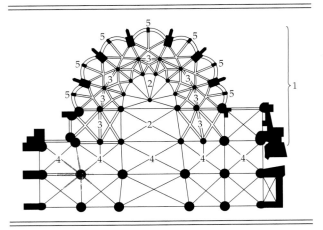

Figure 10.23   Floor Plan, Ambulatory. Church of St. Denis, Paris. Ca. 1145. This floor plan, based on a similar design used in the pilgrimage churches, became the basis for the reordering of interior space in the Gothic choirs. The features include (1) choir, (2) apse, (3) ambulatory, (4) transept, and (5) chapel.

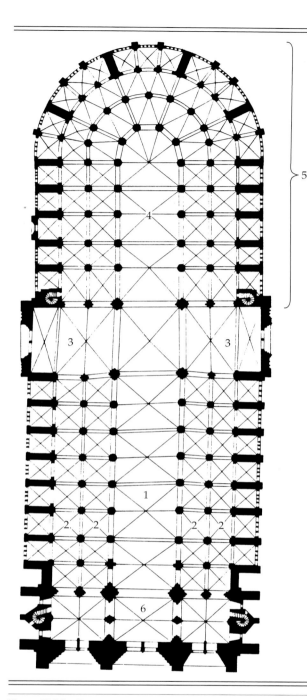

Figure 10.24   Floor Plan of Notre Dame. Paris. 1163–ca. 1250. This drawing shows the principal features of Notre Dame cathedral: (1) nave, (2) aisle, (3) transept, (4) apse, (5) choir, and (6) narthex, or vestibule.

Figure 10.25   Western Facade. Notre Dame. Paris. 1220–1250. In the gallery above the western portals are twenty-eight images of the kings of Judah, including David and Solomon. These sculptures, typical of Gothic churches, are more than decorations: they are reminders that Mary and Jesus were descended from royalty. In the medieval mind, this religious idea was meant to buttress the monarchical style of government.

Inside Notre Dame, which can hold ten thousand people, the spectacular nave reveals the awe-inspiring effects of Early Gothic art at its best (Figure 10.26). The strong vertical lines and the airy atmosphere represent the essence of this style. With its ribbed vaults and pointed arches, the nave rises to a height of 115 feet from the pavement to the vaulting. Like the harmonious western facade, the nave is divided into three equal tiers: the nave and double aisles, the open spectator **gallery** above the aisles, and, at the top, the clerestory—the luminous window zone.

Notre Dame reveals that the choir was coming to dominate the Early Gothic church. Notre Dame's choir is almost as long as the nave, so that the transept virtually divides the church into two halves. At first, the choir's walls had no special external supports, but as cracks began to appear in the choir's walls during the thirteenth century, flying buttresses were added to ensure greater stability—a feature that would later characterize High Gothic churches (Figure 10.27).

The Gothic sculptures that decorate Notre Dame differ from the exuberant Romanesque style. The Romanesque's animated images of Jesus have given way to the Gothic's sober figures. In addition, the Gothic figures are modeled in three dimensions, and their draperies fall in natural folds (Figure 10.28). At the same time, the rise of the cult of the Virgin meant an increased number of images of Mary as well as of female saints. The name "Notre Dame" itself testifies to the appeal of the cult of the Virgin.

Before Notre Dame was finished, its architects began to move in new directions, refining the traditional

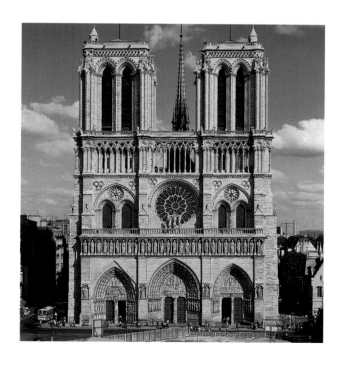

Figure 10.26   Nave. Notre Dame. Paris. View from the height of the western rose window. 1180–1250. Ht. floor to summit of roof, 115′. The nave is clearly not aligned properly. The choir bends perceptibly to the north, which probably reflects the different building times for various parts of the cathedral. The transept and the choir were finished first, after which the nave and the double aisles were added. The western facade was completed last.

features into a new style, called **Rayonnant,** or Radiant. In the Rayonnant style, the solid walls gave way to sheets of stained glass framed by elegant **traceries,** or rich ornamentation, of stone. This radiant effect was especially evident in the north transept facade, which was rebuilt in this new style. With the addition of this transept's imposing rose window, designed to suggest the rays of the sun, the cathedral's interior was bathed in constantly shifting colors, giving it a mystical atmosphere (Figure 10.29).

High Gothic Style, 1194–1300   The High Gothic style is a tribute to the growing confidence of the builders of the thirteenth century, who took the Gothic ingredients and refined them, creating grander churches than had been erected earlier. In comparison with Early Gothic architecture, High Gothic churches were taller and had greater volume; artistic values now stressed wholeness rather than the division of space into harmonious units. Rejecting the restrained decoration of the Early Gothic style, the High Gothic architects covered the entire surface of their churches' western facades with sculptural and architectural designs.

The cathedral in Amiens is a perfect embodiment of the High Gothic style. Amiens was planned so that flying buttresses would surround its choir and march along its nave walls (Figure 10.30). Instead of trying to disguise these supports, the architect made the exterior skeleton central to his overall plan. As a result, more-spacious window openings could be made in the nave and the choir walls than had been the case in Notre Dame. Furthermore, the design of Amiens' nave was also changed so that the entire space was perceived as a homogeneous volume. The division of the nave walls into three equal horizontal bands was eliminated, and the system of arches and bays overhead became less emphatic (see the chapter-opening photo, p. 226). Amiens' overall floor plan was conservative, however, for it resembled that of Notre Dame; for example, its

Figure 10.27   Notre Dame. Paris. View from the east. 1163–1182. Notre Dame's choir, shown on the right, was originally built without chapels and flying buttresses—a sign of its Early Gothic origins. Paris's greatest church caught up with the High Gothic style in the fourteenth century, when these architectural features were added.

Figure 10.28 *The Last Judgment.* **Central portal, western facade, Notre Dame, Paris. Ca. 1210.** This tympanum represents Jesus enthroned and presiding over the Last Judgment. Surrounding him are the apostles, the prophets, the church fathers, and the saints—arranged in descending order of their importance in relation to Jesus. Like all the sculptures of Notre Dame's first story, the entire scene was gilded with gold paint until the mid–fifteenth century.

Figure 10.29 **North Rose Window of Notre Dame. Paris. Ca. 1255.** This masterwork by Jehan de Chelles is the only original of Notre Dame's three rose windows. The nineteenth-century restoration genius Eugène Viollet-le-Duc re-created the other two. Measuring forty-three feet in diameter, the window was installed after workers first removed sections of the existing wall. The bits of predominantly blue glass, encased in iron settings, were then placed inside the stone frame.

Figure 10.30   Amiens Cathedral. Amiens, France. Ca. 1220–1270. This photograph shows the brilliantly articulated exterior skeleton of Amiens cathedral. Gothic churches openly displayed the exterior support system that made their interior beauty possible. In the Renaissance, this aspect of Gothicism was decried for its clumsiness. Renaissance architects preferred classical structures that hid their stresses and strains.

transept bisected a choir and a nave of equal length (Figure 10.31).

The western facade of Amiens shows how decoration changed in the High Gothic style (Figure 10.32). Amiens' western wall and towers are pierced with rich and intricate openings. The elegant tracery has the effect of dissolving the wall's apparent solidity. What surface remains intact is covered with an elaborate tapestry of architectural devices and sculptural figures (Figure 10.33).

The finest stained glass from the High Gothic era is from the cathedral in Chartres, a town fifty miles south of Paris. Chartres has 176 windows, and most are the thirteenth-century originals. Outstanding examples of this art are the Charlemagne panels depicting scenes from the *Song of Roland*, illustrated earlier in this chapter (see Figure 10.10). Each figure is precisely rendered, though many are cropped at the edge of the pictorial space. The glass itself is brilliant, notably in the dominant blue tones.

High Gothic painting survives best in the manuscript illuminations of the late thirteenth century. By that time, these small paintings were being influenced by developments elsewhere in Gothic art. The Gothic illuminators abandoned the lively draperies of the Romanesque and instead showed gowns hanging in a natural manner. More important, they sometimes allowed the architectural frame to dominate the painting, as in the *Psalter of St. Louis IX* of France. Commissioned by the sainted French king, this book contains seventy-eight full-page paintings of scenes from the Old Testament. Of these paintings, *Balaam and His Ass* is a typical representation of the anonymous painter's style (Figure 10.34). The scene unfolds before a High Gothic church; two gables with rose windows are symmetrically balanced on the page. Although this painting owes much to changes in Gothic sculpture, the animated figures of the men, the angel, and the ass are reminiscent of the exuberant Romanesque style.

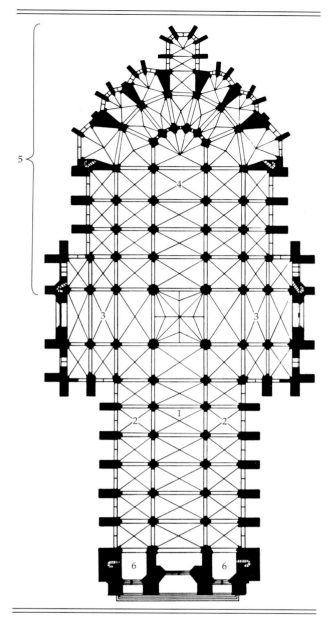

Figure 10.31   Floor Plan of Amiens Cathedral. Amiens, France. Ca. 1220–1236. This drawing shows the principal features of Amiens cathedral: (1) nave, (2) aisle, (3) transept, (4) apse, (5) choir, and (6) narthex.

Figure 10.32   Western Facade. Amiens cathedral. Amiens, France. Ca. 1220–1236. Comparison of Amiens' facade with that of Notre Dame in Paris (see Figure 10.25) shows how the High Gothic differs from the Early Gothic. The basic form remains the same, but Amiens' surface is richer in detail and more splendid overall. The pointed features, such as the arches over the portals and over the openings in the towers, are the most characteristic visual element in the High Gothic style.

Music

As with the other arts, the purpose of music during the High Middle Ages was the glorification of God. At first, the monophonic (single-line) Gregorian chants were still the main form of musical expression, but two innovations—the introduction of tropes and the development of polyphony—led the way to a different sound in the future.

Among the compositions of sacred music written during this period, the works of Hildegard of Bingen have a lasting appeal. Hildegard composed within the tradition of Gregorian chant (see Chapter 8), though she, a devout mystic, claimed ecstatic visions as the inspiration for her musical ideas. The words for her texts

Figure 10.33   *Golden Virgin*. Amiens cathedral. Ca. 1260. Amiens, France. The *Golden Virgin* of Amiens, so called because it was originally covered with a thin layer of gold, is one of the most admired works of Gothic art. The artist has depicted Mary as a loving earthly mother with fine features, a high forehead, and a shy smile. This sculpture shows the new tenderness that was creeping into art during the High Middle Ages as part of the rise of the cult of the Virgin.

Figure 10.34   *Balaam and His Ass. Psalter of St. Louis IX.* 1252–1270. Bibliothèque Nationale de France, Paris. The architectural details in this miniature painting show a correspondence with the Rayonnant architectural style: the two gabled roofs, the two rose windows with exterior traceries, the pointed arches, and the pinnacles. Just as Gothic architects emphasized the decorative aspects of their buildings, so did this anonymous painter of miniatures. The story of Balaam and his ass (Numbers 22:22–35 in the Old Testament) was a beast fable—a popular literary genre in the Middle Ages. In the biblical story, the ass could speak and see things of which his master, Balaam, was ignorant. In the painting, the ass turns his head and opens his mouth as if to speak.

were drawn from the Bible, her theological writings, and the church's liturgy.

Hildegard's works were unusual not only because they were written by a woman but also because they were performed by women singers before audiences of women—Hildegard's fellow nuns. Besides the previously mentioned sung morality play *Ordo Virtutum (The Company of the Virtues)*, Hildegard composed seventy-seven songs, chants, and hymns for the church's liturgy, including such works as "O Pastor Animarum" ("O Shepherd of Souls"), "Spiritui Sancto" ("To the Holy Spirit"), and "O Jerusalem." She also wrote a kyrie (a chant sung during the Mass asking the

Lord for mercy) and an alleluia (a chant sung during the Mass offering praise), as well as two longer works composed specifically for women, one dedicated to virgins and the other to widows.

Hildegard's "O Pastor Animarum" is one of the seventy-seven songs in the collection known as the *Symphonia* (full title: *Symphonia armonie celestium revelationum*, or *Symphony of the Harmony of Celestial Revelations*). *Symphony* here means simply "collection" and should not be confused with the modern symphony, a musical form. "O Pastor Animarum" is an **antiphon**, a short prose text, chanted by an unaccompanied voice or voices during the liturgy. Addressed to God the Father, this antiphon reads, in Latin: *"O Pastor animarum, / et o prima vox, / perquam omnes creati sumus, / nunc tibi, / tibi placeat, / ut degneris nos liberare / de miseries et languoribus nostris"* (in English: "O Shepherd of souls, / and o first voice, / through whom all creation was summoned, / now to you, / to you may it give pleasure and dignity, / to liberate us / from our miseries and languishing"). Typically, Hildegard's antiphon is composed in **plainsong** (also called *plainchant*), the Christian chant that dominated the period. The music shows her personal style: wide leaps of melody and ornamental features, especially **melismas** (groups of notes sung to the same syllable) and, to a lesser extent, **syllabic** singing (one note per syllable).

The **tropes,** or turns, were new texts and melodies inserted into the existing Gregorian chants. Added for both poetic and doctrinal reasons, these musical embellishments slowly changed the plainchants into more elaborate songs. Culminating in about 1150, this musical development coincided with the appearance of the richly articulated Gothic churches. The tropes also gave a powerful impetus to Western drama. From the practice of troping grew a new musical genre, the **liturgical drama,** which at first was sung and performed in the church but gradually moved outdoors. From the twelfth century onward, these works were staged in the area in front of the church as sacred dramas or mystery plays (from Latin *mysterium,* "secret" or "hidden"—i.e., the plays revealed deep truths). As their popularity increased, they began to be sung in the vernacular instead of Latin. Ultimately, the liturgical drama supplied one of the threads that led to the revival of the secular theater.

Gregorian chants were also being modified by the development of **polyphony,** in which two or more lines of melody are sung or played at the same time. In the early eleventh century, polyphony was extremely simple and was known as **organum.** It consisted of a main melody, called the *cantus firmus,* accompanied by an identical melody sung four or five tones higher or lower. By about 1150, the second line began to have its own independent melody rather than duplicating the first. During the thirteenth century, two-voiced organum gave way to multivoiced songs called **motets,** which employed more complex melodies. In the motets, the main singer used the liturgy as a text while up to five other voices sang either commentaries or vernacular translations of the text. The result was a complex blend of separate voices woven into a harmonious tapestry. By about 1250, the motet composers had laid the foundations of modern musical composition.

Notwithstanding these developments in sacred music, the church could not stop the rise of secular music any more than it could prevent the spread of courtly love. Indeed, the first secular music was associated with

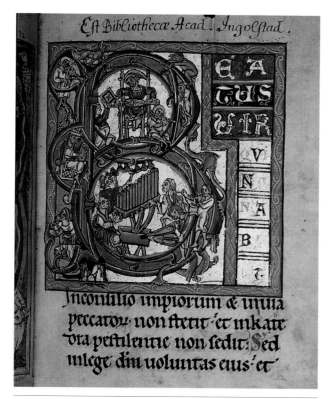

Figure 10.35   Embellished Letter *B*. Psalter from Würzburg-Ebrach. Early thirteenth century. Universitäts Bibliothek, Munich. In illuminated manuscripts, the initial letter of a sentence was often embellished with intricate details, drawn from the artist's imagination and experience. In this example from a thirteenth-century German psalter, the letter *B* is interwoven with a band of musicians playing instruments typical of the era: organ (with bellows), bells, ivory horn, flute, stringed instruments, and an instrument for bows. The artist who painted this miniature scene has captured the liveliness of a musical performance, depicting several players singing.

the same courts where the *chansons de geste* and the troubador songs flourished in the twelfth century. At first, France was the center of this musical movement, but in the early thirteenth century, German poets took the lead. At the same time, music began to be practiced not just by aristocratic poets but also by middle-class minstrels, and new musical instruments—some, such as the **lute** (a multistringed instrument with neck and sound box) and the bagpipe, banned by the church—started to find their way into secular music (Figure 10.35).

Technology

Technology during the High Middle Ages recovered many valuable techniques from ancient Rome, and, by improving on this heritage and borrowing from Islam, the West was able to sustain Europe's burgeoning economy and society, as well as, in a few cases, to take steps forward. Among the largest steps forward was the adoption of papermaking and the astrolabe, both introduced from the Islamic world (see Chapter 9). However, the impact of these new technologies was relatively limited. Technology's strongest impact on the wider culture was made by further advances in warfare, the rise of watermills and windmills in the North, and new tools in farming.

Advances in military technology included

- larger, more powerful warhorses, imported from Spain;
- widespread use of better saddles, stirrups, and spurs, which enhanced the knight's stability on his mount;
- better armor, including head-to-toe chain mail, metal gauntlets (gloves), and helmets;
- the introduction of the powerful, accurate crossbow; and

- the introduction of gunpowder (probably from China), used mainly as an explosive in siege warfare to topple walls.

Advances in agricultural productivity included

- water-driven mills that significantly expanded milling capacity—more grain could be milled faster, producing more flour, and increasing food supplies;
- the proliferation of windmills, probably introduced from the Muslim world, perhaps by crusaders; and
- a widespread shift from the ox to the horse as a plow and draft animal, facilitated by the horse-collar.

SUMMARY

Europe doubled in size and population in the High Middle Ages. Intellectual life grew more intense, with more schools and more masters. Encounters with more classical texts and with Islamic learning pushed thinkers to grapple with the relationship between faith and reason. In the writings of Thomas Aquinas, people learned to believe that some things could be known by human reason alone while other things could be known only through divine revelation. Not all writing was theological or philosophical. Latin continued to be used as a literary language, but writings in many vernaculars appeared in quality and profusion—songs of deeds, lays, lyrics, and romances. Vernacular literature reached its apogee in Dante's *Comedy*. Architecture went through two distinct phases: Romanesque styles embellished Carolingian achievements and carried them into the twelfth century at which point the Gothic style took over, first in the region around Paris and then almost everywhere else in Europe. The beautiful but simple plainchants of the early Middle Ages yielded to polyphony, to multiple voices.

KEY CULTURAL TERMS

feudalism	minstrel	Lombard bands	tracery
chivalry	troubador	Second Romanesque style	antiphon
Investiture Controversy	romance	tympanum	plainsong
friars	lay	cloister	melismas
Crusades	vernacular language	pointed arch	syllabic
cathedral	courtly love	ribbed vault	trope
Scholasticism	*terza rima*	buttress	liturgical drama
realism	stained glass	choir	polyphony
nominalism	Romanesque style	rose window	organum
via media	Gothic style	blind arcade	motet
goliard	narthex	gargoyle	lute
chanson de geste	First Romanesque style	gallery	
canzone	Lombard arcades	Rayonnant style	

The Legacy of the High Middle Ages

In Quentin Tarantino's 1994 film *Pulp Fiction,* one violent character says to a victim, "I'm gonna get medieval on you." The popular image of the Middle Ages may be one of violence, backwardness, and superstition. But that image is wrong in almost every way. Medieval violence, in all its intensity and mayhem, was not, like that of modern times, mechanized and technological. Modern ordered society under law is more a medieval than a classical heritage; for example, the United States archives in Washington display a copy of the Magna Carta. Modern business rests on the practices of Italian merchants. The popes have greatly reduced power today, but there are still a billion Catholics who look to them for guidance. And the theology of Thomas Aquinas ("Thomism") was official in the Catholic Church until very recently. CDs of Gregorian chant and Paris polyphony sell remarkably well. Nineteenth-century Romanticism revived Gothic architecture, and many American cities and universities have Gothic buildings. The university may be the most enduring legacy of the Middle Ages. In popular culture, films like *Braveheart* and *Beowulf* keep medieval themes alive. The beloved tales of *The Lord of the Rings* and *The Hobbit* were written by an Oxford professor of medieval literature, J. R. R. Tolkien. The immensely popular Harry Potter books and films are filled with medieval symbols and images. Chivalry is surely not dead even if "polite" society is near its demise. There is much to think about in the tendency of some radical Islamists to call Westerners who dare to intervene in the Middle East "crusaders."

St. Patrick's Cathedral, New York. Neogothic. Designed by James Renwick and constructed between 1858 and 1878. Pope Pius IX made New York an archbishopric in 1850 and Archbishop John Joseph Hughes decided to build a new cathedral as a proud expression of American Catholicism. To connect the American church with its European heritage, he asked Renwick to build a Gothic building. It will amuse modern New Yorkers to learn that what is now the corner of Fifth Avenue and 51st Street was then out in the country.

Master of the Cité des Dames, Christine de Pizan presenting her book to Queen Isabeau of Bavaria (1410–1415). Illuminated manuscript, tempera and gold on vellum, 5½ × 6¾″. British Library. (Ms. Harley 4431 vol. 1 fol 3r.). Images like this one proliferated in luxurious books on both religious and secular subjects produced for elite owners.

11

The Late Middle Ages

Crisis and Recovery

1300–1500

Preview Questions

1. *Identify* the major crises of the late Middle Ages.

2. *Discuss* the differences between high and late medieval philosophy and theology.

3. *What* is new and distinctive about late medieval literature?

4. *Name* several differences between high and late medieval architecture and painting.

The Four Horsemen of the Apocalypse—Conquest, War, Famine, and Death—rode roughshod over Europe in the late Middle Ages. The Black Death ravaged the population. The economy suffered one shock after another. The church had to relinquish its dream of a united Christendom when faced with the reality of warring European states. New military tactics and weapons rendered chivalry obsolete, and the chivalric code began to seem a romantic fiction. In the universities, new intellectual currents drove a wedge between philosophy and theology, which had been so carefully integrated by Thomas Aquinas. Vernacular literature took off in bold new directions. And the balanced High Gothic style in art and architecture gave way to the florid late Gothic style.

This beautiful painting of Christine de Pizan presents a counterpoint to the horrors of the age. It suggests wealth and luxury, which did indeed mark the lifestyles of the rich and famous. The figures are all women, a rarity in European art before this time, and the centerpiece is a book, probably Christine's *Book of the City of Ladies.* An Italian herself, Christine wrote in French, which points to two trends in the age: the vernacular was increasingly prominent in literature and the world of scholarship was growing more international. Women were beginning to figure in art and to practice one or another of the arts. That the image shown here features a book is significant in another way as well: the production of books exploded in the fifteenth century, aided by the invention of the printing press with movable type. From an artistic point of view, the image shows the artist grappling with mathematical perspective. By the end of the fifteenth century, that problem would be solved.

Learning Through Maps

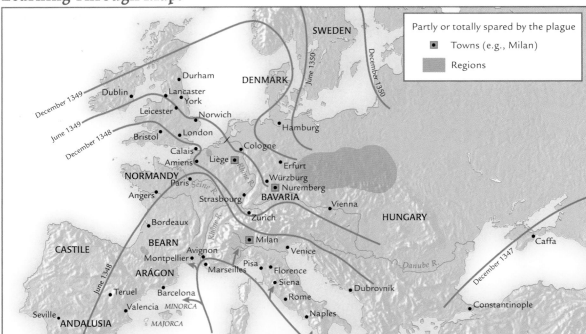

MAP 11.1   PROGRESS OF THE BLACK DEATH ACROSS EUROPE IN THE FOURTEENTH CENTURY

This map shows the spread of the plague across Europe in the mid–fourteenth century. *1. **Notice** how the dark lines mark the progress of the plague at a specific time. 2. **Where** and **when** does the Black Death appear in Europe? 3. **Where** and **when** does it end? 4. **What** regions and cities were partly or totally spared the plague? 5. **Consider** the role of various types of travelers in spreading the Black Death.*

HARD TIMES COME TO EUROPE

Shortly after the opening of the fourteenth century, Europe entered a disastrous period of economic depression, accompanied by soaring prices and widespread famine. Against the backdrop of the Hundred Years' War between England and France (1337–1453), social unrest increased and renegade armies ravaged much of western Europe. The church, in disgrace and disarray for much of this period, was unable to provide moral or political leadership. As old certainties evaporated, the optimistic mood of the High Middle Ages gave way to a sense of impending doom.

Ordeal by Plague, Famine, and War

Of all Europe's calamities, the worst was the plague that ravaged Europe from 1348 to 1351 and then intermittently for another century. In the sixteenth century, writers began to label the epidemic the "Black Death,"

which has become the common term. Scholars used to think confidently that the Black Death was an instance of bubonic plague transmitted to humans by fleas from infected rats, but they are no longer sure of this. Bubonic plague tends to spread slowly and its typical mortality is far less than Europe experienced at the time of the Black Death. So deadly was the disease that more than a third of Europe's seventy million people died in the first epidemic alone. The plague first appeared in Italy in 1347 (Map 11.1). From Italy, the disease spread rapidly over most of Europe, halted by the frost line in the north. The mechanism of disease transmission was not fully understood, and the plague created panic.

The Black Death cast a long shadow over the late Middle Ages. Many writers and artists reflected the melancholy times, occasionally brightening their dark works with an end-of-the-world gaiety. The age's leading image became the Dance of Death, often portrayed

Figure 11.1 *The Dance of Death.* **Fifteenth century.** In the wake of the Black Death, art and literature became filled with themes affirming the biblical message that life is short and death certain. A vivid image of this theme was the *Danse Macabre*, or Dance of Death, which took many artistic and literary forms. In this example, a miniature painting taken from a fifteenth-century Spanish manuscript, the corpses are shown nude, stripped of their human dignity, and dancing with wild abandon.

as a skeleton democratically joining hands with kings, queens, popes, merchants, peasants, and prostitutes as they danced their way to destruction. This symbol forcefully portrayed the folly of human ambition and the transitory nature of life (Figure 11.1).

The plague was compounded by growing famine conditions across the European continent. Starting in 1315, agricultural harvests failed with some regularity for more than a century. These famines braked centuries of steady population growth and weakened the populace by making them more susceptible to diseases.

War also disrupted the pattern of social and economic life. Princes from France and Aragon (northeastern Spain) struggled to control southern Italy. Northern Italian cities waged war among themselves for commercial and political advantage. England and France fought the seemingly endless Hundred Years' War, while the dukes of Burgundy attempted to carve out a "middle kingdom" between France and the German Empire. Farther east, from 1347 on, the Ottoman Turks occupied Greece and the Balkan peninsula, conquered Constantinople in 1453, and menaced eastern Europe. Amid all this constant warfare, bands of mercenaries and marauding renegades only made things worse.

Depopulation and disruption, therefore, were the chief results of the plague and the wars that accompanied it. Old areas, such as France, lost population and prosperity, while new areas, such as eastern Europe and Scandinavia, gained population and prosperity. Florence and Venice, which were initially devastated by the plague, rebounded by the fifteenth century. Disparities between rich and poor grew greater. Wages

fluctuated wildly as workers moved about in search of opportunities and employers competed for their services. Between 1296 and 1381 in Flanders, Florence, France, and England, workers and peasants rose up violently, albeit without durable effect (see Slice of Life). Ironically, in the long term those who survived experienced an elevated standard of living. Political and social unrest did not, however, bring much real change. Serfdom continued to decline in western Europe, but in eastern Europe the lives of peasants grew worse. Urban middle classes still fought with each other and with their royal and ecclesiastical overlords.

THE SECULAR MONARCHIES

France and England maintained their leading positions in Europe, but they exhausted their economies with wasteful wars. The Hundred Years' War, as the group of conflicts between the mid–fourteenth and the mid–fifteenth centuries is called, had three root causes: England's conquest in 1066 by a Norman duke; Henry II's (r. 1154–1189) "Angevin Empire"; and John of England's defeat in 1212 by the French king Philip II (r. 1180–1223) (Timeline 11.1). The war was fought entirely on French soil. The Valois dynasty—successor to the Capetians in 1328—had to contend not only with England but also with the dukes of Burgundy, who threatened to break their ties with the French crown and establish an independent kingdom on France's eastern border. The Burgundian court at Dijon was the most brilliant in northern Europe, attracting the leading artists and humanists of the age. A heroic figure who emerged from this war was Joan of Arc

Timeline 11.1   ROYAL DYNASTIES IN LATE MEDIEVAL FRANCE AND ENGLAND

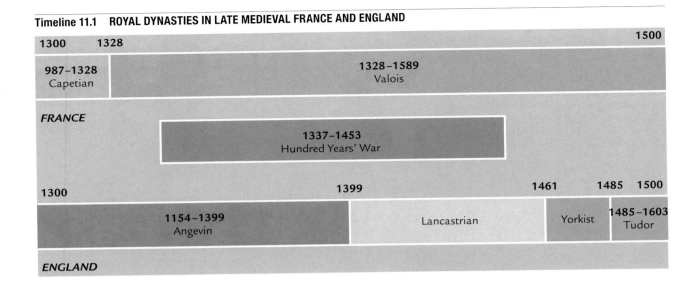

(1412–1431), who rallied the French to victory, only to be burned at the stake by the English; in modern times, she became one of France's national heroines and a Roman Catholic saint.

Despite the ravages of the Hundred Years' War, the Valois kings ultimately increased their territory. Except for the port of Calais in northern France, England was forced to cede its overseas lands to the French crown. The dukes of Burgundy were brought under French control. And the northwestern region of Brittany, the last major territory that had escaped the French crown, was acquired through marriage. The contour of modern France was now complete (Figure 11.2).

While the Hundred Years' War raged on the Continent, life in England was disrupted by aristocratic factionalism, peasant unrest, and urban strife. Like France, England was emerging from feudalism, but it was moving in a different direction. The English Parliament, which represented the interests of the nobles, towns, and rural counties, gained power at the expense of the king.

When Henry VII (r. 1485–1509) became king, however, it became apparent that a key reason for the dominance of Parliament had been the weakness of the kings. This founder of England's brilliant Tudor dynasty avoided the quarrels his predecessors had had with Parliament by abandoning foreign wars, living off his own estates, and relying on his own advisers. Henry VII's policies deflated parliamentary power and made him as potent as his contemporaries in France.

The success of the French and the English kings in centralizing their states attracted many imitators. Their ruling style—with royal secretaries, efficient treasuries, national judiciaries, and representative assemblies—was adopted in part by other states. Spain was the most successful in achieving unity. Dynastic politics and

civil war kept central Europe and Scandinavia from becoming strong and centralized. The Holy Roman Empire was the least successful of these political entities, and Germany remained divided into combative states. And, in the eastern Mediterranean, the Ottoman Turks, devout Muslims, posed a threat to Christian Europe.

THE PAPAL MONARCHY

Following its pinnacle of power and prestige in 1200 under Pope Innocent III, the church entered a period of decline in about 1300, and for the next century it was beset with schism and heresy. From 1309 to 1377, the seat of the papacy was located in Avignon in France, a papal fief on the Rhône River, chosen initially to allow negotiations with the king of France after the disastrous conflict between Boniface VIII and Philip IV (see Chapter 10). Opponents of the relocation of the papacy, claiming the popes were in the pocket of the French king, tagged it the "Babylonian Captivity" (hearkening to the captivity of the ancient Jews in Babylon). The Avignon popes were exceptionally effective administrators, especially in the financial realm, but often worldly and dissolute.

The Avignon papacy had barely ended in 1378 when a new calamity, the Great Schism, threw the church into even more confusion. Gregory XI (pope 1370–1378) returned to Rome in 1377 but he died in 1378, and, in the ensuing election of an Italian pope, some French cardinals alleged intimidation and returned to Avignon. When the French cardinals elected a new pope, Western Christendom was divided with two popes, two colleges of cardinals, and two papal courts. The rising power of the secular states became evident as rulers cast their support for one side or the other: France, Sicily, Scotland, Castile, Aragon, and Portugal

Figure 11.2 *An Archbishop before a King of France. The Grand Coutumes of Normandy, the Coutumes of France.* **Fifteenth century. Law Library, Library of Congress, Washington, D.C.** In addition to wars and marriage, the kings of France consolidated their power by establishing legal and judicial control over their newly acquired regions and territories. One of their tactics was to collect and codify the *coutumes*, or local customary laws. For centuries, provincial lawyers and regional courts had formulated and interpreted these local laws, and, by the fifteenth century, the *coutumes* had become the basis and structure of the legal rulings and procedures in each province. Charles VII (r. 1422–1461) ordered in 1453 that the *coutumes* be codified and brought before him and his grand council for their examination and approval. Unlike other compilations, *The Grand Coutumes of Normandy* (ca. 1450–1470) were embellished with seven miniature paintings depicting various examples of the application and execution of the laws, which were common in Normandy and in England. In this example, the French king gives a document or charter to the archbishop of Normandy. Since such agreements between kings and church leaders were renewed many times in the fourteenth and fifteenth centuries, this miniature is likely symbolic, not representing an actual event. However, its message is clear: the crown holds the real power.

rallied behind the Avignon pope; England, Flanders, Poland, Hungary, Germany, and the rest of Italy stayed loyal to the Roman pope. The papal office suffered the most; the pope's authority diminished as pious Christians became bewildered and disgusted.

The worst was yet to come. In 1409 both sets of cardinals summoned a church council in Pisa to heal the fissure. The Pisan Council elected a new pope and called on the other two popes to resign. They refused, and the church was faced with *three* rulers claiming papal authority. The Great Schism was finally resolved at the Council of Constance (1414–1418), which deposed the Avignon ruler, accepted the resignation of the Roman claimant, ignored the Pisan Council's choice, and elected a new pope, Martin V.

With the success of the Council of Constance, conciliar rule (rule by councils) as a way of curbing the power of the popes seemed to be gaining support in the church. But Martin V (pope 1417–1431) rejected this idea as soon as he was elected to the papal throne. Nevertheless, the conciliar movement remained alive until the mid–fifteenth century, when strong popes reasserted the monarchical power of their office. Although powerful, these popes failed to address pressing moral and spiritual concerns, for they were deeply involved in Italian politics and other worldly interests, ruling almost as secular princes in Papal States.

TECHNOLOGY

As farming life changed because of the growth of urban life, so did Europe's fledgling industrial life, and new technology, for instance the suction pump, increased productivity in some industries. Older inventions, such as eyeglasses, mechanical clocks, and

gunpowder, were improved in this age of rapid change. However, the most significant technological innovation of the late Middle Ages was the development of printing with movable metal type in the mid–fifteenth century.

The Rise of Industries

Hand-loomed textile manufacturing remained the leading industry, but its production and distribution centers shifted. The greatest change in textile manufacturing, however, was precipitated by England's shift from the export of raw wool to the export of finished cloth, a change that disrupted the traditional rural way of life.

Wool merchants organized the new textile industry in England. The merchants, who bought and owned the raw wool, created the "putting-out system," the assigning of tasks (shearing, carding, combing, spinning, weaving, fulling, felting, dyeing, and cutting) to families who worked at home—which came to be defined as the cottage industry. The spinning wheel—imported

SLICE OF LIFE

A Gossip Columnist of the Late Middle Ages

Henry Knighton
A VIEW FROM THE PROVINCES

The Chronicle *of Henry Knighton (?–1396) is an excellent source for the late Middle Ages in England. An attentive observer of public affairs, Knighton recorded the gossip about the political and religious unrest of his age. He lived mainly in Leicestershire, far from London, but he had well-placed contacts and reliable sources. In the first excerpt, Knighton reports on the 1381 rebellion of Wat Tyler. In the second excerpt, he passes along a rumor about religious unrest, which may be related to the Lollards, who believed that women could be priests.*

1

The next day, which was Saturday [15 June 1381], they all came together again in Smithfield, where the king [Richard II] came early to meet them, and showed that although he was young in years he was possessed of a shrewd mind. He was approached by their leader, Wat Tyler, who had now changed his name to Jack Straw. He stood close to the king, speaking for the others, and carrying an unsheathed knife, of the kind people call a dagger, which he tossed from hand to hand as a child might play with it, and looked as though he might suddenly seize the opportunity to stab the king if he should refuse their requests, and those accompanying the king therefore greatly feared what might come to pass. The commons asked of the king that all game, whether in waters or in parks and woods should become common to all, so that everywhere in the realm, in rivers and fishponds, and woods and forests, they might take the wild beasts, and hunt the hare in the fields, and do many other such things without restraint.

And when the king wanted time to consider such a concession, Jack Straw drew closer to him, with menacing words, and though I know not how he dared, took the reins of the king's horse in his hand. Seeing that, [William] Walworth, a citizen of London, fearing that he was about to kill the king, drew his basilard and ran Jack Straw through the neck. Thereupon another esquire, called Ralph Standish, stabbed him in the side with his basilard. And he fell to the ground

on his back, and after rising to his hands and knees, he died.

2

A woman in London celebrates mass. At that time there was a woman in the city of London who had an only daughter whom she taught to celebrate the mass; and she privily set up and furnished an altar in her own bedroom, and there she caused her daughter on many occasions to dress as a priest and in her fashion to celebrate mass, though when she came to the sacramental words she prostrated herself before the altar and did not complete the sacrament. But then she would rise for the rest of the mass and recite it to the end, her mother assisting her and showing her devotion.

That nonsense went on for some time, until it was revealed by a neighbour who had been admitted to the secret, when it came to the ears of the bishop of London. He summoned them to his presence and showed them the error of their ways, and compelled them to display the child's priestly tonsure in public, for her head was found to be quite bald. The bishop greatly deplored and bewailed such misconduct in the church in his time, uttering many lamentations, and put an end to it by enjoining penance upon them.

Interpreting This Slice of Life

1. *What* particular demand did Wat Tyler make of Richard II, the English King?

2. *Why* do you think Knighton singled out this demand in his account?

3. *Why* might Wat Tyler have taken the pseudonym Jack Straw?

4. *How* reliable is Knighton as a reporter?

5. *Why* were the unnamed mother and daughter punished by the bishop of London?

6. *What* bias may have motivated Knighton to report this London gossip to his patron?

7. *What* modern parallel can you draw to Henry Knighton and his *Chronicle*?

from China via the Middle East, perhaps during the Crusades—streamlined the spinning of wool into thread, or yarn. It replaced the ancient method, involving two handheld sticks, called a distaff and a spindle. With the spinning wheel the worker stretched wool from a distaff onto a spindle, turning the wheel constantly so as to create a continuous thread. Women traditionally performed the spinning, hence the medieval terms *spinster* and *distaff side,* meaning "woman's work."

In England, merchant entrepreneurs invested in sites based on available grazing land for sheep and access to fast-flowing streams—the latter to power fulling mills, where wooden paddles washed and beat the cloth before it was stretched to dry outdoors. In some textile-producing areas, merchants recruited skilled workers from Flanders (modern Belgium). The importation of foreign workers could provoke social unrest, as in 1381, during the Peasants' Revolt, when the rioters massacred Flemish workers, accusing them of taking work from the local populace.

Other new industries also emerged. Rag paper, a Chinese invention improved by the Arabs, was manufactured widely in Spain, Italy, France, and Germany. Silk fabrics were woven in impressive patterns in Florence, Venice, and Lucca, from the 1300s and, in England and France, from the late 1400s. Salt was now distributed by Venice and Lisbon and used in the industries of tanning leather and preserving food. The iron industry expanded to meet the demand for weapons, armor, and horseshoes.

The Printing Press

The German craftsman Johannes Gutenberg (1397–1468) is often credited with the invention of the printing press, in about 1450, even though his achievement rests on numerous earlier developments. That is, the model for his printing press came from similar devices used to bind books and to make wine and paper. Gutenberg also had knowledge of printing from woodblocks (though without a printing press), invented in China in perhaps the sixth century CE and developed in the West after 1350, whereby pictures along with a brief text could be impressed onto a paper surface (see the section "The Print," later in the chapter).

Gutenberg's invention gave rise to the printing and publishing industries, with a host of related occupations, such as printers, engravers, compositors, typefounders (designers of typefaces), booksellers, editors, proofreaders, and librarians. Because it was cheaper to print a book than to have a text copied as a manuscript, books became agents of democracy, with huge repercussions for education, literature, and society. Hints of the changes to come may be glimpsed in a survey of the perhaps twenty-eight thousand books, known as **incunabula** (from the Latin, "cradle"), which were printed before 1500 in nearly three hundred cities and in almost two dozen languages: a mass of Christian texts, especially Bibles, prayer books, and lives of saints, in both Latin and vernacular languages; a flood of "how-to" manuals on topics such as etiquette; a horde of fictional works calculated to appeal to literate laypeople; a few books of music, showing lines and notes; and from Jewish-owned presses, an outpouring of works in Hebrew, including Bibles, prayer books, and almanacs.

Global Encounter:
The Dissemination of Technologies

Neither the cloth nor the printing industries could have flourished in the late Middle Ages without two technologies that traveled from China across the Silk Road (see Chapter 8) to the Mediterranean and then to Europe. The spinning wheel was known in China by the eleventh century, may have reached Europe in the thirteenth century, and proliferated in 1400s. This simple invention made it possible to turn vegetable (cotton) and animal (wool) fibers into thread or yarn in vastly greater quantities than ever before. The Chinese learned how to make paper from rags in, probably, the second century BCE. For a long time the Chinese did not discern paper's possibilities as a writing material. They used it for wrapping material, for hygiene (rather like tissue), and for clothing. Legend has it that Arabs learned about papermaking from prisoners in Samarkand, discovered its utility for disseminating writing, and retained the secret about how to make it and what to use it for until Christian merchants stumbled upon the substance in about 1100. Slowly the technique of papermaking spread across the Christian world until, in the late Middle Ages, it became a major industry in many parts of Europe. Paper was so much cheaper than parchment that its spread complemented printing as a feature of the dissemination of books and ideas in late medieval Europe.

• • • • •

THE CULTURAL FLOWERING OF THE LATE MIDDLE AGES

The calamitous political, social, and economic events of the late Middle Ages were echoed in the cultural sphere by the breakdown of the medieval synthesis in religion, theology, literature, and art. New secular voices began to be heard, challenging traditional views, and the interests of the urban middle classes started to influence art and architecture. Although the church remained the principal financial supporter of the arts, rich town dwellers, notably bankers and merchants, were emerging as the new patrons of art (Figure 11.3).

Religion

The waves of monastic reform that had repeatedly brought renewed life to the medieval church largely ceased in the late Middle Ages. Lay piety thus became one of the most significant developments in the religious landscape. By 1400 the Brethren and Sisters of the Common Life and the Friends of God were rising in the Rhineland, the Low Countries, and Flanders.

Figure 11.3   Jacques Coeur's House. 1443–1451. Bourges, France. Coeur was an immensely successful entrepreneur who at one point bankrolled the French kings. His magnificent mansion at Bourges spawned many imitations among wealthy businessmen across Europe. The building's spiky turrets, fanciful balconies, and highly decorated windows are all secular adaptations of the late Gothic style more commonly seen in church architecture. Coeur conducted his Europe-wide financial and commercial dealings from this house, sending messages by carrier pigeons released through holes in the roof.

This lay movement constituted the *devotio moderna,* or the "new devotion," with its ideal of a pious lay society. Disappointed with traditionally trained priests, members of these groups often rejected higher education and practiced the strict discipline of the earlier monastic orders, but without withdrawing into a monastery. Among the most important expressions of this new devotion was *The Imitation of Christ,* by Thomas à Kempis (1380–1471). His manual, with its stern asceticism, reflected the harsh ideals of the Brethren and Sisters of the Common Life, the group of which Thomas was a member. For other groups, however, sober reflections on the life of Christ were not enough. The flagellants, for example, who regarded the plague as God's way to judge and punish an evil society, staged public processions in which they engaged in ritual whippings in an attempt to divert divine wrath from the general population (Figure 11.4).

The flagellants managed to escape official censure, but those more openly critical of the church did not. The leaders who attempted to reform the church in England and Bohemia met stout resistance from the popes. The English reform movement sprang from the teachings of John Wycliffe (about 1320–1384), an Oxford teacher whose message attracted both nobility and common folk. Wishing to purify the church of worldliness, Wycliffe urged the abolition of ecclesiastical property, the subservience of the church to the state, and the denial of papal authority. The most lasting achievement of Wycliffe's movement was the introduction of the first complete English-language Bible, produced by scholars inspired by his teaching. After his followers (known as Lollards, because during religious frenzy, their tongues were said to "loll" out of their mouths) were condemned as heretical, the secular officials launched savage persecutions.

The Bohemian reformers in the Holy Roman Empire were indebted to Wycliffe, whom some had met at Oxford; but, more important, their strength was rooted in the popular piety and evangelical preachers of mid-fourteenth-century Prague. The heresy became identified with Jan Hus (about 1369–1415), a Czech theologian who accepted Wycliffe's political views but rejected some of his religious teachings. Hus was invited to the Council of Constance in 1415, where his ideas were condemned, and he was burned at the stake by state authorities. His death outraged his fellow Czechs, many of whom, including the powerful and wealthy, now adopted his views. Hussite beliefs became a vehicle for Czech nationalism, as Hus's ethnic comrades fought against German overlords. Backed by powerful lay leaders, the Hussites survived into the next century. They gained more followers during the Protestant Reformation and exist today as the Moravian Brethren.

Although the secular authorities, instigated by the church, could usually be counted on to put down the heresies, the church had a more powerful internal weapon at its disposal: the Inquisition (from the Latin *inquisitio,* "inquiry"). Created by the church to seek out Albigensian heretics in the thirteenth century (see Chapter 10), the Inquisition became an adjunct to state power in late medieval Spain, where Jews were most often targeted. Following the basic ideals of Roman law, courts of inquisition allowed suspects to be condemned without facing their accusers and accepted evidence gained under torture. Forbidden by the Bible to shed blood, the leaders of the Inquisition turned convicted heretics over to the state authorities, who then executed them by burning. Hundreds of men and women perished in this way.

Figure 11.4 *Flagellation Scene. Annales of Gilles Le Muisit.* **Bibliothèque Royale de Belgique, Brussels.** This miniature painting represents a familiar scene across Europe during the plague years. The penitents, depicted with bare backs and feet, marched through towns scourging themselves with whips. By this self-punishment, they hoped to atone for their own and society's sins and thus end the plague.

Theology and Philosophy

Alongside all the strife in the wider world, scholars in Europe's universities engaged in intellectual combat. The major disputes were over Thomism, the theological system of Thomas Aquinas, which in the late Middle Ages was drawing increasing criticism. The old philosophical struggle between realism and nominalism finally ended with a nominalist victory.

The Via Antiqua *versus the* Via Moderna   The opening round in the theological war against Thomism began soon after the death of Thomas Aquinas in 1274. In 1277 church officials in Paris condemned the Latin Averroists for their rationalism. As part of their attack on extreme rationalism, the church authorities rejected some of Aquinas's arguments. The censure of Thomism led to a heated controversy that raged among university scholars for much of the late Middle Ages. In particular, Thomas's fellow Dominican friars waged an acrimonious battle with the Franciscan masters, their great rivals in theological studies.

During these theological debates, new labels were invented and assumed by the opposing sides. Aquinas's *via media* came to be termed by his opponents the *via antiqua,* or the "old-fashioned way." Broadly speaking, the *via antiqua* followed Thomism in urging that faith and reason be treated as complementary approaches to divine truth. In contrast, the *via moderna,* or the "modern way," made a complete separation of faith and reason. In time the *via moderna* prevailed, driving the *via antiqua* underground until it was revived by the neoscholastics in the nineteenth century.

Duns Scotus and William of Ockham   The conflict between the *via antiqua* and the *via moderna* was best exemplified in the writings of John Duns Scotus and William of Ockham, respectively. The first of these commentators was sympathetic to the theology of Thomas Aquinas, but the second scholar was unmistakably hostile and tried to discredit Thomism.

Duns Scotus [duhnz SKOAT-us] (about 1265–1308), the most persuasive voice of the *via antiqua,* was a Scottish thinker who was trained as a Franciscan and lectured at the universities in Oxford, Paris, and Cologne. Even though he was a supporter of Thomism, Duns Scotus unwittingly undermined Aquinas's synthesis by stressing that faith was superior to reason, a shift in focus that arose from his belief in God's absolute and limitless power. Pointing out that God's existence could not be proven either through the senses or by reason, he asserted that only faith could explain the divine mystery. Furthermore, Duns Scotus concluded that because the theologian and the philosopher have different intellectual tasks, theology and science (i.e., the study of nature) should be independent fields of inquiry.

What Duns Scotus unintentionally began, William of Ockham (about 1300–1349) purposely completed. Under the assaults of Ockham's keen intellect, the Thomist theological edifice collapsed. An Oxford-trained theologian, he recognized the importance of both reason and faith; but, like Scotus, he did not see how reason could prove God's existence. Both thinkers believed that only personal feelings and mystical experiences could reveal God and the divine moral order. Yet Ockham went further than Scotus by asserting that reason, the senses, and empirical evidence could enable human beings to discover and hence understand the natural world. To Ockham, faith and reason were both valid approaches to truth, but they should be kept apart so that each could achieve its respective end.

In the seemingly endless medieval debate between the realists and the nominalists, Ockham's reasoning swept nominalism to its final victory. Like the nominalists of the twelfth century, Ockham denied the existence of universals and claimed that only individual objects existed. He concluded that human beings can have clear and distinct knowledge only of specific things in the physical world; no useful knowledge can be gained through reason or the senses about the spiritual realm. Ockham's conclusion did not mean that human beings were cast adrift without access to the world of God. A corollary of his approach was that understanding of the spiritual realm rested solely on the truths of faith and theology.

In his reasoning, William of Ockham asserted a principle of economy that stripped away all that was irrelevant: arguments should be drawn from a minimum of data and founded on closely constructed logic. "It is vain to do with more what can be done with fewer," he says in one of his works. Ockham's "razor" of logic eliminated superfluous information that could not be verified, thus enabling a student to cut to the core of a philosophical problem. The Ockhamites, following their mentor's logic and empiricism, challenged the realists and dominated the intellectual life of the universities for the next two hundred years.

Another key development found Greek scholars migrating to Italy. For one example, Manuel Chrysoloras (1353–1415) settled in Florence on the invitation of the city government and began to teach Greek (Figure 11.5). As another example, John Bessarion (1403–1472) settled in Rome in 1437, where he founded a school and taught Greek, philosophy, and science. Greek was not yet widely known in the West and as the ancient tongue spread, Greek scholarship, and eventually the works of Plato, became widely known.

Figure 11.5 PAOLO UCCELLO. *Manuel Chrysoloras Teaching Greek in Florence.* **Drawing. Louvre.** Uccello (1397–1475) was a mathematician as well as a painter and he was among the pioneers in the use of mathematical perspective in painting, but his discoveries are not particularly evident in this undated drawing. Although Chrysoloras's classroom teaching techniques are not known, today's scholars believe he would read aloud, in front of his students, a passage in Greek from some classical text and then analyze the work, drawing on sources from other Byzantine writers, a pedagogical device used in Constantinople.

Science

Ockham's ideas broadened the path to modern science that had been opened by two thirteenth-century thinkers. In that earlier time, Robert Grosseteste [GROSS-test] (about 1175–1253), a Franciscan at Oxford University, had devised a scientific method for investigating natural phenomena; using step-by-step procedures, he employed mathematics and tested hypotheses until he reached satisfactory conclusions. Roger Bacon (about 1220–1292), another Franciscan and a follower of Grosseteste, advocated the use of the experimental method, which he demonstrated in his studies of optics, solar eclipses, and rainbows and in his treatises on mathematics, physics, and philosophy.

In the fourteenth century, other thinkers, with Grosseteste and Bacon as guides and Ockham's logic as a weapon, made further contributions. Outstanding among these men was one bold Parisian scholar who took advantage of the growing interest in the experimental method, Nicholas Oresme [O-REM] (about 1330–1382). Oresme answered all of Aristotle's objections to the idea that the earth moved. Using pure reason and applying theoretical arguments, he concluded that it was as plausible that the earth moved around the sun as that it was fixed. Having used reason to show that the earth may move, however, Oresme then chose to accept church doctrine, denying what he had demonstrated. Nevertheless, Oresme's arguments, along with Ockham's separation of natural philosophy from theology and Bacon's formulation of the experimental method, foreshadowed the approaches of modern science.

Literature

The powerful forces that were reshaping the wider culture—the rising new monarchies, the growing national consciousness among diverse peoples, the emerging secularism, and the developing urban environment—were also transforming literature in the late Middle Ages. The rise of literacy produced a growing educated class who learned to read and write the local languages rather than Latin, and a shift to vernacular literature began to occur (see Chapter 10). Two new groups—the monarchs and their courts, and the urban middle class—joined the nobility and the church as patrons and audiences. And, most important, printing enabled a wider and faster dissemination of knowledge than ever before.

Northern Italian Literature: Petrarch and Boccaccio   Petrarch and Boccaccio—both Florentines, like Dante—grew up in a Christian world that was urban, rapidly secularizing, and had little experience with chivalry. These two writers captured the mood of this transition era as Florence and the other Italian city-states shed their medieval outlook. Both authors looked back to the classical world for inspiration; yet both found, in the bustling world of the nearby towns, the materials and characters for their stories. Of the two, Petrarch was the more dedicated classicist and often used ancient themes in his writings.

Francesco Petrarch [PAY-trark] ("Petracco" in Italian) (1304–1374), though Florentine by birth and in spirit, grew up in the south of France where his father worked at the papal court. As a diplomat for popes and Italian princes, Petrarch won fame and wealth, but his reputation arose from his career as a professional man of letters. He unleashed a torrent of superb Latin scholarship on classical subjects and themes but also earned wide renown for a collection of 366 love lyrics and sonnets called *Canzoniere,* or *Songbook,* in beautiful Italian. Petrarch, despite a clerical training, reveals the complementary Latin and vernacular, secular and spiritual interests of his time.

Petrarch touched on religious themes in *Secretum,* or *Secret Book,* which deals with the state of his soul. In this dialogue, "Augustinus," or St. Augustine, grills "Franciscus," or Petrarch, about his innermost thoughts and desires, charging him with all the deadly sins. Freely admitting his moral lapses, Franciscus pleads that he is the same as any other man—driven by a love of learning, a weakness for fleshly attractions, and an appetite for personal comforts. Despite this confession, with its modern overtones, the dialogue shows that Petrarch could not liberate himself fully from medieval values. Classicism inspired much of his scholarship, but Augustine's *Confessions* called forth the *Secretum.*

Even more than his lifelong friend Petrarch, Giovanni Boccaccio [bo-KACH-e-o] (1313–1375) was a man of the world. The son of a banker, Boccaccio began his literary career by penning prose romances along with poetic pastorals and sonnets, many of which were dedicated to Fiammetta, a young woman who was both his consuming passion and his literary muse. His early efforts, however, are overshadowed by his Italian prose masterpiece, *The Decameron.* Written in about 1351, this work reflects the grim conditions of the Black Death, which had just swept through Florence. In *The Decameron* (from the Greek words for "ten days"), Boccaccio describes how ten young men and women, in their efforts to escape the plague, flee the city to a country villa, where they pass the time, each telling a story a day for ten days. Most of their one hundred tales were based on folk stories and popular legends. Although some tales deal lightly with social mores and a few contain moral messages, the majority simply entertain. Boccaccio, speaking through a cross section of urban voices and relying on well-known stories, helped develop a form of literature that eventually led to the modern short story.

English Literature: Geoffrey Chaucer   Like its Italian counterpart, English literature rapidly matured into its own forms during the late Middle Ages. Until this time, most educated English people read and spoke French, but a rising sense of national consciousness, triggered by the Hundred Years' War and an emerging educated urban class, hastened the spread of English as the native tongue.

After 1300 important works in English appeared, such as *The Vision of Piers Plowman,* a moral allegory, by William Langland (about 1332–1400), that graphically exposes the plight of the poor and calls for a return to Christian virtues. This work provides insight into England's social and economic system and, through the author's anguish, reveals the social tension around the time of the Peasants' Revolt in 1381.

English literature was still establishing its own identity when Geoffrey Chaucer (about 1340–1400) appeared on the scene. He wrote in an East Midland dialect of English that became the standard form for his generation as well as the foundation of modern English. The son of a wealthy London merchant, Chaucer spent his professional life as a courtier, a diplomat, and a public servant for the English crown. The profession of "writer" or "poet" was unknown in Chaucer's day. But his poetry brought him renown, and when he died he was the first commoner to be buried in Westminster Abbey, a favored burial spot for English royalty.

Chaucer began composing his most famous work, *The Canterbury Tales,* in 1385. He set the tales in the context of a pilgrimage to the tomb of Thomas Becket, the twelfth-century martyr. Even though the journey has a religious purpose, Chaucer makes it plain that the travelers intend to have a good time along the way. To make the journey from London to Canterbury more interesting, the thirty-one pilgrims (including Chaucer himself) agree to tell tales—two each going and returning—and to award a prize for the best story told.

Chaucer completed only twenty-three tales and the general Prologue, in which he introduces the pilgrims. Each person on the pilgrimage not only represents an English social type but also is a unique and believable human being. In this poetic narrative about a group of ordinary people, the spiritual is mixed with the temporal and the serious with the comic.

Chaucer drew his pilgrims from nearly all walks of medieval society. The Knight personified much that was noble and honorable in the chivalric code; his bravery could not be questioned, but he was also a mercenary and cruel to his enemies. Certain representatives of the church are also somewhat skeptically treated. The Prioress, the head of a convent and from the upper class, is more concerned about her refined manners and polished language than the state of her soul. Similarly, the Monk lives a life of the flesh and enjoys good food, fine wines, and expensive clothing. The Friar seems the very opposite of his sworn ideals; he is eager to hear a confession for a fee, and he never goes among the poor or aids the sick. However, in the country Parson, Chaucer portrays a true servant of God who preaches to his parish, looks after the infirm and dying, and lives as simply as his church members. Among the secular travelers, the most vivid is the Wife of Bath. A widow five times over, this jolly woman is full of life and loves to talk. She has been on many pilgrimages and not only knows about foreign places but also has a keen insight into people (Figure 11.6).

As for the tales they tell, the pilgrims' choices often reflect their own moral values. The worthy Knight tells a chivalric love story, but the Miller, a coarse, rough man well versed in lying and cheating, relates how a young wife took on a lover and deceived her husband. Thus the pilgrims' stories, based on folk and fairy tales, romances, classical stories, and beast fables, are entertaining in themselves and function as a kind of *summa* of the storyteller's art.

Figure 11.6 *The Wife of Bath.* **Ellesmere Manuscript. Early fifteenth century. Bancroft Library, University of California at Berkeley.** In the Ellesmere Manuscript, an early edition of *The Canterbury Tales* issued soon after Chaucer's death, each story was accompanied by a sketch of the pilgrim who was narrating it. This portrait of the Wife of Bath shows her riding an ambler, a horse that walks with an easy gait, and wearing a wimple, the typical headdress of nuns as well as laywomen of the period.

French Literature: Christine de Pizan   Christine de Pizan [kris-teen duh PEE-zahn], among the leading French writers of the day, began to explore in her works the status and role of women. She also contributed to the triumph of vernacular over Latin by writing in a graceful French with the learnedness of Latin.

Christine de Pizan (1364–about 1430) was by birth an Italian from Pisa whose literary gifts blossomed under the patronage of the French kings and dukes of Burgundy. She began a life of study after the death of her husband, a royal official, in 1389, left her with a family to support. The first known Western woman to earn a living through her writings, Christine blazed the trail for women authors.

Christine wrote on diverse topics, working within the well-established literary genres of her day, including love poems, lays, biography, letters, political tracts, and moral proverbs. Two themes dominate her writing: calls for peace and appeals for the recognition of women's contributions to culture and social life. Both themes reflect the era in which she lived—an age beset by civil strife because of the Hundred Years' War and a time in which women were scarcely allowed to express an opinion in public.

The work of Christine's that has generated the most interest among modern readers is *The Book of the City of Ladies* (1405), which forcefully tries to raise the status of women and to give them dignity. Offering one of the first histories of women and arguing that women have the right to be educated, based on her premise that women are moral and intellectual equals of men, this book seems almost feminist in a modern sense; however, a close reading shows that Christine is writing within a medieval framework. Nowhere in this book or in any other writings does she advocate that women abandon their traditional roles and strike out on a new path. Nevertheless, Christine de Pizan is the first Western writer to raise the issue of women's rights in society and culture.

Architecture and Art

The Gothic style continued to dominate architecture (see Chapter 10), but the balanced and unified High Gothic of the thirteenth century was now replaced with the ornate effects of the **late Gothic style.** Virtuosity became the chief aesthetic goal, as the architects took basic forms and pushed them to the stylistic limits. Virtuosity bordering on excess marked painting and sculpture too. Statues and sculptured figures were given willowy, swaying bodies, rendered in exquisite detail, and illuminated manuscripts and painted wooden panels became more refined. At the same time, in Florence around 1300, Giotto was revolutionizing art with a new approach to painting. The trend toward naturalism embodied in his works was the most significant new artistic development of this period and was destined to be the wave of the future.

Late Gothic Architecture   France—the home of the Gothic style—remained a potent source of architectural innovation. French architects now abandoned the balanced ideal of the High Gothic and made extravagance their guiding principle, creating a late Gothic style typified by ever greater heights and elaborate decoration. In the fifteenth century, this tendency culminated in the **Flamboyant style,** so named for its flamelike effects. French churches built in this style had sky-piercing spires, and their facades were embroidered with lacy or wavy decorations that obscured the buildings' structural components (Figure 11.7). During the fourteenth century, the late Gothic spread, becoming an international style, although with almost infinite local variations.

In England, the late Gothic was called **Perpendicular** because of its dramatic emphasis on verticality.

Figure 11.7   The Church of St. Maclou. 1435–ca. 1514. Rouen, France. St. Maclou's exterior illustrates the ornate late Gothic style. Its west facade, unlike a square High Gothic front, fans out to form a semicircular entrance. There are five portals (rather than the usual three), two of which are blind, and set above them are steeply pitched stone arches of intricate design.

Figure 11.8   Choir of Gloucester Cathedral. Ca. 1330–1357. Gloucester, England. The choir and apse of Gloucester cathedral were rebuilt in the Perpendicular Gothic style in about 1330, when King Edward III chose the church as the burial shrine for his murdered father, Edward II. The architects made the earlier Norman apse into a square and filled the east end with glass panels. Inside, the builders redesigned the support system, using thin vertical piers; these piers were attached to the walls and laced together on the ceiling, creating elaborate patterns that complemented the glass decorations.

This Perpendicular style was characterized by an increased use of paneled decorations on the walls and overhead vaults, resulting in a variation of rib vaulting, called **fan vaulting,** in which stone ribs arch out from a central point in the ceiling to form a delicate pattern. This style also increased the number of window openings, which necessitated additional flying buttresses. The best example of the English Perpendicular is the cathedral in Gloucester. In the choir, the vertical lines, extending from the floor to the ceiling, where the tracery is interwoven, unite the building's interior into an upward-moving volume (Figure 11.8). Just as impressive as the interior is the nearby cloister with its fan vaulting that weaves a pattern overhead while tying the walls and ceiling into a complex unit (Figure 11.9).

A key example of the late Italian Gothic is the cathedral in Siena. Filled with civic pride, Siena's citizens urged their leaders to build a cathedral more splendid than those of their neighbors. Begun in the mid–thirteenth century, the cathedral was constructed over the next one hundred fifty years, and, as a result, the building complex shows a mixture of styles: the **campanile,** or bell tower, is executed in the Italian Romanesque, but the overall cathedral complex is Italian Gothic (Figure 11.10). The facade, for the first time in Italy, incorporated nearly life-size figures into the total design, thus heightening its resemblance to the French Gothic. However, many features distinguish the style of Siena from the French style. For example, the decorative

Figure 11.9   South Cloister of Gloucester Cathedral. Ca. 1370. Gloucester, England. Fan vaulting, an intricate pattern in which ribs arch out from a central point in the ceiling, first appeared at Gloucester cathedral and inspired many imitations. Although the ribs may appear to be structurally necessary, they are really a richly decorative device carved from stone. In Gloucester's south cloister, the tracery fans out from the top of each column and then merges in the center of the ceiling, giving the impression of a delicate screen.

Figure 11.10   Siena Cathedral. 1250–1400. Siena, Italy. Extant records and floor plans show that the Sienese changed their minds several times before deciding on the cathedral's final shape. At one time, in about 1322, a commission of architects advised that the existing cathedral be demolished because the foundations and walls were not strong enough to support new additions. Nonetheless, construction went forward, and the cathedral is still standing after more than six hundred years.

statues on Siena's facade were placed above the gables, not set in niches. Furthermore, the Sienese builders put mosaics into the spaces in the gables and above the central rose window.

Florence, Siena's greatest military and trade rival, refused to be outdone by its nearby competitor. The Florentine city fathers asked Giotto [JAWT-toe] (about 1276–1337), the city's most renowned painter, to design a campanile for their own cathedral. Today, the

first story of the bell tower—with its carvings, interlaced patterns of pink and white marble, and hexagonal inlays—still stands as conceived by Giotto (Figure 11.11). Giotto's plan, as left in a drawing, called for an open tower with a spire on top, as in a French Gothic tower. But later architects constructed a rectangular top instead and decorated it with marble—making it distinctively Italian rather than reminiscent of the French.

Figure 11.11   GIOTTO. Campanile of the Florentine Cathedral. Ca. 1334–1350. Ht. approx. 200′. Florence, Italy. Giotto's Tower, as this campanile is known in Florence, is one of the city's most cherished landmarks. Today, its bells still toll the time. The two sets of windows in the central section and the taller openings at the top give the campanile a strong sense of balanced proportion. Thus, despite being built in the fourteenth century, the tower anticipates the classical ideal that was revived in the Renaissance.

Late Gothic Sculpture   During the late Middle Ages, sculpture, like architecture, continued to undergo stylistic changes, among which two general trends may be identified. One trend centered in Italy, notably in Siena, where the Pisano [pee-SAHN-o] family began to experiment with sculptural forms that foreshadowed Renaissance art, with its return to classical themes and values (see Chapter 12). Outstanding among the members of the gifted Pisano family was Giovanni Pisano (1245–1314), who designed the intricate late Gothic facade of the Siena cathedral (see Figure 11.10). Giovanni's great artistic reputation is largely based on the massive marble pulpit that he carved for the cathedral at Pisa. Using classical themes derived from Roman art (as Renaissance artists were to do), he designed the pulpit to rest on acanthus leaves at the top of eight Corinthian columns (Figure 11.12). The lions that support two of the columns were modeled on those on an ancient Roman sarcophagus. Just as late Roman art blended Christian and classical symbols, so Giovanni's treatment of the pulpit's base mixed images of the cardinal virtues, such as Justice and Temperance, with the figure of the Greek hero Herakles.

Pisano's octagonal pulpit includes eight panels in high relief that depict scenes from the lives of either John the Baptist or Christ. Of these panels, the scene depicting the Nativity ranks as his finest work. In this scene, he portrays a natural vitality through the careful balance and orderly spacing of the animals and people (Figure 11.13). The placement and calm actions of the surrounding figures frame the Virgin and child so that the viewer's attention is focused on these two central figures. Giovanni's swaying figures with their smooth draperies were rooted in late Gothic art, but their quiet serenity attested to his classicizing manner.

The other trend in sculpture during this time centered in Burgundy, where Philip the Bold (r. 1364–1404) supported scholars and artists at his ducal court in Dijon. Preeminent among these was Claus Sluter [SLUE-tuhr] (about 1350–1406), a sculptor of Netherlandish origin who helped to define this last phase of Gothic art. Sluter's masterly sculptures are still housed in a monastery near Dijon, and his most famous work, *The Well of Moses*, was commissioned for the cloister of this monastic retreat.

The Well of Moses, which was designed as a decorative cover for an actual well in a courtyard, is surrounded at its base with Old Testament prophets symbolizing the sacraments of communion and baptism. The most beautifully rendered of the surviving life-size statues is Moses, encased in a flowing robe and standing erect with a finely chiseled head (Figure 11.14). Sluter's sense of the dramatic moment, of the prophet's personal emotions, and of the individual features makes the statue nearly an individual portrait.

Figure 11.12 Giovanni Pisano. **Pulpit in the Pisa Cathedral. Ca. 1302–1310. Pisa, Italy.** Pisano built and carved this massive (17-foot-high) pulpit at the height of his reputation. A superb artist but a quarrelsome man, Pisano recorded his frustrations in the lengthy inscription around the pulpit's base. In it he claimed that he had achieved much, had been condemned by many, and took full responsibility for this work of art. Pisano's advance from anonymity to a position of great artistic repute was typical of a new breed of artist appearing in fourteenth-century Italy.

Sluter rendered Moses's beard and the unfurled scroll in precise detail and carved the figure with the head turned to the side, eyes looking into the future.

Late Gothic Painting and the Rise of New Trends

Of all the arts, painting underwent the most radical changes in the late Middle Ages. Illuminated manuscripts maintained their popularity, but included more secular themes under the patronage of titled aristocrats and wealthy merchants. At the same time, painters of frescoes and wooden panels introduced new techniques for applying paint and mixing colors. Stylistically, painters preferred to work in the extravagant late Gothic manner with its elegant refinement and undulating lines. Nevertheless, Giotto and other Italian painters discovered fresh ways of depicting human figures that started to revolutionize art.

Illuminated Manuscripts　The Burgundian court played a pivotal role in the production of one of the outstanding illuminated manuscripts of the medieval period, the *Très Riches Heures du Duc de Berry*. This famous

Figure 11.13　Giovanni Pisano. Nativity Scene. Pulpit in the Pisa cathedral. Ca. 1302– 1310. 33¹/₂ × 44¹/₂". Pisa, Italy. In this late Gothic sculpture, Pisano cut deeply into the marble's surface to give a nearly three-dimensional effect. His many figures seem involved in their own tasks but are nevertheless linked with one another around the Madonna and child. For example, the two shepherds (the head of one has been lost) in the upper-right corner appear to be listening to the angels approaching from the left, while at the far right, sheep rest and graze. Such balanced placements are evidence of Pisano's classicizing tendencies. Pisano's relief retains a prominent Gothic feature, however, by presenting the Virgin and child twice—in the central scene and in the lower-left corner, where a seated Mary, balancing the baby Jesus on her right leg, stretches her left hand to test the temperature of the water in an elaborate basin.

collection of miniatures was painted by the three Limbourg brothers for the duke of Berry, brother of Philip the Bold of Burgundy. These illustrations stand above the others of their time for their exquisite detail, general liveliness, and intricately designed crowd scenes—some of the marks of the late Gothic style.

The *Très Riches Heures,* or the *Very Rich Hours,* represents a type of small prayer book that was a favorite of nobles and businessmen. These personal books of worship, with their litanies and prayers, were often handsomely hand-illustrated to enhance their value. The duke of Berry's prayer book contained some 130 miniatures, including scenes from the life of Christ and the calendar cycle. In the calendar series, each tiny painting, finely detailed and colored in jewel-like tones, notes a seasonal activity appropriate for the month. Some represent the brilliant court life of the duke, and others depict the drudgery of peasant life, sharply differentiated from the court scenes by their action and color. The illustration for January shows the duke of Berry surrounded by his well-dressed courtiers and enjoying a sumptuous feast (Figure 11.15).

The Print   The print, a new artistic medium, developed in the late Middle Ages in the Austrian-Bavarian regions, eastern France, and the Netherlands. Sparked by the growth of lay piety, the earliest prints were devotional woodcuts to be used as aids to personal meditation. The prints initially featured scenes from the lives of the Virgin and Christ. For the **woodcut,** the artist drew an image on a woodblock, which was then cut by a woodcutter and printed by the artist; some were then hand-tinted by a colorist. By 1500 the new techniques of **engraving** (using a sharp tool to draw an image onto a metal plate overlaid with wax, dipping the plate in acid, and then printing it) and **drypoint** (marking an image onto a copper plate with a metal stylus and then printing it) were becoming increasingly popular.

Probably the outstanding set of prints dating from this period was that in the Medieval Housebook, a late-fifteenth-century German manuscript. The so-called Medieval Housebook was a gathering of 192 prints, of which only 126 remain. Most of the prints are in black and white, though a few are partially colored. The printing techniques vary from drypoint and engraving to simple drawings on vellum. Stylistic differences indicate that at least three artists contributed to the work, thus suggesting that the Housebook may have been produced in a workshop. For convenience, however, the artist is called simply the Housebook Master. Of the surviving 126 prints, the subjects range over late medieval life, from the workaday world to jousting scenes to court life. Some prints offer realistic views of medieval buildings, including barnyards, private dwellings, and palaces; most are highly detailed,

Figure 11.14   CLAUS SLUTER. *Moses,* from *The Well of Moses.* Ca. 1395–1406. Ht. of full figure approx. 6′. Chartreuse de Champmol, Dijon, France.   Sluter followed the allegorical tradition of medieval art in this portrait of the Hebrew prophet Moses. The book in Moses's right hand and the scroll over his left shoulder symbolize the Word of God. Sluter also depicted Moses with "horns" growing out of his forehead, as was characteristic in medieval representations.

showing hair and clothing styles. Others are lively and playful, depicting relations between the sexes and the classes (Figure 11.16).

New Trends In Italy: Giotto   While the illuminated manuscript and the print were popular in northern Europe, a revolution in painting was under way in Italy. The paintings of Giotto are generally recognized as having established a new direction in Western art, one that led into the Renaissance. In Giotto's own day, Dante praised him and the citizens of Florence honored him.

Figure 11.15   LIMBOURG BROTHERS. **Month of January, from the *Très Riches Heures du Duc de Berry*. 1413–1416. Approx. 8¹/₂ × 5¹/₂″. Musée Condé, Chantilly, France.** This miniature painting provides insightful social history in its exquisite details. The duke, seated in the right center, is dressed in a blue patterned cloak and is greeting his guests for what was probably a New Year's celebration. Behind the duke stands a servant, over whose head are written the words "aproche, aproche," a welcome that is the equivalent of "come in, come in." Above this festive scene, the zodiac signs of Capricorn and Aquarius identify the month as January.

Giotto's revolution in painting was directed against the prevailing **Italo-Byzantine style,** which blended late Gothic with Byzantine influences. Giotto turned this painting style, with its two-dimensional, timeless quality, into a three-dimensional art characterized by naturalism and the full expression of human emotions. Partly through the innovative use of light and shade and the placement of figures so as to create nonmathematical **perspective,** or depth, Giotto was able to paint realistic-looking figures, rather than the flat, ornamental depictions found in most illuminated manuscripts or the Italian altar paintings.

A painting by one of Giotto's contemporaries, Cimabue [chee-muh-BU-ay] (about 1240–1302), the *Madonna Enthroned,* reveals the state of Italian painting at this time (Figure 11.17). The angels on the side are

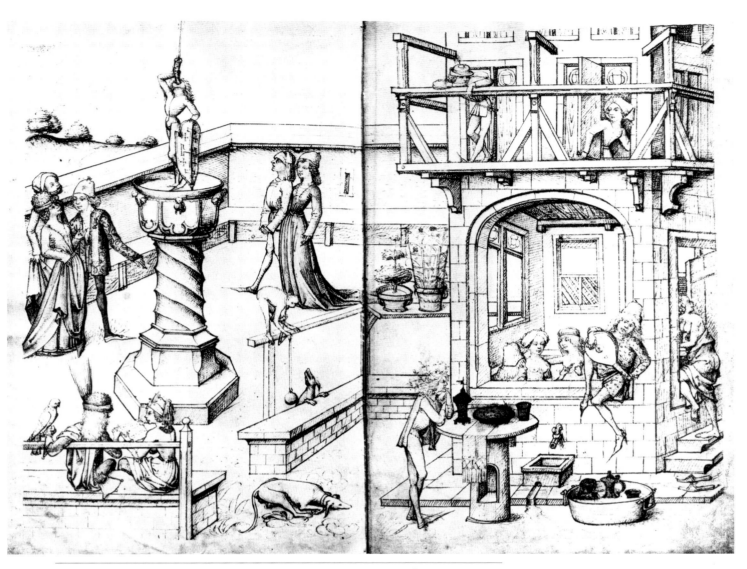

Figure 11.16 HOUSEBOOK MASTER. *Leisure Time at the Bath.* Ca. 1475–1490. Ink on vellum drawing, **partially colored. Private collection.** This print reveals the upper classes at play as well as the strict social order. On the left, young couples converse or flirt around a fountain in a courtyard; the pets (a falcon, two dogs, and a monkey) are indicators of the high status of their owners; a lady-in-waiting holds the skirt of her mistress. On the right, young aristocrats (a man and two women) enjoy bathing, while a third woman is entering the bathhouse. A servant serenades the bathers on a stringed instrument, as another waits in attendance. On the balcony, two servants enjoy a flirtatious moment. This Chaucerian-like scene, with its frank sensuality, indicates that within the increasingly secular world of the late Middle Ages the pleasures of the flesh could be a fit subject for an artist.

rendered stiffly, aligned vertically without any sense of space between them, and placed flat on the wood panel without any precise relationship with the figures below them (the prophets Jeremiah and Isaiah on the outside and the Patriarch Abraham and King David under the throne). Although Cimabue's angels are balanced in their placement and the depiction of the figures of the Madonna and Christ child offers some sense of rounded form, the overall effect of the work confirms its debt to the two-dimensional tradition of Italo-Byzantine art.

In contrast, Giotto's *Madonna Enthroned,* painted about thirty years after Cimabue's, shows how Giotto was transforming Florentine art (Figure 11.18). His Madonna seems to be actually sitting on her throne, and the four angels on either side of her chair are placed to give a sense of spatial depth, or perspective. The angels' distinctive gazes are highly expressive, suggesting feelings of wonder. The Virgin resembles an individual woman and Christ a believable child, not a shrunken adult. Although Giotto uses Gothic touches—the pointed arch, the halos, and the applied gold leaf—the natural rendering of the figures fore-shadows great changes in art.

Giotto was a prolific artist whose paintings adorned churches in Florence and cities all over Italy. At the Arena Chapel in Padua, Giotto painted his masterpiece, two sets of frescoes, one of the life of the Virgin and the other of the life of Christ. These thirty-eight scenes show Giotto at the height of his powers, rendering space with a sense of depth and organizing figures so as to create dramatic tension. An outstanding scene from the Padua frescoes is the *Pietà*, or *Lamentation* (Figure 11.19). This scene, which portrays the grief for the dead Christ, expresses total despair through the mourners' faces and gestures, from Mary, who cradles the body of Jesus, to John, who stands with arms outstretched, to the hovering angels.

Figure 11.17 Cimabue. *Madonna Enthroned.* **Ca. 1280. Tempera on panel, 12′7¹/₂″ × 7′4″. Uffizi Gallery, Florence.** Although Cimabue was experiencing the same desire for freedom in art as the sculptor Giovanni Pisano, this painting of the Madonna shows that he was still strongly under the spell of the Italo-Byzantine tradition. Rather than showing the intense feeling of Giotto's portraits, Cimabue's Virgin and Christ child remain medieval and mystical.

In the fresco's stark and rugged landscape, even nature seems to mourn, notably in the barren tree that refers to the barren fig tree in Luke's Gospel (13:6–9) which itself signified that no fruit, that is good works, are to be found in this world. After Giotto died in 1337, no painter for the rest of the century was able to match his remarkable treatment of nature and human emotions.

Flemish Painting: Jan Van Eyck and Hans Memling
When Philip the Good (r. 1419–1467) became duke of Burgundy, he expanded his territories to include the wealthy counties of Holland, Zeeland, and Luxembourg, known as Flanders. Philip was the greatest secular patron of the arts of his day. Of the artists encouraged by his patronage, the brothers Jan and Hubert van Eyck are the most famous, and their religious

Figure 11.18 Giotto. *Madonna Enthroned.* Ca. 1310. Tempera on panel, 10'8" × 6'8". **Uffizi Gallery, Florence.** Giotto's *Madonna Enthroned*, so revolutionary in its composition and spatial dimensions, has been called the most influential painting of the fourteenth century. Especially innovative in this altarpiece is the realistic treatment of the Virgin's eyes: they are shaped like ordinary eyes and peer out at the viewer rather than gazing into the distance, as in the Italo-Byzantine style.

Figure 11.19   Giotto. *Pietà,* or *Lamentation.* Ca. 1305–1310. Fresco, 7′7″ × 7′9″. **Arena Chapel, Padua, Italy.** Such works gained Giotto his reputation as the modern reviver of realistic art—a tradition that had been lost with the fall of ancient Rome. In this fresco, he created three-dimensional space in ways that even the Greeks and the Romans had not used. Giotto's illusion of depth was conveyed by surrounding the dead Christ with numerous figures and, in particular, by placing two mourners in the foreground with their backs to the viewer. Giotto's use of perspective was convincing to his generation even though it lacked mathematical precision.

works and portraits established the Flemish style of art. Little is known of Hubert, but Jan van Eyck [YAHN van IKE] (about 1370–1441) is considered the founder of the Flemish school.

As a general principle, Flemish art sought reality through an accumulation of precise and often symbolic details, in contrast to Italian art, which tended to be more concerned with psychological truth, as in Giotto's frescoes in the Arena Chapel. This national style, expressed primarily through painting with oils on wood panels, turned each artwork into a brilliant and precise reproduction of the original scene. The finest detail in a patterned carpet, the reflected light on a copper vase, and the wrinkled features of an

elderly patron were laboriously and meticulously recorded. The Flemish style, with its close attention to detail, was widely appreciated and quickly spread to Italy and England.

Jan van Eyck, probably with his brother's help, painted an altarpiece for the cathedral at Ghent, Belgium (Figure 11.20). This large work—commissioned for the main altar—still remains in its original place. The twenty panels are hinged together so that when opened twelve are visible. These twelve panels are divided into two levels—heavenly figures and symbols on the upper level and earthly figures on the lower level. On the ends of the upper level are nude portraits of Adam and Eve, next to angels singing and playing

Figure 11.20 HUBERT AND JAN VAN EYCK. *Ghent Altarpiece.* Ca. 1432. Oil on panel, 11'3" × 14'5". St. Bavo cathedral, Ghent, Belgium. This large altarpiece may seem to be a collection of separate paintings, but the work is united in themes and symbolism. What links the panels is their portrayal of Christ's redemption of humanity. From *The Sin of Adam and Eve* to the mystic *Adoration of the Lamb*, all the paintings touch in some manner on Christ's sacrifice.

musical instruments. Mary on the left and John the Baptist on the right flank a portrayal of God the Father, resplendent in a jewel-encrusted robe and triple crown. Below, on the lower level, are human figures who are depicted as moving toward the center panel. On the left, knights and judges ride on horseback, while, on the right, pilgrims and hermits approach on foot.

The focus of the *Ghent Altarpiece*, when opened, is the lower center panel, the *Adoration of the Lamb*. In this work, the sacrificial death of Jesus is symbolized by the cross, the baptismal font in the foreground, and the blood issuing from the lamb into the communion chalice. The surrounding worshipers include holy virgins, martyrs, and prophets, plus the four evangelists and the twelve apostles, who stand and kneel in groups amid plants and trees (Figure 11.21). Besides mystical subjects, van Eyck could paint secular works, though still filled with symbolism, as in the *Arnolfini Wedding Portrait* (see Interpreting Art).

A second outstanding artist working in Flanders during the late Middle Ages was Hans Memling (about 1430–1494), the most popular painter of his day

in Bruges. Long a northern commercial center, Bruges was now entering a period of decline, hastened by the displacement of the Burgundian ruling house by that of the Hapsburgs and the silting of the River Zwin, which shifted trade to Antwerp. Before settling in Bruges, the German-born Memling studied painting in Cologne and the Netherlands, where he fully absorbed the northern tradition. Memling's painting style, which borrowed heavily from that of Jan van Eyck and his generation, was characterized by serenity and graceful elegance, traits that stand in marked contrast to this turbulent era. After starting his workshop in Bruges, Memling grew wealthy from commissions, mainly for altarpieces and portraits, paid for by church leaders, local businesspeople, and resident foreign merchants. More than eighty of his works survive.

Memling was particularly celebrated for the piety of his Madonna paintings, such as the *Madonna and Child with Angels* (Figure 11.22). Following the Flemish tradition, this painting is filled with religious symbolism, which reinforces the message that Christ died to atone for the sins of humankind. The baby Christ

Figure 11.21   Hubert and Jan van Eyck. *Adoration of the Lamb.* Detail of the *Ghent Altarpiece.* Ca. 1432. St. Bavo cathedral, Ghent, Belgium.   This lower center section of the opened altarpiece dramatically shows how the Flemish school could use religious symbolism to evoke a mystical effect. The refined details, which derive from the tradition of manuscript painting, make this scene both credible and otherworldly.

Figure 11.22 HANS MEMLING. *Madonna and Child with Angels.* After 1479. Oil on panel, 23¹/₈ × 18⁷/₈″. **Andrew W. Mellon Collection. National Gallery of Art, Washington, D.C. (1937.1.41).** Memling, though part of the Flemish tradition, appears to have been aware of developments in Renaissance Italy. He introduced some Italian elements into this painting, such as the *putti,* or small angels (used as decorations on the columns and arch), and the stringed musical instruments held by the angels.

Interpreting Art

Date The inscription on the rear wall reads *Johannes de Eyck fuit hic* [Latin for "Jan van Eyck was here"] 1434.

Subject Traditionally, this painting was thought to portray the 1434 wedding of Giovanni Arnolfini and Giovanna Cenami. But this pair did not marry until 1447. So, rival theories abound over the painting's subject: the Arnolfinis at their betrothal or some other legal transaction; or Giovanni's marriage to an undocumented wife; or a memorial to Giovanni's first wife, Costanza Trenta (d. 1433).

Style Van Eyck used wet-on-wet paints to achieve subtlety and variety of color. Layers of translucent glazes cause the surface to shimmer with light. The use of color, light, and shadow creates three-dimensionality, an effect heightened by the way outside light streams into the room. Van Eyck was the first painter to master photo-like realism.

Religious Symbols The single burning candle functions as a sanctuary lamp in a church, signaling the constant presence of God.

Around the mirror are medallions with scenes of Christ's passion—promises of salvation to the persons represented. The couple do not wear shoes—they are standing on holy ground. The dog symbolizes (marital) fidelity: the common dog's name Fido comes from Latin *fido*, "I trust."

Secular Symbols The lavish attire signifies prosperity, but the bride wears no jewelry—a symbol of the restraint of the merchant classes as opposed to the ostentatious display of the nobles. The man raises his hand in a sign of authority; the woman's hand is shown in a submissive pose—conforming to the period's marriage roles.

Historical Interest This painting is the oldest extant representation of real people in an authentic setting. A historic fashion note: The woman is not pregnant; she wears a stomacher—a fashion of the era that emphasized a woman's stomach. Other items in the room exude wealth: the Turkish carpet on the floor; the oranges, a rarity in this period; and the intricate chandelier.

JAN VAN EYCK. *Arnolfini Wedding Portrait* or *Arnolfini Double Portrait.* 1434. Oil on wood, 33 × 22½″. **National Gallery, London.** The Arnolfinis, originally from Lucca (Italy), were agents of the Medici family. The painting was executed in Bruges, where there was an Italian community. Flanders, like Italy, had banking, commercial, and industrial centers. This work is an expression of the symbolic realism that dominated northern European painting in the late Middle Ages.

1. **Subject** How might the subject of this painting be interpreted?
2. **Style** Discuss the most important stylistic feature of this painting.
3. **Religious Symbols** What conclusions can be drawn from the relative absence of religious symbols?
4. **Secular Symbols** Identify and explain at least three secular symbols in the painting.
5. **Historical Interest** Discuss evidence for wealth and luxury revealed by this painting.

reaches for an apple held by an angel, the fruit symbolizing original sin. The second angel, dressed in a vestment associated with the High Mass, plays a harp, possibly a reference to heavenly music. A carved vine of grapes, depicted on the arch, is an emblem of Holy Communion. On the left column stands David, an ancestor of Christ, and on the right column stands Isaiah, a prophet who foretold the birth of the Messiah. A particular feature of Memling's paintings is their inclusion of Turkish carpets—as in van Eyck's *Arnolfini Wedding Portrait* (see Interpreting Art).

The format and the details of Memling's enthroned Madonna hearken back to Jan van Eyck, but without the intensity or sense of reality. Memling's style is static and somewhat artificial. The painting space is clearly arranged, but the landscape and architectural background function as a stage set; the figures are so composed that they constitute a veritable *tableau vivant*, a staged scene in which costumed actors remain silent as if in a picture. Each of the three figures is treated in similar fashion—thin bodies; oval faces; blank, emotionless stares. Adding to the air of artificiality is the absence of shadows, for the painting is bathed in unmodulated light.

Music

The forces of change transforming Europe in the 1300s also had an impact on the field of music (Figure 11.23). Sacred music began to be overshadowed by secular music, with the rise of new secular forms—such as the ballade and rondeau—based on the **chanson,** a song set to a French text and scored for one or more voices, often with instrumental accompaniment. Polyphony remained the dominant composing style, but composers now wrote secular polyphonic pieces that were not based on Gregorian chants. These changes were made possible by innovations that coalesced into what came to be called the "new art" (**ars nova** in Latin),

particularly in Paris, the capital of polyphonic music. The innovations included a new system of music notation, along with new rhythmic patterns such as **isorhythm**—the use of a single rhythmic pattern from the beginning to the end of a work, despite changes in the melodic structure. The chief exponent of *ars nova* was the French composer and poet Guillaume de Machaut [gee-yom duh mah-show] (about 1300–1377).

Machaut, who trained as a priest and musician, first made his mark as a court official to the king of Bohemia. For his services, he was rewarded with an appointment to the cathedral in Reims (1337), where he worked for much of the rest of his life. His music circulated widely in his day, largely because he made gifts of his music manuscripts to wealthy patrons. Thus, he became one of the first composers whose works have survived. Reflecting the decline in church music, his output consists mainly of secular love themes. His verses influenced Chaucer.

Although Machaut was famous for secular music, his reputation rests on his *Notre Dame* Mass, the first polyphonic version of the Mass Ordinary by a known composer. "Ordinary" refers to the five parts of the Mass that remain unchanged throughout the liturgical year, namely the kyrie ("Lord, have mercy"), gloria ("Glory"), credo ("the Nicene Creed"), sanctus and benedictus ("Holy" and "Blessed"), and Agnus

Figure 11.23 *Music and Her Attendants.* **Fourteenth century. From Boethius,** *De Arithmetica.* **Biblioteca Nazionale, Naples.** This miniature painting, using both secular and religious imagery, artfully surveys the state of music in the late Middle Ages. Court music, which flowered during this period, is represented by the seated lady playing a portable pipe organ, in the center, while around her other ladies perform with various instruments, including, starting from the top right and going clockwise: a lute; clappers; trumpets; nakers, or kettledrums; a shawm, an ancestor of the oboe; bagpipes; a tambourine; and a rebec, a precursor of the viol. Religious music, which had kept the legacy of ancient music alive after the fall of Rome, is represented by King David, visible in the circle at the top center, who is depicted playing a psaltery, a handheld type of harp, which is named after the Psalms—the book attributed to his authorship. As to the source of the instruments on view, Greco-Roman tradition supplied only the pipe organ, clappers, trumpets, and bagpipes, while all the others, including the psaltery, were imports from the Islamic world, either from Muslim Spain or from the Middle East during the Crusades.

Dei ("Lamb of God"). Written for four voices, some of which may have been performed by instrumentalists, Machaut's Mass made liberal use of isorhythm in most of its parts. Following his lead, composers for more than six hundred years made the Mass Ordinary the central point of choral music.

A short analysis of Machaut's Agnus Dei, from the *Notre Dame* Mass, shows the new polyphonic style. Its complex composition—four voices singing four parts simultaneously and using varied rhythms—means that the lead melody (sung by the tenor and based on an existing plainsong) is lost in a web of shifting sounds. The two lower voices, including the tenor, provide the ground for this piece. The two upper voices are the more inventive, ornamenting the text with melismas and syllabic singing, along with shifting rhythms, in-cluding **syncopation**—the accenting of a weak beat when a strong beat is expected. A prayer for mercy and peace, Agnus Dei is highly repetitive—a typical prac-tice in the Christian liturgy. And it is divided into three parts, the symbol of the Trinity. Thus, Agnus Dei fur-thers Christian beliefs through words, musical sounds, and structure.

Agnus Dei reads, in Latin, *"Agnus Dei, qui tollis pec-cata mundi: misere nobis / Agnus Dei, qui tollis peccata mundi: Miserere nobis / Agnus Dei, qui tollis peccata mundi: dona nobis pacem,"* and, in English, "Lamb of God, who taketh away the sins of the world, have mercy on us / Lamb of God, who taketh away the sins of the world, have mercy on us / Lamb of God, who taketh away the sins of the world, grant us peace."

SUMMARY

Despite suffering a series of shocks, late medieval Eu-rope made advances in many areas. The Hundred Years' War was costly but left both France and En-gland poised to strengthen their monarchies. The Black Death was massively but unevenly disruptive and so many parts of Europe actually prospered. The first stirrings of industrialism emerged with textile manu-facturing, papermaking, bookmaking, and printing. The Catholic Church lurched from crisis to crisis but new religious movements like the Brethren and Sisters of the Common Life tapped reservoirs of devotion. Al-though philosophy and theology edged apart, brilliant work was done in both fields. Architects and sculp-tors continued to work in the Gothic mode, but their work became exuberantly decorative without major structural breakthroughs. Painters expanded their repertoire of traditionally religious subjects to treat secular themes, and they began to solve problems of mathematical perspective and photographic realism.

The Legacy of the Late Middle Ages

The Hundred Years' War sealed a mortal enmity between France and England that was not healed until the early twentieth century, although the two nations still vie for European leadership. The modern world is not threatened with pandemics like the Black Death but has not eliminated war and famine. Nevertheless, the Spanish flu after World War I, AIDs, the avian flu, and botulism are reminders of what medieval people experienced. The separation of philosophy and theology hastened secularization as thinkers increasingly abandoned religious explanations for physical reality. So, philosophers today tend not to ask ethical questions about how we should live and theologians rarely try to explain the universe. The "new atheists" claim that science has answered all questions worth asking while some religious believers try to impose "creation science" on schools. The breakdown of the high medieval synthesis that occurred in the late Middle Ages has left people grasping for truth and reality. Wealthy royals and churchmen were common throughout the Middle Ages, but in the late medieval period fantastically wealthy laymen, who sometimes built themselves sumptuous houses, became more and more important as patrons of artists, a tradition that is still prevalent today. Printing launched a media revolution that has been accelerated by the Internet.

The Biltmore Mansion, Asheville, North Carolina. 1889–1895. Built for George Washington Vanderbilt by Richard Morris Hunt in the French Renaissance style, this is still the largest private house in America at 135,000 square feet. Such houses were meant to evoke the great chateaux of Europe and to establish a kind of connection between American plutocrats and European aristocrats.

KEY CULTURAL TERMS

incunabula	Flamboyant style	engraving	*ars nova*
devotio moderna	Perpendicular style	drypoint	isorhythm
via antiqua	fan vaulting	Italo-Byzantine style	syncopation
via moderna	campanile	perspective	
late Gothic style	woodcut	*chanson*	

Donatello. Erasmo da Narni, called "Gattamelata." Bronze, approx. 12 × 13'. Piazza del Santo, Padua. Donatello adorned his figure with Roman armor but with a decidedly medieval sword. His stern countenance represents the Renaissance ideal of the strong commander.

12

The Early Renaissance
Return to Classical Roots
1400–1494

Preview Questions

1. *What* connections can be identified between Italy's political and social life and the styles and interests of early Renaissance architects and artists?

2. *What* were the key intellectual characteristics of the early Renaissance?

3. *Identify* both changes and continuities between the Middle Ages and the early Renaissance.

4. *How* did early Renaissance painting evolve from Masaccio to Leonardo?

In 1860 the Swiss historian Jacob Burckhardt published his masterpiece *The Civilization of the Renaissance in Italy.* Emphasizing the themes of individualism, humanism, and classicism, Burckhardt attempted to capture the spirit of the Renaissance period in all its aspects. He believed that the Renaissance freed people from medieval shackles, that art became a key expression of life and not merely an aesthetic pleasure, and that classical humanism, far from being an elitist and antiquarian exercise, changed people and states for the better. Decades later, the influential art historian Erwin Panofsky claimed that people in the Renaissance "looked back [at the past] as from a fixed point in time." Believing themselves different from their medieval predecessors, they felt kinship with the people of Greek and Roman antiquity, whom they sought to emulate. Curiously, then, Renaissance figures made something new out of their encounter with something old.

Since the nineteenth century, it has been customary to refer to the period from about 1300 to 1550 as "the **Renaissance**" (from a French word meaning "rebirth"). What was born again, in this reckoning, was the culture of classical antiquity. Nevertheless, there has been lively controversy over how to interpret this period. Some scholars consider it as part of the late Middle Ages, a time characterized by decline and calamity, and they deemphasize any interest in the classical period. Other scholars view this period as the beginning of early modern Europe. This "early modern" view maintains that the Renaissance was a limited, elite movement and that scholars should pay more attention to the experiences of ordinary men and women than to those of artists and writers.

Pictured here is the equestrian statue of Erasmo da Narni (1370–1443), called Gattamelata ("Honey Cat"), who was a prominent soldier of fortune in Renaissance Italy, where republican ideals were trumped by despots. The sculptor Donatello, one of the most famous Renaissance artists, portrayed Erasmo as a triumphant Roman. But he could as easily be seen as

1400	1494	1520	1600
Early Renaissance	High Renaissance	Late Renaissance	

a medieval warrior—and he was a soldier by profession. He rose from modest circumstances to serve the Venetians whose Senate paid for this statue, which was erected in Padua, a mainland city dominated by Venice. Equestrian statues had all but vanished in the Middle Ages. In short, this exquisite monument signals the varied tendencies of Renaissance Europe. Today it is generally conceded that the late medieval, or Renaissance, or "early" early modern centuries achieved few innovations in government or the economy. The church, beset by turmoil, was criticized but remained a powerful force. Ironically, despite humanism and classicism, many great Renaissance buildings were churches, many churchmen patronized artists, and religious subjects still provided the majority of artistic themes. Intellectual and artistic life unquestionably took some steps forward. But Renaissance novelty emerged from a subtle blending of the forces of continuity and change (Timeline 12.1).

EARLY RENAISSANCE HISTORY AND INSTITUTIONS

Two great themes dominated the history of Italy during the fifteenth century. One of these was the intense and destructive, but sometimes creative, competition among several Italian powers. The other was a series of international developments that had mainly negative consequences in Italy. It is intriguing to think that Italy's spectacular cultural achievements took place amid war, political strife, and economic upheaval.

Italian City-States during the Early Renaissance

During the early Renaissance, five Italian states competed for dominance: the Republic of Venice, the Duchy of Milan, the Republic of Florence, the Papal States, and the Kingdom of Naples (Map 12.1). In the first half of

Learning Through Maps

MAP 12.1   THE STATES OF ITALY DURING THE RENAISSANCE, CA. 1494

This map shows the many states and principalities of Italy in the early Renaissance. 1. *Consider* how the size of each state affected its role in competing for dominance of the Italian peninsula. 2. *Notice* the large number of states in the north compared to the small number in the south. 3. *Notice* the four forms of government—duchy, republic, kingdom, and papal states. 4. *Identify* the major ports of the Italian state system. 5. *What* geographic advantage made the Papal States such a force in Italian politics?

the fifteenth century, the Italian states waged incessant wars among themselves, shifting sides when it was to their advantage.

The continuous warfare, against a background of economic uncertainty, provided the conditions for the emergence of autocratic rulers called *signori,* who arose from prominent families or popular factions. Taking advantage of economic and class tensions, these autocrats pledged to solve local problems, and in so doing they proceeded to accumulate power. What influence the guilds, the business leaders, and the middle class had wielded in the thirteenth and fourteenth centuries gave way to these despots, ending the great medieval legacy of republicanism in Venice, Milan, and Florence.

Under the *signori,* the conduct of warfare also changed. Technological developments improved weaponry, and battles were fought with mercenary troops led by *condottieri,* soldiers of fortune who sold their military expertise to the highest bidder. But the most significant change in Renaissance warfare was the emergence of diplomacy as a peaceful alternative to arms, a practice that gradually spread throughout the Continent. The Italian regimes began sending representatives to other states, and it soon became customary for these diplomats to negotiate peace settlements. In turbulent fifteenth-century Italy, these agreements seldom lasted long—with the notable exception of the Peace of Lodi. This defensive pact, signed in 1454 by Milan, Florence, and Venice, established a delicate balance of power and ensured peace in Italy for forty years.

Before the Italian city-states were eclipsed by other European powers, however, upper-class families enjoyed unprecedented wealth, which they used to cultivate their tastes in literature and art and thus substantially determine the culture of the early Re-

naissance (Figure 12.1). One reason for the importance these families gave to cultural matters is that they put high value on family prestige and on educating their sons for their predestined roles as heads of family businesses and their daughters as loyal wives and successful household managers (Figure 12.2). The courts of the local rulers, or *grandi,* became places where educated men—and, on occasion, women—could exchange ideas and discuss philosophical issues.

Although the status of women did not improve appreciably, more were educated than ever before. Many ended up behind the walls of a convent, however, if their parents could not afford the costly dowry expected of an upper-class bride. The few upper-class women with an independent role in society were those who had been widowed young. The women at the ducal courts who exercised any political influence

Figure 12.1 Pedro Berruguete (aka Pietro di Spagna). *Federico da Montefeltro and His Son Guidobaldo.* Ca. 1476–1477. Oil on panel, 4′5¹⁄₈″ × 2′5⁷⁄₈″. Galleria Nazionale della Marche, Urbino. Urbino, under the Montefeltro dynasty, was transformed from a sleepy hill town with no cultural history into a major center of Renaissance life. Federico, the founder of the dynasty and one of the greatest *condottieri* of his day, was named duke of Urbino and captain of the papal forces by Pope Sixtus IV in 1474. Federico then devoted his energies to making Urbino a model for Italian Renaissance courts. In this portrait, the seated Federico wears the armor of a papal officer while reading a book—symbols that established him as both a soldier and a scholar, later the ideal of Baldassare Castiglioni's (1478–1529) *Courtier* (1528). At the duke's right knee stands his son and heir, Guidobaldo, wearing an elaborate robe and holding a scepter, a symbol of power. Federico's dream ended with his son, the last of the Montefeltro line. At the Urbino court, artists combined Flemish and Italian styles, as in this double portrait. The internal lighting, emanating from some unseen source on the left, is adopted from the tradition pioneered by Jan van Eyck; the profile portrait of the duke follows the Italian practice, based on portrait heads rendered on medals. This double portrait was probably painted by Pedro Berruguete, Spain's first great Renaissance artist, who studied painting in Naples and worked briefly in Urbino before returning to his homeland.

ARS VTINAM. MORES
ANIMVM QVE EFFINGERE
POSSES PVLCHRIOR IN TER
RIS NVLLA TABELLA FORET
MCCCCLXXXVIII

Figure 12.2 DOMENICO GHIRLANDAIO. *Giovanna degli Albizzi Tornabuoni.* Ca. 1489–1490. Tempera and (?) oil on panel, 29½ × 19¼″. Madrid, Thyssen-Bornemisza Collection. This likeness of Giovanna degli Albizzi Tornabuoni (1468–1486) embodies the Florentine ethos of family, city, and church. Her husband, Lorenzo Tornabuoni, a member of a prominent Florentine family, commissioned it as a memorial. Probably painted after his wife's death, it was much admired by Lorenzo, who, according to household records, kept it hanging in his bedroom, even after his remarriage. The subject's gold bodice is decorated with emblems—interlaced *L*s and diamonds—which are symbolic of Lorenzo and his family. The brooch, the coral necklace, and the prayer book allude to Giovanna's high social status and piety. In the background, the Latin epigram "O Art, if thou were able to depict conduct and the soul, no lovelier painting would exist on earth" evokes the Renaissance ideal that equates physical beauty with moral perfection. It is based on a line from an ancient Roman poet.

did so because of their family alliances. One of the most powerful of these women was Lucrezia Borgia [loo-KRET-syah BOR-juh] (1480–1519), the illegitimate daughter of Pope Alexander VI. Married three times before the age of twenty-one, she held court in Ferrara and was the patron of many writers and artists. Most women, however, found real power unattainable.

Florence, the Center of the Renaissance

Amid Italy's artistic and intellectual centers, Florence, the capital of the Tuscan region, was the most prominent. After 1300 Florence's political system went through three phases, evolving from republic to oligarchy to family rule. Despite political turmoil, however, Florentine artists and writers made their city-state the trendsetter of the early Renaissance (Timeline 12.2).

The republic, which began in the fourteenth century with hopes for political equality, fell into the hands

of a wealthy oligarchy. This oligarchy, composed of rich bankers, merchants, and successful guildsmen and craftsmen, ruled until the early fifteenth century, when the Medici family gained control. The Medicis dominated Florentine politics and cultural life from 1434 to 1494.

The Medicis rose from modest circumstances. Giovanni di Bicci de' Medici [jo-VAHN-nee dee BEET-chee day MED-uh-chee] (1360–1429) amassed the family's first large fortune through banking and close financial ties with the papacy. His son Cosimo (1389–1464) added to the Medicis' wealth and outmaneuvered his political enemies, becoming the unacknowledged ruler of Florence. He spent his money on books, paintings, sculptures, and palaces, and, claiming to be the common man's friend, he was eventually awarded the title *Pater patriae*, Father of His Country—a Roman title revived during the Renaissance.

Cosimo's son, Piero, ruled for only a short time and was succeeded by his son Lorenzo (1449–1492), called the Magnificent because of his grand style of living. Lorenzo and his brother Giuliano controlled Florence until Giuliano was assassinated in 1478 by the Pazzi family, rivals of the Medicis. Lorenzo brutally executed the conspirators and then governed autocratically for the next fourteen years. His brutality notwithstanding, in some years Lorenzo spent half of Florence's budget buying books.

Within two years of Lorenzo's death, the great power and prestige of Florence began to weaken and the buoyant spirit of the early Renaissance was eclipsed. Two events are symptomatic of this decline in Florence's spirit and authority. The first was the iconoclastic crusade against the city led by the Dominican monk Fra Savonarola [sav-uh-nuh-ROH-luh] (1452–1498). He opposed the Medicis' rule and wanted to restore a republican form of government. And he hated everything that the Renaissance stood for. In his fire-and-brimstone sermons, Savonarola denounced Florence's leaders and the city's infatuation with the arts. He eventually ran

Timeline 12.2   THE EARLY RENAISSANCE IN FLORENCE, 1400–1494

1400							1494
			Early Renaissance				

1403–1424 Ghiberti's north doors, Florentine Baptistery	**1425** Invention of linear perspective (Brunelleschi)	**1424–1452** Ghiberti's east doors, Florentine Baptistery	**1438–1445** Fra Angelico's *Annunciation*	**1461** Completion of Pazzi Chapel by Brunelleschi	**1473–1475** Verrocchio's *David*	**1480s** Botticelli's *Primavera* and *The Birth* *of Venus*	**1483** Leonardo da Vinci's *The Virgin* *of the Rocks*
	1425–1428 Masaccio's frescoes for Santa Maria Novella	**1430–1432** Donatello's *David*		**1462** Founding of Platonic Academy, Florence			
		1435 Alberti's *On Painting*					

afoul of the papacy and was excommunicated and publicly executed, but not before he had had an enormous effect on the citizens—including the painter Botticelli, who is said to have burned some of his paintings while under the sway of Savonarola's reforming zeal. The second event was the destructive invasion of Italy by Charles VIII of France (r. 1483–1498) in 1494.

The Resurgent Papacy, 1450–1500

The Great Schism was ended by the Council of Constance in 1418, and a tattered Christendom reunited under a Roman pope (see Chapter 11). By 1447 the so-called Renaissance popes were in command and had turned their attention to consolidating the Papal States and securing their interests among Italy's competing powers. Like the secular despots, these popes engaged in war and, when that failed, diplomacy. They brought artistic riches to the church but also lowered its moral tone by accepting bribes for church offices and filling positions with kinsmen. But above all, these popes patronized Renaissance culture.

Three of the most aggressive and successful of these popes were Nicholas V (pope 1447–1455), Pius II (pope 1458–1464), and Sixtus IV (pope 1471–1484). Nicholas V, who had been librarian for Cosimo de' Medici, founded

the Vatican Library, an institution virtually unrivaled today for its holdings of manuscripts and books (Figure 12.3). He also continued the rebuilding of Rome begun by his predecessors. Pius II, often considered the most representative of the Renaissance popes because of his interest in the Greek and Roman classics and authorship of poetry, rose rapidly through the ecclesiastical ranks. This clever politician practiced both war and

Figure 12.3   Melozzo da Forli, Pope Sixtus IV, Appoints Bartolomeo Platina as Vatican Librarian. 1477. Vatican Museums. Although the Vatican Library was founded by Pope Nicholas V in 1448, Platina (1421–1481) was the first official Vatican librarian. A versatile scholar, he published a cookbook but is best known for his history of the popes. Caught up in the turmoil of the Renaissance, Platina was dismissed and then recalled by Pius II and then charged by that pope with studying the history of all papal privileges (documents according various rights). There is still today a prefect of the Vatican Library, always a distinguished scholar.

diplomacy with astounding success. As a student of the new learning and as a brilliant writer in Latin, Pius II attracted intellectuals and artists to Rome. His personal recollections, or *Commentaries,* reveal much about him and his turbulent times. Sixtus IV came from a powerful family and increased his personal power through nepotism, the practice of giving offices to relatives. He continued the papal tradition of making Rome the most beautiful city in the world. The construction of the Sistine Chapel, later adorned with paintings by Botticelli, Perugini, and Michelangelo, was his greatest achievement (see Chapter 13).

International Developments

For Italy, the chief consequence of Charles's invasion in 1494 was that it shattered the forty-year-old Peace of Lodi. Charles was pressing a somewhat dubious hereditary claim to the Kingdom of Naples, where he was crowned in 1495. His invasion of the north owed much to the connivance of the ruling family of Milan, the old enemies of Florence.

Outside Italy, three events further weakened the region's prospects for regaining its position as a major economic power: the fall of Constantinople in 1453, Portugal's opening of the sea route around Africa to India at the end of the century, and Columbus's Spanish-sponsored voyage to the New World. These events shifted the focus of international trade from the Mediterranean to the Atlantic. The fall of Constantinople to the Ottoman Turks in 1453 temporarily closed the eastern Mediterranean markets to the Italian city-states. At the same time, by virtue of the wide-ranging global explorations they sponsored, some European powers—most notably Portugal and Spain—were extending their political and economic interests beyond the geographic limits of continental Europe.

Alone among Italian powers, the Venetians managed to negotiate the new realities. Within a few decades of the fall of Constantinople, the Venetians negotiated new and lucrative commercial privileges with the Turks. Paintings by van Eyck and Memling (see Chapter 11) included Turkish carpets, indicating an increasing European interest in the exotic. Influences also traveled in the opposite direction. Sultan Mehmet II Fatih ("the Conqueror") (1432–1481) commissioned a portrait of himself by a major Venetian painter, Gentile Bellini (Figure 12.4). Thereafter, European conventions in painting had a profound influence on Turkish art.

THE SPIRIT AND STYLE OF THE EARLY RENAISSANCE

Drawing inspiration from ancient Greek and Roman models, the thinkers and artists of the early Renaissance explored such perennial questions as, What is human nature? How are human beings related to God? and What is the best way to achieve human happiness? Although they did not reject Christian explanations outright, they were intrigued by the secular and humanistic values of the Greco-Roman tradition and the answers they might provide to these questions. They also rightfully claimed kinship with certain fourteenth-century predecessors such as the writer Petrarch and the artist Giotto (see Chapter 11).

Those artists, scholars, and writers who are identified with the early Renaissance and who embodied its spirit were linked, through shared tastes and patronage, with the entrepreneurial nobility, the progressive middle class, and the secular clergy. Until about 1450, most artistic works were commissioned by wealthy

Figure 12.4　**GENTILE BELLINI.** *Mehmet II.* **Ca. 1480. Oil on canvas, 27³/₄ × 20⁵/₈". National Gallery, London.** Bellini's commission for this portrait grew out of a diplomatic exchange between Venice and the Ottoman Empire. As a condition of making peace with Venice after a war, Mehmet II requested that a Venetian portrait painter be sent to his court. Bellini's portrait blends Western technique—the oil medium, the seated subject in profile, and the perspective—with Islamic touches—the rounded arch with an elaborate design, the sumptuous fabric draped over the balustrade, the turban and fur-lined robe, and the black background.

patrons for family chapels in churches and for public buildings; later, patrons commissioned paintings and sculptures for their private dwellings.

Even though artists, scholars, and writers stamped this age with their fresh perspectives, some of the old cultural traits remained. Unsettling secular values emerged in the midst of long-accepted religious beliefs, creating contradictions and tensions within the society. In other ways, however, the past held firm, and certain values seemed immune to change. For example, early Renaissance thought made little headway in science, and church patronage still strongly affected the evolution of the arts and architecture, despite the growing impact of the urban class on artistic tastes.

Humanism, Schooling, and Scholarship

Inspired by Petrarch's interest in Latin literature and language, scholars began to collect, copy, disseminate, and comment upon Roman texts uncovered in monastic and cathedral libraries. There was a shift in emphasis from the church Latin of the Middle Ages to the pure Latin style of Cicero, the first-century BCE Roman writer whose eloquent letters and essays established a high moral and literary standard (see Chapter 5). For centuries Greek works, if they were known at all, were read in Latin translations. Petrarch, who knew no Greek, sponsored a Latin translation of Homer. Gradually, however, the humanists studied Greek and began to acquire and study works in the original. Already in the 1300s, these scholars spoke of their literary interests and new learning as *studia humanitatis.* They coined this term, which may be translated as "humanistic studies," and we call them "humanists."

Humanism, as used in the Renaissance and even today, is a multifaceted term. It may imply a concern with the literary culture of Greco-Roman antiquity. And it may suggest an interest in the humane disciplines: history, rhetoric, poetry, philosophy, for example. And it may connote a tendency to look for natural as opposed to theological explanations. In response to the demand for humanistic learning, new schools sprang up in most Italian city-states. In these schools was born the Renaissance ideal of an education intended to free or to liberate the mind—a liberal education.

Coluccio Salutati [kuh-LOOTCH-ee-o sahl-u-TA-tee] (1331–1406), who was chancellor of Florence, founded and endowed many schools; Florence had no university. He himself wrote letters, orations, and histories praising his city's past. He took Cicero as his ideal, arguing that family life and public service, not penance and retreat from the world, should be held up as exemplary ideals. He also argued that the liberty of free, educated citizens created an environment in which people could flourish.

A little later, Guarino [gwa-REE-no] of Verona (1374–1460) stressed the importance of learning Latin and Greek in their classical purity. He believed that constant reading of and reflection on classical texts would inculcate their values in modern people. He also emphasized the importance of rhetoric, the art of speaking elegantly and persuasively, as opposed to the stress on logic and grammar that had dominated in the Middle Ages.

Finally, Vittorino da Feltre [veet-toe-REE-no dah FEL-tray] (1378–1446) made the most significant contributions. Vittorino favored a curriculum that exercised the body and the mind—the ideal of the ancient Greek schools. His educational theories were put into practice at the school he founded in Mantua at the ruler's request. At this school, called the Happy House, Vittorino included humanistic studies along with the medieval curriculum. A major innovation was the stress on physical exercise, which arose from his emphasis on moral training. At first, only the sons and daughters of Mantuan nobility attended his school, but gradually the student body became more democratic as young people from all social classes were enrolled. Vittorino's reforms were slowly introduced into the new urban schools in northern Europe, and their model—the well-rounded student of sound body, solid learning, and high morals—helped to lay the foundation for future European schools and education.

Two products of this educational program will serve to illustrate its many effects. Leonardo Bruni (1374–1444) typifies the practical, civic humanist—the kind of man who believed that properly educated individuals would make for a better civic community. A one-time chancellor, or chief secretary, of Florence's governing body, or *signoria,* Bruni also worked for both the Medicis and the papacy and wrote *History of the Florentine People.* This work reflected his humanistic values, combining as it did his political experience with his knowledge of ancient history. To Bruni, the study of history illuminated contemporary events. Bruni and the other civic humanists, through their writings and their governmental service, set an example for later generations of Florentines and helped infuse them with love of their city. Moreover, by expanding the concept of humanistic studies, they contributed new insights to the ongoing debate about the role of the individual in history and in the social order. The textual and linguistic interests of the humanists met to perfection in Lorenzo Valla (1406–1457)—the second product of Vittorino's educational program. Valla exposed the Donation of Constantine as a forgery by noting that its vocabulary and grammar could not date from the fourth century. Occasionally during the Middle Ages, this famous document, probably written in the eighth century, had been cited by the popes as proof of their political authority over Christendom.

SLICE OF LIFE

Battle of the Sexes, Fifteenth-Century Style

Laura Cereta
IN DEFENSE OF THE EDUCATION OF WOMEN

In this letter, dated January 13, 1488, eighteen-year-old Laura Cereta (1469–1499) responds fiercely to a male critic whose praise she finds patronizing to her as a woman. She then sets him straight about the intellectual needs of women of that time. There were a few women humanists, but the movement's participants were overwhelmingly male, as were their interests.

My ears are wearied by your carping. You brashly and publicly not merely wonder but indeed lament that I am said to possess as fine a mind as nature ever bestowed upon the most learned man. You seem to think that so learned a woman has scarcely before been seen in the world. You are wrong on both counts. . . .

I would have been silent, believe me, if that savage old enmity of yours had attacked me alone. . . . But I cannot tolerate your having attacked my entire sex. For this reason my thirsty soul seeks revenge, my sleeping pen is aroused to literary struggle, raging anger stirs mental passions long chained by silence. With just cause I am moved to demonstrate how great a reputation for learning and virtue women have won by their inborn excellence, manifested in every age as knowledge. . . .

Only the question of the rarity of outstanding women remains to be addressed. The explanation is clear: women have been able by nature to be exceptional, but have chosen lesser goals. For some women are concerned with parting their hair correctly, adorning themselves with lovely dresses, or decorating their fingers with pearls and other gems. Others delight in mouthing carefully composed phrases, indulging in dancing, or managing spoiled puppies. Still others wish to gaze at lavish banquet tables, to rest in sleep, or, standing at mirrors, to smear their lovely faces. But those in whom a deeper integrity yearns for virtue, restrain from the start their youthful souls, reflect on higher things, harden the body with sobriety and trials, and curb their tongues, open their ears, compose their thoughts in wakeful hours, their minds in contemplation, to letters bonded to righteousness. For knowledge is not given as a gift, but [is gained] with diligence. The free mind, not shirking effort, always soars zealously toward the good, and the desire to know grows ever more wide and deep. It is because of no special holiness, therefore, that we [women] are rewarded by God the Giver with the gift of exceptional talent. Nature has generously lavished its gifts upon all people, opening to all the doors of choice through which reason sends envoys to the will, from which they learn and convey its desires. The will must choose to exercise the gift of reason. . . .

I have been praised too much; showing your contempt for women, you pretend that I alone am admirable because of the good fortune of my intellect. . . . Do you suppose, O most contemptible man on earth, that I think myself sprung [like Athena] from the head of Jove? I am a school girl, possessed of the sleeping embers of an ordinary mind. Indeed I am too hurt, and my mind, offended, too swayed by passions, sighs, tormenting itself, conscious of the obligation to defend my sex. For absolutely everything—that which is within us and that which is without—is made weak by association with my sex.

Interpreting This Slice of Life

1. *Describe* the ways Cereta responds to her critic.
2. *What* are some of the types of women she lists?
3. *How* does she portray herself?
4. According to Cereta, *what* are some of the talents God has given to women?
5. *Compare and contrast* Cereta's arguments with those used by modern feminists.

Supposedly, the Roman emperor Constantine, after he departed for Constantinople, gave the popes his western lands and recognized their power to rule in them.

Thought and Philosophy

The Italian humanists were not satisfied with medieval answers to the perennial inquiries of philosophy because those answers did not go beyond Aristotelian philosophy and Christian dogma. Casting their scholarly nets wider, Renaissance thinkers fell under the influence of a richer array of ancient authors than had been known in the Middle Ages. Some Renaissance scholars advocated a more tolerant attitude toward unorthodox religious and philosophical beliefs than in the past. A few Renaissance thinkers began to stress individual fulfillment instead of social or religious conformity. During the Renaissance, a growing emphasis on the individual resulted in a more optimistic assessment of human nature and capability, which led to a diminution of Christianity's stress on human sinfulness and weakness.

As noted in Chapter 11, a small number of Byzantine scholars, living and working in Rome, Florence, and Venice, added an important new dimension to the Renaissance. As teachers of Greek, these scholars introduced Italy's first generation of humanists to many ancient works not seen in the West for nearly a thousand years. Then, in 1453, with the fall of Constantinople to the Ottoman Turks, a fresh wave of Byzantine scholars, teachers, and intellectuals arrived in Italy, bearing countless manuscripts. Thereafter, the humanists began to focus increasingly on Greek language, literature, and, eventually, philosophy. The philosophy of Plato found a home in Italy in 1462 when Cosimo de' Medici established the Platonic Academy at one of his villas near Florence. Here, scholars gathered to examine and discuss the writings of Plato as well as those of the Neoplatonists, as Plato's followers in late antiquity are called. The academy was under the direction of the brilliant humanist Marsilio Ficino [mar-SILL-e-o fe-CHEE-no] (1433–1499), whom Cosimo commissioned to translate Plato's works into Latin.

In two major treatises, Ficino made himself the leading voice of Florentine Neoplatonism by harmonizing Platonic ideas with Christian teachings. Believing that Platonism came from God, Ficino began with the principle that both thought systems rested on divine authority. Like Plato, Ficino believed that the soul was immortal and that complete enjoyment of God would be possible only in the afterlife, when the soul was in the divine realm. Ficino also revived the Platonic notion of free will—the power of humans to make of themselves what they wish. In Ficino's hands, free will became the source of human dignity because human beings were able to choose to love God or to reject him.

Ficino had the most powerful impact on the early Renaissance when he made Plato's teaching on love central to Neoplatonism. Following Platonism, he taught that love is a divine gift that binds all human beings together. Love expresses itself in human experience by the desire for and the appreciation of beauty in its myriad forms. Platonic love, like erotic love, is aroused first by the physical appearance of the beloved. But Platonic love, dissatisfied by mere physical enjoyment, cannot rest until it moves upward to the highest spiritual level, where it finally meets its goal of union with the Divine. Under the promptings of Platonism, the human form became a metaphor of the soul's desire for God. Many Renaissance writers and artists came under the influence of Ficino's Neoplatonism, embracing its principles and embodying them in their works. Sandro Botticelli [baht-tuh-CHEL-lee] (1445–1510), for example, created several allegorical paintings in which divine love and beauty are represented by an image from pre-Christian Rome—Venus—the goddess of love (Figure 12.5).

Ficino's most talented student, Pico della Mirandola [PEE-koh DELL-lah me-RAHN-do-lah] (1463–1494), surpassed his master's accomplishments by the breadth of his learning and the virtuosity of his mind. Pico—a wealthy and charming aristocrat—impressed everyone with his command of languages, range of knowledge, and spirited arguments. His goal was the synthesis of Platonism and Aristotelianism within a Christian framework that also encompassed Jewish, Arab, and Persian ideas. Church authorities and traditional scholars attacked Pico's efforts once they grasped the implication of his ambitious project—that all knowledge shares basic common truths and that Christians could benefit from studying non-Western, non-Christian writings.

Pico's second important contribution—the concept of individual worth—had been foreshadowed by Ficino. Pico's *Oration on the Dignity of Man* gives the highest expression to this idea, which is inherent in the humanist tradition. According to Pico, human beings, endowed with reason and speech, are created as a microcosm of the universe. Set at the midpoint in the scale of God's creatures, they are blessed with free will, which enables them either to raise themselves to God or to sink lower than the beasts. This liberty to determine private fate makes human beings the masters of their individual destinies and, at the same time, focuses attention on each human being as the measure of all things—a classical belief now reborn. Yet Pico's magnificent *Oration* begins as a commentary on Psalm 8: "What is man that thou art mindful of him?"

Architecture, Sculpture, and Painting

It was in architecture, sculpture, and painting that the Renaissance made its most dramatic breaks with the medieval past. The **early Renaissance style** was launched in Florence by artists who rejected the excesses of the late Gothic style (compare Figures 11.7 and 12.6). Led by the architect Filippo Brunelleschi [brun-uh-LESS-kee] (1377–1446), this group studied the ruins of classical buildings and ancient works of sculpture to unlock the secrets of their harmonious style. They believed that once the classical ideals were rescued from obscurity, new works could be fashioned that captured the spirit of ancient art and architecture without slavishly copying it.

Artistic Ideals and Innovations Inspired by Brunelleschi's achievement, architects, sculptors, and painters made the classical principles of balance, simplicity, and restraint the central ideals of the early Renaissance style. Sculpture and painting, freed from their subordination to architecture, regained their ancient status as independent art forms and in time became the most cherished of the visual arts. Renaissance

Figure 12.5 SANDRO BOTTICELLI. *The Birth of Venus.* 1480s. Tempera on canvas, 5'8" × 9'1". Uffizi Gallery, Florence. With the paintings of Botticelli, the nude female form reappeared in Western art for the first time since the Greco-Roman period. Botticelli's Venus contains many classical echoes, such as the goddess's lovely features and her modest pose. But the artist used these pre-Christian images to convey a Christian message and to embody the principles of Ficino's Neoplatonist philosophy.

Figure 12.6 LEONE BATTISTA ALBERTI. Tempio Malatestiano (Malatesta Temple) (Church of San Francesco). Ca. 1450. Rimini, Italy. Although unfinished, this church strikingly demonstrates the revolution in architecture represented by early Renaissance ideals. Nothing could be further from the spires of late Gothic cathedrals than this simple, symmetrical structure with its plain facade, post-and-lintel entrance, rounded arches, and classical columns. Designed by the leading theoretician of the new style, the Malatesta Temple served as a model for artists and architects of the later Renaissance.

sculptors and painters aspired to greater realism than had been achieved in the Gothic style, seeking to depict human musculature and anatomy with a greater degree of credibility. Whereas architecture and sculpture looked back to ancient Greek and Roman traditions, developments in painting grew from varied sources, including the Islamic world and the late medieval world, though the most important inspiration was the art of the Florentine painter Giotto.

Two technical innovations—linear and atmospheric or aerial perspective—forever changed painting and, to a degree, architecture and sculpture too. The invention of linear perspective was another of Brunelleschi's accomplishments although his work was anticipated by the mathematician and artist Paolo Uccello (see Chapter 11). Using principles of architecture and optics, he conducted experiments in 1425 that provided the mathematical basis for achieving the illusion of depth on a two-dimensional surface (and,

coincidentally, contributed to the enhancement of the status of the arts by grounding them in scholarly learning). Brunelleschi's solution to the problem of linear perspective was to organize the picture space around the center point, or **vanishing point.** After determining the painting's vanishing point, he devised a structural grid for placing objects in precise relation to each other within the picture space. He also computed the ratios by which objects diminish in size as they recede from view, so that pictorial reality seems to correspond visually with physical accuracy. He then subjected the design to a mirror test—checking its truthfulness in its reflected image. Pietro Perugino's [pair-oo-GEE-no] (about 1450–1524) *Christ Giving the Keys to St. Peter* is a splendid example of the new technique (Figure 12.7).

When the camera appeared in the nineteenth century, it was discovered that the photographic lens "saw" nature according to Brunelleschi's mathematical rules. After the 1420s, Brunelleschi's studies led

Figure 12.7 Pietro Perugino. *Christ Giving the Keys to St. Peter.* 1480–1482. Fresco. North Wall, Sistine Chapel, Vatican City. Pope Sixtus IV renovated an old chapel—now known after him as "Sistine"—between 1477 and 1480. He attracted many of the best painters of the day to execute frescoes for the side walls. They were first to make preliminary frescoes to see if their work and subject matter was satisfactory. By early 1482, it was clear that the works were in fact excellent. Perugino took as his theme a topic of great ideological interest to the papacy, namely the "Petrine Text" (Matthew 16:16–18; see Chapter 7). Perugino not only displays virtuosity in his ostentatious use of linear perspective, but he also combines this with ideological, theological, and historical perspectives. Christ tells Peter he is the rock on which the church will be built. So here the church is directly above Peter. The church itself stands between two triumphal arches inspired by the Arch of Constantine (see Figure 7.8). The church has triumphed over the state, it seems. The vast expanse of the background suggests that Peter's authority, conferred by Christ, is limitless.

to the concept of Renaissance space, the notion that a composition should be viewed from one single position. For four hundred years, or until first challenged by Manet in the nineteenth century, linear perspective and Renaissance space played a leading role in Western painting (see Chapter 19).

Atmospheric, or aerial, perspective was perfected by painters north of the Alps in the first half of the fifteenth century, although the Italian painter Masaccio was the first to revive atmospheric perspective in the 1420s, based on the Roman tradition. Through the use of colors, these artists created an illusion of depth by subtly diminishing the tones as the distance between the eye and the object increased; at the horizon line, the colors become grayish and the objects blurry in appearance. When atmospheric perspective was joined to linear perspective, as happened later in the century, a greater illusion of reality was achieved than was possible with either type used independently.

Leone Battista Alberti [ahl-BAIR-tee] (1404–1472) published a treatise in 1435 that elaborated on the mathematical aspects of painting and set forth brilliantly the humanistic and secular values of the early Renaissance. Alberti was an aristocratic humanist with a deep knowledge of classicism and a commitment to its ideals. In his treatise, he praised master painters in rousing terms, comparing their creativity to God's—a notion that would have been considered blasphemous by medieval thinkers. He asserted that paintings, in addition to pleasing the eye, should appeal to the mind with optical and mathematical accuracy. But paintings, he went on, should also present a noble subject, such as a classical hero, and should be characterized by a small number of figures, by carefully observed and varied details, by graceful poses, by harmonious relationships among all elements, and by a judicious use of colors. These classical ideals were quickly adopted by Florentine artists eager to establish a new aesthetic code.

Architecture   The heaviest debt to the past was owed by the architects, for they revived the classical orders—Doric, Ionic, and Corinthian. The new buildings, though constructed to accommodate modern needs, were symmetrical in plan and relied on simple decorative designs. The theoretician of early Renaissance style was Alberti, who wrote at length on Brunelleschi's innovations. Alberti believed that architecture should embody the humanistic qualities of dignity, balance, control, and harmony and that a building's ultimate beauty rests on the mathematical harmony of its separate parts.

In the High Middle Ages, most architects were stonemasons and were regarded as artisans, like shoemakers or potters. But by the fifteenth century, the status of architects had changed. Because of the newly discovered scientific aspects of their craft, the leading architects were now grouped with those practicing the learned professions of medicine and law. By 1450 Italian architects had freed architecture from late Gothicism, as well as from the other arts. Unlike Gothic cathedrals adorned with sculptures and paintings, these new buildings drew on the classical tradition for decorative details. That is, Renaissance architects revived the practice of using simple architectural elements as parts of a building's decoration but not of its structure (see Figure 12.10 and compare Figure 5.12). This transformation became the most visible symbol of early Renaissance architecture.

Although Brunelleschi established the new standards in architecture, most of his buildings have been either destroyed or altered considerably by later hands. However, the earliest work to bring him fame still survives in Florence largely as he had planned it—the dome of the city's cathedral (Figure 12.8). Although the rest of the cathedral—nave, transept, and choir—was finished before 1400, no one had been able to devise a method for erecting the projected dome until Brunelleschi received the commission in 1420.

Figure 12.8   Filippo Brunelleschi. **Cathedral Dome, Florence. 1420–1436. Ht. of dome from floor, 367′.**   After the dome of the Florence cathedral was erected according to Brunelleschi's plan, another architect was employed to add small galleries in the area above the circular windows. But the Florentine authorities halted his work before the galleries were fully installed, leaving the structure in its present state.

Figure 12.9 FILIPPO BRUNELLESCHI. **Design for Construction of Dome of Florence Cathedral.** Brunelleschi designed the dome of the Florence cathedral with an inner and an outer shell, both of which are attached to the eight ribs of the octagonal-shaped structure. Sixteen smaller ribs, invisible from the outside, were placed between the shells to give added support. What held these elements together and gave them stability was the lantern, based on his design, that was anchored to the dome's top sometime after 1446.

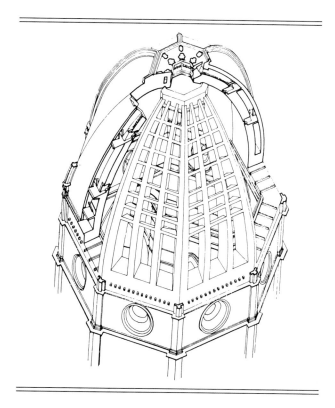

Using the learning he had gained from his researches in Rome as well as his knowledge of Gothic building styles, he developed an ingenious plan for raising the dome, which was virtually completed in 1436.

Faced with a domical base of 140 feet, Brunelleschi realized that a hemispheric dome in the Roman manner, like the dome of the Pantheon, would not work (see Figure 5.10). Traditional building techniques could not span the Florentine cathedral's vast domical base, nor could the cathedral's walls be buttressed to support a massive dome. So he turned to Gothic methods, using diagonal ribs based on the pointed arch. This innovative dome had a double shell of two relatively thin walls held together by twenty-four stone ribs, of which only eight are visible. His crowning touch was to add a lantern that sits atop the dome and locks the ribs into place (Figure 12.9). The dome's rounded windows echo the openings in the upper nave walls, thereby ensuring that his addition would harmonize with the existing elements. But the octagonal-shaped dome was Brunelleschi's own creation and expresses a logical, even inevitable, structure. Today, the cathedral still dominates the skyline of Florence, a lasting symbol of Brunelleschi's creative genius.

Brunelleschi's most representative building is the Pazzi Chapel, as the chapter house, or meeting room, of the friars of Santa Croce is called. This small church embodies the harmonious proportions and classical features that are the hallmark of the early Renaissance style. In his architectural plan, Brunelleschi centered a dome over an oblong area whose width equals the dome's diameter and whose length is twice its width and then covered each of the chapel's elongated ends with a barrel vault. Double doors opened into the center wall on one long side, and two rounded arch windows flanked this doorway. A loggia [LOH-je-uh], or open porch, which Brunelleschi may not have designed, preceded the entrance (Figure 12.10). Inside the

Figure 12.10 FILIPPO BRUNELLESCHI AND OTHERS. **Exterior, Pazzi Chapel, Santa Croce Church. 1433–1461. Florence.** The Pazzi Chapel's harmonious facade reflects the classical principles of the early Renaissance style: symmetry and simplicity. By breaking the rhythm of the facade with the rounded arch, the architect emphasizes its surface symmetry so that the left side is a mirror image of the right side. Simplicity is achieved in the architectural decorations, which are either Greco-Roman devices or mathematically inspired divisions.

chapel, following the classical rules of measure and proportion, Brunelleschi employed medallions, rosettes, **pilasters** (or applied columns), and square panels. In addition to these classical architectural details, the rounded arches and the barrel vaults further exemplify the new Renaissance style (Figure 12.11). His classical theories were shared by Florence's humanist elite, who found religious significance in mathematical harmony. Both they and Brunelleschi believed that a well-ordered building such as the Pazzi Chapel mirrors God's plan of the universe.

The other towering figure in early Renaissance architecture was Alberti. Despite the influence of his ideas, which dominated architecture until 1600, no completed building based on his design remains. A splendid unfinished effort is the Tempio Malatestiano in Rimini (see Figure 12.6), a structure that replaced the existing church of San Francesco. Rimini's despot,

Figure 12.11 FILIPPO BRUNELLESCHI. **Interior. Pazzi Chapel, Santa Croce Church. Ca. 1433–1461. 59'9" long × 35'8" wide. Florence.** Decorations on the white walls of the Pazzi Chapel's interior break up its plain surface and draw the viewer's eye to the architectural structure: pilasters, window and panel frames, medallions, capitals, and dome ribs. The only nonarchitecturally related decorations are the terra-cotta sculptures by Luca della Robbia (1399/1400–1482) of the four evangelists and the Pazzi family coat of arms, mounted below the medallions.

Sigismondo Malatesta (1417–1468), planned to have himself, his mistress, and his courtiers buried in the refurbished structure, and he appointed Alberti to supervise the church's reconstruction.

Alberti's monument represents the first modern attempt to give a classical exterior to a church. Abandoning the Gothic pointed arch, Alberti designed this church's unfinished facade with its three rounded arches after a nearby triumphal arch. He framed the arches with Corinthian columns, one of his favorite decorative devices. Although the architect apparently planned to cover the church's interior with a dome comparable to Brunelleschi's on the Florentine cathedral, Malatesta's fortunes failed, and the projected temple had to be abandoned. Nevertheless, Alberti's unfinished church was admired by later builders and helped to point the way to the new Renaissance architecture.

Sculpture   Like architecture, sculpture blossomed in Florence in the early 1400s. Sculptors, led by this period's genius, Donatello [dah-nah-TEL-lo] (about 1386–1466), revived classical practices that had not been seen in the West for more than a thousand years: the freestanding figure; the technique of contrapposto, or a figure balanced with most of the weight resting on one leg (see Figure 3.19); the life-size nude statue; and the equestrian statue. Donatello was imbued with classical ideals but obsessed with realism. He used a variety of techniques—expressive gestures, direct observation, and mathematical precision—to reproduce what his eyes saw. Donatello accompanied Brunelleschi to Rome to study ancient art, and he adapted linear perspective as early as 1425 into a small **relief**—figures carved to project from a flat surface—called *The Feast of Herod* (Figure 12.12). The subject is the tragic end of John the Baptist, Florence's patron saint, as recounted in Mark 6:20–29. In Donatello's square bronze panel, the saint's severed head is being displayed on a dish to King Herod at the left, while the scorned Salome stands near the right end of the table. A puzzled guest leans toward the ruler, who recoils with upraised hands; two children, at the left, withdraw from the bloody head; and a diner leans back from the center of the table—all depicted under the rounded arches of the new Brunelleschian architecture. The sculpture's rich details and use of linear perspective point up the horror of the scene and thus achieve the heightened realism that was among the artistic goals of this era. The scene's vanishing point runs through the middle set of arches, so that the leaning motions of the two figures in the foreground not only express their inner turmoil but also cause them to fall away from the viewer's line of sight.

Donatello also revived the freestanding male nude, one of the supreme expressions of ancient art. Donatello's bronze *David,* probably executed for Cosimo de' Medici, portrays David standing with his left foot on

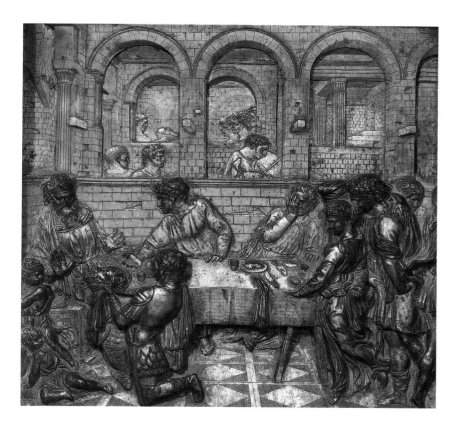

Figure 12.12 DONATELLO. *The Feast of Herod.* **Ca. 1425. Gilt bronze, 23½″ square. Baptismal font, San Giovanni, Siena.** The first low-relief sculpture executed in the early Renaissance style, *The Feast of Herod* is a stunning example of the power of this new approach to art. Its theatrical force arises from the successful use of linear perspective and the orderly placement of the figures throughout the three rooms.

Figure 12.13 DONATELLO. *David.* Ca. 1430–1432. Bronze, ht. 62¼".
Bargello, Florence. The David and Goliath story was often allegorized
into a prophecy of Christ's triumph over Satan. But Donatello's sculpture
undermines such an interpretation, for his *David* is less a heroic figure than
a provocative image of refined sensuality, as suggested by the undeveloped
but elegant body, the dandified pose, and the incongruous boots and hat.
Donatello's *David* is a splendid modern portrayal of youthful male power,
self-aware and poised on the brink of manhood.

the severed head of the Philistine warrior Goliath—
a pose based on the biblical story (Figure 12.13). This
sculpture had a profound influence on later sculptors,
who admired Donatello's creation but produced rival
interpretations of David (Figure 12.14). Donatello and
his successors used the image of David to pay homage
to male power—a major preoccupation of Renaissance
artists and intellectuals.

The only serious rival to Donatello in the early Renaissance was another Florentine, Lorenzo Ghiberti
[gee-BAIR-tee] (about 1381–1455), who slowly adapted
to the new style of art. In 1401 he defeated Brunelleschi in a competition to select a sculptor for the north
doors of Florence's Baptistery. The north doors consist
of twenty-eight panels, arranged in four columns of
seven panels, each depicting a New Testament scene.
These doors, completed between 1403 and 1424, show
Ghiberti still under the influence of the International
Gothic style that prevailed in about 1400. Illustrative of this tendency is the panel *The Annunciation*
(Luke 1:26–38), which depicts the moment when Mary
learns from an angelic messenger that she will become the mother of Christ (Figure 12.15). The Gothic
quatrefoil, or four-leafed frame, was standard for
these panels, and many of Ghiberti's techniques are
typical of the Gothic style—the niche in which the Virgin stands, her swaying body, and the angel depicted
in flight. Nevertheless, Ghiberti always exhibited a
strong feeling for classical forms and harmony, as in
the angel's well-rounded body and Mary's serene face.
Ghiberti's early work reveals the Renaissance synthesis of the Christian and classical, of the classical and
the medieval.

The artistic world of Florence was a rapidly changing one, however, and Ghiberti adapted his art to
conform to the emerging early Renaissance style of
Donatello. Between 1425 and 1452, Ghiberti brought
his mature art to its fullest expression in the east
doors, the last of the Baptistery's three sculptured
portals. These panels, larger than those on the north
doors, depict ten scenes from the Old Testament. Most
of the Gothic touches have been eliminated, including
the framing quatrefoils, which are now replaced with
square panels (Figure 12.16).

One of the sublime panels from the east doors
depicts the story of the brothers Cain and Abel (Figure 12.17), taken from Genesis 4:1–16. This panel shows,
in many ways, Ghiberti's growing dedication to classical ideals, seen, for example, in the graceful contrapposto of the standing figures and their proportional
relationships. This work translates Albertian aesthetics
into bronze by creating an illusion of depth. According
to Ghiberti's *Commentaries,* the sculptor's purpose was
not illusion for illusion's sake but, rather, an articulate
visual presentation of the biblical story. Five incidents
from the story of Cain and Abel are illustrated: (1) Cain

and Abel as children with their parents, Adam and Eve, at the top left; (2) Cain and Abel making sacrifices before an altar, at the top right; (3) Cain plowing with oxen and Abel watching his sheep, in the left foreground and left middle, respectively; (4) Cain slaying Abel with a club, in the right middle; and (5) Cain being questioned by God, in the right foreground.

Painting In the early fourteenth century, Giotto had founded a new realistic and expressive style (see Chapter 11), on which Florentine painters began to build at the beginning of the fifteenth century. Much of Giotto's genius lay in his ability to show perspective, or the appearance of spatial depth, in his frescoes, an illusion he achieved largely through the placement of the figures (see Figure 11.19). Approximately one hundred years after Giotto, painters learned to enhance the realism of their pictures by the use of linear perspective.

The radical changes taking place in architecture and sculpture were minor compared with the changes in painting. Inspired by classicism though lacking significant examples from ancient times, painters were relatively free to experiment and to define their own path. As in the other arts of the 1400s, Florentine painters led the way and established the standards for the new style—realism, linear perspective, and psychological truth (convincing portrayal of emotional states). This movement climaxed at the end of the century with the early work of Leonardo da Vinci.

After 1450 Florence's dominance was challenged by Venetian painters, who were forging their own artistic

Figure 12.14 ANDREA DEL VERROCCHIO. *David.* 1473–1475. Bronze, ht. 4'2". Bargello, Florence. Verrocchio's *David* inaugurated the tradition in Renaissance Florence of identifying the Jewish giant-killer with the city's freedom-loving spirit. A masterpiece of bravado, Verrocchio's boyish hero stands challengingly over the severed head of Goliath. In its virility, this work surpasses the sculpture that inspired it, Donatello's *David* (see Figure 12.13). Florence's ruling council liked Verrocchio's statue so much that they placed it in the Palazzo Vecchio, the seat of government, where it remained until Michelangelo's *David* (see Figure 13.20) displaced it. Verrochio's *David* was restored in 2003, bringing back to the original the gold patina in the locks of hair, the borders of the clothes and boots, and the pupils of the eyes. With the restoration of the gold leaf gilding, restorers have concluded that the statue originally was intended for display indoors.

Figure 12.15 LORENZO GHIBERTI. *The Annunciation.* Panel from the north doors of the Baptistery. 1403–1424. Gilt bronze, 20½ × 17¾". Florence. Ghiberti's rendition of the Annunciation was typical of his panels on the north doors. Mary and the angel are placed in the shallow foreground and are modeled almost completely in the round. The background details, including a sharply foreshortened representation of God on the left, are scarcely raised from the metal. The contrast between these design elements enhances the illusion of depth.

◄ **Figure 12.16** Lorenzo Ghiberti. *Gates of Paradise.* **East doors of the Baptistery. 1424–1452. Gilt bronze, ht. approx. 17'. Florence.** The ten scenes depicted on these doors are based on Old Testament stories, taken from the books of Genesis through Kings. Reading from top left to right, then back and forth, and ending at bottom right, the panels begin with an illustration of the opening chapters of Genesis followed by others representing events in the lives of Cain and Abel, Noah, Abraham, Isaac and Jacob, Joseph, Moses, Joshua, David, and Solomon. Taking heed of medieval artistic tradition, Ghiberti placed several dramatic episodes from the life of each biblical character in a single panel. Each panel was formed into a wax model, then cast in bronze, and gilded with gold. According to Giorgio Vasari, the Renaissance artist and writer, Michelangelo, on first seeing the doors, described them as "worthy of Paradise"—the name by which they are still known—the *Gates of Paradise.* In 1991 Ghiberti's original doors were moved inside to Florence's Duomo Museum and duplicate doors replaced them on the Baptistery.

tradition. Venice, not having won its freedom from the Byzantine Empire until the High Middle Ages, was still in the thrall of Byzantine culture (see Chapter 8). As a result, Venetian painters and their patrons showed a pronounced taste for the stylized effects and sensual surfaces typical of Byzantine art. However, a distinct school of Venetian painters emerged, which eventually would have a major impact on the course of painting in the West.

North of the Alps, a third early Renaissance development was taking place in Burgundy and the Low Countries. There, compared with Italians, painters kept more closely to religious themes and images and departed less from the Gothic. The northern artists concentrated on minute details and landscapes rather than on the problems of depth and composition that concerned Italy's painters.

The guiding genius of the revolution in painting in the earlier Florentine school was the youthful Masaccio [mah-ZAHT-cho] (1401–1428), whose career was probably cut short by the plague. He adopted mathematical perspective in his works almost simultaneously with its elaboration by Brunelleschi. In the history of Western painting, Masaccio's *Holy Trinity* fresco is the first successful depiction in painting of the new concept of Renaissance space. His design for this fresco in the church of Santa Maria Novella, Florence, shows that he was well aware of the new currents flowing in the art of his day. The painting offers an architectural setting in the style of Brunelleschi, and the solidity and vitality of the figures indicate that Masaccio had also absorbed the values of Donatello's new sculpture. Masaccio's fresco portrays the Holy Trinity—the three divine persons in the one Christian God—within a simulated chapel (Figure 12.18). Jesus's crucified body appears to be held up by God the Father, who stands on a platform behind the cross; between the heads of Father and Son is a dove, symbolizing the Holy Spirit and completing the Trinitarian image. Mary and Saint John, both clothed in

contemporary dress, flank the holy trio. Mary points dramatically to the Savior. Just outside the chapel's frame, the donors kneel in prayer—the typical way of presenting patrons in Renaissance art.

In the *Holy Trinity* fresco, Masaccio uses a variety of innovations. He is the first painter to show light falling from a single source, in this instance, from the left, bathing the body of Christ and coinciding with the actual lighting in Santa Maria Novella. This realistic feature adds to the three-dimensional effect of the well-modeled figures. The use of linear perspective further heightens the scene's realism. Finally, the perspective, converging to the midpoint between the kneeling donors, reinforces the hierarchy of beings within the fresco: from God the Father at the top to the human figures at the sides. In effect, mathematical precision is used to reveal the divine order—an ideal congenial to Florence's intellectual elite.

A second fresco by Masaccio, *The Tribute Money,* painted in the Brancacci Chapel of the church of Santa Maria del Carmine, Florence, is recognized as Masaccio's masterpiece (Figure 12.19). This fresco illustrates the Gospel account (Matthew 17:24–27) in which Jesus advises Peter, his chief disciple, to pay the Roman taxes. Because this painting depicts a biblical subject virtually unrepresented in Christian art, it was probably commissioned by a donor to justify a new and heavy Florentine tax. Whether the fresco had any effect on tax collection is debatable, but other artists

Figure 12.17 Lorenzo Ghiberti. *The Story of Cain and Abel.* **Detail from the east doors of the Baptistery (the** *Gates of Paradise***). 1424–1452. Gilt bronze, 31¼ × 31¼". Florence.** This exquisite panel from the Florence Baptistery's east doors is a testament to Ghiberti's absorption of early Renaissance taste. Ghiberti followed Brunelleschi's new rules for linear perspective by placing the vanishing point in the middle of the tree trunks in the center of the panel, and he adhered to Alberti's principle of varied details by adding the oxen, sheep, and altar.

Figure 12.18 MASACCIO. *The Holy Trinity.* **1427 or 1428. Fresco, 21′10½″ × 10′5″. Santa Maria Novella, Florence.** Masaccio achieved a remarkable illusion of depth in this fresco by using linear and atmospheric perspective. Below the simulated chapel, he painted a skeleton in a wall sarcophagus (not visible in this photograph) with a melancholy inscription reading, "I was once that which you are, and what I am you also will be." This *memento mori*, or reminder of death, was probably ordered by the donor, a member of the Lenzi family. His tomb is built into the floor and lies directly in front of the fresco.

were captivated by Masaccio's stunning technical effects: the use of perspective and **chiaroscuro,** or the modeling with light and shade.

The Tribute Money fresco follows the continuous narrative form of medieval art. Three separate episodes are depicted at the same time—in the center, Jesus is confronted by the tax collector; on the left, Peter, as foretold by Jesus, finds a coin in the mouth of a fish; and, on the right, Peter pays the coin to the Roman official. Despite this Gothic effect, the fresco's central section is able to stand alone because of its spatial integrity and unified composition. Like Donatello, Masaccio could synthesize several traditions masterfully. Jesus is partially encircled by his apostles, and the tax gatherer, viewed from the back, stands to the right. In this central group, the heads are all at the same height,

Figure 12.19 MASACCIO. *The Tribute Money.* **Ca. 1425. Fresco, 8′2⅜″ × 19′8¼″. Santa Maria del Carmine, Florence.** This fresco represents the highest expression of the art of Masaccio, particularly in his realistic portrayal of the tax collector. This official, who appears twice, first confronting Christ in the center and then receiving money from Peter on the right, is depicted with coarse features—a typical man of the Florentine streets. Even his posture, though rendered with classical contrapposto, suggests a swagger—a man at home in his body and content with his difficult occupation.

for Masaccio aligned them according to Brunelleschi's principles. Fully modeled in the round, each human form occupies a precise, mathematical space.

Painters such as the Dominican friar Fra Angelico (about 1400–1455) extended Masaccio's innovations. Fra Angelico's later works, painted for the renovated monastery of San Marco in Florence and partially funded by Cosimo de' Medici, show his mature blending of biblical motifs in Renaissance space. The *Annunciation* portrays a reflective Virgin receiving the archangel Gabriel (Figure 12.20). Mary and Gabriel are framed in niches in the Gothic manner, but the other elements—the mastery of depth, the simplicity of gestures, the purity of colors, and the integrated scene— are rendered in the new, simple Renaissance style. The

painting's vanishing point is placed to the right of center in the small barred window looking out from the Virgin's bedroom. The loggia, or open porch, in which the scene takes place was based on a new architectural fashion popular among Florence's wealthy elite. Religious images abound in this painting; the enclosed garden symbolizes Mary's virginity, and the barred window attests to the purity of her life. Because of his gracious mastery of form and space, Fra Angelico's influence on later artists was pronounced.

One of those Fra Angelico influenced was Piero della Francesca [PYER-o DAYL-lah frahn-CHAY-skah] (about 1420–1492), a great painter of the second Florentine generation, who grew up in a Tuscan country town near Florence. His panel painting *The Flagellation*

Figure 12.20 Fra Angelico. *Annunciation.* 1438–1445. Fresco, 7′6″ × 10′5″. Monastery of San Marco, Florence. Fra Angelico's portrayal of the Virgin at the moment when she receives the news that she will bear the baby Jesus is a wonderful illustration of the painter's use of religious symbols. Mary's questioning expression and her arms crossed in a maternal gesture help to establish the painting's subject. Moreover, the physical setting of the scene, bare except for the rough bench on which Mary sits, suggests an ascetic existence—an appropriate detail for the painting's original setting, a monastery.

Figure 12.21 Piero della Francesca. *The Flagellation.* **1460s. Oil on panel, 23 × 32″. Galleria Nazionale della Marche, Palazzo Ducale, Urbino.** A secondary religious message may be found in this work. In 1439 the Orthodox Church discussed union with Rome at the Council of Florence but later repudiated the merger when the Byzantine populace rioted in favor of Turkish rule. The hats on Pilate (seated at the left) and the third man from the right are copies of Greek headdresses that were worn at the council. In effect, these figures suggest that the Greek Church is a persecutor of true Christianity, for the papacy regarded the Greek Orthodox faith as schismatic.

shows the powerful though mysterious aesthetic effects of his controversial style (Figure 12.21). The sunlight flooding the scene unites the figures, but the composition places them in two distinct areas. At the extreme left sits Pilate, the judge, on a dais. The painting's subject—the scourging of Christ before his crucifixion—is placed to the left rear. Reinforcing this odd displacement are the figures on the right, who are apparently lost in their own conversation. Aesthetically this strange juxtaposition arises because Piero has placed the horizon line around the hips of the figures beating Christ, causing the three men on the right to loom in such high perspective; thus the men in the foreground appear to be indifferent to Christ

and unaware of his importance. The effect is distinctly unsettling in a religious scene. The modern world, which loves conundrums, has developed a strong passion for the private vision of Piero della Francesca as represented in his art.

Botticelli is the best representative of a lyrical aspect of this second generation and one of the most admired painters in the Western tradition. One of the first Florentine artists to master both linear and atmospheric perspective, he was less interested in the technical aspects of painting than he was in depicting languid beauty and poetical truth.

Until the 1480s, Botticelli's art was shaped by the Neoplatonic philosophy of the Florentine Academy,

Interpreting Art

Subject The title of the painting, *Primavera*, means "spring" in Italian. The painting is an allegory of the return of the bountiful fruits, flowers, and love that have always been associated with springtime.

Composition To the right, ominous Zephyr grabs beautiful Chloris who, breathing flowers, is being transformed into Flora ("flower"). To Chloris/Flora's left, crowned Spring enters strewing flowers—symbols of spring. Left and behind Spring, Venus, the goddess of love, presides. Above Venus, Eros, portrayed as a *putto* or as Cupid, draws his bow and aims at the Three Graces (Beauty, Chastity, and Pleasure). One of the graces gazes lovingly at the god Mercury, who seems oblivious to the whole scene.

Mythological Sources The scene may be based on Ovid's story of the harsh wind of March, Zephyr, who raped the mortal Chloris but then fell in love with her and transformed her into the goddess Flora.

Philosophical Perspective Thematically, from right to left, the painting contrasts carnal sensuality with pure Platonic love.

Historical Perspective Many scholars think that Lorenzo de' Medici commissioned the painting as a wedding gift for Lorenzo di Pierfrancesco de' Medici (who may be represented as Mercury) as a symbol of pure love as described by Ficino, the Neoplatonist thinker.

Artistic Perspective Despite its exquisitely accurate figures and as many as five hundred plants and flowers, the painting uses a medieval narrative technique—multiple scenes in the same plane—and does not array the foreground and background so as to create linear perspective.

SANDRO BOTTICELLI. *Primavera.* Ca. 1482. Tempera on panel, 6'8" × 10'4". Uffizi Gallery, Florence. Botticelli's lyricism is evident in his refined images of human beauty. His figures' elegant features and gestures, such as the sloping shoulders and the tilted heads, were copied by later artists. The women's blond, ropelike hair and transparent gowns are typical of Botticelli's style.

1. **Content** Identify the figures in the painting and explain their purpose.
2. **Cultural** Why is it significant that an early Renaissance artist turned to classical mythology for his subject matter?
3. **Philosophical Perspective** How does this painting reflect the philosophy of Marsilio Ficino?
4. **Theme** What message might his painting have communicated to a young couple about to be married?
5. **Style** Compare and contrast Botticelli's use of perspective with that of Pietro Perugino (Figure 12.7) and Piero della Francesca (Figure 12.21).

and thus he often allegorized pagan myths, giving them a Christian slant. Especially prominent in Neoplatonic thought was the identification of Venus, the Roman goddess of love, with the Christian belief that "God is love." Botticelli, with the support of his patrons, notably the Medici family, made the Roman goddess the subject of two splendid paintings, *The Birth of Venus* (see Figure 12.5) and the *Primavera*. In this way, female nudes once again became a proper subject for art, though male nudes had appeared earlier, in Donatello's generation (see Figure 12.13).

In the 1480s, Florentine art was moving toward its culmination in the early works of Leonardo da Vinci (1452–1519). Leonardo is the quintessential representative of a new breed of artist: the Renaissance man,

who takes the universe of learning as his province. Not only did he defy the authority of the church by secretly studying human cadavers, but he also rejected the classical values that had guided the first generation of the early Renaissance. He relied solely on empirical truth and what the human eye could discover. His notebooks, encoded so as to be legible only when read in a mirror, recorded and detailed his lifelong curiosity about both the human and the natural worlds. In his habits of mind, Leonardo joined intellectual curiosity with the skills of sculptor, architect, engineer, scientist, and painter.

Among Leonardo's few surviving paintings from this period, the first version of *The Virgin of the Rocks* reveals both his scientific eye and his desire to create a

Figure 12.22   Leonardo da Vinci. *The Virgin of the Rocks.* **1483. Oil on panel, approx. 6′3″ × 3′7″. Louvre.**   Two slightly different versions of this work exist, this one dating from 1483 and a later one done in 1506 and on view in the National Gallery in London. The Louvre painting, with its carefully observed botanical specimens, is the culmination of the scientific side of the early Renaissance. The painting's arbitrary features—the grotto setting and the unusual perspective—point ahead to the High Renaissance; the dramatic use of chiaroscuro foreshadows the "night pictures" of the baroque period (see Figure 15.9).

haunting image uniquely his own (Figure 12.22). In this scene, set in a grotto or cave, Mary is portrayed with the infant Jesus, as a half-kneeling infant John the Baptist prays and an angel watches. The plants underfoot and the rocks in the background are a treasure of precise documentation. Nevertheless, the setting is Leonardo's own invention—without a scriptural or a traditional basis—and is a testimony to his creative genius.

Leonardo's plan of *The Virgin of the Rocks* shows the rich workings of his mind. Ignoring Brunelleschian perspective, Leonardo placed the figures his own way. He also adapted a fairly standard medieval pyramid design for arranging the figures in relation to one another; Mary's head is the pyramid's apex, and her seat and the other three figures anchor its corners. Within this pyramid, Leonardo creates a dynamic tension by using gestures to suggest a circular motion: The angel points to John the Baptist, who in turn directs his praying hands toward Jesus. A second, vertical, line of stress is seen in the gesturing hands of Mary, the angel, and Christ. Later artists so admired this painting that its pyramidal composition became the standard in the High Renaissance.

No prior artist had used **chiaroscuro** to such advantage as Leonardo does in *The Virgin of the Rocks*, causing the figures to stand out miraculously from the surrounding gloom. And unlike earlier artists, he colors the atmosphere, softening the edges of surfaces with a fine haze called **sfumato.** As a result, the painting looks more like a vision than a realistic scene. Leonardo's later works are part of the High Renaissance (see Chapter 13), but his early works represent the fullest expression of the scientific spirit of the second generation of early Renaissance painting.

While the Florentine painters were establishing themselves as the driving force in the early Renaissance, a rival school was beginning to emerge in Venice. The Venetian school, dedicated to exploring the effects of light and air and re-creating the sensuous effects of textured surfaces, was eventually to play a major role in the history of painting in Italy and the West. Founded by Giovanni Bellini, a member of a dynasty of painters, the Venetian school began its rise to greatness.

Giovanni Bellini (about 1430–1516), who trained in the workshop of his father, the late Gothic painter Jacopo Bellini (about 1400–1470), made Venice a center of Renaissance art comparable to Florence and Rome. Ever experimenting, always striving to keep up with the latest trends, he frequently reinvented himself. Nevertheless, there were constants in his approach to painting. He combined the traditions of the Florentine school (the use of linear perspective and the direct observation of nature) and those of the Flemish school (the technique of oil painting, the use of landscape as background, and the practice of religious symbolism). Made aware of the importance of atmosphere by the Venetian setting, Bellini also experimented with a range of colors, variations in color intensity, and changes in light. In particular, Bellini perfected the landscape format as a backdrop for foreground figures. A great teacher, Bellini founded a workshop where his methods were taught to young painters, including Giorgione and Titian (see Chapter 13).

An excellent example of Bellini's use of landscape may be seen in *St. Francis in Ecstasy* (Figure 12.23). This work, which depicts an ecstatic St. Francis displaying the stigmata (spontaneous appearance of open wounds, similar to those of the crucified Christ), shows Bellini's typical treatment of landscape: he divides the painting surface into zones, beginning with the area around the saint in the foreground, continuing through a second zone occupied by a donkey and a crane, to a third zone featuring Italian castles nestled into a hillside, and concluding with a fourth zone marked by a fortress and the sky. To heighten the realism, Bellini uses both a rich palette of colors and numerous objects to lead the viewer's eye into the vast distance. He adds to the realism by suffusing the scene with natural light. The landscape, with its vivid rendering of flora and fauna, expresses the Franciscan belief that humankind should live in harmony with the natural world (see Chapter 10).

Music

The changes affecting the cultural life of fifteenth-century Europe naturally also affected the music of the time. The impetus for a new musical direction, however, did not spring from classical sources, because ancient musical texts had virtually perished. Instead, the new music owed its existence to meetings between English and Continental composers at the church councils that were called to settle the Great Schism (see Chapter 11) and the Continental composers' deep regard for the seductive sound of English music. The English composer John Dunstable [DUHN-stuh-bull] (about 1380–1453) was a central figure in the new musical era that began

with the opening of the fifteenth century. Working in England and in France, he wrote mainly religious works—motets for multiple voices and settings for the Mass—that showed his increasingly harmonic approach to polyphony. The special quality of his music is its freedom from the use of mathematical proportion—the source of medieval music's dissonance.

Dunstable's music influenced composers in France, in Burgundy, and in Flanders, known collectively as the Franco-Netherlandish school. This school, which became the dominant force in fifteenth-century music, blended Dunstable's harmonics with northern European and Italian traditions. The principal works of this group were Latin **Masses** (Figure 12.24), or musical settings of the most sacred Christian rite; motets,

Figure 12.23 GIOVANNI BELLINI. *St. Francis in Ecstasy.* 1470s. Oil in tempera on panel, 49 × 55⅞". Frick Collection, New York. In the foreground, Bellini renders his vision of the grotto at Alvernia, a mountain retreat near Assisi, where St. Francis went to pray and fast for forty days, in imitation of Christ's forty days in the wilderness. The artist reinforces the scene's religious significance through various symbols, such as the grapevine and the stigmata, alluding to the sacrifice of Christ, and the donkey (in the middle distance), emblematic of Jesus's entry into Jerusalem before the Crucifixion.

Figure 12.24 **Mass at the Court of Philip the Good in Burgundy. Bibliothèque Royale de Belgique, Brussels. Fifteenth century.** This miniature painting shows a Mass being conducted at the court of Philip the Good of Burgundy (r. 1419–1467). Philip's patronage of the arts and music attracted leading painters and musicians to his court, which he conducted in cities across his holdings in modern-day Holland, Belgium, and France. John Dunstable, a composer of the Franco-Netherlandish school, was, on occasion, at the duke's court. In the painting, the priest prepares the sacraments at the altar, with his attendant behind him. On the right, the choir, dressed in white robes and gathered in front of the music stand, sings the Latin Mass. In the center background, dressed in black, stands a member of the Burgundian royal court, attended by two servants.

or multivoiced songs set to Latin texts other than the Mass; and secular *chansons,* or songs, with French texts, including such types as the French ballade and the Italian madrigal, poems set to music for two and six voices, respectively. Together, these polyphonic compositions established the musical ideal of the early Renaissance: multiple voices of equal importance singing **a cappella** (without instrumental accompaniment) and stressing the words so that they could be understood by listeners.

Between 1430 and 1500, the Continent's musical life was guided by composers from the Franco-Netherlandish school, the most important of whom was the Burgundian Josquin des Prez [zho-SKAN day PRAY] (about 1440–1521). Josquin was influential in his day and is now recognized as one of the greatest composers of all time. He was the first important composer to use music expressively so that the sounds matched the words of the text, thereby moving away from the abstract church style of the Middle Ages. One of his motets was described at the time as evoking Christ's suffering in a manner superior to painting. Josquin also began to organize music in the modern way, using major and minor scales with their related harmonies. All in all, he is probably the first Western composer whose music on first hearing appeals to modern ears.

Josquin's motet *Ave Maria . . . Virgo Serena* (Hail, *Mary . . . Serene Virgin;* 1502), a musical setting of a prayer to the Virgin Mary, shows the new expressive Renaissance style as it breaks away from the abstract music of the Middle Ages. Based on a Gregorian chant, the opening section quickly gives way to an innovative melody. Divided into seven sections, the motet employs shifting voice combinations in each part. The opening section uses polyphonic **imitation,** a musical technique that functions like a relay race. The soprano begins with the phrase *Ave Maria,* which, in turn, is restated by the alto, tenor, and bass. Next, there follows the second phrase, *gratia plena* ("full of grace"), sung to a different melody, which is also repeated among the voices. The musical effect in the first section is to create an overlapping tapestry of sound. The second section uses a duet of two upper voices, which is then imitated by the lower voices. Next, there is a four-voice ensemble, using expressive music that reflects the text, *nova laetitia* ("new joy"). Then, there follow four sections that shift voice groupings along with alterations in rhythms, ending with a brief pause. The motet ends with the group singing together in sustained chords: *"O mater Dei / memento mei. Amen,"* or "O Mother of God / remember me. Amen."

SUMMARY

Renaissance politics, like all politics, were messy. England and France struggled to recover from the Hundred Years' War. The papacy combated the conciliar movement (see Chapter 11) but failed to attain a high spiritual standard. The Italian cities trumpeted humane and republican values but degenerated into despotisms.

Politics notwithstanding, humanism triumphed in scholarship and the arts. Civic leaders and rich families weaned artists from exclusive dependence on clerical sponsors and religious topics, and the popes brought the Renaissance to Rome. Architects looked to classical antiquity for inspiration in style, technique, and subject matter. Artists captured the natural world as never before. Music grew more harmonic as it moved away from the abstract style practiced by medieval composers. Plato supplanted Aristotle as a guide for philosophers. Philosophers and other writers explored the unlimited potential of free people endowed with free will.

The Legacy of the Early Renaissance

Renaissance education continued, as in the Middle Ages, to be based on the seven liberal arts. Whereas the content and purpose of medieval education was religious and aimed at salvation, the "new learning" aimed to improve human beings in this world, to make them free, responsible and accountable, which has been the goal of liberal education until today. The Renaissance put the classics, not the Bible or the church fathers, at the heart of the curriculum, and until quite recently the classics have maintained that honored place in colleges and universities. When the great poet Alexander Pope (1688–1744) said, "The proper study of mankind is man," he was uttering a sentiment dear to Renaissance humanists. The Renaissance revival of classical architecture spawned a series of neoclassical revivals that have transformed cities, campuses, and private residences. When people speak of "Platonic relationships," they may not be aware that they are not referencing Plato himself but instead his Renaissance interpreter Marsilio Ficino. How many children who grew up watching the Teenage Mutant Ninja Turtles knew that the peaceful one, Donatello, was named for a Renaissance sculptor? In the 1920s and 1930s, African American artists and musicians in New York created a movement that came to be known as the "Harlem Renaissance." In the 1970s General Motors erected a complex of buildings in Detroit called the "Renaissance Center," intending to convey the "rebirth" of a depressed city. In 1981 Philip Lader, former U.S. ambassador to England, launched the "Renaissance Weekends" designed to bring together men and women distinguished in every walk of life for discussions on topics of universal significance. Nobel Prize–winning author Orhan Pamuk's beautiful novel *My Name Is Red* (1998) has as one of its central themes the tensions in Turkish culture generated by the adoption of Western styles. So the "Renaissance Man," with Leonardo da Vinci as the model, is still held up as an ideal—the person (man or woman to be sure) accomplished in every sort of knowledge.

The Renaissance Center, Detroit, Michigan. 1977–1981. John Portman, principal architect. Despite its modernist architecture, the seven buildings that comprise the Center, essentially a towering hotel and six office buildings, were labeled the "Renaissance Center" with the explicit intention of bringing a new birth to downtown Detroit. The very label signals the enduring significance of the word *Renaissance*.

KEY CULTURAL TERMS

Renaissance	early Renaissance style	relief	Mass
studia humanitatis	vanishing point	chiaroscuro	a cappella
humanism	pilaster	sfumato	imitation

MICHELANGELO. *Dying Slave.* **1513–1516. Marble, approx. 7′5″. Louvre, Paris.** Michelangelo's *Dying Slave* was commissioned by Pope Julius II as part of an ensemble of sculptures for his tomb. The slave's appearance—closed eyes and tilted head—suggests that he is in his death throes. Two symbols convey a moral lesson about the dangers of the earthly passions: the band around the chest and a barely sketched figure of a monkey, grasping the left shin.

13

The High Renaissance and Early Mannerism

1494–1564

Preview Questions

1. *What* were the major political developments of the High Renaissance and early mannerism?

2. *What* long-term economic and social trends were under way in the High Renaissance and early mannerism, and *how* did they help reshape Western life and culture?

3. *Compare* and *contrast* the High Renaissance and mannerist styles in the arts and humanities.

Between 1494 and 1564, two cultural styles flourished in Italy, making this one of the West's most brilliantly creative periods. In the **High Renaissance,** 1494–1520, classical principles reached a state of near perfection. After 1520, however, the Renaissance veered away from the humanistic values of classicism toward an antihumanistic vision of the world, labeled **mannerism,** because of the self-conscious, or "mannered," style adopted by its nonconformist artists and intellectuals. Mannerism continued to evolve until 1600, but its first phase ended in 1564, with the death of Michelangelo.

This two-stage cultural flowering occurred as Western life was undergoing rapid changes. Italy's city-states fought one another or fended off foreign invaders, making the Italian peninsula a battle zone. France, England, and Spain emerged as modern nation-states, with only one major power—the Hapsburg Empire—retaining its feudal nature. Rising prosperity, technological changes, and new social trends added to the turbulence of this period.

Michelangelo's *Dying Slave* embodies many of the trends between 1494 and 1564. The statue's idealized traits—the perfectly proportioned figure, the restrained facial expression, and the gentle S-curve of the body—are hallmarks of the High Renaissance. But the figure's overall sleekness and dramatic arm movements—probably based on one figure in the first-century CE *Laocoön Group* (see Interpreting Art on page 99), newly rediscovered in 1506—were portents of early mannerism. The medium in which this statue is carved, Carrara marble from northern Italy, was highly prized by Michelangelo—a taste he shared with ancient Roman sculptors. *Dying Slave*, commissioned for Pope Julius II's tomb, ended up in the possession of the French king, Francis I, with Michelangelo's blessing—thus underscoring another trend of this period: the rise of the modern nation-state.

THE RISE OF THE MODERN SOVEREIGN STATE

The most important political development during this period was the emergence of powerful sovereign states in France, England, and Spain. This process, already under way in the late fifteenth century (see Chapter 11), now began to influence foreign affairs. The ongoing rivalries among these three states led to the concept of the balance of power—a principle that still dominates politics today.

From 1494 to 1569, Europe's international political life was controlled, either directly or indirectly, by France and Spain. France's central role resulted from the policies of its strong Valois kings, who had governed since the early 1300s. Spain's fortunes soared during this era, first under the joint rule (1474–1504) of Ferdinand V and Isabella and then under Charles I (r. 1516–1556). In 1519 Charles I was elected Holy Roman emperor as Charles V (he was of the royal house of Hapsburg), thus joining the interests of Spain and the Holy Roman Empire until his abdication in 1556. England did not get involved in Continental affairs during this time.

After 1591 the French and the Spanish rulers increasingly dispatched their armies into the weaker states, where they fought and claimed new lands. As the sovereign monarchs gained power, the medieval dream of a united Christendom—pursued by Charlemagne, the popes, and the Holy Roman emperors—slowly faded away. These new states were strong because they were united around rulers who exercised increasing central control. Although most kings claimed to rule by divine right, their practical policies were more important in increasing their power. They surrounded themselves with ministers and consultative councils, both dependent on the crown. The ministers were often chosen from the bourgeois class, and they advised the rulers on such weighty matters as religion and war and also ran the developing bureaucracies. The bureaucracies in turn strengthened centralized rule by extending royal jurisdiction into matters formerly administered by the feudal nobility, such as the justice system.

The crown further eroded the status of the feudal nobles by relying on mercenary armies rather than on the warrior class, a shift that began in the late Middle Ages. To pay these armies, the kings had to consult with representative bodies, such as Parliament in England, and make them a part of the royal government.

The Struggle for Italy, 1494–1529

Italy's relative tranquility, established by the Peace of Lodi in 1454, was shattered when the French invaded in 1494 and asserted a hereditary claim to land. For the next thirty-five years, Italy was a battleground where France, Spain, and the Holy Roman Empire fought among themselves, as well as with the papacy and most of the Italian states. The French repeatedly invaded Italy in these years, only to be repelled by varied combinations of local states and foreign rulers. Ironically, the French kings, during these campaigns, grew enamored of the Italian Renaissance, bringing its artistic and intellectual ideals to their court (Figure 13.1).

A far-reaching political effect of this fight for Italy's future was to launch a series of wars between France and the Holy Roman Empire, a struggle that pitted the old Europe against the new. The Holy Roman Empire, ruled by Charles V of the Hapsburg line, was a decentralized relic from the feudal past. France, led by the bold Francis I (r. 1515–1547) of the royal house of Valois, was the epitome of the new sovereign state.

The first Hapsburg-Valois war (1522–1529) was the only one fought in Italy. In 1527 the troops of Charles

Figure 13.1   Jean Clouet. *Francis I.* Ca. 1525. Oil on panel, 37³/₄ × 29¹/₈″. **Louvre, Paris.** During his thirty-two-year reign, Francis I embarked on an extensive artistic program, inspired by the Italian Renaissance, to make his court the most splendid in Europe. Under his personal direction, Italian artworks and artists, including Leonardo da Vinci, were imported into France. Ironically, this rather stylized portrait by Jean Clouet, Francis's chief court artist, owes more to the conventionalized portraits of the Gothic style than it does to the realistic works of the Italian Renaissance.

V ran riot in Rome, raping, looting, and killing. This notorious sack of Rome had two major consequences: (1) it cast doubt on Rome's ability to control Italy—long a goal of the popes—for it showed that secular leaders no longer respected the temporal power of the papacy; and (2) it ended papal patronage of the arts for almost a decade, thus weakening Rome's role as a cultural leader. It also had a chilling effect on artistic ideals and contributed to the rise of mannerism.

In 1529 the Treaty of Cambrai ended the first phase of the Hapsburg-Valois rivalry. And, after years of warfare, Italy was divided and exhausted. Some cities suffered nearly irreparable harm. The Florentine republic fared the worst; in the 1530s, its Medici family resumed control of the city, but they were little more than puppets of foreign rulers who now controlled much of the peninsula. The only Italian state to keep its political freedom was Venice, which became the last haven for artists and intellectuals in Italy for the rest of the sixteenth century.

Charles V and the Hapsburg Empire

By 1530 the struggle between the Valois and the Hapsburgs had shifted to central Europe. The French felt hemmed in by the Spanish to the south, the Germans to the east, and the Dutch to the north—peoples all ruled by the Hapsburg emperor Charles V. In French eyes, Charles had an insatiable appetite for power and for control of the Continent. In turn, the Hapsburg ruler considered the French king a land-hungry upstart who stood in the way of a Europe united under a Christian prince. In 1559, after a number of exhausting wars and a series of French victories, the belligerents signed the Treaty of Cateau-Cambrésis, which ushered in a brief period of peace (Map 13.1).

Charles V, the man at the center of most of these events, lived a life filled with paradoxes (Figure 13.2). Because of the size of his empire, he was in theory one of the most powerful rulers ever to live; but in actuality, again because of the vastness of his lands, he never quite succeeded in gaining complete control of his empire. In some ways, he was the last medieval king; in other ways, he foreshadowed a new age driven by sovereign kings, standing armies, diplomatic agreements, and strong religious differences.

Charles V's unique position at the center of Europe's political storm was the result of a series of timely deaths and births and politically astute arranged marriages. These circumstances enabled the Hapsburg rulers to accumulate vast power, wealth, and land. Charles was born in 1500 to a German father and a Spanish mother, and he was the grandson of both the Holy Roman emperor Maximilian I and the Spanish king Ferdinand V. He held lands in present-day Spain, France, Italy, Germany, and Austria—along with much

Figure 13.2 TITIAN. *Charles V with a Dog.* Ca. 1533. Oil on canvas, 6′3″ × 3′8″. Prado, Madrid. Titian's full-length, standing portrait of Charles V was painted when the Hapsburg emperor was at the height of his power. By rendering the "ruler of the world" in contrapposto, his fingers casually holding the collar of his dog, Titian endows the emperor with a natural grace. The lighting that illuminates Charles from the dark background and the breathless hush that seems to envelop the man and dog are trademarks of Titian's style.

of the New World. By 1519 Charles V—simultaneously Charles I of Spain—ruled the largest empire the world has ever known.

For most of his life, Charles traveled from one of his possessions to another, fighting battles, arranging peace treaties, and attempting to unify his empire of disparate holdings. His attention was often divided, and he found himself caught between two powerful

Learning Through Maps

MAP 13.1 EUROPEAN EMPIRE OF CHARLES V, CA. 1556

This map shows the extensive holdings of the Holy Roman emperor Charles V, also known as King Charles I of Spain. *1. **Notice** the lands inherited and the lands gained by Charles V. 2. **Identify** the boundaries of the Holy Roman Empire. 3. **Who** were Charles V's enemies within the Holy Roman Empire and elsewhere? 4. **Consider** the challenges Charles V faced in governing his widely scattered and culturally diverse empire. 5. **What** impact did geography have on France's attitude toward Charles V's empire?*

foes—especially the French to the west and the Ottoman Turks to the east—who drained both his personal energies and his imperial resources.

Within the Holy Roman Empire, the princes of the German principalities often took advantage of Charles's prolonged absences and his preoccupation with the French and the Turks. Their ability to gain political power at the emperor's expense increased after Martin Luther's revolt and the beginning of the Protestant Reformation (see Chapter 14). Charles also weakened his

own position by his contradictory policies: at times he angered the disaffected German princes by meddling in their affairs and condemning Lutheran doctrines, and at other times he angered the popes by making concessions to the Protestants.

Exhausted and disillusioned by his inability to prevail in Europe, Charles abdicated in 1556 and retired to a monastery. His brother Ferdinand (r. 1558–1564) took control of the German-Austrian inheritance and was elected Holy Roman emperor. His son Philip

Figure 13.3 *Siege of Vienna.* **British Library.** In spring, 1529, Sultan Suleyman launched an assault against Christian Europe from Muslim-dominated Bulgaria. Marching through Hungary and eastern Austria, the Ottoman army was finally stopped at the gates of Vienna in late September 1529. As news of the Turkish invasion spread across Europe, German and Spanish troops poured into Vienna, shoring up its walls, while the Viennese prepared for a long siege. Twenty-five days later, in mid-October, the Turks abruptly retreated. This failed siege marked the Turks' deepest advance into central Europe. It also led to a 150-year struggle between the Ottomans and the West, years filled with mutual suspicion and reciprocal attacks. In this battle scene, the unknown artist depicts both the Turks and the Western forces armed with the latest firearms and military equipment.

(r. 1556–1598) assumed control of the Spanish Hapsburg holdings, including Spain, the New World territories, and the Netherlands. Thus ended Charles's vision of a united Christendom, which had turned into a nightmare of endless meetings, gory battles, and false hopes of peace and unity.

The West and Islam: The Rise of the Ottoman Empire

As the High Renaissance dawned in 1494, Islam's presence in Western Europe had just ended, with the surrender of the last Muslim state in Granada, Spain. Southeastern Europe was a different situation. There, the Ottoman Turks had been expanding their territory since the founding of their empire in 1399. A series of Ottoman rulers deftly reworked the decaying and splintered Muslim world into a well-ordered military and political power. After conquering the feeble Byzantine Empire in 1453, Sultan Mehmet II moved his capital to Constantinople and assumed a new title, *Kayser-I Rum* (Roman emperor)—thereby asserting his claim over the collapsed Roman world.

Under Suleyman the Magnificent (r. 1520–1566), the Ottoman Empire reached its zenith, as it expanded from its base in Anatolia into central Europe. With much of mainland Greece already under Ottoman rule by 1500, Suleyman's troops marched into and conquered the modern states of Bulgaria, Romania, and Hungary, before being stopped at Vienna in 1529 (Figure 13.3).

• • • •

The defeat at Vienna weakened the Ottoman Empire and inaugurated its more than 150 years of bitter rivalry with the West. In 1571 the European Holy League, a coalition of Roman Catholic powers, defeated a Muslim fleet at the Battle of Lepanto, off western Greece—a victory that blocked Ottoman advance into Italy. In 1583 the British signed the first trade treaty with the Ottoman Empire—a potent symbol of the new economic reality. The Western European states, with overseas colonies—notably, England, France, the Netherlands, Portugal, and Spain—were now the leaders in world trade. Further weakening the states on the periphery of the new economy was the discovery of gold and silver in the New World, thus causing an upward price spiral. Unsurprisingly, after 1600, the Ottoman Empire was beset by declining prosperity, a weakened central government, and ethnic unrest among its peoples.

ECONOMIC EXPANSION AND SOCIAL DEVELOPMENTS

By 1500, Europe had nearly recovered from the plague; the sixteenth century continued to be a time of growing population and increasing prosperity. The center of trade shifted from the Mediterranean to the Atlantic coast, making cities like London and Antwerp financial and mercantile capitals. Skilled craftspeople turned out quality products, and enterprising merchants distributed these finished goods across much of northwestern Europe. The daring sailing expeditions of this period provided new raw materials from America. Innovative manufacturing methods spurred economic growth and expanded worldwide markets.

Demographics, Prosperity, and the Beginning of a Global World

Modern research indicates that the population of Europe increased from about forty-five million in 1400 to sixty-nine million in 1500 and to about eighty-nine million by 1600. Society grew more urban, as people migrated from the countryside to urban areas and the number of cities with populations over one hundred thousand rose from five to eight between 1500 and 1600. Rome, for example, grew from about fifty thousand in 1526—the year before the sack—to one hundred thousand by the end of the century.

Prosperity that resulted from economic expansion brought a higher standard of living for the urban middle class, but throughout much of the century prices rose faster than wages. Those who were not profiting from increased economic growth, such as poor peasants and impoverished nobles living on unproductive farms, suffered the most. In areas of Europe hardest hit by inflation or agricultural and commercial stagnation, economic crises often became intertwined with social and religious issues that intensified long-standing regional and local differences.

Yet the boom offered economic opportunities to some. Many merchants made fortunes and provided employment for others. These merchants and the bankers who offered loans were also accumulating capital, which they then invested in various commercial activities. The wars of Charles V were financed by wealthy bankers operating in a well-organized money market. The amassing of surplus capital and its reinvestment ushered in the opening phase of commercial capitalism, which laid the foundation for Europe's future economic expansion.

Global Encounter: The First European Explorers

Spurring on this rising prosperity were the abundant raw materials overseas along with potential markets for Europe's finished products. Portugal sent out the first wave of explorers under the patronage of Prince Henry the Navigator (1394–1460). As governor of the Algarve region in southern Portugal, he founded a school of navigation, encouraged voyages and trade down the west coast of Africa, and hoped to convert the natives to Christianity. By 1487, Portuguese ships had rounded the Cape of Good Hope, and in 1498, Vasco da Gama [VAS-co da GAH-ma] (about 1460–1520) sailed up the east coast of Africa, crossed the Indian Ocean—with the aid of a Muslim mariner—and landed at Calicut (modern Kolkata, formerly Calcutta) India. Da Gama returned to Portugal two years later, his ships laden with spices and pepper. During the 1500s, the Portuguese conquered towns along Africa's east coast and established trading posts on the coasts of modern Indonesia and China and in Nagasaki, Japan. They monopolized the spice and pepper trade, tried to control the sea routes between Europe and the Far East, and extended their holdings into the New World—Brazil.

Although da Gama's achievements were overshadowed by those of later explorers, he was immortalized in Portugal's national memory by its first great poet, Luis Vaz de Camões [LU-ees VAZH th KAE-moish] (about 1524–1580) (Figure 13.4). Camões modeled his epic poem, *The Lusiads* (named for Lusus, the mythical founder of Portugal) on Virgil's *Aeneid*. As in the *Aeneid*, Camões portrays da Gama as he encounters enemies (usually Muslims), meets a friendly king to whom he recounts the glorious history of his land, and returns home a hero. In Camões's poem, Portugal is now a great power, a harbinger of Europe's future, a savior of Europe from foreign enemies, and a global missionary for the Christian faith.

• • • • •

Portugal's day in the sun was brief. In 1580 the Portuguese Empire began to decline when it passed under

 Figure 13.4   Portrait of *Luis Vaz de Camões*. 16th–17th century. Oil on canvas. Portuguese School. Museu Nacional de Arte Antigua, Lisbon, Portugal. In this anonymous portrait, Luis Vaz de Camões is dressed as a soldier and wears the laurel crown of the poet—an honorific symbol from classical culture. The loss of his eye, he wrote, taught him about the expense of war and reminded him of the price he paid for his personal heroism and his country's empire.

Spanish rule, until 1640. At the same time, Spain, the Netherlands, England, and France commenced a bitter rivalry, competing for overseas markets and colonies. After 1650, this rivalry had a dramatic impact on the European economy and social life. The influx of gold and silver into Europe from Spain's mines in Central and South America began to drive prices up. And the introduction of New World farm products led to new manufactured goods, for example, cotton and the rise of the textile industry, while tobacco, cocoa, the tomato, and the potato altered consumer habits.

Technology

The High Renaissance was a period of economic and social transformation, stimulated by advances in technology. Two groups who contributed to this dynamic period were the inventors and tinkerers whose devices and discoveries opened the world for exploration. An especially powerful agent of change was improved firearms, which rendered old forms of warfare obsolete and, gradually, altered the balance of power among the rising nation-states.

Sailing   Europe, starting in 1492, began to explore and then conquer much of the world. The pretext was the spread of the Christian faith, but the motivation was gold, commodities, and other riches. Based on knowledge of the sea and the winds, sailing technology was now advanced for navigational instruments, ships, and sails. Europe had entered the Age of Exploration and, in rapid order, came to dominate the globe until the mid–twentieth century.

The historic developments in navigational instrument technology and seamanship were

- the magnetic compass, to determine direction,
- the astrolabe, to determine latitude, and
- an increased understanding of the path of prevailing winds and currents in the ocean.

These advances empowered mariners to sail farther and farther from Europe. In 1522 a heroic milestone was reached when the first Westerners circumnavigated the globe: the surviving crew of the ships commanded by the Portuguese navigator Fernao de Magalhaes [mah-GAHL-yeesh] (in English, Ferdinand Magellan) (about 1480–1521).

 The dramatic innovations in sailing ship technology included the following:

- The *galley* (a long warship powered by oars and sails; loaded with armed boarding parties) became dominant in naval warfare, after 1400.
- The galley was modified into a square-rigged ship fitted with deck cannons, after 1450.
- The Portuguese and the Spanish perfected a cargo carrying galley called the *caravel* (a three-masted vessel with a small roundish hull and a high stern and bow).
- The caravel was replaced by the larger *galleon*, with greater maneuverability and firepower—the mainstay of Europe's global commerce and navies, from 1550 to 1700.

So successful were the galleons that the outcome of Europe's wars was often determined by battles at sea, as in England's triumph over the Spanish Armada in 1588.

Warfare   One of the most far-ranging agents of technological change occurred with firearms, including

- the cannon (early 1300s); first, as siege cannons, packed with gunpowder and stones or bits of metal—used to batter down walls of castles and towns,
- the lightweight, rustfree bronze cannon, which quickly replaced the iron cannon, and
- arsenals and foundries, turning out guns and shot.

As these advances unfolded, Europe's first arms race began: the Spaniards held the lead, from about 1500, but the Dutch and English moved ahead after 1600. Amassing weapons became a central need for each sovereign state, while new strategies and tactics were reshaping the nature of warfare.

Among those who understood how new weaponry was transforming warfare was the artist-scientist Leonardo da Vinci (see the section "Painting" on page 334). He designed catapults, giant crossbows, and cannons. He calculated the trajectories of missiles fired by mortars and cannons and drew plans for armed land vehicles, underwater craft, and flying machines. As a military engineer, he advised city planners on fortifications. Leonardo's quest for knowledge led him not only to invent engines of war but also to speculate on how these destructive devices brutalized humans and destroyed nature (Figure 13.5).

Science and Medicine

While less pronounced in their immediate impact than the technological innovations, advances in science during this age would have long-lasting effects.

In the natural sciences, Leonardo again led the way, in observation, practices, and understanding. His genius was directed toward the study of nature in all of its forms, especially the human body. In what he learned, he perhaps surpassed all those innovators who had gone before him. He dissected human cadavers and took meticulous notes, describing organs, bones, and muscles, and drawing detailed anatomical studies. Although his writings and anatomical drawings were not made public during his lifetime, Leonardo's contributions to the understanding of the human body and the function of its skeleton, muscles, and organs reflected the Renaissance's desire to understand ourselves and the world.

Between 1400 and 1600, Italy's schools of medicine continued to be among the best in Europe. During this time, Italy took another innovative step in medical care through the creative work of local administrators in the largest cities, officials who personified another characteristic of the Italian Renaissance, **civic humanism.** Civic humanism was an outgrowth of the Renaissance's cultivation of the culture of ancient Greece and Rome. Italy's civic administrators—dedicated men who were trained in the Greek and Latin classics—saw themselves as modern equivalents of civil servants in an ancient *polis,* or city. As such, they tried to establish responsible and efficient city governments. One of their projects, for example, which had a strong impact on medical care, was the setting up of citywide health boards composed of physicians and medical personnel, to deal with public health issues, especially plague and other contagious

Figure 13.5 LEONARDO DA VINCI. *Men Struggling to Move a Large Cannon.* Ca. 1488. Pen and ink, drawing. Windsor, Royal Library. Leonardo's drawing is more than just a scene of a sixteenth-century iron foundry. While much can be learned from its details—the use of winches and pulleys, the tools and equipment, and the differing types of cannons—the artist is also showing how machines are coming to control human life. Leonardo was fascinated by the machines of war, but he also understood their destructive force, as when he wrote: "With its breath it will kill men and ruin cities and castles."

diseases. Although lacking knowledge of the germ theory of disease, the health boards could build on practices that had worked in the past. For example, starting in the 1400s, they used controls and quarantines to isolate plague and prevent the spread of this and other contagious diseases among the populace. The new city health boards had jurisdiction over such matters as keeping records of each death and its cause, inspecting food markets, regulating city health conditions, and supervising burials, cemeteries, hospitals, and even beggars and prostitutes.

FROM HIGH RENAISSANCE TO EARLY MANNERISM

The characteristics of High Renaissance style were largely derived from the visual arts. Led by painters, sculptors, and architects who worshiped ancient

Timeline 13.1   ITALIAN CULTURAL STYLES BETWEEN 1494 AND 1564

1494		1520				1564
	High Renaissance		Early Mannerism			
French invasion of Italy	**1508–1512** Michelangelo's Sistine Chapel ceiling frescoes	**1519** Death of Leonardo da Vinci **1520** Death of Raphael	**1532** Publication of Machiavelli's *The Prince*	**1536–1541** Michelangelo's *Last Judgment* fresco	**1550** Palladio's Villa Rotonda	**1564** Death of Michelangelo

classical ideals, notably those of late-fifth-century BCE Greece, the High Renaissance was filled with images of repose, harmony, and heroism. Under the spell of classicism and the values of simplicity and restraint, artists sought to conquer unruly physical reality by subjecting it to the principle of a seemingly effortless order.

The visual arts dominated the High Renaissance, but literary figures also contributed to this era. From classicism, the High Renaissance authors appropriated two of their chief aesthetic aims, secularism and idealism. Like their ancient predecessors, historians showed that contemporary events arose from human causes rather than from divine action—unmistakable evidence of a mounting secular spirit. Actually, secularism more deeply affected the writing of history than it did the arts and architecture, where church patronage and religious subjects still held sway. A rising secular consciousness can also be seen in the popular handbooks on manners that offered advice on how to become a perfect gentleman or lady. Although they have no counterpart in ancient literature, these books have the classical quality of treating their subject in idealized terms.

What distinguished the High Renaissance preoccupation with the classical past from the early Renaissance's renewed interest in ancient matters was largely a shift in creative sensibility. The early Renaissance artists, in the course of growing away from the late Gothic style, had invented new ways of recapturing the harmonious spirit of ancient art and architecture. The geniuses of the next generation, benefiting from the experiments of the early Renaissance, succeeded in creating masterpieces of disciplined form and idealized beauty. The High Renaissance masters' superb confidence allowed them to produce works that were in harmony with themselves and the physical world—a hallmark of classical art.

In spite of its brilliance, the High Renaissance existed for only a fleeting moment in the history of Western culture—from the French invasion of Italy in 1494 until the death of Raphael in 1520 (preceded by the death of Leonardo in 1519) (Timeline 13.1). In this era, the Renaissance popes spared no expense in their patronage of the arts and letters. After the disasters of the fourteenth century, the papacy seemed to have restored the church to the vitality that it had enjoyed in the High Middle Ages. In reality, however, the popes of the early sixteenth century presided over a shaky ecclesiastical foundation. To the north, in Germany, a theological storm was brewing that would eventually split Christendom and destroy the papacy's claim to rule the Christian world. This religious crisis, coupled with increasing tendencies to exaggeration in High Renaissance art and with the sack of Rome in 1527, contributed to the development of mannerism and its spread through Italy and later across western Europe (Figure 13.6).

Mannerist painters, sculptors, and architects abandoned two of the guiding principles of the High Renaissance: the imitation of nature and the devotion to classical ideals. In contrast to High Renaissance masters, mannerist painters deliberately chose odd perspectives that called attention to the artists' technical effects and their individual points of view. Mannerist sculptors, rejecting idealism, turned and twisted the human figure into unusual and bizarre poses to express their own notions of beauty. Likewise, mannerist architects toyed with the emotions and expectations of their audience by designing buildings that were intended to surprise. Behind the mannerist aesthetic lay a questioning or even a denial of the inherent worth of human beings and a negative image of human nature, along with a sense of the growing instability of the world.

Literature

The leading writers of the High Renaissance in Italy drew their themes and values from the Greco-Roman classics. Their artistic vision sprang from the classical virtue of *humanitas*—a term coined by Cicero in antiquity that can be translated as "humanity," meaning the wisdom, humor, tolerance, and passion of the person who has good sense. With some reservations, these writers also believed in classicism's basic tenet that human nature is inherently rational and good. One of the finest expressions of High Renaissance literature

Figure 13.6 *Pope Clement VII Besieged in Castel Sant'Angelo.* **1554. Engraving, 6¹⁄₆ × 9″. Kunsthalle, Hamburg.** This engraving shows the imperial army of Charles V besieging Castel Sant'Angelo, one of the pope's palaces, during the sack of Rome in 1527. The engraver's sympathies with the pope are revealed by the huge statues of St. Peter (with keys, on the right) and St. Paul (with sword, on the left), who look on disapprovingly. Pope Clement VII, imprisoned in his own fortress, peers down on the scene from a balcony at the center top.

was the poetry of the artist Michelangelo, whose love poems and other lyrical verses adhered closely to the classical tradition. But, even as High Renaissance literature was enjoying its brief reign, the mannerist works of the Florentine author Niccolò Machiavelli began to appear, and at the heart of his thought is an anticlassical spirit. Despite his education in classicism and his strict rationalism, Machiavelli concluded that the human race is irremediably flawed. The contrast between the idealizing spirit of the High Renaissance and the antitraditionalist views of mannerism can be clearly seen by placing the work of the diplomat and courtier Baldassare Castiglione beside that of Machiavelli. Each wrote a book that can fairly be described as a manual of behavior—but there the resemblance ends.

Michelangelo   Like Leonardo da Vinci, Michelangelo embodied the "Renaissance man," the well-rounded cultural ideal of this period. Along with remarkable achievements in architecture, painting, and sculpture, Michelangelo was a dedicated poet. More than three hundred of his short (usually fourteen-line) poems survive, written mainly between 1532 and 1548. His poems, although virtually unknown in his day, did circulate among friends and patrons. In one instance, one poem reached a larger audience, when it served as the focus of an admirer's address to the Florentine Academy, in 1547.

In his poetry, Michelangelo adopted either the Petrarchan sonnet (see Chapter 12) or the **madrigal**—an irregular verse form, not to be confused with the English madrigal (see "Music in Late-Sixteenth-Century Italy and England," Chapter 14). Classicism in his High Renaissance style included the Petrarchan sonnet and the Neoplatonic philosophy that he had absorbed as a youth in Florence, at the Medici court. In his verses, Platonic love, while originating in physical beauty, ultimately leads to the divine. A product of his era, Michelangelo also wrote verses about his life as a working artist and as a man facing aging and death.

Castiglione   The reputation of Castiglione [kahs-teel-YOH-nay] (1478–1529) rests on *The Book of the Courtier* or, simply, *The Courtier,* one of the most influential books of the High Renaissance. Intended for Italian court society, *The Courtier* was published in 1528. Translated into most Western languages, it quickly became the bible of courteous behavior for Europe's upper classes until about 1800.

A Mantuan by birth, Castiglione (Figure 13.7) based his guide to manners on life at the north Italian court of Urbino, where, between 1504 and 1517, he lived under the patronage of its resident duke, Guidobaldo da Montefeltro (see Figure 12.1). Impressed by the graceful conversations of his fellow courtiers and especially taken with the charms of Urbino's duchess, Elisabetta, Castiglione was moved to memorialize his experiences in writing. *The Courtier* is composed as a dialogue, a literary form originated by Plato and favored by Cicero. Castiglione's dialogue is set in Urbino and peopled with actual individuals for whom he invents urbane and witty conversations that suit their known characters. Despite this realistic touch, his book's overall tone is definitely idealistic and hence expressive of High Renaissance style.

Castiglione's idealism shines forth most clearly in the sections in which the invited company try to define the perfect courtier, or gentleman. Under Duchess Elisabetta's eye, the guests debate which aspect of the ideal gentleman's training should take precedence: education in the arts and humanities or skill in horsemanship and swordplay. Eventually, both sides agree that the ideal courtier should be proficient in each of these areas. A sign that the Renaissance had raised the status of painting and sculpture was the group's expectation that a gentleman be knowledgeable about both of these art forms.

The Courtier also describes the perfect court lady. In the minds of the dialogue participants, the ideal lady is a civilizing influence on men, who would otherwise be crude. To that end, the perfect lady should

Figure 13.7 RAPHAEL. *Baldassare Castiglione.* 1514. Oil on canvas, 32¼ × 26½". Louvre, Paris. Castiglione, author of *The Book of the Courtier*, was memorialized in this handsome portrait by the High Renaissance painter, Raphael. Elegantly groomed and completely at ease, Castiglione appears here as the age's ideal courtier—an ideal that he helped to establish.

be a consummate hostess, charming, witty, graceful, physically attractive, and utterly feminine. She ought to be well versed in the same areas as a man, except for athletics and the mastery of arms. With these social attributes, the cultivated lady can then bring out the best in a courtier. But she must not seem his inferior, for she contributes to society in her own way.

Castiglione's book turned away from medieval values and led his followers into the modern world. First, Castiglione argued that social relations between the sexes ought to be governed by Platonic love—a spiritual passion that surpassed physical conquest—and thus he rejected medieval courtly love and its adulterous focus. Second, he reasoned that women in society should be the educated equals of men, thereby sweeping away the barrier that had been erected when women were excluded from medieval universities. In the short run, the impact of Castiglione's social rules was to keep women on a pedestal, as courtly love had done. But for the future, his advice allowed women to participate actively in every aspect of society and encouraged their education in much the same way as men's.

Machiavelli   In contrast to Castiglione's optimism, the Florentine Machiavelli [mak-ee-uh-VEL-ee] (1469–1527) held a negative view of human nature and made human weakness the central message of his writings. If *The Courtier* seems to be taking place in a never-never land where decorum and gentility are the primary interests, Machiavelli returns the reader to political reality. His mannerist cynicism about human weakness sprang from wounded idealism, for life had taught him that his early optimism was wrong. In his writings, the bleak view of human nature is meant to restore sanity to a world that he thought had gone mad.

Except for Martin Luther (see Chapter 14), Machiavelli left a stronger imprint on Western culture than any other figure who lived between 1494 and 1564. Machiavelli's most enduring contribution was *The Prince,* which inaugurated a revolution in political thought. Rejecting the medieval tradition of framing political discussions in Christian terms, Machiavelli treated the state as a human invention that ought not necessarily conform to religious or moral rules. He began the modern search for a science of politics that has absorbed political thinkers and policymakers ever since.

Machiavelli's career in sixteenth-century Italy, like that of many writers in antiquity, was split between a life of action and a life of the mind. Between 1498 and 1513, he served the newly reborn Florentine republic as a senior official and diplomat, learning statecraft firsthand. During these turbulent years, he was particularly impressed by the unscrupulous Cesare Borgia, Pope Alexander VI's son. In 1513, after the fall of the Florentine republic to the resurgent Medici party, Machiavelli was imprisoned, tortured, and finally exiled to his family estate outside the city. There, in exile, he wrote the small work known as *The Prince* (1513), which circulated in manuscript until after his death. In 1532 it was finally published.

Machiavelli had several motives in writing this masterpiece. Despairing over Italy's dismemberment by the French and the Spanish kings, he hoped the book would inspire an indigenous leader to unify the peninsula and drive out the foreigners. Enlightened by his personal experience in Florence's affairs, he wanted to capture in writing the truth of the politics to which he had been a witness. And, of equal importance, by dedicating *The Prince* to the restored Medici ruler, he hoped to regain employment in the Florentine state. Like other writers in this age, Machiavelli could not live by his wits but had to rely on secular or religious patronage.

Machiavelli's work failed in its immediate objectives: the Medici despot brushed it aside, and Italy remained

Figure 13.8 Leonardo da Vinci. *The Last Supper.* (Restored.) 1495–1498. Oil-tempera on wall, 15′1⅛″ × 28′10½″. Refectory, Santa Maria delle Grazie, Milan. Classical restraint is one of the defining characteristics of this High Renaissance masterpiece. Instead of overwhelming the viewer with distracting details, Leonardo reduces the objects to a minimum, from the austere room in which the meal is being celebrated to the simple articles on the dining table. The viewer's gaze is thereby held on the unfolding human drama rather than on secondary aspects of the scene.

fragmented until 1870. But as a work that exposed the ruthlessness needed to succeed in politics, *The Prince* was an instant, though controversial, success. The book was denounced by religious leaders for its amoral treatment of political power and read secretly by secular rulers for its sage advice. In the prevailing worldview of the 1500s, an era still under the sway of Christian ideals, the name "Machiavelli" became synonymous with dishonesty and treachery, and the word Machiavellianism was coined to describe the amoral notion that "the end justifies the means."

From the modern perspective, this negative valuation of Machiavelli is both too simplistic and too harsh. Above all else he was a clear-eyed patriot anguished by the tragedy unfolding in Italy. *The Prince* describes the power politics that the new sovereign states of France and Spain were pursuing in Italian affairs. Machiavelli realized that the only way to rid Italy of foreigners was to adopt the methods of its successful foes. Seeing his countrymen as cowardly and greedy, he had no illusions that a popular uprising would spring up and drive out Italy's oppressors. Only a strong-willed monarch, not bound by a too-restrictive moral code, could bring Italy back from political chaos.

The controversial heart of Machiavelli's treatise was the section that advised the ruler on the best way to govern. Machiavelli counseled the prince to practice conscious duplicity, since that was the only way

to maintain power and to ensure peace—the two basic goals of any state. By appearing virtuous and upright while acting as the situation demanded, the prince could achieve these fundamental ends.

Painting

In the arts, the period between 1494 and 1564 was preeminently an age of painting, though several sculptors and architects created major works in their respective fields. The classical values of idealism, balance, and restraint were translated by High Renaissance painters into harmonious colors, naturally posed figures with serene faces, realistic space and perspectives, and perfectly proportioned human bodies. After 1520, mannerist tendencies became more and more evident, reflected in abnormal subjects, contorted figures with emotionally expressive faces, and garish colors.

Leonardo da Vinci The inauguration of the High Renaissance in painting is usually dated from Leonardo's *The Last Supper,* completed between 1495 and 1498 (Figure 13.8). Commissioned by the Dominican friars of the church of Santa Maria delle Grazie in Milan, *The Last Supper* heralded the lucidity and harmony that were the essence of High Renaissance style. In executing the fresco, Leonardo unfortunately made use of a flawed technique, and the painting began to flake during his lifetime. Over the centuries, the work has been touched up frequently and restored seven times, with the most recent restoration completed in 1999. Nevertheless, enough of his noble intention is evident to ensure the reputation of *The Last Supper* as one of the best-known and most beloved paintings of Western art.

Leonardo's design for *The Last Supper* is highly idealized—a guiding principle of the High Renaissance. The fresco depicts the moment when Jesus says that one of the twelve disciples at the table will betray him (Matthew 26:21). Ignoring the tradition that integrated this symbolic meal into an actual refectory, Leonardo separated the scene from its surroundings so that the figures would seem to hover over the heads of the clergy as they ate in their dining room. Idealism is also evident in Leonardo's straightforward perspective. The artist makes Jesus the focal center by framing him in the middle window and locating the vanishing point behind his head. In addition, the arrangement of the banqueting party—Jesus is flanked by six followers on either side—gives the painting a balanced effect. This harmonious composition breaks with the medieval custom of putting the traitor Judas on the opposite side of the table from the others.

A final idealistic touch may be seen in the way that Leonardo hides the face of Judas, the third figure on Jesus's right, in shadow while illuminating the other figures in bright light. Judas, though no longer seated apart from the rest, can still be readily identified, sitting cloaked in shadows, reaching for the bread with his left hand, and clutching a bag of silver—symbolic of his treason—in the other hand. For generations, admirers have found Leonardo's fresco so natural and inevitable that it has become the standard version of this Christian subject.

Leonardo's setting and placement of the figures in *The Last Supper* are idealized, but his depiction of the individual figures is meant to convey the psychological truth about each of them. Jesus is portrayed with eyes cast down and arms outstretched in a gesture of resignation, while on either side a tumultuous scene erupts. As the disciples react to Jesus's charge of treason, Leonardo reveals the inner truth about each one through bodily gestures and facial expressions. Beneath the visual tumult, however, the artistic rules of the High Renaissance are firmly in place. Since neither biblical sources nor sacred tradition offered an ordering principle, Leonardo used mathematics to guide his arrangement of the disciples. He divides them into four groups of three figures; each set in turn is composed of two older men and a younger one. In his conception, not only does each figure respond individually, but also each interacts with other group members.

Besides mastering a narrative subject like *The Last Supper*, Leonardo created a new type of portrait when he painted a half-length view of the seated *Mona Lisa*

Figure 13.9 Leonardo da Vinci. *Mona Lisa.* 1503. Oil on panel, 30¼ × 21″. Louvre, Paris. Leonardo's *Mona Lisa*, a likeness of the wife of the wealthy Florentine merchant Giocondo, illustrates the new status of Italy's urban middle class. This class was beginning to take its social cues from the fashionable world of the courts, the milieu described by Castiglione. Leonardo treats his middle-class subject as a model court lady, imbuing her presence with calm seriousness and quiet dignity.

(Figure 13.9). As the fame of this work spread, other painters (and, later, photographers) adopted Leonardo's half-length model as a basic format for portraits. Avoiding the directness of *The Last Supper*, Leonardo hints at the sitter's demure nature through her shy smile and the charmingly awkward gesture of having the fingers of her right hand caress her left arm. In her face, celebrated in song and legend, he blends the likeness of a real person with an everlasting ideal to create a miraculous image. Further heightening the painting's eternal quality, the craggy background isolates the figure in space and time, in much the same way that the grotto functioned in Leonardo's *Virgin of the Rocks* (see Figure 12.22). Finally, he enhances the *Mona Lisa*'s mystery by enveloping the subject in the smoky atmosphere called *sfumato*—made possible by the oil medium—which softens her delicate features and the landscape in the background.

During the High Renaissance, Leonardo's great works contributed to the cult of genius—the high regard, even reverence, that the age accorded to a few select artists, poets, and intellectuals. *The Last Supper* earned Leonardo great fame while he was alive. The history of the *Mona Lisa* was more complicated, since it was unseen while he lived and found among his effects when he died in 1519. After his death, as the *Mona Lisa* became widely known, first as a possession of the king of France and later as a jewel in the Louvre collection, Leonardo was elevated to membership among the immortals of Western art.

Michelangelo   While Leonardo was working in Milan during most of the 1490s, Michelangelo Buonarroti [my-kuh-LAN-juh-lo bwo-nahr-ROH-tee] (1475–1564)

was beginning a career that would propel him to the forefront of first the Florentine and later the Roman Renaissance, making him the most formidable artist of the sixteenth century. Michelangelo's initial fame rested on his sculptural genius, which manifested itself at the age of thirteen when he was apprenticed to the early Renaissance master Ghirlandaio and then, one year later, taken into the household of Lorenzo the Magnificent, the Medici ruler of Florence. In time, Michelangelo achieved greatness in painting and architecture as well as in sculpture, but he always remained a sculptor at heart.

Michelangelo's artistic credo was formed early, and he remained faithful to it over his long life. Sculpture, he believed, was the art form whereby human figures were liberated from the lifeless prison of their surrounding material. In this sense, he compared the sculptor's creativity with the activity of God—a notion that would have been judged blasphemous in

prior Christian ages. Michelangelo himself, unlike the skeptical Leonardo, was a deeply pious man given to bouts of spiritual anxiety. His art constituted a form of divine worship.

Central to Michelangelo's artistic vision was his most celebrated image, the heroic nude male. Like the ancient Greek and Roman sculptors whose works he studied and admired, Michelangelo viewed the nude male form as a symbol of human dignity. In the High Renaissance, Michelangelo's nudes were based on classical models, with robust bodies and serene faces. But in the 1530s, with the onset of mannerism, the growing spiritual crisis in the church, and his own failing health, Michelangelo's depiction of the human figure changed. His later nudes had distorted body proportions and unusually expressive faces.

In 1508 Michelangelo was asked by Pope Julius II (pope 1503–1533) to decorate the Sistine Chapel ceiling. Michelangelo tried to avoid this commission, claim-ing that he was a sculptor and without expertise in frescoes, but the pope was unyielding in his insis-tence. The chapel had been built by Julius II's uncle, Pope Sixtus IV (pope 1471–1484), in the late 1400s, and most of the walls had already been covered with fres-coes. Michelangelo's frescoes were intended to bring the chapel's decorative plan closer to completion.

The challenge of painting the Sistine Chapel ceiling was enormous, for it was almost 70 feet from the floor, its sides were curved downward, necessitating numer-ous perspective changes, and its area covered some 5,800 square feet. Michelangelo overcame all these diffi-culties, teaching himself fresco technique and working for four years on scaffolding, to create one of the glories of the High Renaissance and unquestionably the great-est cycle of paintings in Western art (Figure 13.10).

Michelangelo, probably with the support of a papal adviser, designed a complex layout (Figure 13.11) for the ceiling frescoes that combined biblical narrative,

Figure 13.10 Michelangelo. **Sistine Chapel Ceiling. (Restored.) 1508–1512. Full ceiling 45 × 128'. The Vatican.** Michelangelo's knowledge of architecture prompted him to paint illusionistic niches for the Hebrew prophets and the pagan sibyls on either side of the nine central panels. Neoplatonism inspired his use of triangles, circles, and squares, for these geometric shapes were believed to hold the key to the mystery of the universe. These various framing devices give visual order to the more than three hundred figures in his monumental scheme.

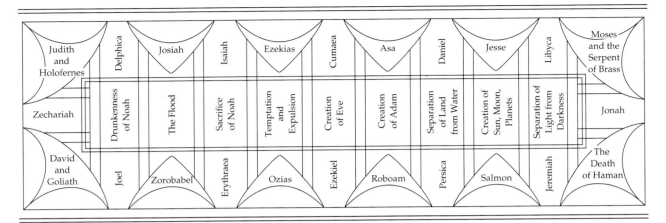

Figure 13.11   Plan of Ceiling Frescoes, Sistine Chapel. 1508–1512. The paintings on the Sistine Chapel ceiling may be grouped as follows: (1) the central section, which presents the history of the world from the Creation (called "The Separation of Light from the Darkness") through the "Drunkenness of Noah"; (2) the gallery of portraits on both sides and at either end, which depict biblical prophets and pagan oracles; and (3) the four corner panels depicting Jewish heroes and heroines who overcame difficulties to help their people survive.

theology, Neoplatonist philosophy, and classical allusions. In the ceiling's center, running from the altar to the rear of the chapel, he painted nine panels that illustrate the early history of the world, encompassing the creation of the universe, the fall of Adam and Eve, and episodes in the life of Noah. Framing these biblical scenes are nude youths, whose presence shows Michelangelo's belief that the male form is an expression of divine power.

On either side of the center panels, Michelangelo depicted Hebrew prophets and pagan sibyls, or oracles—all foretelling the coming of Christ (see Interpreting Art photo). The pagan sibyls represent the Neoplatonist idea that God's word was revealed in the prophecies of pre-Christian seers. At the corners of the ceiling, he placed four Old Testament scenes of violence and death that had been allegorized as foreshadowing the coming of Christ. Michelangelo unified this complex of human and divine figures with an illusionistic architectural frame, and he used a plain background to make the figures stand out.

The most famous image from this vast work is a panel from the central section, *The Creation of Adam* (Figure 13.12), based on a passage in the book of Genesis. Michelangelo reduces the scene to a few details, in accordance with the High Renaissance love of simplicity. Adam, stretched out on a barely sketched bit of ground, seems to exist in some timeless space. Depicted as a pulsing, breathing human being, he possesses wondrous vitality in human flesh, the likes of which had not been seen in Western art since the ancient Greeks. In a bold move, Michelangelo ignored the Genesis story that told of God's molding Adam from dust. Instead, the artist painted Adam as half-awakened and reaching to God, who will implant a

soul with his divine touch—an illustration of the Neoplatonic idea of flesh yearning toward the spiritual.

By the 1530s, Michelangelo was painting in the mannerist style, reflecting his disappointment with Florence's loss of freedom and his own spiritual torment. In this new style, he replaced his heroic vision with a fearful view of the world. A compelling example of this transformation is *The Last Judgment,* painted on the wall behind the Sistine Chapel's altar. This fresco conveys his own sense of sinfulness as well as humanity's future doom (Figure 13.13). Executed twenty-five years after the ceiling frescoes, *The Last Judgment,* with its images of justice and punishment, also reflects the crisis atmosphere of a Europe divided into militant Protestant and Catholic camps. In the center of the fresco, Michelangelo depicts Jesus as the divine and final judge, with right arm raised in a commanding gesture. At the bottom of the fresco, the open graves yield up the dead, and the saved and the damned (on Jesus's right and left, respectively) rise to meet their fate.

In *The Last Judgment,* Michelangelo abandons the architectural framework that had given order to the ceiling frescoes. Instead, the viewer is confronted with a chaotic surface on which a circle of bodies seems to swirl around the central image of Jesus. Michelangelo elongates the bodies and changes their proportions by reducing the size of the heads. There is no classical serenity here; each figure's countenance shows the anguish provoked by this dreaded moment. Faced with judgment, some figures gesture wildly while others look beseechingly to their Savior. In this mannerist masterpiece, simplicity has been replaced by exuberant abundance, and order has given way to rich diversity.

Interpreting Art

Composition Three figures (a female, in foreground, and two boys, in midground), a draped chair, and a large open book are crowded into an illusionistic niche.

Architectural Elements The niche, defined by decorated columns on either side and a running band of lines in the rear, provides a space to frame the central figures.

Female Body The muscular shoulders and back reflect Michelangelo's practice of using male models for female subjects. The resulting image deviates from classical ideals of feminine beauty.

Anatomy Michelangelo was fascinated by the way muscles and bones interacted beneath the skin. In this image, he presents the sibyl, with her back to the viewer, her upraised arms holding her book of sayings, and her lower body balanced on her toes.

Religious Perspective Michelangelo's overall plan, blending Christian theology and Neoplatonic thought, is meant to validate the Christian view of creation and human history.

Color Color is used to heighten the image's three-dimensional look, by using primary colors for the bodies, clothing, and draperies so that they will stand out against the muted hues of the background.

MICHELANGELO. *The Libyan Sibyl.* (Restored.) Detail of the Sistine Chapel ceiling. 1508–1512. 12′11½″ × 12′6″. The Vatican. Michelangelo's subject—the Libyan Sibyl—was an ancient oracle, based in Libya. Neoplatonic thought—which contributed to the plan for the Sistine Chapel ceiling—taught that God, however imperfectly, spoke to all peoples. Thus, the voice of God could be heard in the sibyl's utterances. By 1500 the church had accepted the Libyan Sibyl, along with eleven other pagan seers, as divinely inspired prophetesses foretelling the coming of Christ.

1. **Composition** *How* does Michelangelo place the Libyan Sibyl within the architecture of the Sistine Chapel?

2. **Context** *Discuss* the ways this painting is representative of early-sixteenth-century Rome.

3. **Religious Perspective** *Why* is a pagan figure included within this Christian artwork?

4. **Economic Perspective** *Discuss* the role played by wealth in the creation of this painting.

5. **Cultural Perspective** *What* does this painting suggest about Michelangelo's attitude toward women and his relationship with them?

Raphael The youngest of the trio of great High Renaissance painters is Raphael [RAFF-ee-uhl] Santi (1483–1520). Lacking Leonardo's scientific spirit and Michelangelo's brooding genius, Raphael nevertheless had such artistry that his graceful works expressed the ideals of this style better than did those of any other painter. Trained in Urbino, Raphael spent four years (1504–1508) in Florence, where he absorbed the local painting tradition, learning from the public works of both Leonardo and Michelangelo. Inspired

Figure 13.12   MICHELANGELO. *The Creation of Adam.* **Detail (restored) of the Sistine Chapel ceiling. 1511.**
9′5″ × 18′8″. The Vatican. One of the most celebrated details of this fresco is the outstretched fingers of
God and Adam that approach but do not touch. By means of this vivid symbol, Michelangelo suggests that a
divine spark is about to pass from God into the body of Adam, electrifying it into the fullness of life. The image
demonstrates the restraint characteristic of the High Renaissance style. The Vatican's restoration of the Sistine
Chapel frescoes has revealed the brilliant colors of the original, apparent in this detail.

by what he saw, Raphael developed his artistic ideal of
well-ordered space in which human beauty and spatial harmony were given equal treatment.

Moving to Rome, Raphael had an abundance of
patrons, especially the popes. The secret of Raphael's
success was his talent for blending the sacred and the
secular, and in an age when a pope led troops into battle or went on hunting parties, this gift was appreciated
and rewarded. Perhaps Raphael's most outstanding
work in Rome was the cycle of paintings for the *stanze,*
or rooms, of the Vatican apartment—one of the finest
patronage plums of the High Renaissance. Commissioned by Julius II, the *stanze* frescoes show the same
harmonization of Christianity and classicism that Michelangelo brought to the Sistine Chapel ceiling.

Raphael's plan for the four walls of the Stanza della
Segnatura in the papal chambers had as its subjects
philosophy, poetry, theology, and law. Of these, the
most famous is the fresco devoted to philosophy called
The School of Athens (Figure 13.14). In this work, Raphael
depicts a sober discussion among a group of ancient
philosophers drawn from all periods. Following Leonardo's treatment of the disciples in *The Last Supper,*
Raphael arranges the philosophers in groups, giving
each scholar a characteristic gesture that reveals the essence of his thought. For example, Diogenes sprawls on
the steps apart from the others—a vivid symbol of the

arch Cynic's contempt for his fellow man. In the right
foreground, Euclid, the author of a standard text on geometry, illustrates the proof of one of his theorems. In
his careful arrangement of this crowd scene, Raphael
demonstrates his mastery of ordered space.

The School of Athens has a majestic aura because of
Raphael's adherence to classical forms and ideas. The
architectural setting, with its rounded arches, medallions, and coffered ceilings, is inspired by classical
ruins and also perhaps by contemporary structures.
Perfectly balanced, the scene is focused on Plato and
Aristotle, who stand under the series of arches at the
painting's center. Raphael reinforces their central position by placing the vanishing point just above and
between their heads. The two thinkers' contrasting
gestures symbolize the difference between their philosophies: Plato, on the left, points his finger skyward,
suggesting the world of the Forms, or abstract thought,
and Aristotle, on the right, motions toward the earth,
indicating his practical and empirical method. Raphael also uses these two thinkers as part of his ordering scheme to represent the division of philosophy
into the arts and the sciences. On Plato's side, the poetic thinkers are gathered under the statue of Apollo,
the Greek god of music and lyric verse; Aristotle's half
includes the scientists under the statue of Athena, the
Greek goddess of wisdom.

Figure 13.13 MICHELANGELO. *The Last Judgment.* 1536–1541. 48 × 44′. Sistine Chapel, the Vatican.
This *Last Judgment* summarizes the anticlassicism that was sweeping through the visual arts. Other painters studied this fresco for inspiration, borrowing its seemingly chaotic composition, its focus on large numbers of male nudes, and its use of bizarre perspective and odd postures as expressions of the mannerist sensibility. This fresco has been restored, its colors returned to the vivid primary colors of Michelangelo's original design and the draperies removed (they had been added during the Catholic Reformation).

Figure 13.14 RAPHAEL. *The School of Athens.* 1510–1511. Fresco, 18 × 26′. **Stanza della Segnatura, the Vatican.** Much of Raphael's success stemmed from the ease with which he assimilated the prevailing ideas of his age. For instance, the posture of the statue of Apollo in the wall niche on the left is probably derived from Michelangelo's *Dying Slave* (see the chapter-opening photo). For all his borrowings, however, Raphael could be very generous, as indicated by the conspicuous way he highlights Michelangelo's presence in this fresco: the brooding genius sits alone in the foreground, lost in his thoughts and oblivious to the hubbub swirling about him.

Of even greater fame than Raphael's narrative paintings are his portraits of the Virgin Mary, or his Madonna series–admired for their exquisite sweetness and harmonious composition. Raphael's Madonnas clearly show the influence of Leonardo, whose Virgin and child paintings were well known by then (see Figure 12.22). Like many of the Madonna series, Raphael's *Alba Madonna* (Figure 13.15) is composed in a low pyramidal shape, a design borrowed from Leonardo. But, otherwise, *The Alba Madonna* differs from Leonardo's approach, which placed the Virgin and child either enthroned or in an elaborate setting. Here, Raphael's figures are set within a plain Italian landscape, thus creating a sense of timelessness. The Virgin's head functions as the apex of a pyramid, its left side defined by the leaning body of the infant John the Baptist, and its right side defined by the Virgin's outstretched left arm and billowing cloak. Raphael adds a dash of mystery by having all three figures stare at the cross in Jesus's hand—the symbol of crucifixion. This prophetic touch—showing the Virgin to be aware of her son's future sacrifice—helps explain this painting's alternate title, *Madonna of Humility.*

The Venetian School: Giorgione and Titian   Venice maintained its autonomy during the High Renaissance both politically and culturally. Despite the artistic pull of the Roman and Florentine schools, the Venetian artists stayed true to their Byzantine-influenced tradition of sensual surfaces, rich colors, and theatrical lighting. The two greatest painters of the Venetian High Renaissance were Giorgione [jor-JO-na] (about 1477–1510), who was acknowledged to be Venice's premier artist at the end of his life, and Titian [TISH-uhn] (about 1488–1576), who in his later years was revered as Europe's supreme painter.

Little is known of Giorgione's life until the last years of his brief career. A student of the Bellini workshop, he won early fame, indicated by the rich private and public commissions he was awarded. Although only a few of his works survive, Giorgione's influence on the course of European art was substantial. His two major innovations, the female nude and the landscape, contributed to the growing secularization of European painting. These developments helped to make Venetian art distinctive from that of Rome and Florence.

The Tempest (Figure 13.16) is probably his best-known work. Breaking free of the Bellinis' influence, Giorgione created a dramatic landscape, framed on

Figure 13.15 RAPHAEL. *The Alba Madonna.* Ca. 1510. Oil on wood panel transferred to canvas, overall (diameter) 37'³/₁₆". National Gallery of Art, Washington, D.C. The painting's provenance illustrates how works of art survive. Paolo Giovio (1483–1552), an Italian scholar and historian, commissioned the painting—a **tondo,** or circular painting— which he planned to donate to a church. In the eighteenth century, it was acquired by the House of Alba, an aristocratic Spanish family, whose ownership gave the painting its designated name. In 1836, Nicholas I, the Russian czar, bought the painting, which hung in the Hermitage Museum in St. Petersburg until 1931, when the Soviet government sold it to an American millionaire, Andrew Mellon. In 1937 Mellon donated it to the National Gallery of Art, Washington, D.C.

Figure 13.16 GIORGIONE. *The Tempest.* 1505. Oil on canvas, 31¹/₄ × 28³/₄". Galleria dell'Accademia, Venice. Giorgione's mysterious painting evokes the moment— called an "anxious hush"—that sometimes attends the prelude to a violent thunderstorm. Giorgione creates this tense mood through atmospheric effects that suggest a gathering storm: billowing clouds; a flash of lightning and its watery reflection; and, in particular, the stark color contrasts between the harshly lighted buildings and the somber hues of earth, sky, and river. The mood is also heightened by the presence of two vulnerable figures, especially the nursing mother who gazes quizzically at the viewer, about to be engulfed by the storm. The painting has a typical Venetian feature in its carefully rendered textures—flesh, cloth, wood, stone, and foliage.

Figure 13.17 TITIAN. *Martyrdom of St. Lawrence.* **1550s. Oil on canvas, 16′5¹/₂″ × 9′2″. Chiesa dei Gesuiti, Venice.** Even though Titian worked within the classical rules required by the High Renaissance style, he sometimes deviated from its strict regularity, as in this painting. The temple's columns recede along a diagonal line, creating a sense of deep space in the foreground; within this space, he arranged objects in a triangular outline with the celestial light source at the apex. By using diagonal and triangular lines, as he often did in his religious works, Titian was able to achieve dramatic and emotional effects without forfeiting coherence or meaning. He heightened this effect by bathing the human figures in the light from the sky and the glow from the torches and the fire underneath St. Lawrence.

the left by a soldier and on the right by a partly clothed mother nursing a child, that did not allude to mythology, the Bible, or allegorical stories. Whereas Bellini's *St. Francis in Ecstasy* (see Figure 12.23) made the saint the focus of the painting, in *The Tempest* the framing figures are overshadowed by the menacing storm. Thus, Giorgione's landscape, freed of storytelling elements, becomes the subject and should be appreciated on its own terms.

Titian's paintings were prized not only for their easy grace and natural lighting—characteristics of

the Venetian Renaissance—but also for their dramatic use of color (see Figure 13.2). Titian's adherence to the principles of High Renaissance style is evident in such narrative paintings as his *Martyrdom of St. Lawrence* (Figure 13.17). According to tradition, Lawrence, a Spaniard, served as a deacon in charge of the church's treasures in Rome. When commanded to turn this wealth over to the civil authorities, he instead assembled the poor and distributed the treasures to them. For this act of defiance, the Romans condemned and executed him in 258. Later, as St. Lawrence, he became the patron saint of the poor and downtrodden.

Titian's careful arrangement of this scene of torture and martyrdom reflects his commitment to the principle of simplicity. In the foreground, he shows St. Lawrence being roasted on a grill; to the right, he depicts a pagan temple, rendered in sharply receding perspective, thereby framing the saint's death scene. The juxtaposition of the dying St. Lawrence and the classical temple reminds the viewer that the pagan Romans had failed to eradicate Christianity. Titian's subtle modulations of color, which create a sense of harmony, made him a leading "colorist"—an artist concerned more with color than with form—and an inspiration to future generations of painters.

The School of Parma: Parmigianino Parma, in northern Italy, was another center of High Renaissance art, but the city's best-known artist is a founder of mannerism, Parmigianino [pahr-mee-jah-NEE-noh] (1503–1540). The *Madonna with the Long Neck* shows Parmigianino's delight in ambiguity, distortion, and dissonance and his love of eccentric composition (Figure 13.18). Mary is portrayed with sloping shoulders and long arms in the manner of Botticelli, and her sensuous figure is not quite hidden under diaphanous draperies—a disturbing mix of sacred and profane love. A similar confusion exists in the depiction of the infant Christ: the bald baby Jesus appears more dead than alive, so that the subject invokes the Pietà image of the dead Christ stretched on his mother's lap along with the image of the Virgin and Christ child. On the left, five figures stare in various directions. In the background, unfinished columns and an old man reading a scroll, perhaps an allusion to biblical prophecies of Jesus's birth, add to the feeling of multiple focuses and contradictory scales. Unlike the art of the High Renaissance, which offered readily understood subjects, this mannerist painting, with its uneasy blend of religious piety and disguised sexuality, is enigmatic.

Sculpture

Michelangelo's sculptures, just like his paintings, helped to define High Renaissance style. An early sculpture that helped to inaugurate this style was the *Pietà* executed when he was twenty-one (Figure 13.19).

Figure 13.18 PARMIGIANINO. *Madonna with the Long Neck.* 1534–1540. Oil on panel, 7′1″ × 4′4″. **Uffizi Gallery, Florence.** This Madonna by Parmigianino is one of the landmark works in the mannerist style. Ignoring classical ideals, Parmigianino exaggerates the Virgin's body proportions, especially the slender hands and long neck, and elongates the body of the sleeping Jesus. This anticlassical portrait was greatly at odds with the prevailing High Renaissance image of the Madonna established by Raphael.

The touching subject of the *Pietà*—Mary holding the body of the dead Christ—struck a responsive chord in Michelangelo, for he created several variations on the *Pietà* theme during his lifetime.

The first *Pietà,* executed in 1498–1499, about the same time as Leonardo's *Last Supper,* shows Michelangelo already at the height of his creative powers. He has captured completely a bewildering sense of loss in his quiet rendering of Mary's suffering. Everything about the sculpture reinforces the somber subject: the superb modeling of Jesus's dead body, with its heavy head and dangling legs; Mary's outstretched gown, which serves as a shroud; and Mary's body, burdened by the weight of her son. Like some ancient funeral monument, which the *Pietà* brings to mind, this sculpture of Mary and Jesus overwhelms the viewer with its sorrowful but serene mood.

In 1501, two years after finishing the *Pietà,* Michelangelo was given the commission by the city of Florence

Figure 13.19 MICHELANGELO. *Pietà.* 1498–1499. Marble, ht. 5′8¹/₂″. **St. Peter's, the Vatican.** This *Pietà* is the only one of Michelangelo's sculptures to be signed. Initially, it was exhibited without a signature, but, according to a legend, when Michelangelo overheard spectators attributing the statue to a rival sculptor, he carved his signature into the marble strap that crosses Mary's chest.

SLICE OF LIFE

Artists and Their Critics: Michelangelo's Strategy

Giorgio Vasari
FROM *LIFE OF MICHELANGELO*

Medieval artists were guild members, that is, skilled craftspeople with little social status. In the following vignette, Michelangelo is portrayed as one of a new breed: a proud Renaissance artist, ready to take on critics, even the head of the Florentine republic. The vignette's author, Giorgio Vasari (1511–1574), who studied painting with Michelangelo, is known today primarily as a biographer of Renaissance artists.

Some of his [Michelangelo's] friends wrote to him from Florence urging him to return there as it seemed very probable that he would be able to obtain the block of marble that was standing in the Office of Works. . . . The marble was eighteen feet high, but unfortunately an artist . . . had started to carve a giant figure, and had bungled the work so badly that he had hacked a hole between the legs and left the block completely botched and misshapen. So the wardens of Santa Maria del Fiore (who were in charge of the undertaking) threw the block aside and it stayed abandoned for many years. . . . However, Michelangelo measured it again and calculated whether he could carve a satisfactory figure from the block by accommodating its attitude to the shape of the stone. Then he made up his mind to ask for it. Piero Soderini [the elected head of the Florentine republic] and the wardens decided that they would let him have it, as being something of little value, and telling themselves that since the stone was of no use to their building, either botched as it was or broken up, whatever Michelangelo made would be worthwhile. So Michelangelo made a wax model of the young David with a sling in his hand; this was intended as a symbol of liberty for the Palace, signifying that just as David had protected his people and governed them justly, so whoever ruled Florence should vigorously defend the city and govern it with

justice. He began work on the statue in the Office of Works of Santa Maria del Fiore, erecting a partition of planks and trestles around the marble; and working on it continuously he brought it to perfect completion, without letting anyone see it. . . .

When he saw the David in place Piero Soderini was delighted; but while Michelangelo was retouching it he remarked that he thought the nose was too thick. Michelangelo, noticing that [Soderini] was standing beneath the Giant and that from where he was he could not see the figure properly, to satisfy him climbed on the scaffolding by the shoulders, seized hold of a chisel in his left hand, together with some of the marble dust lying on the planks, and as he tapped lightly with the chisel let the dust fall little by little, without altering anything. Then he looked down at [Soderini], who had stopped to watch, and said:

"Now look at it."

"Ah, that's much better," replied Soderini. "Now you've really brought it to life."

And then Michelangelo climbed down, feeling sorry for those critics who talk nonsense in the hope of appearing well informed.

Interpreting This Slice of Life

1. *Why* was Michelangelo eager to work on this block of marble?
2. *What* does this story reveal about the character of Michelangelo?
3. *What* trick did Michelangelo play on Soderini?
4. *Speculate* as to the motive behind Michelangelo's behavior.
5. *Do* artists today show some of the same traits as those of Michelangelo in this piece? *Explain*.

for the sculpture that is generally recognized as his supreme masterpiece, the *David* (Figure 13.20). He was eager for this commission because it allowed him to test himself against other great sculptors who had tackled this subject, such as Donatello in the early Renaissance (see Figure 12.13). Moreover, Michelangelo, a great Florentine patriot, identified David with the aggressive spirit of his native city. His *David* was instantly successful, and the republic of Florence

adopted the statue as its civic symbol, placing the work in the open square before the Palazzo Vecchio, the town hall. Damage to the statue through weathering and local unrest caused the civic leaders eventually to house Michelangelo's most famous sculpture indoors, where it remains today.

Michelangelo's *David*, rather than imitating Donatello's partly clothed and somewhat effete version, portrays the young Jewish warrior as a nude, classical

Figure 13.20 MICHELANGELO. *David.* **1501–1504. Marble, ht. 14′3″. Accademia, Florence.** Michelangelo's colossal *David*— standing more than 14 feet tall—captures the balanced ideal of High Renaissance art. The "closed" right side with its tensed hanging arm echoes the right leg, which supports the figure's weight; in the same way, the "open" left side with its bent arm is the precise counterpart of the flexed left leg. Further tension arises from the contrast between David's steady stare and the readiness of the right fist, which holds the stone. Through these means, Michelangelo reinforces the image of a young man wavering between thought and action.

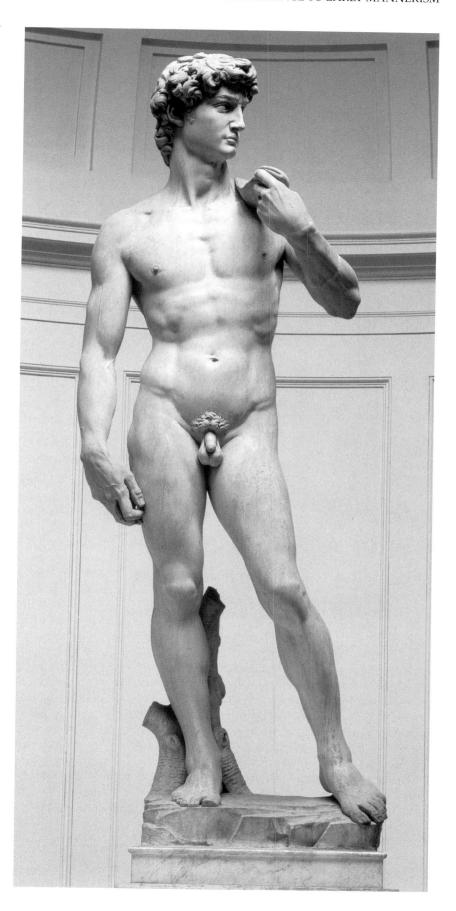

Figure 13.21   MICHELANGELO. *Pietà*. Before 1555. Marble, ht. 7'8". **Santa Maria del Fiore, Florence.** The rage that seemed to infuse Michelangelo's mannerist vision in *The Last Judgment* appears purged in this *Pietà*—the work he was finishing when he died at the age of eighty-eight. Mannerist distortions are still present, particularly in the twisted body of the dead Christ and the implied downward motion of the entire ensemble. But the gentle faces suggest that serenity has been restored to Michelangelo's art.

Michelangelo's later sculpture is mannerist in style, as are his later paintings. A second *Pietà*—with Christ, Mary, Mary Magdalene, and Joseph of Arimathea— shows the change in his depiction of the human form (Figure 13.21). In this somber group, Michelangelo's anticlassical spirit is paramount. Jesus's body is elongated and unnaturally twisted in death; the other figures, with great difficulty, struggle to support Jesus's dead weight. But rather than detracting from the sculpture's impact, the awkward body adds to the scene's emotional interest—an aim of mannerist art, which did not trust the viewer to respond to more orderly images. Joseph, the rich man who, according to the Gospel, donated his own tomb to Jesus, has Michelangelo's face—a face that is more a death mask than a human countenance.

Architecture

The architectural heir to Alberti in the early sixteenth century was Donato Bramante [brah-MAHN-tay] (1444–1514), who became the moving force behind the High Renaissance in architecture. Trained as a painter, Bramante rejected the reigning building style, called **scenographic,** in which buildings are composed of discrete, separate units. Instead, by concentrating on space and volume, Bramante created an architecture that was unified in all its components and that followed the rules of the classical orders.

The clearest surviving expression of Bramante's architectural genius is the Tempietto, or little temple, in Rome (Figure 13.22). This small structure was designed both as a church, seating ten worshipers, and as a building marking the site of the martyrdom of St. Peter. Copied from the circular temples of ancient Rome, this small domed building became the prototype of the central plan church popularized in the High Renaissance and later.

Bramante's design for the Tempietto sprang from ancient classical principles. Foremost was his belief that architecture should appeal to human reason and that a building should present a severe appearance, not seek to please through specially planned effects. Bramante also thought that a building should be unified like a piece of sculpture and that ornamentation should be restricted to a few architectural details.

hero. Taking a damaged and abandoned block of marble, Michelangelo carved the colossal *David* as a muscular adolescent with his weight gracefully balanced on the right leg, in classical contrapposto. The *David* perfectly represents Michelangelo's conception of sculpture; imagining a human figure imprisoned inside marble, he simply used his chisel to set it free.

Michelangelo also made minor deviations from classical principles in his rendition of David in the name of higher ideals, just as ancient artists had done. David's large hands, for example, are outside classical proportions and suggest a youth who has yet to grow to his potential. And David's furrowed brow violates the classical ideal of serene faces but reflects his intense concentration.

Figure 13.22   Bramante. Tempietto. After 1502. Marble, ht. 46′; diameter of colonnade 29′. San Pietro in Montorio, Rome. Bramante's Tempietto is the earliest surviving High Renaissance building and an exquisite example of this style. Fashioned from pure classical forms, the building is almost devoid of decoration except for architectural features, and the separate parts—dome, cylindrical drum, and base—are brought into a harmonious whole.

In accordance with this artistic credo, the Tempietto functions like a work of sculpture; it is raised on a pedestal with steps leading up to its colonnaded porch. In the absence of sculptural decorations, the temple's exterior is accented with architectural details: the columns; the **balustrade,** or rail with supporting posts; and the dome with barely visible ribs. The proportions of its various features, such as the ratio of column widths to column heights, were based on ancient mathematical formulas. Unfortunately, the plan to integrate the small temple into a circular courtyard of a nearby church was never completed—thus deviating from the classical rule that buildings should relate to their surrounding space. Despite the absence of this crowning touch, the Tempietto is one of the jewels of the High Renaissance.

Bramante had been commissioned by Pope Julius II to rebuild St. Peter's Basilica, the world's most famous church, but he died before his plans could be carried out. The supervision of the rebuilding of the church fell to other architects; eventually Michelangelo, at the age of seventy-one, was given this vital task. From 1546 until his death in 1564, Michelangelo, among his other artistic duties, was occupied with St. Peter's, especially with the construction of the dome. Although the dome was completed after his death and slightly modified, it remains Michelangelo's outstanding architectural monument and a splendid climax to his career.

Michelangelo's sculptural approach to architecture was similar to Bramante's. To integrate the dome with the rest of St. Peter's, Michelangelo used double Corinthian columns as a unifying agent. Because the facade was altered in the 1600s, Michelangelo's dome is best observed from the southwest (Figure 13.23). Beginning at ground level, the Corinthian order serves as an artistic feature that gives harmony to the building. Sometimes as columns, sometimes as pilasters, and sometimes as ribs, the double Corinthian units move up the walls, eventually up the dome's drum, and up the dome itself.

St. Peter's plan shows that Michelangelo the architect differed from Michelangelo the painter and sculptor. In painting and sculpture, he had by the 1530s become a mannerist in his use of exaggeration and expressive effects. But in architecture, he stayed faithful to the High Renaissance and its ideal of harmonious design.

The preeminent architect of the mannerist style was Andrea di Pietro (1508–1580), known as Palladio [pah-LAHD-yo], whose base was Vicenza, in northern Italy. The name Palladio derives from Pallas, a name for Athena, the goddess of wisdom. Palladio's artistic creed was rooted in classicism, but his forte was the richly inventive way in which he arranged the classical elements of a building to guarantee surprise. He played with the effects of light and shadow, adding

Figure 13.23 MICHELANGELO. **Dome of St. Peter's. View from the southwest. 1546–1564. (Completed by Giacomo della Porta, 1590.) Ht. of dome 452′. Rome.** Its harmonious design and its reliance on classical forms made Michelangelo's dome an object of universal admiration when it was completed in 1590, after his death. From then to the present day, other architects have used his dome as a model, hoping to reproduce its classical spirit.

feature on top of feature, to create buildings that possess infinite variety in the midst of a certain decorative solemnity.

Palladio's most influential domestic design was the Villa Capra, more commonly called the Villa Rotonda because of its central circular area and covering dome (Figure 13.24). Inspired by ancient Roman farmhouses, the Villa Rotonda is a sixteenth-century country house built of brick and faced with stucco and located on a rise overlooking Vicenza. A dome provides a central axis from which four symmetrical wings radiate. Each of the four wings in turn opens to the outdoors through an Ionic-style porch raised on a pedestal. The porticoes, or covered porches supported by columns, then lead to the ground level through deeply recessed stairways. Statues stand on the corners and peak of each of the four pediments, and others flank the four stairways.

Palladio's mannerist spirit can be seen at work in the design of the Villa Rotonda. Although the coldly formal porches are classical in appearance, no Greek or Roman temple would have had four such identical porches, one on each side of the building (Figure 13.25). Palladio's design incorporates the unexpected and the contradictory within an apparently classical structure.

Besides designing buildings, Palladio wrote the treatise *Quattro libri dell'architettura,* or *The Four Books of Architecture.* This work, in English translation, gained wide currency and led to the vogue of Palladianism in the English-speaking world. English aristocrats in the 1700s commissioned country houses built on Palladian principles, as did plantation owners in America's antebellum South.

Music

No radical break separates High Renaissance music from the music of the early Renaissance.

Choral Music Josquin des Prez, the leading composer of the dominant Franco-Netherlandish school, had previously brought to a climax the early Renaissance style while he was employed in Italy by the popes and the local aristocrats (see Chapter 12). His sixteenth-century pieces, which consist chiefly of religious Masses and motets along with secular *chansons,* or songs, simply heightened the ideal already present in his earlier works: a sweet sound produced by multiple voices, usually two to six, singing a cappella and expressing the feelings described in the text. Despite his interest in music's emotional power, Josquin continued to subordinate the song to the words—thus reflecting the needs of the church, the foremost patron of the age. The clearly sung texts also show the classical restraint of his High Renaissance style. A striking feature of this style was the rich multichoral effect produced when the singers were subdivided into varied groups of voices.

Figure 13.24 PALLADIO. **Villa Rotonda (Villa Capra). Begun 1550. (Completed in about 1592 by Vincenzo Scamozzi [1548–1616].) Ht. of dome 70′; villa 80′ square. Vicenza.** Despite its classical elements, the Villa Rotonda is a mannerist building. Unlike High Renaissance buildings, which were designed to be integrated with their settings, this boxlike country house stands in an antagonistic relationship to its surrounding garden space. Furthermore, the mannerist principle of elongation is apparent in its four long stairways. But the Villa Rotonda's most striking mannerist feature is the surprise inherent in a plan that includes four identical porches.

Experimentation with choral effects was carried into the next generation by Adrian Willaert [VIL-art] (about 1490–1562), a member of the Franco-Netherlandish school and a disciple of Josquin's. After the latter's death, Willaert became Europe's most influential composer. Appointed the chapel master of the cathedral of St. Mark's in Venice, Willaert is considered the founder of the Venetian school of music. Taking advantage of St. Mark's two organs and the Venetian practice of blending instruments with voices, he wrote music for two choirs as well. By various musical techniques, such as alternating and combining voices, contrasting soft and loud, and arranging echo effects, Willaert created beautiful and expressive sounds that were the ancestor of the splendid church concertos of the baroque era. A benefit of Willaert's innovations was that the organ was released from its dependence on vocal music.

Missa Christus resurgens (Mass, the Risen Christ, about 1536), composed for four voices, shows Willaert's beautifully expressive style. Based on a short polyphonic

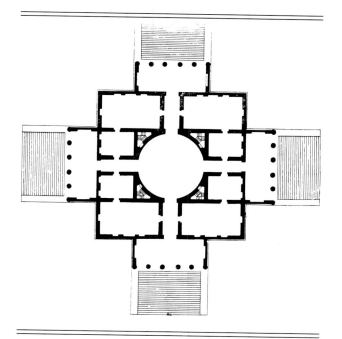

Figure 13.25 PALLADIO. **Floor Plan of the Villa Rotonda.** Palladio designed the Villa Rotonda to further the social ambitions of its wealthy Venetian owner, making its most prominent interior feature a central circular area, an ideal space for concerts, parties, and other gatherings. He surrounded this space with four identically shaped sets of rooms on two levels—to house family and guests. Passageways led to the four porches, where residents could obtain relief from the summer's heat and enjoy diverting views of the countryside.

Figure 13.26   GIOVANNI DI LUTERO, KNOWN AS DOSSO DOSSI. *Apollo and Daphne.* Ca. 1538. Oil on canvas, 6′2″ × 3′9″. **Galleria Borghese, Rome.** Dosso Dossi (about 1490–1542) painted many allegorical and mythological scenes. His sense of color and understanding of light— adapted from the Venetian art of Giorgione and Titian—added to the magic and fantasy of his works. In this painting, Apollo, the patron of poetry and music and leader of the Muses, is placed in the foreground, while Daphne, whom he constantly chased, is in the middle ground, fleeing from her pursuer. An Italian city, perhaps Bologna (identified by its Twin Towers), fills in the background. Apollo, rather than playing the lyre, an ancient Greek string instrument, is holding a violin. This painting may be one of the first to feature the violin, since the violin did not appear until about 1510.

work by the Franco-Flemish composer Jean Richafort (about 1480–1547), Willaert's Mass creates an appealing tapestry of sound, using melismas and imitation, but ensuring faultless understanding of the text—the essence of "modern" sacred polyphony, his legacy. The short Agnus Dei (Lamb of God) begins with all four voices forming an ever-shifting ground, from which the tenor voice emerges, soaring above the rest, giving an ethereal sound and acting as a musical metaphor for Christ's rebirth.

Other Developments   Instrumental music still played a secondary role to the human voice. However, Josquin and Willaert composed a few pieces for specific instruments, either transposing melodies originally intended for singers or adapting musical forms from dance tunes.

Another important step forward occurred with the birth of the violin, an instrument with strings and a bow, which evolved from the Arabic *rebec* and the medieval fiddle and its Italian cousin (Figure 13.26). By 1600, Italian artisans had fixed the violin's basic size and shape, but the number of strings continued to vary for decades. The tradition of making violins of great distinction began with Andrea Amati (about 1520–1578), who founded a workshop in Cremona in the mid–sixteenth century. Antonio Stradivari (about 1644–1737) and Andrea Guarneri (about 1626–1698), two of the most famous violin makers in history, were apprentices of Niccolò Amati (1596–1684), Andrea's grandson. Antonio Stradivari brought violin making to its highest level of perfection, building 540 violins along with many other string instruments. Today, a Stradivari violin is considered one of the most precious musical instruments in the world.

A further development, holding great future promise, was the invention of the **consort,** a set of musical instruments in the same family, ranging from the low bass to the high treble, initially made up of either recorders or viols. The consort represented the principle of the mixed instrumental ensemble, and from this start would emerge the orchestra. And, when human voices were added to the mixture, the conditions were ripe for opera.

SUMMARY

The High Renaissance and early mannerism flourished at the dawn of the modern world.

Politically, France, Spain, and England gradually gave up feudal trappings to become the first modern, centralized nation-states, while the Hapsburg Empire remained stuck in the past with each of its vast territories governed according to local custom. Economically, demographic changes, rising prosperity, and technological innovation triggered a wave of globalization, as Portugal, followed by Spain, England, France, and the Netherlands, jockeyed to initiate contacts with non-Western peoples. Socially, two contradictory trends emerged: the code of courtesy at the Italian courts, which created the social ideal of the gentleman and the lady; and the idea of individualism, to be celebrated in public and private life.

Culturally, Leonardo, Michelangelo, and Raphael perfected the High Renaissance style with its values of balance, proportion, and restraint. And the great Michelangelo pioneered early mannerism—a variant of the High Renaissance style—in which classical forms were given exaggerated poses, odd perspectives, and a dash of playfulness. In philosophy, the mannerist thinker Machiavelli founded modern political thought, based on his bleak view of human nature.

The Legacy of the High Renaissance and Early Mannerism

The notion of nation-statehood evolved from being a European ideal to becoming a political force across the globe, inspiring to this day both reform (currently 193 states comprise the United Nations) and revolution (the 2011 uprisings in the Middle East).

The wave of globalization, launched during this period, led to our interconnected twenty-first-century world. The code of courtesy was adopted by Europe's elite and eventually trickled down to the West's middle classes. Concurrently, individualism became a defining theme of Western culture. The living embodiment of individualism today is Lady Gaga (Stefani Joanne Angelina Germanotta, b. 1986), with her talent for self-celebration. Nevertheless, Miss Manners (Judith Martin, b. 1938)—a syndicated columnist in newspapers and on the Web (http://lifestyle.msn.com)—remains a pervasive force in contemporary culture.

Leonardo, Michelangelo, and Raphael are titanic figures in today's global culture. A newly discovered Leonardo painting, *Salvador Mundi (Savior of the World)* drew crowds when it was exhibited at London's National Gallery (2011), while fierce controversy surrounds the plan in Florence, Italy, to "excavate" behind a mural—and thus destroy a Renaissance artwork—in search of a lost Leonardo fresco. Michelangelo, the quintessential "Renaissance man," has become the gold standard against whom ambitious artists and humanists have been compared for the past five hundred years. And Raphael is a beloved figure in his own right, a tribute to his "sweet madonnas" and his singular mastery of the High Renaissance style. In popular culture, these cultural icons are the names of three of the four Teenage Mutant Ninja Turtles (1984–present), a mainstream franchise of comics, television, video games, clothing, toys, and other merchandise. In 2011, Mattel, the toy maker, introduced the "Mona Lisa" Barbie doll, in homage to Leonardo.

Finally, the great Florentine writer, Machiavelli, inspired later thinkers to invent other models of good government—a staple of the academic discipline, political science. And, in 2008, Machiavelli's ideas were given a populist spin by the British writer Tim Phillips, who argued that *The Prince* could serve as a guide to today's politics and business culture.

Lady Gaga. Getty Images. Lady Gaga expresses both the truth of Andy Warhol's famous dictum, that everyone in a media-saturated culture will get fifteen minutes of fame, and the current craze for "branding"—that is, to sell oneself as a unique commodity. In this photograph, Lady Gaga, dressed in a billowing frock, blond wig, and Hollywood shades, is making a pitch for her own recordings and, at the same time, drawing in potential consumers to Barneys, the Manhattan fashion store, where this media event is taking place.

KEY CULTURAL TERMS

High Renaissance	madrigal	*Pietà*	balustrade
mannerism	Machiavellianism	scenographic	consort
civic humanism	tondo		

Glossary

Italicized words within definitions are defined in their own glossary entries.

abstract art Art that presents a subjective view of the world—the artist's emotions or ideas—or art that presents *line*, *color*, or shape for its own sake.

abstract expressionism Also known as *action painting*, a nonrepresentational artistic style that flourished after World War II and was typified by randomness, spontaneity, and an attempt by the artist to interact emotionally with the work as it was created.

abstraction In modern art, nonrepresentational or nonobjective forms in sculpture and painting that emphasize shapes, *lines*, and *colors* independent of the natural world.

a cappella [ah kuh-PEL-uh] From the Italian, "in chapel style"; music sung without instrumental accompaniment.

action painting Another name for *abstract expressionism*. Action painting referred to an artist's use of agitated motions while applying paint to canvas, such as Jackson Pollock's "drip paintings" or Willem de Kooning's slashing strokes. Inspired by *surrealism's* reliance on automatic responses as a way to release the creative unconscious.

adab [ah-DAHB] An Arabic term. Originally, it meant good manners or good conduct. In the eighth century, it appeared as a literary *genre*; later, it indicated the possession of athletic skills and literary knowledge and applied especially to the elite. Today, *adab* refers to the whole of literature.

aesthete One who pursues and is devoted to the beautiful in art, music, and literature.

aisles The side passages in a church on either side of the central *nave*.

ambulatory [AM-bue-la-tor-e] A passageway for walking found in many religious structures, such as outdoors in a *cloister* or indoors around the *apse* or the *choir* of a church.

Anglicanism The doctrines and practices of the Church of England, which was established in the early sixteenth century under Henry VIII.

angry young men A late 1950s and early 1960s literary movement in Great Britain, composed of novelists and playwrights, whose works expressed frustration and anger over their country's loss of empire and declining status on the world's stage. Most of the angry young men were part of an emerging meritocracy, having been born in the lower classes but educated in the universities, including Oxford and Cambridge.

anthropomorphism [an-thro-po-MOR-fizm] The attributing of humanlike characteristics and traits to nonhuman things or powers, such as a deity.

Antigonids The name of the dynasty that ruled Macedon and Greece after the death of Alexander the Great and down to the Roman conquest. One of Alexander's generals, Antigonus the One Eyed, tried unsuccessfully to secure Macedon and Greece but his grandson Antigonus Gonatas established the dynasty definitively.

antiphon [AN-te-fon] In music, a short prose text, chanted by unaccompanied voices during the Christian *liturgy*.

apocalypse [uh-PAHK-uh-lips] In Jewish and early Christian thought, the expectation and hope of the coming of God and his final judgment; also closely identified with the last book of the New Testament, Revelation, in which many events are foretold, often in highly symbolic and imaginative terms.

apologists From the Greek *apologia*, "in defense of." Christian writers (about 150–300) who differentiated between Christianity, Judaism, and pagan philosophies, and who discussed ways in which Christians could be good citizens of the Roman Empire.

apostolic succession A term for the idea in the Catholic Church that the authority of bishops descends from the authority of the apostles, Christ's twelve followers.

apse In architecture, a large projection, usually rounded or semicircular, found in a *basilica*, usually in the east end; in Christian *basilicas*, the altar stood in this space.

aquatint An early type of color print, made with a metal plate, which attempted to replicate the effect of a watercolor; originated in the Netherlands in about 1650. The golden age of the aquatint was from about 1770 to 1850. The print's name derives from nitrous oxide *(aqua fortis)*, a chemical used in the printmaking process.

arabesque [air-uh-BESK] Literally, "Arabian-like"; a complex figure of decorative lines, patterns, and designs, often floral, in Islamic works of art.

arcade A series of arches supported by *piers* or columns, usually serving as a passageway along a street or between buildings.

Archaic style The *style* in Greek sculpture, dating from the seventh century to 480 BCE, that was characterized by heavy Egyptian influence; dominated by the *kouros* and *korē* sculptural forms.

architectural paintings A type of wall painting which created the optical illusion of either a wall opening or the effect of looking through a window; popular in imperial Rome.

architrave [AHR-kuh-trayv] The part of the *entablature* that rests on the *capital* or column in classical *post-beam-triangle construction*.

arcosolium Arched chambers, usually belowground and carved out along the passageways of the *catacombs*. Many arcosolia have elaborate paintings.

aria [AH-ree-uh] In music, an elaborate *melody* sung as a solo or sometimes a duet, usually in an *opera* or an *oratorio*, with an orchestral accompaniment.

ars nova Latin, "new art"; a style of music in fourteenth-century Europe. It used more secular themes than the "old art" music of earlier times, which was closely identified with sacred music.

art film A film *genre* marked by unusual narrative structures, violent action, and uplifting themes; associated with directors indebted to *auteurist* theory.

art song (lied) In music, a *lyric* song with *melody* performed by a singer and instrumental accompaniment usually provided by piano; made popular by Schubert in the nineteenth century.

ashlar [ASH-luhr] A massive hewn or squared stone used in constructing a fortress, palace, or large building.

assemblage art An art form in which the artist mixes and/or assembles found objects, such as scraps of paper, cloth, or junk, into a three-dimensional work and then adds paint or other decorations to it.

ataraxia [at-uh-RAK-see-uh] Greek, "calmness"; in *Hellenistic* philosophy, the state of desiring nothing.

atonality [ay-toe-NAL-uh-tee] In music, the absence of a *key* note or tonal center and the use of the *tones* of the chromatic *scale* impartially.

atrium [AY-tree-uhm] In Roman architecture, an open courtyard at the front of a house; in Christian *Romanesque* churches, an open court, usually colonnaded, in front of the main doors of the structure.

attic The topmost section or crown of an arch.

audience The group or person for whom a work of art, architecture, literature, drama, film, or music is intended.

aulos In music, a reed woodwind instrument similar to the oboe, usually played in pairs by one player as the double aulos; used in Greek music.

autarky [AW-tar-kee] Greek, "self-sufficient"; in *Hellenistic* thought, the state of being isolated and free from the demands of society.

auteur [oh-TURR] French, "author"; a film director who imposes a personal style. The *auteurist* director "writes" with the camera to express a personal vision.

avant-garde [a-vahn-GARD] French, "advance guard"; writers, artists, and intellectuals who push their works and ideas ahead of more traditional groups and movements.

baldacchino [ball-duh-KEE-no] An ornamental structure in the shape of a canopy, supported by four columns, built over a church altar, and usually decorated with statues and other ornaments.

balustrade In architecture, a rail and the row of posts that support it, as along the edge of a staircase or around a dome.

baptistery A small, often octagonal structure, separated from the main church, particularly in Europe, where baptisms are performed.

bard A tribal poet-singer who composed and recited works, often of the *epic poetry* genre.

baroque [buh-ROKE] The prevailing seventeenth-century artistic and cultural *style*, characterized by an emphasis on grandeur, opulence, expansiveness, and complexity.

barrel vault A ceiling or *vault* made of sets of arches placed side by side and joined together.

basilica [buh-SILL-ih-kuh] A rectangular structure that included an *apse* at one or both ends; originally a Roman building used for public purposes, later taken over by the Christians for worship. The floor plan became the basis of nearly all early Christian churches.

bay A discrete interior or exterior architectural element marked not by walls but by piers, columns, vaulting, or windows.

beat generation A literary movement in the United States, from about 1950 to 1970, made up of poets, novelists, and playwrights, who stood apart from the mainstream literary establishment, as reflected in their use of street language, experimental forms of literary expression, and liberal use of alcohol and drugs. While expressing solidarity with society's downtrodden—the source of the term *beat*—the beats criticized capitalism, bourgeois society and values, and the nuclear arms race.

bel canto [bell KAHN-toe] Italian, "beautiful singing"; a style of singing characteristic of seventeenth-century Italian *opera* stressing ease, purity, and evenness of *tone* along with precise vocal technique.

blank verse Unrhymed iambic pentameter (lines with five feet, or units, each consisting of an unaccented and an accented syllable).

blaxploitation film A crime film *genre*, after 1970, that features a swaggering black hero, catering to black audiences.

blind arcade A decorative architectural design that gives the appearance of an open *arcade* or window but is filled in with some type of building material such as stone or brick.

blues A type of music that emerged around 1900 from the rural African American culture, was originally based on work songs and religious spirituals, and expressed feelings of loneliness and hopelessness.

Byzantine style [BIZ-uhn-teen] In painting, decoration, and architecture, a *style* blending Greco-Roman and oriental components into a highly stylized art form that glorified Christianity, notably in domed churches adorned with *mosaics* and polished marble; associated with the culture of the Eastern Roman Empire from about 500 until 1453.

cadenza [kuh-DEN-zah] In music, a *virtuoso* passage, usually for a solo instrument or voice, meant to be improvised or to have an improvised feeling.

Cajun A descendant of French pioneers, chiefly in Louisiana, who in 1755 chose to leave Acadia (modern Nova Scotia) rather than live under the British crown.

calligraphy Literally "beautiful writing." Penmanship or handwriting, usually done with flowing lines, used as a decoration or as an enhancement of a written work; found in Islamic and Christian writings.

Calvinism The theological beliefs and rituals set forth in and derived from John Calvin's writings, placing emphasis on the power of God and the weakness of human beings.

campanile From the Latin *campana*, "bell"; a bell tower, especially one near but not attached to a church; an Italian invention.

canon A set of principles or rules that are accepted as true and authoritative for the various arts or fields of study; in architecture, it refers to the standards of proportion; in painting, the prescribed ways of painting certain objects; in sculpture, the ideal proportions of the human body; in literature, the authentic list of an author's works; in religion, the approved and authoritative writings that are accepted as divinely inspired, such as the *scriptures* for Jews and Christians; and in religious and other contexts, certain prescribed rituals or official rules and laws. In music, a canon is a *composition* in which a *melody* sung by one voice is repeated exactly by successive voices as they enter.

canzone [kan-ZOH-nee] Latin, "chant"; a type of love poem popular in southern France during the twelfth and thirteenth centuries.

capital In architecture, the upper or crowning part of a column, on which the *entablature* rests.

capitularies From the Latin *capitula* ("chapters"), a term meaning quasi-legislative documents of varying lengths issued by Carolingian kings on a variety of secular and ecclesiastical topics. Some capitularies flowed from the kings, while others emerged from general assemblies of the Franks.

Carolingian minuscule A new, highly legible script that originated in the reign of Charlemagne (768–814). The script served the king's desire for accurate copies of key ancient and contemporary books. It gradually replaced earlier scripts that were difficult to read and led to errors in transcription.

catacomb From Greek, *kata kumbas*, "at the hollows"; the traditional name for the miles and miles of subterranean burial chambers carved into the soft stone around the city of Rome. Though particularly associated with Christian burials, Romans had long used the catacombs.

cathedral The church of a bishop that houses a cathedral, or throne symbolizing the seat of power in his administrative district, known as a diocese.

causality The idea that one event "causes" another; the relation between a cause and its effect.

cella [SELL-uh] The inner sanctum or walled room of a *classical* temple where sacred statues were housed.

chamber work Music for a small ensemble of instruments or voices.

chanson [shahn-SAWN] French, "song"; a fourteenth- to sixteenth-century French song for one or more voices, often with instrumental accompaniment. Similar to a *madrigal*.

chanson de geste [shahn-SAWN duh zhest] A poem of brave deeds in the *epic* form developed in France during the eleventh century, usually to be sung.

character A person in a story or play; someone who acts out or is affected by the *plot*.

chiaroscuro [key-ahr-uh-SKOOR-oh] In painting, the use of dark and light contrast to create the effect of modeling of a figure or object.

Chinese rococo A variation of the European *rococo*, characterized by oriental shapes, materials, techniques, and design elements.

Chinoiserie [shen-WAZ-uh-ree] French, "Chinois," China. A *style* and taste in the West for Chinese culture, embracing the decorative arts and, to a lesser extent, Chinese writings; most influential from 1740 to 1770, but lingering until about 1850.

chivalry The rules of conduct, probably idealized, featuring courage, prowess, loyalty, religious faith, and generosity, that governed the social roles and duties of aristocrats in the Middle Ages.

chivalric novel A late medieval literary form that presented romantic stories of knights and their ladies; the dominant literary form in Spain from the late Middle Ages into the *Renaissance*.

choir In architecture, that part of a *Gothic* church in which the service was sung by singers or clergy, located in the east end beyond the *transept*; also, the group of trained singers who sat in the choir area.

chorus In Greek drama, a group of performers who sang and danced in both *tragedies* and *comedies*, often commenting on the action; in later times, a group of singers who performed with or without instrumental accompaniment.

Christian humanism An intellectual movement in sixteenth-century northern Europe that sought to use the ideals of the *classical* world, the tools of ancient learning, and the morals of the Christian *scriptures* to rid the church of worldliness and scandal.

chthonian deities [THOE-nee-uhn] In Greek religion, earth gods and goddesses who lived underground and were usually associated with peasants and their religious beliefs.

civic humanism An Italian *Renaissance* ideal, characterized by dedicated and educated citizens who served as administrators and civil servants in their cities; inspired by the period's *classical* revival.

civilization The way humans live in a complex political, economic, and social structure, usually in an urban environment, with some development in technology, literature, and art.

cladding In architecture, a covering or overlay of some material for a building's exterior walls.

classic, or classical Having the forms, values, or standards embodied in the art and literature of Greek and Roman *civilization*; in music, an eighteenth-century style characterized by simplicity, proportion, and an emphasis on structure.

classical baroque style A secular variation of the *baroque* style that was identified with French kings and artists, was rooted in *classical* ideals, and was used mainly to emphasize the power and grandeur of the monarchy.

clavier [French, KLAH-vyay; German, KLAH-veer] Any musical instrument having a keyboard, such as a piano, organ, or harpsichord; the term came into general usage with the popularity of Bach's set of studies titled *The Well-Tempered Clavier.*

clerestory windows [KLEER-stor-ee] A row of windows set along the upper part of a wall, especially in a church.

cloister In architecture, a covered walkway, open on one side, which is attached to the four walls of buildings that face a quadrangle; originated in medieval church architecture. Also, a monastery or convent dedicated to religious seclusion.

collage [koh-LAHZH] From the French *coller*, to "glue"; a type of art, introduced by Picasso, in which bits and pieces of materials such as paper or cloth are glued to a painted surface.

color Use of the hues found in nature to enhance or distort the sense of reality in a visual image.

comedy A literary *genre* characterized by a story with a complicated and amusing *plot* that ends with a happy and peaceful resolution of all conflicts.

comedy of manners A humorous play that focuses on the way people in a particular social group or class interact with one another, especially regarding fashions and manners.

commedia dell'arte [kuh-MAY-de-uh del-AR-teh] Italian, "comedy of art"; an Italian theatrical *genre* from the sixteenth to the eighteenth century, using puppets and stock characters, with a strong streak of improvisation. Highly influential later on live theater in Italy and elsewhere.

composition The arrangement of constituent elements in an artistic work; in music, composition also refers to the process of creating the work.

conceptual art A *late modern* art movement in which the concept or idea of the proposed art is more important than the means for its execution.

concerto [kuhn-CHER-toe] In music, a *composition* for one or more soloists and *orchestra,* usually in a symphonic *form* with three contrasting movements.

conch The rounded semi-dome that topped the half-*drum* of an *apse.*

congregational or Friday mosque A type of *mosque* used for Friday prayers, inspired by the prophet Muhammad's original example. Characterized by a central courtyard along with a domed fountain for ablutions; found across the Islamic world.

consort A set of musical instruments in the same family, ranging from bass to soprano; also, a group of musicians who entertain by singing or playing instruments.

constructivism A movement in nonobjective art, originating in the Soviet Union and flourishing from 1917 to 1922 and concerned with planes and volumes as expressed in modern industrial materials such as glass and plastic.

content The subject matter of an artistic work.

context The setting in which an artistic work arose, its own time and place. Context includes the political, economic, social, and cultural conditions of the time; it can also include the personal circumstances of the artist's life.

contrapposto [kon-truh-POH-stoh] In sculpture and painting, the placement of the human figure so the weight is more on one leg than the other and the shoulders and chest are turned in the opposite direction from the hips and legs.

convention An agreed-upon practice, device, technique, or form.

Corinthian The third Greek architectural order, in which temple columns are slender and *fluted,* sit on a base, and have *capitals* shaped like inverted bells and decorated with carvings representing the leaves of the acanthus bush; this style was popular in *Hellenistic* times and widely adopted by the Romans.

cornice In architecture, the crowning, projecting part of the *entablature.*

cosmopolitan From Greek, *cosmos,* "world," and *polis,* "city"; a citizen of the world, that is, an urban dweller with a universal, or world, view.

Counter-Reformation A late-sixteenth-century movement in the Catholic Church aimed at reestablishing its basic beliefs, reforming its organizational structure, and reasserting itself as the authoritative voice of Christianity.

countersubject In music, in the *fugue,* a contrasting variant to the *subject;* played in tandem with the *subject,* either below or above it.

courtly love A new and idealized ethos as the product of noble courts that envisioned "fine love" as the love of an unattainable lady and male refinement in manners and behavior.

covenant In Judaism and Christianity, a solemn and binding agreement or contract between God and his followers.

Creole An ambiguous term, sometimes referring to descendants of French and Spanish settlers of the southern United States, especially Louisiana; used by Kate Chopin in her short stories and novels in this sense. In other contexts, *Creole* can refer either to blacks born in the Western Hemisphere (as distinguished from blacks born in Africa) or to residents of the American Gulf states of mixed black, Spanish, and Portuguese ancestry.

crescendo [krah-SHEN-doh] In music, an increase in volume.

cruciform [KROO-suh-form] Cross-shaped; used to describe the standard floor plan of a church.

Crusades A series of military campaigns launched in 1095 by Pope Urban II to recover the Holy Land from its Muslim conquerors. The name derives from *crucesignati,* Latin for "signed by the cross," signifying the cross that crusaders stitched onto their clothing. The First Crusade (1097–1099) captured Jerusalem and established some small "Crusader States" in the eastern Mediterranean but the movement as a whole failed, over the centuries, in its stated objective.

cubism A *style* of painting introduced by Picasso and Braque in which objects are broken up into fragments and patterns of geometric structures and depicted on the flat canvas as if from several points of view.

culture The sum of human endeavors, including the basic political, economic, and social institutions and the values, beliefs, and arts of those who share them.

cuneiform [kue-NEE-uh-form] Wedge-shaped characters used in writing on tablets found in Mesopotamia and other ancient *civilizations.*

Cynicism A *Hellenistic* philosophy that denounced society and its institutions as artificial and called on the individual to strive for *autarky.*

Dada [DAH-dah] An early-twentieth-century artistic movement, named after a nonsense word that was rooted in a love of play, encouraged deliberately irrational acts, and exhibited contempt for all traditions.

decadence A late-nineteenth-century literary *style* concerned with morbid and artificial subjects and themes.

deconstruction In *postmodern* literary analysis, a set of practices for analyzing and critiquing a text in order to "deconstruct" its actual meaning and language.

deductive reasoning The process of reasoning from the general to the particular—that is, beginning with an accepted premise or first statement and, by steps of logical reasoning or inference, reaching a conclusion that necessarily follows from the premise.

Deism [DEE-iz-uhm] A religion based on the idea that the universe was created by God and then left to run according to *natural laws,* without divine interference; formulated and practiced in the eighteenth century.

de Stijl [duh STILE] Dutch, "the style"; an artistic movement associated with a group of early-twentieth-century Dutch painters who used rectangular forms and primary colors in their works and who believed that art should have spiritual values and a social purpose.

devotio moderna [de-VO-tee-oh mo-DER-nuh] The "new devotion" of late medieval Christianity that emphasized piety and discipline as practiced by lay religious communities located primarily in northern Europe.

Diaspora [dye-AS-puhr-uh] From the Greek, "to scatter"; the dispersion of the Jews from their homeland in ancient Palestine, a process that began with the Babylonian Captivity in the sixth century BCE and continued over the centuries.

Dionysia [DYE-uh-NYSH-ee-ah] Any of the religious festivals held in ancient Athens honoring Dionysus, the god of wine; especially the Great Dionysia, celebrated in late winter and early spring in which *tragedy* is thought to have originated.

divertimento Instrumental work, performed as entertainment, as at social gatherings or banquets.

dominate Term applied to the Roman imperial regime inaugurated by Diocletian (284–305) implying that the emperor was *dominus,* "lord and master," instead of "first citizen" (see *principate*). The dominate persisted in the East into the Byzantine era but became meaningless in the West after the death of Theodosius (395), Rome's last sole emperor.

Doric The simplest and oldest of the Greek architectural orders, in which temple columns have undecorated *capitals* and rest directly on the *stylobate.*

drum In architecture, a circular or polygonal wall used to support a dome.

drypoint In art, the *technique* of incising an image, using a sharp, pointed instrument, onto a metal surface or block used for printing. Also, the print made from the technique.

dynamics In music, changes in the volume of a sound.

early Renaissance style A *style* inspired by *classical* rather than *Gothic* models that arose among Florentine architects, sculptors, and painters in the late fourteenth and early fifteenth centuries.

electronic music Music produced using electronic means, usually with a *synthesizer* and/or a computer.

empiricism The process of collecting data, making observations, carrying out experiments based on the collected data and observations, and reaching a conclusion.

engraving In art, the *technique* of carving, cutting, or etching an image with a sharp, pointed instrument onto a metal surface overlaid with wax, dipping the surface in acid, and then printing it. Also, the print made from the *technique.*

Enlightenment The eighteenth-century philosophical and cultural movement marked by the application of reason to human problems and affairs, a questioning of traditional beliefs and ideas, and an optimistic faith in unlimited progress for humanity, particularly through education.

entablature [en-TAB-luh-choor] In architecture, the part of the temple above the columns and below the roof, which, in *classical* temples, included the *architrave,* the *frieze,* and the *pediment.*

entasis [EN-ta-sis] In architecture, convex curving or enlarging of the central part of a column to correct the optical illusion that the column is too thin.

environmental art A *postmodern* art form that uses the environment, including stone, earth, and water, so as to create a natural-looking artwork. Environmental art is ephemeral, as it tends to revert to its primary elements over time—thus echoing the ever-changing world of nature.

epic A poem, novel, or film that recounts at length the life of a hero or the history of a people.

epic poetry Narrative poetry, usually told or written in an elevated style, that recounts the life of a hero.

epic theater A type of theater, invented by Brecht, in which major social issues are dramatized with outlandish props and jarring dialogue and effects, all designed to alienate middle-class *audiences* and force them to think seriously about the problems raised in the plays.

Epicureanism [ep-i-kyoo-REE-uh-niz-uhm] A *Hellenistic* philosophy, founded by Epicurus and later expounded by the Roman Lucretius, that made its highest goals the development of the mind and an existence free from the demands of everyday life.

episode In music, a short transitional section played between the *subject* and the *countersubject;* used in *fugal* composition.

epistemology The branch of philosophy that studies the nature, extent, and validity of knowledge.

eschatology [es-kuh-TAHL-uh-jee] The concern with final events or the end of the world, a belief popular in Jewish and early Christian communities and linked to the concept of the coming of a *Messiah.*

Etruscans A people of mysterious origins who ruled the territory north of Rome in Italy from the ninth to the sixth century BCE. They dominated the early Romans and influenced their art, architecture, and religion.

evangelicalism Historically, a nineteenth-century Protestant movement, mainly in the United States, which grew out of the Methodist tradition and emphasized personal piety and the working of the Holy Spirit. Evangelicalism dominated mainline Protestant America until about 1870. Today, evangelicalism is a term used for describing Protestants who emphasize *fundamentalism,* biblical inerrancy, and conservative social values.

evangelists From the Greek *evangelion,* a term generally used for those who preach the Christian religion; more specifically, the four evangelists, Matthew, Mark, Luke, and John, who wrote about Jesus Christ soon after his death in the first four books of the New Testament.

evolution The theory, set forth in the nineteenth century by Charles Darwin, that plants and animals, including humans, evolved over millions of years from simpler forms through a process of natural selection.

existentialism [eg-zi-STEN-shuh-liz-uhm] A twentieth-century philosophy focusing on the precarious nature of human existence, with its uncertainty, anxiety, and ultimate death, as well as on individual freedom and responsibility and the possibilities for human creativity and authenticity.

expressionism A late-nineteenth-century literary and artistic movement characterized by the expression of highly personal feelings rather than of objective reality.

fan vaulting A decorative pattern of *vault* ribs that arch out or radiate from a central point on the ceiling; popular in English *Perpendicular* architecture.

Faustian [FAU-stee-uhn] Resembling the character Faust in Goethe's most famous work, in being spiritually tormented, insatiable for knowledge and experience, or willing to pay any price, including personal and spiritual integrity, to gain a desired end.

fauvism [FOH-viz-uhm] From the French *fauve,* "wild beast"; an early-twentieth-century art movement led by Matisse and favoring exotic colors and disjointed shapes.

fête galante [fet gah-LAHNN] In *rococo* painting, the *theme* or scene of aristocrats being entertained or simply enjoying their leisure and other worldly pleasures.

feudalism The customary name for the political regime in much of the medieval West, beginning in the Carolingian period. The term basically pertains to honorable relationships between lords and vassals. Vassals promised to give their lords homage and fealty (i.e, respect and fidelity), as well as aid and counsel (i.e., military service and legal advice). In return, lords promised their vassals protection and maintenance (i.e., military cover and a landed estate), or fief (*feudum* in Latin, whence the name "feudalism.").

The term also signifies the exploitation of peasants by landowners.

First Great Awakening The period of religious revivalism among Protestants that placed emphasis on a direct and personal relationship with God and undermined the traditional role and power of the established churches; centered mainly in the British American colonies during the 1730s and 1740s.

First Romanesque The first stage of *Romanesque* architecture, about 1000–1080. First Romanesque churches had high walls, few windows, and flat wooden roofs, and were built of stone rubble and adorned with *Lombard bands* and *Lombard arcades*. It began along the Mediterranean, in the area ranging from Dalmatia, across northern Italy and Provence, to Catalonia.

Flamboyant style [flam-BOY-uhnt] A late French *Gothic* architectural style of elaborate decorations and ornamentation that produce a flamelike effect.

florid baroque style A variation of the *baroque* style specifically identified with the Catholic Church's patronage of the arts and used to glorify its beliefs.

fluting Decorative vertical grooves carved in a column.

flying buttress An external masonry support, found primarily in *Gothic* churches, that carries the thrust of the ceiling, or *vault*, away from the upper walls of the building to an external vertical column

forms In music, particular structures of arrangements of elements, such as *symphonies*, songs, concerts, and *operas*. In painting and sculpture, **form** refers to the artistic structure rather than to the material of which an artwork is made.

forum In Rome and many Roman towns, the public place, located in the center of the town, where people gathered to socialize, transact business, and administer the government.

forte [FOR-tay] Italian, "loud." A musical term.

fortississimo [fawrh-tis-ISS-e-moh] In music, extremely loud; abbreviated *fff*.

fourth-century style The sculptural *style* characteristic of the last phase of the *Hellenic* period, when new interpretations of beauty and movement were adopted.

fresco A painting done on wet or dry plaster that becomes part of the plastered wall.

friars Members of a thirteenth-century mendicant (begging) monastic order.

frieze [fREEz] A band of painted designs or sculptured figures placed on walls; also, the central portion of a temple's *entablature* just above the *architrave*.

fugue [FEWg] In music, a *composition* for several instruments in which a *theme* is introduced by one instrument and then repeated by each successively entering instrument so that a complicated interweaving of themes, variations, *imitations*, and echoes results; this compositional technique began in the fifteenth century and reached its zenith in the *baroque* period in works by Bach.

fundamentalist movement or fundamentalism Historically, an American Protestant movement that broke free of the *evangelicals* from about 1870 to 1970, stressing biblical inerrancy, "speaking in tongues," and opposition to certain modern scientific trends, such as evolution and higher criticism. Today, fundamentalism is often aggregated with *evangelicalism* and other socially conservative religious movements.

gallery In architecture, a long, narrow passageway or corridor, usually found in churches and located above the *aisles*, and often with openings that permit viewing from above into the *nave*.

gargoyle [GAHR-goil] In architecture, a water spout in the form of a grotesque animal or human, carved from stone, placed on the edge of a roof.

genre [ZHON-ruh] From the French, "a kind, a type, or a class"; a category of artistic, musical, or literary composition, characterized by a particular *style, form,* or *content.*

genre subject In art, a scene or a person from everyday life, depicted realistically and without religious or symbolic significance.

geocentrism The belief that the earth is the center of the universe and that the sun, planets, and stars revolve around it.

ghazal [GUZ-l] A short *lyric*, usually dealing with love, composed in a single rhyme and based on the poet's personal life and loves.

glissando [gle-SAHN-doe] (plural, **glissandi**) In music, the blending of one *tone* into the next in scalelike passages that may be ascending or descending in character.

goliards [GOAL-yuhrds] Medieval roaming poets or scholars who traveled about reciting poems on topics ranging from moral lessons to the pains of love.

Gospels The first four books of the New Testament (Matthew, Mark, Luke, and John), which record the life and sayings of Jesus Christ; the word itself, from Old English, means "good news" or "good tales."

Gothic style A *style* of architecture, usually associated with churches, that originated in northern France and whose three phases—early, High, and late—lasted from the twelfth to the sixteenth century. Emerging from the *Romanesque* style, Gothic is identified by *pointed arches, ribbed vaults, stained-glass* windows, *flying buttresses*, and carvings on the exterior.

Gregorian chant A *style* of *monophonic* church music sung in unison and without instrumental accompaniment and used in the *liturgy*; named for Pope Gregory I (590–604).

groined vault, or cross vault A ceiling, or *vault*, created when two *barrel vaults*, set at right angles, intersect.

happening A *late modern* theatrical development, combining skits with outrageous events and involving performances by painters, actors, musicians, and audience members, so as to give the impression of spontaneity.

hard-edge In *late modern* painting, a technique used in color paintings, by which the areas of *color* are precisely delineated from one another.

harmony The simultaneous combination of two or more *tones*, producing a chord; generally, the chordal characteristics of a work and the way chords interact.

heliocentrism The belief that the sun is the center of the universe and that the earth and the other planets revolve around it.

Hellenic [hell-LENN-ik] Relating to the time period in Greek civilization from 480 to 323 BCE, when the most influential Greek artists, playwrights, and philosophers, such as Praxiteles, Sophocles, and Plato, created their greatest works; associated with the *classical* style.

Hellenistic [hell-uh-NIS-tik] Relating to the time period from about 323 to 31 BCE, when Greek—and later Roman—and

Oriental or Middle Eastern cultures and institutions intermingled to create a heterogeneous and *cosmopolitan civilization.*

henotheism The worship of one god without denying the existence of other gods. Sometimes called "monolatry." Associated with Akhenaten in Egypt.

heresy Greek, literally "to choose," "a choice." In Christian *theology,* any church teaching deliberately chosen that is deemed unacceptable by the majority, by the popes, or by the bishops sitting in a council. By extension, any unorthodox belief or teaching in politics, philosophy, or science.

hieroglyphs [HI-uhr-uh-glifs] Pictorial characters used in Egyptian writing, which is known as hieroglyphics.

high classical style The *style* in Greek sculpture associated with the ideal physical form and perfected during the zenith of the Athenian Empire, about 450–400 BCE.

higher criticism A rational approach to Bible study, developed in German Protestant circles in the nineteenth century, that treated the biblical *scriptures* as literature and subjected them to close scrutiny, testing their literary history, authorship, and meaning.

High Renaissance The period from about 1495 to 1520, often associated with the patronage of the popes in Rome, when the most influential artists and writers of the *Renaissance,* including Michelangelo, Raphael, Leonardo da Vinci, and Machiavelli, were producing their greatest works.

high tech In architecture, a *style* that uses obvious industrial design elements with exposed parts serving as decorations.

hip-hop In *postmodern* popular culture, after 1970, an eclectic trend among African Americans and Hispanic Americans, drawing on break dancing, graffiti art, rap rhyming, and disc jockeys playing with turntables and "scratch" effects; highly influential on today's youth culture, popular music, film, and dance styles.

holiness A nineteenth-century American Protestant movement, which came out of the Methodist tradition, emphasizing holy living and the need to be "born again" as a true disciple of Jesus Christ; part of the *fundamentalist* movement after 1870.

Homeric epithet A recurring nickname, such as "Ox-eyed Hera," used in Homer's *Iliad* or *Odyssey.*

hubris [HYOO-bris] In Greek thought, human pride or arrogance that leads an individual to challenge the gods, usually provoking divine retribution.

humanism An attitude that is concerned with humanity, its achievements, and its potential; the study of the *humanities;* in the *Renaissance,* identified with *studia humanitatis.*

humanities In the nineteenth century, the study of Greek and Roman languages and literature; later set off from the sciences and expanded to include the works of all Western peoples in the arts, literature, music, philosophy, and sometimes history and religion; in *postmodernism,* extended to a global dimension.

hymn From the Greek and Latin, "ode of praise of gods or heroes"; a song of praise or thanksgiving to God or the gods, performed both with and without instrumental accompaniment.

idealism In Plato's philosophy, the theory that reality and ultimate truth are to be found not in the material world but in the spiritual realm.

idée fixe [ee-DAY FEEX] French, "fixed idea"; in music, a recurring musical *theme* that is associated with a person or a concept.

ideogram [ID-e-uh-gram] A picture drawn to represent an idea or a concept.

idyll A relatively short poem that focuses on events and *themes* of everyday life, such as family, love, and religion; popular during the *Hellenistic* period and a standard *form* that has been periodically revived in Western literature throughout the centuries.

illuminated manuscript A richly decorated book, painted with brilliant colors and gold leaf, usually of sacred writings; popular in the West in the Middle Ages.

illusionism The use of painting *techniques* in *florid baroque* art to create the appearance that decorated areas are part of the surrounding architecture, usually employed in ceiling decorations.

imitation In music, a *technique* in which a musical idea, or motif, is presented by one voice or instrument and is then followed immediately by a restatement by another voice or instrument; the effect is that of a musical relay race.

impasto [ihm-PAHS-toe] In painting, the application of thick layers of pigment.

impressionism In painting, a *style* introduced in the 1870s, marked by an attempt to catch spontaneous impressions, often involving the play of sunlight on ordinary events and scenes observed outdoors; in music, a style of *composition* designed to create a vague and dreamy mood through gliding melodies and shimmering *tone colors.*

impressionistic In art, relating to the representation of a scene using the simplest details to create an illusion of reality by evoking subjective impressions rather than aiming for a totally realistic effect; characterized by images that are insubstantial and barely sketched in.

incunabula (singular, **incunabulum**) From the Latin, "cradle"; the collection of books printed before 1500 CE.

inductive reasoning The process of reasoning from particulars to the general or from single parts to the whole and/or final conclusion.

installation art A boundary-challenging type of art born in the 1960s that creates architectural tableaux, using objects drawn from and making references to artistic sources (such as music, painting, sculpture, and theater) and the workaday world (such as everyday tasks, media images, and foodstuffs) and that may include a human presence. Associated with the work of Ann Hamilton.

international style In twentieth-century architecture, a *style* and method of construction that capitalized on modern materials, such as ferro-concrete, glass, and steel, and that produced the popular "glass box" skyscrapers and variously shaped private houses.

Investiture Controversy The long quarrel between the medieval popes and the German emperors over their respective rights and responsibilities. The struggle sprang from the denial by the church, especially by the eleventh century popes, of the right of laypeople to invest clerics with the symbols of their church offices.

Ionic The Greek architectural order, developed in Ionia, in which columns are slender, sit on a base, and have *capitals* decorated with scrolls.

isorhythm In music, a unifying method based on rhythmic patterns rather than *melodic* patterns.

Italo-Byzantine style [ih-TAL-o-BIZ-uhn-teen] The *style* of Italian *Gothic* painting that reflected the influence of *Byzantine* paintings, *mosaics,* and icons.

iwan [eye-van] In Islamic architecture, a vaulted hall. In the 4-*iwan* mosque, one *iwan* was used for prayers and the other three for study or rest.

jazz A type of music, instrumental and vocal, originating in the African American community and rooted in African, African American, and Western musical forms and traditions.

Jesuits [JEZH-oo-its] Members of the Society of Jesus, the best-organized and most effective monastic order founded during the *Counter-Reformation* to combat Protestantism and spread Roman Catholicism around the world.

jihad [JEE-HAD] Originally, this Arabic term meant "to strive" or "to struggle" and, as such, was identified with any pious Muslim combating sin and trying not to do evil. In modern times, radical Islamic states and groups have given the term new meaning as "Holy War" and have used it to justify military and other violent action against their enemies. A central belief in Islam.

key In music, a tonal system consisting of seven *tones* in fixed relationship to a tonic, or keynote. Since the *Renaissance,* key has been the structural foundation of the bulk of Western music, down to the *modernist* period.

keystone The central stone at the top of an arch that locks the other stones in place.

Koine [KOI-nay] A colloquial Greek language spoken in the *Hellenistic* world that helped tie together that *civilization.*

korē [KOH-ray] An *Archaic* Greek standing statue of a young draped female.

kouros [KOO-rus] An *Archaic* Greek standing statue of a young naked male.

late Gothic style A *style* characterized in architecture by ornate decoration and tall cathedral windows and spires and in painting and sculpture by increased refinement of details and a trend toward *naturalism;* popular in the fourteenth and fifteenth centuries in central and western Europe.

late mannerism The last stage of the *mannerist* movement, characterized by exaggeration and distortion, especially in painting.

late modernism The last stage of *modernism,* characterized by an increasing sense of existential despair, an attraction to non-Western cultures, and extreme experimentalism.

lay A short *lyric* or narrative poem meant to be sung to the accompaniment of an instrument such as a harp; based on Celtic legends but usually set in feudal times and focused on courtly love *themes,* especially adulterous passion. The oldest surviving lays are those of the twelfth-century poet Marie de France.

leitmotif [LITE-mo-teef] In music, and especially in Wagner's *operas,* the use of recurring *themes* associated with particular characters, objects, or ideas.

liberalism In political thought, a set of beliefs advocating certain personal, economic, and natural rights based on assumptions about the perfectibility and autonomy of human beings and the notion of progress, as first expressed in the writings of John Locke.

liberation theology A reform movement, which began in the late 1960s among Roman Catholic priests and nuns in Latin America, blending Christian teachings on social and economic justice with Marxist theory. After this movement went global, the Vatican withdrew its support in the 1980s, though liberation theology remains an underground force in some parts of the world today.

libretto [lih-BRET-oh] In Italian, "little book"; the text or words of an *opera,* an *oratorio,* or a musical work of a similar dramatic nature involving a written text.

line The mark—straight or curved, thick or thin, light or dark—made by the artist in a work of art.

Linear A In Minoan *civilization,* a type of script still undeciphered that lasted from about 1800 to 1400 BCE.

Linear B In Minoan *civilization,* an early form of Greek writing that flourished on Crete from about 1400 until about 1300 BCE and lasted in a few scattered places on the Greek mainland until about 1150 BCE; used to record commercial transactions.

liturgical drama Religious dramas, popular between the twelfth and sixteenth centuries, based on biblical stories with musical accompaniment that were staged in the area in front of the church, performed at first in Latin but later in the *vernacular languages;* the mystery plays (*mystery* is derived from the Latin for "action") are the most famous type of liturgical drama.

liturgy A rite or ritual, such as prayers or ceremonies, practiced by a religious group in public worship.

local color In literature, the use of detail peculiar to a particular region and environment to add interest and authenticity to a narrative, including description of the locale, customs, speech, and music. Local color was an especially popular development in American literature in the late nineteenth century.

loggia A porch or gallery open on one or more sides, sometimes at street level, sometimes on a second story, normally placed on the front of a building but could be a self-standing structure.

logical positivism A school of modern philosophy that seeks truth by defining terms and clarifying statements and asserts that metaphysical theories are meaningless.

logos [LOWG-os] In *Stoicism,* the name for the supreme being or for reason—the controlling principle of the universe—believed to be present both in nature and in each human being.

Lombard arcades In architecture, a sequence of decorative *arcades* beneath the eaves of a building. First used in churches in Lombardy (north central Italy). A defining feature of the *First Romanesque.*

Lombard bands In architecture, a web of vertical bands or buttresses along the sides of a building. First used in churches in Lombardy (north central Italy). A defining feature of the *First Romanesque.*

luminism An art movement that emphasized nature rather than the individual. In nineteenth-century American landscape painting, a group of artists, who were inspired by the vastness of the American West and influenced by *transcendentalism,* approached their work by consciously removing themselves from their paintings.

lute In music, a wooden instrument, plucked or bowed, consisting of a sound box with an elaborately carved sound hole and a neck across which the (often twelve) strings pass. Introduced during the High Middle Ages, the lute enjoyed a height of popularity in Europe from the seventeenth to eighteenth century.

Lutheranism The doctrine, *liturgy,* and institutional structure of the church founded in the sixteenth century by Martin Luther, who stressed the authority of the Bible, the faith of the individual, and the worshiper's direct communication with God as the bases of his new religion.

lyre In music, a handheld stringed instrument, with or without a sound box, used by ancient Egyptians, Assyrians, and Greeks. In Greek culture, the lyre was played to accompany song and recitation.

lyric A short subjective poem that expresses intense personal emotion.

lyric poetry In Greece, verses sung and accompanied by the *lyre;* today, intensely personal poetry.

Machiavellianism [mahk-ih-uh-VEL-ih-uhn-iz-uhm] The view that politics should be separated from morals and dedicated to the achievement of desired ends through any means necessary ("the end justifies the means"); derived from the political writings of Machiavelli.

madrasa [mah-DRASS-ah] An Arabic term meaning a religious school for advanced study; a forerunner of the Islamic university. Today, *madrasas* are schools for Islamic youth, and their curriculum is based on the Qur'an.

madrigal [MAD-rih-guhl] A *polyphonic* song performed without accompaniment and based on a secular text, often a love *lyric;* especially popular in the sixteenth century.

magic realism A literary and artistic *style* identified with Latin American *postmodernism* that mixes realistic and supernatural elements to create imaginary or fantastic scenes.

mannerism A cultural movement between 1520 and 1600 that grew out of a rebellion against the *Renaissance's* artistic norms of symmetry and balance; characterized in art by distortion and incongruity and in thought and literature by the belief that human nature is depraved.

maqamah [mah-kah-mah] In Arabic, "assembly." A Muslim literary *genre,* intended for educated readers, that recounted stories of rogues and con men; filled with wordplay, humor, and keen usage of Arabic language and grammar. Created by al-Hamadhani in the tenth century.

Mass In religion, the ritual celebrating the Eucharist, or Holy Communion, primarily in the Roman Catholic Church. The Mass has two parts, the Ordinary and the Proper; the former remains the same throughout the church year, whereas the latter changes for each date and service. The Mass Ordinary is composed of the Kyrie, Gloria, Credo, Sanctus, and Agnus Dei; the Mass Proper includes the Introit, Gradual, Alleluia or Tract, Sequence, Offertory, and Communion. In music, a musical setting of certain parts of the Mass, especially the Kyrie, Gloria, Credo, Sanctus, Benedictus, and Agnus Dei. The first complete Mass Ordinary was composed by Guillaume de Machaut [mah-SHOH] (about 1300–1377) in the fourteenth century.

mass culture The tastes, values, and interests of the classes that dominate modern industrialized society, especially the consumer-oriented American middle class.

matriarchy Greek, literally "mother-rule"; term for historical or mythical societies in which political and social power is in the hands of women.

medallion In Roman architecture, a circular decoration often found on triumphal arches enclosing a scene or portrait; in general architectural use, a tablet or panel in a wall or window containing a figure or an ornament.

medium The material from which an artwork is made.

melisma In music, in *plainsong,* a style of singing in which a group of notes is sung to the same syllable; the opposite of *syllabic* singing.

melody A succession of musical *tones* having a distinctive shape and rhythm.

Messiah A Hebrew word meaning "the Anointed One," or one chosen by God to be his representative on earth; in Judaism, a savior who will come bringing peace and justice; in Christianity, Jesus Christ (*Christ* is derived from a Greek word meaning "the Anointed One").

metaphysical Meaning literally "beyond nature," based on abstract and speculative reasoning, not on empirical observation.

metope [MET-uh-pee] In architecture, a panel, often decorated, between two *triglyphs* on the *entablature* of a *Doric* Greek temple.

mezzotint Also known as halftone. An early type of color print, made with a metal plate, characterized by subtle gradations of shadings and clear definition of *line;* developed in about 1650 in the Netherlands.

microtone In music, an interval, or distance between a sound (pitch) on a scale, that is smaller than a semi*tone*—the smallest interval in mainstream Western music prior to *jazz.* Muslim music uses a microtonal system.

minaret In Islamic architecture, a tall, slender tower with a pointed top, from which the daily calls to prayer are delivered; located near a *mosque.*

minbar [min-bar] In Muslim *mosque* architecture, a pulpit with steps, sometimes on wheels for portability; used by a cleric for leading prayers and giving sermons.

miniature A small painting, usually of a religious nature, found in *illuminated manuscripts;* also, a small portrait.

minimalism A trend in *late modern* and *postmodern* art, architecture, and music that found beauty in the bare essentials and thus stripped art, buildings, and music to their basic elements. The minimalist aesthetic was a strong influence in the architecture of Mies van der Rohe, many art styles, including *conceptual art, environmental art,* and *op art,* and the music of Philip Glass.

minstrel A professional entertainer of the twelfth to seventeenth century; especially a secular musician; also called "jongleur."

minuet and trio In music, a *classical* music form, based on two French court dances of the same name, dating from the seventeenth and eighteenth centuries; often paired in the third section of *symphonies* in the *classical* period. Typically, the minuet was in ¾ time and with a moderate *tempo,* while the trio provided contrast but had no standard form.

modernism A late-nineteenth- and twentieth-century cultural, artistic, and literary movement that rejected much of the past and focused on the current, the secular, and the revolutionary in search of new forms of expression; the dominant style of the twentieth century until 1970.

modes A series of musical *scales* devised by the Greeks and believed by them to create certain emotional or ethical effects on the listener.

monophony [muh-NOF-uh-nee] A *style* of music in which there is only a single line of melody; the *Gregorian chants* are the most famous examples of monophonic music.

monotheism From the Greek *monos*, "single, alone," and the Greek *theos*, "god"; the belief that there is only one God.

montage In film, a technique consisting of highly elaborate editing patterns and rhythms.

mood In music, the emotional impact of a *composition* on the feelings of a listener.

mosaic An art form or decoration, usually on a wall or a floor, created by inlaying small pieces of glass, shell, stone, or metal in cement or plaster to create pictures or patterns.

mosque A Muslim place of worship, often distinguished by a dome-shaped central building placed in an open space surrounded by a wall.

motet A multivoiced song with words of a sacred or secular text, usually sung without accompanying instruments; developed in the thirteenth century.

mural A wall painting, usually quite large, used to decorate a private or public structure.

muse In Greek religion, any one of the nine sister goddesses who preside over the creative arts and sciences.

music drama An *opera* in which the action and music are continuous, not broken up into separate *arias* and *recitatives*, and the music is determined by its dramatic appropriateness, producing a work in which music, words, and staging are fused; the term was coined by Wagner.

myth A traditional story about gods, heroes, or ancestors that serves to exemplify essential moral, political, social, or psychological characteristics believed to exist in a given society.

narrative voice In literature, the *narrator,* a key element in fiction. An omniscient narrator, usually in the third person, knows everything about the *plot* and *characters,* regardless of time and place—typical of nineteenth-century novels. In *modernist* fiction, the narrative voice tends to be disjointed, unreliable, and often in the first person.

narrator The speaker whose voice we hear in a story or poem.

narthex The porch or vestibule of a church, usually enclosed, through which worshipers walk before entering the *nave.*

naturalism In literature, a late-nineteenth-century movement inspired by the methods of science and the insights of sociology, concerned with an objective depiction of the ugly side of industrial society.

natural law In *Stoicism* and later in other philosophies, a body of laws or principles that are believed to be derived from nature and binding on human society and that constitute a higher form of justice than civil or judicial law.

natural philosophy Science based on philosophical speculation and experiments or data, founded in Ionian Greece in the sixth century BCE; a term that embraced both science and philosophy until about 1800 CE.

nave The central longitudinal area of a church, extending from the entrance to the *apse* and flanked by *aisles.*

neoclassical style In the late eighteenth century, an artistic and literary movement that emerged as a reaction to the *rococo* style and that sought inspiration from ancient *classicism.* In the twentieth century, between 1919 and 1951, *neoclassicism* in music was a style that rejected the emotionalism favored by *romantic* composers as well as the dense orchestral sounds of the *impressionists*; instead, it borrowed features from seventeenth- and eighteenth-century music and practiced the ideals of balance, clarity of texture, and non-programmatic works.

neoclassicism In the late third century BCE, an artistic movement in the disintegrating *Hellenistic* world that sought inspiration in the Athenian Golden Age of the fifth and fourth centuries BCE; and, since 1970, neoclassicism has been a highly visible submovement in *postmodernism,* particularly prominent in painting and architecture, that restates the principles of *classical* art—balance, harmony, idealism.

neoexpressionism A submovement in *postmodernism,* associated primarily with painting, that offers social criticism and is concerned with the expression of the artist's feelings.

Neolithic Literally, "new stone"; used to define the New Stone Age, when human *cultures* evolved into agrarian systems and settled communities; dating from about 10,000 or 8000 BCE to about 3000 BCE.

neoorthodoxy A twentieth-century Protestant movement, dedicated to recentering orthodox theology in Christian thought and emphasizing the central role played by God in history. Founded after World War I in opposition to the *Social Gospel.*

Neoplatonism A philosophy based on Plato's ideas that was developed during the Roman period in an attempt to reconcile the dichotomy between Plato's concept of an eternal World of Ideas and the ever-changing physical world; in the fifteenth-century *Renaissance,* it served as a philosophical guide for Italian humanists who sought to reconcile late medieval Christian beliefs with *classical* thinking.

neorealism A submovement in *postmodernism* that is based on a photographic sense of detail and harks back to many of the qualities of nineteenth-century *realism.*

neoromanticism A *postmodern* movement in music, starting after 1970, which rejects *atonality* and draws inspiration from the music of the *romantic* period.

neumes From the Greek *neuma*, a "gesture," or "sigh"; a system of musical notation (a written pattern of dots and squiggles), used from the Carolingian period to the fourteenth century, inserted into *plainchant* manuscripts to signal pitch and to a lesser degree the shape of the *melody.*

New Comedy The *style* of comedy favored by *Hellenistic* playwrights, concentrating on gentle satirical *themes*—in particular, romantic *plots* with stock *characters* and predictable endings.

nihilism The denial of any objective ground of truth and, in particular, of moral truths.

nominalism [NAHM-uh-nuhl-iz-uhm] In medieval thought, the school that held that objects were separate unto themselves but could, for convenience, be treated in a collective sense because they shared certain characteristics; opposed to *realism.*

northern Renaissance The sixteenth-century cultural movement in northern Europe that was launched by the northward spread of Italian *Renaissance* art, culture, and ideals. The northern Renaissance differed from the Italian Renaissance largely because of the persistence of the *late Gothic style* and the unfolding of the *Reformation* after 1520.

Nouvelle Vague French, "New Wave"; a *late modern* movement in French film, featuring innovative narrative structures and various experimental cinematic techniques.

French word for "New Wave" films in the post–World War II period that experimented with new ways to capture scenes and events.

octave In music, usually the eight-tone interval between a note and a second note of the same name, as in C to C.

oculus [AHK-yuh-lus] The circular opening at the top of a dome; derived from the Latin word for "eye."

Old Comedy The *style* of *comedy* established by Aristophanes in the fifth century BCE, distinguished by a strong element of political and social satire.

oligarchy From the Greek *oligos*, "few"; a state ruled by the few, especially by a small fraction of persons or families.

Olympian deities In Greek religion, sky gods and goddesses who lived on mountaintops and were worshiped mainly by the Greek aristocracy.

op art A *late modern* art movement, using *abstract*, mathematically based forms to create stimulating images for the eyes, such as optical patterns, lingering images, and whirling effects.

opera A drama or play set to music and consisting of vocal pieces with *orchestral* accompaniment; acting, scenery, and sometimes *choruses* and dancing are used to heighten the dramatic values of operas.

oratorio A choral work based on religious events or *scripture* employing singers, *choruses*, and *orchestra*, but without scenery or staging and performed usually in a church or a concert hall.

orchestra In Greek theaters, the circular area where the *chorus* performed in front of the audience; in music, a group of instrumentalists, including string players, who play together.

organum [OR-guh-nuhm] In the ninth through the thirteenth centuries, a simple and early form of *polyphonic* music consisting of a main *melody* sung along with a *Gregorian chant*; by the thirteenth century it had developed into a complex multivoiced song.

Paleolithic Literally, "old stone"; used to define the Old Stone Age, when crude stones and tools were used; dating from about 2,000,000 BCE to about 10,000 BCE.

pantheism The doctrine of or belief in multitudes of deities found in nature; a recurrent belief since prehistoric times. Prominent in nineteenth-century *romanticism*.

pantomime In Roman times, dramatic productions featuring instrumental music and dances, favored by the masses; later, a type of dramatic or dancing performance in which the story is told with expressive or even exaggerated bodily and facial movements.

paradigm shift The exchange of one worldview or perspective for another, as, for example, the shift from earth-centered astronomy to sun-centered astronomy between 1550 and 1700; a **paradigm** is an unconsciously agreed-on pattern of thought in a scientific discipline and, by extension, any shared set of beliefs and habits of thought; a term coined by Thomas Kuhn.

parchment A writing surface, prepared from calf-, sheep-, and goatskins, developed in ancient Pergamum. Parchment's supple surface allowed the storing of writing on both sides of a page and thus opened the door to the first books.

pastoral A type of *Hellenistic* poetry that idealized rural customs and farming, especially the simple life of shepherds, and deprecated urban living.

paterfamilias Latin, literally "the father of the family"; the term applied to the male head of a Roman household who possessed life and death authority over all in his residence, family members and servants alike.

patricians From Latin, *pater*, "father"; the patricians were the well-born, landholding class that dominated the Roman republic for centuries.

Pax Romana Latin, the "Roman Peace." A term applied to the first two centuries of the Roman Empire when the Mediterranean was at peace, albeit on Roman terms.

pediment In *classical*-style architecture, the triangular-shaped area or gable at the end of the building formed by the sloping roof and the *cornice*.

pendentive [pen-DEN-tiv] In architecture, a triangular, concave-shaped section of *vaulting* between the rim of a dome and the pair of arches that support it; used in Byzantine and Islamic architecture.

performance art A democratic type of mixed-media art born in the 1960s that ignores artistic boundaries, mixing high art (such as music, painting, and theater) and popular art (such as rock and roll, film, and fads), to create a unique, nonreproducible, artistic experience. Associated with the work of Laurie Anderson.

peristyle [PAIR-uh-stile] A colonnade around an open courtyard or a building.

Perpendicular style The highly decorative *style* of *late Gothic* architecture that developed in England at the same time as the *late Gothic* on the European continent.

Persian miniature A *style* of *miniature* painting that flourished in Persia from the thirteenth to seventeenth century; characterized by rectangular designs, the depiction of the human figure as about one-fifth the height of the painting, and refined detail.

perspective A technique or formula for creating the illusion or appearance of depth and distance on a two-dimensional surface. **Atmospheric perspective** is achieved in many ways: by diminishing color intensity, by omitting detail, and by blurring the lines of an object. **Linear perspective,** based on mathematical calculations, is achieved by having parallel lines or lines of projection appearing to converge at a single point, known as the *vanishing point*, on the horizon of the flat surface and by diminishing distant objects in size according to scale to make them appear to recede from the viewer.

Petrine Idea In Catholic *theology*, the idea that as Christ had made St. Peter the leader of the apostles (Matthew 16: 18–19), his successors, the bishops of Rome (or popes), inherited his authority.

philosophes [FEEL-uh-sawfs] A group of European thinkers and writers who popularized the ideas of the *Enlightenment* through essays, novels, plays, and other works, hoping to change the climate of opinion and bring about social and political reform.

phonogram A symbol used to represent a syllable, a word, or a sound.

photomontage An art *medium* in which photographs, from varied sources, but especially from newspapers, are cut up, rearranged, and pasted onto a surface, such as a poster board. When done, the photomontage usually sent a political or social message. Starting in 1918, the photomontage was part of the *Dada* movement's assault against traditional art.

Physiocrats [FIZ-ih-uh-kratz] A group of writers, primarily French, who dealt with economic issues during the *Enlightenment*, in particular calling for improved agricultural productivity and questioning the state's role in economic affairs.

piano Italian, "soft." In music, softly. Also, the usual term for *pianoforte*.

pianissimo Italian, "very softly," a musical term.

pianoforte [pee-an-o-FOR-tay] A piano; derived from the Italian for "soft/loud," terms used to describe the two types of sound emitted by a stringed instrument whose wires are struck with felt-covered hammers operated from a keyboard.

picaresque novel From the Spanish term for "rogue." A type of literature, originating in sixteenth-century Spain, that recounted the comic misadventures of a roguish hero who lived by his wits, often at the expense of the high and mighty; influenced novel writing across Europe, especially in England, France, and Germany, until about 1800; the anonymous *Lazarillo de Tormes* (1554) was the first picaresque novel.

pictogram A carefully drawn, often stylized, picture that represents a particular object.

pier In architecture, a vertical masonry structure that may support a *vault*, an arch, or a roof; in *Gothic* churches, piers were often clustered together to form massive supports.

Pietà [pee-ay-TAH] A painting or sculpture depicting the mourning Virgin and the dead Christ.

Pietism A religious reform movement among German Lutherans, which stressed personal piety, along with support for social programs for the poor; part of the general religious ferment of western Europe in the late 1600s and early 1700s and a catalyst for the *First Great Awakening* in British Colonial America in the 1700s.

pilaster [pih-LAS-tuhr] In architecture, a vertical, rectangular decorative device projecting from a wall that gives the appearance of a column with a base and a *capital;* sometimes called an applied column.

Pinteresque In the theater, a dramatic style, attributed to the British playwright Harold Pinter; characterized by enigmatic *plots* and, especially, long pauses in the dialogue.

Platonism The collective beliefs and arguments presented in Plato's writings stressing especially that actual things are copies of Ideas.

plainsong Also called *plainchant.* In music, the *monophonic* chant sung in the *liturgy* of the Roman Catholic Church.

plebeians The great mass of the Roman people who eventually attained political but never social equality with the patricians.

plot The action, or arrangement of incidents, in a story.

podium In architecture, a low wall serving as a foundation; a platform.

poetry Language that is concentrated and imaginative, marked by meter, rhythm, rhyme, and imagery.

pointed arch A key element of *Gothic* architecture, probably introduced from the Muslim world, which permitted the joining of two arches of identical height but different width. Pointed arches led to complex designs and reduced the need for thick walls to support the massive *vaults* and roofs typical of the *Romanesque style.*

pointillism [PWANT-il-iz-uhm] Also known as divisionism, a *style* of painting, perfected by Seurat, in which tiny dots of paint are applied to the canvas in such a way that when they are viewed from a distance they merge and blend to form recognizable objects with natural effects of color, light, and shade.

polyphony [puh-LIF-uh-nee] A style of musical *composition* in which two or more voices or melodic lines are sung or played at the same time.

polytheism [PAHL-e-the-iz-uhm] The doctrine of or belief in more than one deity.

pop art An artistic *style* popular between 1960 and 1970 in which commonplace commercial objects drawn from *mass culture,* such as soup cans, fast foods, and comic strips, became the subjects of art.

portico In architecture, a covered entrance to a building, usually with a separate roof supported by columns.

porticus A covered, usually colonnaded, porch or walkway. A porticus might complement one building or serve to join two or more buildings together.

post-and-lintel construction A basic architectural form in which two vertical posts, or columns, support a horizontal lintel, or beam.

post-beam-triangle construction The generic name given to Greek architecture that includes the post, or column; the beam, or lintel; and the triangular-shaped area, or *pediment.*

postimpressionism A late-nineteenth-century artistic movement that extended the boundaries of *impressionism* in new directions to focus on structure, composition, fantasy, and subjective expression.

postmodernism An artistic, cultural, and intellectual movement, originating in about 1970, that is more optimistic than *modernism,* embraces an open-ended and democratic global *civilization,* freely adapts elements of high culture and *mass culture,* and manifests itself chiefly through revivals of earlier styles, giving rise to *neoclassicism, neo-expressionism,* and *neorealism.*

poststructuralism In analytical theory, a set of *techniques,* growing out of *structuralism,* which were used to show that meaning is shifting and unstable.

Praxitelean curve [prak-sit-i-LEE-an] The graceful line of the sculptured body in the *contrapposto* stance, perfected by the *fourth-century style* sculptor Praxiteles.

primitivism In painting, the "primitives" are those painters of the Netherlandish and Italian schools who flourished before 1500, thus all Netherlandish painters between the van Eycks and Dürer and all Italian painters between Giotto and Raphael; more generally, the term reflects modern artists' fascination with non-Western art forms, as in Gauguin's Tahitian-inspired paintings. In literature, primitivism has complex meanings; on the one hand, it refers to the notion of a golden age, a world of lost innocence, which appeared in both ancient pagan and Christian writings; on the other hand, it is a modern term used to denote two species of cultural relativism, which either finds people isolated from civilization to be superior to those living in civilized and urban settings, as in the cult of the noble savage (Rousseau), or respects native peoples and their cultures within their own settings, yet accepts that natives can be as cruel as Europeans (the view expressed by Montaigne).

principate Term applied to the Roman imperial regime inaugurated by Augustus Caesar (31 BCE–14 CE), who was designated "princeps," meaning "first citizen." The principate lasted until the death of Marcus Aurelius in 180 CE.

problem play A type of drama that focuses on a specific social issue; the Swedish playwright Ibsen was a pioneer of this *genre,* as in *A Doll's House* (1879), concerning women's independence.

program music Instrumental music that depicts a narrative, portrays a *setting,* or suggests a sequence of events; often based on other sources, such as a poem or a play.

prose The ordinary language used in speaking and writing.

prosimetric A literary work in both *prose* and verse. Developed in antiquity, this literary *genre* was popularized in the Middle Ages by Boethius's *Consolation of Philosophy* and adapted for the vernacular by Dante's *La Vita Nuova (The New Life).*

Ptolemies The name of the dynasty—descended from Ptolemy, one of Alexander the Great's generals—that ruled Egypt down to the Roman conquest.

Puritanism The beliefs and practices of the Puritans, a small but influential religious group devoted to the teachings of John Calvin; they stressed strict rules of personal and public behavior and practiced their beliefs in England and the New World during the seventeenth century.

qasida [kah-SEE-dah] In Arabic, "ode." An ode composed in varied meters and with a single rhyme; that is, all lines end in the same rhyming sound. The leading poetic *genre* in Muslim literature.

qiblah [kee-blah] In Islamic *mosque* architecture, a niche, often richly decorated, pointing the direction for prayer, that is, toward the Kaaba in Mecca.

ragtime A type of instrumental music, popularized by African Americans in the late nineteenth and early twentieth centuries, with a strongly syncopated rhythm and a lively *melody.*

Rayonnant [ray-yo-NAHNN] A decorative *style* in French architecture associated with the High *Gothic* period, in which walls were replaced by sheets of *stained glass* framed by elegant stone *traceries.* Also called "Radiant."

realism In medieval philosophy, the school that asserted that objects contained common or universal qualities that were not always apparent to the human senses but that were more real or true than the objects' physical attributes; opposed to *nominalism.* In art and literature, a mid- to late-nineteenth-century style that focused on the everyday lives of the middle and lower classes, portraying their world in a serious, accurate, and unsentimental way; opposed to *romanticism.*

recitative [ress-uh-tuh-TEEV] In music, a rhythmically free but often stylized declamation, midway between singing and ordinary speech, that serves as a transition between *arias* or as a narrative device in an *opera.*

Reformation The sixteenth-century religious movement that looked back to the ideals of early Christianity, called for moral and structural changes in the church, and led ultimately to the founding of the various Protestant churches.

refrain In music, a recurring musical passage or phrase; called *ritornello* in Italian.

regalia Plural in form, often used with a singular verb. The emblems and symbols of royalty, as the crown and scepter.

relief In sculpture, figures or forms that are carved so that they project from the flat surface of a stone or metal background. **High relief** projects sharply from the surface; **low relief,** or **bas relief,** is more shallow.

Renaissance [ren-uh-SAHNS] From the French for "rebirth"; the artistic, cultural, and intellectual movement marked by a revival of *classical* and *humanistic* values that began in Italy in the mid–fourteenth century and had spread across Europe by the mid–sixteenth century.

representational art Art that presents a likeness of the world as it appears to the naked eye.

res publica Latin, literally "the public thing"; the term the Romans applied to their government and society, signaling that civic life and duty were the business of all—at least of all male citizens.

restrained baroque style A variation of the *baroque* style identified with Dutch and English architects and painters who wanted to reduce *baroque* grandeur and exuberance to a more human scale.

revenge tragedy A type of play popular in sixteenth-century England, probably rooted in Roman *tragedies* and concerned with the need for a family to seek revenge for the murder of a relative.

ribbed vault A masonry roof with a framework of arches or ribs that reinforce and decorate the *vault* ceiling.

rocaille [roh-KYE] In *rococo* design, the stucco ornaments shaped like leaves, flowers, and ribbons that decorate walls and ceilings.

rococo style [ruh-KOH-koh] An artistic and cultural *style* that grew out of the *baroque* style but that was more intimate and personal and emphasized the frivolous and superficial side of aristocratic life.

romance A story derived from legends associated with Troy or Celtic culture but often set in feudal times and centered on *themes* of licit and illicit love between noble lords and ladies.

Romanesque style [roh-muhn-ESK] A *style* of architecture, usually associated with churches built in the eleventh and twelfth centuries, that was inspired by Roman architectural features, such as the *basilica,* and was thus Roman-like. Romanesque buildings were massive, with round arches and *barrel* or *groined vault* ceilings, and had less exterior decoration than *Gothic* churches.

romanticism An intellectual, artistic, and literary movement that began in the late eighteenth century as a reaction to *neoclassicism* and stressed the emotional, mysterious, and imaginative side of human behavior and the unruly side of nature.

rondeau [RON-doh] (plural, **rondeaux**) A French verse form, consisting of thirteen lines, or sometimes ten lines, dating from the late Middle Ages.

rose window A large circular window, made of *stained glass* and held together with lead and carved stones set in patterns, or *tracery,* and located over an entrance in a *Gothic cathedral.*

sacred music Religious music, such as *Gregorian chants, Masses,* and hymns.

sarcophagus [sahr-KAHF-uh-guhs] (plural, **sarcophagi**) From the Greek meaning "flesh-eating stone"; a marble or stone coffin or tomb, usually decorated with carvings, used first by Romans and later by Christians for burial of the dead.

satire From the Latin, "medley"—a cooking term; a literary *genre* that originated in ancient Rome and was characterized by two basic forms: (a) tolerant and amused observation of the human scene, modeled on Horace's style, and (b) bitter and sarcastic denunciation of all behavior and thought outside a civilized norm, modeled on Juvenal's style. In modern times, a literary work that holds up human vices and follies to ridicule or scorn.

satyr-play [SAT-uhr] A comic play, often featuring sexual *themes,* performed at the Greek drama festivals along with the *tragedies.*

scale A set pattern of *tones* (or notes) arranged from low to high.

scenographic [see-nuh-GRAF-ik] In *Renaissance* architecture, a building style that envisioned buildings as composed of separate units; in the painting of stage scenery, the art of *perspective* representation.

scherzo [SKAIRT-so] From the Italian for "joke"; a quick and lively instrumental *composition* or movement found in *sonatas* and *symphonies.*

Scholasticism In medieval times, the body or collection of knowledge that tried to harmonize Aristotle's writings with Christian doctrine; also, a way of thinking and establishing sets of arguments.

Scientific Revolution The seventeenth-century intellectual movement, based originally on discoveries in astronomy and physics, that challenged and overturned medieval views about the order of the universe and the theories used to explain motion.

scripture The sacred writings of any religion, as the Bible in Judaism and Christianity.

Second Romanesque The second and mature stage of *Romanesque* architecture, about 1080–1200. Second Romanesque churches were richly decorated and built on a vast scale, including such features as double *transepts,* double *aisles,* crossing towers, and towers at the ends of the *transepts;* associated with Cluniac monasticism.

secular music Nonreligious music, such as *symphonies,* songs, and dances.

Seleucids The name of the dynasty (most of whose rulers were called Seleucus or Antiochus) that ruled Syria and Mesopotamia after the death of Alexander the Great and down to the Roman conquest. Seleucus I was one of Alexander's generals.

senate From Latin *senex,* "old man"; the senate was the assembly of former officeholders at Rome. The senate could not pass laws but often issued opinions that were influential.

serenade In music, a lighthearted piece, intended to be performed outdoors in the evening; popular in the eighteenth and nineteenth centuries.

serial music A type of musical composition based on a *twelvetone scale* arranged any way the composer chooses; the absence of a tonal center in serial music leads to *atonality.*

setting In literature, the background against which the action takes place; in a representational artwork, the time and place depicted.

seven liberal arts Essentially, the curriculum of the ancient schools. Canonized by Martianus Capella in *The Marriage of Mercury and Philology* (late fifth century CE), the arts were grammar, rhetoric, dialectic (logic), arithmetic, geometry, astronomy, and music. In medieval schools, the arts were often divided into the Trivium (grammar, rhetoric, and dialectic) and the Quadrivium (arithmetic, geometry, astronomy, and music).

Severe style The first sculptural *style* of the *classical* period in Greece, which retained stylistic elements from the *Archaic* style.

sfumato [sfoo-MAH-toh] In painting, the blending of one *tone* into another to blur the outline of a form and give the canvas a smokelike appearance; a technique perfected by Leonardo da Vinci.

shaft graves Deep pit burial sites; the dead were usually placed at the bottom of the shafts; a burial practice in Mycenaean Greece.

skene [SKEE-nee] A small building behind the *orchestra* in a Greek theater, used as a prop and as a storehouse for theatrical materials.

Skepticism A *Hellenistic* philosophy that questioned whether anything could be known for certain, argued that all beliefs were relative, and concluded that *autarky* could be achieved only by recognizing that inquiry was fruitless.

slave narrative A literary *genre,* either written by slaves or told by slaves to secretaries who wrote them down, which emerged prior to the American Civil War; the genre was launched by the *Narrative of the Life of Frederick Douglass, an American Slave* (1845); the harsh details of the inhumane and unjust slave system, as reported in these narratives, contributed to *realist* literature.

social contract In political thought, an agreement or contract between the people and their rulers defining the rights and duties of each so that a civil society might be created.

Social Gospel A Protestant movement, mainly in the United States, whose heyday was from 1880 to 1945, which stressed social improvement rather than personal piety; the religious equivalent of *liberal* politics.

socialism An economic and political system in which goods and property are owned collectively or by the state; the socialist movement began as a reaction to the excesses of the factory system in the nineteenth century and ultimately called for either reforming or abolishing industrial capitalism.

socialist realism A Marxist artistic theory that calls for the use of literature, music, and the arts in the service of the ideals and goals of socialism and/or communism, with an emphasis in painting on the realistic portrayal of objects.

solipsism In philosophy, the sense that only one's self exists or can be known.

sonata [soh-NAH-tah] In music, an instrumental *composition,* usually in three or four movements.

sonata form A musical *form* or structure consisting of three (or sometimes four) sections that vary in *key, tempo,* and *mood.*

squinch In architecture, an arch, or a set of gradually wider and projecting arches placed diagonally at the internal angles of towers in order to mount a round or polygonal superstructure on a square plan, used in Gothic, Byzantine, and Islamic architecture (cf. *pendentives*).

stained glass An art form characterized by many small pieces of tinted glass bound together by strips of lead, usually to produce a pictorial scene of a religious theme; developed by *Romanesque* artists and a central feature of *Gothic* churches.

stele [STEE-lee] A carved or inscribed vertical stone pillar or slab, often used for commemorative purposes.

stereobate In Greek architecture, the stepped base on which a temple stands.

Stoicism [STO-ih-sihz-uhm] The most popular and influential *Hellenistic* philosophy, advocating a restrained way of life, a toleration for others, a resignation to disappointments, and a resolution to carry out one's responsibilities. Stoicism appealed to many Romans and had an impact on early Christian thought.

stream of consciousness A writing technique used by some modern authors in which the narration consists of a *character's* continuous interior monologue of thoughts and feelings.

structuralism In *postmodernism,* an approach to knowledge based on the belief that human behavior and institutions can be explained by reference to a few underlying structures that themselves are reflections of hidden patterns in the human mind.

studia humanitatis [STOO-dee-ah hu-man-ih-TAH-tis] **(humanistic studies)** The Latin term given by *Renaissance* scholars to new intellectual pursuits that were based on recently discovered ancient texts, including moral philosophy, history, grammar, rhetoric, and poetry. This new learning stood in sharp contrast to medieval *Scholasticism.*

Sturm und Drang [STOORM oont drahng] German, "storm and stress"; a German literary movement of the 1770s that focused on themes of action, emotionalism, and the individual's revolt against the conventions of society.

style The combination of distinctive elements of creative execution and expression, in terms of both *form* and *content.*

style galant [STEEL gah-LAHNN] In *rococo* music, a *style* of music developed by French composers and characterized by graceful and simple *melodies.*

stylobate [STY-luh-bate] In Greek temples, the upper step of the base that forms a platform on which the columns stand.

subject In music, the main *theme.*

sublime [suh-BLIME] In *romanticism,* the term used to describe nature as a terrifying and awesome force full of violence and power.

suprematism [suh-PREM-uh-tiz-uhm] A variation of *abstract art,* originating in Russia in the early twentieth century, characterized by the use of geometric shapes as the basic elements of the composition.

surrealism [suh-REE-uhl-iz-uhm] An early-twentieth-century movement in art, literature, and theater, in which incongruous juxtapositions and fantastic images produce an irrational and dreamlike effect.

swing band A fifteen- or sixteen-member orchestra, which plays ballads and dance tunes; dominated popular music in the United States and in large cities in western Europe, from the early 1930s until the early 1950s.

syllabic In music, in *plainsong,* a style of musical setting in which one note is set to each syllable.

symbolic realism In art, a *style* that is realistic and true to life but uses the portrayed object or person to represent or symbolize something else.

symphony A long and complex *sonata,* usually written in three or four movements, for large *orchestras;* the first movement is traditionally fast, the second slow, and the third (and optional fourth) movement fast.

syncopation [sin-ko-PAY-shun] In music, the technique of accenting the weak beat when a strong beat is expected.

syncretism [SIN-kruh-tiz-uhm] The combining of different forms of religious beliefs or practices.

synthesizer [SIN-thuh-size-uhr] An electronic apparatus with a keyboard capable of duplicating the sounds of many musical instruments, popular among *postmodernist* composers and musicians.

tabula rasa [TAB-yuh-luh RAH-zuh] "Blank tablet," the Latin term John Locke used to describe the mind at birth, empty of inborn ideas and ready to receive sense impressions, which Locke believed were the sole source of knowledge.

technique The systematic procedure whereby a particular creative task is performed.

tempera A permanent, fast-drying painting *medium* consisting of colored pigment and a water-soluble binder, usually egg yolk; widely used in early Christian art and then continuously used until the development of oil paints in the fifteenth century.

tempo In music, the relative speed at which a *composition* is to be played, indicated by a suggestive word or phrase or by a precise number such as a metronome marking. (A metronome is a finely calibrated device used to determine the exact tempo for a musical work.)

tenebrism In painting, a style of *chiaroscuro* that uses bright, sweeping light to illuminate figures against an intense dark background.

terza rima [TER-tsuh REE-muh] A three-line stanza with an interlocking rhyme scheme (*aba bcb cdc ded,* and so on), used by Dante in his *Divine Comedy.*

tetrarchy Greek, "rule by four." A term applied to the institutional arrangements created by Diocletian, in which rule in the Roman Empire was shared among two Augustuses and two Caesars.

texture In a musical composition, the number and nature of voices or instruments employed and how the parts are combined.

theater of the absurd A type of theater that has come to reflect the despair, anxieties, and absurdities of modern life and in which the characters seldom make sense, the *plot* is nearly nonexistent, bizarre and fantastic events occur onstage, and *tragedy* and *comedy* are mixed in unconventional ways; associated with *late modernism.*

theme The dominant idea of a work; the message or emotion the artist intends to convey; used in music, literature, and art.

themes The name for administrative and military districts created in the Byzantine Empire in the eighth and ninth centuries. Soldiers were settled on the land and served under the local commander, the *strategos.* The system provided for defense without that state's having to raise tax revenues to pay soldiers.

theme and variations In music, a *technique* in which a musical idea is stated and then repeated in variant versions, with modifications or embellishments; used in independent works or as a single movement in a *symphony, sonata,* or chamber work.

theocracy From the Greek *theos,* "god"; a state governed by a god regarded as the ruling power or by priests or officials claiming divine sanction.

theology The application of philosophy to the study of religious truth, focusing especially on the nature of the deity and the origin and teachings of an organized religious community.

tondo From the Italian *rotondo,* "round"; a circular artwork containing a painting or a sculpture, originating in ancient Greece and Rome and revived during the Renaissance.

tone A musical sound of definite pitch; also, the quality of a sound.

tone color In music, the quality of a sound, determined by the overtones; used for providing contrasts.

tracery Ornamental architectural work with lines that branch out to form designs, often found as stone carvings in *rose windows*.

tragedy A serious and deeply moral drama, typically involving a noble protagonist brought down by excessive pride (hubris) and describing a conflict between seemingly irreconcilable values or forces; in Greece, tragedies were performed at the festivals associated with the worship of Dionysus.

transcendentalism A literary and philosophical movement that emphasized the spiritual over the material, the metaphysical over the physical, and intuition over empiricism. Its central tenet identified God or the divine spirit (transcendence) with nature; popular in early- and mid-nineteenth-century New England.

transept In church architecture, the crossing arm that bisects the *nave* near the *apse* and gives the characteristic *cruciform* shape to the floor plan.

tremolo In music, the rapid repetition of two pitches in a chord, so as to produce a tremulous effect.

triclinium (plural, **triclinia**) In the Roman world, a dining room with three couches for diners to recline on while eating. In the Middle Ages, the term for a formal reception chamber, which could be used for dining or other festive occasions.

triconch A prestigious building type developed by the Romans and inherited by medieval builders. The three (tri-) *conches* constituted an *apse* at one end and two *apse*-like extrusions along the building's long sides.

triglyph [TRY-glif] In Greek architecture, a three-grooved rectangular panel on the *frieze* of a *Doric* temple; triglyphs alternated with *metopes*.

trill In music, the rapid alternation of two notes, a step apart; used as a musical embellishment.

triptych [TRIP-tik] In painting, a set of three hinged or folding panels depicting a religious story, mainly used as an altarpiece.

trope [TROHP] In *Gregorian chants*, a new phrase or *melody* inserted into an existing chant to make it more musically appealing; also called a turn; in literature, a figure of speech.

troubador [TROO-buh-door] A composer and/or singer, usually an aristocrat, who performed *secular* love songs at the feudal courts in southern France.

twelve-tone scale In music, a fixed *scale* or series in which there is an arbitrary arrangement of the twelve *tones* (counting every half tone) of an octave; devised by Arnold Schoenberg.

tympanum [TIM-puh-num] In medieval architecture, the triangular space over a doorway set above the lintel, usually decorated with carvings depicting biblical themes; in *classical* style architecture, the recessed face of a *pediment*.

ukiyo-e [oo-key-yoh-AY] A type of colorful Japanese print, incised on woodblocks, that is characterized by simple design, plain backgrounds, and flat areas of color. Developed in seventeenth-century Japan; admired by late-nineteenth-century Parisian artists, who assimilated it to a Western style that is most notable in the prints of Mary Cassatt.

utilitarianism [yoo-til-uh-TARE-e-uh-niz-uhm] The doctrine set forth in the social theory of Jeremy Bentham in the nineteenth century that the final goal of society and humans is "the greatest good for the greatest number."

vanishing point In linear *perspective*, the point on the horizon at which the receding parallel lines appear to converge and then vanish.

vault A ceiling or roof made from a series of arches placed next to one another.

vernacular language [vuhr-NAK-yuh-luhr] The language or dialect of a region, usually spoken by the general population as opposed to the wealthy or educated elite.

vernacular literature Literature written in the language of the populace, such as English, French, or Italian, as opposed to the language of the educated elite, usually Latin.

via antiqua [VEE-uh ahn-TEE-kwah] The "old way," the term used in late medieval thought by the opponents of St. Thomas Aquinas to describe his *via media*, which they considered outdated.

via media [VEE-uh MAY-dee-ah] The "middle way" that St. Thomas Aquinas sought in reconciling Aristotle's works to Christian beliefs.

via moderna [VEE-uh moh-DEHR-nah] The "new way," the term used in late medieval thought by those thinkers who opposed the school of Aquinas.

video art A type of art made with a video monitor or monitors; produced using either computerized programs or handheld cameras; can be ephemeral or permanent.

virtuoso [vehr-choo-O-so] An aristocratic person who experimented in science, usually as an amateur, in the seventeenth century, giving science respectability and a wider audience; later, in music, a person with great technical skill.

voussoir [voo-SWAR] A carved, wedge-shaped stone or block in an arch.

Vulgate Name for the edition and translation of the Bible into Latin prepared by St. Jerome (345–420). The term derives from Latin *vulgus*, meaning "the crowd" or "the people generally," but specifically those who spoke Latin, not Greek.

westwork The exterior western end of a church; originated by the Carolingians, whose churches were given tall, impressive western ends. *Romanesque* and *Gothic* builders retained Carolingian height but added sculptural and architectural details so as to create ornate, intricate facades.

woodcut In art, the technique of cutting or carving an image onto a wooden block used for printing; originated in the late Middle Ages. Also, the print made from the technique.

word painting In music, the illustration of an idea, a meaning, or a feeling associated with a word, as, for example, using a discordant *melody* when the word *pain* is sung. This technique is especially identified with the sixteenth-century *madrigal*; also called word illustration or madrigalism.

ziggurat [ZIG-oo-rat] A Mesopotamian stepped pyramid, usually built with external staircases and a shrine at the top; sometimes included a tower.

Credits

TEXT CREDITS

Index

Page numbers in *italics* indicate pronunciation guides; page numbers in **boldface** indicate illustrations.